THE
MENTAL
HEALTH
DESK
REFERENCE

THE MENTAL HEALTH DESK REFERENCE

A Practice-Based Guide to Diagnosis, Treatment, and Professional Ethics

Edited by

Elizabeth Reynolds Welfel

R. Elliott Ingersoll

WILEY

John Wiley & Sons, Inc.

Library of Congress Cataloging-in-Publication Data:

The mental health desk reference / Elizabeth Reynolds Welfel, R. Elliott Ingersoll [editors].
    p. cm.
  Includes bibliographical references.
   ISBN 0-471-39572-2 (cloth : alk. paper); 0-471-65296-2 (pbk. : alk. paper)
   1. Mental health counseling. I. Welfel, Elizabeth Reynolds, 1949– II. Ingersoll, R.
Elliott.
 RC466.M464 2001
 616.89'14—dc21   2001017830

To Fred and Brandon who make it all worthwhile.

To my wife Jenn for offering her critical thinking skills.

To my students for the great questions I hope these chapters will address.

PREFACE

This book is designed to be an accessible and authoritative resource for mental health professionals seeking to provide effective, responsible, and up-to-date services to their clients. In the current economic, political, and social climate, mental health professionals from every discipline struggle to provide competent and caring services to their clients, but feel hindered in that endeavor by the limits imposed by third-party payors, the shrinkage in governmental funding for their work, and the lack of public understanding or support for their work. At the same time, they are being held to a higher standard of accountability to demonstrate that their services are effective, efficient, and in keeping with the best practices identified by research. They are at more risk than ever for malpractice claims and ethics complaints against them but also feel so overwhelmed by the bureaucracy of serving clients with managed care insurance that they often are not able to be as diligent as they want to be. When they turn to the professional literature to guide them, all too often they find complex and lengthy research papers that seem too removed from day-to-day practice to be helpful, or simplistic theories and models of service that have so flimsy a scientific basis that they cannot feel confident in their use. This book provides a concise resource that gives up-to-date, scientifically sound, and

practical guidance to practitioners in serving their clients. The brief chapters are written by many of the best scholars in the field, are informed by current research, and are presented in a straightforward and practical format that busy practitioners can readily access.

The book is unique in several ways. First, it combines in a single source both recommendations for effective practice and guidance for ethical community practice. Second, it addresses issues related to multicultural counseling and psychotherapy in a concise but rigorous way. Third, it is inclusive of all mental health professions that serve clients in the community and is not limited to one type of practitioner. Its authors, chosen for their expertise and not their professional identification, span virtually all the mental health professions including (in alphabetical order) clinical psychology, counseling psychology, counselor education, psychiatry, and social work. Fourth, this book addresses mental health service across the life span and across a diversity of settings, with the major focus always on recommendations for effective and responsible services to clients in those settings.

Because the authors come from a variety of disciplines, they do not use identical terminology to refer either to mental health professionals or to the people whom they serve. Some use the terms clinician or therapist and patient, others use counselor and client. As editors, we have decided to honor the terminology the authors chose and not impose a conformity. We believe that allowing them to speak "in their own voices" has resulted in a better book. At the very least, it mirrors more closely the multidisciplinary nature of mental health practice in the community. It also reflects our philosophy that the provision of competent and caring service to clients takes precedence over disciplinary differences.

The book is divided into nine major parts. The first 58 chapters focus on effective practice with sections on assessing and treating adult and child disorders; good practice with adjustment issues and normal developmental concerns; crisis intervention; competent service with diverse populations and group and family treatment; and practice management. The second major portion of the book—Chapters 59 through 72—explores the ethical and legal dimensions of practice with attention both to standards for practice and recommendations for acting responsibly with emerging technology and third-party payors. The book ends with an appendix containing codes of ethics and guidelines for readers to access as needed.

ACKNOWLEDGMENTS

A task as comprehensive in scope as this book could only be completed with the commitment of a team of people, the most important of whom are the chapter authors. These authors succeeded in a daunting task—producing a concise, accurate, and up-to-date discussion of the issues in the field in a very confined format—and the ultimate value of this book lies primarily in their hands, although we as editors take all responsibility for any errors found herein. We also wish to thank our colleagues at Cleveland State who supported us (and took on extra work at times to help us complete this project on schedule) and our graduate assistants, Ann O'Neill and Laura Burns, who diligently attended to all the work we gave them. We also wish to thank our editor at Wiley, Tracey Belmont, who expertly assisted us at every stage of the process and Publications Development Company of Texas. Finally, we owe a debt to our families who supported us in every possible way to complete this project.

ELIZABETH REYNOLDS WELFEL
R. ELLIOTT INGERSOLL
Cleveland, Ohio

CONTENTS

EDITORS

Elizabeth Reynolds Welfel is Professor and Coordinator of Counselor Education at Cleveland State University. She earned a doctorate in counseling psychology at the University of Minnesota in 1979 and is licensed as a psychologist in Ohio. Prior to her position at Cleveland State, she was on the faculty of the counseling psychology program at Boston College. Dr. Welfel is author of two books, *The Counseling Process* and *Ethics in Counseling and Psychotherapy,* and numerous articles in the professional literature. Dr. Welfel's major research and teaching activities have centered on promoting responsible mental health practices. Her most recent research explores the ethics of Internet counseling and psychotherapy.

R. Elliott Ingersoll is an Associate Professor and Chairperson of the Department of Counseling, Administration, Supervision, and Adult Learning at Cleveland State University. He is licensed as a Professional Clinical Counselor and a psychologist in the state of Ohio. He earned his PhD in counselor education at Kent State University in 1995. He is the coauthor of two books, *Explorations in Counseling and Spirituality* and *Becoming a 21st Century Agency Counselor* as well as numerous articles. His research activities are focused on psychopharmacology and the interface between counseling and spirituality.

CONTRIBUTORS

Howard S. Adelman
Department of Psychology
University of California at Los Angeles

Ferdinand Arcinue
Division of Counseling Psychology
University of Southern California

Donald R. Atkinson
Graduate School of Education
University of California at Santa Barbara

Ann Bauer
Department of Psychology and Counseling
Arkansas State University

Susan Bichsel
Jewish Family Services Association of
   Cleveland
Beachwood, OH

Gerald J. Bostwick Jr.
School of Social Work
University of Cincinnati

Christiane Brems
Department of Psychology
University of Alaska

Paula J. Britton
Department of Counseling and Human
   Services
John Carroll University

Robert E. Brodie II
Graduate School of Education
University of California, Santa Barbara

Laura Burns
PhD Program in Urban Education
Cleveland State University

Jason J. Burrow
Counseling Psychology Program
University of Oregon

David Michael Coe
Portage Path Behavioral Health Center
Akron, OH

Robert K. Conyne
Department of Counseling
University of Cincinnati

Tony D. Crespi
Department of Psychology
University of Hartford

Paula R. Danzinger
Department of Special Education and
   Counseling
William Paterson University

Judith A. DeTrude
Department of Educational Leadership
   and Counseling
Sam Houston State University

Jim Evans
Department of Psychology
University of Alberta

Christopher M. Faiver
Department of Counseling and Human
    Services
John Carroll University

Donna L. Fleming
Director of Counseling and Research
University of North Texas

Patricia Frazier
Department of Psychology
University of Minnesota

Stephen J. Freeman
Department of Family Sciences
Texas Women's University

Gerald L. Gandy
Department of Rehabilitation Counseling
Virginia Commonwealth University

Noni K. Gaylord
Department of Psychology
University of Memphis

Michele Getzelman
Division of Counseling Psychology
University of Southern California

Earl J. Ginter
Counseling and Human Development
    Services
University of Georgia

Gary G. Gintner
Department of Educational Leadership,
    Research and Counseling
Louisiana State University

Ann Glauser
Counseling and Human Development
    Services
University of Georgia

Harriet L. Glosoff
Department of Counselor Education
University of Virginia

Rodney K. Goodyear
Division of Counseling Psychology
University of Southern California

Darcy Haag Granello
Counselor Education
The Ohio State University

Paul F. Granello
Counselor Education
The Ohio State University

Christopher Habben
Department of Human Development
Virginia Polytechnic Institute and State
    University

Mitchell M. Handelsman
Department of Psychology
University of Colorado at Denver

Richard J. Hazler
Department of Counselor Education
Ohio University

Kathleen T. Heinlen
PhD Program in Urban Education
Cleveland State University

Barbara Herlihy
Department of Educational Leadership,
    Counseling and Foundations
University of New Orleans

Alvin E. House
Department of Psychology
Illinois State University

R. Elliott Ingersoll
Counseling, Administration, Supervision,
    and Adult Learning
Cleveland State University

Seth C. Kalichman
Department of Psychiatry and Behavioral
    Medicine
Medical College of Wisconsin

Cynthia R. Kalodner
College of Human Resources and Education,
    Counseling
West Virginia University

Christopher A. Kearney
Department of Psychology
University of Nevada, Las Vegas

Katherine M. Kitzmann
Department of Psychology
University of Memphis

Jeffrey A. Kottler
Department of Counseling
California State University, Fullerton

John F. Kugler
Bay Ridge Preparatory School
Brooklyn, NY

Timothy M. Lane
Counseling and Testing Services
University of North Texas

Ellen B. Lent
Department of Counseling and Personnel
    Services
University of Maryland, College Park

Monique C. Liddle
Department of Counseling and Educational
    Psychology
Indiana University

Lisa M. Linning
Department of Psychology
University of Nevada at Las Vegas

Neal E. Lipsitz
Director of Counseling Services
Holy Cross College

Katy L. Lynch
Department of Psychology
University of Montana

Kathryn C. MacCluskie
Counseling, Administration, Supervision,
    and Adult Learning
Cleveland State University

E. Davis Martin Jr.
Department of Rehabilitation Counseling
Virginia Commonwealth University

Benedict T. McWhirter
Counseling Psychology Program
University of Oregon

Janet Melcher
School of Social Work
University of Cincinnati

Cindy L. Miller-Perrin
Social Sciences Division
Pepperdine University

Jane E. Myers
Department of Counseling and Educational
    Development
University of North Carolina at Greensboro

Joel T. Nigg
Department of Psychology
Michigan State University

Nancy A. Orel
Gerontology Program
Bowling Green State University

Cynthia J. Osborn
Counseling and Human Development
    Services
Kent State University

Thomas V. Palma
Counseling, Administration, Supervision,
    and Adult Learning
Cleveland State University

Charles Palmer
Counselor Education Program
University of Montana

John Joseph Peregoy
Department of Educational Psychology
University of Utah

Megan L. Petruzzi
Counseling and Human Development
    Services
Kent State University

Boyd W. Pidcock
Department of Counseling Psychology
Lewis and Clark College

Joan Polansky
Northern Arizona University
Statewide Programs

Susan B. Previts
Counseling and Human Development
    Services Program
Kent State University

Anne M. Prouty
Family Therapy Center
Virginia Polytechnic Institute and State
    University

Rose M. QuinonesDelValle
Counseling, Administration, Supervision,
    and Adult Learning
Cleveland State University

Carl F. Rak
Director, PhD Program in Urban Education
Cleveland State University

Marsha D. Rappley
Department of Pediatrics
Michigan State University

Pam Remer
Department of Psychology
University of Kentucky

Theodore P. Remley Jr.
Department of Counseling, Educational
    Leadership and Foundations
University of New Orleans

James R. Rogers
Department of Counseling and Special
    Education
The University of Akron

John L. Romano
Department of Educational Psychology
University of Minnesota

Ronald H. Rooney
Department of Social Work
University of Minnesota

Susan Rosenberger
Department of Psychology
University of Minnesota

Sharon Rostosky
Department of Psychology
University of Kentucky

Valerie L. Schwiebert
Department of Counselor Education
Western Carolina University

Margot Schofield
University of New England
Armidale, Australia

Thomas L. Sexton
Department of Counseling and Educational
    Psychology
Indiana University

Howard B. Smith
American Counseling Association
Alexandria, VA

John Sommers-Flanagan
Families First
Missoula, MT

Rita Sommers-Flanagan
Counselor Education Program
University of Montana

Michael J. Sporakowski
Department of Human Development
Virginia Polytechnic Institute and State
    University

Holly A. Stadler
Counseling and Counseling Psychology
Auburn University

Jason Steward
Department of Psychology
University of Minnesota

Larry S. Stokes
Private Practice
Metairie, LA

David Sue
Department of Psychology
Western Washington University

Lisa A. Suzuki
Department of Applied Psychology
New York University

Thomas P. Swales
Director, Psychological Assessment Center
MetroHealth Medical Center
Cleveland, OH

Mei Tang
Department of Counseling
University of Cincinnati

Ty Tashiro
Department of Psychology
University of Minnesota

Linda Taylor
Los Angeles Public Schools and
University of California at Los Angeles

Derek Truscott
Department of Psychology
University of Alberta

Jeffrey S. Van Lone
College of Human Resources and Education,
    Counseling
West Virginia University

Laura J. Veach
Counselor Education Program
Wake Forest University

Melanie A. Warnke
Counseling and Human Development
  Services Program
Kent State University

Albert L. Watson
Department of Counseling
University of Cincinnati

Elizabeth Reynolds Welfel
Counseling, Administration, Supervision,
  and Adult Learning
Cleveland State University

John D. West
Counseling and Human Development
  Services Program
Kent State University

Lori R. Wicker
Graduate School of Education
University of California at Santa Barbara

Carmen Braun Williams
Division of Counseling Psychology and
  Counselor Education
University of Colorado at Denver

Michael Windle
Department of Psychology
University of Alabama

Margaret Laurie Comer Wright
Department of Psychology
University of Kentucky

PART I
Counseling for Adjustment Disorders and Life Stress

1 PREVALENCE OF ADULT DISORDERS

R. Elliott Ingersoll and Laura Burns

The notion of prevalence occurs in medical and psychological research but the methods used to estimate prevalence yield far more general results than many clinicians may suppose. Prevalence is determined through statistical probability and, as the mathematician Morris Kline (1972) noted, statistics are first and foremost a confession of ignorance. The statistics with which mental health professionals estimate the prevalence of mental/emotional disorders are drawn from epidemiological research. Epidemiological research is the study of the incidence, distribution, and consequences of particular problems in one or more specified populations as well as factors that affect distribution of the problems in question (Barlow & Durand, 1999; U.S. Department of Health, Education, and Welfare, 1978).

Gathering accurate statistics on mental and emotional disorders has always been a challenging task. The Association of Medical Superintendents of American Institutions for the Insane (later renamed the American Psychiatric Association—APA) first initiated this task in 1917. The responsibility for gathering statistics was shifted to the Biometrics branch of the National Institute of Mental Health (NIMH) in 1949 (American Psychiatric Association, 2000a). The APA relies heavily on the epidemiological research of others for the prevalence estimates found in the various Diagnostic and Statistical Manuals. Epidemiologic research may be carried out by one or two persons or in massive projects like the NIMH Epidemiologic Catchment Area Program (Eaton & Kessler, 1985).

DuPont, DuPont, and Spencer (1999) stated that the epidemiology of mental/emotional disorders was really begun in the 1970s in the Epidemiologic Catchment Area (ECA) study that used large samples from five communities in the United States. From this data, generalizations were extrapolated to the U.S. population in general producing the first national estimates for specific disorders. They noted that the first "truly national sample" was the National Comorbidity Study (NCS) conducted between 1990 and 1992 that used *DSM-III-R* criteria.

Since statistics are first and foremost a confession of ignorance, prevalence data based on statistics are always works in progress to be understood as "best guesses" given available methodologies. Several problems challenge researchers to make accurate estimates regarding the prevalence of a particular disorder. First, there is a significant time lag between the refinement of an edition of the *DSM*, and the gathering and analysis of data. For example, studies are still being published estimating prevalence based on *DSM-III-R* criteria (Kessler et al., 1997) that was replaced in 1994 by *DSM-IV* (which was replaced in 2000 by *DSM-IV-TR*). When the *DSM* is updated, additional disorders may be added and criteria or descriptors associated with a disorder may change. For example the *DSM-IV* (APA, 1994) added Bipolar II Disorder to describe individuals who suffered from major depressive episodes and a low-grade mania (hypomania) but not mania proper. *DSM-IV-TR* (APA, 2000b) went on to make changes in the narrative section describing the relationship between Bipolar I Disorder and Bipolar II disorder.

A second problem associated with estimating prevalence has to do with the methods used. As any researcher knows, some research methods are better than others. There is a paucity of research comparing various methods or data gathering instruments (Boyle et al., 1997; Regier, 2000) and reported prevalence rates may vary study by study (Regier et al., 1998). Methods of epidemiological research on mental disorders have varied over time. Kohn, Dohrenwend, and Mirotznik (1998) stated that there have been three generations of evolving, large-scale epidemiological research using two strategies. Each generation has used different psychiatric nosologies and data collection tools. The first generation relied primarily on institutional records and key informants but no real standardized procedures for data collection. The second generation utilized structured interviews in the community by nonclinical interviewers that were subsequently rated by a psychiatrist. The third generation (starting around 1980) used clinician and trained nonclinician interviewers in the community to obtain information necessary to determine the presence of mental disorders as categorized in the *DSM*. This present generation utilizes explicit diagnostic criteria as well as structured clinical interview schedules (Dohrenwend, 1998; Eaton & Kessler, 1985; Kohn et al., 1998). Currently, all epidemiologic approaches are based on personal interviews and there is still controversy over the accuracy of the interview method particularly over whether it is appropriate to use lay-interviewers (Dohrenwend, 1998). Dohrenwend noted ". . . classification systems in psy-

chiatry have been and will continue to be tentative as long as disorders are grouped on the basis of signs and symptoms elicited in interviews" (pp. 146–147).

Perhaps the most substantial problem with epidemiological data is summarized by Blazer and Kaplar (2000) who stated that a central conflict is whether or not symptoms reported by community residents in structured interviews are clinically significant or not. On one side of the debate, Regier (2000) noted that the conflict could be resolved with better research methods that would allow a diagnosis to be made from the results of a structured clinical interview. On the other side, Spitzer (1998) and Frances (1998) have asserted that data from epidemiological studies cannot replace clinical judgment. Blazer and Kaplar (2000) contended that the conflict could not be resolved because the methodologies of both sides are plagued with measurement error.

In this chapter, we briefly review the prevalence of the most common adult disorders. We have organized the chapter so the disorders are presented in the same order as they appear in the *DSM*. Disorders usually first diagnosed in infancy, childhood, or adolescence can be found in Chapter 20. Mental disorders due to or related to general medical conditions are omitted as are many subtypes of larger syndromes (e.g., dementia due to head trauma). There are numerous disorders for which there are no clear epidemiological data (e.g., Pain Disorder, Factitious Disorder, and all of the Dissociative Disorders). These have also been omitted from this chapter.

Some disorders are discussed in terms of point prevalence, some in terms of lifetime prevalence, and some in terms of both. Point prevalence refers to the estimated proportion of people in the population thought to suffer from the disorder at any given time. Lifetime prevalence is an estimate at a given time of all individuals who have ever suffered from the disorder. Incidence refers to the rate of new cases in a specified period of time (usually annually) (LaBruzza, 1997). Which of these types of prevalence or incidence data should be cited depends on the availability of data. Unless otherwise noted, estimates of prevalence are taken from *DSM-IV-TR* (APA, 2000b).

Attention Deficit Hyperactivity Disorder (ADHD). Although there is limited prevalence data on ADHD in adults, it is estimated that of the 3% to 9% of children suffering from the disorder, the disorder will persist into adulthood for 10% to 50% of these afflicted children (Levin & Donaldson, 1999). Barkely (1998) has noted that the *DSM* criteria sets are developmentally insensitive so he believes that the percentages of afflicted children who will continue to suffer from the disorder in adulthood range from 3% to 68%. Barkley's point is that patients may outgrow the diagnosis but not the disorder.

Delirium. The point prevalence is estimated at 0.4% in adults 18-years-old and older. The point prevalence for adults 55 and older is estimated at 1.1%. In hospitalized patients with medical illness, the point prevalence ranges from 10% to 30% and up to 60% of nursing home residents age 75 and older may be delirious at any given time.

Dementia. Dementia may have one of 75 or more etiologies. 1% to 5% of these are reversible while approximately 95% are progressive (Alzheimer's type being the most common progressive dementia) (Nussbaum, 1998). Prevalence figures vary study by study and range from 1.4% to 1.6% for individuals between the ages of 65 to 69. The prevalence increases with age and rises to 16% to 25% for individuals over 85 years of age.

Dementia of the Alzheimer's Type (ALZ). Like progressive dementias in general, ALZ incidence increases with the age of the cohort under study. At age 65, the prevalence is 0.6% in males and 0.8% in females. Respectively, these increase to 11% and 14% at age 85 and 21% and 25% at age 90.

Substance Use Disorders (SUDs). It is difficult to make estimates of substance use disorders with adults particularly when the use of numerous licit and illicit substances may be common and even culturally reinforced. In addition, the very notion of substance abuse as a syndrome meriting inclusion in *DSM* is still debated (Helzer, 1994). Mirin et al. (2000) estimated that approximately 15% of regular users of any substance will become psychologically dependent on that substance, that is, they come to believe they are unable to function without it. Data on physical dependence varies depending on the substance. It should be noted that although each subcategory below bears the generic label for disorders related to a substance (e.g., Alcohol-Related Disorders), for most subcategories, all we have are estimates of use which give us no clue as to how many users would meet the criteria for abuse or dependence.

Alcohol Dependence (AD). Estimates of prevalence vary markedly across studies for both alcohol abuse and dependence. Using *DSM-III-R* and *DSM-IV* criteria, it is estimated that the lifetime risk for alcohol dependence in the mid-1990s was approximately 15% with the point prevalence being 5%. According to the ECA survey, 37% of people with an alcohol disorder had another comorbid mental/emotional disorder (Gallant, 1994).

Amphetamine-Induced Disorders. The *DSM-IV-TR* notes that the patterns of amphetamine use differ geographically and over time in the general population. More recent estimates report approximately 5% of adults ever using stimulant drugs to get "high" with 1% reporting such activities in the prior year. A national epidemiological study in the early 1990s reported a lifetime prevalence of 1.5%. Although these estimates are thought to address amphetamines proper and amphetamine-like substances, they probably do not address the full chemical diversity of the amphetamine molecule and the chemical variations that are produced and sold illegally. For example, 3,4-methylenedioxymethamphetamine ("Ecstasy") is technically an amphetamine derivative but is classed as a hallucinogen.

Caffeine-Related Disorders. It is estimated that 80% to 85% of adults consume caffeine within any given year and larger numbers of youth are thought to be using caffeine products. The prevalence of caffeine-related disorders is unknown.

Cannabis-Related Disorders. Marijuana is estimated to be the most frequently abused illicit psychoactive drug in the United States. Because of the legal issues involved and the variable patterns of use, it is difficult to estimate the number of users meeting the criteria for abuse or dependence. A 1992 survey estimated that lifetime rates of cannabis dependence or use are approximately 5%. Use has been estimated for adults 18 to 29 who ever used (26%), to used in the last 30 days for high school seniors (14%), to daily use in high school seniors and young adults (3.7% of adult males and 1.6% of adult females (Millman & Beeder, 1994).

Cocaine-Related Disorders. The patterns of cocaine use are believed to fluctuate with the times. A 1996 national survey estimated that 10% of the population had ever used cocaine and 2% had used it in the previous year. Crack use was less prevalent with 2% of the population estimated to have ever used and 0.6% using in the last year.

Hallucinogen-Related Disorders. The estimation of hallucinogen-related disorders is complicated by the disagreement over which substances are hallucinogens proper. The current category includes 3,4-methylenedioxymethamphetamine which is chemically an amphetamine derivative and experientially an empathogen rather than a hallucinogen. Until current disagreements regarding classification are resolved, it is unlikely that we will have accurate prevalence estimates. According to the 1996 survey used by the writers of the *DSM-IV-TR*, 10% of the population age 10 and older is estimated to have ever used a hallucinogen.

Inhalent-Related Disorders. It is difficult to estimate the prevalence of these because it is thought their use might be underrepresented in surveys. The current estimates from the 1996 survey indicate that around 6% of the U.S. population is thought to have ever used an inhalant with 1% reporting use in the past year.

Nicotine-Related Disorders. As of the 1996 data, 72% of the U.S. population is thought to have ever used cigarettes with 32% using in the past year. Lifetime prevalence is highest for those 35 and older (78%) but use in the prior year was highest in the 18 to 25 year old age group (45%). It is estimated that 80% to 90% of regular smokers have nicotine dependence, which equals an estimate of 25% of Americans. Greater decreases in smoking are seen for Caucasians than African Americans or Hispanics. Increases in smoking have been reported since the mid-1990s for women with less than a high school education. It is estimated that 17% of Americans have ever used smokeless tobacco products but there are no estimates for dependence in this group.

Opioid-Related Disorders. In 1996, 4% of men and 6% of women were estimated to have ever used an analgesic drug in a manner other than that for which it was prescribed (2% in the past year). The 18- to 25-year-old cohort had the highest prevalence of ever using an analgesic in this manner (9%). The lifetime prevalence for heroin use is around 1%.

Phencyclidine-Related Disorders. Data from 1996 reported that 3% of Americans ages 12 and older have ever used phencyclidine (PCP) with the highest lifetime prevalence (4%) being reported in the 26 to 34 year old age group. Phencyclidine is thought to account for about 3% of substance-related deaths.

Sedative, Hypnotic, or Anxiolytic-Related Disorders. More than 15% of Americans use these medications in any given year. Most take as directed without any misuse. 1996 data estimate that 6% of Americans have ever taken these drugs illicitly. The age group with the highest estimated illicit use was 26- to 34-year-olds (3% using "sedatives" and 6% using "tranquilizers").

Schizophrenia. Schizophrenia is observed across cultures, worldwide. The prevalence among adults is thought to be between 1% and 1.5% of adults.

Delusional Disorder. This disorder is thought to be uncommon in outpatient clinical settings. It is estimated that the disorder is prevalent in 1% to 2% of inpatient mental health facilities.

Major Depressive Disorder (MDD). The lifetime prevalence of MDD varies between 10% to 25% for females and 5% to 12% for males. The point prevalence varies from 5% to 9% for females and 2% to 3% for males.

Dysthymic Disorder (DD). Estimates vary regarding DD. Lifetime prevalence is estimated to be 6% while the point prevalence is thought to be around 3%. Keller and Russell (1996) have noted that chronic depression is generally common in community samples with 2.7% to 4.3% being diagnosed with DD.

Bipolar I Disorder. The estimated lifetime prevalence of Bipolar I disorder in community samples fluctuates between 0.4% to 1.6%.

Bipolar II Disorder. There is scant data on Bipolar II disorder partially because of its newness (first listed in *DSM-IV*) and because of difficulties making the diagnosis accurately. Current estimates of lifetime prevalence are 0.5% of the population.

Cyclothymic Disorder. Studies estimate the prevalence to be between 0.4% and 1% of the population. The prevalence in mood disorders clinics is higher, between 3% and 5%.

Panic Disorder (with or without Agoraphobia). Most studies report rates between 1% and 2% although some estimate as high as 3.5% of the general population. The one-year prevalence rates range between 0.5% and 1.5% of the population.

Specific Phobia. Phobias are common in the general population although they rarely reach the level of distress or impairment necessary to qualify as a mental and emotional disorder. Estimated prevalence varies depending on the threshold used to determine distress and impairment. In community samples prevalence estimates range between 4% and 8.8%. Lifetime prevalence estimates range between 7.2% and 11.3%.

Social Phobia (SB). The estimated lifetime prevalence is 3% to 13%. The 6-month prevalence is estimated to be 0.9% to 1.7% for males and 1.5% to 2.6% for females (Myers et al., 1984). In the general population most people with SB have a fear of public speaking.

Obsessive-Compulsive Disorder (OCD). Lifetime prevalence is estimated at 2.5% and 1-year prevalence between 0.5% to 2.1%. The average age of onset ranges from early adolescence to the mid-twenties.

Posttraumatic Stress Disorder (PTSD). The lifetime prevalence for PTSD ranges from 1% to 14% and the variability is related to the methodology used and the population sampled. Studies of at-risk individuals (e.g., combat veterans, victims of volcanic eruption or criminal violence) yield even broader prevalence rates ranging from 3% to 58%.

Acute Stress Disorder. The prevalence of Acute Stress Disorder in the general population is not known. However, for victims of severe trauma, it is estimated to be between 14% and 33%.

Generalized Anxiety Disorder (GAD). The point prevalence for GAD has been estimated at 2% for females and 4% for males (Wittchen, Zhao, Kessler, & Eaton, 1994) Lifetime prevalence is estimated at 5%.

Somatization Disorder. Studies have reported widely variable prevalence rates ranging from 0.2% to 2% for women and less than 0.2% for men.

Conversion Disorder. Reported rates for Conversion Disorder vary widely and are not well defined. They range from 11 people out of every 100,000 to 500 people in every 100,000.

Hypochondriasis. The incidence of hypochondriasis is estimated to be 2% to 7% in general medical practice. The prevalence for the general population is estimated at 1% to 5%.

Sexual Disorders. Scant epidemiological data exists on the sexual disorders. The *DSM-IV-TR* relies on one comprehensive study that summarizes sexual complaints that may be related to particular disorders. There is no way of knowing if the complaints would reach the levels of distress and impairment necessary to actually make the diagnosis.

Hypoactive Sexual Desire Disorder. The one comprehensive study to date has estimated that as many as 33% of women may suffer from complaints in this category at any given time. Clearly this high number may include complaints related to the context of the person's life that may never qualify as the disorder proper.

Arousal Problems. The problems in this category could be prominent in Female Sexual Arousal Disorder and Male Erectile Disorder. It is estimated that at any given time, 20% of females may have complaints related to arousal problems and 10% of males would have complaints related to erectile dysfunction.

Orgasm-Related Problems. The problems in this category could be related to Female Orgasmic

Disorder, Male Orgasmic Disorder, and Premature Ejaculation. At any given time, 25% of females and 10% of males are estimated to have complaints related to orgasms.

Dyspareunia. Problems that may fit this category given sufficient impairment and distress are estimated to be experienced by 3% of males and 15% of females.

Anorexia Nervosa. Lifetime prevalence among females is estimated to be 0.5% of the population although there are many more women who are suffering from related symptoms that are sub-threshold for the disorder. Prevalence in males is thought to be $\frac{1}{10}$ that of women.

Bulimia Nervosa. The general prevalence is estimated to be 1% to 3% among adolescent and young adult females. Male occurrence is thought to be $\frac{1}{10}$ of that.

Primary Insomnia. Primary Insomnia is thought to afflict 1% to 10% of the general population and up to 25% of elderly people.

Narcolepsy. Studies estimate that between 0.02% and 0.16% of the population is afflicted with Narcolepsy.

Breathing-Related Sleep Disorders. The most common of these is Obstructive Sleep Apnea Syndrome which is thought to afflict between 1% and 10% of the population.

Sleepwalking Disorder. The prevalence of sleepwalking disorder is thought to be in the range of 1% to 5% while incidents of sleepwalking (not the disorder per se) are more common for up to 7% of adults.

Pathological Gambling. This is the only disorder in the category of Impulse-Control Disorders Not Elsewhere Classified with any community estimates. For adults, the estimated prevalence is 0.4% to 3.4%.

Adjustment Disorders (AD). It is estimated that between 10% and 30% of clients in mental health outpatient settings suffer from adjustment disorders of some type. One would suspect that the prevalence in the general population would be higher although there are no epidemiological studies to support that hypothesis.

Personality Disorders. The personality disorders in the *DSM* are the least validated in the

manual. One problem is great comorbidity where 50% of people meeting the criteria for one personality disorder also meet the criteria for at least one more. Tyrer (1995) stated that "the degree of overlap between and among the different personality disorders is far too great, and the specious use of the term "comorbidity" hides diagnostic confusion" (p. 29). He concluded that even if the categories were more valid, there is no way to classify a person meeting the criteria for more than one personality disorder. Without going further into the debate about the validity of these categories, suffice it to say that one should be mindful of the debate while reading current prevalence data. Disorders for which there is no prevalence data (e.g., Schizoid Personality Disorder) have been omitted from this chapter.

Paranoid Personality Disorder. Estimated to be present in between 0.5% and 2.5% of the general population.

Schizotypal Personality Disorder. Estimated to be present in 3% of the general population.

Antisocial Personality Disorder. Estimated to be present in 3% of males and 1% of females in the general population.

Borderline Personality Disorder. Estimated to be present in 2% of the general population.

Histrionic Personality Disorder. Limited data allow for estimates of about 2% to 3% of the general population.

Narcissistic Personality Disorder. Estimated to exist in less than 1% of the general population.

Avoidant Personality Disorder. Estimated to exist in between 0.5% and 1% of the general population.

Obsessive-Compulsive Personality Disorder. Estimated to be present in approximately 1% of the general population.

References

American Psychiatric Association. (1987). *Diagnostic and statistical manual of mental disorders* (3rd ed., rev.). Washington, DC: Author.
American Psychiatric Association. (1994). *Diagnostic and statistical manual of mental disorders* (4th ed.). Washington, DC: Author.

American Psychiatric Association. (2000a). *DSM: A brief historical note* [Online]. Available: www .psych.org/htdocs/pnews/98-04-03/hx.html.

American Psychiatric Association. (2000b). *Diagnostic and statistical manual of mental disorders* (4th ed., text rev.). Washington, DC: Author.

Barkley, R.A. (1998). Attention deficit hyperactivity disorder: Long-term course, adult outcome, and comorbid disorder. In *NIH consensus development conference: Diagnosis and treatment of attention deficit disorder* (pp. 57–59). Bethesda, MD: National Institutes of Health.

Barlow, D.A., & Durand, V.M. (1999). *Abnormal psychology* (2nd ed.). Pacific Grove, CA: Brooks/ Cole.

Blazer, D.G., & Kaplar, B.H. (2000). Controversies in community-based psychiatric epidemiology: Let the data speak for themselves. *Archives of General Psychiatry, 57,* 227.

Boyle, M.H., Offord, D.R., Racine, Y.A., Szatmari, P., Sanford, M., & Fleming, J.E. (1997). Adequacy of interviews vs. checklists for classifying childhood psychiatric disorders based on parents' reports. *Archives of General Psychiatry, 54,* 793–799.

Dohrenwend, B.P. (1998). A psychosocial perspective on the past and future of psychiatric epidemiology. *American Journal of Epidemiology, 147,* 222–231.

DuPont, R.L., DuPont, C.M., & Spencer, E. (1999). Generalized anxiety disorder: A clinician's guide to "the worry disease." *Directions in Psychiatry, 19,* 133–144.

Eaton, W.W., & Kessler, L.G. (1985). *Epidemiologic field methods in psychiatry: The NIMH epidemiologic catchment area program.* Orlando, FL: Academic Press.

Frances, A. (1998). Problems in defining clinical significance in epidemiologic studies. *Archive of General Psychiatry, 55,* 119.

Gallant, D. (1994). Alcohol. In M. Galanter & H.D. Kleber (Eds.), *Textbook of substance abuse treatment* (pp. 67–90). Washington, DC: American Psychiatric Press.

Helzer, J.E. (1994). Psychoactive substance abuse and its relation to dependence. In T.A. Widiger, A.J. Frances, H.A. Pincus, R. Ross, M.B. First, & W. Wakefield Davis (Eds.), *DSM-IV sourcebook: Volume 1* (pp. 21–33). Washington, DC: American Psychiatric Press.

Keller, M.B., & Russell, C.W. (1996). Dysthymia. In T.A. Widiger, A.J. Frances, H.A. Pincus, R. Ross, M.B. First, & W. Wakefield Davis (Eds.), *DSM-IV sourcebook: Volume 2* (pp. 21–35). Washington, DC: American Psychiatric Press.

Kessler, R.C., Crum, R.M., Warner, L.A., Nelson, C.B., Schulenberg, J., & Anthony, J.C. (1987). Lifetime co-occurrence of *DSM-III-R* alcohol abuse and dependence with other psychiatric disorders in the National Comorbidity Survey. *Archives of General Psychiatry, 54,* 313–318.

Kline, M. (1972). *Mathematical thought from ancient to modern times.* New York: Oxford University Press.

Kohn, R., Dohrenwend, B.P., & Mirotznik, J. (1998). Epidemiological findings on selected psychiatric disorders in the general population. In B.P. Dohrenwend (Ed.), *Adversity, stress and psychopathology* (pp. 235–284). New York: Oxford University Press.

LaBruzza, A.L. (1997). *Using DSM-IV: A clinician's guide to psychiatric diagnosis.* Northvale, NJ: Aronson.

Levin, F.R., & Donaldson, P.L. (1999). Diagnosis and treatment of ADHD in drug dependent adults. *Directions in Psychiatry, 19,* 251–268.

Millman, R.B., & Beeder, A.B. (1994). Cannabis. In M. Galanter & H.D. Kleber (Eds.), *Textbook of substance abuse treatment* (pp. 91–100). Washington, DC: American Psychiatric Press.

Mirin, S. L., Bukstein, O., Isbell, P.G., Kleber, H., Schottenfeld, R.S., Weiss, R.D., & Yandrow, V.W. (2000). Practice guideline for the treatment of patients with substance use disorders: Alcohol, cocaine, opiods. In *American Psychiatric Association Practice guidelines for the treatment of psychiatric disorders* (pp. 139–238). Washington, DC: Author.

Myers, J.L., Weissman, M.M., Tischler, G.L., Holzer, C.E., Leaf, P.J., Orvaschel, H., Anthony, J.D., Boyd, J.H., Burke, J.D., Krammer, M., & Stolzman, R. (1984). Six month prevalence of psychiatric disorders in three communities. *Archives of General Psychiatry, 41,* 939–957.

Nussbaum, P.D. (1998, October). *Aging of the brain, aging of the mind.* Unpublished lecture delivered in Akron, OH.

Reiger, D.A. (2000). Community diagnosis counts. *Archives of General Psychiatry, 57,* 223.

Reiger, D.A., Kaelber, C.T., Rae, D.S., Farmer, M.E., Knauper, B., Kessler, R.C., & Norquist, G.S. (1998). Limitations of diagnostic criteria and assessment instruments for mental disorders: Implications for research and policy. *Archives of General Psychiatry, 55,* 109–115.

Spitzer, R. (1998). Diagnosis and need for treatment are not the same. *Archives of General Psychiatry, 55,* 120.

Tyrer, P. (1995). Are personality disorders well classified in *DSM-IV*? In W.J. Livesley (Ed.),

The DSM-IV personality disorders (pp. 29–44). New York: Guilford Press.

U.S. Department of Health, Education, and Welfare. (1978). *Epidemiology, health systems research, and statistics/data systems: Report of an ADAMHA workgroup.* Washington, DC: Author.

Wittchen, H-U., Zhao, S., Kessler, R.C., & Eaton, W. (1994). *DSM-III-R* generalized anxiety disorder in national comorbidity survey. *Archives of General Psychiatry, 51,* 355–364.

2 COUNSELING CLIENTS WITH UNDERLYING MEDICAL PROBLEMS

Christiane Brems

In recent years, studies have documented a strong link between medicine and psychology, as many clients with mental health concerns actually suffer from medical illness and vice versa. Tomb (1995) found that 50% to 80% of patients treated in medical clinics actually had a diagnosable psychiatric disorder; 60% of patients treated by general medical practitioners actually needed mental health care; and 50% of patients in psychiatric clinics had undiagnosed medical illnesses. Wickramasekera, Davies, and Davies (1996) showed that over half of patient visits to primary care physicians were related to psychosocial problems, although presented to the provider in the form of physical complaints. Klonoff and Landrine (1997) accumulated evidence that as many as 41% to 83% of psychiatric patients instead suffer from an undiagnosed medical illness.

These numbers show that counselors must be aware of clients' physical needs as much as medical providers need to consider patients' emotional state. Both medical and psychological providers often fail to consider the possibility that clients presenting for one reason (e.g., medical concerns or psychological problems) may also or instead suffer from a condition in the realm of the other provider (Wickramasekera et al., 1996). These oversights could be prevented if both providers were more willing to consider the importance of the other and more open to working collaboratively (Brems, 2000). Doubtless, such collaboration enhances the quality of treatment (and life) of clients who are in need of medical *and* psychological interventions. Not surprisingly, lawsuits increasingly are brought against psychological providers who failed to investigate possible underlying physical diagnoses that would have explained a client's psychological symptoms (Klonoff & Landrine, 1997). Thus, for the sake of their clients and to minimize their own risk of being sued for malpractice, counselors need to be knowledgeable about medical referrals and have collaborative relationships with medical providers. This means raising their awareness of physical and psychological symptoms that should stimulate referrals (Samson, Levin, & Richardson, 1998; White, Marans, & Krengel, 1998).

PSYCHOLOGICAL SYMPTOMS THAT REQUIRE MEDICAL DIFFERENTIAL DIAGNOSIS

Not making appropriate medical referrals when psychological symptoms have medical causes can lead to lack of problem resolution at best and life-threatening situations at worst. Thus, it is crucial that counselors be aware of possible differential medical diagnoses. Psychological symptoms that should stimulate data gathering for possible medical referral follow, with medical causes to be ruled out in parentheses:

- Anorexia Nervosa (e.g., Crohn's disease, hypopituitarism, systemic lupus erythematosus).
- Delirium (e.g., drug toxicity or withdrawal, metabolic disease, psychosocial trauma or stress, postoperative and postictal states, CNS trauma, infection).
- Delusional Disorder (e.g., metabolic/endocrine disorder such as thyroid disturbance, CNS lupus, hypopituitarism, Cushing's syndrome; neurological disorders such as temporal lobe epilepsy; Wilson's disease).
- Dementia (e.g., primary dementia such as Alzheimer's disease, Pick's disease, Creutzfeldt-Jakob disease; endocrine disorder; infections, including HIV; tumors, mainly in central nervous system; neurological disorder such as Huntington's Chorea, Parkinson's disease, palsy, subdural hematoma; nutritional deficiencies; vascular disorders; toxicities; head trauma).
- Generalized Anxiety (e.g., cardiovascular disease such as arrhythmias, coronary artery disease, hypertension, mitral valve prolapse; respiratory disease such as asthma, hyperventilation, chronic obstructive lung disease, pulmonary embolus; endocrine/metabolic disorders such as hypoglycemia, hyper- or hypothyroidism, hyponatremia; neurological disorders such as

tumors, infection, complex partial seizures, migraines; peptic ulcers and ulcerative colitis).
- Major Depression (e.g., malignancies; CNS impairment such as uremia, demyelination, hypoxia, hepatic encephalopathy, infections such as hepatitis, mononucleosis, syphilis; nutritional deficiencies; endocrine disorders such as hypo- and hyperthyroidism, diabetes, pituitary insufficiency, Cushing's syndrome, Addison's disease).
- Mania (e.g., hypo- or hyperthyroidism, diencephalic or frontal stroke, multiple sclerosis, complex partial seizures, brain tumors).
- Panic Disorder (e.g., cardiovascular disease, especially mitral valve prolapse; respiratory disease; neurological disease; endocrine disorder; pheochromocytoma).
- Psychogenic Amnesia (e.g., organic amnestic disorder, epilepsy, postconcussion amnesia, substance-induced amnesia).
- Psychogenic Fugue (e.g., organic mental disorder, complex partial seizures, malingering).
- Schizophrenia (e.g., epilepsy, partial complex seizures, CNS tumor or infection, CNS degenerative disease, B_{12} and/or folic acid deficiency, endocrine/metabolic disease, toxicity, multiple sclerosis).
- Sexual Dysfunction (e.g., neurophysiological factors, side effect of drug or medication use, general medical illness).
- Insomnia (e.g., organic factors such as Parkinson's disease; cardiovascular insufficiency; respiratory disease).
- Parasomnia (e.g., endocrine disorders, diabetes mellitus, vascular disorder, neural disorders, epileptic seizures).

ADDITIONAL HINTS TO IDENTIFY THE NEED FOR MEDICAL REFERRAL

Beyond using symptoms, several hints help identify the need for medical referral. When a client presents with *inconsistent symptoms,* physical disorder needs to be suspected. For example, if a client complains of fatigue, lack of appetite, and sexual disinterest, but claims no other symptoms consistent with depressive disorder, medical evaluation is indicated given the lack of consistency to support a pure psychiatric diagnosis of depression (i.e., never use "atypical" diagnoses without medical corroboration). When a client who has been seen for a while suddenly develops *new, more, or more severe symptoms*, a medical referral is warranted. Morrison (1997) warns that counselors must "think outside the mental health box" (p. 2), especially with clients they have seen for some time. When sudden symptomatic changes occur, it is the responsibility of the counselor to begin to question whether the pure mental health diagnosis truly accounts for the entire clinical picture. Another cue to the need for medical referral can be *unusual or changing appearance or mannerisms* (Morrison, 1997). Examples include features such as premature or nonmale pattern thinning of hair (e.g., hypothyroidism, malnutrition, or liver failure), darkening of skin (e.g., adrenal insufficiency or hypothyroidism), stiff or halting movements (e.g., fibromyalgia or Creutzfeldt-Jakob disease), shortness of breath (e.g., B_1 deficiency or congestive heart failure), or tremors (e.g., Parkinson's disease, multiple sclerosis, or hypoglycemia). Any *alarming symptoms*, such as blood in sputum or stool, persistent headaches, or similar severe or sudden physical manifestations also always warrant medical referral, even if the client does not connect them to the psychological presenting symptoms. Klonoff and Landrine (1997) suggest that *"visual illusions or hallucinations always have an organic, rather than functional or psychiatric, etiology"* (p. 59), and hence always require a medical referral. In fact, these authors indicate that basic physical exams should be required of all psychotherapy clients. Finally, when in doubt, refer.

FEATURES OF THE SUCCESSFUL REFERRAL PROCESS

If a client meets a criterion for medical referral, counselors need to explore whether the client received a recent (within the past one to three months) medical evaluation that assessed *relevant* medical disorders. If so, the counselor requests a release of information (ROI) from the client to access this medical information. Only a medical provider can make a medical diagnosis, especially as many differential diagnoses rely not solely on a simple medical exam, but require in-depth and protracted medical testing and evaluation. Table 2.1, based on Morrison's (1997) *When Psychological Problems Mask Medical Disorders* and Klonoff and Landrine's (1997) *Preventing Misdiagnosis of Women*, lists the most common physical disorders with psychological manifestations and actions necessary to rule them out. Knowing which medical tests are typically used helps counselors decide whether the client's medical exam targeted the current presenting symptoms. This is necessary to confirm that at the time of the physical exam the medical professional was aware of the psychological symptoms and ruled out the relevant medical issues. This thoroughness is suggested because not all clients are truthful and not all medical providers are equally qualified.

The referral process itself is straightforward. The client is made aware of the need for the medical referral, prepared for the medical contact, given a referral name if he or she does not have a regular medical provider, and asked to sign an ROI to allow communication between the medical provider and counselor. When making referrals to physicians, physician's assistants, nutritionists, nurse practitioners, and so forth, counselors have the responsibility to coordinate and facilitate this process for their clients. To prepare for their role as facilitators, counselors should enhance communication with physicians. First, it is recommended that counselors *identify medical specialists* with whom they can collaborate easily. Klonoff and Landrine (1997) recommend that this list optimally include an endocrinologist, a neurologist, a gynecologist, and an internist. Counselors need to be prepared to *provide hypotheses* about what might be going on with the client, providing concrete ideas of differential diagnoses based on physical data. To do so, they need to *learn basic medical jargon* that allows for communication and engenders respect. Medical providers will take a nonmedical referral source more seriously if he or she

TABLE 2.1 Physical Disorders with Psychological Symptoms

Disorder	Psychological Symptoms	Physical Symptoms	Medical Tests
Adrenal insufficiency (Addison's disease)	Fatigue, apathy, depression, social withdrawal, anxiety, suicidality, psychosis, poverty of thought, recent memory impairment	Weakness, darkening skin, nausea, abdominal pain, fainting, vomiting, weight loss, anorexia (loss of appetite)	History of salt cravings, urine or sputum test measuring cortisol levels
Amyotropic lateral sclerosis (Lou Gehrig's disease)	Depression, dementia	Muscle weakness, weight loss, ataxia (inability to coordinate voluntary muscle movement), dysarthria (inability to articulate words), cramping	Electromyography (to show muscle twitching)
Brain abscess	Lethargy, cognitive changes and symptoms	Headache, fever, stiff neck, seizures, nausea, vomiting, focal neurological symptoms	CT scan, MRI
Brain tumor	Loss of memory, cognitive changes, dementia, depression, psychosis, dissociation, personality changes	Headaches, vomiting, dizziness, seizures, focal neurological symptoms	CT scan, MRI, brain biopsy
Carcinoid syndrome	Flushing of the face and body (blushing)	Diarrhea, abdominal pain, blood-containing stool	Urine sample to assess high levels of serotonin breakdown products
Cardiac arrhythmia	Anxiety, delirium	Fatigue, dizziness, delirium, palpitations	Electrocardiogram
Chronic obstructive lung disease	Anxiety, panic, depression, insomnia, delirium	Cough, shortness of breath, tremor, headache, dark skin hue	Pulmonary function studies, blood-gas determination
Congestive heart failure	Anxiety, panic, insomnia, delirium, depression	Shortness of breath, fatigue, edema, cold, weakness, cyanosis	Chest X-ray, echocardiogram
Cryptococcus	Irritability, disorientation, mania, dementia, psychosis	Headache, fever, stiff neck, blurred vision, nausea, staggering gait	Search for causative yeast organism in cerebrospinal fluid bathed in india ink
Cushing's syndrome	Emotional lability, depression, anxiety, loss of libido, delirium, irritability, paranoid delusion, suicidality (high risk)	Hypertension, amenorrhea (cessation of menstruation), oily skin, increased body hair, weakness, facial and truncal obesity, buffalo hump	Physical exam, corticosteroid level in 24-hour urine specimen, history of steroid-containing substances
Diabetes mellitus	Fatigue, lethargy, panic, depression, poor concentration, delirium	Increased hunger, thirst, and urine output; rapid weight loss; blurred vision	At least two abnormal glucose tolerance tests
Fibromyalgia	Chronic fatigue, depression, anxiety	Muscle pain, stiffness, and tenderness	By history and symptom presentation

(continued)

TABLE 2.1 *Continued*

Disorder	Psychological Symptoms	Physical Symptoms	Medical Tests
Head trauma	Personality change, delirium, dementia, amnesia, mood swings, psychosis, anxiety	Headache, dizziness, fatigue, paralysis, seizures, anosmia (loss of sense of smell)	Skull X-ray, MRI, CT scan
Herpes encephalitis	Forgetfulness, anxiety, psychosis	Fever, headache, stiff neck, vomiting, focal neurological symptoms	Electroencephalogram, brain biopsy, CT scan
Homocystinuria	Mental retardation, dementia, behavioral problems	Impaired vision, shuffling gait, blotchy skin	Blood or urine test to check for elevated levels of homocysteine and methionine
Huntington's disease	Apathy, depression, irritability, impulsive behavior, personality changes, cognitive changes, suicidality, dementia	Insomnia, restlessness, ataxia, inarticulate speech, good appetite with weight loss, clumsiness, writhing motions of the limbs	Family history of this fatal disease, genetic testing
Hyperparathyroidism (Hypercalcemia)	Personality change, depression, anxiety, suicidality, delirium, psychosis; often mistaken for hypochondriasis	Urinary tract infections, weakness, tiredness, anorexia, nausea, vomiting, thirst, constipation, muscle and abdominal pain	Blood test to establish high serum calcium and parathyroid hormone levels
Hypertensive encephalopathy	Paranoia, delirium	Headache, nausea, paralysis, vomiting, visual impairment, seizures	Measurement of blood pressure (presence of hypertension)
Hyperthyroidism	Agitated depression, depression, anxiety, panic, delirium, psychosis; often mistaken for Bipolar Disorder	Goiter, red and puffy eyelids, bulging eyes, weakness, palpitations, hunger, tremor, warm, increased appetite with weight loss, diarrhea	Thyroid panel (blood test) to check for elevation of serum thyroxine levels and drop in thyroid stimulating hormone
Hypoglycemia	Anxiety, depersonalization, lethargy, fatigue	Sweating, palpitations, tremulousness, headache, confusion	Food diary, 5-hour fasting glucose tolerance test
Hypoparathyroidism (Hypocalcemia)	Irritability, mental retardation, depression, anxiety, paranoia, delirium, dementia	Numbness, tingling, and spasms in hands, feet, and throat; headaches; thin, patchy hair; poor tooth development	Blood test to establish low serum calcium and parathyroid hormone levels
Hypopituitarism	Apathy, indifference, fatigue, depression, decreased libido, drowsiness; often mistaken for Dependent Personality Disorder or psychotic depression	Waxy skin, loss of body hair, inability to tan, loss of appetite and weight, loss of nipple pigmentation, premature wrinkles around eyes and mouth	X-ray, CT scan, or MRI to establish structural pituitary abnormality; blood test to establish hormonal deficiencies

TABLE 2.1 *Continued*

Disorder	Psychological Symptoms	Physical Symptoms	Medical Tests
Hypothyroidism	Apathy, depression, suicidality, slowed cognitive function, dementia; mistaken for rapid-cycling Bipolar Disorder	Dry and brittle hair, dry skin, hair loss, edema, cold intolerance, appetite loss with weight gain, goiter, constipation, hoarseness, hearing loss, slow heartbeat	Blood test to establish drop in serum thyroxine and elevation in thyroid stimulating hormone levels; measurement of basal body temperature on five consecutive mornings
Lyme disease	Depression, psychosis, anxiety, mild cognitive symptoms	Headache, fever, chills, fatigue, stiff neck, malaise, achiness	History of tick bite, serum antibody response to B. Burgdorferi
Meniere's syndrome	Anxiety, panic, depression, poor concentration	Dizziness, nausea, vomiting, tinnitus (ringing in the ears), nystagmus (rapid, involuntary eyeball oscillation), deafness	Diagnosis based on symptoms
Mitral valve prolapse	Panic (do not use anxiolytics)	Chest pain, fainting, palpitations, breathlessness	Echocardiogram
Multiple sclerosis	Depression, mania, sudden emotionality, cognitive impairment, dementia; misdiagnosed as somatization or Histrionic Personality Disorder	Ataxia, numbness, weakness, fatigue, visual problems, incontinence, trouble walking, paresthesias (tingling or prickling of skin)	MRI to show areas of plaque; birthplace north of 55° latitude; hot bath test (weakness and faintness after hot bath)
Myasthenia gravis	Anxiety, memory loss, minor cognitive symptoms	Muscle weakness	Tensilon test (injection of edrophonium to check for briefly improved muscle strength)
Niacin deficiency (Pellagra)	Depression, anxiety, delirium, dementia	Weakness, anorexia, headache, diarrhea, red and rough skin	Food diary, based on symptoms, urine test
Pancreatic cancer	Depression, initial insomnia, crying spells, suicidality, anxiety, hypersomnia	Weight loss, weakness, abdominal pain, insomnia, hypersomnia	Ultrasound, CT scan, or endoscopic retrograde pancreatography; needle biopsy
Parkinson's disease	Depression, anxiety, impaired attention, cognitive deficits, paranoia; visual hallucinations as side effect of medications	Tremor, muscle rigidity, decreased mobility, masked facies, trouble walking, poor fine motor coordination	Based on symptoms and physical exam
Pernicious anemia	Forgetfulness, depression, dementia, psychosis	Anemia, dizziness, tinnitus, glossy tongue, palpitations	Blood test
Pheochromocytoma	Anxiety, panic	Headache, sweating, palpitations, nausea, high blood pressure	24-hour urine test for high catecholamine levels

(continued)

TABLE 2.1   *Continued*

Disorder	Psychological Symptoms	Physical Symptoms	Medical Tests
Porphyria	Depression, mania, euphoria, anxiety, delirium, psychosis	Abdominal pain, muscle weakness, tremors, dark urine, vomiting, seizures, sweating	Blood or urine test to check for high levels of porphobilinogen
Posterolateral sclerosis	Anxiety, weakness, memory impairment, psychosis; mistaken for Conversion Disorder	Heavy limbs, stocking and/or glove sensory loss, alteration in reflexes	Electromyography
Prion disease	Anxiety, fatigue, poor concentration, slowed mental function	Difficulty walking, tremors, muscle rigidity, hypokinesia (decreased muscle movement)	Electroencephalogram, history of ingestion of infected meat
Progressive supranuclear palsy	Slowed mental function, forgetfulness, apathy, labile mood	Double vision, unsteady gait, muscle stiffening	CT scan showing atrophy of pons and midbrain
Protein energy malnutrition	Apathy, lethargy, cognitive changes	Weight loss; loss of skin elasticity; dry, thin hair; low body temperature, heart rate, and blood pressure	Food diary, physical exam, blood test for low serum protein levels
Sleep apnea	Insomnia, depression, drowsiness, irritability, poor concentration	Snoring, morning headache, nocturia (nighttime urination)	Sleep polysomnography
Syphilis	Personality changes, fatigue, irritability, grandiosity, cognitive symptoms, psychosis	Ulcerous chancre, fever, headache, sore throat, skin rash, swollen lymph nodes	Serum screening test and serum fluorescent treponeme antibody absorption test
Systemic lupus erythematosus	Severe depression, cognitive symptoms, anorexia, psychosis (thorazine exacerbates symptoms)	Muscle and joint pain, butterfly rash, fatigue, fever, loss of appetite, nausea, vomiting, weight loss	Blood test to establish elevation of antinuclear antibodies
Thiamine deficiency (Beriberi)	Fatigue, irritability, anxiety, delirium, amnesia	Shortness of breath, edema, rapid heartbeat, nystagmus, trouble walking, fever, vomiting	History of alcoholism, food diary, MRI, CT scan, blood/urine tests
Wilson's disease (Inherited copper toxicosis)	Anxiety, personality change, irritability, anger, loss of inhibition, psychosis, depression, cognitive symptoms	Dysarthria, tremor, spasticity, rigidity, trouble swallowing, dystonia (poor tonicity of tissue), drooling	Liver function test (excess copper), blood tests (deficient copper-protein ceruloplasmin), MRI, CT scan

Source: From *Dealing with Challenges in Psychotherapy and Counseling,* 1st ed., by C. Brems © 2000. Reprinted with permission of Wadsworth, an imprint of Wadsworth Group, a division of Thomson Learning. Fax (800) 730-2215.

refers to the *client as patient* (Klonoff & Landrine, 1997). Obtaining *basic preliminary physical data* from the client also expedites the referral and increases the likelihood of correct medical diagnosis. Preliminary physical data may be gleaned through an interview and consists of information such as weight patterns, sleep patterns, changes in physical functioning, substance use, and specific physical symptoms and their context (Brems, 1999). The more physical data counselors can offer, the more seriously they and the referral will be taken by the physician (Klonoff & Landrine, 1997). Presenting this wealth of medical information in the most *concise and brief* manner, as opposed to embedded in a lengthy psychosocial history, will reap the greatest benefit (Diamond, 1998). Finally, it is important that counselors *never pretend to understand information* when in reality they do not. Asking questions to be informed about clients' medical conditions and the medical tests they may be facing is essential for optimal rapport. If counselors do not understand what their clients will encounter, they cannot help them prepare.

PLANNING TREATMENT AFTER A
COMPLETED MEDICAL REFERRAL

If the medical provider rules out physical or medical causes for the client's presenting concerns, the counselor makes a proper mental health treatment plan focusing on the client's psychological symptoms, comfortable in the knowledge that no medical concerns are present. If, however, an underlying medical diagnosis completely or partially causes the psychological symptoms, counselor and physician collaborate to determine the optimal course of action. Medical symptoms are best treated by the medical provider; however, the sequellae of having a medical disorder that has emotional consequences are best treated by the counselor. Psychological treatment with a client who has an underlying medical illness will be different from counseling a client with psychological symptoms without medical causes. For the client with both concerns, counseling requires different goals and will largely be influenced by the severity, acuity,

and chronicity of the medical illness. Close monitoring of the client's physical condition will be necessary, as will the counselor's need to learn more about the client's particular illness. Again, collaboration with the medical provider in this regard is emphasized.

References

Brems, C. (1999). *Psychotherapy: Processes and techniques.* Boston: Allyn & Bacon.

Brems, C. (2000). *Dealing with challenges in psychotherapy and counseling.* Pacific Grove, CA: Brooks/Cole.

Diamond, R.J. (1998). *Instant psychopharmacology: A guide for the nonmedical mental health professional.* New York: Norton.

Klonoff, E.A., & Landrine, H. (1997). *Preventing misdiagnosis of women: A guide to physical disorders that have psychiatric symptoms.* Thousand Oaks, CA: Sage.

Morrison, J. (1997). *When psychological problems mask medical disorders: A guide for psychotherapists.* New York: Guilford Press.

Samson, J.A., Levin, R.M., & Richardson, G.S. (1998). Psychological symptoms in endocrine disorders. In P.M. Kleespies (Ed.), *Emergencies in mental health practice* (pp. 332–354). New York: Guilford Press.

Tomb, D.A. (1995). *Psychiatry.* Baltimore: Williams & Wilkins.

White, R.F., Marans, K.S., & Krengel, M. (1998). Psychological/behavioral symptoms in neurological disorders. In P.M. Kleespies (Ed.), *Emergencies in mental health practice* (pp. 312–331). New York: Guilford Press.

Wickramasekera, I., Davies, T.E., & Davies, S.M. (1996). Applied psychophysiology: A bridge between the biomedical model and the biopsychosocial model in family medicine. *Professional Psychology: Research and Practice, 27,* 221–233.

COUNSELING WITH UNEMPLOYED AND UNDEREMPLOYED CLIENTS

Ellen B. Lent

And when we have time on our hands,
We have a pastime
Wherein we try to have a good time,
Even a grand time,
Or perhaps the time of our life.

(Bolles, 2000, p. xii)

In the best of all worlds, our work is the time of our life. The emotional experience of satisfying work may protect us from negative mental health outcomes and physical health complaints (Lent, 1995). When work fails to be the time of our clients' lives, a counseling intervention may be useful. The purpose of this chapter is to focus attention on what is known about responsible and ethical practices in counseling adult clients who have lost a job or who complain of being underemployed.

Underemployment is defined here as less-than-optimum use of an individual's capacities at work. Possible companions of underemployment include boredom and loss of dignity (Hansen, 1997), uncertainty (Landy, 1992), anxiety (Osipow & Fitzgerald, 1996), and low self-confidence (Shullman & Carder, 1983). Depression, anxiety, substance use, and other unwanted behaviors have been seen with chronic and acute joblessness and job dissatisfaction (Locke & Latham, 1990). *Unwanted unemployment* and underemployment can themselves be life stressors and can reduce people's ability to handle other stressors. In addition, the absence of income is an important stressor for most unemployed clients.

Concepts related to unemployed and underemployed individuals fall into one of the following categories: *internal*, or unique to the person; and *external*, including availability of work, development opportunities, bias and other unjust barriers related to clients' demographic features, and access to technology.

INTERNAL ISSUES

Factors often included in models of job and career psychology include interests, values, skills, decisiveness, and maturity. When a client is at liberty to choose among available and attractive work options, these factors can be very useful in counseling. However, when clients are in distress about work, additional internal factors such as well-being, self-efficacy, work strain, and other emotional and cognitive stressors may be more prominent.

Well-being is defined as the belief that one is living a good and worthwhile life, accompanied by the presence of positive feelings and the relative absence of negative feelings (Diener, 2000). Job satisfaction is a component of well-being. Satisfaction with one's job, more than working conditions or supervision, may be closely related to clients' mental health (Osipow & Fitzgerald, 1996).

A facet of well-being relevant to work roles is the ability to be flexible in setting goals. Because becoming and staying employed relies partly on factors outside of one's individual control, the willingness to adjust and change goals is an important factor in difficult circumstances (Diener, 2000). How people adapt to changing conditions helps to indicate their ability to benefit from counseling and reach their goals.

Clients' level of *self-efficacy,* or belief in their ability to complete certain actions, can indicate their willingness to engage in a job search. They may doubt their own competence and worth and question their ability to find a new job or improve their present working conditions. Underemployed clients may believe that their talents are not valued. Job search self-efficacy has been found to predict actual job searching better than general self-esteem and sense of control (Saks & Ashforth, 1999). The setting of specific goals and a belief in positive outcomes are important aspects of job search self-efficacy that may help predict the success of counseling interventions.

Reduced self-efficacy and self-esteem can interfere with individuals' plans to identify and act on their interests in the workplace (Betz, 1999). If clients are not confident of their "match" with particular jobs or work settings, they risk giving up in the face of barriers such as discrimination or lack of training.

Work strain refers to problems with work tasks, demands, and relationships. It can include being over- or underworked; having conflict in work relationships, feeling unprepared for new work tasks, and having multiple demands at work and in other life roles. Workers with outdated skills may describe being underutilized or bored. Clients may sometimes report lack of interest when they are actually feeling depressed or anxious about their work or the upcoming job search. Use of caffeine and nicotine may alleviate boredom due to monotonous work tasks (Landy, 1992).

Other Emotional and Cognitive Stressors

A significant proportion of recipients of public assistance are homeless, have chronic physical or mental health problems or drug or alcohol problems, and are survivors of serious abuse (Edwards, Rachal, & Dixon, 1999). Intellectual and cognitive deficits may be present as well. Because many of these adults are now entering the workforce, it is more likely that counselors will see these issues in clients presenting with employment concerns. In addition, the loss of a job or chronic underemployment may be stressful enough to contribute to a depressed or anxious mood, behavior disruptions, and other negative symptoms.

The state of being employed can itself be significant: "Almost any type of work, regardless of how much of an underload or overload it represents, has the capacity to relieve depression in some people" (Landy, 1992, p. 137). Unemployment can precipitate depression, anxiety, substance abuse, and other serious disorders in some people.

For clients experiencing an unwanted job loss or chronic underemployment, searching for a new position may propel them into counseling. After issues such as those above are resolved or ruled out, general factors in job transition are useful to address.

Interests

There is a huge literature on assessing and measuring vocational interests, underscoring the perceived importance of interests when counseling adults on work transitions. Interests are measured by a variety of available inventories that can help clients to "focus attention, arouse feelings, and steer a direction" (Savickas & Spokane, 1999, p. 6). The reliability and validity of interest inventories for various cultural and ethnic groups is still under study. Interests can also be assessed by card sorts and other methods of self-report (cf. Peterson, 1998). Research has amply demonstrated their stability—and there is a strong genetic component to individual interests (cf. Betsworth & Fouad, 1997; Swanson & Gore, 2000)—but it is not yet known how much change in interests is possible over time and across different activity settings. Understanding clients' interests does not tell the entire story in a counseling intervention. Individual *values* are also important factors in work transition. Status, comfort, and safety may rank higher than altruism, achievement, and autonomy in a job change decision, citing one set of values often applied to the work setting (Dawis & Lofquist, 1984). The role of meaning in work also plays a part in many people's cognitive and emotional responses to unwanted job loss or underutilization.

People's *skill* levels are often deduced by examining test scores, academic grades, letters of reference, and other unique indicators. Standardized scores of aptitude and achievement are also used in some settings. Prediction of future job performance can be attempted by these means, but concerns exist about the effects on disadvantaged job candidates (Osipow & Fitzgerald, 1996). The variable nature of performance appraisals in the workplace, with multiple raters of uncertain quality and motivation, makes skill level a factor that may straddle internal and external categories. It is clear, however, that ability and skill feedback contributes importantly to people's self-concepts and beliefs about their work interests and choices.

The level of *decidedness* with which clients approach job and career choice has received significant attention. Less is known about the role of decidedness in adults who have been employed but are seeking a new job. Theories of coping methods in responding to chronic stress include an emphasis on decision making (cf. Folkman & Moskowitz, 2000). Indecisiveness can signal emotional conflicts or obstacles to making choices (Savickas, 1996). Self-efficacy for making decisions can help or hinder the process; for instance, beliefs in one's ability to find acceptable job options and choose among them predicts employment (Saks & Ashforth, 1999).

A well-known definition of *vocational maturity* encompasses a number of tasks relevant to choosing an occupation or work setting. Defined by Donald Super and his colleagues, it includes an evaluation of interests, behaviors, values, and knowledge said to aid in vocational planning and choice (Thompson, Lindeman, Super, Jordaan, & Myers, 1981).

EXTERNAL ISSUES

A variety of factors external to clients may impact on counseling assessment and treatment. *Availability of work* is relevant to everyone, but is even more important as the U.S. and the global economy shift further toward information technology and biotechnology and away from manufacturing and many service occupations. Two million white-collar jobs change dramatically or disappear in the United States every year, and a significant number of blue-collar jobs incorporate new levels of computer-related skills (Rifkin, 1995).

Access to job networks and promotional opportunities is a crucial factor relevant to counseling the unemployed and underemployed. Bias, discrimination, and other barriers can affect a significant proportion of hopeful workers. Persons of low social class represent one such vulnerable group. A home address from a poor neighborhood can destine a job application for the recycling bin (Wilson, 1996). Discrimination on the basis of age, gender, race, disability, sexual orientation, and other demographics renders many others vulnerable as well. These conditions can lower self-efficacy and expectations for success.

Access to learning and new skill development is crucial to remaining employable and having a positive work experience. Persons reporting no on-the-job development, training, or learning are at risk of unemployment or underemployment due to skill obsolescence.

Technology access increasingly dictates the amount of job information available and the speed with which it is obtained. Many potential employers request resumes strictly by electronic transmission, containing key words that are recognizable by computer programs that route them to the most appropriate recipient. With sufficient economic means, people can subscribe to services that remotely search job listings throughout the World Wide Web, delivering the most relevant openings directly to their e-mail address on a daily basis. Clients with little or no technology access may be left out of this avenue of job searching.

Social support has been shown to reduce the effects of stress in many different domains. Gaining the support of important others is a significant aspect of lessening the stress and overcoming the barriers of underemployment and unemployment. It has been suggested that aiding clients in finding and gathering supportive others yields more benefit than focusing on removing barriers in job search and work transitions (Brown & Krane, 2000).

COUNSELING PROCESS FACTORS

What counselors bring to the counseling relationship—their assumptions, values, methods, and intervention choices—deserve mention in this discussion. Evaluating clients nondirectively aids in keeping counselor biases and assumptions at a minimum (Lent, 1996). Structural obstacles such as discrimination must be explored from the client's perspective. The type of intervention recommended may be highly informational, highly therapeutic, or a combination of both. Counselors may find that collaboration with bachelor's-level career development facilitators (Splete & Hoppin, 2000) and other trained personnel works to their advantage in efficient provision of services.

Confidentiality and privacy must be clearly described and carefully guarded, especially when telephone or computer lines are involved (including telephone counseling and coaching and inventories completed via Web sites). The validity and reliability of inventories and other instruments must be determined and delivered by those trained and competent in their use.

There is some evidence that in establishing and maintaining a counseling relationship, the focus on a specific task and goals for clients to accomplish is of greater import than a therapeutic bond between counselor and client (Warwar & Greenberg, 2000). On the other hand, a resurgence of interest in therapeutic empathy encourages focus on counselor-client interactions. Narrative counseling techniques highlight the stories that clients tell and suggest methods for actively "writing" new portions in the context of counseling.

COUNSELING RECOMMENDATIONS

One definition of counseling for work concerns encompasses a number of the themes mentioned in this chapter: "Helping people make goal-congruent work or career choices that will allow them to experience work,

career, and life satisfaction in a changing society" (Brown & Krane, 2000, p. 740). A client-centered assessment aids in understanding the full scope of clients' needs, goals, satisfiers, and interests in the world of work. It can also encourage discussion of external and internal obstacles that may be holding clients back from feeling confident and taking action. Counselors can evaluate sense of competence or self-efficacy by asking clients if they believe they can perform actual job search behaviors, such as revising a resume or finding job leads. This can lead to specific action steps that should improve clients' belief in their abilities.

Counselors can initiate discussion of bias, discrimination, and other societal obstacles in their assessment. Expectations about salary, benefits, promotion and training opportunities, and level of autonomy or responsibility may be affected by clients' social class, race, gender, age, and other demographic features.

Many clients seeking work transition counseling expect to be given testing, which will indicate their best work choices. Placing responsibility for this process on an external resource can be indicative of anxiety regarding the task. Because a major cause of early termination from career counseling is anxiety, it is advisable to engage clients in a thorough assessment and explore potential emotional barriers before embarking on a structured exploration of interests, skills, and work values. At the end of this process, the match between clients' needs and talents should be maximized, "so that their aspirations are aimed as high as their ability will take them" (Brown & Krane, 2000, p. 751).

Two Notes of Caution

Clients may inform you that they have completed career inventories on the Internet and that they have taken action based on the results. Remote administration of these instruments can be fraught with pitfalls (cf. Sampson & Lumsden, 2000):

• Clients' unique issues may not have been assessed initially.

- The norm groups for the instrument may not represent the client demographically.
- The person who administered or scored the instrument may not be adequately trained.
- Clients may have completed the instrument in an environment not conducive to reliable results; for instance, with interruptions or other challenges to concentration.
- Clients' privacy may not have been protected, and they may begin to receive unsolicited marketing materials linked to their individual responses.
- The inventory results might not have been reported in a way that allowed clients' full understanding or follow-up discussion.

A second cautionary topic is the unanswered question of the long-term usefulness of counseling adults in work transitions. Studies have shown that people using counseling and allied services are more satisfied with job choice, values clarification, and other immediate outcomes. However, research has not effectively demonstrated that people who obtain career or job counseling are more satisfied with their work, their life, or other related outcomes in the long run (Brown & Krane, 2000). This question deserves further study to determine the ideal amount of effort that should be expended on program design, counseling processes, structured activities and instruments, and other services designed to help people have the time of their lives in the workplace.

Tests and Inventories

Published instruments often enrich the counseling process for clients who have minimal conflicts and obstacles. Among the many instruments in use for adults making work transitions, the following titles may be useful after a careful assessment:

Adult Career Concerns Inventory (Super, Thompson, & Lindeman (1987).

Campbell Interests and Skills Survey (Campbell, 1994).

Career Attitudes and Strategies Inventory—Career Obstacles Checklist and Job

Satisfaction Scale (Holland & Gottfredson, 1994).

Career Decision-Making Self-Efficacy Scale (Betz, Klein, & Taylor, 1996).

Kuder Career Search (Zytowski, 1999).

Myers-Briggs Type Indicator (Myers, Mc-Cauley, Quenk, & Hammer, 1998).

Occupational Stress Inventory (Osipow & Spokane, 1987).

Self-Directed Search (Holland, 1994).

Strong Interest Inventory (Strong, Hansen, & Campbell, 1994).

Card sorts offer another structured way for counselors and clients to explore occupational interests. Manipulating cards with occupational titles can provide a novel activity in the counseling process. The following titles may be useful:

Deal Me In Cards (Farren, Kaye, & Leibowitz, 1985).

Occupational Interest Card Sort (Knowdell, 1993).

Missouri Occupational Card Sort (Krieshok, Hansen, & Johnston, 1989).

Slaney Vocational Card Sort (Slaney, 1978).

Vocational Exploration and Insight Kit (Holland & Associates, 1980).

Other resources worthy of attention follow:

Careerhub: www.careerhub.org. This Web site was designed in consultation with the University of California, Berkeley, as a stand-alone resource for career and job searchers. It offers free inventories that do not require a trained counselor's interpretation and provides guidance on when to seek a counselor. Access to copyrighted instruments and materials is available for a fee.

Joint special issue, *The Career Development Quarterly* and *The Journal of Employment Counseling:* Collaboration, Partnership, Policy, and Practice in Career Development. 48, June 2000: National Career Development Association.

Special issue, *Journal of Career Assessment: Career Assessment and the Internet.* 8, Winter 2000: Psychological Assessment Resources, Inc.

Handbook of Career Counseling Theory and Practice (2000). Edited by M.L. Savickas and W.B. Walsh. Palo Alto: Davies-Black.

What Color Is Your Parachute? (2000). Richard Bolles. Berkeley, CA: Ten Speed Press.

SUMMARY

Clients can report significant difficulty facing the stressors of underemployment or unemployment. Although not enough is known about the long-term effects of counseling for these issues, it is highly desirable to do a complete assessment and intervene promptly, addressing both internal and external factors related to work transitions. When emotionally ready, clients can benefit from structured adjuncts in counseling and targeted discussion of supports and obstacles to achieving satisfaction in their work lives.

References

Bettsworth, D.G., & Fouad, N.A. (1997). Vocational interests: A look at the past 70 years and a glance at the future. *Career Development Quarterly, 46,* 23–47.

Betz, N.E. (1999). Getting clients to act on their interests: Self-efficacy as a mediator of the implementation of vocational interests. In M.L. Savickas & A.R. Spokane (Eds.), *Vocational interests: Meaning, measurement and counseling use* (pp. 327–344). Palo Alto, CA: Davies-Black.

Betz, N.E., Klein, K.L., & Taylor, K.M. (1996). Evaluation of a short form of the Career Decision-Making Self-Efficacy Scale. *Journal of Career Assessment, 1,* 21–34.

Bolles, R.N. (2000). *What color is your parachute? A practical manual for job-hunters and career-changers.* Berkeley, CA: Ten Speed Press.

Brown, S.E., & Krane, N.E.R. (2000). Four (or five) sessions and a cloud of dust: Old assumptions and new observations about career counseling. In S.D. Brown & R.W. Lent (Eds.), *Handbook of counseling psychology* (3rd ed., pp. 740–766). New York: Wiley.

Campbell, D.P. (1994). *The Campbell Interests and Skills Survey.* Minneapolis, MN: National Computer Systems.

Dawis, R.V., & Lofquist, L.H. (1984). *A psychological theory of work adjustment: An individual-differences model and its applications.* Minneapolis: University of Minnesota Press.

Diener, E. (2000). Subjective well-being: The science of happiness and a proposal for a national index. *American Psychologist, 55,* 34–43.

Edwards, S.A., Rachal, K.C., & Dixon, D.N. (1999). Counseling psychology and welfare reform: Implications and opportunities. *The Counseling Psychologist, 27,* 263–284.

Farren, C., Kaye, B., & Leibowitz, Z. (1985). *Deal me in.* Silver Spring, MD: Career Systems.

Folkman, S., & Moskowitz, J.T. (2000). Positive affect and the other side of coping. *American Psychologist, 55,* 647–654.

Hansen, L.S. (1997). *Integrative life planning: Critical tasks for career development and changing life patterns.* San Francisco: Jossey-Bass.

Holland, J.L. (1994). *Self-directed search.* Odessa, FL: Psychological Assessment Resources.

Holland, J.L., & Gottfredson, G.D. (1994). *Career Attitudes and Strategies Inventory: An inventory for understanding adult careers.* Odessa, FL: Psychological Assessment Resources.

Holland, J.L., & Associates. (1980). *Counselor's guide to the Vocational Exploration and Insight Kit (VEIK).* Palo Alto, CA: Consulting Psychologists Press.

Knowdell, R.L. (1993). *Manual for Occupational Interests Card Sort Kit.* San Jose, CA: Career Research and Testing.

Krieshok, T.S., Hansen, R.N., & Johnston, J.A. (1989). *Missouri Occupational Card Sort manual.* Columbia: University of Missouri, Career Planning and Placement Center.

Landy, F.J. (1992). Work design and stress. In G.P. Keita & S.L. Sauter (Eds.), *Work and well-being: An agenda for the 1990s* (pp. 119–158). Washington, DC: American Psychological Association.

Lent, E.B. (1995, August). *Worklife efficacy: Prevention and intervention.* Paper presented at the third conference on Work Stress and Health, American Psychological Association and National Institute for Occupational Safety and Health, Washington, DC.

Lent, E.B. (1996). The person focus in career theory and practice. In M.L. Savickas & W.B. Walsh (Eds.), *Handbook of career counseling theory and practice* (pp. 109–120). Palo Alto, CA: Davies-Black.

Locke, E.A., & Latham, G.P. (1990). Work motivation and satisfaction: Light at the end of the tunnel. *Psychological Science, 1,* 240–246.

Myers, I.B., McCaulley, M.H., Quenk, N.L., & Hammer, A.L. (1998). *Myers-Briggs Type Indicator manual.* Palo Alto, CA: Consulting Psychologists Press.

Osipow, S.H., & Fitzgerald, L.F. (1996). *Theories of career development* (4th ed.). Boston: Allyn & Bacon.

Osipow, S.H., & Spokane, A.R. (1987). *Occupational Stress Inventory manual, research version.* Odessa, FL: Psychological Assessment Resources.

Peterson, G.W. (1998). Using a vocational card sort as an assessment of occupational knowledge. *Journal of Career Assessment, 6,* 49–67.

Rifkin, J. (1995). *The end of work: The decline of the global labor force and the dawn of the post-market era.* New York: Putnam.

Saks, A.M., & Ashforth, B.E. (1999). Effects of individual differences and job search behaviors on the employment status of recent university graduates. *Journal of Vocational Behavior, 54,* 335–349.

Saks, A.M., & Ashforth, B.E. (2000). Change in job search behaviors and employment outcomes. *Journal of Vocational Behavior, 56,* 277–287.

Sampson, J.P., Jr., & Lumsden, J.A. (2000). Ethical issues in the design and use of internet-based career assessment. *Journal of Career Assessment, 8,* 21–35.

Savickas, M.L. (1996). A framework for linking career theory and practice. In M.L. Savickas & W.B. Walsh (Eds.), *Handbook of career counseling theory and practice* (pp. 191–208). Palo Alto, CA: Davies-Black.

Savickas., M.L., & Spokane, A.R. (Eds.). (1999). *Vocational interests: Meaning, measurement and counseling use.* Palo Alto, CA: Davies-Black.

Shullman, S.L., & Carder, C.E. (1983). Vocational psychology in industrial settings. In W.B. Walsh & S.H. Osipow (Eds.), *Handbook of vocational psychology: Applications* (Vol. 2, pp. 141–180). Hillsdale, NJ: Erlbaum.

Slaney, R.B. (1978). Expressed and inventoried vocational interests: A comparison of instruments. *Journal of Counseling Psychology, 25,* 520–529.

Splete, H.H., & Hoppin, J.M. (2000). The emergence of career development facilitators. *Career Development Quarterly, 48,* 340–347.

Strong, E.K., Jr., Hansen, J.C., & Campbell, D. (1994). *Strong Interest Inventory.* Palo Alto, CA: Consulting Psychologists Press.

Super, D., Thompson, A., & Lindeman, R. (1987). *Manual for the Adult Career Concerns Inventory.* Palo Alto, CA: Consulting Psychologists Press.

Swanson, J.L., & Gore, P.A., Jr. (2000). Advances in vocational theory and research. In S.D. Brown & R.W. Lent (Eds.), *Handbook of counseling psychology* (3rd ed., pp. 233–269). New York: Wiley.

Thompson, A.S., Lindeman, R.H., Super, D.E., Jordaan, J.P., & Myers, R.A. (1981). *Career development inventory: Users manual.* Palo Alto, CA: Consulting Psychologists Press.

Warwar, S., & Greenberg, L.S. (2000). Advances in theories of change and counseling. In S.D. Brown & R.W. Lent (Eds.), *Handbook of counseling psychology* (3rd ed., pp. 571–600). New York: Wiley.

Watts, A.G. (2000). Career development and public policy. *Career Development Quarterly, 48,* 301–312.

Wilson, W.J. (1996). When work disappears: The world of the new urban poor. New York: Alfred A. Knopf.

Zytowski, D. (1999). *Kuder career search: Preview manual.* Adel, IA: National Career Assessment Services.

4 EFFECTIVE COLLEGE COUNSELING

Neal E. Lipsitz

The primary goal of the college environment is to promote learning and growth in students; such personal change requires adjustment, and the unique role of college counselors is to assist students in dealing with the developmental challenges that accompany personal growth. (Davis & Humphrey, 2000, p. 43)

COLLEGE COUNSELING CENTER MISSIONS AND FUNCTIONS

Addressing college counseling as a whole is difficult because just as every institution of higher education is distinct, so is every college counseling center. Counseling centers differ according to the type of college in which they reside (four-year/two-year, public/private, large/small), the school's mission, and the resources available to them. Five distinct types of centers were first identified by Whiteley, Mahaffey, and Geer (1987):

1. *Macrocenter.* Provides a wide range of clinical services such as personal and career counseling and testing, along with special functions including training and consultation with limited advising.
2. *Career planning and placement.* Career-oriented services with minimal counseling and other functions.
3. *Counseling orientation.* Similar to macrocenters but with fewer career services.
4. *General-level service.* Wider functions including "dean of students"-type functions, more services to a greater number of students than a conventional counseling center.

5. *Minimal service.* Minimal service provided in all areas.

More recently, however, Stone and Archer (1990) emphasize the wide variation in college counseling center design and function even within each category. For example, variation occurs when centers of the same type operate from different theoretical orientations (e.g., psychodynamic vs. cognitive-behavioral) or with various service limits (e.g., short-term vs. open-ended treatment modalities).

Because college counseling centers are not independent operations and serve only members of a college community, their success in meeting the needs of the community depends on the degree to which they focus their activities to mesh with the mission of the particular college (Bishop, 1991). Clearly, centers themselves also need an explicitly articulated philosophy to function well. As these philosophies are set in the context of different institutional histories, mission statements, and service offerings, counseling centers necessarily differ significantly.

Finally, there is great variation in college students themselves. Some schools are more homogeneously populated (e.g., in terms of student ages and cultural backgrounds) and others are more diverse. Because counseling centers must meet the needs of the students they serve, this too contributes to the differences among them.

Regardless of this variability, essential roles and functions for college counseling centers have been articulated and standardized. For example, the Standards and Guidelines for

Counseling Programs and Services by the Council for the Advancement of Standards in Higher Education (CAS, 1997) outline three major functions for college counseling centers: developmental, remedial, and preventive. The developmental function is aimed at helping students mature and succeed academically; the remedial function is designed to provide professional clinical services to students with significant personal adjustment problems; and the preventive function focuses on neutralizing environmental conditions that interfere with student welfare. The Accreditation Standards for University and College Counseling Centers by the International Association of Counseling Services (IACS) (Kiracofe et al., 1994) parallel those listed above. Stone and Archer (1990), CAS (1997), and IACS (Kiracofe et al., 1994) also suggest more specific recommendations, including consultation and outreach to a variety of groups in the campus community, staff development, crisis intervention, psychological and career testing, research, and evaluation of services.

THE SCOPE AND INTENSITY OF STUDENT NEEDS AND PROBLEMS

College students typically bring four kinds of issues with them to the college experience (Chandler & Gallagher, 1996):

> *Personal and social adjustment issues* involving relationship difficulties, self-esteem, existential concerns, depression, sexual abuse and harassment.
>
> *Academic and career concerns.*
>
> *Stress and psychosomatic symptoms,* including anxiety.
>
> *Distressing symptoms* related to substance abuse, sexual dysfunction, eating disorders, and unusual behavior.

Generally, the most prevalent issues include relationship difficulties, depression, anxiety, low self-esteem, stress, academic problems, and career concerns (Chandler & Gallagher, 1996). Even college counseling centers with

fairly homogeneous student populations now find themselves challenged by the array of student problems because students on every campus today show a wider range of previous life experiences, cultural backgrounds, socioeconomic levels, interests, needs, developmental issues, and family structures. For example, a 31-year-old immigrant from Cambodia with a full-time job, an extended family to help support, and English as a second language is a more likely member of the first-year class today than in the past. In addition, a greater proportion of students are likely to have experienced mental health problems prior to college and to have sought professional help for those problems, including the use of medications (Altschuler, 2000). A recent study by the World Health Organization (2000) that examined 30,000 people from seven countries concluded that mental disorders are, in fact, becoming more widespread across every age level. The Cooperative Institutional Research Program survey (Sax, Astin, Korn, & Mahoney, 2000) found that among first-year students a sense of being "frequently" overwhelmed has grown steadily over the past 15 years (from 16% in 1985 to 31% in 1999).

Whether psychopathology among college students is truly more common has been extensively debated in the professional literature (Erickson Cornish, Riva, Henderson, Kominars, & McIntosh, 2000; Gilbert, 1992; O'Malley, Wheeler, Murphey, O'Connell, & Waldo, 1990; Pledge, Lapan, Heppner, Kivlighan, & Roehlke, 1998; Sharkin, 1997; Stone & Archer, 1990). R. Gallagher, Gill, and Sysko's (2000) survey of counseling center directors revealed that 222 of 286 (77.6%) believed that severe psychological problems have increased in students over the past five years. On the other hand, Pledge, et al., (1998) found that levels of student psychopathology had not increased since the late 1980s in their study of 2,000 college students between 1989 and 1995. These authors do suggest, however, that the mental health issues college students present to college counselors have become more consistently severe since the late 1980s. Sharkin (1997) argued that increased pathology in college students is not supported by empirical data but is actually a reflection of the perception of college mental health clinicians. Cornish et al. (2000) concluded that it was not the overall level of distress of students that had increased, but a small increase in the amount of extremely distressed students accounted for the perceptions of a widespread increase in psychopathology among staff. Intuitively, this argument makes a lot of sense given the greater overall diversity of college students today, their varied backgrounds, and their potential for previous emotional health issues. A common challenge for college counselors today, then, is the successful management of what is perceived to be, and may in fact be, a more demanding clinical caseload than in the past (Davis & Humphrey, 2000; Stone & Archer, 1990).

Whatever the true figure for its frequency, effective treatment for students who present more serious psychopathology is possible only if counseling center staff are adequately trained to conduct thorough assessment, treatment planning, and direct intervention. Otherwise, referral into the community, or even refusal to treat, may be more in keeping with the best interests of the client. Moreover, the need for psychiatric consultation remains high for both assessment of psychopathology and medication evaluation/monitoring.

COMPETENCIES AND CHALLENGES FACING COLLEGE COUNSELORS

A related challenge is created by the breadth of service expected of college counseling center staff. The demands of clinical work are strong, yet it would not be prudent for staff to sit behind closed doors and wait for students to appear. In fact, a wide array of competencies are required of counseling center staff. Spooner, in Davis and Humphrey (2000), suggests that college counselors need to be professionally trained, multiculturally and technologically competent, creative at problem solving, and capable of maintaining their own physical, emotional, and spiritual equilibrium. Because of the increased diversity of the student body, Archer and Cooper (1998)

identify a number of specific populations with whom college counselors need to exhibit competency:

Multicultural/international students.

Students with learning disabilities and attention deficits.

Older and nontraditional students, especially women returning to education.

Gay, lesbian, bisexual, and transgendered students.

College counselors also need the ability to be effective consultants to faculty, staff, parents, and the community, to provide meaningful and effective outreach to the campus community, and to provide helpful career counseling for students making the school-to-work transition. The suggestion that college counseling centers "move beyond the therapy office" is an often echoed theme (Davis & Humphrey, 2000; Stone & Archer, 1990; P. Gallagher & Demos, 1983) because it is so crucial to success in the competencies listed above. When students see staff doing outreach, consultation, crisis intervention, training, and the like, they tend to feel more comfortable about using the counseling center. This may be especially true for students from diverse cultural backgrounds, for whom trust may be more easily established after a significant exposure on a more informal basis. In other words, the major benefit from outreach is that it provides multiple ports of entry to the counseling center.

SPECIAL ETHICAL CHALLENGES IN COLLEGE COUNSELING

The diverse roles of the college counselor and the closed nature of the community this profession services present several important ethical challenges. Dual relationships are a distinct hazard, especially for counselors playing more than one role on campus (e.g., also teaching, advising a student organization, living on campus). Counselors must be cognizant of their role in each setting and set appropriate boundaries around their immediate interactions with students. Maintaining confidentiality can be challenging when parents, deans, professors, or concerned peers are looking for information regarding a student they care about. If confidentiality is not adequately explained to other campus professionals, counselors can appear to be uncooperative and difficult. "Duty to warn" can provide a potential safeguard for a third party when a client reveals that he or she is immanently going to hurt the third party physically. Amada (1994) speaks to the unique issues that arise when college administrators refer disruptive students to the campus counseling center. Attempts to enact mandatory counseling by deans, judicial affairs officers, alcohol education personnel, and residence life staff, for example, are probably best met with offers to provide "information sessions" to these students if they would like to find out what the counseling center has to offer them. The guiding principle is to protect the privacy and dignity of the students as the highest priority but also to recognize the rights and responsibilities of faculty and administrators to the campus community.

INNOVATIONS AND EMERGING ISSUES

Brief therapy is a mode that has shown some efficacy in helping college counselors deal with the demand for services (Archer & Cooper, 1998). Even clients with more serious presenting problems appear to benefit from this approach, at least as a way to become prepared for more extensive therapy. And brief intermittent therapy is a natural approach for college students, as they are in a position to work on various issues in short order as they progress through their college years. In fact, the National Survey of Counseling Center Directors (P. Gallagher, Gill, Goldstrohm & Sysko, 1999) indicated that the average number of sessions per client was five, whether or not session limits were in place. As a fairly standard finding across college counseling centers nationwide, this statistic illustrates the developmental readiness that enables

most college students to resolve rather quickly the problems that brought them into counseling. Of course, some college students are seen for longer-term counseling, and although that group generally uses up a relatively large portion of staff resources, they also represent a relatively small portion of each center's clinical population.

Crisis intervention plays a central role in the services rendered by college counseling centers. When students are in the midst of emotional crises (e.g., psychotic breaks, suicidal gestures or attempts, major grief reactions, sexual assaults, substance abuse crises), the campus community looks to professional staff from the counseling center to intervene. Therefore, it is imperative that an effective crisis response system be in place. This is often accomplished through a pager system enabling at least one member of the counseling center staff to be accessible at all times. Following a major catastrophe on campus (e.g., death of a student, multiple deaths in an accident, residence hall fire), it is helpful to have a crisis-catastrophic emergency and postvention plan. Counseling center staff should be prepared to play a central role in the response to such events. Of the 311 counseling center directors surveyed by P. Gallagher et al. (1999), 214 (70.4%) had a procedure in place for dealing with such incidents. A common model of response to traumatic incidents that can be adapted for use on a college campus is the Critical Incident Stress Management model (Mitchell & Everly, 1993).

College counseling centers have long been committed to viewing student issues in the context of the life transitions students are experiencing. This developmental perspective assumes that students approach their problems in a manner that is consistent with their level of development. Our job as college counselors, then, is to help students mature as they progress through the transitional issues they are facing. This is a health-oriented perspective rather than a psychopathological one. For example, first-year college students are generally dealing with issues related to leaving home and establishing a life independent of their families. Sophomores, having left the novelty of first year behind, can feel lost, not knowing what direction to choose academically and/or relationally as they work to define themselves intrapersonally. Juniors often begin to feel the press of their adult lives after college starting to make an impact and deal with issues of commitment to potential career paths as well as relationships. Seniors, for whom graduation is in sight, often deal with issues related to leaving their college lives behind, moving into their career, and facing financial independence.

Counseling centers have long been encouraged to engage in research for accountability purposes (Stone & Archer, 1990). Bishop (1991) suggested that "successful efforts at strategic planning will . . . require the systematic collection of data about what a counseling center staff actually does and how well it performs its functions" (p. 408). He goes on to suggest that maintaining a database for self-study can help clarify problem areas so they can then be rectified. At a more basic level, data are necessary so that counseling centers can describe their activities to the decision makers at their institutions as well as understand student culture and the related demand on counseling services (Bishop, 1995).

In their follow-up to Stone and Archer's article on the challenges that college and university counseling centers faced in the 1990s, Guinee and Ness (2000) indicated that counseling centers are paying increased attention to accountability issues. They also report that centers can no longer compete for tight resources simply through data on students served or evidence of high levels of client satisfaction. These authors suggest that centers must assess the efficacy of their practices, study the demographics of their clients, and chart the actual severity of problem presentations in counseling center clients. However, Guinee and Ness also point out that little progress has actually been made in conducting systematic research in these areas over the past 15 years. More centers are beginning to use outcome questionnaires such as the Outcome Questionnaire-45.2 (OQ-45.2) (Lambert et al., 1996) or the Psychotherapy Outcome Assessment and Monitoring System (POAMS) (Kopta & Lowry, 2000). As this practice continues, along with the need to conduct needs assessments of students, perhaps increased attention to accountability issues will translate into informative research in this area.

Counseling centers will also need to assess the effectiveness of the many innovations that seem to be developing into standard practice. For example, national mental health screening days are more common on college campuses every year, and the breadth of screenings is increasing. Many campuses now offer depression, anxiety, alcohol, and eating disorders screening days on a yearly basis. Currently, little independent research on the impact of these events has been conducted.

Partnerships between college counseling centers and community agencies account for another innovation. To provide adequate services to students presenting with substance abuse, eating disorders, or sexual assault issues, ancillary services in the community are often warranted. Such services may include:

- A substance abuse center with detoxification capabilities for substance abusing students.
- Nutritional counseling, medical monitoring, and a support group for eating disordered students.
- Medical and legal resources for student survivors of sexual assault through contacts with the local hospital, the rape crisis center, or the sexual assault unit of the local police department.

Still another innovation is related to increased accessibility of mental health providers on campus. Recognizing that students do not function on an ordinary, business hours schedule, counseling centers are having success meeting student needs by expanding hours of operation. Accessibility is further extended with a 24-hour, seven days/week emergency coverage system with a pager service and counseling center Web site with links that can provide psychoeducation to an unlimited number of students anytime anyone is interested. Examples of Web sites that include relevant information about college student mental health issues are:

- Dr. Bob's Mental Health Links at the University of Chicago (www.uhs.bsd.uchicago.edu/~bhsiung/mental.html).
- Counseling Center Village at the University of Buffalo, with links to university and college counseling center Web sites worldwide, self-help Web pages, and a virtual pamphlet collection (www.ub-counseling.buffalo.edu/ccv.html).
- Self-help brochures at the University of Illinois at Urbana-Champaign (www.couns.uiuc.edu/brochure.htm).

Clearly, computer technology accounts for a large proportion of the recent innovations in college counseling. Computer list-serves, such as the directors' list-serve of the Association of University and College Counseling Center Directors (AUCCCD), are an example of computer-based innovations. Davis and Humphrey (2000) point out various forms of high-technology communications that have the potential to extend counseling service delivery itself if counselors adopt them (e.g., chat rooms, bulletin boards, Web sites, e-mail, Web counseling, and simultaneous audio and video transmission).

RESOURCES FOR COLLEGE COUNSELORS

How can college counselors keep up with developments in the field of college mental health? As is true with all professions, the professional associations and related journals are excellent sources of information. Organizations worth joining include the American Psychological Association (APA), the American Counseling Association (ACA), and the American College Health Association (ACHA). Of specific interest in APA is Division 17, which is devoted to the field of Counseling Psychology, clearly the most directly related professional training program for doctoral-level college counselors. *The Counseling Psychologist* is published by Division 17 of APA. Affiliated with ACA is the American College Counseling

Association (ACCA). The *Journal of College Counseling* is published by ACCA. The *Journal of American College Health* is published by the ACHA. Other journals related to the work of college counselors include *Journal of College Student Development, Journal of College Student Psychotherapy,* and *Journal of College Mental Health.*

SUMMARY

These are challenging times for college and university counseling centers. The current trend demands that competent and professional services be rendered on a wide range of mental health issues, for a more clinically demanding population, in ways that effectively reach a diverse group of students with increased accountability and fewer resources. Fortunately, standards, guidelines, and a wide variety of tools exist to help us with this task. Many of these resources have been addressed in this chapter. Standards such as those published by CAS and IACS help us to define our roles and functions clinically and administratively. Competency requirements, professional ethics, and common practices guide us toward the appropriate application of our trade. Tools made available through administrative innovation, accountability measures, professional affiliations, and improved communication and computer technology help us to serve our campus communities more effectively and efficiently. With sufficient awareness of these resources, and by working cooperatively, we can meet the challenges of today and realize our goals for tomorrow.

References

Altschuler, G.C. (2000, August 6). Adapting to college life in an era of heightened stress. *New York Times,* pp. 12, 16.

Amada, G. (1994). *Coping with the disruptive college student: A practical model.* Asheville, NC: College Administration Publications.

Archer, J., & Cooper, S. (1998). *Counseling and mental health services on campus: A handbook of contemporary practices and challenges.* San Francisco: Jossey-Bass.

Bishop, J.B. (1991). Managing demands on counseling services: A process of change (A response to Dworkin and Lyddon). *Journal of Counseling and Development, 69,* 408–410.

Bishop, J.B. (1995). Emerging administrative strategies for college and university counseling centers. *Journal of Counseling and Development, 74,* 33–38.

Chandler, L.A., & Gallagher, R.P. (1996). Developing a taxonomy for problems seen at a university counseling center. *Measurement and Evaluation in Counseling and Development, 29,* 4–12.

Council for the Advancement of Standards in Higher Education. (1997). *The CAS book of professional standards for higher education.* Washington, DC: Author.

Davis, D.C., & Humphrey, K.M. (Eds.). (2000). *College counseling: Issues and strategies for a new millennium.* Alexandria, VA: American Counseling Association.

Erickson Cornish, J.A., Riva, M.T., Henderson, M.C., Kominars, K.D., & McIntosh, S. (2000). Perceived distress in university counseling center clients across a six-year period. *Journal of College Student Development, 41,* 104–109.

Gallagher, P.J., & Demos, G.D. (1983). *Handbook of counseling in higher education.* New York: Praeger.

Gallagher, R.P., Gill, A.M., Goldstrohm, S.L., & Sysko, H.B. (1999). *National survey of counseling center directors.* Alexandria, VA: International Association of Counseling Services.

Gallagher, R.P., Gill, A.M., & Sysko, H.B. (2000). *National survey of counseling center directors.* Alexandria, VA: International Association of Counseling Services.

Guinee, J.P., & Ness, M.E. (2000). Counseling centers of the 1990's: Challenges and changes. *The Counseling Psychologist, 28,* 267–280.

Gilbert, S.P. (1992). Ethical issues in the treatment of severe psychopathology in University and college counseling centers. *Journal of Counseling and Development, 70,* 695–699.

Kiracofe, N.M., Donn, P.A., Grant, C.O., Podolnick, E.E., Bingham, R.P., Bolland, H.R., Carney, C.G., Clementson, J., Gallagher, R.P., Grosz, R.D., Handy, L., Hansche, J.H., Mack, J.K., Sanz, D., Walker, L.J., & Yamada, K.T. (1994). Accreditation standards for university and college counseling centers. *Journal of Counseling and Development, 73,* 38–43.

Kopta, S.M., & Lowry, J.L. (2000). *The Psychotherapy Outcome Assessment and Monitoring System: College counseling center version.* Unpublished manuscript.

Lambert, M.J., Hansen, N.B., Umphress, V., Lunnen, K., Okiishi, H., Burlingame, G.M., Heufner, J.C., & Reisinger, C.R. (1996). *Administration and Scoring manual for the Outcome Questionnaire (OQ-45.2).* Wilmington, DE: American Professional Credentialing Services LLC.

Mitchell, J.T., & Everly, G.S. (1993). *Critical incident stress debriefing (CISD): An operations manual for the prevention of traumatic stress among emergency services and disaster workers.* Elliott City, MD: Chevron Corporation.

O'Malley, K., Wheeler, I., Murphey, J., O'Connell, J., & Waldo, M. (1990). Changes in levels of psychopathology being treated at college and university counseling centers. *Journal of College Student Development, 31,* 464–465.

Pledge, D.S., Lapan, R.T., Heppner, P.P., Kivlighan, D., & Roehlke, H.J. (1998). Stability and severity of presenting problems at a university counseling center: A 6-year analysis. *Professional Psychology: Research and Practice, 29,* 386–389.

Sax, L.J., Astin, A.W., Korn, W.S., & Mahoney, K.M. (1999). *The American freshman: National norms for fall 1999.* Los Angeles: UCLA, Higher Education Research Institute.

Sharkin, B.S. (1997). Increasing severity of presenting problems in college counseling centers: A closer look. *Journal of Counseling and Development, 75,* 275–281.

Stone, G.L., & Archer, J., Jr. (1990). College and university counseling centers in the 1990's: Challenges and limits. *The Counseling Psychologist, 18,* 539–607.

Whiteley, S.M., Mahaffey, P.J., & Geer, C.A. (1987). The campus counseling center: A profile of staffing patterns and services. *Journal of College Student Personnel, 28,* 71–81.

World Health Organization International Consortium in Psychiatric Epidemiology. (2000). Cross-national comparisons of the prevalences and correlates of mental disorders. *Bulletin of the World Health Organization, 78,* 413–426.

5 DIVORCE COUNSELING

Katherine M. Kitzmann and Noni K. Gaylord

Divorce rates in the United States reached historically high levels in the 1980s, making divorce a normative experience in American society (National Center for Health Statistics, 1995). Although the divorce rate showed a downward trend in the 1990s, at least 50% of recent marriages are expected to end in divorce (Cherlin, 1992), and about 60% of current divorces involve children (National Center for Health Statistics, 1995). The transition to divorce is often a significant stressor for both adults and children. Members of divorced families are two to three times as likely to receive psychological treatment compared to members of married families (Howard et al., 1996). Family members seek help both for dealing with psychological disorders, which are more common among children and parents in divorced families, but also for help in dealing with subclinical problems, such as painful feelings, unhappy memories, and ongoing distress associated with the family disruption (Emery, 1999).

Research shows that adults and children show a range of outcomes associated with the divorce transition. Among adults, anxiety, depression, alcohol abuse, loneliness, impulsivity, and emotional lability may emerge or increase in the aftermath of divorce (Bloom, Asher, & White, 1978; Hetherington, 1993). Separated and divorced adults, especially men, are also at increased risk for compromised immune system functioning and physical illness (Burman & Margolin, 1992; Dura & Kiecolt-Glaser, 1991). Compared to children from nondivorced families, children from divorced families are at higher risk for academic problems, externalizing and internalizing disorders, low social competence, low self-esteem, and problems in close relationships (Amato & Keith, 1991b). However, it should be noted that although the divorce transition is associated with significant distress for many, the normative outcome is resilience, with most children and adults eventually showing good psychological adjustment to the stressor of divorce (Emery, 1999).

It is probably most helpful to think of divorce as a process of life transitions rather than as a single event. Longitudinal research shows that much of the distress observed after divorce actually begins prior to divorce and can be attributed to the strains of unhappy marital and family relationships (Cherlin et al., 1991). The first two years following divorce are associated with significant distress and disruption in family life. By two years after divorce, however, most adults and children are adapting reasonably well (Hetherington, 1989). For both men and women, psychological well-being increases after the formation of a new mutually caring, intimate relationship, such as a successful remarriage (Hetherington, 1993). However, remarriage can present its own set of stressors when children are involved. The fact that divorce rates are even higher in remarriages than in first marriages means that many adults and children actually undergo multiple divorce-related transitions (Cherlin, 1992).

COUNSELING ADULTS DURING THE DIVORCE TRANSITION

Men and women going through divorce seek therapy at much higher rates than do married adults (Howard et al., 1996). These adults show a wide range of responses to divorce, including painful emotions of anger and sadness, feelings of guilt and remorse, and relief and excitement about the termination of a difficult marriage. Counseling can provide a safe place to express these feelings and to experience grief related to the multiple losses associated with the dissolution of a marriage. These include loss of a partner, loss of the dream of being happily married, and loss of roles, including one's role as spouse and as a member of the spouse's extended family. For many adults, divorce also involves significant changes in parent-child relationships and diminished contact with children, an especially important stressor for the noncustodial parent (Kitson, 1992). In some cases, parents who have difficulty accepting the reality of divorce will engage in drawn-out litigation as a way to maintain connection with the spouse (Emery, 1994). Counseling can assist these individuals to find more effective ways to deal with issues of loss and acceptance.

Counselors can provide an important element of social support during the divorce transition and can help the divorced adult problem-solve about ways to make use of other forms of support. Divorced adults commonly report social isolation and loneliness; in one study, 30% of divorced adults still experienced severe loneliness even 16 months after the divorce (Spanier & Thompson, 1983). Counseling can also address the multiple life changes that accompany divorce, which might include moving, establishing an independent household, and finding employment. These stressors are especially relevant for women, as the economic impact of divorce is significantly more negative for women than for men (McLanahan & Booth, 1989). Even small changes in coping strategies can be helpful in the face of these many stressors. One helpful resource for clients is Weiner-Davis's (1992) book *Divorce Busting*, which describes brief, solution-focused techniques for adults dealing with divorce-related distress.

Many divorcing adults seek help through support groups and group-based intervention programs. These programs typically involve 6 to 24 hours of group meetings and address topics such as finding a new support system, feelings of isolation and diminished self-esteem, running a household alone, financial planning, and dating (Lee, Picard, & Blain, 1994). These programs appear to be helpful in decreasing symptoms of depression and overall distress, with average improvement levels comparable to typical psychotherapy outcomes (Lee et al., 1994). Programs that have proven effective in improving participants' psychological adjustment and parenting skills include the Colorado Separation and Divorce Project (Hodges & Bloom, 1986), the Divorce Adjustment Project (Stolberg & Cullen, 1983), the Children of Divorce Parenting Intervention (Wolchik et al., 1993), and the Parenting through Change program (Forgatch & De-Garmo, 1999).

Many divorcing adults participate in short-term workshops designed to improve family functioning during the divorce transition. Although parents report high consumer satisfaction with these programs, research using control groups suggests little objective benefit either in terms of parenting or child functioning (Emery, Kitzmann, & Waldron, 1999). The strong interest in short-term programs, both on the part of community members and the court system, provides an opportunity for researchers to evaluate what works and what does not (Emery et al., 1999).

COUNSELING CHILDREN AFFECTED BY DIVORCE

The transition to divorce is one that affects all members of the family, and many children are referred for counseling during this difficult period. Children often have to cope simultaneously with painful emotions about their parents' divorce and with other transitions such as moving, changing schools, and making new friends. The child's ability to cope with these stressors can be compromised by parents' expression of hostility toward one another, ongoing interparental conflict surrounding visitation or joint custody, or decreased or unpredictable contact with the noncustodial parent. Many children show problems during this transition, the most common being aggression and conduct problems (Amato & Keith, 1991b). Boys and girls appear to be equally affected, but may be differentially impacted by a parent's subsequent remarriage. For example, research in mother-custody families has shown that boys' problems tend to decrease with the addition of a stepfather, whereas this transition can entail new stressors for girls, who may have become closer to their mothers after the divorce (Hetherington, Bridges, & Insabella, 1998).

Developmental factors are critical in the discussion of counseling for children of divorce. Most children are younger than 6 when their parents divorce (Emery, 1999), and a great deal of the clinical literature focuses on the needs of these very young children. Among preschoolers from divorced homes, conduct problems are most prevalent (Amato & Keith, 1991b), and preschoolers also show significant confusion about being to blame for the divorce and about whether divorce means that a parent no longer loves them (Knoff & Bishop, 1997). In general, however, children in elementary and high school show more problems after divorce than do preschoolers or college students (Amato & Keith, 1991b). School-age children are more likely than younger children to try to mediate their parents' conflict, and although they may be better able to understand that divorce is not their fault, they may still feel responsible for fixing the problem (Knoff & Bishop, 1997). For adolescents, parental divorce may highlight struggles with the transition to young adulthood (Hodges, 1991). As adults, children of divorce are at higher risk for depression and life dissatisfaction (Amato & Keith, 1991a) and are much more likely than other adults to divorce themselves (Amato, 1996).

Individual counseling can provide a safe environment for the child to grieve the multiple losses inherent to divorce, express both love for and anger toward both parents, discuss misconceptions about the cause of divorce and who is to blame, and then begin to learn skills to overcome divorce-related fears and to cope with the divorce transition. Play therapy is commonly used with younger children, whereas older children and adolescents are more able to talk openly about their experiences related to their parents' divorce. Wallerstein (1989) has noted that regardless of the child's age, adaptation to divorce involves several psychological tasks. First, children must acknowledge the reality of the marital rupture and disengage from parental conflict and distress. With time, children resume a routine and customary activities and experience some resolution of their feelings of loss, self-blame, and anger. Finally, children must accept the permanence of the divorce and achieve realistic hopes about relationships.

Counselors can play an important role in encouraging parents to talk honestly with their children about the divorce at a level appropriate for the child's age. Parents can assure their children that they are not to blame and are not responsible for helping the parents to get along. At the same time, parents should be encouraged not to discuss with their children topics that are more appropriately discussed with other adults, such as feelings of hostility toward the ex-spouse, conflict over visitation or joint custody arrangements, and insecurities about finances. Parents can be helped to make the child's life as stable and consistent as possible, both within the custodial household and between households in cases of frequent visitation or joint custody. Books that may be helpful to parents include *Mom's House, Dad's House: A Complete Guide for Parents Who Are Separated, Divorced, or Remarried* (Ricci, 1997), *How It Feels When Parents Divorce* (Krementz, 1999), *Don't Divorce Us! Kids' Advice to Divorcing Parents* (Sommers-Flanagan, Elander, & Sommers-Flanagan, 1999), and *Dinosaurs Divorce: A Guide for Changing Families* (Brown & Krasny, 1999).

In addition to individual counseling, school-based group therapy programs are a common intervention for children of divorce.

Groups typically meet for 6 to 16 weeks and are designed to lessen children's isolation and loneliness, foster support and trust, and clarify misconceptions about divorce. As a whole, these groups show considerably lower effectiveness than psychotherapy in general (Lee et al., 1994). Two exceptions are the Children of Divorce Intervention Project, a 12-week intervention for children from kindergarten through sixth grade (Pedro-Carroll & Cowen, 1985), and the Divorce Adjustment Project, a 12- to 14-week program for children age 7 to 13 (Stolberg & Mahler, 1994).

COUNSELING COUPLES AND FAMILIES AFFECTED BY DIVORCE

Although most divorce-related counseling targets individual adjustment, interventions with two or more family members can also be helpful during the transition to divorce. Child custody mediation is an increasingly common alternative to litigation that many hope can act as a preventive intervention by improving coparenting and minimizing children's exposure to poorly resolved conflict (Emery & Wyer, 1987). Mediation is associated with faster resolution and fewer court hearings (Emery, 1994), higher participant satisfaction (Emery, Matthews, & Kitzmann, 1994), and increased compliance with child support agreements as well as greater involvement by noncustodial fathers in their children's lives (Dillon & Emery, 1996). However, mediation has not been shown to be associated with any mental health benefits, either for parents or children (Emery et al., 1994; Kitzmann & Emery, 1994).

Family therapy is another resource that may be helpful during divorce-related transitions. Although parents may be divorced and living apart, they may still meet regularly with their children in family therapy, especially in cases of joint physical custody or frequent visitation (Isaacs, Montalvo, & Abelsohn, 1986). Family therapy can help parents learn to shelter their children from poorly resolved interparental conflict and to provide consistent expectations and rewards in the two households, and can help maintain and strengthen children's relationships with both parents. Family therapy may also be helpful during the transition to remarriage and stepparenting, a period in which family roles and rules can be in flux (Crosbie-Burnett & Ahrons, 1985; Visher & Visher, 1988).

SUMMARY

Members of divorced families are two to three times as likely as members of married families to receive psychological treatment (Howard et al., 1996). Common interventions during the transition to divorce include individual therapy for adults and for children, support groups for adults, school-based intervention programs for children, mediation for couples, and family therapy.

Several points should be highlighted. First, little research has been conducted on the effectiveness of individual counseling for adults or children affected by divorce, or of family therapy for divorced and remarried families. Whereas group-based interventions for divorced adults have been found to be about as effective as individual therapy for improving psychological adjustment (Lee et al., 1994), most "weekend workshop" programs have not proven effective. With some high-quality exceptions, most school-based programs for children also show limited effectiveness. Mediation, although beneficial in several respects, is not associated with significant improvement in family members' mental health and is not a substitute for traditional forms of intervention.

Second, it is most helpful to think of divorce not as a single event, but as a process of transitions. Longitudinal research suggests that many of the problems thought to be caused by divorce are actually present well before the divorce occurs. After divorce, the first two years are the most stressful, but most adults and children show great improvement by two years. Several years after the divorce, however, many divorced adults remarry, a transition that can bring both benefits and additional stressors. Because the divorce rate is even higher in second marriages than in first marriages, many adults and children are actually going through multiple transitions over the course of several years.

Finally, although the risk for psychological problems and involvement in therapy are both significantly higher in divorced families, most adults and children affected by divorce can be described as resilient, as most do not show mental health problems and most do not seek therapy (Emery et al., 1999). This is not to say that divorce has no impact, as many people affected by divorce report significant painful emotions, even years afterwards (Laumann-Billings & Emery, 2000). However, it would be a mistake to conclude that divorce by itself is the sole cause of the adjustment problems seen in adults and children from divorced families, as members of nondivorced high-conflict families have psychological problems comparable to those seen in families of divorce (Amato,1999). It is most helpful to view clients' problems as a response to multiple stressors, including marital conflict and problematic family relationships.

References

Amato, K. (1996). Explaining the intergenerational transmission of divorce. *Journal of Marriage and the Family, 58,* 628–640.

Amato, K. (1999). Children of divorced parents as young adults. In E.M. Hetherington (Ed.), *Coping with divorce, single parenting, and remarriage* (pp. 147–163). Mahwah, NJ: Erlbaum.

Amato, K., & Keith, B. (1991a). Parental divorce and adult well-being: A meta-analysis. *Journal of Marriage and the Family, 53,* 43–58.

Amato, K., & Keith, B. (1991b). Parental divorce and the well-being of children: A meta-analysis. *Psychological Bulletin, 110,* 26–46.

Bloom, B.L., Asher, S.J., & White, S.W. (1978). Marital disruption as a stressor: A review and analysis. *Psychological Bulletin, 85,* 867–894.

Brown, M.T., & Krasny, L. (1999). *Dinosaurs divorce: A guide for changing families* (2nd ed.). New York: Little, Brown.

Burman, B., & Margolin, G. (1992). Analysis of the association between marital relationships and health problems: An interactional perspective. *Psychological Bulletin, 112,* 39–63.

Cherlin, A. (1992). *Marriage, divorce, remarriage.* Cambridge, MA: Harvard University Press.

Cherlin, A., Furstenberg, F.F., Chase-Lansdale, P.L., Kiernan, K.E., Robins, P.K., Morrison, D.R., & Teitler, J.O. (1991). Longitudinal studies of effects of divorce in children in Great Britain and the United States. *Science, 252,* 1386–1389.

Crosbie-Burnett, M., & Ahrons, C.R. (1985). From divorce to remarriage: Implications for therapy with families in transition. *Journal of Psychotherapy and the Family, 1,* 121–137.

Dillon, P., & Emery, R.E. (1996). Divorce mediation and resolution of child custody disputes: Long-term effects. *American Journal of Orthopsychiatry, 66,* 131–140.

Dura, J.R., & Kiecolt-Glaser, J.K. (1991). Family transitions, stress, and health. In P.A. Cowan & E.M. Hetherington (Eds.), *Family transitions* (pp. 59–76). Hillsdale, NJ: Erlbaum.

Emery, R.E. (1994). *Renegotiating family relationships: Divorce, child custody, and mediation.* New York: Guilford Press.

Emery, R.E. (1999). *Marriage, divorce, and children's adjustment* (2nd ed.). Newbury Park, CA: Sage.

Emery, R.E., Kitzmann, K.M., & Waldron, M. (1999). Psychological interventions for separated and divorced families. In E.M. Hetherington (Ed.), *Coping with divorce, single parenting, and remarriage* (pp. 323–344). Hillsdale, NJ: Erlbaum.

Emery, R.E., Matthews, S., & Kitzmann, K.M. (1994). Child custody mediation and litigation: Parents' satisfaction and functioning a year after settlement. *Journal of Consulting and Clinical Psychology, 62,* 124–129.

Emery, R.E., & Wyer, M.M. (1987). Divorce mediation. *American Psychologist, 42,* 472–480.

Forgatch, M.S., & DeGarmo, D.S. (1999). Parenting through change: An effective prevention program for single mothers. *Journal of Consulting and Clinical Psychology, 67,* 711–724.

Hetherington, E.M. (1989). Coping with family transitions: Winners, losers, and survivors. *Child Development, 60,* 1–14.

Hetherington, E.M. (1993). An overview of the Virginia Longitudinal Study of Divorce and Remarriage with a focus on early adolescence. *Journal of Family Psychology, 7,* 39–56.

Hetherington, E.M., Bridges, M., & Insabella, G.M. (1998). What matters? What does not? Five perspectives on the association between marital transitions and children's adjustment. *American Psychologist, 53,* 167–184.

Hodges, W., & Bloom, B. (1986). Preventive intervention program for newly separated adults: One year later. *Journal of Preventive Psychiatry, 3,* 35–49.

Hodges, W.F. (1991). *Interventions for children of divorce: Custody, access, and psychotherapy* (2nd ed.). New York: Wiley.

Howard, K.I., Cornille, T.A., Lyons, J.S., Vessey, J.T., Lueger, R.J., & Saunders, S.M. (1996). Patterns of service utilization. *Archives of General Psychiatry, 53,* 696–703.

Isaacs, M.B., Montalvo, B., & Abelsohn, D. (1986). *The difficult divorce.* New York: Basic Books.

Kitson, G.C. (1992). *Portrait of divorce.* New York: Guilford Press.

Kitzmann, K.M., & Emery, R.E. (1994). Child and family coping one year after mediated and litigated child custody disputes. *Journal of Family Psychology, 8,* 150–157.

Knoff, H.M., & Bishop, M.D. (1997). Divorce. In G.G. Bear, K.M. Minke, & A. Thomas (Eds.), *Children's needs: II. Development, problems, and alternatives* (pp. 593–604). Bethesda, MD: National Association of School Psychologists.

Krementz, J. (1999). *How it feels when parents divorce.* New York: Knopf.

Laumann-Billings, L., & Emery, R.E. (2000). Distress among young adults from divorced families. *Journal of Family Psychology, 14,* 671–687.

Lee, C., Picard, M., & Blain, M. (1994). A methodological and substantive review of intervention outcome studies for families undergoing divorce. *Journal of Family Psychology, 8,* 3–15.

McLanahan, S., & Booth, K. (1989). Mother-only families: Problems, prospects, and politics. *Journal of Marriage and the Family, 51,* 557–580.

National Center for Health Statistics. (1995). Advance report of final divorce statistics 1989 and 1990: Supplement. *Monthly Vital Statistics Report, 43*(9). Hyattsville, MD: Author.

Pedro-Carroll, J.L., & Cowen, E.L. (1985). The Children Cope with Divorce program: An investigation of the efficacy of a school-based prevention program. *Journal of Consulting and Clinical Psychology, 53,* 603–611.

Ricci, I. (1997). *Mom's house, dad's house: A complete guide for parents who are separated, divorced, or remarried* (2nd ed.). New York: Simon & Schuster.

Sommers-Flanagan, R., Elander, C., & Sommers-Flanagan, J. (1999). *Don't divorce us! Kids' advice to divorcing parents.* Alexandria, VA: American Counseling Association.

Spanier, G.B., & Thompson, L. (1983). Relief and distress after marital separation. *Journal of Divorce, 7,* 31–49.

Stolberg, A., & Cullen, P. (1983). Preventive interventions for families of divorce: The Divorce Adjustment Project. In L.A. Kurdek (Ed.), *New directions in child development: Children and divorce* (Vol. 19, pp. 71–81). San Francisco: Jossey-Bass.

Stolberg, A., & Mahler, J. (1994). Enhancing treatment gains in a school-based intervention for children of divorce through skill training, parental involvement, and transfer procedures. *Journal of Consulting and Clinical Psychology, 62,* 147–156.

Visher, E., & Visher, J. (1988). *Old loyalties, new ties: Therapeutic strategies with stepfamilies.* New York: Brunner/Mazel.

Wallerstein, J.S. (1989). *Second chances: Men, women, and children a decade after divorce.* New York: Ticknor and Fields.

Weiner-Davis, M. (1992). *Divorce-busting.* New York: Summit Books.

Wolchik, S.A., West, S.G., Westover, S., Sandler, I.N., Martin, A., Lustig, J., Tein, J., & Fisher, J. (1993). The Children of Divorce parenting intervention: Outcomes evaluation of an empirically based program. *American Journal of Community Psychology, 21,* 293–331.

6 DEATH AND BEREAVEMENT

Stephen J. Freeman

Those in the counseling profession often have as their guiding light, and rightly so, the idea that counseling and therapy should instill hope. In light of this view, there may be a hesitancy to venture into the perceived hope-defeating realm of death and bereavement. The question arises, Why study such topics? The answer is simple: Death is a natural part of life and bereavement is an inescapable concomitant part of that life and of our natural inclination to relate to and bond with others.

A death loss is a disruption in the attachment bond a person has with a significant other in his or her environment. As such, the system must reorganize to a different level. The self is a system whose task is to regulate behavior designed to maintain contact with a significant other. The goal of the system is to maintain comfort and security through connectedness. This reorganization process generally follows four phases (Bowlby, 1980):

Phase I: Phase of numbing. This phase is characterized by an initial disbelief that the death has actually occurred and usually lasts from a few hours to a week and may be interrupted by outbursts of extreme emotion.

Phase II: Phase of yearning and searching. Survivors may be restless, preoccupied with thoughts of the deceased, and prone to initially interpret events (phone ringing, door opening) as coming from the deceased person.

Phase III: Phase of disorganization and despair. It will become apparent that attachment behaviors that were effective in maintaining the attachment bond while the deceased was alive are no longer working. The person begins to wonder if any part of prior life is salvageable. This can create despair. The self without the deceased person must be reevaluated and redefined, requiring full acceptance of the loss.

Phase IV: Phase of greater or lesser degree of reorganization. Now that the bereaved individual has come to a realization that life must go on, various changes may begin to take place. Thoughts of the deceased begin to take a different place in the bereaved's life. Social relationships and responsibilities may also be changing to accommodate a world without the person who was lost. (p. 85)

THE GRIEF EXPERIENCE

In addition to Bowlby's phases, Westberg (1962) lists ten fairly common stages for people in grief. These are described below. It should be understood, however, that grief is fluid and most people do not begin with stage 1 and proceed in an orderly fashion to stage 10. There is a great deal of movement among and within the stages, and often, bereaved individuals will comment that after a week or two of "progress," they have reverted back to the beginning. It is important to remember that grief contains the emotional illusion of regression when, in fact, movement is always forward. At worst, one is merely standing still. As long as the grieving process is not diluted or interrupted, there is progress:

1. *Shock.* The shock of death is to be expected even after a long illness and months of anticipatory grief. People often describe the first few weeks of grief as having been on autopilot. There is little actual memory of specific details, merely the knowledge that one did what had to be done. Shock usually wears off after five or six weeks, but may last much longer, depending on the person's skill at self-protection from painful feelings and the significance of the relationship.

2. *Emotional Release.* It is not uncommon to see intense emotional release at the time of the death, and then have it seem to dry up for a number of weeks. When the shock finally dissipates, the bereaved will often feel strong emotions such as anger, fear, remorse, and extreme loneliness. Lives are reviewed during this period, and people are amazed to discover the degree of dependence they felt for the person who died. This can lead to loss of self-esteem and feelings of inadequacy.

3. *Depression.* Depression takes the emotions mentioned above and intensifies them, adding feelings of helplessness and hopelessness. The bereaved will complain of not feeling their loved one close to them anymore, of wanting to be with him or her. There are fears of suicide from friends and family, but the bereaved will usually express it as "I won't do anything to myself, but if death comes for me tonight, I won't fight it."

4. *Physical Symptoms of Distress.* This is a very common phenomenon, especially in children. If the deceased died of a heart attack, the survivor(s) may experience tightness in the chest, pain radiating to the jaw and down the left arm, and other symptoms associated with a heart attack.

5. *Anxiety.* The bereaved experience vivid dreams, waking and sleeping, in which they see or hear their loved one. There is also spiritual anxiety, expressed as "Where is my loved one now? Is he or she happy?

How can he or she be at peace knowing I am suffering so much?" There is also the fear that the anger being felt toward God will bring about punishment in the form of additional losses. Many experience deep anxiety over the possibilities of forgetting their loved one and will express concern that they can no longer recall how the person smiled or how his or her voice sounded.

6. *Hostility.* Anger usually surfaces in the sixth or eighth week after death. This rage is sometimes random, sometimes specific. God, medical professionals, clergy, and the deceased are frequent targets. Usually, the individual is confused by the intensity of the anger, seeing it as inappropriate but feeling unable to defuse it.

7. *Guilt.* Guilt is sometimes real, often imaginary or exaggerated, but should always be taken with great seriousness. Death amplifies whatever problems existed in the relationship, and even minor life issues that had been virtually ignored are now insurmountable obstacles for the survivor. The "shoulds" seem to rule the world of the bereaved: "I should have done this. I should not have done that." Rational explanations may soothe for a time, but usually the guilt will return until resolution is achieved. No one can punish us better that we can punish ourselves, and the instrument is guilt.

8. *Fear.* Fear wears many faces with the bereaved. There may be a fear of sleeping in the same bed or room. There may be a fear of leaving the house or of staying in it. People are afraid of the aloneness that comes after a death, and they are also afraid of beginning new relationships, however platonic these may be. There is a fear of never knowing joy again or not being able to laugh without guilt. The act of living becomes fearful for the person who feels so lost without his or her loved one, and each day is a burden to be endured.

9. *Healing through Memories.* The bereaved move back and forth between good memories and bad. At times, it seems that there is a need for self-punishment, and so all the negative aspects of the relationship are

resurrected and relived. The happier moments often seem too painful, and it may
take many months before these can be
faced, but there is healing in remembering. As the memories become less painful,
there is an ability to begin to face the
world once again.

10. *Acceptance.* There is a difference between
accepting the reality of death (thereby letting go) and forgetting the person who has
died. As with the healing of any serious
wound, there will always be a scar to remind one of the injury. With time will
come a lessening of the pain, until finally
the injury can be touched, remembered,
and accepted as a new part of the life being
lived. This acceptance may take two years
or more to achieve, depending on the
depth of emotional investment one made
in the relationship with the deceased.

Within these phases and stages, there is a
continuum of behaviors ranging from normal
and healthy to dysfunctional for the person
who is grieving. Westberg's (1962) theory
suggests that the patterns of loss following a
death are similar (but not identical in duration or intensity) regardless of age, gender, or
relationship to the deceased.

THE NORMAL EXPERIENCE OF GRIEF: FACILITATING GRIEF COUNSELING

A helpful concept for both the mourner and
the caregiver is the tasks of mourning. The
mourner's awareness of these needs or tasks
of grief work can give a participative, action-
oriented outlook to the experience of grief as
opposed to a perception of grief being a phenomenon experienced in a passive manner.
This also provides a framework for outlining
a significant portion of the helper's role.

Tasks of Mourning

The first task of mourning is to experience and
express outside of oneself the reality of the
death (Lindemann, 1944; Parks & Weiss, 1983;
Worden, 1991). This involves confronting the

reality that the person has died and will not be
coming back. Questions to ask yourself as a
counselor working with the bereaved:

Where is the person in terms of confronting the reality that his or her loved
one has died?

Do I need to respect the person's need to
avoid the full reality of the loss for a period of time while attempting to help him
or her cautiously confront this new reality?

Is the person using unhealthy defense
mechanisms such as overuse of alcohol,
overeating, the traveling cure, or similar
behaviors?

The second task of mourning is to tolerate
the emotional suffering that is inherent in the
grief while nurturing oneself both physically
and emotionally (Parks & Weiss, 1983;
Shuchter & Zisook, 1990; Worden, 1991). The
thoughts and feelings (pain of grief) resulting
from this encounter with death must be ab-
sorbed. If avoided or denied, the movement
toward resolution is inhibited. Questions to
ask yourself as a counselor working with the
bereaved:

Has the person allowed himself or herself
to experience the pain of grief? If so, with
whom has he or she shared their grief?

Was the person provided with a sense of
feeling understood in the expression of his
or her grief?

The third requisite of mourning is to con-
vert the relationship with the deceased from
one of presence to one of memory (Lindemann,
1944; Parks & Weiss, 1983; Rando, 1987, 1993;
Ruskay, 1996; Sable, 1991; Worden, 1991). The
mourner works to modify and detach the emotional ties to the person who has died in preparation to live in an altered relationship with
the dead person. The mourner should not be
expected to relinquish all ties to the person
who died. However, an alteration of the relationship must be accomplished. Accomplishing
an evolution of this type often provides a
sense of meaning to the bereaved. Questions

to ask yourself as a counselor working with the bereaved:

Where is the person in the process of converting the relationship from one of presence to one of memory?

Is the bereaved resisting any change in viewing the relationship as one of presence? If so, what contributing factors may be influencing this (e.g., nature of the relationship with the deceased, personality of the deceased or of the bereaved)?

Does the bereaved think he or she must give up all forms of bonding with the deceased?

What can I do as a counselor to help facilitate a new type of relationship rooted in memory (e.g., stimulation of memories, new rituals, expression of dreams)?

The fourth task of mourning is to develop a new sense of self-identity based on a life without the deceased (Lindemann, 1944; Parks & Weiss, 1983; Ruskay, 1996; Worden, 1991). Role confusion involves the struggle between the *we* and the *I* and fears associated with one's new autonomy. Research suggests that women have more difficulty in this struggle than men; however, women are much more likely than men to seek support and guidance as they struggle with the development of this new identity.

Questions to ask yourself as a counselor working with the bereaved:

Where is the bereaved in the process of forming a new self-identity?

Is time a factor influencing where this person is currently?

What are the role changes that this person is experiencing?

Are role models of persons who have gone through similar experiences available to the bereaved?

To complete the grief work, one must relate the experience of loss to a context of meaning. The bereaved will typically question their philosophy of life, their values in seeking an answer to the question "Why?" As Nietzsche (1968) said, "It was not the suffering that was his problem but that the question was wanting to the outcry, Why the *suffering*?"

Questions to ask yourself as a counselor working with the bereaved:

Where is the person in the process of relating the experience of loss to a context of meaning?

What were the person's religious and philosophical beliefs about life before the loss?

How has the loss altered these beliefs?

What is standing between the bereaved and their accepting their fate?

TIME INTERVALS AND IMPLICATIONS FOR COUNSELORS

The time guide for counselors is as fluid as the stages of grief. People move within the stages quickly, sometimes going back to the first hours and then jumping well ahead of where they actually are, feeling as though they have finally finished. This is normal and to be expected. The following is only a descriptive guide (Freeman & Ward, 1998).

First 48 hours. The shock of the death can be intense, and denial is often strong in the first hours. The emotional response can be frightening to the bereaved and friends and family members.

First week. The necessity of planning the funeral and making other arrangements usually takes over, and the bereaved may function in an automatic manner. This may be followed by a feeling of letdown and emotional and physical exhaustion.

2 to 5 weeks. There is a general feeling of abandonment as family and friends return to their own lives after the funeral. Employers often expect the bereaved to have recovered and to be fully functional on the job. The insulation of shock may still be in effect, and there may be a sensation of "This isn't going to be as bad as I first thought."

6 to 12 weeks. It is during this time that the shock finally wears off and the reality of the loss sets in. Emotions range widely, and the person feels out of control and lack support of family or friends, who may think, "That was three months ago. Why are you feeling bad now?" Some of the experiences during this time are:

- Radical changes in sleep patterns.
- Onset of fear, sometimes paranoia.
- Changes in appetite with significant weight gain or loss.
- Changes in libido.
- Periods of uncontrollable weeping.
- Loss of motivation.
- Fatigue and generalized weakness.
- Physical symptoms of distress.
- Muscle tremors.
- Increased need to talk about the deceased.
- Extreme mood swings.
- Desire for isolation.
- Inability to concentrate or remember.

3 to 4 months. The cycle of good and bad days begins. Irritability increases and there is a lowering of frustration tolerance. There may be verbal and physical acting out of anger, feelings of emotional regression, and an increase in somatic complaints, especially flu and colds, as the immune system is depressed.

6 months. Depression sets in as the sixth-month anniversary approaches. The event of loss is relived and the emotional upheaval seems to be starting all over again. Anniversaries, birthdays, and holidays are especially difficult, bringing about renewed depression.

12 months. The first anniversary of the death can be traumatic or the beginning of resolution, depending on the amount and quality of grief work done during the year.

18 to 24 months. This is the time for resolution. The pain of separation becomes bearable, and the bereaved is able to proceed with the living of their own life. There is an emotional letting go of the deceased, a recognition that, although the person will never be forgotten, the pain of the death will no longer need to be the focal point of the life of the bereaved. It is during this phase that the terms bereaved and grieving are eased from the vocabulary, and the process of living begins in earnest.

Bowlby (1980) suggests that clinicians sometimes have unrealistic expectations about the progress people should be making as they grieve. He quotes one widow: "Mourning never ends: only as time goes on it erupts less frequently" (p. 101). Rando (1983) describes a v configuration, with bereavement intensity decreasing in the second year and increasing in the third year. This suggests that patterns of grieving fluctuate over time in a nonlinear fashion (Gray, 1987). Grief and mourning are uniquely individual processes and no one has the correct timetable for their completion.

PATHOLOGICAL GRIEVING: ABNORMAL GRIEF RESPONSE

Pathological or abnormal grief is the intensification of grief to the level where the person is overwhelmed, resorts to maladaptive behavior, or remains interminably in the state of grief without progression of the mourning process toward completion. It involves processes that do not move progressively toward assimilation or accommodation but, instead, lead to stereotyped repetitions or extensive interruptions of healing (Horowitz, Wilmer, Marmar, & Krupnick, 1980, p. 1157).

Research (de Vries, 1997; Grad & Zavasnik, 1996; Horowitz et al., 1980; Rubin & Schechter, 1997; Worden, 1991) suggests that complicated bereavement has to do with four primary factors: relational, circumstantial, historical, and personality factors.

Relational Factors

Relational factors define the type of relationship the person had with the deceased. The most frequent type of relationship that hinders people from adequate grieving is one involving extreme ambivalence coupled with unexpressed hostility. Highly narcissistic relationships, in which the deceased represents an extension of the bereaved, necessitate confronting a loss of part of oneself, thus making for complications. Highly dependent relationships are also difficult to grieve. In this type of relationship, the bereaved loses the source of strength that has sustained them, and the result is an overwhelming sense of abandonment and helplessness. The sense of overwhelming helplessness and loss of self-concept tend to overwhelm any other feelings, including feelings related to healthy grief.

Circumstantial Factors

Circumstances surrounding a loss may preclude or make completion of the grieving process difficult or impossible. Uncertainty of the loss, not knowing if a person is truly dead, precludes adequate grieving (e.g., missing children, soldier who is listed MIA, or disaster victims whose bodies are not recovered). Where no concrete evidence of death is found, mourning can be unresolved. Situations where multiple losses occur (e.g., Oklahoma City bombing) can make grieving nearly impossible due to the sheer volume involved. Where there are multiple losses in close proximity, it becomes easier to shut down completely.

Historical Factors

Individual history involving prior experience of complicated grief results in a higher probability of having complications again. Additionally, past losses and separations have an affect on current losses and separations and the capacity for future attachments. History of mental illness can predispose one to complications that prevent adequate grief response.

Personality Factors

Grief resolution requires the experiencing of universal feelings of helplessness in the face of existential loss; personality factors are related to how well or poorly a person copes with emotional distress. Inability to tolerate extreme emotional distress leads to defensive withdrawal and can short-circuit the grieving process.

SUMMARY

When an attachment bond is broken, people experience a grief response. A loss through death is a normal and universal phenomenon that requires everyone who experiences it to reevaluate and reorganize their attachments to significant others. Bowlby (1980) posited that reorganization of attachment progresses through four phases. Reorganization and resolution of the grieving process require time for successful completion of the tasks of mourning.

References

Bowlby, J. (1980). *Loss, sadness and depression*. New York: Basic Books.
de Vries, B. (1997). Kinship bereavement in later life: Understanding the variations in cause, course, and consequence. *Omega: Journal of Death and Dying, 35,* 141–157.
Freeman, S., & Ward, S. (1998). Death and bereavement: What counselors should know. *Journal of Mental Health Counseling, 20*(3), 216–226.
Grad, O., & Zavasnik, A. (1996). Similarities and differences in the process of bereavement after suicide and after traffic fatalities in Slovenia. *Omega: Journal of Death and Dying, 33,* 243–251.
Gray, R. (1987). Adolescent response to the death of a parent. *Journal of Youth and Adolescence, 16*(6), 511–525.
Horowitz, M., Wilmer, N., Marmar, C., & Krupnick, J. (1980). Pathological grief and the activation of latent self-images. *American Journal of Psychiatry, 137,* 1157–1162.
Lindemann, E. (1944). Symptomology and management of acute grief. *American Journal of Psychiatry, 101,* 141–148.
Nietzsche, F. (1967). *The genealogy of morals and ecco homo* (Walter Kaufmann, Trans.). New York: Vintage Books.
Parks, C., & Weiss, R. (1983). *Recovery from bereavement*. New York: Basic Books.
Rando, T.A. (1983). An investigation of grief and adaptation in parents whose children have died from cancer. *Journal of Pediatric Psychology, 8*(1), 3–20.

Rando, T.A. (1987). The unrecognized impact of sudden death in terminal illness and in positively progressing convalescence. *Israeli Journal of Psychiatry and Related Sciences*, 24(1/2), 125–135.

Rubin, S., & Schechter, N. (1997). Exploring the social constructs of bereavement: Perceptions of adjustment and recovery in bereaved men. *American Journal of Orthopsychiatry*, 67, 279–289.

Ruskay, S. (1996). Saying hello again: A new approach to bereavement counseling. *Hospice Journal, 11,* 5–14.

Sable, P. (1991). Attachment, loss of spouse, and grief in elderly adults. *Omega: Journal of Death and Dying, 23*(2), 129–142.

Shuchter, S.R., & Zisook, S. (1990). Hovering over the bereaved. *Psychiatric Annals, 20*(6), 327–333.

Westberg, G. (1962). *Goodgrief.* Philadephia: Fortress Press.

Worden, J.W. (1991). *Grief counseling and grief therapy.* New York: Springer.

7   STRESS, COPING, AND WELL-BEING

Applications of Theory to Practice

John L. Romano

Stress, coping, and well-being are three constructs that have received much attention in the psychological literature and mass media markets. The concepts are applicable to children and adolescents, as well as adults. In this chapter, I present an overview of how each of these terms has been conceptualized. The overview is followed by a conceptual framework describing how psychological practitioners may interact with clients to help them reduce stress, strengthen coping strategies, and promote overall well-being.

STRESS

Although the layperson may have a general understanding of the meaning of stress, stress has been conceptualized and defined differently by scholars. Physiologist Hans Selye (1976) defined stress as the "nonspecific response of the body to any demand" (p. 1). Selye's work followed in the tradition of two other physiologists, Claude Bernard and Walter Cannon, who studied the ability of living organisms to maintain internal physiological constancy despite changes in their external environments. Cannon (1932) referred to this internal balance as homeostasis. The phrase "flight or fight," referring to responses to survive a dangerous situation, requires an adaptation of the organism to meet the danger, thus changing the organism's internal balance. Although the flight-or-fight response helps us to survive life-threatening situations (e.g., a pedestrian rapidly moving away from an approaching vehicle), prolonged arousal that upsets internal physiological balance can lead to negative health consequences (Rice, 1999).

Physiological adaptation to stressful life events is the theoretical basis for the development of the popular Social Readjustment Rating Scale (SRRS; Holmes & Rahe, 1967). This scale is made up of 43 life events ranked in order of degree of personal difficulty, from 1 ("death of a spouse") to 43 ("minor violations of the law"). Holmes and Rahe hypothesized that the onset of physical illness was associated with the number and severity of life events. The life events conceptual framework and variations of life event scales have been developed for other populations, including children and adolescents (Coddington, 1972; Masten, Neemann, & Andenas, 1994) and college students (Marx, Garrity, & Bowers, 1975). Although the Holmes and Rahe research brought attention to life events, physiological adaptation, and their impact on health, the research has been criticized for yielding low correlations between life events and illness (Dohrenwend & Dohrenwend, 1984; Somerfield & McCrae, 2000). Sarafino (1998) summarized the literature highlighting other limitations of the SRRS, including the ambiguity of some of the items, variations in importance that people attach to the events, and the lack of consideration of contextual factors related to the life events and onset of illness. For example, financial reserves and job satisfaction will impact the significance of a job loss, and genetic factors may influence the onset of disease. Lazarus (1992) also argues that it is difficult to demonstrate psychosocial influences on health for some of these same reasons.

As a response to the early and almost exclusive attention to physiological changes that accompany stressful events, and also to account for individual differences, Lazarus and his colleagues (Lazarus & Folkman, 1984) present a transactional, cognitive model of stress. They conceptualize stress as "a particular relationship between the person and the environment that is appraised by the person as taxing or exceeding his or her resources and endangering his or her well-being" (p. 19). A person's appraisal of the event and his or her ability to cope with the event are central to Lazarus's formulation. During a stressful encounter, a person makes "primary" and "secondary" appraisals of the situation. Primary appraisal refers to the amount of threat the person perceives, and secondary appraisal is the person's evaluation of his or her ability to cope with the threat. These appraisals are sometimes fleeting, and the person can reappraise a situation as new information is learned. Lazarus furthered our understanding of stress by considering both the person and the stressful event, whereas previous work focused primarily on either the person or the stressful event.

Stevan Hobfoll (1989), critical of Lazarus's conceptualization of stress for being circular and overly emphasizing perceptions, brought a different perspective to psychological stress. In his "conservation of resources" model, Hobfoll defined stress "as a reaction to the environment in which there is (a) the threat of a net loss of resources, (b) the net loss of resources, or (c) a lack of resource gain following the investment of resources" (p. 516). Therefore, stress occurs because of an actual or perceived loss of resources or lack of gain of resources following investment. Resources can include "objects, personal characteristics, conditions, or energies that are valued by the individual or that serve as a means for attainment of these objects, personal characteristics, conditions, or energies" (p. 516).

Rice (1999) has summarized other models of stress, including those based on learning, psychodynamic, and social theory. Although each theory of stress has limitations, collectively they offer different opportunities and options to intervene with clients who are experiencing stress reactions.

COPING

Closely aligned to the study of stress are conceptual models of how people cope with stress. The study of coping, as with stress, offers different theoretical approaches. Aldwin

(1994) placed the study of coping into three broad categories: person-, situation-, and cognitive-based approaches. Person-based approaches hypothesize that personality characteristics are major determinants of how people cope with stress. These approaches have their roots in psychoanalytic theory and the use of defense mechanisms to cope with stress. Situational approaches argue that coping behaviors are largely influenced by the contextual factors surrounding the stressor; people cope differently depending on the nature of the stressor. Cognitive approaches, exemplified by Lazarus's (1993) work, are based on the person's cognitive appraisal of the situation.

Lazarus (1993) defines coping "as ongoing cognitive and behavioral efforts to manage specific external and/or internal demands that are appraised as taxing or exceeding the resources of the person" (p. 237). According to Lazarus, coping behaviors can be problem-focused or emotion-focused. Problem-focused coping functions to alter the person-environment relationship to improve a stressful situation, whereas emotion-focused coping attempts to moderate the emotional distress associated with a stressful event. An example of the former is seeking legal advice during a marital separation; joining a support group during the separation would be an example of the latter. Obviously, as these examples show, problem- and emotion-focused coping are not mutually exclusive, and they are both utilized to cope with many stressful situations.

The research on stress and coping has grown exponentially during the past 30 years (Somerfield & McCrae, 2000). However, some have argued that much of the research offers little of practical value to clinicians (Coyne & Racioppo, 2000). Others are less pessimistic but acknowledge the necessity of bridging the gap between stress and coping research and clinical practice (Lazarus, 2000).

WELL-BEING

Psychology has been dominated by research and clinical practice focusing on negative affect, psychopathology, and remediation. In recent years, there has been a resurgence of interest and scholarly attention to positive affect, health and well-being, and prevention. Seligman and Csikszentmihalyi (2000), introducing a special issue of *American Psychologist*, describe positive psychology as "a science of positive subjective experience, positive individual traits, and positive institutions . . . to improve the quality of life" (p. 5). Lightsey (1996) presents an extensive literature review of subjective well-being and psychological resources and concludes by offering several recommendations for counselors (e.g., helping clients develop positive beliefs about themselves and teaching active problem-solving skills to mediate stress reactions). Romano (1997) conceptualized "student well-being" as "the development of knowledge, attitudes, skills, and behaviors that maximize students' functioning" (p. 246). A large body of literature has investigated competence, resiliency, and stress resistance in children (Garmezy, Masten, & Tellegen, 1984; Masten & Coatsworth, 1998; see also Rak, this volume). After reviewing the literature, Benard (1993) concluded that resilient children have four attributes: social competence, problem-solving skills, autonomy, and a sense of purpose. Folkman and Moskowitz Tedlie (2000) point out that negative affect and distress have dominated the stress and coping literature. They argue for greater attention to the study of positive affect and positive outcomes associated with stressful events. Romano and Hage (in press) strongly recommend that greater attention be given to the prevention of psychological disturbances and problematic lifestyle behaviors in the training and practice of psychologists and counselors.

FRAMEWORK TO HELP CLIENTS MANAGE STRESS, IMPROVE COPING, AND ENHANCE WELL-BEING

Mental health practitioners can be instrumental in helping clients reduce stress, improve coping, and strengthen overall well-being to improve the client's psychological, occupational, and social functioning. The framework here presented is appropriate for individual and group work, as well as for preventive and remedial interventions.

Clients often seek counseling only after other alternatives to manage a stressor have been tried and found lacking (e.g., advice from family/friends, self-help books). Sometimes, the stressors are manifested in physical symptoms such as muscular pain, stomach distress, or headaches. When clients present physical symptoms, it is necessary for therapists to make a referral to a physician to eliminate organic causes for the symptoms. In other words, it should not be assumed that psychological stress is the primary cause of the physical symptoms. Excessive stress can also be manifested in sleep and eating disturbances, increased use of alcohol and other drugs (i.e., legal and illegal and over-the-counter and prescribed medications), and interpersonal difficulties at home and work. During initial sessions, counselors and psychologists need to assess how the client is currently coping with the stressful situation. This assessment should include questions about alcohol and drug use, episodes of depression, suicidal ideation, and incidences of violent behaviors. In addition, questions about sleep patterns, eating behavior, and physical activity should be asked.

The framework includes three components: (1) increase awareness of behaviors and reactions associated with a stressful situation, (2) improve coping strategies, and (3) strengthen well-being.

Increase Awareness

One goal of many preventive and remedial psychological interventions is to increase the participant's or client's personal awareness. When a presenting issue is stress-related, it is important that clients gain increased awareness of their personal responses to the stressful situation.

Physiological Awareness. Selye's (1976) contributions made us acutely aware of physiological changes that accompany stressful events.

Because of these physiological reactions, it is important that mental health professionals help clients understand physical changes that may occur during stressful events. Therapists can explain the flight-or-fight response and the physiology of stress, including descriptions of the sympathetic and parasympathetic nervous systems and hormonal changes that occur during a stress response. Clients are usually aware of the physical reactions because they have experienced many of them, for example, muscle tension, rapid heartbeat, cold fingers, and shallow breathing. Greater understanding of the reasons for these changes helps clients reduce their fears about them and appreciate the value of coping interventions (e.g., relaxation training) designed to moderate the physical effects of stress. A related benefit is a greater sense of physiological control. Biofeedback therapy can help clients learn more subtle physiological information about themselves. In the absence of sophisticated biofeedback equipment (e.g., electromyograph), clients can be encouraged to be aware of physiological changes that accompany stressful situations (e.g., an excessively tight grip on a telephone during an important call).

Cognitive Awareness. Cognitive psychology has made us very aware of the role of private thoughts in emotional disturbance (Beck & Weishaar, 2000; Ellis, 2000). Cognitions contribute significantly to stress reactions, and a discussion of the role of private thoughts in stress reactions should take place with the client. As with the physiological dimension above, clients usually understand from their own experience how thinking behaviors influence their emotions.

In Lazarus's (1984) conceptualization of stress, a person's cognitive appraisal of a situation is related to a stress reaction. Clients can be instructed to monitor their thoughts surrounding stressful situations; in this way, they record their stress appraisals and become aware of irrational and distorted self-talk. A thoughts diary helps clients monitor their self-talk by recording over several days their strong emotional responses (e.g., anxiety, anger, sadness), the events that precipitated the emotions, and the thoughts that accompanied the emotions and events. A client examines with the counselor this record of self-talk and how it may be contributing to stress reactions.

Lifestyle Awareness. Lifestyle patterns contribute to stress reactions. For example, excessive caffeine, limited physical activity, lack of proper nutrition, poor sleep habits, weak social networks, and time mismanagement may not only add to the distress of a situation, but interfere with a person's ability to cope with the situation. Clients need to learn how lifestyle behaviors contribute to stress. For example, excessive caffeine contributes to overstimulation of the nervous system; poor sleep habits and low social support interfere with healthy coping behaviors; poor nutrition increases the risk of illness. Different types of record-keeping or diaries help clients become aware of these and other lifestyle behaviors. Examples include asking clients to record all that they eat and drink over several days and keeping a time diary to monitor use of time.

The major goals of this component are to (1) teach an understanding of the relationship of physiology, thoughts, and lifestyle to stress; (2) encourage clients to increase their awareness of their reactions to stressful situations; and (3) monitor how they are presently coping with the situation. Self-awareness is important as an initial step in the change process.

Improve Coping Strategies

The second component of this framework is helping clients change, improve, or strengthen their coping strategies to better manage a stressful situation. Various interventions are available in the three domains of physiology, cognition, and lifestyle. Interventions related to these domains may overlap and are not mutually exclusive. Interventions can be utilized for remedial and preventive purposes and in individual and group applications.

Physiological Change. The flight-or-fight response disrupts physiological homeostasis during a stressful encounter. The sympathetic nervous system predominates during the response. Interventions such as relaxation training, diaphragmatic breathing, and meditation

engage the parasympathetic nervous system, creating a relaxation response. These interventions give clients tools or strategies to help the body return to an increased level of homeostasis. As the parasympathetic nervous system becomes engaged, physiological changes occur; for example, heart rate is slowed, hands and fingers become warmer, and muscle tension is reduced. A major advantage of teaching clients strategies to influence their physiology is the sense of control they experience over their physiological reactions to a stressful encounter. One example is teaching clients the difference between stress-induced breathing (i.e., upper chest movement, shallow breaths) and relaxed breathing (i.e., abdomen movement, deeper breaths). One form of relaxed breathing is called diaphragmatic breathing because it utilizes the diaphragm, a muscle at the bottom of the chest cavity, to regulate the flow of oxygen into and out of the body. Diaphragmatic breathing is sometimes referred to as natural breathing because newborn infants instinctively breathe with the diaphragm. Stress reactions disrupt this natural tendency to breathe with the diaphragm. Clients can be given instruction and practice in diaphragmatic breathing and asked to utilize this strategy during stressful encounters. Diaphragmatic breathing and other forms of psychophysiological interventions have the effect of inducing emotional calmness as they engage the parasympathetic nervous system. Breathing techniques have advantages over other forms of psychophysiological interventions because they can be implemented with little or no notice from others. However, clients must remember to utilize them; I have encouraged people to make notes to themselves ("breathe with my diaphragm") in anxiety-producing situations (e.g., public speaking).

Cognitive Change. Cognitive-behavior theory (Beck & Weishaar, 2000; Ellis, 2000) has provided numerous techniques and strategies to help clients change thinking patterns that contribute to stress reactions. One type of strategy is cognitive restructuring, in which clients learn to replace irrational and distorted beliefs and thoughts with self-statements that are more rational and realistic. Changing self-defeating and stress-producing thoughts to those that are more self-enhancing will reduce stress reactions. In terms of Lazarus's (1984) concepts of stress and coping, cognitive restructuring strategies have the potential to help clients appraise stressful situations more accurately. If a client regularly uses words such as "should," "always," "never," "everybody/nobody," and "can't," these are signs that the client's thought patterns may be self-defeating. Suggesting that clients utilize more appropriate language (e.g., "some," "most people," "I chose" rather than "I should") will reduce stress. Other cognitive strategies include thought stopping and cognitive rehearsal, which are techniques to discourage the use of self-defeating thoughts and promote self-enhancing thoughts.

One stress management intervention utilizing cognitive strategies along with other techniques is called stress inoculation training (SIT). SIT was developed by Meichenbaum and his colleagues (Meichenbaum & Jaremko, 1983) to help people prepare for stressful events. SIT inoculates people against the effects of stress situations through education, coping skills training, and application.

Lifestyle Change. Mental health professionals are well positioned to inform people about lifestyle behaviors that contribute to stress and those that may buffer the effects of stress. As behavior change experts, counselors are well qualified to initially assess problematic lifestyle behaviors and suggest possible change strategies. Psychologists and counselors may need to refer to other professionals for consultation in areas that are beyond their expertise (e.g., nutritionist, chemical dependency counselor, exercise physiologist). At times, referral to a clergy person may be necessary. Most important, however, counselors need to teach clients how lifestyles that promote well-being will help to manage stress and enhance overall health. For example, people are bombarded in the national media about the health benefits of physical exercise and diets low in sugar and saturated fats. However, clients may be less informed about the potential benefits of physical exercise as a stress management strategy (Long & Flood,

1993). They also may underestimate how misuse of time and weak social support networks may contribute to stress.

Lifestyle changes must be introduced gradually so that clients do not become discouraged and lose motivation to change. Discuss with clients changes that they are most motivated to make. Once the focus of change has been decided on, a change strategy can be developed, implemented, and regularly evaluated for effectiveness.

Strengthen Well-Being

The final component of this model teaches clients behaviors and strategies to enhance their overall well-being to buffer the effects of future stressors and life changes. In addition to physiological, cognitive, and lifestyle domains, it is recommended that clients periodically review other areas of their lives, including spiritual, family, and career. Included in these areas are themes of personal values, life meaning, hope, optimism, and life satisfaction (e.g., family, career, and interpersonal relationships).

Kobasa (1979) has studied people who are resistant to the negative health effects of stressful life events. She hypothesized that these people are characterized by a "hardy personality"; that is, they are people who exhibit a sense of personal control, are committed to their endeavors, and feel challenged by them. According to Kobasa, these characteristics serve as protective factors in stressful situations.

A holistic model of personal development, addressing several dimensions of the human condition, is highly recommended to strengthen well-being. Romano (1984) developed a holistic model of stress management in the form of a university course and reported promising results. Recently, Hoffman and Driscoll (2000) articulated a broadly conceptualized biopsychosocial model of health promotion and disease prevention to address health needs. Coping styles and stress management are important components of the model. The Wheel of Wellness is another comprehensive example of a holistic model for health and well-being presented by Myers, Sweeney, and Witmer (2000).

Stress, coping, and well-being are important psychological constructs that have enjoyed a rich theoretical and applied history. Although much more needs to be learned about them, there is sufficient research evidence to recommend the application of these constructs for preventive and remedial applications by mental health practitioners.

References

Aldwin, C.M. (1994). *Stress, coping, and development: An integrative perspective.* New York: Guilford Press.

Beck, A.A., & Weishaar, M.E. (2000). Cognitive therapy. In R.J. Corsini & D. Wedding (Eds.), *Current psychotherapies* (pp. 241–272). Itasca, IL: Peacock.

Benard, B. (1993, November). Fostering resiliency in kids. *Educational Leadership,* 44–48.

Cannon, E.B. (1932). *The wisdom of the body.* New York: Norton.

Coddington, R.R. (1972). The significance of life events as etiologic factors in the diseases of children: II. A study of a normal population. *Journal of Psychosomatic Research, 16,* 205–213.

Coyne, J.C., & Racioppo, M.W. (2000). Never the twain shall meet? Closing the gap between coping research and clinical intervention research. *American Psychologist, 55,* 655–664.

Dohrenwend, B.S., & Dohrenwend, B.P. (1984). Life stress and illness: Formulation of the issues. In B.S. Dohrenwend & B.P. Dohrenwend (Eds.), *Stressful life events and their contexts.* New York: Prodist.

Ellis, A. (2000). Rational emotive behavior therapy. In R.J. Corsini & D. Wedding (Eds.), *Current psychotherapies* (pp. 168–204). Itasca, IL: Peacock.

Folkman, S., & Moskowitz Tedlie, J. (2000). Positive affect and the other side of coping. *American Psychologist, 55,* 647–654.

Garmezy, N., Masten, A.S., & Tellegen, A. (1984). The study of stress and competency in children: A building block for developmental psychopathology. *Child Development, 55,* 97–111.

Hobfoll, S.E. (1989). Conservation of resources: A new attempt at conceptualizing stress. *American Psychologist, 44,* 513–524.

Hoffman, M.A., & Driscoll, J.M. (2000). Health promotion and disease prevention: A concentric biopsychosocial model of health status. In S.D. Brown & R.W. Lent (Eds.), *Handbook of counseling psychology* (3rd ed., pp. 532–567). New York: Wiley.

Holmes, T.H., & Rahe, R.H. (1967). The social readjustment rating scale. *Journal of Psychosomatic Research, 11,* 213–218.

Kobasa, S.C. (1979). Stressful life events, personality and health: An inquiry into hardiness. *Journal of Personality and Social Psychology, 37,* 1–11.

Lazarus, R.S. (1992). Four reasons why it is difficult to demonstrate psychosocial influences on health. *Advances, the Journal of Mind-Body Health, 8,* 6–7.

Lazarus, R.S. (1993). Coping theory and research: Past, present, and future. *Psychosomatic Medicine, 15,* 234–247.

Lazarus, R.S. (2000). Toward better research on stress and coping. *American Psychologist, 55,* 665–673.

Lazarus, R.S., & Folkman, S. (1984). *Stress, appraisal, and coping.* New York: Springer.

Lightsey, O.S. (1996). What leads to wellness? The role of psychological resources in well-being. *The Counseling Psychologist, 24,* 589–735.

Long, B.C., & Flood, K.R. (1993). Coping and work stress: Psychological benefits of exercise. *Work and Stress, 7,* 109–119.

Marx, M.B., Garrity, T.F., & Bowers, F.R. (1975). The influence of recent life experiences on the health of college freshmen. *Journal of Psychosomatic Research, 19,* 87–98.

Masten, A.S., & Coatsworth, J.D. (1998). The development of competence in favorable and unfavorable environments: Lessons from research on successful children. *American Psychologist, 53,* 185–204.

Masten, A.S., Neemann, J., & Andenas, S. (1994). Life events and adjustment in adolescents: The significance of event independence, desirability, and chronicity. *Journal of Research on Adolescence, 4,* 71–97.

Meichenbaum, D., & Jaremko, M.E. (1983). *Stress reduction and prevention.* New York: Plenum Press.

Myers, J.E., Sweeney, T.J., & Witmer, J.M. (2000). The Wheel of Wellness counseling for wellness: A holistic model for treatment planning. *Journal of Counseling and Development, 78,* 251–266.

Rice, P.L. (1999). *Stress and health.* Pacific Grove, CA: Brooks/Cole.

Romano, J.L. (1984). Stress management and wellness: Reaching beyond the counselor's office. *Personnel and Guidance Journal, 62,* 533–536.

Romano, J.L. (1997). School personnel training for the prevention of tobacco, alcohol, and other drug use: Issues and outcomes. *Journal of Drug Education, 27,* 245–258.

Romano, J.L., & Hage, S.M. (in press). Prevention and counseling psychology: Revitalizing commitments for the 21st century. *The Counseling Psychologist.*

Sarafino, E.P. (1998). *Health psychology: Biopsychosocial interactions* (3rd ed.). New York: Wiley.

Seligman, M.E.P., & Csikszentmihalyi, M. (2000). Positive psychology: An introduction. *American Psychologist, 55,* 5–14.

Selye, H. (1976). *The stress of life.* New York: McGraw-Hill.

Somerfield, M.R., & McCrae, R.R. (2000). Stress and coping research: Methodological challenges, theoretical advances, and clinical applications. *American Psychologist, 55,* 600–625.

8   THE FAT CLIENT

Janet Melcher and Gerald J. Bostwick Jr.

On a daily basis, people in the United States are bombarded with images of ideal personal appearance. Mass media communications suggest that achieving the correct appearance will lead to acceptance, success, and overall happiness in life. The current standards for attractiveness include size specifications. It is not surprising, then, that some people who seek mental health care may be concerned about food and weight issues either because their actual size is different from what society deems desirable, or because they have become obsessed with maintaining a body size that already meets or exceeds societal standards. Concerns about food and weight bring anguish in many forms. The following discussion focuses specifically on providing help to those persons who are truly considered heavier than average or obese by the mental health practitioner.

The word "fat" will be used in this chapter when referring to clients. As Barron and Lear (1989) point out, the word "obese" is used in a medical context and therefore suggests that fat is a disease. "Overweight" suggests that there is really a correct weight that one is over. The word fat is used to acknowledge and honor the most accurate description of the client, in the hope that the word's derogatory connotation will fade.

If the fat person expresses concern about food and weight, the mental health practitioner needs to expand the scope of the assessment and intervention plan by considering the following:

- The influence of social/cultural beliefs and messages about size.
- Biological factors that affect size.

- Psychological ramifications of being heavier than average in a society that values thinness.

SOCIAL/CULTURAL BELIEFS AND MESSAGES ABOUT SIZE

Today in Western culture, the slender body shape is placed before the public as a standard to achieve, particularly for women. This preoccupation with thinness is a relatively recent phenomenon. Prior to the late 1800s and early 1900s, thinness was often considered unhealthy and unattractive. One factor that brought about the change in attitude was the expansion of women's roles around the turn of the century. In the late 1800s, feminist ideas emerged. Some women were attending college and many were finding jobs outside the home. At the same time, the view that women were too frail to be physically active was supplanted by the view that healthy women should be athletic. Thus, women began to enjoy more overall physical freedom. The expansion in women's roles necessitated changes in women's fashions. The cumbersome clothing styles of the past were simply no longer practical. The fashion industry responded by designing more functional clothing. The new styles were more revealing, making it more difficult for women to use clothing for body shape enhancement. Because clothing could no longer be used to cosmetically shape the body, the body became the object to be shaped (Bennett & Gurin, 1982; Seid, 1989, 1994).

By the middle of the century, the changing attitudes about appropriate weight and size were reinforced by a Metropolitan Life Insurance Company retrospective study (as cited in Bennett & Gurin, 1982) that examined the relationship between weight and mortality rates. Despite the biased samples and questionable data analyses, the findings were generalized to the entire population. The proliferation of papers generated by this insurance company's scientist was instrumental in accelerating the change in attitudes about weight and health. By the early 1950s, obesity was identified as

the number one health problem in this country. Obesity became a disease to be treated by physicians; the remedy for the disease was the weight-loss diet (Bennett & Gurin, 1982; Seid 1989).

While the health care industry was busy embracing the notion that lower body weight was healthy for all, the fashion industry came along to firmly implant an association between thinness and beauty in the consciousness of the culture (Seid, 1989). In the 1960s, the appearance of the famous fashion model Twiggy (5'7" and 98 pounds) marked the beginning of a more severe standard for thinness, which continues to be idealized today (Seid, 1994).

In the decades after the 1960s, the models for female beauty became increasingly thinner and less likely to resemble what the average American woman could realistically achieve. For example, Garner, Garfinkel, Schwartz, and Thompson (1980) found that the Miss America contestants during the period from 1959 to 1978 showed a trend toward decreasing weights at the same time that American women were increasing in weight. In an update of this research, Wiseman, Gray, Mosimann, and Ahrens (1992) found that the Miss America contestants' body weights continued to decrease between 1979 and 1988. During this period, the reported Miss America body weights were 13% to 19% below the weights that would be expected for women of their ages. These authors point out that maintaining a weight of 15% below the expected weight is one criterion for the diagnosis of anorexia nervosa.

Today, the pursuit of thinness remains quite popular. For instance, results of a recent survey of U.S. college students (Centers for Disease Control and Prevention, 1997) indicated that 41.6% of students considered themselves to be overweight, even though only 20.5% were classified as overweight. Female students were more likely to consider themselves overweight than male students. The report states that 46.4% of the college student respondents were attempting to lose weight. Overall, one-third of college students have used dieting as a means to control weight and about one-half have used exercise.

Media messages continue to promote the concept that weight loss is a goal that the acceptable person will achieve. The messages mainly affect females. Levine and Smolak (1996) found that weight loss is glorified in magazines and through televised messages that adolescent girls and young women are likely to see. Wertheim, Paxton, Schutz, and Muir (1997) found that girls responded to the thin ideal pictured in the media by feeling pressured to be thin. Pinhas, Toner, Ale, Garfinkel, and Stuckless (1999) report that the women in their study felt angrier and had an increase in depressed mood after looking at pictures of the thin models from common fashion magazines. While conducting a content analysis of popular magazines, Malkin, Wornian, and Chrisler (1999) discovered that 94% of women's magazines showed thin females on the cover. They also found that the magazine covers displayed messages about weight that were positioned next to other messages with the implication that weight loss will lead to an improved life.

When reviewing the literature on weight loss issues, several themes emerge (Kilbourne, 1994; Nichter & Nichter, 1991; Seid, 1989):

- Advertisers have an interest in keeping consumers dissatisfied with themselves because profit depends on selling something that the consumer lacks. There is no incentive to tell consumers, especially women, that they are perfectly acceptable just as they are.
- To ward off uncomfortable reminders that life is full of uncertainties, great value is placed on "being in control" in our culture. Weight has become symbolically linked to control. Those considered fat are viewed as violators of the mandate for control and are consequently judged as lacking in virtue.
- Satisfying versus suppressing the appetite for food has become a moral issue for persons of all sizes, especially for fat people.

Naturally, the impact of living in this social context may be quite significant for the fat person. As early as 1962 researchers found that there was a correlation between obesity and socioeconomic status, with the highest percentage of obese women falling into the lowest socioeconomic status group. Men showed a similar trend to a lesser degree (Moore, Stunkard, & Srole, 1962). More recently, a seven-year follow-up of subjects who were overweight during adolescence and early adulthood found that the women had completed fewer years of school, were not as likely to be married, and were more likely to live in poverty than women who had not been overweight. These researchers believe that their findings support the position that socioeconomic status is a consequence of being overweight, and they question the assumption that being overweight is due to socioeconomic status (Gortmaker, Must, Perrin, Sobol, & Dietz, 1993).

Rothblum and associates (1990) found that the very obese participants in their research reported experiencing various types of employment discrimination. Both obese and very obese people also reported school victimization, including being called negative weight-related names, being excluded from sports or social activities, and being victims of discrimination by teachers.

Access to appropriate medical care is a concern for obese people. Some have been denied health insurance because of their weight (Rothblum, Brand, Miller, & Oetjen, 1990). Some may not have adequate health care simply because they are poor and cannot afford health insurance and preventive care (Rothblum, 1994). Some are reluctant to seek medical care because they anticipate receiving abuse and admonitions about weight from their physicians, regardless of the symptom for which treatment is sought (Burgard & Lyons, 1994).

Finally, Seid (1989) notes that the cruelest and most damaging thing the fashion industry did in the 1960s was to convey the idea that anyone could become thin. The health care industry supported this notion as well. The assumption that thinness is attainable by everyone persists. This view is particularly distressing given the evidence that biological realities are in conflict with the cultural mandate to be thin.

BIOLOGICAL FACTORS THAT AFFECT SIZE

The set point theory holds that the body has a built-in system that determines how much fat is needed (Nisbett, 1972). When a person tries to reduce the fat stores through a weight-loss diet, biological changes occur. These changes are actually designed to help the body survive through times of famine. Metabolic rates decrease and calories are burned more slowly to defend the fat stores. The dieter may notice that weight loss slows or stops altogether. Soon, the dieter will experience intense hunger and may feel compelled to eat. When eating occurs, weight is gained more easily because the metabolic rate is lowered (Bennett & Gurin, 1982; Leibel, Rosenbaum, & Hirsch, 1995). Most dieters will regain the weight lost within two to five years and many will weigh more than they did before the diet (Garner & Wooley, 1991).

When working with the fat client, the mental health practitioner should keep the following in mind:

- Fat people do not eat more than lean people. A fat person may need to eat considerably less than the lean person to maintain an average body size (Garner & Wooley, 1991).
- Different people can eat the same amount of food and have very different body sizes (Bouchard et al., 1990).
- Genes appear to influence body fatness, and the childhood environment has little or no effect (Stunkard et al., 1986).
- A body mass index (BMI) in the 26 to 28 range is considered over the ideal weight. BMI is weight in kilograms divided by the square of height in meters (kg/m^2). Longitudinal studies show that BMIs in this range do not necessarily result in increased mortality rates (Ernsberger & Haskew, 1987; Troiano, Frongillo, Sobal, & Levitsky, 1996).
- Weight loss can reduce cholesterol and blood pressure and improve glucose tolerance, but these health benefits disappear with the regaining of weight and often are more problematic than prior to the weight loss (Garner & Wooley, 1991).
- Weight cycling (repeatedly losing and regaining weight) is associated with higher rates of death from coronary heart disease and death from all causes (Brownell & Rodin, 1994; Lissner et al., 1991).
- Persons who gain a modest amount of weight during adulthood have the lowest mortality rates, and weight loss is associated with higher mortality rates (Andres, Muller, & Sorkin, 1993; Pamuk et al., 1992).
- Normal daily calorie intake for adults may range from 2,400 to 3,000 calories per day. Most weight-loss diets prescribe 945 to 1,200 calories per day. The World Health Organization states that 900 or fewer calories qualifies as starvation (*www.naafa.org*).
- Hunger is managed best through eating at regular, predictable intervals (Wooley, Wooley, & Dyrenforth, 1979).

Because there are hazards associated with weight loss, experts recommend lifestyle changes that promote health for persons of any size (I. Kedd, 2000). This involves incremental, moderate changes in eating and exercise habits that can be realistically sustained over time. The health benefits are immediate. For example, a study comparing fitness levels in overweight and normal-weight men found a lower risk of mortality in the physically fit regardless of size (Barlow, Kohl, Gibbons, & Blair, 1995). Although there is much conflicting information about healthy eating, authorities seem to agree that eating a varied diet that incorporates favorite foods, fruits, vegetables, and whole grains is most beneficial; they also recommend limiting portions of foods high in fat (Berg, 1993; Burgard & Lyons, 1994). Research indicates that blood pressure can be reduced by diet content (Appel et al., 1997). Also, risk factors for coronary artery disease can be reduced by using a combination of dietary content and exercise even for people who remain fat (Barnard, Ugianskis, Martin, & Inkeles, 1992).

PSYCHOLOGICAL RAMIFICATIONS OF BEING FAT IN A SOCIETY THAT VALUES THINNESS

In both the general and professional literature, there has been a tendency to view a person's weight-loss failures as the result of a psychological defect. Of course, fat people have the same range of difficulties and disturbances as people of any size, but studies have found that the rate of psychopathology in the obese population is similar to the rate in the nonobese population. So the idea that people are fat because they have psychological disturbance has been refuted (Stunkard & Wadden, 1992). However, some psychological symptoms that fat people present to mental health professionals are actually the offshoots of being fat in a society that values thinness. Symptoms that are really the psychological ramifications of being fat include distorted relationships with food, problematic emotions associated with food deprivation, and self-deprecating responses to the prejudices about size.

Many fat people have tried weight-loss diets. Often, they want very much to comply with societal expectations. For some, the repeated efforts to lose weight have resulted in distorted relationships with food, which may become manifest in the following ways:

- Binge eating and some overeating can be a consequence of the body's push to restore fat after restrictions in food intake. This particular eating compulsion is a biological survival mechanism and is not necessarily indicative of psychological pathology (Polivy, 1996; Telch & Agras, 1993).
- The fat person has been trained and encouraged to limit food intake, so that normal eating (eating in response to internal hunger signals) seems forbidden (Polivy, 1996).
- Even when not overeating, the fat person may be apologetic about the amount of food consumed and may even feel the need to hide when eating (Polivy, 1996).

Unfortunately, the amount of food required to stabilize eating patterns and improve emotions will often lead to fears of weight gain. Weight gain is perceived as failure. For the perennial dieter, the decision to stop dieting is a significant psychological step that means parting with the dream of being thin. The fat client may need time to accept the fact that permanent size reduction is an unattainable goal and to develop a new way of thinking about self and food.

For some people, even with adequate food intake over time, significant overeating or binge eating may continue. When the person has experienced food deprivation, even if intermittently, food can take on exaggerated importance. The good feeling one gets by satisfying hunger seems to get confused with soothing emotional pain. Overeating consistently used to ease emotional pain does not occur in all cases, as the popular media suggests. When overeating does occur in this manner, however, it can be quite alarming for the individual.

Many unpleasant emotional reactions are associated with food deprivation. These include irritability, anxiety, mood swings, and depressive symptoms (Garner & Wooley, 1991; Polivy, 1996). Adequate nourishment is needed for optimal psychological functioning. When eating returns to normal, these emotional changes may subside.

Finally, fat people have different psychological reactions to societal prejudice and discrimination. Those who subscribe to the view that weight is under their control accept society's condemnation of their size and consider themselves at fault for their own condition. In contrast, some fat people recognize the distortions in the media and in the public's thinking about weight and do not accept the view that they are defective or deficient (Crocker, Crornwell, & Major, 1993). Responses to this hostile environment range from total self-deprecation to fat activism.

ASSESSMENT

For clients of any size, especially females, food and weight issues may be a concern. The fat client may or may not express concern about these issues. As part of the usual assessment process, the mental health practitioner may mention that food and weight issues are of great concern to many people living in this culture and then may ask if these issues are a concern for the client. If the client indicates that there are no concerns in this area, the exploration is ended. The mention of the subject gives the client permission to revisit the topic at a later time. If the client expresses concern about food and weight issues, the assessment should be expanded to include a discussion of dieting history, current eating patterns, level of physical activity, and expectations about any problems that will be solved as a result of resolving food and weight issues.

Dieting History

The dieting history provides some indication of clients' long-term relationship with food as well as their understanding of why past attempts at resolving food and weight issues have not been successful. The following questions can be used to explore the dieting history:

- How many diets have been tried?
- What types of diets were tried?
- Approximately when did the dieting take place?
- How much weight was regained after each diet?
- Were there any emotional changes when dieting?
- What is your understanding of the reason for lack of success with weight loss?

Current Eating Patterns

Clients' eating patterns may range from normal to somewhat problematic to so troubled that a formal eating disorder diagnosis is warranted. The practitioner may discover that a client's eating falls within a normal pattern even when the client defines the eating as problematic: The client believes that something must be wrong with the eating pattern because a heavy weight is maintained. Clients may express some conflicts about food because eating has been discouraged. Some clients may be engaging in binge-purge

behaviors that would put the eating pattern in the bulimic category.

For many practitioners and clients as well, there can be a great temptation to focus on how much food the client is eating with little attention to the overall pattern of eating. If the person is truly binge eating or consistently overeating, the usual pattern includes some period of deprivation that precedes the overeating. The client could be experiencing a rebound from a recent weight-loss diet or perhaps the client does not eat all day and then eats continuously at night. The deprivation must be understood and addressed to help the client become free of food obsessions. To obtain the pertinent information about eating patterns, the following questions may be asked:

- It is helpful to know the details about the most recent diet. What type of diet did you try and when did it occur? What have you noticed about eating patterns since the diet?
- Describe the way you eat on a typical day. What do you consider to be a good eating day? What is a bad day? Do you have foods that you consider good or bad? If so, please explain.
- Do you see a connection between your emotions and your eating pattern?
- Most people overeat at times. Some people feel that they overeat constantly. How would you describe your overeating?
- Do you ever binge eat? If so, how often, when does the binge occur, and what is consumed?
- Sometimes, people try to maintain a lower weight by trying not to eat, by vomiting after eating, by using laxatives, or by exercising extensively. Have you used any of these methods to control weight?

Exercise

A review of the exercise history and current activity level is important for several reasons. Some clients may be supporting their own health currently by engaging in regular physical activity, but they may be discouraged because significant weight loss has not occurred. Some may have gained weight after an injury or illness resulted in a need to limit activity, so accommodations may be needed for the person to remain active. Some may be reluctant to exercise because they fear being ridiculed if exposed to the public eye. The questions related to exercise include:

- Do you exercise or engage in any type of physical activity?
- Do you have any physical problems that require you to limit your physical activity?
- If you are not currently engaged in any kind of regular physical activity, do you have any concerns that prevent you from being active (e.g., don't want to put on a leotard and go to the aerobics class with all the thin women)?

Goals Accomplished by Losing Weight

People of all sizes focus energy on losing weight in part because being thinner may be the means by which another goal is attained. Perhaps the weight loss is intended to bring greater social acceptance or improved health. Questions should be designed to help clients reveal the goal(s) that are ultimately to be accomplished by losing weight. Responses to the following questions will help the practitioner to further clarify the clients' goals:

- What was happening in your life that made you decide to try to lose weight?
- How would your life be better if you lost weight?

When the information about dieting, eating patterns, exercise, and goals to be accomplished by weight loss is added to the information gathered in the usual assessment process, the client's issues usually fall into one of five categories. As we delineated in an earlier article (Melcher & Bostwick, 1998) the categories are:

- *Normal but Doesn't Know It*—she functions well in all or most areas of her life and eating is actually normal. She believes that

she must be doing something wrong because she is heavier than average. She may be asking for help at this moment in her life because of some normal developmental shift, which causes her to reflect upon where she is in life. For example, she may turn 30 and become more concerned about the fact that she's not married. She believes that weight loss is required in order to meet this and other life goals;
- *Well-Adjusted Overeater*—this person functions well. However, she may be overeating or perhaps binge eating because she has been dieting and/or excessively exercising;
- *Emotionally Troubled Normal Eater*—this person is not overeating, but believes that an eating problem exists because she is heavier than average. She has emotional issues that cause problems in functioning but these are not necessarily related to her weight;
- *Emotionally Troubled Overeater*—this person is involved in overeating or problematic eating and has co-existing emotional problems. In this case, the social worker still needs to know whether there has been recent food deprivation because, as in the other cases, the effort to diet is contributing to the eating problem. For this individual, when food deprivation no longer exists there may be continued use of food to help with managing a variety of emotions (e.g., anxiety, depression); and,
- *Normal and Knows It*—this person is heavier than average, has accepted her size, functions well, and does not overeat. However, she may feel lonely because few people understand her situation and she may feel exhausted by societal discrimination. (p. 200)

INTERVENTION

With the possible exception of the "normal and knows it" client, all of the clients in the four remaining categories need information about the arbitrary nature of size stipulations in Western culture, about the pitfalls of weight-loss dieting, and about the option of living in a manner that promotes health regardless of size. An ideal way to transmit such information is through a psychoeducational group. In a psychoeducational group, clients receive information, have the opportunity to discuss how the information applies to their own situation, and receive group support (Ciliska, 1998).

If no group is available, the mental health practitioner may certainly share this information with individual clients. When working with an individual, the delivery of the information is paced to address the specific concerns of that client. Time is allowed for discussion of the client's reactions to the information and for therapeutic input from the practitioner.

If the client's eating pattern is in the normal range, this assessment should be shared with the client. Clients may respond to this news with mixed feelings of relief for not being at fault for their size, and sadness because thinness has eluded them.

If the client's eating pattern is problematic, intervention calls for some discussion of how this individual might plan to schedule meals at regular intervals. The client needs to work toward knowing that food will be available at regular intervals (e.g., breakfast, lunch, and dinner, or lunch, dinner, and evening snack) to stop overeating. Some of the overeating may be an attempt to hoard food before the next famine. Techniques such as sitting comfortably at a place designated only for eating and avoiding other activities, such as watching TV or reading while eating, can help the person focus on eating in response to internal signals. Some clients may want to give up the effort to improve eating patterns if episodes of overeating occur, so they need reassurance that returning to their old, familiar eating pattern is expected. Following the plan perfectly may be essential for losing weight, but it is not required for developing a more satisfying relationship with food (Roth, 1984).

Assessment of emotional difficulties is an ongoing process if the eating is restricted. Some dysphoria may be the result of inadequate nourishment. When there are diagnosable emotional problems, proceed with treatment as usual. If one mental health practitioner is working with the food and weight issues as well as the more general mental health concerns, discussion of the two areas can be blended. If overeating is truly used to cope with emotional upsets, then the connection between each precipitating event and eating must be explored to help the client find a more productive way of responding.

Finally, a few other things to consider:

- A referral can be made to a dietitian who agrees with a size acceptance philosophy for help with the problem eating.
- A consultation with a physical therapist or exercise physiologist might be useful to the person who has physical problems that interfere with becoming physically active.
- Sometimes, meetings that include the client and family members or significant others may be useful for educating all involved and for helping clients communicate their needs about food and weight issues to those who are closest to them.
- Contact with a support group or with a size acceptance organization can help clients maintain self-acceptance and feel less isolated. One helpful resource is the National Association to Advance Fat Acceptance (NAAFA—www.naafa.org).

References

Andres, R., Muller, D.C., & Sorkin, J.D. (1993). Long-term effects of change in body weight on all-cause mortality. *Annals of Internal Medicine, 119*(7, Pt. 2), 737–743.

Appel, L.J., Moore, T.J., Obarzanek, E., Vollmer, W.M., Svetkey, L.P., Sacks, F.M., Bray, G.A., Vogt, T.M., Cutler, J.A., Windhauser, M.M., Lin, P., Karanja, N. (1997). A clinical trial of the effects of dietary patterns on blood pressure. *New England Journal of Medicine, 336*(16), 1117–1124.

Barlow, C.E., Kohl, H.W., III, Gibbons, L.W., & Blair, S.N. (1995). Physical fitness, mortality and obesity. *International Journal of Obesity, 19*(Suppl. 4), 41–44.

Barnard, R.J., Ugianskis, E.J., Martin, D.A., & Inkeles, S.B. (1992). Role of diet and exercise in the management of hyperinsulinemia and associated atherosclerotic risk factors. *American Journal of Cardiology, 69,* 440–444.

Barron, N., & Lear, B.H. (1989). Ample opportunity for fat women. In L. Brown & E. Rothblum (Eds.), *Fat oppression and psychotherapy: A feminist perspective.* Binghamton, NY: Haworth Press.

Bennett, W., & Gurin, J. (1982). *The dieter's dilemma.* New York: Basic Books.

Berg, F.M. (1993). *The health risks of weight loss.* Hettinger, ND: Obesity and Health.

Bouchard, C., Tremblay, A., Després, J., Nadeau, A., Lupien, P., Thériault, G., Dussault, J., Moorjani, S., Pinault, S., & Fournier, G. (1990). The response to long-term overfeeding in identical twins. *New England Journal of Medicine, 322*(21), 1477–1482.

Brownell, K.D., & Rodin, J. (1994). Medical, metabolic, and psychological effects of weight cycling. *Archives of Internal Medicine, 154,* 1325–1330.

Burgard, D., & Lyons, P. (1994). Alternatives in obesity treatment: Focusing on health for fat women. In P. Fallon, M.A. Katzman, & S.C. Wooley (Eds.), *Feminist perspectives on eating disorders.* New York: Guilford Press.

Centers for Disease Control and Prevention. (1997). *Youth risk behavior surveillance: National college health risk behavior survey—United States, 1995,* 46(ss-6), 1–54. Retrieved May 10, 2000. Available: www.cdc.gov/nccdphp/dash/MMWRFiles/ss4606.html.

Ciliska, D. (1998). Evaluation of two nondieting interventions for obese women. *Western Journal of Nursing Research, 20*(1), 119–135.

Crocker, J., Cornwell, B., & Major, B. (1993). The stigma of overweight: Affective consequences of attributional ambiguity. *Journal of Personality and Social Psychology, 64*(1), 60–70.

Ernsberger, P., & Haskew, P. (1987). *Rethinking obesity: An alternative view of its health implications.* New York: Human Sciences Press.

Garner, D.M., Garfinkel, P.E., Schwartz, D., & Thompson, M. (1980). Cultural expectations of thinness in women. *Psychological Reports, 47,* 483–491.

Garner, D.M., & Wooley, S.C. (1991). Confronting the failure of behavioral and dietary treatments for obesity. *Clinical Psychology Review, 11,* 729–780.

Gortmaker, S.L., Must, A., Perrin, J.M., Sobol, A.M., & Dietz, W.H. (1993). Social and economic consequences of overweight in adolescence and young adulthood. *New England Journal of Medicine, 329*(14), 1008–1012.

Ikedd, J.P. (2000, January/February). Health promotion: A size acceptance approach. *Healthy Weight Journal, 14,* 12–14.

Kilbourne, J. (1994). Still killing us softly: Advertising and the obsession with thinness. In P. Fallon, M.A. Katzman, & S.C. Wooley (Eds.), *Feminist perspectives on eating disorders.* New York: Guilford Press.

Leibel, R.L., Rosenbaum, M., & Hirsch, J. (1995). Changes in energy expenditure resulting from altered body weight. *New England Journal of Medicine, 332*(10), 621–628.

Levine, M.P., & Smolak, L. (1996). Media as a context for the development of disordered eating. In L. Smolak, M.P. Levine, & R. Striegel-Moore (Eds.), *The developmental psychopathology of eating disorders: Implications for research, prevention, and treatment.* Mahwah, NJ: Erlbaum.

Lissner, L., Odell, P.M., D'Agostino, R.B., Stokes, J., III, Kreger, B.E., Belanger, A.J., & Brownell, K.D. (1991). Variability of body weight and health outcomes in the Framingham population. *New England Journal of Medicine, 324*(26), 1839–1844.

Malkin, A.R., Wornian, K., & Chrisler, J.C. (1999). Women and weight: Gendered messages on magazine covers. *Sex Roles, 40*(7/8), 647–655.

Melcher, J., & Bostwick, G.J., Jr. (1998). The obese client: Myths, facts, assessment, and intervention. *Health and Social Work, 23*(3), 195–202.

Moore, M., Stunkard, A., & Srole, L. (1962). Obesity, social class, and mental illness. *Journal of the American Medical Association, 181*(11), 962–966.

National Association to Advance Fat Acceptance. *Weight loss: Fact and fiction.* Sacramento, CA: Author. Retrieved June 20, 2000. Available: www.naafa.org

Nichter, M., & Nichter, M. (1991). Hype and weight. *Medical Anthropology, 13,* 249–284.

Nisbett, R.E. (1972). Hunger, obesity, and the ventromedial hypothalamus. *Psychological Review, 79*(6), 433–453.

Pamuk, E.R., Williamson, D.F., Madans, J., Serdula, M.K., Kleinman, J.C., & Byers, T. (1992). Weight loss and mortality in a national cohort of adults, 1971–1987. *American Journal of Epidemiology, 136*(6), 686–697.

Pinhas, L., Toner, B.B., Ali, A., Garfinkel, P.E., & Stuckless, N. (1999). The effects of the ideal of female beauty on mood and body satisfaction. *International Journal of Eating Disorders 25*(2), 223–226.

Polivy, J. (1996). Psychological consequences of food restriction. *Journal of the American Dietetic Association, 96*(6), 589–592.

Roth, G. (1984). *Breaking free from compulsive eating.* New York: Signet Book.

Rothblum, E.D. (1994). "I'll die for the revolution but don't ask me not to diet": Feminism and the continued stigmatization of obesity. In P. Fallon, M.A. Katzman, & S.C. Wooley (Eds.), *Feminist perspectives on eating disorders.* New York: Guilford Press.

Rothblum, E.D., Brand, P.A., Miller, C.P., & Oetjen, H.A. (1990). The relationship between obesity, employment discrimination, and employment related victimization. *Journal of Vocational Behavior, 37,* 251–266.

Seid, R.P. (1989). *Never too thin: Why women are at war with their bodies.* New York: Prentice Hall Press.

Seid, R.P. (1994). Too "close to the bone": The historical context for women's obsession with slenderness. In P. Fallon, M.A. Katzman, & S.C. Wooley (Eds.), *Feminist perspectives on eating disorders.* New York: Guilford Press.

Stunkard, A.J., Sorensen, T.I.A., Hanis, C., Teasdale, T.W., Chakraborty, R., Schull, W.J., & Schulsinger, F. (1986). An adoption study of human obesity. *New England Journal of Medicine, 314*(4), 193–198.

Stunkard, A.J., & Wadden, T.A. (1992). Psychological aspects of severe obesity. *American Journal of Clinical Nutrition, 55*(Suppl.), 524–532.

Telch, C.F., & Agras, W.S. (1993). The effects of a very low calorie diet on binge eating. *Behavior Therapy, 24,* 177–193.

Troiano, R.P., Frongillo, E.A., Jr., Sobal, J., & Levitsky, D.A. (1996). The relationship between body weight and mortality: A quantitative analysis of combined information from existing studies. *International Journal of Obesity, 20,* 63–75.

Wertheim, E.H., Paxton, S.J., Schutz, H.K., & Muir, S.L. (1997). Why do adolescent girls watch their weight? An interview study examining sociocultural pressures to be thin. *Journal of Psychosomatic Research, 42*(4), 345–355.

Wiseman, C.V., Gray, J.J., Mosimann, J.E., & Ahrens, A.H. (1992). Cultural expectations of thinness in women: An update. *International Journal of Eating Disorders, 11*(1), 85–89.

Wooley, S.C., Wooley, O.W., & Dyrenforth, S.R. (1979). Theoretical, practical, and social issues in behavioral treatments of obesity. *Journal of Applied Behavior Analysis, 12*(1), 3–25.

9 GUIDELINES FOR COUNSELING CLIENTS WITH HIV SPECTRUM DISORDERS

Paula J. Britton

Over 800,000 AIDS cases have been reported in the United States, and the numbers of persons infected with HIV continue to rise (Centers for Disease Control and Prevention [CDC], 1999). Counselors are needed to treat clients and their family and friends who are impacted by this disease, including those who are newly diagnosed, those who are challenged with multiple opportunistic infections, and those facing end-of-life issues. It thus becomes increasingly important for counselors to be aware of the unique issues involved with persons living with HIV/AIDS and to possess some conceptualizations and tools with which they can effectively interface with their clients.

DEFINITIONS AND KEY CONCEPTS

HIV (Human Immunodeficiency Virus) is the retrovirus that causes AIDS. Infection with HIV leads to changes in the immune system that can result in a cluster of symptoms recognized as *AIDS (Acquired Immunodeficiency Syndrome)*, a viral disease that impairs the body's ability to fight other diseases. Persons who test positive for HIV have the virus in their system; however, they may or may not be symptomatic. As the disease progresses and the immune system becomes further compromised, the *HIV-positive* person becomes more susceptible to certain unique opportunistic infections. To be *diagnosed with AIDS*, a person must have a T-helper lymphocyte blood count of less than 200 and have had one or more opportunistic infections. The infections often can be treated, but there is no current cure for the underlying immune deficiency caused by HIV. The course of the illness can be unpredictable; some persons progress from being HIV positive and asymptomatic to developing full-blown AIDS very quickly; others remain asymptomatic indefinitely.

Early intervention, referring to the identification of people with HIV and procurement of corresponding medical and psychological treatment, is encouraged. This has become especially salient since the newer class of drugs, protease inhibitors, used in combination with other drugs (e.g., AZT), has been found to slow the progression of the disease significantly. However, the new drug treatment, often referred to as a drug cocktail, has its own set of complex issues (Britton, 2000). HIV-positive people may be required to take many drugs on a rigid schedule and experience debilitating side effects. Moreover, unless prescriptions are adhered to strictly, the virus develops a resistance to the drugs very quickly. These resistant forms of the virus may then be transmitted to others who will not respond to the drug treatments.

In an infected person, the virus can be found in body fluids, including blood, semen, vaginal and cervical secretions, and breast milk. It is most often transmitted by direct exposure to blood by certain acts of sexual intercourse and by needle sharing. Although it is possible for a woman to infect her fetus during gestation, birth, or nursing, the numbers of infection in this manner have decreased due to preventive treatments during pregnancy and birth.

MULTICULTURAL ISSUES

There is a disproportionate percentage of AIDS cases among people belonging to minority cultures, including drug use cultures, racial and ethnic minorities (particularly African Americans and Latinos), women (especially women of color), youth (the highest rate of transmission is among adolescents), gay and bisexual men, and people who are homeless or mentally disabled. Of new cases of persons with diagnosed HIV (not AIDS) reported to the CDC in 1999, 32% were women, and 77% of these women were African Americans or Latinas. Among men, African Americans and Latinos accounted for 59% of the new cases (CDC, 1999).

Counselors need to be informed about different cultures and maintain a perspective that honors and respects diversity. Winiarski (1997) has recommended that counselors working with persons with HIV disease expand their skills and knowledge regarding different cultures, paying special attention to:

Issues around stigmatization: People from oppressed groups frequently have difficulty trusting outsiders and institutions. Thus, it is important not to interpret problems with self-disclosure as resistance or avoidance.

Nontraditional healing methods: It is important to consider how the culture conceptualizes illness, death, and dying.

Views on counseling: Some cultures view counseling as supportive, but others may be very uncomfortable discussing personal information with someone outside the family or church.

UNIQUE ISSUES RELATED TO HIV/AIDS

Although many of the issues that clients impacted by HIV/AIDS deal with are similar to those of people with other chronic illnesses, there are some unique variables that set HIV/AIDS apart from other diseases:

1. *Stigma.* As HIV/AIDS has disproportionately impacted socially stigmatized populations and its transmission involves stigmatized activities (sexual activity and drug use), people with HIV disease are often perceived negatively.
2. *Unpredictability.* With most other diseases, there is a somewhat predictable course of the disease, and people are given information as to what to expect at certain stages. However, with AIDS, people have little guidance as to what to expect, often vacillating from wellness to illness. Subsequently, they can make decisions such as leaving their job, selling their home, and preparing for death, only to find themselves feeling healthy again. This unpredictability has been compared to a roller-coaster ride, with emotions fluctuating from despair to hope and back again to despair. As a result, clients report chronic apprehension and a feeling of being out of control.
3. *Isolation.* Due to the nature of transmission, HIV can be an isolating disease. People frequently struggle with maintaining healthy sexual and intimate relationships and as a result may end up feeling intensely alone.
4. *Age and Stage Differences.* HIV/AIDS tends to infect younger people who are being asked to deal with developmental concerns that most often do not impact people until they are in their later stages of life. It is common for a 75-year-old person to be dealing with end-of-life planning; however, most 25-year-olds are not prepared to deal with these issues but instead are facing career and life-planning issues.

COUNSELING AND HIV TESTING

Testing for HIV has become a complicated issue. Although there has been a push for early identification of people with HIV based on medical advances, there are psychosocial complexities around testing. There is real potential for discrimination in finding out one's HIV status, such as denial of insurance, housing, and employment.

Things to Know about HIV Antibody Testing

The HIV antibody tests are very accurate. They determine whether antibodies are present in the bloodstream; however, they do not make a diagnosis of AIDS. The two most common tests are the preliminary screening test, ELISA (enzyme linked immunosorbent assay), and the confirmatory test, Western Blot.

Home testing kits are now available; however, they are more accurately described as at-home collection kits. They have made testing more accessible to people in rural communities, but raise concern regarding the adequacy of posttest counseling. Rapid tests, available at some labs, allow for results in 5 to 30 minutes; however, a major drawback of this type of testing is the higher rate of false positives until confirmatory tests are administered.

Testing can be *confidential* or *anonymous.* Confidential testing is similar to other medical tests and accessible within certain limitations. Anonymous testing is done without use of names or identifiable information and is inaccessible to anyone but the recipient. Many who get tested do not return for results. In most settings, pre- and postcounseling accompany testing.

Counseling Issues Associated with Testing

Counselors can play a very salient role around testing issues. Common counseling themes include:

Dealing with feelings about being tested (e.g., ambivalence, fear).

Supporting clients while they wait for results.

Education about HIV/AIDS.

Dealing with results of test and acute distress that may result.

DEVELOPMENTAL MODEL OF TREATMENT

This model is based on several development models, including readiness models (e.g., Prochaska, DiClemente, & Norcross, 1992) and crisis models (e.g., Nichols, 1985). The model's central idea is that AIDS is a disease of adjustment and change. Thus, certain counseling interventions may be more effective than others during different phases of adjustment. (The model serves only as a guide; the unique needs of each client will interface with the efficacy of any intervention.)

Stage 1: Crisis

When first discovering their HIV status, most infected people will experience acute distress; however, their reaction to the crisis is a unique process. Many report depression, anxiety, and preoccupation with illness, including intense fatalism or the belief that they will die soon. Denial is another common initial reaction characterized by a description of feeling "nothing" or "numb." Many present with symptoms of an adjustment disorder; however, people can have other reactions that are within the range of "normal."

At this stage, the counselor's task is to provide crisis intervention and supportive counseling to facilitate coping. It is helpful to normalize clients' responses and assist them in managing their emotional reactions. This may include assessing support networks and making referrals, such as pastoral counseling, Alcoholics Anonymous, legal guidance, medical/dental health care, testing sites, gay community resources, and methadone clinics.

This is not the time to delve into emotional responses, nor is it the best time for educa-tion, as a person in crisis usually cannot clearly process new information. However, it may be one of the few times a person with HIV disease has access to counseling (e.g., posttest counseling), so it can be helpful to provide persons with information that they can refer to later (such as written material or pamphlets). It is also not the best time for a psychological assessment. The client's acute reaction may not reflect premorbid diagnosis but a natural reaction to crisis. Instead, a counselor should provide support, resources, and a calming presence.

Stage 2: Adjustment

Although acute distress is almost universal at beginning stages of HIV/AIDS, it usually decreases after a few weeks. The next phase involves digesting the information about oneself and finding ways to handle it. The tasks involve making some decisions about work and living arrangements as well as personal relationships.

As in phase 1, this process is unique for each individual. Some people do not experience any emotional problems during the asympotmatic phases of HIV disease. Others remain in denial, which can be a necessary and beneficial means of coping. However, denial that persists for extended periods of time can delay the onset of medical treatment and may have deleterious health effects.

Stage 2 is often characterized by a decrease in denial. Instead, people may be faced with a vacillation of denial with acute symptoms. It is also a time of high risk for substance abuse and suicide.

Disclosure Issues. A common theme during this stage involves issues around who and how to tell about one's HIV status. Counselors need to be cognizant of and sensitive to the dilemmas around disclosure, including potential for prejudice, challenges to sexual and intimate relationships, being labeled an unfit parent, vulnerability to violence, loss of job and insurance, and disclosure of sexual orientation or past drug behavior. The counseling relationship is a helpful place for clients to explore disclosure issues and subsequently be more planful and prepared.

Issues around Medical Treatment. As people more deeply acknowledge their HIV status or when confronted with their first HIV symptoms, they are often faced with difficult medical decisions. Many are encouraged to take medications early, often prior to any symptoms. The strategy is a challenge because of the potential for side effects. Issues of compliance and adherence are critical. Counseling can assist clients in processing and making decisions around their medical care, including helping people:

- Take responsibility for their own health.
- Observe and report symptoms to physician.
- Develop partnerships with physicians.
- Comply with treatment.
- Understand and keep track of medications.
- Prepare for and utilize medical appointments.
- Become good consumers of treatment.
- Assert rights.

Suicide. People with HIV infection have higher levels of suicidal ideation and more frequent attempts when compared with their non-HIV-infected counterparts. Risk of suicide appears higher in people relatively early on in the HIV disease (Marzuk et al., 1997). Unique correlations to suicidal ideation in persons with HIV disease include: onset of symptoms, number of close friends diagnosed with HIV, knowing someone who died from AIDS, and perceived risk of developing AIDS.

Counseling Interventions. A counselor's role during this stage is to provide ongoing and unconditional support. Counselors should continue to accept the affective experiences of clients, normalizing their range of feelings, such as fear, anxiety, depression, and pleasure. This is a good time to refer clients for group work, as groups can provide identification and expression of feelings, social involvement, security in the continuity and structure of a group, safety, modeling of adaptation to disease, opportunity for touch, new perspectives, and education (e.g., medical information, derailing myths).

Stage 3: Acceptance

During this phase, people begin to form a new sense of equilibrium: the formation of a new, more stable identity. Clients begin to accept their limitations but still manage their lives. They may talk about living with AIDS versus dying from AIDS.

Interpersonal and insight therapy is appropriate at this stage and may involve a multitude of themes, including:

- Family of origin work.
- Establishing emotional, physical, and sexual contact with others.
- Boundary development and setting healthy limits.
- Coming-out issues.
- Self-awareness and attending to one's own experiences.
- Exploration of meanings and purpose.
- Communication work.
- Spiritual exploration (e.g., finding appreciation for small pleasures, a capacity to live life in the present and to its fullest, focusing on quality versus quantity of life).

Diagnosing Depression and Anxiety. During this phase, psychological assessments are indicated. However, assessment is complicated because of the overlapping symptoms of HIV disease with depression/anxiety. Thus, characteristics of HIV disease should be taken into account and diagnosis made after considering overlapping symptoms, including symptoms of AIDS-related infections, other illnesses, side effects of medications, and symptoms of distress. For example, symptoms often associated with anxiety or depression, such as problems concentrating and making decisions, difficulties in social or occupational functioning, negative changes in physical appearance, fatigue and sleep disturbances, loss of appetite, declining sexual interest, and weight loss, can be associated with HIV disease, especially if the neurological system has been impacted by the disease.

Employment Issues. Persons with HIV often are faced with difficult employment decisions. Many rely on their employment for their health insurance. Often, they feel too ill to work and choose to go on disability. This option may offer them time to boost their immune system, but conversely, it also is recognition that HIV has gained control of their lives, which is especially difficult for those strongly tied to their careers. Moreover, with the success of new drug treatments, many who feel ready to return to work fear losing their disability benefits.

Stage 4: End-of-Life Issues

During this stage, clients are interested in talking about end-of-life concerns. These may include making decisions regarding final medical treatment, estate planning and wills, dealing with unresolved relationships and saying goodbye, making video/audiotapes or journals, discussing spiritual questions, planning for their funeral, and making rational suicide plans.

Clients may or may not be ill when they desire to process these issues. The counselor needs to be able to tolerate his or her own anxiety about death and dying and monitor personal beliefs and values around end-of-life decisions. This can be particularly salient while dealing with the issue of rational suicide, the decision to rationally end one's life to avoid the protracted pain, dependence, and economic decline associated with advanced HIV disease (Werth, 1996). As there has been debate surrounding the role of mental health practitioners around hastened death requests, counselors are encouraged to be familiar with the professional literature regarding this controversial area (Silverman, 2000; Rogers & Britton, 1994; Werth, 1992; Werth & Holdwick, 2000).

AIDS Dementia. HIV brain infection and AIDS-related opportunistic infections of the central nervous system are some of the most feared health problems for persons with HIV disease. Significant deterioration in cognitive abilities can occur prior to systemic illness; however, these neurological deficits most often coexist with other opportunistic infections. Unfortunately, the protease inhibitors are not successful in slowing neurological impairment, and thus there are more cases of AIDS dementia surfacing in otherwise healthy individuals. Counseling can be a forum for clients to process their fears and learn adaptive techniques when faced with early symptoms. With the onset of late-stage dementia, more complicated caregiving issues surface, and family and friends frequently need assistance in dealing with their feelings and making appropriate caretaking plans.

Multiple Bereavement. Given that HIV is principally spread through sexual behavior and needle sharing, people with HIV infection often experience multiple losses because of the prevalence of HIV in their social networks (Neugebauer et al., 1992). As a result, people may experience bereavement overload, a syndrome that occurs when a person has not completed the process of mourning the loss of one person when another dies. The pervasive, unrelenting feelings of sorrow, loss, and abandonment can be overwhelming.

SUMMARY

Although this model was presented as linear, a spiral more accurately reflects it. Due to the frequent and many losses and crises associated with HIV, persons will frequently return to earlier stages of adjustment (e.g., after a recent death of someone with AIDS, during acute relational conflicts, when symptoms begin or change, around appointments with physicians, or after episodes of discrimination). The process of adjustment and adaptation is ongoing and frequently laborious.

In counseling persons with HIV disease, counselors need to be cognizant of many unique and challenging issues, as well as display sensitivity to multicultural issues. It also requires a monitoring and management of the counselor's own reaction to the often difficult issues. Using a developmental model can guide counselors in choosing effective and appropriate interventions.

References

Britton, P.J. (2000). Staying on the roller coaster with clients: Implications of the new HIV/AIDS medical treatments for counseling. *Journal of Mental Health Counseling, 22*, 85–94.

Centers for Disease Control and Prevention. (1999). *HIV/AIDS surveillance report, 11*(no. 2).

Marzuk, P.M., Tardiff, K., Leon, A., Hirsch, C., Hartwell, N., Portera, L., & Iqbal, M. (1997). HIV seroprevalence among suicide victims in New York City, 1991–1993. *American Journal of Psychiatry, 154*, 1720–1725.

Neugebauer, R., Rabkin, J., Williams, J., Remien, R., Goetz, R., & Gorman, J. (1992). Bereavement reactions among homosexual men experiencing multiple losses in the AIDS epidemic. *American Journal of Psychiatry, 149*, 1374–1379.

Nichols, S.E. (1985). Psychosocial reactions of persons with the acquired immunodeficiency syndrome. *Annals of Internal Medicine, 103*, 765–767.

Prochaska, J.O., DiClemente, C.C., & Norcross, J.C. (1992). In search of how people change. *American Psychologist, 47*, 1102–1114.

Rogers, J., & Britton, P. (1994). AIDS and rational suicide: A counseling psychology perspective or a slide on the slippery slope. *The Counseling Psychologist, 22*, 171–178.

Silverman, M.M. (2000). Rational suicide, hastened death, and self-destructive behaviors. *The Counseling Psychologist, 28*, 540–550.

Werth, J.L., Jr. (1992). Rational suicide and AIDS: Considerations for the psychologist. *The Counseling Psychologist, 20*, 645–659.

Werth, J.L., Jr. (1996). *Rational suicide? Implications for mental health professionals.* Bristol, PA: Taylor & Francis.

Werth, J.L., Jr., & Holdwick, D.J., Jr. (2000). A primer on rational suicide and other forms of hastened death. *The Counseling Psychologist, 28*, 511–539.

Winiarski, M.G. (1997). *HIV mental health for the 21st century.* New York: New York University Press.

Suggested Reading

Hoffman, M.A. (1996). *Counseling clients with HIV disease: Assessment, intervention, and prevention.* New York: Guilford Press.

Kain, C.D. (1996). *Positive: HIV affirmative counseling.* Alexandria, VA: American Counseling Association.

Kalichman, S.C. (1998). *Understanding AIDS: Advances in research and treatment* (2nd ed.). Washington, DC: American Psychological Association.

Kelly, J.A. (1995). *Changing HIV risk behavior: Practical strategies.* New York: Guilford Press.

Odets, W., & Shernoff, M. (1994). *The second decade of AIDS: A mental health practice handbook.* New York: Haterleigh Press.

Rabkin, J., Remiem, R., & Wilson, C. (1994). *Good doctors, good patients: Partners in HIV treatment.* New York: NCM.

PART II

Diagnosis and Treatment of Adults with Mental and Emotional Disorders

10 EFFECTIVE USE OF THE *DSM* FROM A DEVELOPMENTAL/ WELLNESS PERSPECTIVE

Earl J. Ginter and Ann Glauser

The authors of this chapter identify with the developmental/wellness paradigm traditionally associated with counseling (Ginter, 1999). In this chapter, we review a number of diagnostic issues (e.g., cultural factors and the axis system) related to effective use of the *Diagnostic and Statistical Manual of Mental Disorders,* fourth edition, text revision (*DSM-IV-TR*) (APA, 2000). The chapter concludes by providing a review of two models (i.e., Ginter, 1999; Ivey & Ivey, 1998) that will assist any mental health professional interested in adopting and applying a developmental/wellness approach to therapy.

THE *DSM* AND ITS ROLE IN TREATMENT

Hohenshil (1996) indicated that a segment of counselors hold a negative perception of diagnosis because they see diagnosis as either unnecessary or, at its worst, as a contraindicated labeling process that hinders the full effectiveness of counseling—a process that can even psychologically damage some clients. In truth, there are cases where diagnosis has proven to be of little value, and there are other cases where it has resulted in harm to the recipient of the diagnosis, but to a large degree, such outcomes reside less with the process of diagnosis itself and more with how

the diagnostic information was applied after diagnosis (Ginter, 1999). Effective use of the *DSM* depends on an understanding of that system, skill in applying it, and the development of a treatment approach that both recognizes the current role of the *DSM* in practice and is congruent with the defining features of counseling (Ginter, 1999).

Hohenshil (1996) argues in favor of *DSM* diagnosis and presents several points to support his position. Two of his arguments deserve mention in this chapter. First, Hohenshil has indicated that "diagnosis is not a process that occurs at a fixed point in time during the counseling process, nor is it a static concept" (p. 65) and, second, that diagnosis is not confined to just one stage of the counseling process but permeates the entire process from beginning to end and makes a unique contribution at each stage. Finally, Hohenshil asserts that the antidiagnostic position found to linger in counseling is aligned with the following beliefs: Counselors work with less severe client problems than those that elicit a *DSM* diagnostic label; the unique developmental emphasis found in counseling results in counselors focusing on issues of "normality" and "wellness" rather than the type of pathology identified via the *DSM;* and specific counseling models (i.e., client-centered, humanistic, and family systems) espouse certain types of

client-counselor relationships that do not necessitate *DSM* diagnosis. Whether one agrees
or disagrees with Hohenshil's position, the
prevailing reality of what constitutes contemporary counseling practice places those counselors who reject the role played by *DSM*
diagnosis in a tenuous position that they will
find increasingly difficult to defend.

Ignorance of the *DSM* system is not congruent with current expectations concerning
counseling practice. Even those counselors
not traditionally associated with reliance on
DSM language cannot afford to be ignorant of
it if they hope to maintain a certain level of
professionalism and effectiveness. For example, elementary school counselors who possess knowledge of the *DSM* are better able to
collaborate with other professionals and to
make effective referrals that are consistent
with relevant ethical considerations. Finally,
evidence for the pivotal role this diagnostic
system has acquired in counseling was revealed in a 1990s survey in which counselors
reported that the *DSM* served as the "most
frequently used" resource to obtain information related to practice (Hohenshil, 1994).
This finding agrees with Seligman's (1999) assessment of the number of counselor training
programs that devote attention to teaching
use of the *DSM*. What follows is an overview
of the *DSM* system that concludes with a brief
discussion of how it can be used in a manner
consistent with the developmental perspective that is unique to counseling.

DSM-IV-TR: CONTRIBUTING PRECURSORS

The current and prior versions of the *DSM*
represent a concise explanation of a specialized language that possesses its own set of
rules to determine when to apply its nomenclature. Implied in the full title of the book is
the idea that its nomenclature represents a
professional understanding of what delineates a mental disorder, and with each edition we are provided a glimpse of what
constitutes the prevailing professional understanding of various mental disorders at different historical points in time. This
historical progression represents a diagnostic

journey of sorts that has not reached its final
destination. Diagnosticians should remember
that the *DSM* will always be anchored to the
cultural-time period marked by its publication date and as such will continue to provide
an incomplete understanding (or a complete
cultural appreciation) of mental disorders.

Providing a brief history of what had led up
to the fourth edition (APA, 1994, 2000) enables
its users to better identify the strengths and
weaknesses possessed by the newest edition.
As indicated in the 2000 edition of the *DSM*,
various nomenclatures used throughout the
ages have relied to differing degrees on "phe-
nomenology, etiology, and course" (p. xxiv) to
define and isolate the appropriate diagnosis.
The *DSM* system itself is just one of many
historical documents that offered a technical
language intended to convey a packet of information to better understand the thoughts and
behaviors of others. Even a cursory examination of the various systems developed during
different time periods reveals considerable
variation in complexity. Some systems provided relatively short (e.g., "handful") diagnostic listings; other systems provide long
(e.g., "thousands") diagnostic listings, listings
that have been used for a multitude of reasons
(APA, 2000). Beginning in the first half of the
1800s and leading up to the fourth edition of
DSM, several events (APA, 2000, p. xxv–xxvi)
serve as important markers that contribute to a
fuller appreciation of the details contained in
the *DSM-IV-TR:*

• The impetus for developing a classification
  system can be traced to the 1840 U.S. census,
  when information about mental disorders
  was collected via the category "idiocy/in-
  sanity."

• The mental disorders category was expanded to seven "labels" by the 1880 census
  (i.e., dementia, dipsomania, epilepsy, mania,
  melancholia, monomania, and paresis).

• In 1917, three groups (American Medico-
  Psychological Association, Bureau of the
  Census, National Commission on Mental
  Hygiene) combined efforts to collect statis-
  tical data from mental hospitals.

• The American Medico-Psychological Association changed its name in 1921 to the

American Psychiatric Association (APA). APA and the New York Academy of Medicine both contributed to the development of a nomenclature that was printed in the first edition of the American Medical Association's *Standard Classified Nomenclature of Disease*.

- Nomenclature developed by the U.S. Army and the Veterans Administration (e.g., acute mental disturbances where onset of the condition was sudden and relatively short in duration and conditions where the mental disturbance involved both psychological and physiological factors that contributed directly to behaviors and/or thoughts of the patient) and the World Health Organization (primarily its publication of the *International Classification of Diseases* [*ICD*]) greatly influenced the first edition of the *Diagnostic and Statistical Manual: Mental Disorders*. (Similarly, the creation of the *DSM-IV* was largely motivated by the anticipated publication of the tenth edition of the *ICD*; Hohenshil, 1992.)

- Various editions of the *DSM* reflect shifts in the basic foundational issues that have professionally validated the nomenclature relied on in each edition. For example, the term "reaction" used in the *DSM-I* was associated with the particular psychobiological view advocated by Adolf Meyer that mental disorders represented a patient's reaction to factors of a biological, social, and psychological nature. Subsequent editions of the *DSM* were not only developed to coincide with changes in the *ICD*, but also were designed (and written) in a manner to move away from a *theory-influenced* diagnostic system (e.g., Freudian influences found in the *DSM II* were largely expunged in subsequent editions) to a system of classification that is "neutral with respect to theories of etiology" (APA, 1994, p. xviii).

With each new edition (i.e., *DSM-II* to *DSM-IV-TR*), the aim has been to increase the exactness and thoroughness of the diagnostic categories based on all relevant available information. For example, Hohenshil (1994) reports that the *DSM-IV* is approximately 300 pages longer than the *DSM-III-R* (despite the *DSM-IV*'s better organization and apparent effort at greater clarity, it does use medical terminology that may lack meaning for those without previous knowledge). The general revision approach adopted in creating the *DSM-IV* resulted in many significant changes, especially in the area of disorders typically diagnosed in infancy, childhood, or adolescence as well as other noteworthy changes in the areas of Adjustment Disorders, Mood Disorders, Substance-Related Disorders, Anxiety Disorders, and Personality Disorders (Hohenshil, 1994).

The result is "an optimal balance in the *DSM-IV* with respect to historical tradition (as embodied in the *DSM-III* and the *DSM-III-R*), compatibility with *ICD-10*, evidence from reviews of the literature, analyses of unpublished data sets, results of field trials, and consensus of the field" (APA, 2000, p. xxviii). As one would expect and as is articulated by Hohenshil (1994), the *DSM-IV* "is considerably more sensitive to bias issues, more scientific, more logically organized, and better written than any of its four predecessors" (p. 105).

Finally, "to bridge the span between the *DSM-IV* and *DSM-V*" (APA, 2000, p. xxix) the APA published the *DSM-IV-TR*, which introduces a number of important changes. Although most of the descriptive paragraphs in the *DSM-IV* were not revised, the current text revision does reflect new research into schizophrenia, Asperger's Disorder, and other conditions. Expanding knowledge of Asperger's Disorder since 1994 necessitated a fairly extensive revision for that section. Some of the diagnostic criteria related to Personality Change Due to General Medical Condition, Paraphilias, and Tic Disorders were also updated. The *DSM-IV-TR* represents an effort to update the ninth revision, clinical modification of the *ICD* (*ICD-9-CM*) codes used since 1994 that are found in the *DSM* (including Conduct Disorder, Dementia, and Somatoform Disorders). Finally, changes were made to include more up-to-date information about age, culture, gender, course, associated features, and familial patterns of mental disorders to be consistent with recent research findings.

EFFECTIVE USE OF THE *DSM:* POINTS OF CLARIFICATION

The authors of the *DSM-IV-TR* are careful to clarify several aspects of the manual that are both open to misunderstanding and are crucial determinants of effective use. Specifically, the authors address the use of the term "mental disorder," a categorical system of diagnosis, and culture as a mediating diagnostic factor. Of these areas, culture as a factor in effective diagnosis deserves special attention.

The label *"mental disorder* unfortunately implies a distinction between 'mental' disorders and 'physical' disorders that is a reductionistic anachronism of mind/body dualism. A compelling literature documents that there is much 'physical' in 'mental' disorders and much 'mental' in 'physical' disorders" (APA, 2000, p. xxx). The authors of the *DSM-IV-TR* further state that "each of the mental disorders is conceptualized as a clinically significant behavioral or psychological syndrome or pattern that occurs in an individual and that is associated with present distress (e.g., a painful symptom) or disability (i.e., impairment in one or more important areas of functioning) or with a significantly increased risk of suffering death, pain, disability, or an important loss of freedom" (p. xxxi). Also, the position advocated in the *DSM* is that counselors use specifiers when evaluating the presence of symptoms, symptoms used to identify those particular characteristics that coalesce in a defining pattern that denotes a certain mental disorder's occurrence. Symptoms are best viewed as falling along a continuum rather than existing in some fixed amount. Such gradation (i.e., mild, moderate, severe) of symptoms is an essential component of arriving at an accurate diagnosis and effective treatment.

Another caveat related to effective use is introduced early in the fourth edition of the *DSM.* This caveat is linked with the long-standing criticism of the *DSM* system

regarding the misuse of labels, the type of diagnostic label that is a central element to the system comprising the *DSM*'s categorical approach to mental disorders. The authors of the *DSM-IV-TR* point out that users must keep in mind that a particular mental disorder is not the same for everyone placed in that particular category. For example, although certain features of schizophrenia might place a large number of individuals into a particular diagnostic category, a closer inspection of this group would reveal an amazing amount of within-group variability and would lead to the realization that all individuals cannot be reduced to a single diagnostic label (a key reason for relying on the multiaxial approach found in the *DSM*). In other words, it is simply wrong to believe that in any diagnostic group, clinical variability does not exist. To deny such variability is to reduce the *DSM* system to a cookbook approach to diagnosis that will inevitably introduce deleterious effects into treatment.

Sometimes, the misuse of categorical information is difficult to detect and has an almost invisible quality during the period it is misused because of the dominant social climate. What may seem correct and ethical during one period in history is later identified as a form of "oppression" (Glauser & Bozarth, 2001). For example, prior to emancipation of the slaves in America, "running away" from one's abusive owner was considered a symptom of a *mental illness* (Ginter et al., 1996; Weisskopf-Joelson, 1980). The authors of the *DSM* clearly indicate that its nomenclature is to be applied in conjunction with a prudent combination of clinical judgment and cultural sensitivity that recognizes that client behaviors may be tied to specific cultural dynamics typical of a group rather than to a symptom of a particular mental disorder.

Effective treatment planning can occur only if the client is truly understood, and in many cases, a client can be understood only if the counselor rendering the diagnosis possesses cultural sensitivity. The *DSM-IV-TR* represents a significant improvement over earlier editions in its incorporation of cultural considerations for the counselor to ponder before rendering a diagnosis. It should also be noted that several authors believe the developers of the most recent edition of the *DSM* did not go far enough in weaving all the available multicultural information needed into the *DSM*'s diagnostic framework of guidelines.

Ivey and Ivey (1998) and others (e.g., Smart & Smart, 1997) have been very critical of the *DSM*'s efforts to incorporate cultural sensitivity into its diagnostic scheme. Smart and Smart provide a critical but balanced review of the *DSM*'s shortcomings and strengths as they pertain to five areas:

1. *Cultural-Specific Sections.* Seventy-nine of the 400 *DSM-IV* disorders provide specific cultural information. This inclusion represents a vast improvement over earlier editions, but an assessment of the scope devoted to each section reveals an inconsistent approach in terms of the depth of coverage. The inconsistency is evident in that in some cases only a few words are used as cultural qualifiers, while in other cases the text devoted to a disorder covers several paragraphs.

2. *Glossary of Culture-Bound Syndromes.* Twenty-five syndromes are reported in an appendix and are described in the *DSM* as "locality-specific troubling experiences that are limited to certain societies or cultural areas" (Smart & Smart, 1997, p. 394). The means of reporting this information has received somewhat heated criticism and has been referred to by Smart and Smart as a sort of "tourist" approach to reviewing a very important area of consideration. Furthermore, Smart and Smart suggest a Western cultural bias exists that results in Western cultural-bound categories being treated differently from those listed in this appendix. The result of the differential treatment is an inconsistent formatting used in the *DSM*. For example, Smart and Smart argue there is reason to believe anorexia nervosa represents a Western culture-bound syndrome and, as with any other culture-bound syndrome, deserves to be listed with the other 25 found in the glossary. (Currently, there is no consensus concerning whether anorexia nervosa is a Western culture-bound syndrome.)

3. *Outline for Cultural Formulation.* Although criticized for being relegated to the appendix, the outline for evaluating cultural factors is considered by Smart and Smart (1997) as "essential and marks an important step forward in the cultural sensitivity of the" *DSM* (p. 395). We also believe the outline offers a ready-made means to systematically consider a host of factors related to culture. These include cultural identity, cultural explanations for an illness, contributing psychosocial factors, level of functioning, and the client-counselor relationship.

4. *Culturally Sensitive Changes on Axis IV.* The focus of this axis is psychosocial and other forms of stress, and Smart and Smart (1997) point out that in their view, the changes appearing in the *DSM*, "although minor, do in fact, broaden the concept of psychosocial-environmental influence and make Axis IV more sensitive to issues likely to be presented by minorities" (p. 395). When used as part of the diagnosis, Axis IV results in a better understanding of the diagnostic value of considering discrimination, migration, assimilation, and acculturation as potentially defining features of a client's life.

5. *Addition of Culturally Sensitive V Codes.* Smart and Smart (1997) call attention to "acculturation problems" and "religious or spiritual problems" found in the V Codes and suggest that such additions represent an improvement over the *DSM-III*. Acculturation is listed in the V Codes in a manner to help the counselor consider the degree of impact of cultural adjustment on client symptoms. Also, according to Smart and Smart, the structure provided "leaves the counselor great latitude in deciding how to diagnose this issue" (p. 396). Similarly, the means by which a client's spirituality is viewed reflects the greater cultural sensitivity found in the *DSM-IV-TR*. Compared to *DSM-III-R*, which consistently tied religion to psychopathology, the *DSM-IV* recognizes the positive role that religion

can play in one's life and allows the counselor to view this central concern as "detached from other mental disorders as the case may warrant" (Smart & Smart, 1997, p. 396). For example, a Tibetan Buddhist going for a long walk on a well-established pathway might be observed to stop and pick up every earthworm encountered on the heavily traveled pathway, carefully placing each earthworm a safe distance away from the path. This behavior might appear to one unfamiliar with the Tibetan form of Buddhism as an unusual form of excessive compulsive behavior rather than a devotion to respecting all reincarnated life forms and protecting the myriad life forms that inhabit earth from harm, injury, or death.

THE AXIS SYSTEM

The axial approach used in the *DSM* results in isolating the most pertinent information in different domains or information (Fong, 1995).

Axis I: Clinical Disorders

These are typically the presenting problems and include disorders of the following types: Anxiety Disorders; Disorders Usually First Diagnosed in Infancy, Childhood, or Adolescence; Delirium, Dementia, and Amnestic and Other Cognitive Disorders; Mood Disorders; and Substance-Related Disorders. Axis I also is used to report "other conditions that may be a focus of clinical attention." Most clients seek or are referred for counseling due to an Axis I or a V-Code problem (Fong, 1995).

Axis II: Personality Disorders and Mental Retardation

When an Axis II diagnosis is the primary clinical concern, it is indicated by the qualifier "reason for visit" or "principal diagnosis." Even though personality disorders are not always initially apparent during a standard intake interview, their potential to disrupt an otherwise effective treatment program requires the counselor to be sensitive to their

existence (Fong, 1995). Also, if relevant to diagnosis (and treatment), any repetitive pattern that relies on a *defense mechanism* that is believed to interfere with a person's level of environmental adjustment is also noted on Axis II. Defense mechanisms are defined as "Automatic psychological processes that protect the individual against anxiety and from awareness of internal and external dangers or stressors" (APA, 2000, p. 807). Factors such as inflexibility, intensity, and the environmental situation that fixes the meaning of defense mechanisms must be considered when noting reliance on defense mechanisms. In addition, other personality features that fail to meet the criteria for an established Personality Disorder can be noted here (Hohenshil, 1994).

Axis III: General Medical Conditions

These conditions can be very relevant for both treatment and prognosis, especially in terms of pharmacotherapy. Also, it is important to note that if a mental disorder is the result of a medical condition, this will be indicated on *both* Axes III and I (e.g., a mood disorder due to hypothyroidism).

Axis IV: Psychosocial and Environmental Circumstances

These include economic issues, education, health care services, housing, legal system/victim of crime, occupation, social environment, primary support group (familial), and other environmental problems (e.g., natural disasters, war, discord with a mental health professional or agency).

Axis V: Global Assessment of Functioning (GAF) Scale

This scale addresses the dimensions of psychological, social, and occupational well-being and provides a score ranging from 0 (inadequate information) to 100 (superior functioning). The *DSM-IV-TR* provides information about other assessments, specifically the Defensive Functioning Scale, the Global Assessment of Relational Functioning Scale, which many family practitioners will find useful, and the Social and Occupational Functioning Assessment Scale, which can be used to facilitate career counseling.

EFFECTIVE PRACTICE AND THE *DSM*

Nelson and Neufeldt (1996) capture the view held by many practitioners concerning the *DSM*'s use in actual practice when they write that although the *DSM* "is necessary for providing diagnosis-related information to third-party payers in terms of pathology, its primary application in treatment planning is for the identification of disorders such as depression and psychosis that required psychotropic medication . . . [it] appears to have little utility for actual selection of counseling strategies. Research has shown that practitioners seldom use it as a guide to counseling strategies because they do not find it useful. Thus . . . identification of 'pathology' is not necessarily useful in determining what kind of counseling interventions to pursue" (p. 609). The authors of the *DSM-IV-TR* themselves indicate that it is not the intent of the *DSM* to serve as a ready-made resource for recommended treatment.

We believe the *DSM-IV-TR*'s avoidance of the treatment arena is a strength, allowing counselors considerable flexibility in matching a treatment approach to a particular disorder as long as the treatment approach is supported empirically and with sound clinical judgment. We also believe that it is possible to stay true to counseling's unique defining feature of relying on a developmental perspective in working with clients. (There are other defining features [Ginter, 1999], but the developmental aspect is widely recognized as a key feature.) Ivey and Ivey (1998) and Ginter (2001) offer examples of such developmentally based approaches.

Ivey and Ivey (1998) believe that Developmental Counseling and Therapy (DCT) bridges the gap between counseling's unique developmental perspective and the *DSM* diagnostic perspective. They contrast the way the *DSM* and the DCT approaches view the issues of locus of the client's problem, pathology,

developmental and etiological constructs, culture, helper role, causes for client's complaint, client's family, and treatment. Of these, it is the issue of pathology that Ivey and Ivey discuss at length. A condition that would be considered pathological when based only on a *DSM* perspective is represented by DCT as a condition that is best viewed as a "logical response to developmental history" (p. 336). In their article, Ivey and Ivey explain how DCT's treatment interventions are organized around the types of information-processing systems labeled sensorimotor, concrete, formal, and dialectic/systemic. These information-processing systems allow effective client-counselor communication to occur, and thus effective treatment. DCT not only offers a strongly rooted developmental system of intervention but also offers the counselor a means for reframing *DSM* "pathologizing" terminology into positive terminology that better enables the client to build on latent developmental strengths. For example, Ivey and Ivey list 11 personality styles (e.g., paranoid, antisocial, borderline, dependent) and review each in terms of its positive aspect, the behavior/thoughts that are likely to display themselves during a counseling session, probable link to a particular family history, how the style is predicted to affect current relationships outside of counseling, and a possible treatment approach that will enable the client to free latent strengths. For example, the positive aspect of the dependent personality style is "We all need to depend on others." In the early stages of counseling, the client can be expected to display "dependency on the therapist even outside of session and indecision, little sense of self." The family history obtained on such a client will probably reveal that family can be described as an "engulfing, controlling family, [where the client is] not allowed to make decisions, [is] rewarded for inaction, [and is] told what to do." Current interpersonal relationships for the client can be expected to reflect the following: "dependent on friends, drives people away with demands." The probable treatment approach to adopt in working with the dependent client, according to Ivey and Ivey, involves the following:

"reward action, support efforts for self, use paradox, [and] assertiveness techniques" (see Ivey & Ivey, 1998, p. 338).

Ivey and Ivey's (1998) DCT model is much more comprehensive than is evident in any brief review (e.g., they discuss how various personality styles are related to Axis I diagnoses) and deserves a more thorough study of its merits than is available in this chapter. Another model that bridges the gap between *DSM* diagnosis and counseling's developmental approach is based on the work of George Gazda (Ginter, 1999). Ginter (2001) provides a review of the theory and a case study to illustrate how a client with a *DSM* diagnosis of depression can be effectively worked with by utilizing the Life-Skills Model (LSM) (Ginter, 1999). The LSM is based on decades of theory building based on empirical support. Following a *DSM* diagnosis, a client's treatment plan is developed in relation to both the diagnosis and an appropriate life-skills assessment (assessment measures have been developed for children, adolescents, adults, college students, and incarcerated adolescents). LSM treatment is not only a developmentally dependent approach that recognizes the contributions of major developmental theories but is an approach devoted specifically to exploring problems and arriving at solutions based on four all-encompassing developmental dimensions (i.e., interpersonal communication/human relations skills, problem-solving/decision-making skills, physical fitness/health maintenance skills, and identity development/purpose-in-life skills). Again, as with Ivey and Ivey, the reader is referred to published works in this area to ascertain a more thorough description of the LSM.

SUMMARY

The authors of the *DSM* have aimed for greater thoroughness and clarity of presentation with each revision. The authors of the *DSM-IV-TR* (APA, 2000) acknowledge the heterogeneous temperament of individuals within categories of mental disorders and the fact that diagnosis is a "probabilistic" endeavor (p. xxxi). There are no assumptions of absolute categories, "no

assumption that all individuals described as having the same mental disorder are alike in all important ways" (p. xxxi). Thus, users are encouraged to gather supplemental information on each client to capture the complexities inherent in rendering a diagnosis. Simply stated, the *DSM* system can be an effective tool for counselors when they also keep in mind the following considerations:

- The *DSM* classifies mental disorders; it does not classify people.
- Diagnosis is an evolving process that occurs throughout each stage of the counseling process.
- The *DSM* system possesses various limitations, and the users must be knowledgeable about these limitations.
- Effective treatment planning depends on whether the client is fully understood, and effective diagnosis always reflects careful consideration of cultural contexts.
- Ignorance of the *DSM* system is incongruent with current definitions of effective counseling practice.
- A developmental approach to practice (e.g., DCT, LSM) can provide an effective bridge between use of the *DSM* system and the theoretical foundation of counseling.

References

American Psychiatric Association. (1994). *Diagnostic and statistical manual of mental disorders* (4th ed.). Washington, DC: Author.

American Psychiatric Association. (2000). *Diagnostic and statistical manual of mental disorders* (4th ed., text rev.). Washington, DC: Author.

Fong, M.L. (1995). Assessment and *DSM-IV* diagnosis of personality disorders: A primer for counselors. *Journal of Counseling & Development, 73,* 635–639.

Ginter, E.J. (1999). David K. Brook's contribution to the developmentally based life-skills approach. *Journal of Mental Health Counseling, 21,* 191–202.

Ginter, E.J. (2001). Private practice: The professional counselor. In D.C. Locke, J.E. Myers, & E.L. Herr (Eds.), *The handbook of counseling* (pp. 355–372). Thousand Oaks, CA: Sage.

Ginter, E.J., (Chair), Ellis, A., Guterman, J.T., Ivey, A.E., Locke, D.C., & Rigazio-DiGilio, S.A. (1996, April). *Ethical issues in the postmodern era.* World conference of the American Counseling Association, Panel discussion, Pittsburgh, PA.

Glauser, A., & Bozarth, J.D. (2001). Person-centered counseling: The culture within. *Journal of Counseling & Development, 79,* 142–147.

Hohenshil, T.H. (1992). *DSM-IV* progress report. *Journal of Counseling & Development, 71,* 249–251.

Hohenshil, T.H. (1994). *DSM-IV:* What's new. *Journal of Counseling & Development, 73,* 105–107.

Hohenshil, T.H. (1996). Editorial: Role of assessment and diagnosis in counseling. *Journal of Counseling & Development, 75,* 64–67.

Ivey, A.E., & Ivey, M.B. (1998). Reframing *DSM-IV:* Positive strategies from developmental counseling and therapy. *Journal of Counseling & Development, 76,* 334–350.

Nelson, M.L., & Neufeldt, S.A. (1996). Building on an empirical foundation: Strategies to enhance good practice. *Journal of Counseling & Development, 74,* 609–615.

Seligman, L. (1999). Twenty years of diagnosis and the *DSM. Journal of Mental Health Counseling, 21,* 229–239.

Smart, D.W., & Smart, J.F. (1997). *DSM-IV* and culturally sensitive diagnosis: Some observations for counselors. *Journal of Counseling & Development, 75,* 392–398.

Weisskopf-Joelson, E. (1980). Value: The infant terrible of psychotherapy. *Psychotherapy: Theory, Research and Practice, 17,* 459–466.

11 CLINICAL AND DIAGNOSTIC INTERVIEWING

Timothy M. Lane and Donna L. Fleming

Conducting a skillful diagnostic interview is a fundamental and essential tool for the mental health clinician. Diagnostic skills are indispensable in therapeutic relationships, as well as in forensic assessments and social science research. Furthermore, a major trend toward treatment or practice guidelines for specific diagnoses underscores the importance for every clinician to have well-developed diagnostic skills. Expert clinical interviewing requires the clinician to have (1) solid counseling and communication skills; (2) a working knowledge of the *Diagnostic and Statistical Manual of Mental Disorders,* text revision (*DSM-IV-TR*) (APA, 2000) diagnostic criteria; (3) empirically based knowledge of

psychopathology, including clinical presentation, prevalence, course, and treatment options for the diagnostic categories; (4) the ability to skillfully apply the diagnostic process; and (5) an awareness of the ethics, pitfalls, and limitations of the diagnostic process. On the surface, the diagnostic process can appear deceptively simple, but human psychopathology is far from simple. With over 200 *DSM-IV* diagnostic possibilities, solid diagnostic skills are needed to serve clients well. This chapter briefly reviews the basics of the clinical interview, the diagnostic process and components, the benefits of interview tools, the limitations and pitfalls of the diagnostic interview, and suggested readings.

OVERVIEW OF THE CLINICAL INTERVIEW

The clinical interview is a focused, time-efficient process typically consisting of a single 50-minute session. Occasionally, more time or a second interview is required for complex cases. Empathy, warmth, and good communication skills are foundations for a smooth clinical interview and prevent it from becoming a cold, detached interrogation of the client. The major components of the clinical interview usually consist of (1) warming up and building rapport, (2) screening for the problem with an empathic understanding of the client's pain, (3) gathering and integrating the empirical database, (4) formulating a theoretical and diagnostic conceptualization, (5) giving feedback tailored to the client's ability to understand it, and (6) determining prognosis and treatment recommendations. A more detailed summary of the clinical interview components is listed in Table 11.1.

The interview may be tailored to each client, setting, and situation. Clinicians must surmise the current state of the client so as to fine-tune the interview for maximal effectiveness (Hersen & Turner, 1994). The preparation and postinterview follow-up components of the interview are also important. Advanced preparations can enhance the efficiency, effectiveness, and focus of the clinical interview. Preparations include review of referral information, intake forms, mental health or medical records, and assessment results. Additionally, the clinician should ensure privacy, adequate uninterrupted time, and freedom from distractions. The postinterview phase should allow time for tasks such as notes and reports, referrals, consultations, and formulation of plans or questions for the next session.

Multidimensional Context of Human Functioning

Clinicians need to be ever mindful of the multidimensional context of behavior, thought, and emotion by utilizing a biopsychosocial or human ecology perspective (Millon & Davis, 1999). Both current and historic factors may affect behavior. Complex cultural, environmental, biological, genetic, personality, and developmental factors and interactions among factors are but samples of the myriad components that may contribute to human behavior. Readers are referred to Millon and Davis for further study of the current state of knowledge concerning the developmental influences on the etiology of pathological conditions.

THE DIAGNOSTIC PROCESS

The diagnosis should be made in the most heuristic and parsimonious manner (Maxmen & Ward, 1995). Amchin (1991) likened the diagnostic process to that of a funnel that is wide open with diagnostic possibilities at the beginning of the process, but continually and systematically narrows as information is found to support or rule out diagnoses. The clinician gathers, explores, and organizes information in ways that help first to identify the diagnostic possibilities most consistent with the data and then to rule out the remainder of possibilities until a single parsimonious diagnostic picture emerges (Othmer & Othmer, 1994). A framework of logical steps can help make the complexity manageable. Maxmen and Ward suggested the following steps in the diagnostic process: (1) collect data, (2) identify the pathology (if present), (3) evaluate the reliability of the data, (4) determine overall distinctive features of the symptom picture, (5) check diagnostic *DSM-IV* criteria against the client's symptom picture, and (6) resolve diagnostic

TABLE 11.1   Components of the Clinical Interview

1. Introductions, warmup, and screening for problems.
2. Presenting problems and symptoms (with behavioral examples).
3. Mental Status Exam (MSE) and level of functioning.
4. History of the presenting problems.
5. Personal, medical, and psychiatric history (and family history as relevant).
6. Biopsychosocial information (i.e., culture, race, religion, social stressors).
7. Differential diagnoses systematically considered and eliminated.
8. Diagnoses most consistent with all data.
9. Client feedback, questions, concerns, and prognosis.
10. Treatment recommendation and treatment agreement.

uncertainty. For medical safety, prognostic, and treatment reasons, eliminating possible disorders can be as important as identifying probable disorders.

Appendix A of the *DSM-IV* is a compendium of decision trees for differential diagnoses that illustrate the specific criteria and logic of the differential diagnostic process. While *DSM-IV* generally requires specific behavioral criteria, symptom duration and severity, and certain temporal relationships among symptoms to be present in order to make a diagnostic decision, the following process is also necessary. All alternative explanations for the symptoms and problems must have been considered and ruled out before a definitive diagnosis is achieved. Some diagnostic rules can help organize and guide the diagnostic decision-making process.

Diagnostic Rules

The *Rule of Parsimony* suggests that the clinician seek the single most elegant, economical, and efficient diagnosis that accounts for all the available data. If a single diagnosis is insufficient, seek the fewest number that best explain the symptoms (Maxmen & Ward, 1995).

The *Rule of Diagnostic Hierarchy*, as explained by Morrison (1995), suggests that the most severe diagnoses that could account for the symptoms must be ruled out in descending order. The hierarchy declines in medical severity: medical or pharmacologic > psychotic > mood > anxiety > somatic > sexual > personality > adjustment > no mental disorder (Maxmen & Ward, 1995). Sudden clinically significant changes in cognition, mood, anxiety, or personality unexplained by environmental or social factors may be harbingers of undiagnosed medical or neurological problems and must be ruled out through an immediate referral to appropriate medical specialists (i.e., primary care physician, psychiatrist, or neurologist).

The *Rule of Chronology* suggests that the disorder that is present the longest will tend to have priority if it can account for the current symptoms (Morrison, 1995).

The *Rule of Safety* applies when the former rules do not. When the diagnostic picture is unclear, the "safest" diagnosis is the diagnosis that ranks highest for treatability, positive outcome and prognosis, and the least serious pathology and social stigma (Morrison, 1995).

The *Principle of Percentages* suggests that between two or more diagnostic options, consideration is given to the diagnosis that is more frequently found in the population from which the client is drawn (Morrison, 1995).

The *Principle of the Best Data* suggests that the relative decision-making influence of the data should be based on the validity, reliability, objectivity, and longitudinal nature of that data.

The Empirical Database

Components of the empirical database include, but are not limited to, presenting problems, history of those presenting problems, mental status, mental health history, family mental health history, personal and family medical history, social history, educational and military history, work history, relationship and marital history, sexual history, alcohol and drug history, legal history, and leisure time activities (Hersen & Turner, 1994). These areas can be addressed adequately in most interviews through the use of a flexible interviewing approach. Some areas may not be relevant to the clinical picture and may be eliminated from further exploration by only one question; others will need to be addressed in depth. The database can benefit from the additional objective information from family members, friends, police reports, medical or treatment records, and other sources.

The initial screening of the problem focuses on recent primary and secondary symptoms, symptom severity, temporal relationships among data, client explanation of the problems, client level of functioning (in family, social, work, and education realms), and biopsychosocial factors affecting the client. All data are compared with the most applicable syndromes for goodness of fit. More specificity and history will help clarify the current and recent clinical picture and symptom presentation. The history of the presenting problem is a natural extension of the initial screening of the problem. It is important to remember to assess three time periods in the client's history—

premorbid (the period before any symptoms are experienced), prodromal (the period from first symptom onset until clinical severity), and syndromal (the period from which clinical severity of symptoms is first reached to the present)—as each may contain important clues. The history of the presenting problem should describe the earliest onset of the current symptom picture, with dates of onset, symptoms, and course, and note any temporal relationship between symptoms and other factors (i.e., stress, trauma, medical problems). Note recent changes in level of functioning, distress, and insight. The empirical database information must vary flexibly, led by the client's symptoms and clues. Thoroughness is an important quality of the interview because a single fact can change the entire diagnostic picture.

The remainder of the history is gathered in as efficient a manner as possible. The history should paint a longitudinal picture of the client's life in a cultural context. A complete personal history includes such background as developmental history, educational issues, major events, family dynamics, social development, accomplishments, strengths, and protective factors. The medical and psychiatric history should specify previous medical or psychiatric problems, care providers, treatments, medication trials with specific dosages, outcomes, compliance, and side effect problems. Familial history is important for both dynamic and developmental contexts as well as genetic vulnerabilities. Clues to the current clinical picture, latent problems, prognosis, and most promising treatment approaches can lie in any area of history.

MENTAL STATUS EXAM (MSE)

The MSE is at the heart of the diagnostic interview and should capture the individual's immediate mental status at the time of the interview. The MSE assesses a wide range of psychological and neurological functions. The exam can range from a formal exam to a very informal assessment, depending on many variables. A formal exam (where every aspect of the mental status is examined in a standardized manner) is considered the safest option, as some problems (i.e., soft neurological signs) are revealed only through systematic testing. Some clinicians tailor the MSE to the particular client based on the overall data obtained from the interview and referral source.

As with any single piece of information, when used alone, the MSE is sorely insufficient as a basis for making a diagnosis. The MSE must be combined with a thorough and reliable examination of all current symptoms and a history of all systems and symptoms to arrive at a valid diagnostic formulation. In fact, there are many diagnostic categories for which the client will have a "normal" MSE. The major components of the MSE include the following (Othmer & Othmer, 1994):

General observations:

1. Appearance: self-care and hygiene: neat, clean, disheveled, body odor; presentation: manner and appropriateness of clothing, odd or eccentric appearance; weight-to-height ratio; nutritional cues; scars or markings; recent injury or signs of medical problems.
2. Reaction to the interviewer: friendly, compliant, terse, argumentative, socially appropriate.
3. Psychomotor behavior: peculiar mannerisms, extrapyramidal movement, nonverbal symptoms of anxiety, observable energy level, pressured movements or immobility, odd posturing, grimacing, nonverbal signs of hypervigilance.
4. Energy level: normal, manic, lethargic/depressed.

Cognitive and affective aspects:

5. Consciousness: responsiveness and awareness, lethargic, stuporous, variable.
6. Attention and concentration: maintains and shifts attention fluidly, concentrates and focuses on relevant stimuli.
7. Orientation: person, place, and time.
8. Memory: immediate, short-term, remote.
9. Speech: mute, pressured, speeding or slow, loud, timid, shaky, unintelligible, fluency.

10. Content of thinking: delusions, hallucinations, illusions, anxious, obsessive, paranoid, suicidal, homicidal thoughts, somatic preoccupations.
11. Process of thinking: abstract, concrete, linear, logical, flexible, tangential, speeding, odd, ruminative, intrusive thoughts or thought insertion.
12. Mood and affect: flat, blunted, volatile, hostile, incongruent, euthymic.
13. Intelligence: compare to best premorbid level and note temporal changes.
14. Executive functioning: decision making, organizing and planning ability (critical for self-care).
15. Insight and judgment: reflects insight into current problems, use of good judgment by testing reactions to questions requiring social and logical judgment.

It is important for clinicians to commit to memory the components and procedures of conducting the MSE. Equally important is gaining the knowledge of what various results to each MSE component might indicate in light of each syndrome or disorder. In some cases, the MSE may be used to monitor client mental status from time to time and can be one measure of client change. Because time and efficiency are often issues, some clinicians opt to use a short form of the MSE interview such as the Mini-Mental State Exam (Folstein, Folstein, & McHugh, 1975), with good results. Whether the MSE is formal or informal, short or long, it is important that the interviewer be able to reliably determine the MSE results after the diagnostic interview. There are many excellent books currently available that give specific instruction on how to utilize the clinical interview and mental status exam in a diagnosis-specific manner. Those works with which we are most familiar are listed under Recommended Reading at the end of the chapter.

DIAGNOSTIC TOOLS

The more complex the diagnostic scenario, the more important objective data become.

Assessment tools such as objective tests, symptom checklists, and structured interviews can significantly enhance the empirical database with accurate and reliable information. Assessment tools include personality inventories such as the Minnesota Multiphasic Personality Inventory, second edition (Butcher, Dahlstrom,Graham, Tellegen, & Kaemmer, 1989), symptom measures such as the Beck Depression Inventory-II, (Beck, Steer, & Brown, 1996), and symptom checklists such as the Symptoms Checklist-90-R (Derogatis, 1983). Neuropsychiatric tests, which include the Mini-International Neuropsychiatric Inventory-2 (Sheehan et al., 1998), are very useful and sometimes invaluable, but may require specific training and skills to administer and interpret. One detracting feature of some tools is that they may take a significant amount of time to administer or add considerable expense. Often, these are administered after the first session, when a clinician needs to gain more objective information. Structured interviews have significantly increased the reliability (interrater, test-retest, and internal consistency) of the diagnostic interview over that of the unstructured interview (Segal, 1997). There are structured interviews for virtually every Axis I and Axis II diagnostic category. A widely used structured interview for *DSM-IV* Axis I disorders is the Structured Clinical Interview for *DSM-IV* (First, Spitzer, Gibbon, & Williams, 1995). For Axis-II, the Structured Clinical Interview for *DSM-IV* Axis II Personality Disorders (SCID-II, Ver. 2.0) (First, Spitzer, Gibbon, Williams, & Lorna, 1994) is a prime example of a flexible interview schedule that helps work through differential diagnoses.

Choice of assessment tools and structured interviews may depend on many variables, such as the specific information desired by the clinician, relative psychometric properties of each instrument, time of administration, ability of the client to participate in testing, ease of scoring, specific training or educational background needed to administer or interpret the findings, and the benefit-to-cost ratio. As with all tools, the cost- (time and expense) to-benefit ratio must be considered.

One caution is given: Except as pure research criteria or unless otherwise specified, these instruments should be used only as a supplement to the professional diagnostic interview, as most are not designed to be used alone as the sole determinant of a diagnosis. These tools can be powerful additions to the clinician's diagnostic armament and are strongly recommended when used judiciously.

LIMITATIONS AND PITFALLS IN THE DIAGNOSTIC PROCESS

Some common problems we've observed in supervision that may contribute to misdiagnoses include the following:

1. Failure to acknowledge one's limitations: Inevitably, some cases will be beyond one's area of expertise, and ethics may mandate consultation, supervision, or a referral to other experts in respective fields.
2. Not recognizing the limitations of the data: Data must be valid, reliable, pertinent, objective, and complete. A diagnosis is only as good as the data on which it is based; incomplete information will impact on diagnostic accuracy.
3. Jumping to conclusions: Intuition and first impressions, although helpful when developing diagnostic hypotheses, are not objective data and can lead to a dangerous process of taking evaluative shortcuts and relying excessively on compromised data. A single important overlooked fact can lead to misdiagnosis.
4. Stereotyping: Unsupported assumptions about race, culture, gender, age, and diagnostic categories can lead to judgment errors similar to those of jumping to conclusions. Great heterogeneity often exists among persons with the same diagnosis.

SUMMARY

A large number of clinical skills must be integrated effectively for the clinical interview and diagnostic process to proceed smoothly. "Textbook cases" of mental health problems seem much more abundant in textbooks than in real-world practice, and there is no shortage of complex cases readily available to baffle even the most experienced clinician. The clinical interview is often the first step toward helping clients who may have suffered a great deal. Therefore, the time and energy invested in developing sound clinical and diagnostic skills will pay clinicians many dividends in the empathic understanding of clients and increasing clinical effectiveness.

References

Amchin, J. (1991). *Psychiatric diagnosis: A biopsychosocial approach using DSM-III-R.* Washington, DC: American Psychiatric Press.

American Psychiatric Association. (2000). *Diagnostic and statistical manual of mental disorders* (4th ed., text rev.). Washington, DC: Author.

Beck, A.T., Steer, R.A., & Brown, G.K. (1996). *Beck Depression Inventory* (2nd ed.). San Antonio, TX: Psychological Corporation.

Butcher, J.N., Dahlstrom, W.G., Graham, J.R., Tellegen, A., & Kaemmer, B. (1989). *Minnesota Multiphasic Personality Inventory-2 (MMPI-2).* Minneapolis: University of Minnesota Press.

Derogatis, L.R. (1983). *Symptom Check List 90–Revised Version, manual 1.* Baltimore: Johns Hopkins University School of Medicine.

First, M.B., Spitzer, R.L., Gibbon, M., & Williams, J.B.W. (1995). *Structured Clinical Interview: For Axis I DSM-IV disorders–patient edition* (SCID-I/P, Ver. 2.0). New York: New York State Psychiatric Institute, Biometrics Research Department.

First, M.B., Spitzer, R.L., Gibbon, M., Williams, J.B.W., & Lorna, B. (1994). *Structured Clinical Interview for DSM-IV Axis II personality disorders* (SCID-II, Ver. 2.0). New York: New York State Psychiatric Institute, Biometrics Research Department.

Folstein, M.F., Folstein, P.R., & McHugh, P.R. (1975). Mini-Mental State: A practical method for grading the cognitive state of patients for the clinician. *Journal of Psychiatric Research, 12,* 189–198.

Hersen, M., & Turner, S. (1994). The interviewing process. In M. Hersen & S. Turner (Eds.), *Diagnostic interviewing.* New York: Plenum Press.

Maxmen, J., & Ward, N. (1995). *Essential psychopathology and its treatment: Second edition for DSM-IV.* New York: Norton.

Millon, T., & Davis, R.D. (1999). Developmental pathogenesis. In T. Millon, P.H. Blaney, & R.D.

Davis (Eds.), *Oxford textbook of psychopathology.* New York: Oxford University Press.

Morrison, J.R. (1995). *The first interview: Revised for DSM-IV.* New York: Guilford Press.

Othmer, E., & Othmer, S. (1994). *The clinical interview using DSM-IV: Vol. 1: Fundamentals.* Washington, DC: American Psychiatric Press.

Segal, D.L. (1997). Structured interviewing and *DSM* classification. In S. Turner & M. Hersen (Eds.), *Adult psychopathology and diagnosis* (3rd ed.). New York: Wiley.

Sheehan, D.V., Lecrubier, Y., Sheehan, K.H., Amorim, P., Janavs, J., Weiller, E., Hergueta, T., Baker, R., & Dunbar, G.C. (1998). The Mini-International Neuropsychiatric Interview (MINI): The development and validation of a structured diagnostic psychiatric interview for *DSM-IV* and ICD-10. *Journal of Clinical Psychiatry, 59*(Suppl. 20), 22–33.

Hersen, M., & Turner, S. (Eds.). (1994). *Diagnostic interviewing* (2nd ed.). New York: Plenum Press.

Maxmen, J., & Ward, N. (1995). *Essential psychopathology and its treatment: Second edition for DSM-IV.* New York: Norton.

Morrison, J.R. (1995). *The first interview: Revised for DSM-IV.* New York: Guilford Press.

Othmer, E., & Othmer, S. (1994). *The clinical interview using DSM-IV: Vol. 1: Fundamentals.* Washington, DC: American Psychiatric Press.

Othmer, E., & Othmer, S. (1994). *The clinical interview using DSM-IV: Vol. 2: The difficult patient.* Washington, DC: American Psychiatric Press.

Shea, S.C. (1998). *Psychiatric interviewing: The art of understanding. A practical guide for psychiatrists, psychologists, counselors, social workers, nurses, and other mental health professionals* (2nd ed.). Philadelphia: Saunders.

Recommended Readings

Carlat, D. (1999). *The psychiatric interview: A practical guide.* New York: Lippincott, Williams & Wilkins.

12 EFFECTIVE TREATMENT PLANNING

Christopher M. Faiver

Effective treatment planning is one of two tangible end results of a thorough intake assessment of the client. The other result is the determination of an appropriate diagnosis. Actually, the intake assessment may be viewed as a process and a vital component of counseling and therapy. Often the first contact clients have with the mental health arena, assessment sets the tone for the treatment

that follows. Moreover, good listening skills are essential to the derivation of a thorough and accurate intake with the consequent treatment plan.

There are a variety of approaches to effective assessment and treatment planning. These range from the use of psychological tests and inventories (Dougherty & Chamblin, 1999; Fisher, Beutler, & Williams,

1999; Maruish, 1999) to determine the most efficacious treatment to those that couple diagnosis with corresponding treatment modalities (DeGood, Crawford, & Jongsma, 1999; Frances & Ross, 1996; Jensen, 1999; Kadden & Skerker, 1999; King & Scahill, 1999; Klassen, Miller, Raina, Lee, & Olsen, 1999; Othmer & Othmer, 1994; Paleg & Jongsma, 2000; Seligman, 1990; Spitzer, Gibbon, Skodel, Williams, & First, 1994). The counselor's theoretical orientation influences choice of treatment and case disposition, and the exigencies of third-party payment and the managed care environment delimit the need for a precise and measurable treatment plan.

Intake procedures range from the extensive and elaborate to the minimal and concise compilation of data. Nonetheless, a basic structure for assessment emerges. This intake assessment process includes several components: (1) client description, (2) problem description, (3) psychosocial history, (4) mental status examination, (5) diagnosis, and (5) treatment recommendations. First, data are gathered on the client and the presenting concern. Next, background information, called the psychosocial history, is noted, paying special attention to any anomalies—anything out of the ordinary—in the client's past. Finally, the counselor evaluates how the client is functioning presently in the consulting room in what is termed the mental status exam. These data provide the necessary information from which to draw the diagnostic conclusion from the *Diagnostic and Statistical Manual of Mental Disorders,* fourth ed. (APA, 1994), as well as to provide suggested treatment recommendations (Faiver, 1988, 1992; Faiver & O'Brien, 1993; Faiver, Eisengart, & Colonna, 2000; Othmer & Othmer, 1994).

THE INTAKE PROCESS

With the understanding that treatment recommendations emerge from the process of intake, it makes sense to describe this process in some detail.

Client and Concern Description

Generally, the formula denoting age, race, gender, and marital status in adults, followed by the words "complaining of . . . " or "reporting . . . " is standard. For example: A 30-year-old Asian female, divorced, complaining of anxiety and depression following divorce proceedings. In the case of children or those forced to seek treatment, the formula remains the same, with the exception of "whose parents report . . . " or "whom school (or other) officials report . . . " in lieu of the client self-reporting.

Psychosocial History

Next, one examines the past history of the client by performing a psychosocial history. Relevant historical data are gathered on the client, including childhood and adolescence, current and family of origin history, legal history, medical history, religious (belief system) history, employment history, educational/vocational history, avocational history, military history, history of mental health contacts, and relational/social history.

Mental Status

Ascertaining of mental status differs from psychosocial history in that the counselor makes clinical inferences about the client based on present observations of the client rather than on client-reported self-history.

Another simple formula denotes whether the client appeared alert and oriented as to person (who he or she is), place (where he or she is), and time (what the date and time are). Called "orientation in the three spheres," some clinicians simply write "Ox3" to note that the client appeared alert and oriented. Of course, the opposite notation of "disoriented" would be recorded for those clients who fit that description.

Three other areas of mental status assessment merit attention:

- *Cognitions.* Here the counselor explores current functioning in the cognitive arena, including recent and remote memory, intellectual level (below average, average, or above average), concrete versus abstract thinking abilities, judgment, guilt, evidence of hallucinations, delusions.

- *Affect.* The counselor notes current type, appropriateness, level, and intensity of emotions, including depression, anxiety, and mania.
- *Behaviors.* The counselor takes notice of any behavioral anomalies, including tics, psychomotor agitation or retardation, pressured speech, and unusual gestures.

Additionally, the counselor assesses risk of harm to self or others to determine level of lethality, ideation, plans, and means. It behooves the counselor to become familiar with agency and ethical policies in this area.

Finally, the counselor may find it useful to ask the client the question: "Is there anything I haven't asked you that you think I should know?" Often, other pertinent information may result.

Diagnostic Impression (*DSM-IV*)

The counselor draws a diagnostic conclusion based on data provided or self-reported by the client and the clinical inferences observed by the counselor. Note that the diagnosis is merely an impression and, as such, is subject to modification. Data are reported in five areas, called axes. They include:

Axis I   Clinical Syndromes
          Other Conditions That May Be a Focus of Clinical Attention
Axis II   Personality Disorders
          Mental Retardation
Axis III General Medical Conditions
Axis IV   Psychosocial and Environmental Problems
Axis V   Global Assessment of Functioning

Treatment Recommendations

As with the diagnostic impression, treatment recommendations are conclusional data result-ing from the process of the interview and, thus, are tentative and subject to modification. Possible recommendations include psychological testing; psychiatric referral; referral to another professional; a specific type of therapy, such as individual, group, family, or marital; a specific modality, such as stress management, biofeedback, cognitive-behavioral; hospitalization; or even no treatment.

THE TREATMENT PLAN

Formulation of a treatment plan follows intake. Ideally, the client is as involved in the process of treatment planning as possible (Chinman et al., 1999). This involvement helps ensure the investment of the client in his or her treatment. By including the client in the decision-making process, we teach the client that counseling is a shared process in which clients not only have contributions to make, but also have accountability regarding the results of their therapy (Faiver et al., 2000). Of course, the level of client involvement depends on the severity of diagnosis, level of client insight, age, issues of fitness, and the ability, skills, and theoretical orientation of the counselor. Moreover, conclusions regarding treatment recommendations are as individualized as the diagnosis, respecting the uniqueness of the client.

The treatment plan generally follows a management-by-objective format and, as such, is specific, time-limited, and concise. Goals are usually the inverse of the problems stated and are measurable. For example, a client indicating a problem with controlling her anger may have as a goal increased control of outbursts, as evidenced by a specific numerical reduction from five per day to two. The client signs the treatment plan along with the counselor, thus providing further investment in the treatment process as a social contract. We recommend that clients who are minors sign along with their parents to engender their participation. (How often are minors asked to sign anything?)

A simple treatment plan is illustrated in Table 12.1.

TABLE 12.1   Treatment Plan Illustration

Problem/ Concern	Problem/ Goal	Treatment	Treatment of Achievement	Expected Date Results	Follow-Up
1. Anxiety	Decrease tension	Teach progressive muscle relaxtion	12/2002	Ct. reports less stress	In 2 months

TABLE 12.2   Intake Form with Treatment Plan

Client Name _____   Counselor Name _____

Date _____   Length of Interview _____

   I. Client and problem description:

 II. Psychosocial history:

III. Mental status:
    Cognitions:
    Affect:
    Behaviors:
    Risk of harm to self or others:

IV. Diagnostic impression *(DSM-IV)*
    Axis I:
    Axis II:
    Axis III:
    Axis IV:
    Axis V:

 V. Treatment recommendations:

VI. Treatment plan:

Problem/Concern	Goal	Treatment Methods	Expected Date of Achievement	Results	Follow-Up
1.					
2.					
3.					
4.					
5.					

VII. Additional remarks:

In formulating the treatment plan, counselors should pay attention to factors that may affect both therapy planning and process. These include whether client problems are acute or chronic; any socioeconomic limitations; the amount of structure needed (within the context of least restrictive environment); legal system considerations; the conforming of treatment to a specific diagnosis; collaboration with other professionals; the counselor's time constraints and schedule; the counselor's competency to deal with specific problems; any constraints placed by managed care companies; the agency's capacity for dealing with certain problems; the client's ability to deal with his or her problem; and any special client needs that must be addressed (Faiver et al., 2000).

We encourage counselors to be creative as they work with clients in the design of a treatment plan, with the end goal of assisting clients in achieving their ideal level of functioning. Do your best to meet the client's needs within the bounds of the code of ethics, of course. Be frank with clients about what you and your agency are able to do for them, offering referral and assistance in finding appropriate clinical resources as necessary.

Table 12.2 illustrates a basic process outline for the clinical intake with focus on treatment recommendations and treatment plans.

SUMMARY

Effective treatment planning is the culmination of the process of a thorough intake assessment on the part of the counselor. The basic components of any intake include descriptions of the client and his or her concern, a psychosocial history, and a mental status examination. These areas of assessment result in the *DSM-IV* diagnosis and the treatment plan itself. This plan, by necessity, is precise, to the point, and measurable. Clients should be as involved as possible in this process of treatment planning.

References

American Psychiatric Association. (1994). *Diagnostic and statistical manual of mental disorders* (4th ed.). Washington, DC: Author.

Chinman, M.J., Allende, M., Weingarten, R., Steiner, J., Tworkowski, S., & Davidson, L. (1999). On the road to collaborative treatment planning: Consumer and provider perspectives. *Journal of Behavioral Health Services and Research, 26*(2), 211–218.

DeGood, D.E., Crawford, A.L., & Jongsma, A.E. (1999). *The behavioral medicine treatment planner.* New York: Wiley.

Dougherty, L.M., & Chamblin, B. (1999). Assessment as and adjunct in psychotherapy. In P.A. Lichtenberg (Ed.), *Handbook of assessment in clinical gerontology* (pp. 91–110). New York: Wiley.

Eisengart, S., Eisengart, S., Faiver, C., & Eisengart, J. (1996). Respecting physical and psychosocial boundaries of the hospitalized patient: Some practical tips on patient management. *Rural Community Mental Health, 23*(2), 5–7.

Faiver, C. (1988). An initial client contact form. In P.A. Keller & S.R. Heyman (Eds.), *Innovations in clinical practice: A source book* (Vol. 7, pp. 285–288). Sarasota, FL: Professional Resource Exchange.

Faiver, C. (1992). Intake as process. *CACD Journal, 12,* 83–85.

Faiver, C., & O'Brien, E. (1993). Assessment of religious beliefs form. *Counseling and Values, 37*(3), 176–178.

Faiver, C.M., Eisengart, S.P., & Colonna, R. (2000). *The counselor intern's handbook* (2nd ed.). Pacific Grove, CA: Brooks/Cole.

Fisher, D., Beutler, L., & Williams, O. (1999). Making assessment relevant to treatment planning: The STS clinician rating form. *Journal of Clinical Psychology, 55*(7), 825–842.

Frances, A., & Ross, R. (1996). *DSM-IV case studies: A clinical guide to differential diagnosis.* Washington, DC: American Psychiatric Press.

Jensen, P.S. (1999). Fact versus fancy concerning the multimodal treatment study for attention-deficit/hyperactivity disorder. *Canadian Journal of Psychiatry, 44*(10), 975–980.

Kadden, R.M., & Skerker, P.M. (1999). Treatment decision making and goal setting. In B.S. McCrady & E.E. Epstein (Eds.), *Addictions: A comprehensive guidebook* (pp. 216–231). New York: Oxford University Press.

King, R.A., & Scahill, L. (1999). The assessment and coordination of treatment of children and adolescents with OCD. *Child and Adolescent Psychiatric Clinics of North America, 8*(3), 577–597.

Klassen, A., Miller, A., Raina, P., Lee, S.K., & Olsen, L. (1999). Attention-deficit/hyperactivity disorder in children and youth: A quantitative systematic review of the efficacy of different management strategies. *Canadian Journal of Psychiatry, 44*(10), 1007–1016.

Maruish, M.E. (1999). *The use of psychological testing for treatment planning and outcomes assessment* (2nd ed.). Mahwah, NJ: Erlbaum.

Othmer, E., & Othmer, S.C. (1994). *The clinical interview using DSM-IV.* Washington, DC: American Psychiatric Press.

Paleg, K., & Jongsma, A.E., Jr. (2000). *The group therapy treatment planner.* New York: Wiley.

Seligman, L. (1990). *Selecting effective treatments.* Alexandria, VA: American Counseling Association.

13 THE NONMEDICAL THERAPIST'S ROLE IN PHARMACOLOGICAL INTERVENTIONS WITH ADULTS

R. Elliott Ingersoll

In the past 40 years, conceptualizations and treatments of emotional disorders have changed drastically. In the recent past, the theoretical base regarding the etiology and treatment of mental and emotional disorders was strongly psychodynamic (Gabbard, 1994). Despite trends in brief and cognitive therapies, this base has become increasingly medical (Cohen, 1993). The medical model emphasizes the biological bases of behavior and pharmacological manipulation of these biological bases to achieve behavior change (Gabbard, 1994; Schatzberg, Cole, & DeBattista, 1997). At the time of this writing, the core treatment for many of the mental and emotional disorders listed in the *Diagnostic and Statistical Manual* (*DSM-IV*) of the American Psychiatric Association (1994) is pharmacological (Victor, 1996), and there are more pharmacological treat-ments available for these disorders than ever before (Littrell & Ashford, 1995).

According to the American Psychiatric Association, it is difficult to get an exact count of psychotropic prescriptions written in the United States at any given time (T. Tanielian, Associate Director, Office of Research, personal communication, February 8, 1999). Psychotropic medications accounted for 8.8% of the total prescription drug market in 1994 and that number is rising (Pincus et al., 1998). The number of visits for psychotropic medication to primary care physicians and psychiatrists has increased (Pincus et al., 1998), and much of the increase is attributable to newer antidepressants and the increased use of stimulants to treat children and adolescents with Attention-Deficit/Hyperactivity Disorder (ADHD).

The goal of this chapter is to describe the roles of nonmedical mental health professionals dealing with clients taking psychotropic medications. The roles discussed include collaborator, information broker, and support person. Before discussing the roles, the chapter begins with a discussion of why it is important for nonmedical mental health professionals to acquire knowledge about psychopharmacology and an overview of the ethical and legal issues.

Because this chapter does not provide basic pharmacological training, it is important to emphasize that mental health professionals should take at least one course in psychopharmacology and pursue continuing education in that area. Courses designed for nonmedical mental health professionals should follow the level 1 guidelines for psychopharmacology education set forth by the American Psychological Association (APA, 1995). See Ingersoll (in press) for a description of such a course.

WHY LEARN ABOUT PSYCHOTROPIC MEDICATIONS?

A general, working knowledge of psychopharmacology is important for several reasons. First, all mental health professionals should be able to help their clients understand the treatment options they are likely to encounter (Meyer & Dertsch, 1996), and psychotropic medications are increasingly considered treatment options in settings where counseling and psychotherapy take place (Buelow, Herbert, & Buelow, 2000; Faiver, Eisengart, & Colonna, 2000). Many clients of master's-level counselors, social workers, and school psychologists are taking some form of psychotropic medication, but research studies have noted that these professionals lack training in psychopharmacology (Bentley, Farmer, & Phillips, 1991; Kratochwill, 1994; West, Hosie, & Mackey, 1988). Second, mental health professionals need an understanding of how taking medications or noncompliance with medication prescriptions can affect a client's progress in counseling. Understanding these issues can help therapists decide when referral back to the

professional prescribing the client's medication is necessary.

ETHICAL AND LEGAL CONSIDERATIONS

Assuming a mental health professional has at least basic education in psychopharmacology, is there a legal or ethical problem with such a therapist discussing medications with clients? There are no clear prohibitions against a nonmedical mental health professional talking with clients about psychotropic medications (Patterson, 1996), although this is still a gray area. Littrell and Ashford (1995) explored the issue of psychologists discussing psychotropic medications with clients. They noted the history of court decisions on this topic related to the nursing and pharmacy professions and concluded, "Given the precedent established in other professions, it is unlikely that a psychologist's discussion of medication could be construed as practicing medicine without a license" (p. 241). They concluded that there was no basis in case law for assuming that psychologists sharing information about psychotropic medication is illegal. It should be noted that psychologists' situation might change, as there is a movement to train them to prescribe psychotropic medications. Currently, only one U.S. jurisdiction (Guam) has passed legislation allowing limited prescription privileges for clinical psychologists (Foxhall, 1999; Rabasca, 1999).

There is no literature exploring related ethical issues for counselors, social workers, and other mental health professionals, and research in this area is needed. It is important to note that in the American Counseling Association (ACA) Code of Ethics and Standards of Practice, section A.1 states that a primary responsibility of counselors is to promote clients' welfare. This includes being knowledgeable about treatment options, which can include supplementing counseling with psychotropic medication prescribed by a physician. Counselors who may discuss psychotropic medications with clients need to closely observe the ethical principles for collaborating with cooperating agencies and professionals (see

Glosoff, this volume; Patterson, 1996). More and more, it seems that the increasing use of psychotropic medications to treat mental and emotional disorder leads scholars to conclude that legal problems may result from a therapist's *not* pursuing basic knowledge in psychopharmacology (Buelow, Herbert, & Buelow, 2000; Patterson, 1996).

IMPORTANT ROLES FOR THE NONMEDICAL THERAPIST

Mental Health Professional as Collaborator

Seeing a client who may be taking a psychotropic medication raises several possible collaboration situations. Assuming the client has signed the appropriate release of information form, therapists may find themselves collaborating with physicians, psychiatrists, significant others, or members of extended family.

Collaborating with Prescribing Professionals. When considering prescribing professionals in mental health, psychiatrists are usually the first professionals to come to mind. Some therapists may have the luxury of choosing a particular psychiatrist to collaborate with, but the majority of mental health professionals do not. These professionals are often working with a psychiatrist who has a heavy caseload and may get to spend only 10 minutes with the client. In those instances, psychiatrists may rely more on the nonmedical therapist for updates regarding the client's progress. Although psychiatrists specialize in the prescription of medications for mental and emotional disorders, general practitioners write a significant number of prescriptions for psychotropic medications. Whatever the specialty of the prescribing professional, a thoughtful, well-planned collaborative relationship can facilitate the client's treatment (Imhorf, Altman, & Katz, 1998).

Collaboration strategies may be said to fall on a general continuum between taking a "one-down" position to being perceived and treated as an informed colleague. The strategy one chooses depends on the disposition of the medical doctor in question and the

doctor's attitude toward counseling and psychotherapy.

Doctors who view psychotropic medications and therapy as complementary (and trust the credentials of the therapist) typically appreciate the informed colleague strategy. In this type of relationship, the doctor is as interested in what the therapist knows about the client's progress as the therapist is in what the doctor knows about the client's medication regimen. Doctors who are skeptical about the benefits of complementing psychotropic medication with therapy (or who mistrust the credentials of a particular therapist) are best approached through the "one-down" strategy. In this strategy, the therapist presents as one who needs to learn from the doctor and graciously (if not genuflectively) absorbs whatever expertise the doctor can share in the collaboration.

In the collaborative relationship with physicians, therapists have the opportunity to check their understanding of the prescribed medication, ask informed questions, and provide feedback about the client's progress in therapy. The collaborative relationship with medical personnel is an excellent opportunity to gain a greater understanding of clients' responses to medication. This is particularly important if the client is on multiple medications. Although informed questions are appropriate regarding whether a certain client would benefit from a particular medication, it is not appropriate to lobby doctors to prescribe clients certain medications. Such lobbying presumes a medical knowledge that is usually outside the expertise of a nonmedical therapist. As Patterson (1996) noted, the therapist's role is to "support, not supplant" the medical professional's role.

Collaborating with Family Members and Significant Others. Mental health therapists whose clients are taking medications often will be approached by significant others and family members who may hold a variety of attitudes toward medication, ranging from polite curiosity to unbounded hostility. In many cases, loved ones do not have access to as much time with the prescribing professional as with the mental health therapist. Again, assuming the appropriate releases of information have been signed by the client, therapists can provide an important service by helping loved ones understand why a client is on a medication and what it is hoped that the medication will do for the client. It is important to be alert to misinformation that client's loved ones may have regarding what a medication can and cannot do. One woman whose father was suffering from the early stages of Alzheimer's type dementia believed that a medication prescribed (in this case, donepezil) could cure the condition. Although the prescribing physician had already explained that the medication could only slow the progress of the disease, the woman still held firm to the belief that it would cure her father. In this case, the therapist (a clinical counselor) worked several sessions helping the woman through the emotional pain that came with conscious awareness of her father's condition and helped her make the most of the extra time she got with her father because of the benefits of the medication.

Mental Health Professional as Information Broker

Suppose you have a client who comes in and says, "I decided not to talk to my doctor about an antidepressant. I am going to drink tea made from St. John's Wort instead. I saw a great article on it on the Internet." One thing there is no shortage of in our society is information, and that includes information on psychotropic medications. What is important is knowing where to go for *good* information and how to evaluate that information.

Advances in the number and understanding of psychotropic medications are increasing at a dizzying pace. Most clients taking psychotropic medications could use an information broker to assist them in understanding those medications. I use the term "broker" here in the sense of one who acts as an intermediary to arrange information about psychotropic medications. Obviously, to be a good information broker with clients, nonmedical mental health professionals need basic training in understanding psychotropic medications

and interpreting research studies. For quick updates and summaries of research, mental health professionals can turn to newsletters such as *Psychopharmacology Update* published by Manisses Corporation or the electronic newsletter *Medscape* (pharmacotherapy.medscape.com). As with any information, though, it is preferable to get as close to the source as possible.

Taking the role of information broker does not translate into blind support and endorsement of the medical model. Rather, this role helps clients understand what the science of the medical model can and cannot offer them. Regarding the client above who wants to try St. John's Wort, there may be no harm in his trying it if postponing medication does not put him at risk. A good information broker would want to know that herbal compounds are notoriously variable regarding their potency and ingredients (Gutherie, 1999), that the results of studies of St. John's Wort are currently mixed (Health, 2000; Volz, 1997), and that St. John's Wort may have harmful interactions with other drugs. Clearly, the safest course of action for the client in question is to talk to his physician to be certain that St. John's Wort is not contraindicated. Certainly, the herb may have beneficial effects or may act as a placebo for the client in question. Clients will make their own choices on these matters and many never share their use of herbaceuticals with their physicians (Gutherie, 1999). The nonmedical therapist as information broker is in a good position to steer the client toward quality information as well as explore the possibility of a medical consultation before trying the herbal preparation.

Mental Health Professional as Support Person

Clients taking medication often need support for a variety of issues. Consider the case of a woman who was suffering antidepressant-induced sexual dysfunction and waited six months before mentioning it because she was embarrassed to talk about sexuality. Although the client was seeing the therapist (a clinical social worker) to change life situations correlated with her depressive episodes, dealing with the side effect became a therapeutic concern. The client's difficulty talking about sexuality was similar to many other areas of her life where she had difficulty "finding her voice" and stating what she wanted. Her case had a positive outcome and she was able to speak to her physician about the problem and have her medication adjusted to alleviate it.

Supporting Compliance with Medication Regimens. Noncompliance with medication regimens varies greatly across populations, but it is estimated that between 25% and 80% of patients with various disorders are noncompliant with their medications (Sackett, 1980). Patterson (1996) has noted that noncompliance may be defined as "any departure from the instructions for proper use of the medication" (p. 70). Patterson wrote that the role of nonmedical professionals in supporting compliance includes talking regularly with clients about whether they are in fact taking the medication as prescribed, whether the medication seems to be relieving symptoms, and whether the client is suffering from any side effects.

Supporting Culturally Diverse Clients. The field of psychopharmacology is just beginning to investigate the relevance of cultural variables as they may relate to differential attitudes toward and responses to medication. This has been described as ethnopharmacotherapy (Lawson, 1999) and includes looking at variables of diversity and their relationship to medication. Variables of diversity include race, ethnicity, gender, age, ability/disability, and sexual orientation. Lawson noted that most psychiatric journals publishing biological research do not include data regarding the race of the subjects. This despite the fact that different ethnic groups may require different doses, may have different risks for certain side effects, and may receive misdiagnoses due to symptom expression that deviates from the dominant cultural expression.

Probably the most developed body of research on differential effects of medication examines gender. It is estimated that 70% of the psychotropic medications prescribed in the United States are prescribed to women (Ogur, 1986). Newer research is shedding light on such topics as how medications may work differently in women (Yaeger & Hendrick, 1998) and the effects of medications on breast-feeding women (Stowe et al., 1997). The research on racial differences that does exist is in its infancy and typically looks at effects between Caucasians and African Americans or Asians and Asian Americans. There are many issues to be dealt with, including the inaccurate classifying of different groups under the same label (such as "Hispanic") (Jacobsen & Comas-Diaz, 1999).

Differences in physiology are important to such research, and cultural attitudes toward taking medication or herbaceuticals and lifestyle issues from culture to culture are equally important. One example cited by Jacobsen and Comas-Diaz (1999) is the rate of coffee consumption among Latinas and how caffeine's sympathomimetic effects can worsen many symptoms of mental illness as well as affect the hepatic enzymes responsible for drug metabolism.

SUMMARY

In this era of biological psychiatry, the nonmedical mental health professional has important roles to play when clients' therapy is complemented with psychotropic medication. As collaborator, information broker, and support person, the nonmedical mental health professional provides services necessary for quality mental health care. With proper training, continuing education, and ethical practice, the nonmedical mental health professional will continue to be an indispensable part of the total treatment team.

References

American Psychiatric Association. (1994). *Diagnostic and statistical manual of mental disorders* (4th ed.) Washington, DC: Author.

American Psychological Association. (1995). *Curriculum for level one training in psychopharmacology.* Washington, DC: Author.

Bentley, K.J., Farmer, R., & Phillips, M.E. (1991). Student knowledge of and attitudes toward psychotropic drugs. *Journal of Social Work Education, 27,* 279–289.

Buelow, G., Herbert, S., & Buelow, S. (2000). *Psychotherapist's resource on psychiatric medications: Issues of treatment and referral.* Pacific Grove, CA: Brooks/Cole.

Cohen, C.I. (1993). The biomedicalization of psychiatry: A critical overview. *Community Mental Health Journal, 29,* 509–521.

Faiver, C.M., Eisengart, S., & Colonna, R. (2000). *The counselor intern's handbook* (2nd ed.). Pacific Grove, CA: Brooks/Cole.

Foxhall, K. (1999). Town hall meeting focuses on gaining prescription privileges. *APA Monitor, 30,* 30.

Gabbard, G.O. (Ed.). (1994). *Treatment of the DSM-IV psychiatric disorders.* Washington, DC: American Psychiatric Press.

Gutherie, S.K. (1999, September 24). *Herbaceuticals in psychiatry.* Unpublished lecture given at the Medical College of Ohio, Toledo.

Imhof, J.E., Altman, R., & Katz, J.L. (1998). The relationship between psychotherapist and prescribing psychiatrist. *American Journal of Psychotherapy, 52,* 261–272.

Ingersoll, R.E. (in press). Teaching a course in psychopharmacology to counselors: Justification, structure, and methods. *Counselor Education and Supervision.*

Jacobsen, F.M., & Comas-Diaz, L. (1999). Psychopharmacologic treatment of Latinas. *Essential Psychopharmacology, 3,* 29–42.

Kratochwill, T.R. (1994). Psychopharmacology for children and adolescents: Commentary on current issues and future challenges. *School Psychology Quarterly, 9,* 53–59.

Lawson, W.B. (1999). The art and science of ethnopharmacotherapy. In J.M. Herrera, W.B. Lawson, & J.J. Sramek (Eds.), *Cross-cultural psychiatry.* New York: Wiley.

Littrell, J., & Ashford, J. (1995). Is it proper for psychologists to discuss medications with clients? *Professional Psychology: Research and Practice, 238,* 238–244.

Meyer, R.G., & Deitsch, S.E. (1996). *The clinician's handbook: Integrated diagnostics, assessment, and*

intervention in adult and adolescent psychopathology. Boston: Allyn & Bacon.

Ogur, B. (1986). Long day's journey into night: Women and prescription drug abuse. *Women and Health, 11,* 99–115.

Patterson, L.E. (1996). Strategies for improving medication compliance. *Essential Psychopharmacology, 1,* 70–79.

Pincus, H.A., Tanielian, T.L., Marcus, S.C., Olfson, M., Zarin, D.A., Thompson, J., & Zito, J.M. (1998). Prescribing trends in psychotropic medications. *Journal of the American Medical Association, 279,* 526–531.

Rabasca, L. (1999). Guam psychologists gain right to prescribe. *APA Monitor, 30,* 6.

Sackett, D. (1980). Is there a compliance problem? If so, what do we do about it? In L. Lasagna (Ed.), *Controversies in therapeutics.* Philadelphia: Saunders.

Schatzberg, A.F., Cole, J.O., & DeBattista, C. (1997). *Manual of clinical psychopharmacology* (3rd ed.). Washington, DC: American Psychiatric Press.

Stowe, Z.N., Owens, M.J., Landry, J.C., Kilts, C.D., Ely, T., Llewellyn, A., & Nemeroff, C.B. (1997). Sertraline and desmethylsertraline in human breast milk and nursing infants. *American Journal of Psychiatry, 154,* 1255–1260.

Victor, B.S. (1996). Transpersonal psychopharmacology and psychiatry. In B.W. Scotton, A.B. Chinen, & J.R. Battista (Eds.), *Textbook of transpersonal psychiatry and psychology.* New York: Basic Books.

Volz, H.P. (1997). Controlled clinical trials of hypericum extracts in depressed patients: An overview. *Pharmacopsychiatry, 30*(Suppl. 2), 72–76.

West, J.D., Hosie, T.W., & Mackey, J.A. (1988, March). The counselor's role in mental health: An evaluation. *Counselor Education and Supervision,* 233–239.

Yeager, D., & Hendrick, V. (1998). *The faces of depression throughout the female life cycle* [video]. (Available from Interactive Medical Networks, 1375 Piccard Drive, Suite 325, Rockville, MD 20850)

14 GUIDELINES FOR COUNSELING MANDATED AND NONVOLUNTARY CLIENTS

Ronald H. Rooney

Mental health counselors frequently assess or treat clients who did not choose to work with the counselor. Such clients have often been considered resistant, as if their reluctance were part of their pathology rather than a reflection of their coerced circumstances. There is reason to believe that coerced or pressured contact will increase, as the number of clients legally mandated to receive treatment is increasing. This chapter outlines constructs and skills designed to assist you in increasing voluntarism with mandated and nonvoluntary clients.

MAJOR CONSTRUCTS

Constructs Related to Clients

Mental health counselors provide assessments or treatments for *legally mandated* or *court-ordered* clients who seek assistance under the pressure of a court order. They also provide services for *nonvoluntary* clients who seek assistance under formal pressures from agencies, officials, and employers and informal pressures from parents, spouse, partner, and children (as in the case of the elderly) (Rooney, 1992). For example, it has been noted that clients receiving services under managed care, though not legally mandated, often find lim-

ited options covered under their plan (Strom-Gottfried, 1998).

Constructs Related to Process and Outcome

Outcomes can be improved to the extent that there is *motivational congruence* or a fit between the involuntary client's own concerns and those of external sources of pressure. Failing agreement, the oppositional behavior exhibited by court-ordered and nonvoluntary clients is often labeled *resistance.* That oppositional behavior might better be reframed as disagreement with the views of their problems held by others. Fruitful sources of intervention come from reframing expectable opposition from pejorative labels such as resistance to *reactance,* or the normal response that occurs when a person experiences a threat to valued beliefs and behaviors (Brehm, 1976). In addition, involuntary clients often manifest *self-presentation strategies* designed to put themselves in the best light to influence the counselor's recommendation. For example, it is common for a person to ingratiate, supplicate, or attempt to intimidate a counselor considered to have power over important decisions such as child custody (Jones & Pittman, 1982).

Efforts to influence involuntary client beliefs and behaviors often include forms of *confrontation* designed to show clients inconsistencies between their own values and behaviors. Efforts to achieve long-lasting changes often require *persuasion* methods designed to influence those values and behaviors and

The author wishes to thank Michael Chovanec and Carol Kuechler for their useful comments on earlier drafts of this chapter.

aimed at achieving *self-attribution*, in which clients come to acknowledge changes as being in their own best interest rather than simply ways to avoid punishment or attain rewards (Rooney, 1992).

Constructs Related to Ethics

The helping professions are often committed to the empowerment of vulnerable clients, assisting them in reaching greater capacity to influence decisions important to them. Ethical conflicts arise when intervention with involuntary clients involves *paternalism* or actions considered to be in a client's best interest, whether or not the client chooses it. Similarly, *beneficence* refers to interventions designed to enhance a vulnerable client's quality of life whether or not the client chooses it (Murdach, 1996). Limited beneficence applies to selected abrogation of wishes, such as when a psychiatric nurse temporarily limits visits for the welfare of a hospitalized patient. When there is more severe impairment and the effects are longer lasting, selective beneficence applies; for example, physically ill patients might not have the right to refuse treatment. Extensive beneficence occurs when the limitation to functioning is substantial, as when the person has a psychotic condition. In these instances, interference with wishes for best interest may occur relating to many behaviors while suffering with a condition uncontrolled by medication. The challenge for mental health counselors is hence to respect self-determination to the extent possible while also acting with appropriate paternalism and beneficence.

FINDINGS FROM THEORY, RESEARCH, AND PRACTICE

Court-ordered clients have been shown to experience gains from required participation in helping programs. For example, court-ordered recipients of drug treatment have had significantly fewer arrests at 30-month follow-up than matched probationers not receiving the drug treatment (Peters & Murrin, 2000). Participants in welfare-to-work programs, faced with penalties for failure to participate, have participated at a high rate without significant alienation from counselors utilizing the penalties (Riccio & Hasenfeld, 1996).

Similarly, nonvoluntary clients mandated to receive counseling services from an employee assistance program under a "last-chance contract" have fared better at 13- to 25-month follow-up in terms of fewer absences and sick days than other voluntary participants in the program (Keaton & Yamatani, 1993). On the other hand, clients believed to be mentally ill and imminently violent who have been involuntarily hospitalized have been likely to commit assault and battery one day after release (Catalano & McConnell, 1996). Hence, coercion sometimes results in decreases in negative behavior, but concerns are raised about effectiveness when impairment is high. The following three sections summarize research findings on nonvoluntary clients related to client characteristics, program characteristics, and treatment outcome.

Findings Related to Client Characteristics

Persons of color are overrepresented in more restrictive forms of treatment, such as juvenile treatment and out-of-home care. Hence, involuntary clients are more likely to be culturally different from counselors than in most voluntary circumstances (Rooney, 1992).

Involuntary clients coerced into program participation have, in some cases, approved of the mandate and not experienced the kind of alienation from helpers that might be expected (Kramer & Washo, 1993; Riccio & Hasenfeld, 1996).

Clients of all levels of voluntarism vary on a range of readiness for change (Prochaska, DiClemente, & Norcross, 1992). Precontemplators have not considered the problem serious and have not attempted to change. Contemplators, on the other hand, are aware that others consider the problem serious and have considered making changes. One study at intake indicated that involuntary clients were overrepresented, as would be expected, in the precontemplation and contemplation phases (O'Hare, 1996). However, equally significant is the fact that as many as 25% of initially involuntary clients had already moved at first contact to considering decisions or taking action to change. Hence, the counselor should not assume that legally mandated clients necessarily lack motivation for change.

Concerns are raised about whether informed consent is actually possible with involuntary clients when available choices contain significant rewards and punishments. Informed consent with involuntary clients should include honest information that the results of an assessment may not result in the outcome desired by the client and should include disclosure of responsibilities to other parties besides the client. For example, a counselor who does a custody assessment must ethically inform parents that a primary responsibility is to the court in assisting the judge to make a decision in the best interest of the child (Regehr & Angle, 1997).

Findings Related to Program Characteristics

Interviewing that resembles interrogation, including asking an involuntary client to explain his or her behavior, may be less useful than stating the information available to the counselor about the reason for contact (Brodsky & Lichtenstein, 1999). For example, the counselor might say: "You were referred to me for an evaluation by your employer. I would like to hear how you feel about this referral."

Programs that are primarily based on the threat of coercion face the problem of needing extensive surveillance of client acts and the ability to respond rapidly and decisively to violations to be effective (Riccio & Hasenfeld, 1996).

Programs that emphasize personal motivation for success through persuasion methods have also been successful in generating strong participation (Riccio & Hasenfeld, 1996). Such methods may produce longer-lasting changes through self-attribution than those based primarily on compliance.

Confrontation methods that demean and disrespect the involuntary client run the risk of reinforcing abusive beliefs that "might makes right." In working with sexual offenders and domestic violence perpetrators, it has been suggested that those confrontation methods that assist involuntary clients in examining their own behavior and values for inconsistencies in a nonjudgmental, caring manner are more likely to stimulate dissonance (Kear-Colwell & Pollock, 1997; Murphy & Baxter, 1997).

Involuntary clients are more likely to be effected by a confrontive message if the value confronted is strong, their current behavior is inconsistent with what they consider to be ideal behavior, and they are dissatisfied with their current behavior (Sawa & Sawa, 1988). For example, conflicting parents who are engaged in child custody concerns might be influenced about talking negatively about their former spouse to the children if the effects can be seen as inconsistent with their value of loving and protecting their children.

Involuntary clients can be expected to experience a less negative reaction to contact if they can choose among alternatives, even when those choices are constrained (Rooney, 1992). That is, the choice among alternative forms or locations for receiving chemical dependency evaluations or domestic violence treatment is more of a choice than deciding between treatment and prosecution.

Findings Related to Treatment Outcome

Outcomes are improved when involuntary clients are socialized to roles such that they are clear about what to expect from counselors and the helping process and what will be expected from themselves as clients (Rooney, 1992).

Clients are also more likely to be invested in treatment alternatives when they have participated in the construction of the treatment plan (Rooney, 1992). If the treatment plan is constructed by the counselor or developed by rote in a program, the risk is that the involuntary client will feel powerless, experience reactance, and oppose those plans in part because he or she did not have a significant part in developing them.

The long-lasting effects of treatment contacts based on coercion and the appropriate use of persuasive methods designed to facilitate self-attribution with lower-functioning persons remain unanswered questions.

SPECIFIC RECOMMENDATIONS FOR THERAPISTS

Assessment and Initial Contact

Mental health counselors should consider in their assessment of all clients that their motivation to seek help may emerge at least initially from pressure—formal, informal, or legally mandated—from outside themselves. For example, children and adolescents are rarely voluntary in the sense of seeking assistance for concerns of their own (Berman-Rossi & Rossi, 1990).

Initially, try hearing out involuntary clients' view of the situation, their story, and conveying empathically that this view is understood. This should help the counselor achieve motivational congruence (De Jong & Berg, 1999). Once a relationship is established, therapists can explore the involuntary client's view of how the situation would look if the problem, as if by a miracle, were no longer present. This variation of the Adlerian "magic questions" is useful in helping the client reach motivational congruence and self-attribution (De Jong & Berg, 1999).

With many nonvoluntary clients, there will be legally mandated and nonnegotiable options. These should be presented in a matter-of-fact, nonjudgmental fashion. For example, stating "These are the legal requirements for what you and I have to do" at least acknowledges the legal parameters of the situation. Given the legal parameters, therapists can then explore all options available to the client to pursue informed consent and reduce reactance. For example, stating "Within those requirements, we have some choices about how we proceed" may facilitate more exploration within clients regarding their situation.

It should be remembered that involuntary clients can be assisted in group settings as well as in individual work. Dropout rates appear to decrease when involuntary clients feel understood by group leaders and information pertinent to client concerns is shared (Saunders & Hanusa, 1986; Thomas & Caplan, 1999).

Recommendations for Dealing with Difficult Behaviors

Client opposition in the form of hostility, passivity, or passive-aggressive behavior is to be expected when a client feels faced with undesirable alternatives. Labeling this behavior negatively is less useful than empathizing with the feeling of pressure in affirming the involuntary client's sense of reality as a person in a difficult situation. For example, a statement such as "I know this situation is difficult for you. I don't like it when I am pressured to do things either" may help the client feel more understood and diminish urges to act aggressively.

Behavior often labeled as resistance can also be reframed as ambivalent, in the sense that the involuntary client has not made a decision to act. The counselor can support statements that draw on the involuntary client's own motivation (Rollnick & Morgan, 1995). For example, a counselor might say "Part of you is drawn to wait and see whether you can handle this problem on your own. Another part of you wants to make a decision to seek help that might be difficult for you but that you also think could be best for your family."

Of course, there will be situations where the counselor feels a need to use confrontation. Confrontation should be carried out sparingly, in the context of a respectful, trusting relationship. Confrontations often occur when the involuntary client has severely harmed another, broken the law, or plans to do either of these. Confrontations will be more effective if there is a conflict between the behavior and the person's own goals. Rather than confronting in the form of a statement, asking a question about conflict among attitudes, values, and behavior may be more likely to stimulate dissonance (Rooney, 1992). For example, a counselor meeting with a parent who has left a small child without supervision might say "You say that you would never do anything to harm or endanger your child. If a fire had broken out, what would the child do?"

Recommendations for Contracting with Clients

A contracting process that includes both nonnegotiable requirements and negotiable alternatives is recommended for seeking motivational congruence and enhancing self-attribution. As a first priority in exploring contracting, it is recommended that the counselor explore agreements that are *agreeable mandates* or reframed options that permit involuntary clients to reach both their own goals and those of the referral source (Rooney, 1992). For example, "You want to raise your children as you see fit without agency interference. By collaborating with the agency in carrying out a parenting assessment, you can reach your goal of being left alone."

A second priority in contracting is to explore a *let's make a deal* or quid pro quo contract, in which the involuntary client can receive an incentive in exchange for working on the problem of concern to the referral source. For example, a nonvoluntary client can work on an additional voluntary problem of his or her own choosing; a court-ordered client can be offered an incentive to make compliance more attractive (Rooney, 1992).

A third priority in contracting is to explore a *get rid of the pressure* contract, in which the involuntary client contracts to get rid of the unwanted pressure from others. For example, "It sounds as if you would like to get the county off your back, is that right? What do you have to do to get the county off your back?"

When involuntary clients agree to work on a contract, sometimes that work entails agreeing to carry out one or more *disagreeable tasks* or actions that may be experienced as inherently punishing. Involuntary clients can be assisted to enhance their willingness to comply by participating in the selection of the order in which the tasks are completed. For example, they can suggest which task they would like to begin with. They can also plan to reward themselves for completing the task, and they can consider the consequences of failure to complete the disagreeable task (Rooney, 1992).

SUMMARY

Many clients have been mislabeled as resistant, reluctant, unmotivated, and hostile when in fact they never chose to become clients. By being sensitive to legal and nonvoluntary pressures, the counselor can take concrete steps to enhance voluntarism and empower involuntary clients to improve their situation.

References

Berman-Rossi, T., & Rossi, P. (1990, April). Confidentiality and informed consent in school social work. *Social Work in Education*, 195–207.

Brehm, S.S. (1976). *The application of social psychology to clinical practice*. New York: Wiley.

Brodsky, S.L., & Lichtenstein, B. (1999). Don't ask questions: A psychotherapeutic strategy for treatment of involuntary clients. *American Journal of Psychotherapy*, 53(2), 215–220.

Catalano, R., & McConnell, W. (1996). A time-series test of the quarantine theory of involuntary commitment. *Journal of Health and Social Behavior*, 37, 381–387.

De Jong, P., & Berg, I.K. (1999, March 10–13). *Co-constructing cooperation with mandated clients*. Presentation at annual program meeting of Council on Social Work Education, San Francisco.

Jones, E.E., & Pittman, T.S. (1982). Toward a general theory of strategic self-presentation. In J. Sals (Ed.), *Psychological perspectives on the self*. Hillsdale, NJ: Erlbaum.

Kear-Colwell, J., & Pollock, P. (1997). Motivation or confrontation: Which approach to the child sex offender? *Criminal Justice and Behavior*, 24, 20–33.

Keaton, B., & Yamatani, H. (1993). Benefits of mandatory EAP participation: A study of employees with last chance contracts. *Employee Assistance Quarterly*, 9(1), 67–77.

Kramer, L., & Washo, C.A. (1993). Evaluation of a court-mandated prevention program for divorcing parents: The Children First Program. *Family Relations*, 42, 179–186.

Murdach, A.D. (1996). Beneficence re-examined: Protective intervention in mental health. *Social Work*, 41(1), 26–32.

Murphy, C.M., & Baxter, V.A. (1997). Motivating batterers to change in the treatment context. *Journal of Interpersonal Violence*, 12(4), 607–619.

O'Hare, T. (1996). Court-ordered versus voluntary clients: Problem differences and readiness for change. *Social Work, 41*(4), 417–422.

Peters, R.H., & Murrin, M.R. (2000). Effectiveness of treatment-based drug courts in reducing criminal recidivism. *Criminal Justice and Behavior, 27*(1), 72–96.

Prochaska, J., DiClemente, C.C., & Norcross, J.C. (1992). Transtheoretical therapy: Toward a more integrative model of change. *Psychotherapy: Theory, Research and Practice, 19,* 276–288.

Regehr, C., & Angle, B. (1997). Coercive influences: Informed consent in court-mandated social work practice. *Social Work, 42*(3), 300–306.

Riccio, J., & Hasenfeld, Y. (1996). Enforcing a participation mandate in a welfare-to-work program. *Social Service Review, 70,* 516–542.

Rollnick, S., & Morgan, M. (1995). Motivational interviewing: Increasing readiness for change. In A. Washton (Ed.), *Psychotherapy and substance abuse: A practitioner's handbook* (pp. 179–191). New York: Guilford Press.

Rooney, R.H. (1992). *Strategies for work with involuntary clients.* New York: Columbia University Press.

Saunders, D., & Hanusa, D. (1986). Cognitive-behavioral treatment of men who batter: The short-term effects of group therapy. *Journal of Family Violence, 1,* 357–372.

Sawa, S.L., & Sawa, G.H. (1988, April). The value confrontation approach to enduring behavior modification. *Journal of Social Psychology, 128* 207–215.

Strom-Gottfried, K. (1998). Informed consent meets managed care. *Health and Social Work, 23*(1), 25–33.

Thomas, H., & Caplan, T. (1999). Spinning the group process wheel: Effective facilitation techniques for motivating involuntary client groups. *Social Work with Groups, 21*(4), 3–21.

Resources for Further Study

Ivanoff, A., Blythe, B.J., & Tripodi, T. (1994). *Involuntary clients in social work practice: A research-based approach.* New York: Aldine De Gruyter.

Rooney, R.H. (1992). *Strategies for work with involuntary clients.* New York: Columbia University Press.

Training and consultation for work with involuntary clients and videotapes on practice with involuntary clients are available from Ronald Rooney, School of Social Work, 1404 Gortner Avenue, University of Minnesota, St. Paul, MN. 55108, rrooney@che.umn.edu.

Videotape entitled *Talking Solutions with Mandated Clients* is available from the Brief Family Treatment Center, P.O. Box 13736 Milwaukee, WI 53213.

15 USING TEST DATA IN COUNSELING AND CLINICAL PRACTICE

Kathryn C. MacCluskie

Assessing client problems, strengths, and interpersonal functioning is an inherent component of counseling and clinical activity. The term *assessment* refers to procedures as unstructured as intake or mental status interviews, and as highly structured as standardized intelligence instruments. There are myriad occasions when it may be beneficial for a client to participate in structured clinical assessments using standardized tests. This chapter describes these occasions and how the data generated from standardized instruments can be applied to ongoing work with clients. A counselor may choose to use test data to inform or influence treatment in any of the following circumstances:

- To clarify diagnostic possibilities and assess psychopathology.
- To generate insights about a client's strengths or coping abilities.
- To gather information for treatment planning.
- To understand a client's lack of progress in counseling.
- To determine whether a client meets eligibility requirements for inclusion in a particular program. For example, a client may be under consideration for a community-based group living arrangement that requires a minimum skill level in activities of daily living. Using test data, a clinician may determine whether the client possesses the requisite level of independence and remission of symptoms to be able to benefit from the program.

Counselors may administer and interpret the tests with their own clients, may be the referral source and subsequent recipient of data gathered by other clinicians, or may conduct testing for individuals in counseling with others. The information in this chapter is applicable in all these circumstances, but the emphasis is on integrating data from test scores into treatment planning and process. Integration of test data into treatment is both an art and a science that involves incorporation of the client's unique background data and observations of the client's behavior during the testing with test findings. This chapter is to be read with the caution that competence in using test data in practice requires both knowledge of the psychometric properties of the test and supervised experience in its use in the clinical setting. Using test data in clinical practice without this background is unethical.

MAJOR CONSTRUCTS AND TERMINOLOGY

In the medical fields, measurements are often made on specific, identifiable physical entities, such as a red blood cell count or blood pressure. In mental health, in contrast, measurements are based largely on *hypothetical constructs*. A hypothetical construct is a framework of assumptions, developed by theorists and researchers, intended to enable subsequent observations to be understood. Another term for construct is *domain*. For example, intelligence and personality are defined as constructs because neither exists as a physical entity that can be directly measured. Instead, behaviors or attributes considered to be the result of or expression of intelligence or personality must be measured. There is no irrefutable proof that intelligence or personality per se exist within people, but there are individual differences in people's behavior that are measurable. Some of those differences are assumed to be the result of varying levels and types of intelligence or personality.

All of those domains are presumed to exist on a continuum. That is to say, whether we are talking about a specific cognitive ability, a personality attribute, or symptoms of a diagnosable psychological disorder, there is no absolute presence or absence of the attribute being measured. The construct extroversion exemplifies this continuum. Extroversion refers to the extent to which an individual prefers frequent or constant social and interpersonal contact, at one end of the continuum, or solitary activities, at the other end of a continuum. Most people prefer some combination of both, but even those individuals at the far ends of the continuum would not be considered to have absolute absence or absolute presence of the trait of extroversion.

There are three other terms used frequently in the context of standardized assessment. The term *norm* refers to a sample of people on whom the test has been standardized. That standardization sample is referred to as the *norm group*, meaning that test developers have carefully researched patterns of responses that are common. When a test is administered to a client, that client's responses (raw scores) are compared to the responses of those people in the norm group, thus yielding a comparison of the client to the norm, which, theoretically, equates to typical or average among the general population. The term *validity* refers to whether the test does, in fact, measure the construct the test developer was trying to measure. Finally, *reliability* refers to stability of test scores over time. In other words, when a test has high reliability, we can be reasonably certain that if the same test could be administered to the same person many times, his or her raw score would be approximately the same every time. A test can be reliable without necessarily being valid, but a valid test will always be reliable.

Regardless of the particular construct the test seems to measure, clinicians need answers to the following questions before selecting any particular measure:

- What is the evidence regarding the reliability and validity of test scores (i.e., does the test measure the construct it purports to measure and does it do so consistently)? How much confidence can I place in the accuracy of the results?
- What is the norm group for the test, and is it sufficiently comparable to my client to justify its use? Does it include adequate representation of the cultural group of my client? (See Chapter 40 for a discussion of multicultural assessment.)
- Is my client able to cooperate with the test administration process based on current physical, psychological, and intellectual characteristics?
- How effectively can the test identify uncooperative, dishonest, or confused test takers?

TYPES AND APPLICATIONS OF TESTS

Tests can be categorized by the domains (or constructs) they assess, such as cognitive ability, personality characteristics, career interests, academic achievement, learning disabilities, and adaptive behavior. Cognitive ability, personality, and career interest measures are commonly administered in community mental health settings (Watkins,

Campbell, & McGregor, 1988). Within each of those domains, there are numerous ways testing can be used to creatively enhance the diagnostic or treatment process.

Certainly, one traditional and valuable way that psychological test results have been used is to help confirm a diagnosis (though test scores can never be the sole source of data for a diagnosis). However, test scores can also be used in ways that do not emphasize diagnosis. An alternative approach is to describe a client's traits, abilities, and symptoms, and to then consider those descriptions and preferences in the broader context of how to be most helpful to that person.

Cognitive Ability Tests (Intelligence and Achievement)

Following is a partial list of cognitive ability tests commonly encountered in a community mental health setting:

Wechsler Intelligence Scale for Children, third revision (WISC-III) (Wechsler, 1991)

Wechsler Adult Intelligence Scale, third revision (WAIS-III) (Wechsler, 1997)

Kaufman Assessment Battery for Children (Kaufman & Kaufman, 1983)

Kaufman Adolescent and Adult Intelligence Test (Kaufman & Kaufman, 1993)

Wechsler Individual Achievement Test (Wechsler, 1992)

Wide Range Achievement Test—3 (Wilkinson, 1993)

Peabody Individual Achievement Test (Markwardt-Frederick, 1989)

Shipley Institute of Living Scale (Shipley & Zachary, 1986)

In the realm of cognitive ability testing, test scores may be used to inform a decision about whether to include a client in some type of program. For instance, there may be a minimum degree of auditory processing and attention necessary for a client to benefit from a group therapy setting for a substance abuse problem. A cognitive ability test such as the

Shipley Institute of Living Scale (Shipley & Zachary, 1986) might be used to determine whether a client is demonstrating the minimum cognitive ability necessary. Similarly, cognitive ability testing might help a therapist make an informed prediction about a client's ability to benefit from some facet of treatment, such as partial hospitalization. Consider the following case example:

Joe is a 35-year-old man diagnosed with Schizophrenia. He has lived with his parents since his first psychotic break 15 years ago. Joe's case manager has been insistent that he participate in a partial hospitalization program, despite previous failed attempts at such groups. Joe has historically complained that he did not find the partial program beneficial. On standardized measures, Joe demonstrates markedly elevated scores on tests of verbal functioning and slightly below average auditory/motoric functioning. Despite his serious psychiatric diagnosis, his ability level is such that the partial program is not only unhelpful, but might actually be detrimental to the process of his learning to manage his illness.

For a client who has scored markedly higher or markedly lower on a cognitive ability test in comparison to other group members, the format of the group might be either too simplistic or too complex. In either case, that client might experience a degree of frustration or sense of failure that could be detrimental to the treatment process, as Joe's case illustrates. Cognitive ability testing can also give clinicians data about therapeutic approaches that will maximize client's integration of new information. For instance, a client's test scores may reveal the client's preferred learning style in performing verbal, auditory tasks, or visual, motoric tasks. Clinicians can use such information to design future interventions in counseling to improve the efficiency and effectiveness of interventions.

Cognitive testing can also generate information to assist clinicians in appreciating a client's level of cognitive flexibility, the rapidity with which a person is able to switch mental sets and generate alternative solutions to a problem. Cognitive flexibility is necessary to adapt to environmental stressors. Knowing that a client has difficulty with cognitive flexibility can help a clinician to target expanding flexibility as an intermediate treatment goal to increase the potential for the client to deal effectively with environmental stressors.

Data gathered from a client's approach to the testing experience also has therapeutic value. The behavioral observations made during testing can reveal how clients respond to environmental ambiguity, time pressure, frustrations in problem solving, and risks of making erroneous choices. They can also inform us about the client's persistence in challenging tasks and level of self-acceptance. All of these characteristics have direct bearing on a person's functioning in a work setting, in interpersonal relationships, and as part of a community. Thus, astute clinicians can glean valuable information from a cognitive ability test far beyond the obvious data about how many vocabulary words are known or how many novel arithmetic problems are solved correctly.

Personality Tests

Personality tests measure client traits and states related to intrapsychic and interpersonal functioning. Personality tests are divided into two categories: objective and projective formats. Objective personality tests have limited response options, such as true or false. Projective tests use neutral stimuli such as inkblots and then ask the test taker to generate elaborate responses. Examples of projective instruments include the Rorschach Inkblot Test (Rorschach, 1951) and the Thematic Apperception Test (Murray, 1943). Because of space limitations, this chapter focuses exclusively on objective personality tests. Commonly used objective personality assessment instruments include:

Millon Clinical Multiaxial Inventory (MCMI) (Millon, 1987)

Minnesota Multiphasic Personality Inventory, second revision (MMPI-2) (Butcher, Dahlstrom, Graham, Tellegen, & Kaemmer, 1989)

Minnesota Multiphasic Personality Inventory, Adolescent version (MMPI-A) (Butcher, Williams, Graham, Archer, Tellegen, Ben-Porath, & Kaemmer, 1992)

Neuroticism Extroversion Openness Personality Inventory—Revised (NEO PI-R) (Costa & McCrae, 1992)

Personality Assessment Inventory (PAI) (Morey, 1991)

Sixteen Personality Factor questionnaire (16PF) (Cattell, Cattell, & Cattell, 1993)

In addition to the information personality test scores provide regarding intrapsychic dynamics, scores can generate information regarding a client's functioning in social and intimate relationships. Sometimes, questions about interpersonal functioning arise in forensic settings where a typical referral question might be "What can the test reveal about the likelihood client X will again assault her child?" or "What can the test reveal about the extent to which client Y actually intended to harm someone when he lost his temper?" Data from personality inventories will assist in making subsequent decisions regarding child custody or whether incarceration is an appropriate consequence for the client. Again, it is crucial to remember that, because of the limits of reliability and validity, test findings cannot ethically be used as the sole criterion for decision making about these important matters. Multiple sources of data confirming the test finding must be available as well (Welfel, 1998).

Information about a person's intrapersonal dynamics can illuminate the connection between conflicting emotions within an individual and thus why certain emotional symptoms are being generated and how personality attributes and behavior are maintaining the symptoms. Several of the personality inventories incorporate validity scales, which yield information about test takers' inclination to either emphasize or de-emphasize their experiencing of their symptoms.

Some of the above listed instruments are used primarily to describe relative degrees of personality traits such as extroversion (e.g.,

NEO PI-R [Costa & McCrae, 1992]; 16PF [Cattell et al.,1993]); others identify symptoms and suggest possible *DSM-IV* diagnoses to consider (MMPI-2 [Butcher et al., 1989]; PAI [Morey, 1991]). The PAI, for example, includes norms for specific diagnostic categories, including anxiety disorders, thought disorders, mood disorders, antisocial personality disorders, and substance abuse.

When using a multiscaled personality inventory such as the MMPI-2, clinicians can discuss with their client how specific scores/traits not directly connected to the presenting problems still contribute to distress. Conversely, counselors can help clients take advantage of other traits identified by the test that can be assets to recovery. Consider the following case example.

Bob is referred to counseling for panic attacks and demonstrates a high level of anxiety, with an onset following being passed over for a promotion. His NEO PI-R (Costa & McCrae, 1992) profile reveals that he tends to use a rigid cognitive style and is extremely competitive (although his competitiveness is mainly within himself, setting extremely high standards for himself), which seem to contribute substantially to decreased effectiveness in his work performance. However, despite his rigidity, he also demonstrates cooperativeness and agreeableness. After working on cognitive restructuring and assertiveness in counseling, he is able to discuss the promotion situation with his boss and, owing to his high level of cooperation, receives a favorable response from his boss about a new position.

Finally, test results showing a client's need for external structure, level of anxiety about disclosing personal information, and degree of autonomy and initiative can be used to help select appropriate treatment strategies. For example, a client who experiences anxiety or discomfort in ambiguous interpersonal situations may find an unstructured experiential counseling approach less comfortable than a directive, behavioral approach. Much has been written recently about rationales for choosing treatment strategies, with emphasis on using empirically validated treatments (Chambless et al., 1998; Seligman, 1998). Nevertheless, personal preferences and characteristics of the client are also important variables to consider in the treatment process. For instance, outcome research suggests that, generally, the most efficacious treatment for a specific phobia is an exposure and response-prevention treatment protocol. However, if a clinician has access to personality inventory information, he or she may find test scores suggesting that the client would feel more comfortable in an alternative treatment approach. In that case, the clinician may find some creative way to integrate an empirically valid treatment approach with the client's preferred approach. Such integration would be highly respectful of the client and increase the probability for benefit from therapy.

Symptom Cluster Tests

There are many instruments developed to assess presence and intensity of particular forms of distress. A few examples include:

Beck Depression Inventory, second revision (Beck, Steer, & Brown, 1996)

Trauma Symptom Inventory (Briere, 1995)

State-Trait Anger Expression Inventory (Spielberger, 1983)

These instruments assist clinicians in ruling in or out particular disorders in the case of a questionable differential diagnosis. For example, a client may be complaining of a high degree of anxiety, yet on the Beck Depression Inventory, she is endorsing many items indicative of a clinical depression. This finding may have bearing on the type of medication prescribed and the type of treatment plan developed.

Second, instruments that focus on specific symptoms are especially valuable in quantifying the degree of client response to treatment. For example, a therapist can administer the Beck Depression Inventory 2 (Beck et al., 1996) at the beginning of treatment and periodically during treatment to evaluate changes in depressive symptoms.

Symptom cluster instruments also have applications in research on treatment efficacy, particularly in differentiating between those participants with the disorder and those without it. One reliable way to make that differentiation is to use an instrument developed specifically to confirm a particular diagnosis (along with other data, of course).

CLIENT FEEDBACK AS PART OF THE THERAPY PROCESS

Active client involvement in the testing process is important. Initially, a clinician who is arranging for a client to be tested must honestly communicate to the client, in language understandable to the client, what is hoped to be gained from the testing. If the client has been referred from another professional, it is important to begin the assessment process by asking the client to explain his or her understanding of why the testing referral came about. Client understanding of the evaluation process is important for two reasons. First, the greatest likelihood of getting valid, usable client responses occurs when clients clearly understand the importance of cooperating with testing and believe that a concerted effort will be beneficial to them. Second, as part of the ordinary ethical obligation of informed consent, the clinician needs to thoroughly discuss the testing process.

In general, beyond the specific test scores and results obtained, the testing process can be used to enhance both the therapeutic alliance and client responsiveness to therapy. Test data can help clinicians respond more empathetically to clients, thereby increasing rapport and client motivation to continue therapeutic work. In addition, clients may find tests results confirming of their internal experience and may thereby experience relief to find that their level of symptoms is in the clinically significant range. Such scores can lend credence to their suffering, and clients may experience a sense of validation. One adult client, Sue, was vastly relieved to receive a diagnosis of Attention-Deficit Disorder (ADD), because it enabled her to "make sense" of the academic troubles she had experienced her entire life. Prior to this evidence, she had concluded that she was not "very smart," but the diagnosis of ADD enabled her to realize that her symptoms were instead the result of a neuropsychological condition. Thus, the test findings, coupled with other evidence of ADD, led to a breakthrough in counseling for Sue. Perhaps adding to the "aha" experience for her was the counselor's willingness to focus on how the disorder influenced the development of her self-image and the parts of that self-image she now hoped to change.

Sources for Additional Information

For a broad-brush description of many different types of tests, readers are referred to textbooks on assessment such as *The Handbook of Psychological Assessment* (Groth-Marnat, 1999), *Psychological Testing* (Anastasi & Urbina, 1997), and *Tests and Assessment* (Walsh & Betz, 1995). Additionally, many books are available that help readers learn the subtleties of test interpretation for particular instruments, such as *The Revised NEO Personality Inventory: Clinical and Research Applications* (Piedmont, 1998), *Intelligent Testing with the WAIS-III* (Kaufman, 1996), *Essentials of WISC-III and WPPSI-R Assessment* (Kaufman & Lichtenberger, 2000), and *An Interpretive Guide to the Personality Assessment Inventory* (Morey, 1996).

Another source of training and developing expertise in the use of clinical instruments is workshops or seminars. There are often advertisements in professional publications such as the APA *Monitor* or the ACA *Counseling Today* for training workshops, sometimes presented by the author of a test or by representatives of a test publishing company.

References

Anastasi, A., & Urbina, S. (1997). *Psychological testing* (7th ed.). Upper Saddle River, NJ: Prentice-Hall.

Beck, A.T., Steer, R.A., & Brown, G. (1996). *Beck Depression Inventory* (2nd ed.). San Antonio, TX: Psychological Corporation.

Briere, J. (1995). *Trauma Symptoms Inventory*. Odessa, FL: Psychological Assessment Resources.

Butcher, J.N., Dahlstrom, W.G., Graham, J.R., Tellegen, A., & Kaemmer, B. (1989). *Minnesota Multiphasic Personality Inventory–2* (MMPI-2). Minneapolis: University of Minnesota Press.

Butcher, J.N., Williams, C.L., Graham, J.R., Archer, R.P., Tellegen, A., Ben-Porath, Y.S., & Kaemmer, B. (1992). *Minnesota Multiphasic Personality Inventory for Adolescents: Manual for administration, scoring, and interpretation*. Minneapolis: University of Minnesota Press.

Cattell, R.B., Cattell, A.K.S., & Cattell, H.E.P. (1993). *Sixteen Personality Factor Questionnaire* (5th ed.). Champaign, IL: Institute for Personality and Ability Testing.

Chambless, D.L., Baker, M.J., Baucom, D.H., Beutler, L.E., Calhoun, K.S., Crits-Christoph, P., Daiuto, A., DeRebeis, R., Detweiler, J., Haaga, D.A.F., Johnson, S.B., McCurry, S., Mueser, K.T., Pope, K.S., Sanderson, W.C., Shoham, V., Stickle, T., Williams, D.A., & Woody, S.R. (1998). Update on empirically validated therapies, II. *The Clinical Psychologist, 51*(1), 3–16.

Costa, P.I., & McCrae, R.R. (1992). *Neuroticism Extroversion Openness Personality Inventory–Revised*. Odessa, FL: Psychological Assessment Resources.

Groth-Marnat, G. (1999). *Handbook of psychological assessment* (3rd ed.). New York: Wiley.

Kaufman, A.S. (1996). *Intelligent testing with the WAIS-III*. New York: Wiley.

Kaufman, A.S., & Kaufman, N.L. (1983). *Kaufman Assessment Battery for Children*. Circle Pines, MN: American Guidance Service.

Kaufman, A.S., & Kaufman, N.L. (1993). *Kaufman Adolescent and Adult Intelligence Test*. Circle Pines, MN: American Guidance Service.

Kaufman, A.S., & Lichtenberger, E.O. (1999). *Essentials of WAIS-III assessment*. New York: Wiley.

Kaufman, A.S., & Lichtenberger, E.O. (2000). *Essentials of WISC-III and WPPSI-R assessment*. New York: Wiley.

Markwardt-Frederick, C., Jr. (1989). *Peabody Individual Achievement Test-Revised*. Circle Pines, MN: American Guidance Services.

Millon, T. (1987). *Manual for the Millon Clinical Multiaxial Inventory* (MCMI). Minneapolis: National Computer Systems.

Morey, L. (1991). *Personality Assessment Inventory*. Odessa, FL: Psychological Assessment Resources.

Morey, L. (1996). *An interpretive guide to the Personality Assessment Inventory*. Odessa, FL: Psychological Assessment Resources.

Murray, H.A. (1943). *Thematic Apperception Test manual.* Cambridge, MA: Harvard University Press.

Piedmont, R.L. (1998). *The Revised NEO Personality Inventory: Clinical and research applications.* New York: Plenum Press.

Rorschach, H. (1951). *Rorschach Inkblot Test. Psychodiagnostics: A diagnostic test based on perception.* New York: Grune & Stratton.

Seligman, L. (1998). *Selecting effective treatments: A comprehensive, systematic guide to treating mental disorders* (Rev. ed.). San Francisco: Jossey-Bass.

Shipley, W.C., & Zachary, R.A. (1986). *Shipley Institute of Living Scale.* Los Angeles: Western Psychological Services.

Spielberger, C.D. (1983). *Manual for the State-Trait Anxiety Inventory (Form-Y).* Palo Alto, CA: Mind Garden.

Walsh, W.B., & Betz, N.E. (1995). *Tests and assessment* (3rd ed.). Englewood Cliffs, NJ: Prentice-Hall.

Watkins, C.E., Jr., Campbell, V.L., & McGregor, P. (1988). Counseling psychologists' uses of the opinions about psychological tests: A contemporary perspective. *The Counseling Psychologist, 16,* 476–486.

Wechsler, D. (1991). *The Wechsler Intelligence Scales for Children–III.* New York: Psychological Corporation.

Wechsler, D. (1992). *Wechsler Individual Achievement Test.* New York: Psychological Corporation.

Wechsler, D. (1997). *Wechsler Adult Intelligence Scale* (3rd ed.). New York: Psychological Corporation.

Welfel, E.R. (1998). *Ethics in counseling and psychotherapy: Standards, research, and emerging issues.* Pacific Grove, CA: Brooks/Cole.

Wilkinson, G.S. (1993). *Wide Range Assessment Test 3.* Wilmington, DE: Jastak Associates-Wide Range.

16   TREATING ANXIETY DISORDERS IN ADULTS

Paul F. Granello and Darcy Haag Granello

Anxiety is an emotional and physiological state that all people feel and that can be either normal or pathological. Anxiety can be defined as a feeling of unpleasant apprehension typically accompanied by bodily sensations such as a tightness in the chest, a feeling of choking, perspiring, and trembling or shaking. Often, anxious individuals feel restless or confused or think they are not in control or even that they are dying (APA, 2000). Normal anxiety serves an adaptive function if it motivates the individual to behave in a way that forestalls danger. Anxiety is pathological when, due to its intensity or duration, it impedes the client's ability to

function. More than 16 million Americans between the ages of 15 and 24 have anxiety disorders (National Institute of Mental Health [NIMH], 1999), and an estimated 80% of persons diagnosed with anxiety disorders experience panic attacks.

Several theories have been generated to explain the causes of pathological anxiety. Cognitive-behavioral theorists believe that when a stimulus is observed, perceived, or otherwise experienced as frightening, future threats of that stimulus are also perceived with apprehension or avoidance (Seligman, 1998). Psychoanalytic theory suggests that anxiety is a warning to the ego that unacceptable unconscious material is pressing for expression and that the ego must take action, usually in the form of a defense mechanism to cope (Kaplan & Sadock, 1998). Existential theory is useful in explaining "free-floating" anxiety, often associated with generalized anxiety disorder. This form of anxiety is thought to stem from an individual's sense of purposelessness and meaninglessness in life (Savolaine & Granello, 2000). Finally, biological theories suggest that the autonomic nervous system, limbic system, and regions of the cerebral cortex may have dysfunctions in relation to pathological anxiety. Specific neurotransmitters, such as norepinephrin, y-aminobutric acid (GABA), and serotonin, have been linked to anxiety (Kaplan & Sadock, 1998).

The *Diagnostic and Statistical Manual*, fourth edition, text revised (*DSM-IV-TR*), of the American Psychiatric Association (APA, 2000) names the following under the heading of anxiety disorders: Panic Disorder with and without Agoraphobia, Specific Phobia, Social Phobia, Obsessive-Compulsive Disorder, Posttraumatic Stress Disorder, Acute Stress Disorder, Generalized Anxiety Disorder, Anxiety Disorder Due to a Medical Condition, Substance-Induced Anxiety Disorder, and Anxiety Disorder NOS. These disorders are classified together because anxiety is a significant presenting symptom in all of them. However, each disorder responds differently to pharmacological interventions, leading researchers to suspect that they are really a heterogeneous group of disorders (Kaplan & Sadock, 1998).

STATUS OF THE AVAILABLE RESEARCH

Anxiety disorders are some of the most well-researched psychiatric disorders, and several of them, particularly Panic Disorder and the phobias, have large bodies of rigorous efficacy studies associated with their treatment. The National Institute of Health (NIH) issued a consensus statement for the treatment of panic disorder in 1991, the first psychological disorder to be included in a consensus statement of this type. There is less consensus arising from

the research on Obsessive-Compulsive Disorder and Posttraumatic Stress Disorder, although these disorders also have many rigorous studies associated with them. Research to date on generalized anxiety disorder has demonstrated only modest treatment gains, and thus the choice of intervention remains more open to question for this disorder than for any of the other anxiety disorders.

GENERAL TREATMENT APPROACH

Although the treatment for the various types of anxiety disorders differs, there are some generalized treatment approaches that have been found to be successful across the spectrum of anxiety disorders. In their landmark meta-analysis, Smith, Glass, and Miller (1980) found effect sizes for the treatment of anxiety disorders to be 1.78 for cognitive-behavioral approaches, 1.67 for cognitive approaches alone, and 1.12 for behavioral approaches alone. Unlike the null hypothesis, which simply measures whether or not a relationship exists, effect sizes measure the strength of a relationship, with higher numbers indicating greater strength. All of these effect sizes are considered large (Stevens, 1992). Subsequent research has supported the meta-analytic results on the treatment of anxiety disorders (Barlow, Esler, & Vitali, 1998; Franklin & Foa, 1998; Keane, 1998). There is growing support in the research for the use of pharmacological interventions as an adjunct to psychosocial treatments, particularly for severe cases when debilitating anxiety limits the initial success of psychosocial interventions (NIMH, 1999). For all the anxiety disorders, a medical referral is strongly encouraged to rule out a medical condition that might mimic the symptoms of anxiety (Beamish, Granello, Granello, McSteen, & Stone, 1997).

SPECIFIC TREATMENT
RECOMMENDATIONS BY DISORDER

Panic Disorder with and without Agoraphobia

Panic Disorder is one of the most common mental disorders for which people seek treatment, with up to 4 million people, or 1.5% of the U.S. population, meeting the criteria for this disorder. Panic Disorder is characterized by the existence of panic attacks that are not cued by external stimuli. These panic attacks can lead to the development of agoraphobia, and thus panic disorder can occur without (PD) or with agoraphobia (PDA). There is high comorbidity with mood disorders (50% to 65%; Agras, 1993) and substance abuse disorders (15%; Barlow & Shear, 1988), and up to 20% of individuals with panic disorder attempt suicide (Agras, 1993).

Treatment interventions that have been supported by the research (Beamish et al., 1997; NIH, 1991) include:

Cognitive therapy

- Cognitive restructuring to counter the catastrophic misinterpretations of bodily sensations or psychological experiences that occur during panic attacks.
- Focused cognitive therapy to recreate panic symptoms in the therapy session and then reattribute the physical sensations to the proper causes.
- Panic education as an adjunct to inform clients about the nature of panic disorder.

Behavioral therapy

- Best when combined with cognitive therapy.
- Breathing retraining, biofeedback, stress inoculation training, meditation, applied relaxation (but not progressive relaxation), and graduated exposure (to prevent the development of agoraphobia in PD clients or to treat agoraphobia in PDA clients).

Family therapy

- Less supported by the research, but probably an important component of PDA, as family members often engage in enabling behaviors that allow the agoraphobia to continue.

Pharmacological interventions

- Tricyclic antidepressants, MAOIs, benzodiazepines, and SSRIs have all been used in conjunction with psychological interventions, but overreliance on medication can limit the success of psychotherapy by artificially lowering anxiety levels, which rebound when medication is withdrawn (Beamish et al., 1996).

Specific Phobia and Social Phobia

Lifetime prevalence for specific phobias is 11%, with significant gender differences (females = 16%, males = 7%) (Kessler et al., 1994). Specific phobias, although very common overall, tend to be distinct. That is, when a client presents with a specific phobia, it is unlikely that other Axis I or Axis II diagnoses will be comorbid. Social phobia is very common and is the third most prevalent of all mental disorders, exceeded only by Major Depressive Disorder and alcohol dependence. Comorbidity of social phobia and Axis I disorders is common, most often with Agoraphobia (45%), alcohol abuse (19%), major depression (17%), drug abuse (13%), Dysthymia (13%), and Obsessive-Compulsive Disorder (11%) (Schneier, Johnson, Hornig, Liebowitz, & Weissman, 1992). Additionally, up to 70% of persons who meet the criteria for social phobia also meet the criteria for Avoidant Personality Disorder.

Treatment interventions that have been supported in the research include (Barlow et al., 1998):

Behavioral therapy

- Exposure therapy: There is broad consensus in the research literature for treatment of specific phobias that is exposure-based, particularly in vivo exposure. Many clients show improvement after only one to three sessions. High therapist involvement is a key component of this treatment.
- Imaginal exposure has been shown to be effective in reducing fear when in vivo exposure is unavailable, but in vivo is preferred.
- Hypnosis has received some support in the research literature (Kaplan & Sadock, 1998).
- Relaxation techniques are particularly important for the treatment of social phobia.

Cognitive therapy

- Cognitive restructuring and social skills training are important components for the treatment of social phobia.

Pharmacological interventions
(Roy-Byrne & Cowley, 1998)

- Pharmacological treatments have not been proven effective for the treatment of specific phobias.
- For the treatment of social phobia, there has been support for MAOIs and SSRIs. Benzodiazepines also have demonstrated some success, but their use is complicated by high rates of substance abuse comorbidity with social phobia.

Obsessive-Compulsive Disorder (OCD)

The prevalence rate for OCD is 2.5% in adults, and it appears that this disorder occurs at approximately that rate in children and adolescents (Valleni-Basile et al., 1994). Because of the nature of this disorder, clients with severe OCD often have difficulty maintaining employment and have extreme dysfunctions in their marital and interpersonal relationships (Franklin & Foa, 1998).

Treatment interventions that have been supported in the research include:

Behavioral therapy

- Behavioral intervention is considered the "gold standard" for treatment of OCD and has received much empirical support in highly controlled efficacy studies (e.g., Franklin, Abramowitz, Kozak, Levitt, & Foa, 2000). Supported interventions include in vivo exposure, imaginal exposure, ritual prevention, and systematic desensitization to the source of the anxiety (e.g., germs or dirt).

Cognitive therapy

- Cognitive interventions, in conjunction with behavioral techniques, appear to be supported by the research literature, although this is a relatively new area of study and no consensus has yet been reached. The use of Rational Emotive Therapy (e.g., understanding the realistic consequences of not engaging in rituals) and Socratic questioning to challenge clients' dysfunctional beliefs appear to be an important component of treatment (Franklin & Foa, 1998).

Family therapy

- Because of the high degree of family dysfunction and marital discord associated with OCD, family therapy is considered an important adjunct to therapy (Amir, Freshman, & Foa, 2000).

Pharmacological interventions

- Drugs may be an important adjunct to treatment, particularly for clients for whom psychotherapy or behavioral therapy alone has been ineffective. Pharmacological interventions appear to be more successful in treating the compulsions than the obsessions. With OCD, there is often a medication lag of up to two months before any noticeable improvement, and thus medication trials should last 6 to 12 months before attempts are made to taper off the medication (Kaplan & Sadock, 1998).
- The tricyclic antidepressant clomipramine (Anafranil) has become the standard medication for OCD. Recent research has supported the efficacy of SSRIs, although these have not been as extensively studied with this population, and no research exists to suggest that they are more effective for OCD than clomipramine (den Boer, Bosker, & Slaap, 2000).

Posttraumatic Stress Disorder (PTSD) and Acute Stress Disorder (ASD)

Prevalence rates for PTSD and ASD range from 1% to 14% in various studies. This broad range can be accounted for by fluctuations in the occurrences and nature of disasters that affect large populations (e.g., bombings, earthquakes) and traumatic events that affect individuals (e.g., rapes, assaults). PTSD has significant comorbidity with other Axis I disorders, particularly alcohol abuse (70%) and depression (68%), as well as Axis II disorders (26%) (Roth & Fonagy, 1996). ASD is diagnosed when the symptoms last for less than one month; PTSD is diagnosed when the symptoms last for more than one month.

Treatment interventions that have been supported by the research include:

Critical incident stress debriefing (CISD)

- As soon as possible after the trauma, CISD is recommended to try to prevent the development of PTSD. It is intended to help the client learn to tolerate and process the trauma, express feelings surrounding the trauma, and learn increased control and coping (see Carlier, 2000).

Behavioral therapy

- Systematic desensitization (gradual exposure to reminders of the trauma), habituation, and anxiety management (biofeedback, relaxation) (Tarrier, Sommerfield, Pilgrim, & Humphreys, 1999).

Cognitive therapy

- To modify cognitive distortions about the trauma (e.g., self-blame, impact of the trauma).
- Stress inoculation training (thought stopping, guided self-dialogue) (Keane, 1998).

Family therapy

- This is less supported by the research, but may be helpful in sustaining relationships through acute symptom periods.

EMDR (eye movement desensitization and reprocessing) (Shapiro, 1995)

- The pairing of kinesthetic stimulation, such as eye movement, with recall of the stressor. (This technique has been supported primarily through case studies, although one efficacy study demonstrated improvement that was superior to biofeedback for PTSD.)

Pharmacological interventions

- No specific class of medications has been demonstrated to be the treatment of choice, although SSRIs, particularly fluoxetine, are gaining in popularity and have demonstrated

significant treatment success (Meltzer-Brody, Connor, Churchill, & Davidson, 2000). Other pharmacological interventions that have received empirical support include tricyclic antidepressants, MAOIs, and benzodiazepines (these should be used with caution, given the high rates of comorbidity with substance abuse) (Yehuda, Marshall, & Giller, 1998).

Generalized Anxiety Disorder (GAD)

GAD is characterized by excessive worry about several circumstances on more days than not for a period of more than six months (APA, 2000). GAD is a chronic disorder that may have biological and characterological bases that are not completely amenable to psychotherapy (Barlow et al., 1998). GAD has a prevalence of 5.1% in the general population and is twice as common in women as men. More than 90% of clients with GAD have a lifetime history of the disorder (Roy-Byrne & Cowley, 1998). Although research to date has not uncovered a treatment that is effective in eliminating the symptoms of GAD, several interventions have shown moderate success in reducing the severity of the symptoms.

Treatments that have been demonstrated to show improvement include:

Cognitive-behavioral therapy (CBT) (Barlow et al., 1998)

- CBT has been shown to be more effective than analytic, nondirective, or relaxation training, with significant improvements for up to 75% of clients, with continued improvements at six-month follow-up.
- Behavioral therapy alone (e.g., exposure, relaxation, biofeedback) is not as effective as when combined with a cognitive component.

Pharmacological interventions

- Some success has been shown with the following medications, all used in conjunction with psychological interventions: benzodiazepines (Roth & Fonagy, 1996); buspirone (reduces the cognitive anxiety symptoms to a greater extent than the physical symptoms; Feighner & Cohn, 1989); and antidepressants (imipramine or SSRIs; den Boer et al., 2000).

SUMMARY

Anxiety disorders are some of the most common clinical mental health diagnoses, and there is a substantial body of research relating to their treatment. In general, the research supports a cognitive-behavioral approach to treatment, although this is less supported for Generalized Anxiety Disorder. Many different types of pharmacological interventions also have been demonstrated to be effective in the treatment of anxiety, and the mental health practitioner should work closely with the client's physician in the treatment of these cases.

References

Agras, W.S. (1993). The diagnosis and treatment of panic disorder. *Annual Review of Medicine, 44,* 39–51.

American Psychiatric Association. (2000). *Diagnostic and statistical manual of mental disorders* (4th ed., text rev.). Washington, DC: Author.

Amir, N., Freshman, M., & Foa, E.B. (2000). Family distress and involvement in relatives of obsessive-compulsive disorder patients. *Journal of Anxiety Disorders, 14,* 209–217.

Barlow, D.H., Esler, J.L., & Vitali, A.E. (1998). Psychosocial treatments for panic disorders, phobias, and generalized anxiety disorder. In P.E. Nathan & J.M. Gorman (Eds.), *A guide to treatments that work* (pp. 288–318). New York: Oxford University Press.

Barlow, D.H., & Shear, M.K. (1988). Panic disorder: Foreword. In A.J. Frances & R.E. Hales (Eds.), *Review of psychiatry* (Vol. 7, pp. 5–9). Washington, DC: American Psychiatric Press.

Beamish, P.M., Granello, D.H., Granello, P.F., McSteen, P., & Stone, D. (1997). Emerging standards of care in the diagnosis and treatment of panic disorder. *Journal of Mental Health Counseling, 19,* 99–113.

Beamish, P.M., Granello, P.F., Granello, D.H., McSteen, P., Bender, B.A., & Hermon, D. (1996). Outcome studies in the treatment of panic disorder: A review. *Journal of Counseling and Development, 74*(5), 460–467.

Carlier, I.V.E. (2000). Critical incident stress debriefing. In A.Y. Shalev & R. Yehuda (Eds.), *International handbook of human response to trauma* (pp. 379–387). New York: Kluwer Academic/Plenum Publishers.

den Boer, J.A., Bosker, F.J., & Slaap, B.R. (2000). Serotonergic drugs in the treatment of depressive and anxiety disorders. *Human Psychopharmacology Clinical and Experimental, 15,* 315–336.

Feighner, J.P., & Cohn, J.B. (1989). Analysis of individual symptoms in generalized anxiety: A pooled, multistudy, double-blind evaluation of buspirone. *Neuropsychobiology, 21,* 124–130.

Franklin, M.E., Abramowitz, J.S., Kozak, M.J., Levitt, J.T., & Foa, E.B. (2000). Effectiveness of exposure and ritual prevention for obsessive-compulsive disorder: Randomized compared with nonrandomized samples. *Journal of Consulting and Clinical Psychology, 68,* 594–602.

Franklin, M.E., & Foa, E.B. (1998). Cognitive-behavioral treatments for obsessive-compulsive disorder. In P.E. Nathan & J.M. Gorman (Eds.), *A guide to treatments that work* (pp. 339–357). New York: Oxford University Press.

Kaplan, H.I., & Sadock, B.J. (1998). *Synopsis of psychiatry: Behavioral sciences/clinical psychiatry* (8th ed.). Baltimore: Williams & Wilkins.

Keane, T.M. (1998). Psychological and behavioral treatments of post-traumatic stress disorder. In P.E. Nathan & J.M. Gorman (Eds.), *A guide to treatments that work* (pp. 398–407). New York: Oxford University Press.

Kessler, R.C., McGonagle, K.A., Zhao, S., Nelson, C.B., Hughes, M., Eshleman, S., Wittchen, H-U., & Kendler, K.S. (1994). Lifetime and 12-month prevalence of *DSM-II-R* psychiatric disorders in the United States: Results from the national comorbidity survey. *Archives of General Psychiatry, 56,* 77–84.

Meltzer-Brody, S., Connor, K.M., Churchill, E., & Davidson, J.R.T. (2000). Symptom-specific effects of fluoxetine in post-traumatic stress disorder. *International Journal of Psychopharmacology, 15,* 227–231.

Nathan, P.E., & Gorman, J.M. (1998). *A guide to treatments that work.* New York: Oxford University Press.

NIH. (1991, September). *Treatment of panic disorder: NIH consensus statement.* Bethesda, MD: Department of Health and Human Services.

NIMH. (1999, August). *Anxiety disorders research.* Bethesda, MD: Department of Health and Human Services.

Roth, A., & Fonagy, P. (1996). *What works for whom?* New York: Guilford Press.

Roy-Byrne, P.P., & Cowley, D.S. (1998). Pharmacological treatment of panic, generalized anxiety, and phobic disorders. In P.E. Nathan & J.M. Gorman (Eds.), *A guide to treatments that work* (pp. 319–338). New York: Oxford University Press.

Savolaine, J., & Granello, P. (2000). *The function of spirituality in individual wellness.* Unpublished manuscript, Ohio State University.

Schneier, F.R., Johnson, J., Hornig, C.D., Liebowitz, M.R., & Weissman, M.M. (1992). Social phobia: Comorbidity and morbidity in an epidemiologic sample. *Archives of General Psychiatry, 48,* 282–288.

Seligman, L. (1998). *Selecting effective treatments.* San Francisco: Jossey-Bass.

Shapiro, F. (1995). *Eye movement desensitization and reprocessing: Basic principles, protocols, and procedures.* New York: Guilford Press.

Smith, M.L., Glass, G.V., & Miller, T.I. (1980). *The benefits of psychotherapy.* Baltimore: Johns Hopkins University Press.

Stevens, J. (1992). *Applied multivariate statistics for the social sciences* (2nd ed.). Hillsdale, NJ: Erlbaum.

Tarrier, N., Sommerfield, C., Pilgrim, H., & Humphreys, L. (1999). Cognitive therapy or imaginal exposure in the treatment of post-traumatic stress disorder. *British Journal of Psychiatry, 175,* 571–575.

Valleni-Basile, L.A., Garrison, C.Z., Jackson, K.L., Waller, J.L., McKeown, R.E., Addy, C.L., & Cuffe, S.P. (1994). Frequency of obsessive-compulsive disorder in a community sample of young adolescents. *Journal of the American Academy of Child and Adolescent Psychiatry, 33,* 782–791.

Yehuda, R., Marshall, R., & Giller, E.L., Jr. (1998). Psychopharmacological treatment of post-traumatic stress disorder. In P.E. Nathan & J.M. Gorman (Eds.), *A guide to treatments that work* (pp. 377–397). New York: Oxford University Press.

Recommended Reading and Additional Information

Antony, B.A., Craske, M.G., & Barlow, D.H. (1995). *Mastery of your specific phobia.* Albany, NY: Graywind Publications.

Beamish, P.M., Granello, D.H., Granello, P.F., McSteen, P., and Stone, D. (1997). Emerging standards of care in the diagnosis and treatment of panic disorder. *Journal of Mental Health Counseling, 19,* 99–113.

Granello, D.H. (1996). Current trends in the treatment alternatives for panic disorder with agoraphobia. *Psychotherapy in Private Practice, 14*(4), 17–33.

Mental Health Net. (2000). www.anxiety.mentalhelp.net/anxiety/anxietytoc.htm

Street, L.L., & Barlow, D.H. (1994). Anxiety disorders. In L.W. Craighead & E.E. Craighead (Eds.), *Cognitive and behavioral interventions: An empirical approach to mental health problems* (pp. 71–87). Boston: Allyn & Bacon.

Treatment of Panic Disorder. (1991, September 25–27). *NIH Consent Statement* [Online]. Available: ww.odp.od.nih.gov/consensus/cons/085/085_statement.htm

17 DIAGNOSIS AND TREATMENT OF ADULT DEPRESSIVE DISORDERS

Gary G. Gintner

One in five Americans will experience a clinically significant episode of depression sometime in his or her lifetime (American Psychiatric Association [APA], 1994). According to the World Health Organization, depression is the fourth leading cause of disability-adjusted life years and premature death (Murray & Lopez, 1996). The extent of disability is directly related to the severity of the depression (Maxmen & Ward, 1995). In this regard, both antidepressant medications and psychotherapy have been shown to be effective interventions for treating depression and reversing its disabling consequences (APA, 2000).

This chapter addresses two major issues in the treatment of adult depression. First, diagnostic issues are discussed relative to accurately diagnosing depressive disorders and their common comorbid conditions. Second, established practice guidelines are reviewed as a way of selecting empirically supported treatments. Although psychosocial treatments are emphasized, the role of somatic treatments such as antidepressant medications also is discussed.

DIAGNOSTIC ISSUES

Major Depressive Disorder (MDD) and Dysthymic Disorder are the two principle depressive disorders listed in the *Diagnostic and Statistical Manual of Mental Disorders,* fourth edition (*DSM-IV-TR;* APA, 2000). In this section, each disorder is examined with regard to symptom presentation, differential diagnosis, range of subtypes, and common co-occurring disorders.

Major Depressive Disorder

MDD is characterized by the occurrence of one or more major depressive episodes and the absence of any history of manic, mixed, or hypomanic episodes (APA, 2000). To meet criteria for a major depressive episode, five symptoms must be present for at least two weeks, with one of the symptoms being either depressed mood (sad or empty) or loss of interest or pleasure. Other symptoms include weight loss or gain, insomnia or hypersomnia, psychomotor retardation or agitation, loss of energy, concentration problems, feelings of worthlessness or excessive guilt, and recurrent suicidal thoughts or a suicide attempt. In terms of suicidality, factors that increase risk

include psychotic features, hopelessness, a past attempt, access to lethal means, and poor social support (APA, 2000). Inventories such as the Beck Depression Inventory (Beck, 1976) and the Hamilton Rating Scale (Hamilton, 1960) can be quite useful in assessing depressive symptomatology. These inventories can be readministered periodically to evaluate therapeutic progress.

Differential Diagnosis. Common rule-out conditions that can induce depressive symptoms include certain medical conditions, medication side effects, substance use, bereavement, and certain other psychiatric disorders. Medical conditions to consider include endocrine problems (e.g., hypothyroidism and diabetes), chronic infections, strokes, and neurological disorders (e.g., Parkinson's disease; Gintner, 1995). Depressive symptoms can also be caused by medications such as antihypertensives (e.g., reserpine, beta blockers, and mytheldopa), hormone-enhancing drugs (e.g., oral contraceptives, estrogen replacement therapy, and steroids), benzodiazapines (e.g., Xanax), and pain medications (Maxmen & Ward, 1995).

A variety of substances can induce depressive symptoms as a result of prolonged use or withdrawal. Probably the most important to rule out is alcohol abuse or dependence (APA, 2000). In fact, it takes at least four to six weeks of abstinence for alcohol-induced depressive symptoms to clear (APA, 2000).

Another important rule-out is bereavement, which is the reaction to the death of a loved one (APA, 2000). According to *DSM-IV* criteria, MDD should not be diagnosed during the first two months following a loss unless the symptoms are not typical of normal bereavement (e.g., worthlessness, suicidal preoccupation, excessive guilt, and psychotic symptoms). In the year following the loss, about 30% of bereaved individuals go on to develop MDD (APA, 2000).

Finally, other psychiatric disorders with depressive symptoms need to be ruled out, such as Bipolar Disorders, Schizoaffective Disorder, and Schizophrenia. A depressive episode in the context of Bipolar II Disorder is especially problematic because clients may not recognize or report past hypomanic episodes (APA,

2000). In terms of differential diagnosis, bipolar depression in comparison to depression in MDD is more likely to be severe and to have psychotic or atypical features (i.e., eating and sleeping more).

Subtypes and Specifiers. DSM-IV expanded the coding of MDD to better capture the symptomatic variations that have been shown to be clinically significant as far as course and treatment selection. First, MDD can be coded as either a single episode (first lifetime occurrence) or recurrent (more than one episode). Episodes can be further differentiated as melancholic, atypical, chronic, catatonic, seasonal, or with postpartum features. There are also specifiers available for noting the severity of the episode, remission status, and the presence of psychotic symptoms.

Comorbid Disorders. Anxiety disorders, personality disorders, and substance dependence disorders are common comorbid conditions for both MDD and Dysthymic Disorder. As many as a third of those with MDD will also have a personality disorder, especially Borderline Personality Disorder (Maxmen & Ward, 1995). Panic Disorder co-occurs in about a quarter of the cases (APA, 2000). Common substances that are abused include alcohol, cocaine, and stimulants. It is not unusual for users to gravitate toward these drugs as a way of "medicating" an underlying depression (Maxmen & Ward, 1995).

Dysthymic Disorder

Dysthymic Disorder is characterized by the presence of a depressed mood plus two other depression symptoms that persists for at least two years in adults (APA, 2000). Those with a late onset (i.e., after age 21) have a better prognosis than those with an earlier onset. Like MDD, atypical features can be coded. Because of the chronic nature of their symptoms, individuals with Dysthymic Disorder tend to have more impaired social and emotional functioning than those with MDD (Roth & Fonagy, 1996).

About 80% of individuals with Dysthymic Disorder will eventually develop MDD, a condition known as double depression (Roth & Fonagy, 1996). These individuals tend to have a shorter major depressive episode but relapse more rapidly than those with MDD alone.

RECOMMENDED TREATMENTS

Once the diagnostic information has been collected, decisions need to be made about the most appropriate interventions. In this section, empirically supported treatments are reviewed for the various forms of depression.

Both psychotherapeutic and somatic treatments have been extensively tested in the treatment of both MDD and Dysthymic Disorder (APA, 2000; DeRubeis & Crits-Christoph, 1998). In fact, practice guidelines or recommended treatments have been published by APA (2000), the American Psychological Association (DeRubeis & Crits-Christoph, 1998), and the Agency for Healthcare Policy and Research (AHCPR, 1993). These recommendations are primarily based on findings from numerous randomized clinical trials. In the future, these evidence-based guidelines may be adopted by managed care companies and other utilization review agencies as a preferred standard of care (Persons, Thase, & Chrits-Christoph, 1996). In this section, these recommendations are integrated to suggest treatments for the various forms of MDD and Dysthymic Disorder.

Mild to Moderate MDD

MDD with mild (i.e., symptoms just meet criteria) to moderate (i.e., excess symptoms but no marked impairment) symptomatology has been shown to respond equally well to psychotherapy and antidepressant medications (APA, 2000). Three major psychotherapeutic approaches have been empirically supported: cognitive therapy (CT; Beck, 1976), interpersonal therapy (IPT; Weissman, Markowitz, & Klerman, 2000), and behavior therapy (BT; Lewinsohn & Gotlib, 1995).

Cognitive Therapy. Of the psychotherapies, CT has the most extensive empirical support as an effective and specific treatment for MDD (APA, 2000; AHCPR, 1993; DeRubeis & Crits-Christoph, 1998). Basically, CT attempts to modify negative views of the self, the environment, and the future through cognitive techniques and behavioral exercises (Beck, 1976). Treatment is highly structured and consists of about 16 to 20 sessions (see Young, Beck, & Weinberger, 1993, for session-by-session protocol). The first stage of therapy aims at symptom reduction by challenging negative thoughts and increasing recognition of mastery experiences. The second phase of treatment targets more basic depressogenic assumptions such as perfectionism. Numerous studies have shown that CT is at least equally as effective as antidepressant medications, but may be better at preventing or delaying the occurrence of subsequent episodes (see Roth & Fonagy, 1996, for review). In comparison to other psychotherapies, CT has been found to be equal or superior to the other empirically supported treatments and superior to other verbal therapies (DeRubeis & Crits-Christoph, 1998; Roth & Fonagy, 1996). CT appears best suited for those with mild to moderate cognitive distortions who are able to abstract and be introspective (Young et al., 1993).

Interpersonal Therapy. IPT assumes that by dealing with interpersonal difficulties, depression can be effectively treated and prevented from recurring (Weissman et al., 2000). Therapy focuses on four potential problem areas: unresolved grief, interpersonal disputes with others, role transitions (e.g., becoming a parent, starting work), and interpersonal deficits (e.g., social isolation). Treatment generally entails 12 to 16 sessions of weekly therapy (see Weissman et al., 2000, for session-by-session protocols). In the first phase of therapy, the clinician orients the client to the interpersonal model and identifies one of the four problem areas to target. In the next phase, interventions are selected that specifically address this area. Commonly used techniques include elicitation of feelings, communication analysis, use of the therapeutic relationship, decision making, and role playing. Controlled studies have shown that IPT equals or nearly equals other empirically supported treatments (AHCPR, 1993; APA, 2000; DeRubeis & Crits-Christoph, 1998). It appears that IPT is less indicated for those with severe interpersonal problems such as Avoidant Personality Disorder (APA, 2000; Weissman et al., 2000).

Behavior Therapy. From a behavioral perspective, depression can result from too few regular reinforcing events (Lewinsohn & Gotlib, 1995). Treatment focuses on reducing the occurrence of unpleasant events and increasing participation in regular pleasant activities. Commonly used techniques include self-monitoring, contracting, activity scheduling, and skill building (e.g., assertion). This is the most systematically studied behavioral approach, but it should be noted that there are other variations (see Craighead, Craighead, & Ilardi, 1999).

Research has shown that BT is an effective treatment for MDD and compares favorably to other empirically supported treatments (AHCPR, 1993; APA, 2000; DeRubeis & Crits-Christoph, 1998). BT may be particularly indicated for those who show deficits in pleasant events and who demonstrate the capacity to comply with behavioral assignments.

Somatic Treatments. The primary somatic treatments that have been systematically examined include antidepressant medication, electroconvulsive therapy (ECT), and light therapy. In terms of medication, there is very little difference in efficacy among the four major classes of antidepressants: tricyclics (TCAs), selective serotonin reuptake inhibitors (SSRIs), monoamine oxidase inhibitors (MAOIs), and the atypical antidepressants (APA, 2000). Rather, preference for a particular class or drug is based largely on its more benign side-effect profile. The older class TCAs and MAOIs have significant side effects. As a result, APA (2000) guidelines generally recommend the SSRIs (e.g., Prozac, Paxil, and Zoloft) and the atypical antidepressants (e.g., Wellbutrin and Effexor) as first-line antidepressants. Studies show that medications are comparable to empirically supported psychotherapies, but may reduce depression more rapidly (about two weeks sooner; APA, 2000). However, side effects may prompt dropout, and relapse is considerable once the medications are discontinued (APA, 2000).

Psychotherapy or Medication? APA (2000) provides two sets of guidelines for selecting treatments for mild to moderate MDD. First, psychotherapy alone is indicated when the clinical picture includes a significant psychosocial stressor, intrapsychic conflict, interpersonal problems, or an Axis II disorder. Other important factors to consider are patient preference, pregnancy, lactation, or the wish to become pregnant. On the other hand, medication alone is recommended when there is a history of a prior positive response or when there is significant sleep or appetite disturbance.

Combined treatment (i.e., psychotherapy and medication) is generally recommended for moderately severe MDD by both APA (2000) and AHCPR (1993). However, the data for this recommendation are mixed at best (Persons et al., 1996). An emerging alternative is a sequential approach in which psychotherapy is offered first and medication is added only if there is minimal gain. Frank et al. (2000) found that remission rates were better for this sequential approach (79%) than for the standard combination treatment (66%). APA (2000) recommends that if there is not at least moderate improvement within eight weeks of using either medication or psychotherapy alone, a combination treatment should be considered.

Severe MDD

Severe MDD is associated with marked functional impairment (e.g., inability to work or socialize) and significant symptomotogy (e.g., suicidal gestures). Both the APA (2000) and AHCPR (1993) guidelines indicate that a somatic treatment (primarily an antidepressant) is the indicated intervention with or without psychotherapy. ECT may be used when there is an urgent need for a more immediate

response or if it was found to be beneficial in the past.

Data are mixed as far as the role of psychotherapy alone with this population (Craighead et al., 1999; Persons et al., 1996). Roth and Fonagy's (1996) exhaustive review of MDD literature concludes that the weight of evidence favors a combined approach for those with severe MDD.

Subtypes of MDD

Recurrent MDD. Many of those with the recurrent pattern will have another episode within two years of remission (Roth & Fonagy, 1996). As a result, greater emphasis on prophylactic treatment is required for this group. In terms of medication regimes, APA (2000) guidelines recommend sustained use of antidepressants with tapering occurring in the month or so prior to discontinuation. In terms of psychotherapy, the recommended treatment should be followed by maintenance sessions spaced biweekly and then monthly for approximately one year.

Psychotic Features. A combination of antidepressants and antipsychotic medication is recommended for MDD with psychotic symptoms (APA, 2000). The primary role of psychotherapy has not been established, but adjunctive work can be useful, especially after acute symptoms subside.

Melancholic Features. This is a severe form of depression that is particularly responsive to antidepressants (e.g., Effexor) or ECT (AHCPR, 1993; APA, 2000). Psychotherapy is also recommended, but not by itself.

Atypical Features. Symptoms such as eating and sleeping more are treated effectively with MAOIs and SSRIs (APA, 2000). The role of psychotherapy has not been established for this subtype. However, if the clinical picture includes rejection sensitivity, which is a potential atypical symptom, CT or IPT may be a useful adjunctive treatment component.

Postpartum Onset. MDD following childbirth is generally treated by antidepressant medication and/or psychotherapy. Because antidepressants may cause complications for those who breast-feed, clients need sound medical information for reaching a decision on how to proceed (APA, 2000). If the MDD is in the mild to moderate range with no complicating features, an empirically supported psychotherapy alone may be indicated.

Seasonal Pattern. The seasonal pattern occurs in about 10% of cases of MDD. Antidepressants alone or in combination with light therapy is the generally recommended treatment regime (APA, 2000). There are no data on the role of psychotherapy, but the general indications for psychotherapy discussed above should be consulted on a case-by-case basis.

Dysthymic Disorder

There are far fewer treatment studies on this milder but more chronic depressive disorder. Studies have shown that CT, IPT, and BT are effective treatment options (APA, 2000). Antidepressant medications also have been found to be effective (APA, 2000), but as many as 50% of dysthymics do not respond to or refuse this option (Roth & Fonagy, 1996). Furthermore, combined treatment has been shown to be more effective than medication alone (APA, 2000). Despite the less severe nature of this disorder overall, outcome is not as favorable as that for MDD (APA, 2000; Roth & Fonagy, 1996). Because of the chronic nature of this disorder, treatment may need to be more protracted than for MDD (APA, 2000).

Comorbidity

Double Depression. Antidepressant medication has been shown to reduce symptoms of both MDD and the underlying Dysthymic Disorder (APA, 2000). The selection of a psychotherapy should follow the guidelines discussed above. Combined treatment approaches are commonly employed (APA, 2000).

Substance Dependence. Detoxification from the substance problem is recommended prior to initiating treatment for depression to assess the degree to which depressive symptoms are substance-induced (APA, 2000). Treatment should then attempt to address both problems either sequentially (with substance dependence targeted first) or concurrently if a dual diagnosis program is available.

Anxiety Disorders. A number of very effective psychotherapies are available for both panic and other anxiety disorders (see DeRubeis & Crits-Christoph, 1998, for review). In addition, antidepressant medications have been shown to reduce symptoms of both depression and anxiety (APA, 2000). Treatment for depression should follow the recommended guidelines, but the anxiety disorder must also be treated or relapse rates for both conditions are quite high (APA, 2000).

Personality Disorders. Those who have a comorbid personality disorder show a less positive response to antidepressant medication (APA, 2000). As a result, psychotherapy is especially indicated in the overall treatment plan. CT in particular shows some advantage over other approaches in the treatment of depression for those with a personality disorder (Craighead et al., 1999).

SUMMARY

An accurate diagnosis that includes subtype features is critical in selecting the optimal treatment package. For MDD in the mild to moderate range, CT, IPT, and BT are considered empirically supported treatments. Antidepressants alone or in combination with psychotherapy are other alternatives, depending on past response. Medications are considered more the first-line treatments for severe MDD and MDD with special features such as psychosis, melancholia, and atypical symptoms. Treatments for Dysthymic Disorder follow many of the guidelines established for MDD. Comorbid conditions are common and treatment plans should attempt to address the range of disorders that are present.

Although the recommended guidelines are useful in making treatment decisions, they have several limitations. First, clients from diverse backgrounds are underrepresented in clinical trials, so the generalization of findings needs to be done cautiously. Second, although the empirically supported treatments outperform comparison treatments, a sizable proportion of clients relapse. This suggests the need for follow-up and maintenance sessions. Finally, the highly structured nature of these treatments assumes that clients are ready to take action and follow instruction. However, it is not unusual for depressed clients to be ambivalent about change or to be averse to strong direction. Thus, clinicians need to be sensitive to client differences and flexible in applying these recommendations.

References

Agency for Health Care Policy and Research (AHCPR) of the Department of Human Services. (1993). New federal guidelines seek to help primary care providers recognize and treat depression. *Hospital and Community Psychiatry, 44,* 598.

American Psychiatric Association. (2000). *Diagnostic and statistical manual of mental disorders* (4th ed., text rev.). Washington, DC: Author.

American Psychiatric Association. (2000). Practice guideline for the treatment of patients with major depressive disorder (rev.). *American Journal of Psychiatry, 157*(4), 1–45.

Beck, A.T. (1976). *Cognitive therapy and the emotional disorders.* New York: International Universities Press.

Craighead, W.E., Craighead, L.W., & Ilardi, S.S. (1999). Psychosocial treatments for major depressive disorder. In P.E. Nathan & J.M. Gorman (Eds.), *A guide to treatments that work* (pp. 226–239). New York: Oxford University Press.

DeRubeis, R.J., & Crits-Christoph, P. (1998). Empirically supported individual and group psychological treatments for adult mental disorders. *Journal of Consulting and Clinical Psychology, 66*(1), 37–52.

Frank, E., Grochocinski, V.J., Spanier, C.A., Buysse, D.J., Cherry, C.R., Houck, P.R., Stapf, D.M., & Kupfer, D.J. (2000). Interpersonal psychotherapy and antidepressant medication: Evaluation of a sequential treatment strategy in women with recurrent major depression. *Journal of Clinical Psychiatry, 61*(1), 51–57.

Gintner, G.G. (1995). Differential diagnosis in older adults: Dementia, depression, and delirium. *Journal of Counseling and Development, 73*(3), 346–351.

Hamilton, M. (1960). A rating scale for depression. *Journal of Neurology, Neurosurgery, and Psychiatry, 23,* 56–62.

Lewinsohn, P.M., & Gotlib, I.H. (1995). Behavioral theory and treatment for depression. In E.E. Becker & W.R. Leber (Eds.), *Handbook of depression* (pp. 352–375). New York: Guilford Press.

Maxmen, J.S., & Ward, N.G. (1995). *Essential psychopathology and its treatment* (2nd ed.). New York: Norton.

Murray, C.J.L., & Lopez, A.D. (1996). *The global burden of disease* (Vol. 1). Geneva, Switzerland: World Health Organization.

Persons, J.B., Thase, M.E., & Crits-Christoph, P. (1996). The role of psychotherapy in the treatment of depression: Review of two practice guidelines. *Archives of General Psychiatry, 53,* 283–290.

Roth, A., & Fonagy, P. (1996). *What works for whom? A critical review of psychotherapy.* New York: Guilford Press.

Weissman, M.M., Markowitz, J.C., & Klerman, G.L. (2000). *Comprehensive guide to interpersonal psychotherapy.* New York: Basic Books.

Young, J.E., Beck, A.T., & Weinberger, A. (1993). Depression. In D.H. Barlow (Ed.), *Clinical handbook of psychological disorders: A step-by-step treatment manual* (pp. 240–277). New York: Guilford Press.

18 EATING DISORDERS

Guidelines for Assessment, Treatment, and Referral

Cynthia R. Kalodner and Jeffrey S. Van Lone

Eating disorders are serious psychological disorders that affect predominately females during adolescence and adulthood. Despite the relatively low prevalence of clinically diagnosed anorexia nervosa (AN) and bulimia nervosa (BN), these disorders continue to receive a great deal of attention in the media. Perhaps this is reflective of societal obsession with thinness and the individuals who commit themselves to the pursuit of the thinnest bodies. Or perhaps it is the disbelief that women will vomit and exercise for hours after eating. The prevalence of eating and body image problems not reaching the criteria established for AN and BN is astounding (Kalodner & Scarano, 1992; Shisslak, Crago, & Estes, 1995; Tylka & Subich, 1999). These eating problems affect a tremendous number of women and an increasing number of men and include people of diverse ethnic and cultural backgrounds.

There are two major types of eating disorders: bulimia nervosa and anorexia nervosa. Eating disorders not otherwise specified (EDNOS) is a term used for people with eating problems who do not fit the specific criteria for either BN or AN. Binge eating disorder, under investigation as a possible additional formal diagnostic category, is an example of EDNOS. A description of BN, AN, and additional eating problems considered EDNOS are presented. See the *DSM-IV* (APA, 1994) for the diagnostic criteria for these eating disorders.

BULIMIA NERVOSA

BN is a disorder noted for binge eating, inappropriate compensatory behavior, and negative self-evaluation. Binge eating is defined as eating an amount of food that is definitely larger than most people would eat under similar circumstances, along with a sense of lack of control over eating during the episode. There are two subtypes of BN: purging and nonpurging type. In the more common purging type (Walsh & Garner, 1997), the individual regularly engages in self-induced vomiting or the misuse of laxatives, diuretics, or enemas. In the nonpurging type, the person uses fasting or excessive exercise, but does not regularly engage in self-induced vomiting or the misuse of laxatives, diuretics, or enemas. One does not have to vomit to meet the criteria for BN. Prevalence for BN ranges from 1% to 3% of adolescent and young adult females (APA, 1994).

ANOREXIA NERVOSA

A key feature of AN is refusal to maintain a minimally normal weight. People with AN have an intense fear of gaining weight or becoming fat. It is common to deny the seriousness of low body weight. AN also falls into two subtypes: restricting and binge eating/purging. Those who fall into the restricting type do not regularly engage in binge eating or purging behavior. Those who fall into the binge eating/purging type binge-eat. AN has a prevalence rate ranging from .05% to 1% of females in late adolescence and early adulthood (APA, 1994).

EATING DISORDERS NOT OTHERWISE SPECIFIED AND THE CONTINUUM OF EATING DISTURBANCES

Eating problems exist on a continuum, with normal eaters on one end and those with clinical eating disorders on the other. The midpoint intervals on the continuum may be referred to as subthreshold, partial syndrome, subclinical, or symptomatic (see Kalodner & Scarano, 1992; Shisslak, Crago, & Estes, 1995; Tylka & Subich, 1999).

Serious eating problems can exist in individuals who do not meet the criteria of BN or AN. In addition to understanding these eating disorders, it is important to attend to subclinical presentations that are assigned to the more heterogeneous EDNOS category. It is noteworthy that NOS might be misinterpreted as connoting eating problems that are not serious or in need of attention. This is not at all the case, as individuals with EDNOS can be quite distressed and in need of attention to the eating issues and associated psychological concerns. Binge eating disorder is an example of an EDNOS; it involves recurrent episodes of binge eating in the absence of regular use of purging, fasting, or excessive exercise characteristic of BN. Binges are characterized by some of the following: rapid eating, eating until uncomfortably full, eating when not hungry, eating alone to avoid embarrassment about the quantity of food consumed, and feeling disgusted, depressed, or guilty when overeating.

EDNOS are much more prevalent than BN or AN, especially among adolescent girls and college women. The prevalence of partial-syndrome eating disorders is approximately twice that of full-syndrome eating disorders (Shisslak et al., 1995). Subclinical BN is reported in 17% to 27% of college women (Kalodner & Scarano, 1992). Additionally, it

has been demonstrated that 50% of college women may be considered symptomatic (Kalodner & Scarano, 1992). Binge eating disorder is also more prevalent than AN or BN; among individuals presenting at weight loss programs, 30% meet the criteria for the disorder (APA, 1994). Less is known about the prevalence of this disorder in the general population.

WHO IS AT RISK?

Ninety percent of cases of AN and BN occur in females (APA, 1994). Adolescence is a critical time for the development of eating problems in girls. With the onset of adolescence, body dissatisfaction increases; this may be a result of physical changes during puberty, especially an increase in body fat. Almost 70% of a sample of female high school students reported that they were presently trying to lose weight (Rosen, Tacy, & Howell, 1990).

Though eating disorders in males are not common, it has been noted that eating problems in males are becoming more prevalent, especially among some special groups of men, such as wrestlers (Enns, Drewnowski, & Grinker, 1987) and gay men (Williamson, 1999). Likewise, until recently, eating disorders had been described as a Western cultural phenomenon facing primarily middle- to upper-class White females. However, eating disorders exist among various ethnic and cultural minority groups in the United States and the world (see Kalodner, 1996). The assumption that eating disorders do not exist in non-White females may lead professionals to miss early warning signs.

COMORBIDITY

Eating disorders are often concurrent with other psychological issues. Depressive symptoms may be found in individuals with AN and BN; obsessive-compulsive issues are more often associated with AN (APA, 1994). A genetic link between depression and eating disorders continues to be explored. One-third to one-half of all individuals with BN also meet the criteria for a personality disorder (APA, 1994). To be sure that associated issues are addressed in treatment, a global assessment of psychological functioning is recommended as a part of all clinical work with individuals who describe concerns with eating-related problems.

Comorbidity with substance abuse is also an issue. The prevalence of comorbid alcohol abuse and/or dependence in women requesting treatment for an eating disorder ranges from under 3% to over 59%, with a median of 22% (Holderness, Brooks-Gunn, & Warren, 1994). Other work indicates that 34% of a sample of bulimic outpatients had a history of problems with alcohol or drugs, and 21% had been in treatment for substance dependence (Mitchell, Specker, & Edmonson, 1997); 33% of individuals with BN also meet criteria for substance abuse or dependence (APA, 1994). It is advisable to assess for both eating disorders and substance abuse in individuals seeking treatment for either, as treatment issues may be further complicated by this dual diagnosis. It is a common recommendation that individuals who have both an eating disorder and a comorbid substance use problem receive treatment for the substance abuse first (Mitchell, Specker, et al., 1997). However, this is an assumption that has not been empirically tested. Mitchell et al. present a model designed to treat patients with both substance abuse and eating disorders.

ASSESSMENT

Assessment of individuals with eating problems requires a comprehensive evaluation of eating and eating-related behaviors, attitudes, and associated affect, as well as a global assessment of psychological functioning (Crowther & Sherwood, 1997). Assessment may include clinical interviews, client self-reports of behaviors, attitudes, and thoughts, self-monitoring, and behavioral observation. Assessment should be considered an essential part of the therapeutic experience. Various self-report measures are used;

two recommended self-report measures are the Eating Attitudes Test (EAT-26) (Garner & Garfinkel, 1979) and Eating Disorders Inventory-2 (EDI-2) (Garner, 1991). The EAT-26 is used as a screening instrument for maladaptive eating attitudes and behaviors in both applied and research settings. The EDI-2 yields eleven subscales: drive for thinness, bulimia, body dissatisfaction, ineffectiveness, perfectionism, interpersonal distrust, interoceptive awareness, maturity fears, asceticism, impulse regulation, and social insecurity. These subscales reflect important areas of concern for individuals with eating and body image concerns. The Eating Disorder Examination (EDE, 12th ed.; Fairburn & Cooper, 1993) is a structured interview that operationally defines the *DSM* criteria for eating disorders. For more information on assessment, see the excellent chapter by Crowther and Sherwood (1997).

SEXUAL ABUSE

The relationship between sexual abuse and eating disorders has received a great deal of attention (cf. Fallon & Wonderlich, 1997; Wooley, 1994). Determining whether sexual abuse constitutes a specific risk for eating disorders or whether sexual abuse represents a risk for any psychiatric problem remains an important question (Kearney-Cooke & Striegel-Moore, 1994). Childhood sexual abuse is associated with increased risk for a variety of psychiatric problems, including eating disorders (Pope & Hudson, 1992; Welch & Fairburn, 1994). Several psychological factors are associated with both eating disorders and sexual abuse, such as diminished self-esteem, self-blame, dissociation, issues with control, and personality disorders (Waller, Everill, & Calam, 1994). The dissociation link is a particularly interesting one (cf. Heatherton & Baumeister, 1991); it posits that dissociation may be a part of the binge eating experience as well as part of the repression of memories of sexual abuse. The issue of the link between sexual abuse and eating disorders, however, remains a topic of continued attention.

TREATMENT AND EFFECTIVENESS

Eating disorders are psychological problems that often require collaboration between mental health professionals and physicians (especially primary care practitioners, pediatricians, and psychiatrists). Referrals from physicians to mental health workers occur when medical professionals suspect that an eating disorder may be present. It is important for mental health providers to refer individuals with eating disorders to physicians for an evaluation of physical health and nutritional status. This referral for physical evaluation may become a therapeutic issue framed by the therapist as a part of the recovery process. Treatment for serious eating disorders may require hospitalization, which requires mental health workers to collaborate with other health care professionals. Dentists and dietitians are often essential to the effective identification and treatment of eating disorders. Because treatment of individuals with eating disorders is complex, it is highly recommended that novice therapists work closely with a skilled supervisor.

A particular issue likely to be faced by mental health counselors as well as medical professionals working with individuals with eating problems is denial of the seriousness of the problem. Treatment refusal is a factor in the treatment of AN (see Goldner, Birmingham, & Smye, 1997). Psychoeducational interventions (Garner, 1997) may be less threatening than traditional counseling, and providing accurate information about the consequences of food restriction, binge eating, and methods of purging, along with the effects of starvation may be a place to start with resistant clients. Self-help books (see Fairburn & Carter, 1997, for a list) are another way to provide help to clients who may be unwilling to commit to counseling.

MEDICAL ISSUES

Eating disorders are associated with a variety of physical health problems and medical complications. In AN, the medical issues that arise are the result of starvation and malnutrition. AN is associated with a 10% mortality rate;

this rate is higher than for most other psychiatric problems. Death may occur due to starvation, suicide, or electrolyte imbalance (APA, 1994). The physical symptoms of AN may affect most major organ systems and have serious implications for cardiovascular and renal functioning. Starvation itself may be the cause of several medical problems, such as constipation, abdominal pain, cold intolerance, lethargy, and excess energy. (For a description of the effects of starvation on human functioning, see Garner, 1997.)

The medical complications associated with BN are related to the methods of compensation used to avoid the weight gain associated with binge eating. Metabolic complications are associated with vomiting and laxative and diuretic abuse. Vomiting is responsible for dental erosion, pharyngeal/esophageal inflammation, and esophageal and gastric tears. An additional warning about the use of syrup of ipecac is important: When it is used repeatedly to induce vomiting, it may accumulate and become harmful to the heart. Chronic laxative use may lead to dependence on laxatives to stimulate colon functioning. Diuretic use is associated with dehydration that can lead to loss of kidney function. For complete information on medical complications, see Mitchell, Pomeroy, and Adson (1997) or Sansone and Sansone (1994).

The importance of nutritional education in working with individuals who exhibit any eating issues cannot be overlooked. Because the impact of nutrition on eating behavior and health is not typically part of the educational experience of the majority of mental health professionals, referrals to registered dietitians are necessary. To provide comprehensive care, it is important for mental health providers to consult with registered dietitians, thus ensuring that treatment issues relevant to health and nutritional status are addressed.

TREATMENT

Treatment for eating disorders may include hospitalization, self-help education, family therapy, cognitive-behavioral psychotherapy, interpersonal psychotherapy, psychodynamic psychotherapy, group therapy, and psychotropic medication. We briefly discuss each of these treatment modalities and provide resources for additional information for each modality presented.

Hospitalization

Hospitalization is more often needed for individuals with AN who reach a body weight that causes physical complications, although individuals suffering from BN who are unresponsive to psychological treatment may also be hospitalized. Inpatient hospitalizations may be warranted for the following reasons:

- To manage medical emergencies such as severe weight loss, electrolyte imbalances, and hypertension.
- To prevent increased weight loss by interrupting patterns of bingeing, purging, and the use of laxatives.
- To manage associated psychological complications such as depression, family crises, risk of self-harm, and substance abuse disorders.

Day treatment programs provide an economical alternative to inpatient hospitalization, allowing clients medical monitoring, intensive psychotherapy, and structured meal programs without removing them from home. Such programs may also provide a transition from inpatient to outpatient treatment.

Self-Help

Support or self-help groups are common in the treatment of eating disorders. Support groups usually are free of charge, held in a nontherapy setting, and often are led by persons who have recovered from an eating problem rather than a mental health professional (Enright, Butterfield, & Berkowitz, 1985; Fairburn & Carter, 1997). Many self-help groups are associated with national organizations (a list of Web sites is included in Table 18.1). These organizations may provide newsletters,

TABLE 18.1   Organizations and Other Sources of Help for Individuals with Eating Disorders

American Anorexia Bulimia Association (AABA)
www.aabainc.org/home.html

American Academy of Family Physicians (AAFP)
www.aafp.org/patientinfo/anorexia.html

Anorexia Nervosa and Related Eating Disorders, Inc. (ANRED)
www.anred.com

National Association of Anorexia Nervosa and Associated Disorders (ANAD)
www.anad.org

National Institute of Mental Health (NIMH)
www.sis.nlm.nih.gov/aids/nimh.html

National Eating Disorders Organization (NEDO)
www.kidsource.com/nedo/index.html

Eating Disorder Referral and Information Center
www.edreferral.com

National Eating Disorder Information Center (NEDIC)
www.nedic.on.ca

Academy for Eating Disorders (AED)
www.acadeatdis.org

Eating Disorders Awareness and Prevention, Inc. (EDAP)
www.edap.org

Food Addicts Anonymous
www.users.erols.com/randrc/faa

HUGS International, Inc.
www.hugs.com

telephone hotlines, and consultation to parents and professionals. There is tremendous variation on the kinds of support groups offered and little evidence to indicate which kinds of groups are of most benefit to various kinds of eating problems. Referrals to support groups may be useful, however, as an adjunct to counseling or as continued support after formal therapy has ended.

Family Therapy

There is more literature on family therapy for AN than for BN, although evaluations of the efficacy of family interventions have not been studied to the same extent as for individual and group interventions. Family therapy is a treatment of choice for patients under 18 years old who live at home. Families of individuals with AN may have characteristics of enmeshment, overprotectiveness, and rigidity. Enmeshment and overprotectiveness refer to boundaries that are not well established and often leave persons with AN feeling as though they cannot separate themselves from the family. Rigidity within the family system involves persistence in behaviors that are not adaptive. There are also issues around conflict, typically involving the family's inability to tolerate disagreement and avoidance of topics that are likely to spark controversy. In family therapy, it is essential to treat the entire family as a unit, rather than allowing the individual with AN to be the identified patient. Families are often in a great deal of distress over the low weight and food refusal of the person with AN. Because consistent weight gain is an important part of treatment for AN, this aspect of treatment must be addressed with the entire family. Although it is the responsibility of the person with AN to gain weight, parents and family are encouraged to assist by allowing the individual to eat foods of his or her choosing.

Cognitive-Behavioral Psychotherapy

Cognitive-behavioral therapy is described as a treatment of choice for BN (Chambless et al., 1998; Wilson & Fairburn, 1993; Wilson, Fairburn, & Agras, 1997). A primary focus is to change cognitive distortions related to body image and other maladaptive cognitions that exist in individuals with BN (e.g., perfectionism and low self-esteem). With modifications, cognitive-behavioral therapy may be successfully used to treat EDNOS, especially binge eating disorder. Cognitive-behavioral therapy attempts to modify behaviors by:

- Using strategies such as self-monitoring and stimulus control.
- Educating patients about own body weight regulation and the hazards of purging.
- Presenting nutritional information.

For AN, Garner, Vitousek, and Pike (1997) describe a cognitive-behavioral program that contains some components of the empirically

validated program for treatment of BN and addresses issues specific to AN, such as the effects of starvation and the need for weight gain. Specific issues that require attention in the treatment of AN include (Goldner & Birmingham, 1994):

- Medical stabilization.
- Establishment of therapeutic alliance.
- Weight restoration.
- Promotion of healthy eating attitudes, behaviors, and activity levels.
- Psychotherapeutic treatment.
- Family and community interventions.

Interpersonal Psychotherapy

Interpersonal therapy, originally developed to address depression, focuses on a detailed analysis of the interpersonal context within which the eating disorder developed and has been maintained (Fairburn, Jones, Peveler, Hope, & Connor, 1993; Fairburn, 1997). Treatment involves identifying and modifying specific interpersonal problems that accompany the eating disorder. According to Fairburn, these interpersonal problems typically fall under the following categories: grief, interpersonal role disputes, role transitions, and interpersonal deficits.

The goal of interpersonal therapy is the resolution of the individual's interpersonal problems. No attention is given to eating habits or behavior. Although cognitive-behavioral studies have dominated the research literature, controlled outcomes studies assessing the effectiveness of interpersonal therapy for BN are also impressive and are included as an empirically supported treatment (Chambless et al., 1998). It has been demonstrated that whereas cognitive-behavioral therapy may more rapidly achieve positive outcomes, interpersonal therapy continues to produce more positive change at follow-up assessments, when cognitive-behavioral outcomes level off (Fairburn et al., 1993). An integration of cognitive-behavioral and interpersonal psychotherapy may provide effective intervention for long-term psychotherapy, allowing treatment to focus on eating behaviors, faulty cognitions, and significant disturbances within the individual's interpersonal milieu.

Psychodynamic Psychotherapy

Long-term psychodynamic therapy may be useful as an alternative treatment for eating disorders when cognitive-behavioral and interpersonal therapies prove ineffective. Crisp (1997) provides a well-articulated modality that integrates psychodynamic and behavioral management techniques in the treatment of AN. However, this therapy for eating disorders has not been scientifically validated (Chambless et al., 1998). Additionally, there are currently no controlled studies comparing long-term psychodynamic therapy and other short-term therapies, such as cognitive-behavioral therapy. Therefore, psychodynamic therapies may be implemented in cases when current, empirically validated therapies have failed.

Group Therapy

Counseling groups provide a promising modality for treatment of BN and EDNOS. Groups reduce the secrecy and shame associated with eating problems, supply a place for reality testing of distorted beliefs and self-perceptions among others who also facing eating disorders, and provide an interpersonal context to facilitate links between eating disorders and interpersonal relationships (Fettes & Peters, 1992; Oesterheld, McKenna, & Gould, 1987). Approaches to group work with this population vary, but most often, groups are active and symptom- and affect-focused. Common features include a focus on the here-and-now, use of journals, cognitive restructuring, incremental goal setting, and support. Interestingly, group treatment in combination with additional therapy was found to be more effective than group therapy alone (Fettes & Peters, 1992). No particular type of group treatment has consistently demonstrated better results than other types (Polivy & Federoff, 1997). It is likely that the nonspecific factors of group interventions

(e.g., universality, interpersonal learning, and other therapeutic factors; Yalom, 1995) contribute to the power of group treatment.

Due to difficulties doing group work with individuals who have AN, considerably less is known about these group interventions. Hall (1985) noted that anorexics are often withdrawn, anxious, rigid, egocentric, preoccupied with body weight and food, and have extreme difficulty identifying and expressing feelings in group counseling. Some therapists do not use group approaches at all for the treatment of AN.

There is a growing body of literature on the use of groups with EDNOS. McNamara (1989) presented an example of a group intervention for repeat dieters. This structured group program was designed to replace dieting with healthier eating and regular, moderate exercise and to increase body esteem by encouraging self-acceptance. Eating behaviors and weight preoccupation were also addressed in addition to psychological issues common in chronic dieters, such as perfectionism, assertiveness, and depression. Polivy and Herman (1992) developed a similar program called "undieting," aimed at reducing dieting behavior in overweight women. The undieting program led to a significant reduction on various EDI subscales, indicating that the program was able to reduce some maladaptive attitudes and behaviors related to body and weight issues.

Psychotropic Medication

Medication should not be the exclusive mode of treatment for eating disorders. There is no evidence that antidepressant or other medications are effective treatments for AN (Garfinkel & Walsh, 1997; Leach, 1995). Furthermore, the side effects of antidepressant medications are especially problematic with AN. In contrast, BN has been responsive to treatment with antidepressant medications. Antidepressants may be useful, independent of the presence of depression. There is no demonstrated efficacy of a particular antidepressant over others; choice of a particular medication should be based on minimizing side effects (Garfinkel & Walsh, 1997). At the same time, medications should be viewed as part of a comprehensive treatment package and should not be prescribed without attention to psychological issues that are addressed in individual, group, or family therapy.

SUMMARY

Eating disorders represent one of the most complicated and complex of psychological disorders. Although AN and BN are the most commonly recognizable and the most attended to of eating disorders in our society, the most common clinical classification is EDNOS. In fact, more than half of young adolescent and early adult females may be classified as partial syndrome or symptomatic. There are many points to consider when developing an integrative plan for the treatment of an eating disorder. In working with clients with eating disorders, mental health practitioners should practice careful assessment, consider medical and comorbidity issues, and consider referral to an expert in this area. This chapter offered information to aid in the selection of appropriate treatment and the development of individual treatment plans that integrate appropriate therapeutic approaches.

References

American Psychological Association. (1994). *Diagnostic and statistical manual of mental disorders* (4th ed.). Washington, DC: Author.

Chambless, D.L., Baker, M.J., Baucom, D.H., Beutler, L.E., Calhoun, K.S., Crits-Christoph, P., Daiuto, A., DeRebeis, R., Detweiler, J., Haaga, D.A.F., Bennett-Johnson, S.B., McCurry, S., Muesser, K.T., Pope, K.S., Sanderson, W.C., Shoham, V., Stickle, T., Williams, D.A., & Woody, S.R. (1998). Update on empirically validated therapies, II. *The Clinical Psychologist, 51*(1), 3–16.

Crisp, A.H. (1997). Anorexia nervosa as flight from growth: Assessment and treatment based on the model. In D.M. Garner & P.E. Garfinkel (Eds.), *Handbook of treatment for eating disorders* (2nd ed., pp. 25–33). New York: Guilford Press.

Crowther, J.H., & Sherwood, N.E. (1997). Assessment. In D.M. Garner & P.E. Garfinkel (Eds.), *Handbook of treatment for eating disorders* (2nd ed., pp. 34–39). New York: Guilford Press.

Enns, M.P., Drewnowski, A., & Grinker, J.A. (1987). Body composition, body size estimation and attitudes toward eating in male college athletes. *Psychosomatic Medicine, 49,* 56–64.

Enright, A.B., Butterfield, P., & Berkowitz, B. (1985). Self-help and support groups in the management of eating disorders. In D.M. Garner & P.E. Garfinkel (Eds.), *Handbook of psychotherapy for anorexia nervosa and bulimia* (pp. 491–512). New York: Guilford Press.

Fairburn, C.G. (1997). Interpersonal psychotherapy for bulimia nervosa. In D.M. Garner & P.E. Garfinkel (Eds.), *Handbook of treatment for eating disorders* (2nd ed., pp. 25–33). New York: Guilford Press.

Fairburn, C.G., & Carter, J.C. (1997). Self-help and guided self-help for binge eating problems. In D.M. Garner & P.E. Garfinkel (Eds.), *Handbook of treatment for eating disorders* (2nd ed., pp. 494–499). New York: Guilford Press.

Fairburn, C.G., & Cooper, Z. (1993). The Eating Disorder Examination. In C.G. Fairburn & G.T. Wilson (Eds.), *Binge eating: Nature, assessment and treatment* (pp. 317–360). New York: Guilford Press.

Fairburn, C.G., Jones, R., Peveler, R.C., Hope, R.A., & O'Connor, M. (1993). Psychotherapy and bulimia nervosa: Longer-term effects of interpersonal psychotherapy, behavior therapy, and cognitive behavior therapy. *Archives of General Psychiatry, 50,* 419–428.

Fallon, P., & Wonderlich, S.A. (1997). Sexual abuse and other forms of trauma nervosa. In D.M. Garner & P.E. Garfinkel (Eds.), *Handbook of treatment for eating disorders* (2nd ed., pp. 394–414). New York: Guilford Press.

Fettes, P.A., & Peters, J.M. (1992). A meta-analysis of group treatment for bulimia nervosa. *International Journal of Eating Disorders, 11*(2), 97–110.

Garfinkel, P.E., & Walsh, B.T. (1997). Drug therapies. In D.M. Garner & P.E. Garfinkel (Eds.), *Handbook of treatment for eating disorders* (2nd ed., pp. 372–380). New York: Guilford Press.

Garner, D.M. (1991). *Eating Disorders Inventory–2.* Odessa, FL: Psychological Assessment Resources.

Garner, D.M. (1997). Psychoeducational principles in treatment. In D.M. Garner & P.E. Garfinkel (Eds.), *Handbook of treatment for eating disorders*

(2nd ed., pp. 145–177). New York: Guilford Press.

Garner, D.M., & Garfinkel, P.E. (1979). The Eating Attitudes Test: An index of the symptoms of anorexia nervosa. *Psychological Medicine, 9,* 273–279.

Garner, D.M., Vitousek, K.M., & Pike, K.M. (1997). Cognitive-behavioral therapy for anorexia nervosa. In D.M. Garner & P.E. Garfinkel (Eds.), *Handbook of treatment for eating disorders* (2nd ed., pp. 94–144). New York: Guilford Press.

Goldner, E.M., & Birmingham, C.L. (1994). Anorexia nervosa: Methods of treatment. In L. Alexander-Mott & D.B. Lumsden (Eds.), *Understanding eating disorders* (pp. 135–157). Washington, DC: Taylor & Francis.

Goldner, E.M., Birmingham, C.L., & Smye, V. (1997). Addressing treatment refusal in anorexia nervosa. In D.M. Garner & P.E. Garfinkel (Eds.), *Handbook of treatment for eating disorders* (2nd ed., pp. 437–461). New York: Guilford Press.

Hall, A. (1985). Group psychotherapy for anorexia nervosa. In D.M. Garner & P.E. Garfinkel (Eds.), *Handbook of psychotherapy for anorexia nervosa and bulimia* (pp. 213–239). New York: Guilford Press.

Heatherton, T.F., & Baumeister, R.F. (1991). Binge eating as escape from self-awareness. *Psychological Bulletin, 110,* 86–108.

Holderness, C.C., Brooks-Gunn, J., & Warren, M.P. (1994). Co-morbidity of eating disorders and substance abuse: Review of the literature. *International Journal of Eating Disorders, 16*(1), 1–34.

Kalodner, C.R. (1996). Eating disorders from a multicultural perspective. In J.L. DeLucia-Waack (Ed.), *Multicultural counseling competencies: Implications for training and practice* (pp. 197–216). Alexandria, VA: Association for Counselor Education and Supervision.

Kalodner, C.R., & Scarano, G.M. (1992). A continuum of nonclinical eating disorders: A review of behavioral and psychological correlates and suggestions for intervention. *Journal of Mental Health Counseling, 14*(1), 30–41.

Kearney-Cooke, A., & Striegel-Moore, R.H. (1994). Treatment of childhood sexual abuse in anorexia nervosa and bulimia nervosa: A feminist psychodynamic approach. *International Journal of Eating Disorders, 15,* 305–319.

Leach, A.M. (1995). The psychopharmacotherapy of eating disorders. *Psychiatric Annals, 25,* 628–633.

McNamara, K. (1989). A structured group program for repeat dieters. *Journal for Specialists in Group Work, 14,* 141–150.

Mitchell, J.E., Pomeroy, C., & Adson, D.E. (1997). Managing medical complications. In D.M. Garner & P.E. Garfinkel (Eds.), *Handbook of treatment for eating disorders* (2nd ed., pp. 383–393). New York: Guilford Press.

Mitchell, J.E., Specker, S., & Edmonson, K. (1997). Management of substance abuse and dependence. In D.M. Garner & P.E. Garfinkel (Eds.), *Handbook of treatment for eating disorders* (2nd ed., pp. 415–423). New York: Guilford Press.

Oesterheld, J.R., McKenna, M.S., & Gould, N.B. (1987). Group psychotherapy of bulimia: A critical review. *International Journal of Group Psychotherapy, 37*(2), 163–185.

Polivy, J.E., & Federoff, I. (1997). Group psychotherapy. In D.M. Garner & P.E. Garfinkel (Eds.), *Handbook of treatment for eating disorders* (2nd ed., pp. 462–475). New York: Guilford Press.

Polivy, J.E., & Herman, C.P. (1992). Undieting: A program to help people stop dieting. *International Journal of Eating Disorders, 11*(3), 261–268.

Pope, H.G., Jr., & Hudson, J.I. (1992). Is childhood sexual abuse a risk factor for bulimia nervosa? *American Journal of Psychiatry, 149,* 455–463.

Rosen, J.C., Tacy, B., & Howell, D. (1990). Life stress, psychological symptoms and weight reducing behavior in adolescent girls: A prospective analysis. *International Journal of Eating Disorders, 9,* 17–26.

Sansone, R.A., & Sansone, L.A. (1994). Bulimia nervosa: Medical complications. In L. Alexander-Mott & D.B. Lumsden (Eds.), *Understanding eating disorders* (pp. 181–201). Washington, DC: Taylor & Francis.

Shisslak, C.M., Crago, M., & Estes, L.S. (1995). The spectrum of eating disturbances. *International Journal of Eating Disorders, 18,* 209–219.

Tylka, T.L., & Subich, L.M. (1999). Exploring the construct validity of the eating disorder continuum. *Journal of Counseling Psychology, 46,* 268–276.

Waller, G., Everill, J., & Calam, R. (1994). Sexual abuse and the eating disorders. In L. Alexander-Mott & D.B. Lumsden (Eds.), *Understanding Eating Disorders* (pp. 135–157). Washington, DC: Taylor & Francis.

Walsh, B.T., & Garner, D.M. (1997). Diagnostic issues. In D.M. Garner & P.E. Garfinkel (Eds.), *Handbook of treatment for eating disorders* (2nd ed., pp. 25–33). New York: Guilford Press.

Welch, S.L., & Fairburn, C.G. (1994). Sexual abuse and bulimia nervosa: Three integrated case control comparisons. *American Journal of Psychiatry, 151,* 402–407.

Williamson, I. (1999). Why are gay men a high risk group for eating disturbance? *European Eating Disorders Review, 7,* 1–4.

Wilson, G.T., & Fairburn, C.G. (1993). Cognitive treatments for eating disorders. *Journal of Consulting and Clinical Psychology, 61,* 261–279.

Wilson, G.T., Fairburn, C.G., & Agras, W.S. (1997). Cognitive-behavioral therapy for bulimia nervosa. In D.M. Garner & P.E. Garfinkel (Eds.), *Handbook of treatment for eating disorders* (2nd ed., pp. 67–93). New York: Guilford Press.

Wooley, S.C. (1994). Sexual abuse and eating disorders: The concealed debate. In P. Fallon, M. Katzman, & S. Wooley (Eds.), *Feminist perspectives on eating disorders* (pp. 171–212). New York: Guilford Press.

Yalom, I.D. (1995). *The theory and practice of group psychotherapy* (4th ed.). New York: Basic.

19 CLINICAL PRACTICE ISSUES IN ASSESSING FOR ADULT SUBSTANCE USE DISORDERS

Boyd W. Pidcock and Joan Polansky

Substance use disorders represent the most frequently occurring mental health problem in the United States (Miller & Brown, 1997; Regier et al., 1990). For example, between 1992 and 1995, there were more than one million substance abuse-related clinic admissions per year (Margolis & Zweben, 1998). Consistently, surveys show that 10% of adults develop significant negative consequences resulting from the use of alcohol (Miller & Brown, 1997). Furthermore, approximately 7% of Americans will develop drug dependence during their lifetime (Brown, 1995). Given the frequency and severity of substance use disorders in mental health settings, it is essential that clinicians develop a high degree of competence in assessing and treating substance use disorders (Margolis & Zweben, 1998; Miller & Brown, 1997).

Because drug and alcohol use often lead to behaviors mimicking a majority of mental disorders, assessment for substance abuse and dependence should be a regular part of the diagnostic interview (Margolis & Zweben, 1998; Miller & Brown, 1997; Perkinson, 1997). Therefore, caution is in order when diagnosing individuals who are currently abusing or dependent on substances or for whom abstinence is recent. The *Diagnostic and Statistical Manual of Mental Disorders* (*DSM-IV-TR*; American Psychiatric Association, 2000) criteria provide the framework for diagnosing substance abuse and dependence. Abuse is characterized by continued substance use despite the presence of significant negative consequences. Because a diagnosis of abuse entails exhibiting only one symptom within a 12-month period, the criteria for abuse are more easily met. The symptoms of abuse include: (1) substance use being responsible for failure at work or in the home; (2) continued use despite negative physiological consequences; (3) ongoing use related to legal problems; and (4) significant relational problems resulting from continued use. The criteria for substance dependence require that at least three symptoms be present within a 12-month period. In contrast to the symptoms for abuse, dependence presents a compulsive pattern of substance use. Dependence symptoms are (1) tolerance; (2) unsuccessful attempts to cut down or quit using; (3) spending a lot of time acquiring the substance; (4) diminishing of relationships, work, or leisure activities because of use; and (5) continued use despite negative physiological or psychological consequences.

DUAL DIAGNOSIS

In addition to developing an awareness of substance disorders, clinicians should also note that the coexistence of substance abuse and mental disorders, known as dual diagnosis or comorbidity, is common (Miller & Brown, 1997; Nace, 1995; Sowers & Golden, 1999). Depending on the treatment specialization and setting, extant research suggests that 25% to 85% of client populations that present for treatment for mental health issues are also experiencing the impacts of substance use disorders (Kiesler, Simpkins, & Morton, 1991; Miller & Brown, 1997; Minkoff, 1991; Sowers & Golden, 1999). Research also consistently indicates that dual diagnosis clients evidence poorer treatment outcomes when compared to clients with mental health issues alone (Margolis & Zweben, 1999; Miller & Brown, 1997). Additionally, the dually diagnosed experience higher levels of affective and anxiety disorders, marital problems, personality disorders, psychoses, sleep disorders, sexual dysfunctions, and posttraumatic stress disorders (Margolis & Zweben, 1999; Miller & Brown, 1997; Sowers & Golden, 1999). Clearly, clinicians who work with the dually diagnosed should be well trained and prepared to work effectively with the complex manifestations that result from the interaction of mental health problems and substance use disorders.

Understanding the relationship between coexisting disorders is essential to accurately assessing potential client risk factors and developing effective treatment plans. These relationships may manifest themselves in a number of ways. The presence of a mental disorder may put the individual at greater risk for developing substance use disorders. In other cases, the substance use disorder precipitates or exacerbates the mental disorder. Once present, the symptoms that began with a substance disorder may continue through abstinence. Sometimes the mental disorder and substance use disorder are totally unrelated (Nace, 1995). Overall, patients with coexistent mental disorders are at greater risk for relapse, and concomitantly, those who relapse are more likely to develop depression. In both cases, these individuals have an increased risk for suicide (Brown, Irwin, & Schuckit, 1991; Galanter, Castanada, & Ferman, 1988; Kessler et al., 1994; Nace, 1995).

ASSESSING SUBSTANCE USE DISORDERS

Given the frequency and complexity of substance use disorders, clinicians should be knowledgeable in the use of a variety of reliable and valid assessment tools to allow successful scrutiny of their clients' substance use. Fortunately, a number of easily administered written and oral tools with demonstrated utility across a wide variety of research, clinical, and medical contexts are available for the practitioner. Although an exhaustive review of the full range of instruments is beyond the purview of this chapter, the assessment tools included are those of demonstrated reliability, validity, simplicity, and efficacy.

The CAGE Questionnaire

Perhaps the most widely used of these tools is also the simplest. Quick and easily administered, the CAGE (Ewing, 1984, as cited in Margolis & Zweben, 1999) includes four questions each with key assessment dimensions forming the acronym that gives the device its name. Figure 19.1 represents the

1. Have you ever felt you should *cut* down on your drinking or drug use?
2. Have people ever *annoyed* you by criticizing your drinking/drug use?
3. Have you ever felt *guilty* about your drinking?
4. Have you ever had a drink or used drugs first thing in the morning (an *eye* opener) to steady your nerves or get rid of a hangover or residual drug effect?

FIGURE 19.1 The CAGE Questionaire (Ewing, 1984). *Source:* Reprinted with permission from *Journal of the American Medical Association,* vol. 252, pp. 1905–1907. Copyright 1984, American Medical Association.

CAGE questionnaire. Each of the four questions assesses a domain of client information indicative of problematic behaviors associated with alcohol use. The CAGE can also be adapted to screen for the presence of problematic substance use. Designed to avoid client confusion and resistance, the questions are unambiguous, direct, and simple. Question 1 assesses for clients' awareness and reaction to the potential loss of control over their substance use. Question 2 assesses the impact of clients' substance use on others, as well as their level of denial and reaction to criticism of their substance use behaviors. Question 3 addresses clients' affective reactions and responses to their substance use. Finally, question 4 scrutinizes the potential physiological impact of clients' substance use by screening for tolerance and withdrawal symptoms. Affirmative responses to any two or more of the questions are considered indicative of client substance use problems. This short instrument has demonstrated efficacy in a diverse variety of assessment settings, such as initial client interviews, hospital emergency rooms, and detox centers, where simplicity and unobtrusive techniques are highly desirable (Margolis & Zweben, 1999; Perkinson, 1997).

The Short Michigan Alcoholism Screening Test (SMAST)

The short form of the Michigan Alcoholism Screening Test (MAST, Selzer, 1971; SMAST; Selzer, Vinokur, & van Rooijen, 1975) is a 13-item yes/no paper-and-pencil scale that has demonstrated its utility in clinical and research contexts (Cooney, Zweben, & Fleming,

1995; Pidcock & Fischer, 1998; Pidcock, Fischer, Forthun, & West, 2000; Sher, Wood, Crews, & Vandiver; 1995). Figure 19.2 is a reproduction of the SMAST. Similar to the CAGE, it is easy to adapt the instrument to include substance use (e.g., "Do you feel your alcohol and drug use is normal?" and "Have you ever attended a meeting of Alcoholics Anonymous or Narcotics Anonymous?") (Pidcock & Fischer, 1998). Scores range from 0 to 13, with 3 or above indicative of substance use problems (Selzer et al., 1975). Reported internal consistency reliability coefficients range from .78 to .82 (Pidcock et al., 2000), .76 to .93 (Selzer et al., 1975), and .96 to .99 (Pokorny, Miller, & Kaplan, 1972). Validity has also been recognized

---

Please answer the following as either yes or no.

1. Do you feel your alcohol and drug use is normal? (By normal, we mean you drink alcohol or use drugs less than or as much as most other people.)
2. Do your parents, boyfriend, girlfriend, husband, wife, or other near relatives ever worry or complain about your alcohol or drug use?
3. Do you ever feel guilty about your alcohol or drug use?
4. Do friends or relatives think you are a normal drinker/drug user?
5. Are you able to stop drinking alcohol or using drugs when you want to?
6. Have you ever attended a meeting of Alcoholics Anonymous or Narcotics Anonymous?
7. Has your alcohol or drug use ever created problems between you and your girlfriend, boyfriend, a parent, or other near relative?
8. Have you ever gotten into trouble at school or work because of your alcohol or drug use?
9. Have you ever neglected your obligations, your family, school, or work for two or more days in a row because of your alcohol or drug use?
10. Have you ever gone to anyone for help about your alcohol or drug use?
11. Have you ever been in a hospital or treatment center because of your alcohol or drug use?
12. Have you ever been arrested for driving under the influence of alcohol or drugs?
13. Have you ever been arrested, even for a few hours, because of other alcohol- or drug-related behaviors?

FIGURE 19.2 The SMAST-D (Pidcock & Fischer, 1998; Selzer, Vinokur, & van Rooijen, 1975). *Source:* Reprinted with permission from *Journal of Studies on Alcohol,* vol. 36, pp. 117–126, 1975. Copyright by Journal of Studies on Alcohol, Inc., Rutgers Center of Alcohol Studies, Piscataway, NJ 08854.

as acceptably high in studies by Zung and Charalmpous (1975). Also of interest to clinicians and researchers, adapted versions have been developed and are available for use with males and females (SMAST-M and SMAST-F; Crews & Sher, 1992; Sher et al., 1995) and older adults (SMAST-G; Blow, Young, Hill, Singer, & Beresford, 1991, as cited in Cooney et al., 1995). Overall, the SMAST is easier to administer, score, and interpret than the 25-item MAST (Selzer, 1971), and the instrument is copyright-free and open to public use (Margolis & Zweben, 1999; Perkinson, 1997).

FAMILY HISTORY OF SUBSTANCE
USE DISORDERS

A substantial body of research strongly supports the finding that substance use disorders tend to run in families (McGue, 1999; Thombs, 1999). The intergenerational linkage is transmitted through both genetic and psychosocial pathways. However, the manner in which the susceptibility is passed through families and the specific contribution of genetic versus environmental factors remains open to much debate (Thombs, 1999). Because of these family-related factors, any substance use assessment should include a careful scrutiny of the intergenerational family history of substance use disorders. Of additional note, research has also demonstrated that children raised in families with alcoholic parents are at greater risk as adults for anxiety, depression, antisocial traits, relationship difficulties, issues with trust, and behavioral problems when compared with children raised in households where parental alcoholism was not a factor (Brown & Schmid, 1999). Importantly, the family history assessment can provide the clinician with a full range of information relevant to mental disorders that goes well beyond risk factors for substance use disorders (Margolis & Zweben, 1999).

**The Children of Alcoholics Screening
Test (CAST)**

The CAST (Jones, 1981/82) identifies latency-age children, adolescents, and adults who are living with or have lived with alcoholic parents. The CAST is a 30-item inventory with scores tabulated by all "yes" responses given. Scores range from 0 to 30, with 6 or above indicating the presence of negative life events associated with parental alcoholism (Jones, 1985). The areas of negative life events measured by the CAST are (1) emotional distress associated with parental alcoholism; (2) perceptions related to marital discord; (3) attempts to control parental drinking; (4) efforts to escape from alcoholism; (5) exposure to drinking-related family violence; (6) tendencies to perceive parents as alcoholic; and (7) desire for help (Pilat & Jones, 1984, 1985). Support for the reliability of the CAST is reported by Clair and Genest (1987), Dinning and Berk (1989), Roosa, Sandler, Beals, and Short (1988), and Yeatman, Bogart, Geer, and Sirridge (1994), in which they reported internal consistency reliability estimates from .88 to .94.

Another option for clinicians and researchers is the CASTD (Pidcock et al., 2000). The instrument has been shortened to 14 items from the original version and adapted to include the presence of parental substance use (e.g., "Have you ever thought that one of your parents had a drinking or drug problem?" and "Have you ever worried about a parent's health because of his or her alcohol or drug use?"). Scores of 3 or above are indicative of the presence of negative life events associated with problematic parental substance use (Pidcock & Fischer, 1998; Pidcock et al., 2000). For the clinician, the CAST and shorter CASTD are effective diagnostic tools that measure and identify specific areas of client functioning impacted by the presence of parental substance use disorders. Both instruments are copyright-protected (CAST; Jones, 1981, 1982); permission for use should be obtained from the author prior to use.

TREATMENT PLANNING

Because a large proportion of clients with substance use problems also have additional coexisting disorders, therapists often need to coordinate care with other helping professionals. Obtaining client consent in the form of signed written releases provides the foundation for contacting treatment programs and physicians prescribing medications. Contacting the appropriate resources is an essential step in the assessment and treatment planning process because it provides collateral data about the client and an ability to engage in hypothesis testing with other professionals.

As with any treatment planning, clearly defining the problem is paramount. However, with substance use disorders, problem identification is often further complicated by the presence of client denial and the dynamic nature manifest in dual diagnosis. With dually diagnosed individuals, the early focus of treatment should be on substance use issues, but other mental health concerns also should be addressed. Despite the movement advocating for controlled use (Sobell & Sobell, 1978, 1993), the majority of research consistently supports abstinence as a primary treatment goal (Brown, 1995; Goldsmith, 1997; Schuckit, 1994; Wallace, 1989, 1996). The most effective treatment strategies prioritize and integrate both substance use and mental health treatment goals and objectives (Brown, 1995; Margolis & Zweben, 1998; Miller & Brown, 1997; Nace, 1995). Additional research demonstrates that optimal treatment planning successfully addresses dual diagnosis and the individual's readiness for change (Prochaska, DiClemente, & Norcross, 1992). Accordingly, treatment is appropriately matched with the client's disorder (Margolis & Zweben, 1999; Miller & Brown, 1997).

Processes of Change

Prochaska et al.'s (1992) transtheoretical model for assessing the processes of change provides treatment recommendations for individuals at each stage. The overall model can be used to help facilitate the clinician's understanding that clients can simultaneously be at different stages of change in relation to their co-occurring substance and mental disorders and, thus, improve treatment planning efficacy (Brady et al., 1996; Miller, 1995). Perhaps the most salient features of the transtheoretical model are realized in its simplicity

and ease of implementation across diverse treatment models and staffs representing multiple levels of education and training (Brady et al., 1996).

Prochaska et al. (1992) define each of the five stages as a series of predictable experiences and tasks that need to be accomplished prior to progressing to the next stage. As with most developmental models, the stages of change overlap in some areas and maintain discrete categories in others. The model postulates a potential to become stuck in one or more stages. Additionally, the model integrates a systems-based spiral pattern accounting for relapse as an integral part of the change process.

With the key features of the model in mind, a closer examination of the stages is in order. The first stage, *precontemplation,* is characterized by the absence of motivation to change because the individual does not believe he or she has a problem. Precontemplative clients are helped to become aware of their emotional response to the negative consequences associated with the behaviors in question. Consciousness-raising interventions will help the client move to the *contemplative stage* (Prochaska & Norcross, 1999). Contemplative clients understand they have a problem and begin evaluating their options. Often, individuals in the contemplative stage are far from committing to actual change. Prochaska, DiClemente, and Norcross (1994) propose that an awareness of the problem and solution is necessary before a successful commitment to the process of change can occur. Therapists should engage clients in activities enhancing both the cognitive and emotional awareness of the problem.

The third stage, *preparation,* involves both client intentions and behaviors. Individuals in the preparation stage should be encouraged to continue small changes while carefully planning detailed schemes for action. Therapists need to provide support and encouragement for clients in the preparation phase so that they can develop a sense of self-efficacy (i.e., they believe that through their own actions they can change their lives in key ways) (Prochaska & Norcross, 1999). The *action stage* is the initiation of plans made during the preparation stage. The plans should modify the behaviors, experiences, and environments of the individual engaged in the change process. Maladaptive behaviors are not simply extinguished but countered with healthier, proactive behaviors mediated by such means as counterconditioning, stimulus control, and contingency management. During this stage, therapists should assist clients in evaluating their change process in order to continue and reinforce the momentum generated by implementing changes.

The first few months of the *maintenance stage* are the most likely time for relapse and for old behaviors to reoccur (Prochaska et al., 1994). Therefore, much of the work to be accomplished during this stage is the continued replacement of old behaviors, experiences, and environments with a healthier lifestyle. Given the increased risk of relapse during this stage, consolidation of gains and continued vigilance to the possibility of relapse is in order. Clinicians need to be especially supportive of client gains, as well as continuing to monitor for signs of relapse-related behaviors.

Relapse prevention interventions grew from the understanding that the skills needed to initiate abstinence differ from those utilized in effective abstinence maintenance (Carroll, 1997; Marlatt & Gordon, 1985). Prevention begins with an assessment for the precipitating factors leading to relapse. Studying episodes of relapse, Marlatt and Gordon (1985) identified the key precipitants: negative affect, interpersonal conflicts, and social pressure. Effective prevention strategies intervene by specifically addressing the individual's relapse precipitants. Overall, understanding the processes that lead to relapse has improved the efficacy of treatment strategies utilized with dually diagnosed clients (Carroll, 1997; Katz & Ney, 1995; Margolis & Zweben, 1998).

SUMMARY

There are a number of key points that clinicians should bear in mind when assessing for substance use disorders:

- Clinicians should routinely assess for substance use disorders and the possibility of dual diagnosis.
- Substance use disorders result from a complex interaction among biopsychosocial factors unique to each client.
- Substance abuse is a maladaptive pattern of substance use leading to significant negative consequences.
- Substance dependency is a generalized loss of control of the substance leading to negative consequences in key areas of functioning.
- Clinicians should routinely use reliable and valid assessment tools when screening for substance use disorders.
- With substance use disorders, clearly defining the problem is essential for effective treatment planning.
- Clinicians should utilize the processes of change for treatment planning and delivery.
- Effective relapse prevention strategies are a vital component of effective treatment of substance use disorders and working with dual-diagnosed clients.

References

American Psychiatric Association. (2000). *Diagnostic and statistical manual of mental disorders* (4th ed., text rev.). Washington, DC: Author.

Blow, F., Young, J., Hill, E., Singer, K., & Beresford, T. (1991). *Predictive value of brief alcoholism tests in a sample of hospitalized adults.* Fifth annual NIMH International Research Conference proceedings. Washington, DC: U.S. Government Printing Office.

Brady, S., Hiam, M.C., Saemann, R., Humbert, L., Fleming, M.Z., & Dawkins-Brickhouse, K. (1996). Dual diagnosis: A treatment model for substance abuse and major mental illness. *Community Mental Health Journal, 32,* 573–578.

Brown, S. (1995). A developmental model of alcoholism and recovery. In S. Brown & I.D. Yalom (Eds.), *Treating alcoholism* (pp. 27–56). San Francisco: Jossey-Bass.

Brown, S., & Schmid, J. (1999). Adult children of alcoholics. In P.J. Ott, R.E. Tarter, & R.T. Ammerman (Eds.), *Sourcebook on substance abuse: Etiology, epidemiology, assessment, and treatment* (2nd ed., pp. 416–429). Boston: Allyn & Bacon.

Brown, S.A., Irwin, M., & Schuckit, M.A. (1991). Changes in anxiety among abstinent male alcoholics. *Journal of Studies on Alcohol, 52,* 55–61.

Carroll, K.M. (1995). Relapse prevention as a psychosocial treatment: A review of controlled clinical trials. In G.A. Marlatt & G.R. VandenBos (Eds.), *Addictive behaviors: Readings on etiology, prevention, and treatment* (pp. 697–717). Washington, DC: American Psychological Association.

Cooney, N.L., Zweben, A., & Fleming, M.F. (1995). Screening for alcohol problems and at-risk drinking in health-care settings. In R.K. Hester & W.R. Miller (Eds.), *Handbook of alcoholism treatment approaches: An effective approach* (2nd ed., pp. 45–60). Boston: Allyn & Bacon.

Clair, D., & Genest, M. (1987). Variables associated with the adjustment of offspring of alcoholic fathers. *Journal of Studies on Alcohol, 48,* 345–355.

Crews, T.M., & Sher, K.J. (1992). Using adapted short MASTs for assessing parental alcoholism: Reliability and validity. *Alcoholism: Clinical and Experimental Research, 16,* 576–584.

Dinning, W.D., & Berk, L.A. (1989). The Children of Alcoholics Screening Test: Relationship to sex, family environment, and social adjustment in adolescents. *Journal of Clinical Psychology, 45,* 335–339.

Ewing, J.A. (1984). Detecting alcoholism: The CAGE Questionnaire. *Journal of the American Medical Association, 252,* 1905–1907.

Galanter, M., Castanada, R., & Ferman, J. (1988). Substance abuse among general psychiatric patients: Place of presentation, diagnosis, and treatment. *American Journal of Drug and Alcohol Abuse, 14,* 211–235.

Goldsmith, R.J. (1997). The elements of contemporary treatment. In N.S. Miller (Ed.), *The principles and practice of addictions in psychiatry* (pp. 392–399). Philadelphia: Saunders.

Jones, J.W. (1981–1982). *Preliminary test manual: The Children of Alcoholics Screening Test.* Chicago: Family Recovery Press.

Jones, J.W. (1985). *Children of Alcoholics Screening Test.* Chicago: Camelot Unlimited.

Katz, R.S., & Ney, N.H. (1995). Preventing relapse. In S. Brown & I.D. Yalom (Eds.), *Treating alcoholism* (pp. 231–276). San Francisco: Jossey-Bass.

Kessler, R.C., McGonagle, K.A., Zhao, S., Nelson, C.B., Hughes, M., Eshleman, S., Wittchen, H-U., & Kendler, K.S. (1994). Lifetime and twelve-month prevalence of *DSM-III-R* psychiatric disorders in the United States. *Archives of General Psychology, 51,* 8–19.

Kiesler, C.A., Simpkins, K.G., & Morton, T.L. (1991). Prevalence of dual diagnosis of mental and substance abuse disorders in general hospitals. *Hospital and Community Psychiatry, 42,* 400–403.

Margolis, R.D., & Zweben, J.E. (1998). *Treating patients with alcohol and other drug problems: An integrated approach.* Washington, DC: American Psychological Association.

Marlatt, G.A., & Gordon, J.R. (1985). *Relapse prevention: Maintenance strategies in the treatment of addictive behaviors.* New York: Guilford Press.

McGue, M. (1999). Behavioral genetic models of alcoholism and drinking. In K.E. Leonard & H.T. Blane (Eds.), *Psychological theories of drinking and alcoholism* (2nd ed., pp. 372–421). New York: Guilford Press.

Miller, W.R. (1995). Increasing motivation for change. In R.K. Hester & W.R. Miller (Eds.), *Handbook of alcoholism treatment approaches: An effective approach* (2nd ed., pp. 89–104). Boston: Allyn & Bacon.

Miller, W.R., & Brown, S.A. (1997). Why psychologists should treat alcohol and drug problems. *American Psychologist, 52*(12), 1269–1279.

Minkoff, K. (1991). Program components of a comprehensive integrated care system for seriously mentally ill patients with substance abuse disorders. *New Directions for Mental Health Services, 50,* 3–12.

Nace, E.P. (1995). The dual diagnosis patient. In S. Brown & I.D. Yalom (Eds.), *Treating alcoholism* (pp. 163–193). San Francisco: Jossey-Bass.

Perkinson, R.R. (1997). *Chemical dependency counseling: A practical guide.* Thousand Oaks, CA: Sage.

Pidcock, B., & Fischer, J.L. (1998). Parental recovery as a moderating variable of adolescent addictive behaviors. *Alcoholism Treatment Quarterly, 16,* 45–57.

Pidcock, B., Fischer, J.L., Forthun, L.F., & West, S. (2000). Hispanic and Anglo college women's risk factors for substance use and eating disorders. *Addictive Behaviors: An International Journal, 25*(5), 705–723.

Pilat, J.M., & Jones, J.W. (1984-1985). Identification of children of alcoholics: Two empirical studies. *Alcohol Health and Research World, 9,* 27–36.

Pokorny, A.D., Miller, B.A., & Kaplan, H.B. (1972). The brief MAST: A shortened version of the Michigan Alcoholism Screening Test. *American Journal of Psychiatry, 129,* 118–121.

Prochaska, J.O., DiClemente, C.C., & Norcross, J.C. (1992). In search of how people change:

Applications to addictive behaviors. *American Psychologist, 47*, 1102–1114.

Prochaska, J.O., DiClemente, C.C., & Norcross, J.C. (1994). *Changing for good.* New York: Morrow.

Prochaska, J.O., & Norcross, J.C. (1999). *Systems of psychotherapy: A transtheoretical analysis.* Pacific Grove, CA: Brooks/Cole.

Regier, D.A., Farmer, M.E., Rae, D.S., Locke, B.Z., Keith, S.J., Judd, L.L., & Goodwin, F.K. (1990). Co-morbidity of mental disorders with alcohol and other drug abuse. *Journal of the American Medical Association, 264*, 2511–2518.

Roosa, M.W., Sandler, I.N., Beals, J., & Short, J.L. (1988). Risk status of adolescent children of problem-drinking parents. *American Journal of Community Psychology, 16*, 225–239.

Schuckit, M.A. (1994). Goals of treatment. In M. Galanter & H.D. Kleber (Eds.), *Textbook of substance abuse treatment* (pp. 3–10). Washington, DC: American Psychiatric Press.

Selzer, M.L. (1971). The Michigan Alcoholism Screening Test: The quest for a new diagnostic instrument. *American Journal of Psychiatry, 127*, 1653–1658.

Selzer, M.L., Vinokur, A., & van Rooijen, L. (1975). A self-administered Short Michigan Alcoholism Screening Test (SMAST). *Journal of Studies on Alcohol, 36*, 117–176.

Sher, K.J., Wood, M.D., Crews, T.M., & Vandiver, P.A. (1995). The Tridimensional Personality Questionnaire: Reliability and validity studies and derivation of a short form. *Psychological Assessment, 7*(2), 195–208.

Sobell, M.B., & Sobell, L.C. (1978). *Behavioral treatment of alcohol problems.* New York: Plenum Press.

Sobell, M.B., & Sobell, L.C. (1993). *Problem drinkers: Guided self-change treatment.* New York: Guilford Press.

Sowers, S., & Golden, S. (1999). Psychotropic medication management in persons with co-occurring psychiatric and substance use disorders. *Journal of Psychoactive Drugs, 31*, 59–70.

Thombs, D.L. (1999). *Introduction to addictive behaviors* (2nd ed.). New York: Guilford Press.

Wallace, J. (1989). *Writings: The alcoholism papers.* Newport, RI: Edgehill.

Wallace, J. (1996). Theory of 12-step oriented treatment. In F. Rotgers, D. Keller, & J. Morgenstern (Eds.), *Treating substance abuse: Theory and technique* (pp. 117–137). New York: Guilford Press.

Yeatman, F.R., Bogart, C.J., Geer, F.A., & Sirridge, S.T. (1994). Children of Alcoholics Screening Test: Internal consistency, factor structure, and relationship to measures of family environment. *Journal of Clinical Psychology, 50*, 931–936.

Zung, B.J., & Charalampous, K.D. (1975). Item analysis of the Michigan Alcoholism Screening Test. *Journal of Studies on Alcohol, 36*, 127–132.

20 MANAGEMENT OF PERSONALITY DISORDERS

Darcy Haag Granello and Paul F. Granello

The *Diagnostic and Statistical Manual,* fourth edition, text revised (*DSM-IV-TR*), of the American Psychiatric Association (APA) defines personality disorders as "enduring patterns of perceiving, relating to, and thinking about the environment and oneself that are exhibited in a wide range of social and personal contexts" (APA, 2000, p. 685). These patterns have an onset of no later than early adulthood and are inflexible and maladaptive, resulting in significant impairment in social or occupational functioning. The personality disorders are coded on Axis II, and the *DSM-IV* includes 10 specific diagnoses, grouped into three clusters: Cluster A, the odd-eccentric cluster (paranoid, schizoid, schizotypal); Cluster B, the dramatic-emotional cluster (antisocial, borderline, histrionic, narcissistic); and Cluster C, the anxious-fearful cluster (avoidant, dependent, obsessive-compulsive). There is also a classification for Personality Disorder, Not Otherwise Specified (NOS), that is not included in any specific cluster. The NOS diagnosis is intended for persons who meet the general criteria for a personality disorder but whose symptoms do not meet the criteria for any specific disorder. Additionally, maladaptive personality traits that do not meet the threshold for a personality disorder can be coded on Axis II, with the proper notation that differentiates traits from the full-blown disorder; for example, the clinician would record: Axis II: V71.09, no diagnosis, with borderline personality traits.

With the exception of Avoidant Personality Disorder, the personality disorders tend to be *ego-syntonic*. That is, persons with these disorders typically do not perceive their actions to be problematic, blaming the actions of those around them for their distress. This differs significantly from most of the major Axis I disorders, which are typically *ego-dystonic*, or troubling to the person with the diagnosis. Thus, persons with personality disorders often make poor historians, and it may be necessary to solicit supplementary information from other sources when making a diagnosis.

PREVALENCE AND COMORBIDITY ISSUES

Personality disorders have high rates of prevalence, although accurate rates are difficult to measure. One problem is with assessment, as there are no instruments available to accurately diagnose a personality disorder.

There is also a lack of clinical focus, with treatment typically focusing on Axis I disorders, and comorbid Axis II disorders remaining undiagnosed. In addition, people with personality disorders seldom seek treatment for their personality disorder, given the ego-syntonic nature of the disorders. Only about one-fifth of people with an Axis II diagnosis receive treatment for the disorder, and most who enter treatment do so because of coexisting Axis I disorders. Thus, estimates of prevalence are imprecise, and range from 10% to 13% in community samples (Crits-Christoph, 1998) to up to 60% in clinical samples (Kaplan & Sadock, 1998).

People with personality disorders are notoriously difficult to treat, and most of the literature focuses on helping people to manage their disorders or controlling the behaviors or symptoms associated with their disorders. Clients with personality disorders often terminate treatment prematurely (Seligman, 1998). In one study with persons with Paranoid Personality Disorder, more than 90% of the participants dropped out before the completion of treatment (Mavissakalian & Hamann, 1987).

Treatment with clients with personality disorders is often long term, with clients entering and leaving therapy many times during their lives. Comorbidity with Axis I disorders is very high. For example, between 36% and 76% of clients with anxiety disorders and 36% to 65% of clients with mood disorders also have a coexisting personality disorder (Ruegg & Frances, 1995). In other studies, 39% of clients with bulimia had a comorbid personality disorder (Fahy, Eisler, & Russell, 1993), and 20% of clients with Obsessive-Compulsive Disorder also fit the criteria for Borderline Personality Disorder (Hermesh, Shahar, & Munitz, 1987).

These comorbidity rates underscore the importance of accurate diagnosis of a coexisting personality disorder when treating Axis I disorders. The presence of a personality disorder can significantly impact the treatment of other disorders, but because they are often not the focus of treatment, they can go undetected. Many studies have found that the presence of a personality disorder can severely limit the treatment effectiveness of Axis I disorders (e.g., Granello, Granello, & Lee, 1999).

Additionally, the high rates of comorbidity among Axis I and Axis II disorders can significantly affect the ability of clients to manage their personality disorders. For example, substance abuse is very high among clients with Axis II disorders, often as an attempt to self-medicate. Thus, management of the personality disorder often cannot begin until the substance abuse issues are under control. Using data from the Epidemiological Catchment Area Program, Swartz, Blazer, George, and Winfield (1990) found that for people with the diagnosis of Borderline Personality Disorder, many had coexisting Axis I disorders that interfered with their ability to manage their personality disorder. These included Generalized Anxiety Disorder (56%), Major Depression (41%), Agoraphobia (37%), Social Phobia (35%), Posttraumatic Stress Disorder (34%), and alcohol/substance abuse (22%).

A final difficulty with comorbidity is the high rates of coexisting disorders within the personality disorders themselves. Although the diagnostic categories appear discreet in the *DSM-IV-TR* (APA, 2000), in reality, many clients have overlapping symptoms and meet the criteria for several personality disorders simultaneously. For example, between 30% and 56% of clients with Paranoid Personality Disorder also meet the criteria for Narcissistic Personality Disorder, and up to 50% of clients with Avoidant Personality Disorder also meet the criteria for Schizotypal Personality Disorder (Zimmerman & Coryell, 1990). It is uncertain whether Axis II overlaps such as these represent true comorbidity or whether they occur because of deficiencies in the current conceptualizations of personality disorders or because of limitations in currently available measures of assessment (Alden, 1989). Regardless of the cause, the overlap between the personality disorders makes controlled studies of individual personality disorders extremely difficult to conduct and makes the findings of such research difficult to apply to clients with multiple Axis II diagnoses.

OVERALL TREATMENT CONSIDERATIONS

Despite the high prevalence of personality disorders in both the clinical and general population, there is a lack of empirical research on treatment. The vast majority of writing is in the form of theoretical analysis or case report. Thus, from a research perspective, very little can be said about the management of the individual personality disorders.

In general, a multifaceted approach that emphasizes cognitive and behavioral interventions is the strategy emerging in the literature. Cognitive interventions, focusing on identifying and challenging irrational thoughts, are gradually shifted from the thoughts that trigger the presenting symptoms to the core thoughts that underlie the dysfunction of the personality disorder (Beck & Freeman, 1990). Behavioral therapy has been reported to enhance treatment success, particularly to modify extremely dysfunctional and self-destructive behavioral patterns (Seligman, 1998). These approaches appear to be more effective in the overall management of the disorder than the psychodynamic approach, although this preference has not been validated by research. There is some concern that a psychodynamic approach may be ineffective, given the lack of insight evidenced by most people with personality disorders (Armstrong, Cox, Short, & Allman, 1991). Psychoeducational groups that emphasize life skills training may be appropriate, with a focus on social skills, life management (e.g., personal care, time management, cooking, nutrition), problem-solving training, and self-control skills (e.g., emotion regulation, distress tolerance). In-patient or day treatment programs may be necessary during acute exacerbations (Piper, Joyce, Azim, & Rosie, 1994).

Clinicians may want to use adjuncts to individual therapy, including family and couples counseling. The behaviors exhibited by the client with a personality disorder are often maintained in relationships that allow the dysfunction to continue. Therefore, these same relationships must be altered to allow the dysfunction to diminish (Benjamin, 1993). Additionally, the use of self-help groups (e.g.,

Alcoholic Anonymous) may be useful for clients struggling with substance abuse in addition to their personality disorder. Finally, because of disruptions in occupational functioning, career counseling may be an important adjunct to therapy.

SPECIFIC TREATMENT RECOMMENDATIONS BY DISORDER

Paranoid Personality Disorder

There are no controlled studies for treatment of Paranoid Personality Disorder, but case reports and nonrandomized studies have shown support for several interventions. A behavioral deficit and skills training approach that teaches clients to monitor their behavioral deficits (e.g., infrequent eye contact, flat affect) and specific skills to overcome these deficits has met with some success, as have cognitive interventions. However, it should be noted that clients with Paranoid Personality Disorder have extremely high dropout rates, and treatment gains for those who remain come very slowly. Challenging the underlying defenses may lead to a loss of self-esteem, and clinicians must take care not to engage in the client's argumentative or threatening style. Because trust and intimacy are core concerns to these clients, clinicians should be honest and straightforward in all interactions and limit their interpretations of client behaviors, which may prove to be too threatening. A professional stance, rather than an overly warm one, will benefit the therapeutic relationship.

Schizoid Personality Disorder

Individuals with Schizoid Personality Disorder are rarely motivated to enter treatment. When they do, therapy should be aimed at achieving modest reductions in social isolation and in promoting more effective adjustment to new circumstances. Anecdotal reports suggest some success with cognitive interventions and social skills interventions (Kalus, Bernsteing,

& Siever, 1995). Individuals with this disorder use fantasy as a defense and have extreme difficulty establishing and maintaining relationships. Thus, these clients need a quiet, reassuring clinician who can maintain interest in them without requiring a reciprocal response. Although they can join group counseling with more success than clients with Paranoid Personality Disorder, they must be protected from aggressive group members who challenge their silence (Kaplan & Sadock, 1998).

Schizotypal Personality Disorder

A combination of social skills training, including attention to interpersonal boundaries, and educative therapy, including reality testing, has been advocated in the literature on this disorder (Stone, 1985), although no controlled studies exist. Anecdotal reports suggest that these clients tend to decompensate in unstructured psychotherapy, and it should be noted that as many as 25% of people with Schizotypal Personality Disorder develop schizophrenia. There have been some reports that clients with moderately severe symptoms can benefit from the use of neuroleptics, although problems may arise with medication compliance. Case management issues are particularly important, as many struggle to maintain housing, food, and employment.

Antisocial Personality Disorder

These clients are typically involuntary and therefore have limited motivation for treatment. Because of their ability to manipulate others, it is essential that clinicians develop and maintain firm limits and frequently analyze the client's actions and statements for the possibility that they are part of the manipulation of the therapist. Although there are no randomized, controlled studies, there are many uncontrolled studies and narrative reports. This emphasis in the literature underlies the importance of finding effective treatment interventions for these clients and reveals the intractability of the disorder. There seems to be no intervention that yields consistently positive results. Suggested interventions include reality therapy to promote an understanding of consequences of behavior, behavioral therapy to promote problem-solving and decision-making skills, and cognitive therapy to promote moral development, abstract thinking, and modification of dysfunctional thoughts (Seligman, 1998). Medication, primarily to address anger and underlying mood disorders, is sometimes recommended (Sperry, 1995), but must be used with caution, given the propensity of these individuals toward substance abuse.

Borderline Personality Disorder

There are few empirical studies but many anecdotal reports of attempts to manage this disorder. All authors emphasize the importance of boundaries and the use of the therapeutic relationship to provide a corrective emotional experience. Linehan's Dialectical Behavioral Therapy (DBT) (1993) has been promoted for the treatment of clients with severe Borderline Personality Disorder; it includes goal setting to increase safety and stability and emotional containment. Others advocate a combination of affect facilitation (learning that emotional expression does not necessarily lead to harm), holding without overcontaining (setting firm boundaries and structure only about important issues), safety contracts, and an up-front understanding of time-limited treatment (Miller, 1995). Cognitive therapy also has been promoted, but must be done within the context of an extremely supportive relationship. Hospitalizations for periods of acute exacerbations may be necessary to keep these clients alive.

Histrionic Personality Disorder

Uncontrolled studies and reports from the field underscore the importance of addressing the underlying defenses of denial and repression. Feelings identification and clarification is important to the therapeutic process (Kaplan & Sadock, 1998) for those with this disorder. Two

important components of treatment are helping clients define the onset of the repression and clarifying the reality of their relationships with others, rather than allowing clients' feelings to define that reality (Andrews, 1984). Clinicians are cautioned to monitor the erotic transference that is common with histrionic clients (Seligman, 1998). Cognitive therapy may be effective, but reliance on cognitions and logic is likely to be a very new experience for these individuals (Beck & Freeman, 1990). Helping clients search for and define reality and blocking attempts to "play games" with the clinician can help build transferable skills and aid in problem solving and decision making. To prevent premature termination, cognitive therapy should be attempted only after a strong therapeutic alliance has been formed, and challenges to irrational thoughts must never be perceived as an attack. Finally, some clients may benefit from medications to ease the symptoms of mood disorders that often accompany this disorder. However, the distribution of the medication must be tightly monitored, as clients with Histrionic Personality Disorder are prone to substance abuse and suicidal gestures.

Narcissistic Personality Disorder

With no controlled studies and very little research or field-based accounts available, limited inferences can be made about treatment of this disorder. Some anecdotal reports have indicated that a psychodynamic approach may be more warranted with these clients than with the other personality disorders. However, this insight-oriented approach would be warranted only for those with a mild dysfunction who have some motivation to engage in therapy (Seligman, 1998). One approach includes gentle cognitive reorientation to establish a baseline of rapport between the client and clinician; then a more direct approach can be gradually integrated. The goal is to probe and modify self attitudes and social habits. Millon (1996) suggested group or family therapy to provide feedback to the client, but cautions that intensive feedback can be very wounding to their highly defended egos and must be integrated slowly.

Avoidant Personality Disorder

There is a strong overlap in the *DSM-IV-TR* (APA, 2000) criteria between Avoidant Personality Disorder and Social Phobia, and many of the same interventions are used. Behavioral therapy, common to treatment of all the phobias, is a cornerstone of treatment for clients with Avoidant Personality Disorder. However, because of their fragility, behavior therapy must not be attempted until there is a strong and trusting therapeutic alliance (Kaplan & Sadock, 1998). Behavioral tasks that encourage social contact must be taken in very small increments, as failure can reinforce feelings of humiliation and low self-esteem. Group therapy may be useful to help clients understand their interpersonal sensitivity, and assertiveness training has received some attention as an important adjunct to therapy. Cognitive therapy has been supported anecdotally, with therapeutic interventions reinforcing the idea that the catastrophizing thoughts of the client seldom come to fruition in real-world contacts.

Dependent Personality Disorder

Although the diagnosis of all personality disorders must be made in culturally appropriate ways, this is particularly true of the diagnosis of Dependent Personality Disorder, where care must be taken not to diagnose a woman who is acting in a culturally appropriate sex role. Treatment of the disorder depends on a strong therapeutic relationship in which the clinician can gradually encourage independence and self-assertion within the counseling relationship. Small steps toward establishing more independence can be reinforced with relaxation techniques to help lessen the anxiety that comes with decision making. More than with other disorders, the person with Dependent Personality Disorder relies on relationships that support and maintain the dysfunctional behavior. Therefore, family and couples counseling is particularly important to help significant

others accept and reinforce the changes the client is making. These clients respond well to therapy that is directive and active, but the clinician must take care not to become the object of the client's attachment.

Obsessive-Compulsive Personality Disorder

No outcome studies on this disorder have been conducted, and reports from the field suggest that treatment of these clients is long and complex, with many clinicians experiencing strong countertransference. Cognitive therapies have met with some success, and clients with Obsessive-Compulsive Personality Disorder tend to respond well to interventions that are cognitive, nonemotional, structured, problem-focused, and present-oriented (Beck & Freeman, 1990). Others have recommended a combination of cognitive therapy (e.g., self-monitoring, thought stopping) with behavioral interventions (e.g., guided imagery, relaxation, self-practice) (Sperry, 1995). Group therapy also may be used as an adjunct, but clinicians may find that they have to keep these clients from monopolizing the group.

SUMMARY

Although personality disorders remain very difficult to treat, there is evidence that therapeutic interventions can help clients manage many of the symptoms of these disorders. Research is extremely limited, but generally suggests a cognitive-behavioral approach that focuses on symptom management rather than insight-oriented therapy. Common therapy adjuncts include psychoeducational groups, life skills groups, problem-solving training, and family therapy. Clinicians working with these clients are cautioned to make thorough diagnositic assessments to check for comorbid Axis I and Axis II disorders that can significantly affect treatment. Finally, clinicians are reminded that therapy with these clients can be a long-term endeavor, with clients entering treatment during acute exacerbations of the disorder and leaving when these symptoms are in remission.

References

Alden, L. (1989). Short-term structured treatment for avoidant personality disorder. *Journal of Consulting and Clinical Psychology, 57*, 756–764.

American Psychiatric Association. (2000). *Diagnostic and statistical manual of mental disorders* (4th ed., text rev.). Washington, DC: Author.

Andrews, J. (1984). Psychotherapy with the hysterical personality: An interpersonal approach. *Psychiatry, 47*, 211–232.

Armstrong, H.E., Cox, G.B., Short, B.A., & Allmon, D.J. (1991). A comparative evaluation of two day treatment programs. *Psychosocial Rehabilitation Journal, 14*, 53–67.

Beck, A.T., & Freeman, A. (1990). *Cognitive therapy of personality disorders.* New York: Guilford Press.

Benjamin, L.S. (1993). *Interpersonal diagnosis and treatment of personality disorders.* New York: Guilford Press.

Crits-Christoph, P. (1998). Psychosocial treatments for personality disorders. In P.E. Nathan & J.M. Gorman (Eds.), *A guide to treatments that work* (pp. 544–553). New York: Oxford University Press.

Fahy, T.A., Eisler, I., & Russell, G.F. (1993). Personality disorder and treatment response in bulimia nervosa. *British Journal of Psychiatry, 162*, 765–770.

Granello, D.H., Granello, P.F., & Lee, F. (1999). Measuring treatment outcomes and client satisfaction in a partial hospitalization program. *Journal of Behavioral Health Services and Research, 26*, 50–63.

Hermesh, H., Shahar, A., & Munitz, H. (1987). Obsessive-compulsive disorder and borderline personality disorder. *American Journal of Psychiatry, 144*, 120–121.

Kalus, O., Bernstein, D.P., & Siever, L.J. (1994). Schizoid personality disorder. In W.J. Livesley (Ed.), *The DSM-IV personality disorders* (pp. 58–70). New York: Guilford Press.

Kaplan, H.I., & Sadock, B.J. (1998). *Synopsis of psychiatry: Behavioral sciences/clinical psychiatry* (8th ed.). Baltimore: Williams & Wilkins.

Linehan, M.M. (1993). *Cognitive-behavioral treatment of borderline personality disorder.* New York: Guilford Press.

Mavissakalian, M., & Hamann, M.S. (1987). *DSM-III* personality disorder in agoraphobia: II. Changes with treatment. *Comprehensive Psychiatry, 28*, 356–361.

Miller, B.C. (1995). Characteristics of effective day treatment programming for persons with borderline personality disorder. *Psychiatric Services, 46*, 605–608.

Millon, T.E. (1996). *Disorders of personality: DSM-IV and beyond.* New York: Wiley.

Piper, W.E., Joyce, A.S., Azim, H.F.A., & Rosie, J.S. (1994). Patient characteristics and success in day treatment. *Journal of Nervous and Mental Disease, 182*, 381–386.

Ruegg, R., & Frances, A. (1995). New research on personality disorders. *Journal of Personality Disorders, 9*, 1–48.

Seligman, L. (1998). *Selecting effective treatments.* San Francisco: Jossey-Bass.

Sperry, L. (1995). *Handbook of diagnosis and treatment of the DSM-IV personality disorders.* New York: Brunner/Mazel.

Stone, J. (1985). Schizotypal personality: Psychotherapeutic aspects. *Schizophrenia Bulletin, 11*, 576–589.

Swartz, M., Blazer, D., George, L., & Winfield, I. (1990). Estimating the prevalence of borderline personality disorder in the community. *Journal of Personality Disorders, 4*, 257–272.

Zimmerman, M., & Coryell, W.H. (1990). *DSM-III* personality disorder dimensions. *Journal of Nervous and Mental Diseases, 178*, 686–692.

Recommended Readings and Additional Information

Beck, A.T., & Freeman, A. (1990). *Cognitive therapy for personality disorders.* New York: Guilford Press.

Mental Health Net. (2000). www.personalitydisorders.mentalhelp.net

Millon, T.E. (1996). *Disorders of personality: DSM-IV and beyond.* New York: Wiley.

Sperry, L. (1995). *Handbook of diagnosis and treatment of the DSM-IV personality disorders.* New York: Brunner/Mazel.

Sperry, L. (1999). *Cognitive-behavior therapy of DSM-IV personality disorders: Highly effective interventions for the most common personality disorders.* Philadelphia: Brunner/Mazel.

21 SCHIZOPHRENIA AND SEVERE MENTAL ILLNESS

Guidelines for Assessment, Treatment, and Referral

Susan Bichsel

The focus of this chapter is on the severe mental illnesses, more recently referred to as neurobiological disorders. The term severe mental illness was defined in 1993 by the National Mental Health Advisory Council, an arm of the National Institute of Mental Health, as including "disorders with psychotic symptoms such as schizophrenia, schizoaffective disorder, manic depressive disorder, autism, as well as severe forms of other disorders such as major depression, panic disorder, and obsessive compulsive disorder" (National Mental Health Advisory Council, 1993). The National Mental Health Advisory Council has determined that in any one-year period, 2.8% of the adult population in the United States is affected by severe mental illness. This means that in any given year in the United States, approximately 5.5 million individuals are diagnosed with a neurobiological disorder.

ARE MENTAL ILLNESSES TREATABLE?

It is a persistent myth that there are no effective forms of treatment for individuals with severe mental illness. However, according to the 1993 report of the National Mental Health Advisory Council, the efficacy of many treatments for severe mental disorders is comparable to that of other branches of medicine, including surgery. For example, in the treatment of schizophrenia and Schizoaffective Disorder, research has shown that traditional antipsychotic medication is effective in reducing psychotic symptoms in 60% of patients and in 70% to 85% of those experiencing symptoms for the first time (National Mental Health Advisory Council, 1993). The "second-generation" antipsychotics, such as clozapine, risperidone, and olanzapine, are effective for an additional 33% of individuals with psychosis who do not respond to the traditional antipsychotics. In the treatment of Bipolar Disorder, approximately 75% of individuals respond to lithium, carbemazepine, or a combination of several medications. For severe depression, at least 80% of individuals respond to tricyclics (Elavil, Norpramine), selective serotonin reuptake inhibitors (SSRIs) such as Prozac and Zoloft, or monoamine oxidase inhibitors (MAOIs) such as Nardil and Parnate. For severe Panic Disorder, between 70% and 90% of individuals respond to an antidepressant or benzodiazapine class of medication. Of all the severe mental illnesses, only autism has no effective medication options at this time (Torrey, 1997).

In addition to pharmacological treatment, many individuals benefit from rehabilitative and supportive counseling (Carter, 1998; Fenton & McGlashon, 1997; Hellkamp, 1993; Kates & Rockland, 1994; Kopelowicz & Liberman, 1998; Mueser & Gingerich, 1994; Mueser & Glynn, 1993). In fact, contrary to the prevailing myths surrounding severe mental illness, there are effective treatments for the majority of individuals who are diagnosed with these disorders. In many instances, multiple interventions are most effective when done conjointly, although the timing of various interventions should be adjusted in accordance with individual need (Fenton & McGlashon, 1997; Kates & Rockland, 1994). Most forms of mental illness require a careful coordination of drug therapy accompanied by social work, nursing, case management, family education, and counseling interventions. Most promising, in a 30-year longitudinal study, Harding, Zubin, and Strauss (1992) reported that 66% of individuals treated for severe mental illness were capable of achieving considerable improvement and recovery. These individuals were eventually capable of integrating successfully into the community with jobs, families, friends, and homes.

Nonetheless, according to the National Mental Health Advisory Council, only 60% of adults diagnosed with severe mental illness receive treatment in any given year. For schizophrenia, the treatment rate is even lower, with only 50% of affected individuals receiving necessary treatment (Von Korff et al., 1985). One of the most serious problems in the treatment of schizophrenia is the refusal to take prescribed medications, largely because of their unpleasant side effects. Although only a few patients refuse medications entirely, nearly 50% stop taking them in the first year and nearly 75% in the first two years (Harvard Medical School, 1992). These data are of particular concern, as research shows that an individual's acceptance or rejection of prescribed medications is the single greatest determinant of effective treatment (Fenton, Blyler, & Heinssen, 1997). Patients who do not take antipsychotic medications will probably receive little benefit from any other kind of treatment.

Torrey (1995) argues that low treatment rates are a direct effect of changes in state laws that made involuntary hospitalization and treatment more difficult to utilize for individuals with little insight into their illnesses. Indeed, debate persists among civil rights lawyers, patient advocates, family members, and providers about an individual's "right" to be psychotic (Torrey, 1997; Woolis, 1992). Whatever the cause of

treatment and medication rejection by patients, individuals with mental illness who are not following prescribed treatment regimens are more likely to be at risk for self-neglect, combativeness, and/or aggressiveness (Torrey, 1997). Studies have shown that the vast majority of individuals with schizophrenia are not violent towards others; a small number of them, however, when left untreated, are.

THE SOCIAL COSTS OF SEVERE MENTAL ILLNESS

Schizophrenia is one of the most common and serious of the mental illnesses. In the United States alone, there are approximately 2.5 million people diagnosed with the disease (Mueser & Gingerich, 1994, NARSAD, 1987; Regier, Farmer, Lock, Keith, & Rae, 1993). While the diagnosis of schizophrenia is complicated by a wide variance in symptomatology, individual difference, and outcome, epidemiological research consistently reports its incidence in the general population at between 0.5% to 2.5%, regardless of culture, gender, or time in history (APA, 1994). Approximately 20% of all individuals with chronic disability (including physical and mental illnesses) are diagnosed with schizophrenia (Mueser & Gingerich, 1994). In this country alone, more than 1 million people with schizophrenia account for 75% of all mental health expenditures (Harvard Medical School, 1995). These numbers do not include the additional 1.1 million individuals in the United States diagnosed with Bipolar Disorder, and the even larger number with severe depression or Obsessive-Compulsive Disorder (Torrey, 1995).

The annual cost of treating severe mental illness for patients, family members, and the community is extraordinary. In the United States, the cost each year is believed to exceed $48 billion for schizophrenia alone (NARSAD, 1987). This total includes the costs of medical treatment, social security payments, and wages lost because of illness for every person diagnosed with the disease. The shift from treating people with mental illness in institutions to treating them in outpatient mental health centers, although fiscally appealing, has further complicated the treatment of this complex illness (Rose, 1979). As a result of deinstitutionalization, illnesses such as schizophrenia have been thrust into the political and social spheres with related issues such as housing discrimination, homelessness, poor medical access and care, patient civil rights, poverty, and social stigma compounding what is already a devastating experience for people who are ill.

Studies show that after several psychotic episodes, many individuals diagnosed with schizophrenia are found on the street, in a public shelter, or in jail (Koegel, Burnam, & Farr, 1988). According to most estimates, 25% to 30% of homeless individuals have severe mental illness (Harvard Medical School, 1992). A 1992 survey of American jails reported that 7.2% of the inmates were seriously mentally ill with acute symptoms. A shocking 29% of the jails acknowledged holding these individuals without any charges against them, often awaiting a bed in a psychiatric hospital. The vast majority of individuals with charges against them had been charged with misdemeanors such as trespassing (Torrey, 1995). Without adequate resources, these individuals are more likely to become victimized by engaging in unsafe sexual practices (AIDS) or using and abusing drugs and alcohol. Indeed, data from the National Institute of Mental Health's (NIMH) Epidemiologic Catchment Area Survey of 1992 established a lifetime rate of substance abuse among people with schizophrenia at 47% (Harvard Medical School, 1995).

The suicide rate in the general population is around 1%; it is 10% to 13% for individuals diagnosed with schizophrenia (Caldwell & Gottesman, 1990; Roy, 1992). A staggering 50% of people with schizophrenia attempt suicide at one point in their lives (Mueser & Glynn, 1993). Suicide is also the most frequent cause of premature death for individuals with schizophrenia (Saarinen, Lehtonen, & Lonnqvist, 1999). According to the NIMH, an additional 20% of individuals with untreated Bipolar Disorder die of suicide; 75% of these victims are men.

THE DIAGNOSIS OF SCHIZOPHRENIA

The schizophrenia spectrum disorders are a group of psychiatric disorders that are thought to be similar in onset, symptoms, levels of impairment, and response to treatment (Mueser & Gingerich, 1994). These disorders include Schizophrenia, Schizophreniform Disorder, Schizoaffective Disorder, and Schizotypal Personality Disorder. The schizophrenias are broken down by the *Diagnostic and Statistical Manual* of the American Psychiatric Association (*DSM-IV*) into four distinct types: paranoid, undifferentiated, disorganized, and catatonic. The four subtypes of schizophrenia are thought to vary somewhat in etiology, course, treatment response, and outcome. For example, people diagnosed with paranoid schizophrenia are thought to have a later onset and better prognosis, whereas individuals diagnosed with the disorganized subtype tend to have an earlier onset, poor premorbid functioning, and a less significant remission or recovery.

Many individuals experience a mix of symptoms and do not fall neatly into one of the four subtypes. For example, Schizoaffective Disorder is the presence of both the symptoms characteristic of schizophrenia and of a concurrent mood disorder. Individuals with schizotypal Personality Disorder, though experiencing milder symptoms, function only marginally better than patients with schizophrenia. A significant number of individuals who have Schizotypal Personality Disorder at a younger age gradually develop Schizophrenia or Schizoaffective Disorder later in life (Mueser & Gingerich, 1994).

Identifying the Illness

Schizophrenia is a complex and confusing illness for mental health professionals, family members, and patients. It is an episodic and unpredictable illness with symptoms that vary in intensity at different times during its course. The specific symptoms of schizophrenia are well documented, including the presence of positive symptoms, negative symptoms, or both. The positive symptoms of schizophrenia describe the presence of hallucinations, delusions, loose associations, disordered thinking, and impairment in reality testing. The negative symptoms include affective flattening (a restriction in the range and intensity of emotional response), alogia (poverty of speech and content), and avolition, or non-goal-directed behavior (Andreasen & Olsen, 1982). Severe negative symptoms are strongly associated with poor social functioning and are relatively stable over time (Mueser & Glynn, 1993). Cognitive disorganization (confused thought and speech) has at times been regarded as both a positive and negative symptom, as well as being in a distinct category of its own (Harvard Medical School, 1995).

Symptoms of all of the schizophrenia spectrum disorders are most likely to appear from late adolescence to the late twenties, with the emergence of symptoms in males generally appearing earlier than in females (Angermeyer & Kuhn, 1988; Kopelowicz & Liberman, 1998). There is a form of late-onset schizophrenia that begins after the age of 40. The exact incidence of late-onset schizophrenia is unclear, but it is not rare (Torrey, 1995). Clinically, late-onset schizophrenia is similar to the other schizophrenias except for the fact that more females than males are affected. It is generally believed that childhood schizophrenia also resembles the adult disease, although it is much more rare. Only 2% of individuals with schizophrenia have the onset of their disease in childhood, with two males affected for every one female (Torrey, 1995). However, in the United States, nearly 75% of individuals with schizophrenia experience their first symptoms between the ages of 17 and 25.

Just prior to an initial psychotic break, individuals can experience a prodromal phase to their illness. During this period of time, there is a growing deterioration in the functioning of the individual, increased eccentricity, odd ideation, and withdrawal from others (Mueser & Glynn, 1993). Counselors who do not specialize in the treatment of severe mental illness should be aware of these early signs of mental illness in some people. Increasingly bizarre, withdrawn, or paranoid behavior on the part of a young adult who presents for individual or marital counseling may denote the early signs of an emerging mental illness. Other signs indicating the onset of severe mental illness include dramatic changes in sleep pattern, severe depression, confused thinking, and extreme highs and lows (Carter, 1994). The individual may sleep less, or more, or at unusual times. As Torrey (1995) states, "Some patients simply begin talking in a vague way in the early stages of their illness, with tangential thoughts that sound almost, but not quite, logical" (p. 96). An early and accurate diagnosis of mental illness is critical, as there is evidence to suggest that long delays in treating early episodes of schizophrenia contribute to a poor outcome (Wiersma, Nienhaus, Slooff, & Giel, 1998). Recent studies indicate that individuals who receive no drug therapy during their first psychotic episode will spend more time in mental hospitals during the next three to five years (Harvard Medical School, 1995).

THE ROLE OF THE COUNSELOR

Many mental health professionals are led to believe that there is no role for counseling and psychotherapy in the treatment of people with mental illness (Fenton & McGlashon, 1997; Hellkamp, 1993; Kates & Rockland, 1994). This is probably one result of the stigma still surrounding these illnesses. Nonetheless, there are a number of critical roles for counselors in the treatment of mental illness, including work with the individuals who experience the illness as well as with the family members affected by it. Moreover, there is evidence that a therapeutic relationship, when used in addition to drug therapy, is helpful in reducing the rehospitalization rate for schizophrenia (Fenton & McGlashon, 1997; Hogarty et al., 1995; Kopelowicz & Liberman, 1998; Rapp, 1998).

One critical role for the counselor is that of making an accurate differential diagnosis. Prior to diagnosing a client with schizophrenia or other psychotic disorder, other physical illnesses should first be ruled out by the treating medical professional (Kopelowicz & Liberman, 1998; Torrey, 1995). Some of the most common illnesses that can mimic symptoms of schizophrenia include tumors of the pituitary gland, viral encephalitis, temporal lobe epilepsy, cerebral syphilis, multiple sclerosis, Huntington's disease, and, most recently, AIDS. The most effective way to rule out these diseases is by referring the patient for a complete diagnostic workup, including basic laboratory work (blood count, urinalysis), a neurological examination, an MRI scan, a mental health exam, and psychological tests.

Childbirth can also lead to severe depression in a minority of women. Once in approximately 1,000 births, a new mother can develop schizophrenia-like symptoms. These symptoms typically develop three to seven days postpartum and dissipate rather quickly with appropriate medication (Torrey, 1995). This disorder appears related to schizophrenia in its biochemical and hormonal properties, but is not considered to be a form of schizophrenia. Most women recover within two weeks of onset.

A number of street drugs will also cause an individual to experience psychotic symptoms that may be difficult to differentiate from thought disorders such as schizophrenia and Bipolar Disorder (Rosenthal & Miner, 1997). Drugs such as LSD, PCP, and amphetamines such as speed will produce hallucinations, delusions, and disorders of thinking. It can be difficult to accurately diagnose an individual before the presence of these substances completely leaves the body. Even then, such as with amphetamine psychosis, recurrent psychotic symptoms may be observed many months after the last use of the drug (Kopelowicz & Liberman, 1998). Prescription drugs have also been known to cause symptoms that mimic schizophrenia and other disorders. Side effects of certain medications in some individuals can include depression, hallucinations, and paranoid delusions. In most cases, these side effects appear when a new drug is introduced and will quickly disappear when the drug is discontinued (Torrey, 1995). A thorough medical evaluation and physical should help clarify the origin of these symptoms in most cases.

It is generally considered sound clinical practice to work as one member of an interdisciplinary team in the treatment of severe mental illness (Hellkamp, 1993; Kopelowicz & Liberman, 1998). Given the exceedingly complex nature of these illnesses (including biological, social, and psychological factors), the client, the family, and the counselor benefit from being part of a larger team of professionals. The vast majority of individuals with severe mental illness are referred to many different agencies to access the services they need (Harvard Medical School, 1995; Mueser & Gingerich, 1994). These agencies and organizations are frequently governed and funded by different local, state, and federal bodies, who in turn may or may not have any relationship with each other. For the most part, this translates into poor communication among agencies on behalf of any particular client, and clients as well as family members frequently lose their way working through this tangled web.

Case management services were designed in part to address these challenges. Case managers, also known as community support workers, typically work out of community mental health centers that were developed in the 1960s to address the needs of patients discharged from state institutions (Mueser, Bond, Drake, & Resnick, 1998; Rapp, 1998; Rapp & Chamberlain, 1985). Case managers are responsible for addressing the social and medical needs of their clients as well as coordinating and monitoring overall treatment (Mueser & Gingerich, 1994). Case managers also refer clients to appropriate housing and to agencies that can assist with financial and medical benefits, such as the Social Security Administration and Medicare. Case management services also provide direct assistance with managing the client's illness, including medication monitoring, family education, and assistance with the tasks of daily living (Kopelowicz & Liberman, 1998). Thus, it is imperative that the case manager work collaboratively with the patient and the other members of the treatment team such as the counselor, psychiatrist, and vocational specialist.

Recent research on treating severe mental illness includes an understanding of these illnesses that takes into consideration an interactive developmental perspective (Strauss, 1989). This way of looking at mental illness seeks not only to understand how the illness unfolds, but also how the illness is affected and influenced by interaction with the environment. Strauss suggests that individuals have a relationship with their illnesses that has the potential to influence course and outcome. As Estroff (1989) writes, schizophrenia is an "I am" illness, one that can take over and define the identity of the person touched. As a cultural anthropologist, Estroff is concerned, too, that the relationships between self and sickness have not been adequately researched with reference to their influence on prognosis. Estroff suggests that the degree to which a person's identity is eroded by schizophrenia may rest on how the person locates or situates the illness in relation to his or her sense of self. She writes, "It seems entirely possible that for some individuals the illness is experienced as an object, and for others it is more of a self-object, while for others it is inseparable from the self" (p. 194). Estroff asks a series of questions: Who and what existed before the illness, and who or what endures after? Is there an after with schizophrenia, or only a before? Is there an identity after mental illness? Is it inevitable that a person with schizophrenia becomes schizophrenic? These researchers propose that the ways in which patients and their treating professionals respond to and address the above issues may significantly influence the course and outcome of these illnesses.

This type of conceptualization of the *experience* of mental illness provides a framework for counselors in this field. As opposed to treating the biological illness itself, counselors can serve a critical adjunctive function by helping the ill individual adapt to the concept of having a chronic illness and its impact on the self. As Rapp (1998) points out, one goal of supportive counseling is to encourage individuals with mental illness to adopt a self-perception where the illness is "one and only one part of me" (p. 66). Rapp believes that in many instances, mental health professionals and the systems in which they work have institutionalized low expectations for people with mental illness. He depicts the role of the helper as being one that empowers individuals with mental illness by being sensitive to their abilities, as well as to the courage and resilience they have demonstrated in coping with their illness.

The timing of counseling in the treatment of individuals with mental illness is also important. Individuals in the earliest stages of their illness are generally not prepared to address the concept of chronic illness. In addition, as an intervention, counseling is generally not considered appropriate or effective with someone whose psychotic symptoms are not well controlled with drug therapy (Kates & Rockland, 1994). As a client begins to improve after an acute psychotic episode, the likelihood of experiencing depression increases. This depression comes with the realization that mental illnesses are lifelong and may impact the person's previously held future life plans. Individuals in this fragile stage of recovery need to be paced so as not to become overwhelmed by the enormity of what chronic mental illness can mean for their future. Indeed, depression and suicide are serious threats when individuals with schizophrenia realize they have lost so many years of their lives to the illness (Carter, 1994; Roy, 1992; Saarinen et al., 1999). Individuals who are most at risk for suicide are those who have a remitting and relapsing course to their illness, good insight (they know they are sick), a poor response to medication, and a gross discrepancy between their earlier achievements in life and their current level of functioning (Kopelowicz & Liberman, 1998; Torrey, 1995). Counselors should be particularly alert for signs of potential suicide immediately following a relapse, when the client is in a remission (Caldwell & Gottesman, 1990).

Counseling Interventions

Many different psychotherapeutic approaches have been explored for individuals with severe mental illness (Hellkamp, 1993; Mueser & Glynn, 1993; Kopelowicz & Liberman, 1998). In general, psychodynamic or insight-oriented counseling approaches are not considered helpful for people with schizophrenia, and may even cause greater stress for some (Lehman & Steinwachs, 1998; Mueser & Berenbaum, 1990; Mueser & Gingerich, 1994). The limited research that has been conducted on psychodynamic therapy with this population suggests that forms of therapy that promote regression and transference can be particularly harmful to people with schizophrenia (Lehman & Steinwachs, 1998). As

Fenton and McGlashon (1997) point out, the counselor should respect the fact that ambitious counseling interventions, when misapplied, can cause "destabilizing cognitive overload" (p. 1494).

Conversely, individual and group therapies that utilize specific combinations of support, education, and behavior and cognitive skills training should be offered over time to improve functioning. These approaches should be designed to address the specific deficits exhibited in individuals with schizophrenia and should be targeted at specific problems, such as medication noncompliance (Lehman & Steinwachs, 1998). Token economy systems, though effective, have been limited in practice due to ethical and legal concerns with adult patients (Mueser & Glynn, 1993).

However, cognitive therapies, such as cognitive remediation and cognitive enhancement therapy, also offer promise (Hogarty et al., 1995; Hogarty & Flesher, 1992). A related technique is known as personal therapy. Personal therapy models regard mood as a major cause of relapse and poor social adjustment, and attempt to reduce patient anguish by using behavioral, educational, and supportive techniques to help individuals detect the onset of psychotic symptoms (Hogarty et al., 1995). Cognitive remediation strategies focus on improving or normalizing cognitive functions such as signal detection, sustained attention, and memory (Green, 1993; Hogarty & Flesher, 1992). One example of this type of therapy involves the use of social skills training where individuals are repeatedly helped to accurately perceive and interpret social situations.

Counseling methods that are geared toward the practical and attempt to teach ill individuals how to cope more effectively with the concrete problems of living appear to be most helpful (Kopelowicz & Liberman, 1998; Mueser & Gingerich, 1994). Torrey (1995) states that supportive counseling can provide a patient with encouragement and practical advice, such as how to access community resources, develop social support, and minimize friction with family members. Kopelowicz and Liberman (1993) describe supportive

counseling as characterized by a positive, therapeutic alliance, a focus on reality issues and solving problems of everyday life, and encouragement and education of the patients and family for proper use of psychotropic medications. Supportive group counseling can also play a critical role in improving individual functioning, social skills, quality of life, and motivation to stay on medication. Group counseling can be particularly helpful in offering support to individuals as they attempt to readjust to social life (Bellack & Mueser, 1993).

Working with Family Members

The deinstitutionalization of individuals from hospital settings to the community has profoundly affected the lives of family members who provide care to a relative with mental illness. Current research shows that two-thirds of individuals diagnosed with schizophrenia return to live with their families after their first hospitalization (Mueser & Gingerich, 1994; Harvard Medical School, 1995). As informal service providers, families have become a primary source of care for their relatives. As a result, researchers and, more recently, counselors have become interested in the family's experience of living with a mentally ill relative.

Families are generally unprepared for a diagnosis of severe mental illness. Unlike other emotional and psychological disorders, illnesses like schizophrenia and Bipolar Disorder can emerge during the peak of a young adult's successful life. Very often, these illnesses strike with little warning when individuals are away at college or just becoming first-time parents. They are illnesses that evoke feelings of disbelief, denial, guilt, loss, and anger for those with the illness as well as for those close to the ill individual. Unfortunately, for many years, professionals erroneously held the family responsible for the illness and thus intensified the pain (Hatfield, 1982). As a result of this belief, practitioners and treatment providers were slow to offer family education or counseling to family members, who were viewed as difficult, demanding, and responsible for their relative's illness. In 1984,

Grunebaum wrote, "Too often family therapists have worked in ways that have implicitly blamed the family" (p. 421). The historical roots of this perspective permeate the literature throughout this century in the belief that mental illnesses are one of the few disorders where "culturally transmitted hypotheses of family pathogenesis" are accepted as precipitants of the illness (Hatfield & Lefley, 1987, p. 30). In the past, professional training and research both have relied heavily on psychogenic theories of mental illness, which attribute the disorder to family dysfunction.

Today, the mental health field is more knowledgeable about major psychiatric disorders such as schizophrenia. Practitioners now know that families do not "cause" schizophrenia and more readily acknowledge its biological and genetic components. However, researchers and practitioners both accept that as one aspect of the social environment, family behavior has the potential to influence the course of mental illness and perhaps even affect relapse rates for the identified patient (Hatfield, 1979; Lefley & Johnson, 1990; Vaughn & Leff, 1985; Winefield & Burnett, 1996). In fact, research indicates that the strongest support for effective psychotherapeutic treatment for schizophrenia has been for various forms of family therapy (Madanes, 1983; Mueser & Glynn, 1993). Randomized clinical trials have repeatedly demonstrated that family interventions that provide some combination of illness education, support, problem-solving training, and crisis intervention reduce one-year relapse rates from a range of 40% to 50% to one of 2% to 23% (Lehman & Steinwachs, 1998).

Providing care to a family member with mental illness has some positive effects, yet it can also be costly to the caregiver (Biegel, Sales, & Schultz, 1991; Hatfield & Lefley, 1987; Goldman, 1982; Solomon & Marcenko, 1992). Indeed, families report that caregiving can be emotionally, physically, and financially burdensome, with some caregivers experiencing high levels of depression (Biegel et al., 1991). Providing care and support to an individual with mental illness can lead to enormous stress and strain on the family system and

affect the health of individual family members (Hatfield, 1979; Kriesman & Joy, 1974). Prominent issues related to the experience of caregiver burden are managing a mentally ill relative's symptomatology and behavior; the isolation of caregivers due in part to the stigma still attached to mental illness; the inability of the patient at times to carry out the tasks of daily living; improper use of medication by the ill person; and the tendency for family members to feel blamed by professionals for their relative's illness (Biegel et al., 1991). Families also feel unprepared to cope with the unpredictable behavior exhibited by their relative, often feeling that he or she has been discharged to the community too quickly and without adequate supports (Francell, Conn, & Gray, 1988; Solomon & Draine, 1995).

In many instances, because the family was seen as a cause of the problem, family members were offered psychotherapy to address their own problematic behavior (Hatfield & Lefley, 1987; Lefley & Johnson, 1990). Although this is no longer viewed as appropriate or helpful to family members, there is still a critical role for counselors to play in the lives of family members. Family members are in need of support in dealing with the intense feelings of grief, guilt, and loss that accompany these illnesses. They also need help in making good decisions for themselves regarding when to offer help to their ill family member and when it is best to offer support from the background. As family caregivers age, it is also necessary to plan for the future. Counselors can be helpful in assisting family members with the emotional task of planning for the long-term care of their relative. These can be complex and difficult issues for caregivers to address without the additional support of a professional.

CONSUMER AND FAMILY ADVOCACY

The use of consumer providers, or case manager aides, represents a new and promising trend in the treatment of people with severe mental illness (Mowbray & Moxley, 1997). Consumer providers are individuals who have themselves experienced severe mental illness and have been trained to provide support to others who are ill. Consumers as providers of mental health services are often willing to undertake vital and important efforts to make supports accessible, usable, and effective (Mowbray, Moxley, Jasper, & Howell, 1997). There are currently numerous consumer-run services operating around the country. These include consumer-run businesses, drop-in centers, residential services, statewide advocacy organizations, and consumer case management programs (Silverman, Blank, & Taylor, 1997). The Clubhouse, a related model of treatment, provides social, recreational, educational, vocational, and housing opportunities to individuals with severe mental illness in a nonthreatening environment (Kopelowicz & Liberman, 1998). One unique aspect of this model is that it is run entirely by individuals with mental illness, with minimal assistance from mental health professionals. A primary expectation of the Clubhouse model is that everyone will work together to keep the program going (Torrey, 1995). These types of opportunities provide consumers with peer support from others with similar experiences, while allowing consumers to take a step forward in their own recovery by providing leadership and support to others.

Services for people with serious mental illness are not likely to improve without the organized input from those who have been most affected. One goal for the mental health professional is to speak on behalf and alongside this vulnerable and often ignored population. The National Alliance for the Mentally Ill (NAMI) has emerged as one of the most visible and influential organizations offering leadership for individuals affected with mental illness. Since its inception in 1979, NAMI has grown to over 140,000 members with 1,000 local chapters providing education, referral, support, and advocacy to needy families. NAMI chapters throughout the country offer family support groups and family-to-family education programs. One strength of this organization is that it presents a unified voice for politicians, professionals, and the community on issues important to people struggling

with mental illness. NAMI has been at the forefront of fighting sensationalism in the media about people with mental illness and fighting for critical issues such as insurance parity for neurobiological brain disorders. Families and professionals can find out about NAMI and the closest chapter to them by going on the Internet to www.nami.org or by calling (800) 950-NAMI.

SUMMARY

The past 20 years have witnessed tremendous growth in research on the efficacy of psychotherapy for the treatment of schizophrenia and other chronic mental illnesses (Glick et al., 1990; Glynn, 1990; Halford & Hayes, 1991; Hellkamp, 1993; Hogarty et al., 1995; May, 1984; Mueser & Glynn, 1993). Family therapy, personal therapy, and supportive psychotherapy models have been found to be effective as one component of multidisciplinary treatment for individuals with mental illness (Fenton & McGlashon, 1997; Hogarty et al., 1995; Kates & Rockland, 1994; Kopelowicz & Liberman, 1998; Mueser & Glynn, 1993). Cognitive deficits and environmental stressors can impose some limitations on growth for those still struggling with basic needs, such as safe housing and affordable medical care; for others, psychotherapy can be vital to recovery. Fenton and McGlashon write that as clinicians, we are challenged with each individual to find "the specific combination of interventions that will be most helpful for this particular patient with this particular type of schizophrenia at this particular phase of illness or recovery" (p. 1495). Keeping this in mind, exciting innovations in the treatment of individuals with severe mental illness are providing hope to patients, practitioners, and families that individuals diagnosed with mental illness can improve both their functioning and their quality of life.

References

American Psychiatric Association. (1994). *Diagnostic and statistical manual of mental disorders* (4th ed.). Washington, DC: Author.

Andreasen, N.C., & Olsen, S. (1982). Negative vs. positive schizophrenia: Definition and validation. *Archives of General Psychiatry, 39,* 789–794.

Angermeyer, M.C., & Kuhn, L. (1988). Gender differences in age at onset of schizophrenia: An overview. *European Archives of Psychiatry and Neurological Sciences, 237,* 351–364.

Bellack, A.S., & Meuser, K.T. (1993). Psychosocial treatment for schizophrenia. *Schizophrenia Bulletin, 19*(2), 317–336.

Biegel, D., Sales, E., & Schulz, R. (1991). *Family caregiving in chronic illness.* London: Sage.

Caldwell, C., & Gottesman, I. (1990). Schizophrenics kill themselves too: A review of risk factors for suicide. *Schizophrenia Bulletin, 16,* 571–589.

Carter, R. (1998). *Helping someone with mental illness.* New York: Random House.

Estroff, S. (1989). Self, identity, and subjective experiences of schizophrenia: In search of the subject. *Schizophrenia Bulletin, 15,* 189–196.

Fenton, W.S., Blyler, C.R., & Heinssen, R.K. (1997). Determinants of medication compliance in schizophrenia: Empirical and clinical findings. *Schizophrenia Bulletin, 23*(4), 637–651.

Fenton, W.S., & McGlashan, T.H. (1997). We can talk: Individual psychotherapy for schizophrenia. *American Journal of Psychiatry, 154*(11), 1493–1495.

Francell, C., Conn, V., & Gray, D. (1988). Families' perceptions of burden of care for chronically mentally ill relatives. *Hospital and Community Psychiatry, 39*(12), 1296–1300.

Glick, I., Spencer, J., Clarkin, J., Haas, G., Lewis, A., Peyser, J., DeMane, N., Good-Ellis, M., Harris, E., & Lestelle, V. (1990). A randomized clinical trial of inpatient family interventions: IV. Follow-up results for subjects with schizophrenia. *Schizophrenia Research, 3,* 187–200.

Glynn, S.M. (1990). Token economy approaches to psychiatric patients: Progress and pitfalls over 25 years. *Behavior Modification, 14,* 383–407.

Goldman, H. (1982). Mental illness and family burden: A public health perspective. *Hospital and Community Psychiatry, 33*(7), 557–559.

Green, M.F. (1993). Cognitive remediation in schizophrenia. *American Journal of Psychiatry, 150,* 178–187.

Grunebaum, H. (1984). Comments on Terkelson's "Schizophrenia and the family: Adverse effects on family therapy." *Family Process, 23,* 421–428.

Halford, W.K., & Hayes, R. (1991). Psychological rehabilitation of chronic schizophrenia patients: Recent findings on social skills training and family psychoeducation. *Clinical Psychology Review, 11,* 23–44.

Harding, C.M., Zubin, J., & Strauss, J.S. (1992). Chronicity in schizophrenia revisited. *British Journal of Psychiatry, 161,* 27–37.

Harvard Medical School. (1992). Schizophrenia: The present state of understanding, Part II. *Harvard Mental Health Letter, 8*(12), 1–5.

Harvard Medical School. (1995). *Harvard Mental Health Letter, 11*(12), 1–4.

Hatfield, A.B. (1979). The family as partner in the treatment of mental illness. *Hospital and Community Psychiatry, 30,* 338–340.

Hatfield, A.B. (1982). Commentary: Therapists and families: Worlds apart. *Hospital and Community Psychiatry, 33,* 513.

Hatfield, A.B., & Lefley, H. (1987). *Families of the mentally ill: Coping and adaptation.* New York: Guilford Press.

Hellkamp, D.T. (1993). Severe mental disorders. In G.S. Stricker & J.R. Gold (Eds.), *Comprehensive handbook of psychotherapy integration* (pp. 385–398). New York: Plenum Press.

Hogarty, G.E., & Flesher, S. (1992). Cognitive remediation in schizophrenia: Proceed . . . with caution. *Schizophrenia Bulletin, 18*(1), 51–57.

Hogarty, G.E., Kornblith, S.J., Greenwald, D., DiBarry, A., Cooley, S., Flesher, S., Reiss, D., Carter, M., & Ulrich, R. (1995). Personal therapy: A disorder-relevant psychotherapy for schizophrenia. *Schizophrenia Bulletin, 21*(3), 379–393.

Kates, J., & Rockland, L. (1994). Supportive psychotherapy of the schizophrenic patient. *American Journal of Psychotherapy, 48*(4), 543–561.

Koegel, P., Burnam, A.M., & Farr, R.K. (1988). The prevalence of specific psychiatric disorders among homeless individuals in the inner city of Los Angeles. *Archives of General Psychiatry, 45,* 1085–1092.

Kopelowicz, A., & Liberman, R.P. (1998). Psychosocial treatments for schizophrenia. In P. Nathan & J. Gorman (Eds.), *A guide to treatments that work* (pp. 190- 211). New York: Oxford University Press.

Kriesman, D., & Joy, V. (1974). Family response to the mental illness of a relative: A review of the literature. *Schizophrenia Bulletin, 1*(10), 34–57.

Lefley, H.P., & Johnson, D. (1990). *Families as allies in the treatment of the mentally ill.* Washington, DC: American Psychiatric Press.

Lehman, A.F., & Steinwachs, D.M. (1998). At issue: Translating research into practice: The schizophrenia patient outcomes research team (PORT) treatment recommendations. *Schizophrenia Bulletin, 24*(1), 1–10.

Madanes, C. (1983). Strategic therapy of schizophrenia. In W. McFarlane (Ed.), *Family therapy in schizophrenia* (pp. 209–225). New York: Guilford Press.

May, P.R. (1984). A step forward in research on psychotherapy of schizophrenia. *Schizophrenia Bulletin, 10,* 604–607.

Mowbray, C.T., & Moxley, D.P. (1997). Consumers as providers: Themes and success factors. In C.T. Mowbray, D.P. Moxley, C.A. Jasper, & L.L. Howell (Eds.), *Consumers as providers in psychiatric rehabilitation* (pp. 504–517). Columbia, MD: International Association of Psychosocial Rehabilitation Services.

Mowbray, C.T., Moxley, D.P., Jasper, C.A., & Howell, L.L. (Eds.). (1997). *Consumers as providers in psychiatric rehabilitation.* Columbia, MD: International Association of Psychosocial Rehabilitation Services.

Mueser, K.T., & Berenbaum, H. (1990). Psychodynamic treatment of schizophrenia: Is there a future? *Psychological Medicine, 20,* 253–262.

Mueser, K.T., Bond, G.R., Drake, R.E., & Resnick, S.G. (1998). Models of community care for severe mental illness: A review of research on case management. *Schizophrenia Bulletin, 24*(1), 37–74.

Mueser, K.T., & Gingerich, S. (1994). *Coping with schizophrenia: A guide for families.* Oakland, CA: New Harbinger.

Mueser, K.T., & Glynn, S.M. (1993). Efficacy of psychotherapy for schizophrenia. In T.R. Giles (Ed.), *Handbook of effective psychotherapy* (pp. 325–354). New York: Plenum Press.

NARSAD. (1997). *Understanding schizophrenia; A guide for people with schizophrenia and their families.* New York: NARSAD Research.

National Mental Health Advisory Council. (1993). Health care reform for Americans with severe mental illness: Report of the National Advisory Mental Health Council. *American Journal of Psychiatry, 150,* 1447–1465.

Rapp, C.A. (1998). *The strengths model: Case management with people suffering from severe and persistent mental illness.* New York: Oxford University Press.

Rapp, C.A., & Chamberlain, R. (1985). Case management services for the chronically mentally ill. *Social Work, 30*(5), 417–422.

Regier, D.A., Farmer, M.E., Lock, B.Z., Keith, S.J., & Rae, D.S. (1993). The de facto United States mental and addictive disorders service system. *Archives of General Psychiatry, 51,* 492–499.

Rose, S. (1979). Deciphering deinstitutionalization: Complexities in policy and program analysis. *Health and Society, 57*(4), 429–459.

Rosenthal, R.N., & Miner, C.R. (1997). Differential diagnosis of substance-induced psychosis and schizophrenia in patients with substance use disorders. *Schizophrenia Bulletin, 23*(2), 187–193.

Roy, A. (1992). Suicide in schizophrenia. *International Review of Psychiatry, 4,* 205–209.

Saarinen, P.I., Lehtonen, J., & Lonnqvist, J. (1999). A suicide risk in schizophrenia: An analysis of 17 consecutive suicides. *Schizophrenia Bulletin, 25*(3), 533–542.

Silverman, S.H., Blank, M.B., & Taylor, L.C. (1997). On our own: Preliminary findings from a consumer-run service model. *Psychiatric Rehabilitation Journal, 21*(2), 151–159.

Solomon, P., & Draine, J. (1995, July). Subjective burden among family members of mentally ill adults: Relation to stress, coping and adaptation. *American Journal of Orthopsychiatry, 65*(3), 419–427.

Solomon, P., & Marcenko, M. (1992). Families of adults with severe mental illness: Their satisfaction with inpatient and outpatient treatment. *Psychosocial Rehabilitation Journal, 16*(1), 121–134.

Strauss, J. (1989). Subjective experiences of schizophrenia: Toward a new dynamic psychiatry. *Schizophrenia Bulletin, 15,* 179–187.

Torrey, E.F. (1995). *Surviving schizophrenia: A manual for families, consumers and providers* (3rd ed.). New York: HarperCollins.

Torrey, E.F. (1997). *Out of the shadows: Confronting America's mental illness crisis.* New York: Wiley.

Vaughn, C., & Leff, J. (1985). *Expressed emotions in families.* New York: Guilford Press.

Von Korff, M., Nestadt, G., Romanoski, A., Anthony, J., Eaton, W., Merchant, A., Chahal, R., Kramer, M., Folstein, M., & Gruenberg, E. (1985). Prevalence of treated and untreated DSM-III schizophrenia. *Journal of Nervous and Mental Disease, 173,* 577–581.

Wiersma, D., Nienhaus, F., Slooff, C., & Giel, R. (1998). Natural course of schizophrenic disorders: A 15-year followup of a Dutch incidence cohort. *Schizophrenia Bulletin, 24*(1), 75–85.

Winefield, H.R., & Burnett, P.L. (1996). Barriers to an alliance between family and professional caregivers in chronic schizophrenia. *Journal of Mental Health, 5*(3), 223–232.

Woolis, R. (1992). *When someone you love has a mental illness.* New York: Putnam Press.

PART III
Diagnosis and Treatment of Children with Mental and Emotional Disorders

22 PREVALENCE OF CHILDHOOD DISORDERS

R. Elliott Ingersoll and Susan B. Previts

The notion of prevalence is common in medical and psychological research, although the methods used to estimate prevalence are less commonly explored in the professional literature. Prevalence is determined through statistical probability, and, as the mathematician Morris Kline (1972) noted, statistics are first and foremost a confession of ignorance. The statistics with which mental health professionals estimate the prevalence of mental/emotional disorders are drawn from epidemiological research. Epidemiological research is the study of the incidence, distribution, and consequences of particular problems in one or more specified populations as well as factors that affect distribution of the problems in question (Barlow & Durand, 1999; U.S. Department of Health, Education, and Welfare, 1978).

The effort to gather accurate statistics was initiated by the Association of Medical Superintendents of American Institutions for the Insane (later renamed the American Psychiatric Association, APA). The responsibility for gathering statistics was shifted to the biometrics branch of the National Institute of Mental Health (NIMH) in 1949 (American Psychiatric Association, 2000a). The APA relies heavily on the epidemiological research of others for the prevalence estimates found in the various *Diagnostic and Statistical Manuals (DSMs)* (personal communication,

L. McQueen, September 26, 2000). Epidemiologic research may be carried out by one or two persons or in massive projects, such as the NIMH Epidemiologic Catchment Area Program (Eaton & Kessler, 1985).

Because statistics are first and foremost a confession of ignorance, prevalence data based on statistics are always a work in progress to be understood as "best guesses" given available methodologies. Several problems challenge researchers to make accurate estimates regarding the prevalence of a particular disorder. First, there is a significant time lag between the refinement of an edition of the *DSM* and the gathering and analysis of data. For example, studies are still being published estimating prevalence based on *DSM-III-R* criteria (Kessler et al., 1997), which was replaced in 1994 by *DSM-IV* (which was replaced in 2000 by *DSM-IV-TR*). When the *DSM* is updated, criteria or descriptors associated with a disorder may change. For example the *DSM-IV* added symptoms to the symptom list in *DSM-III-R* for Conduct Disorder (CD) (APA, 1994). The description of CD was again expanded in *DSM-IV-TR* to include more risk factors and to discuss the relationship between CD and Oppositional Defiant Disorder (ODD) (APA, 2000b).

A second problem associated with estimating prevalence has to do with the methods used. As any researcher knows, some research

155

methods are better than others. There is a paucity of research comparing various methods or data-gathering instruments (Boyle et al., 1997; Regier, 2000), and reported prevalence rates may vary study by study (Regier et al., 1998). Methods of epidemiological research on mental disorders have varied over time. There have been three generations of large-scale epidemiological research using two strategies. Each generation has used different psychiatric nosologies and data collection tools (Kohn, Dohrenwend, & Mirotznik, 1998). The first generation relied primarily on institutional records and key informants but no real standardized procedures for data collection. The second generation utilized structured interviews in the community by nonclinical interviewers that were subsequently rated by a psychiatrist. The third generation (starting around 1980) used clinician and trained non-clinician interviewers in the community to obtain information necessary to determine the presence of mental disorders as categorized in the *DSM*. This present generation utilizes explicit diagnostic criteria as well as structured clinical interview schedules (Dohrenwend, 1998; Eaton & Kessler, 1985; Kohn et al., 1998). Currently, all epidemiologic approaches are based on personal interviews, although there is still controversy over the accuracy of the interview method, particularly whether it is appropriate to use lay interviewers (Dohrenwend, 1998). Dohenwend noted, "Classification systems in psychiatry have been and will continue to be tentative as long as disorders are grouped on the basis of signs and symptoms elicited in interviews" (pp. 146–147).

Perhaps the largest problem with epidemiological data is summarized by Blazer and Kaplar (2000), who stated that a central conflict is whether or not symptoms reported by community residents in structured interviews are clinically significant or not. On one side of the debate, Regier (2000) noted that the conflict could be resolved with better research methods that would allow a diagnosis to be made from the results of a structured clinical interview. On the other side, Spitzer (1998) and Frances (1998) have asserted that data from epidemiological studies cannot replace clinical judgment. Blazer and Kaplar

contended that the conflict could not be resolved because the methodologies of both sides are plagued with measurement error.

Estimating prevalence in children and adolescents is a relatively new undertaking. Prevalence estimates for mental disorders in children are further complicated by the fact that many disorders thought to apply primarily or exclusively to adults (e.g., Bipolar I Disorder) are now being applied to children (McClellan & Werry, 1997). In addition, developmental considerations and comorbidity make diagnosis of children and adolescents much more difficult (House, 1999; U.S. Department of Health and Human Services, 1999; also see House and Swales, this volume). The problems of shifting criteria and refinement of data-gathering instruments exist to a greater degree when attempting to estimate the prevalence of mental/emotional disorders in children (Shaffer et al., 1996). To add to the variables making prevalence estimates difficult to attain, the self-reports of children younger than 8 or 9 years tend to be less reliable than those of older children and adults and often require corroboration from adults in the children's lives. In addition, children are more influenced by factors in their immediate environment, including parent pathology, abuse, neglect, and family discord (Kazdin, 2000).

Given these caveats, this chapter briefly summarizes some of the more common disorders seen in children and adolescents and the prevalence rates from the *DSM* and occasionally other sources. The aim is to organize the disorders from most to least prevalent, although this too is merely an estimation given the caveats already discussed regarding prevalence rates in general. In many cases, we have not found prevalence rates specific to children and adolescents and reproduced the estimated lifetime prevalence rates.

Some disorders are discussed in terms of point prevalence, some in terms of lifetime prevalence, and some in terms of both. Point prevalence refers to the estimated proportion of people in the population thought to suffer from the disorder at any given point in time. Lifetime prevalence is an estimate at a given point in time of all individuals who have ever suffered from the disorder. Incidence refers to the rate of new cases in a specified period of time (usually annually) (LaBruzza, 1997). Which of these types of prevalence or incidence data are sited depends on the availability of data. Diagnoses considered to be rare or with little or no epidemiological data (e.g., Asperger's syndrome) were omitted from this chapter. Unless otherwise noted, the prevalence rates cited are paraphrased from the *DSM-IV-TR* (APA, 2000b).

Dysthymic Disorder (DD). In children, DD seems to occur equally in both sexes and often results in impaired school performance and social interaction. Children and adolescents with DD are usually irritable and cranky as well as depressed. They have low self-esteem and poor skills and are pessimistic. The lifetime prevalence of DD (with or without superimposed Major Depressive Disorder) is approximately 6%. The point prevalence of DD is approximately 3%. Rapoport and Ismond (1996) noted that the diagnosis is probably underutilized with children. Keller and Russell (1996) stated that there have been no epidemiologic studies of DD in children or adolescents.

Conduct Disorder (CD). Prevalence (or at least the diagnosis) of CD seems to have increased in the past 10 years and may be higher in urban than in rural settings. Rates vary widely from 6% to 10% for males and 2% to 9% for females. CD is one of the most frequently diagnosed conditions in all mental health facilities for children.

Adjustment Disorder (AD). AD may occur in any age group, with males and females being equally affected. Prevalence rates in samples of children and adolescents range from 2% to 8%.

Learning Disorders (LDs). Estimates of the prevalence of LD range from 2% to 10%. It is thought that around 5% of students in public schools in the United States are identified as having an LD.

Reading Disorder (RD). "The prevalence of RD is difficult to establish because many studies focus on the prevalence of LD without careful separation into specific disorders of Reading, Mathematics, or Written Expression" (APA, 2000b, p. 52). RD, by itself or combined with Mathematics Disorder or Disorder of the Written Expression, accounts for approximately four of every five cases of LD. The prevalence of RD in the United States is estimated to be 4% of schoolchildren.

Attention-Deficit/Hyperactivity Disorder (ADHD). The prevalence of ADHD in school-age children is estimated variably at 3% to 7% (APA, 2000b) and 3% to 9% (Szatmari, 1992).

Expressive Language Disorder (ELD). Estimates suggest that the developmental type of ELD may affect 3% to 5% of school-age children. There are two subtypes (acquired and developmental), and the acquired type is less common.

Mixed Receptive-Expressive Language Disorder (MRELD). It is estimated that the developmental type of MRELD may occur in up to 3% of school-age children but is probably less common than ELD.

Oppositional Defiant Disorder (ODD). Rates of ODD range from 2% to 16% but vary depending on the nature of the population sample and methodology. The fact that many of the symptoms may be normal developmental behaviors makes diagnosis and prevalence estimates of this disorder difficult (Rapoport & Ismond, 1996).

Developmental Coordination Disorder (DCD). Prevalence of DCD has been thought to be as high as 6% for children in the age range of 5 to 11 years.

Phonological Disorder (PD). For children 6 and 7 years old, prevalence for moderate to severe PD is estimated at approximately 2% to 3%, although the prevalence of milder forms of the disorder is higher. By age 17, the prevalence falls to 0.5%.

Mathematical Disorder (MD). The prevalence of MD is harder to establish than many other disorders because many studies focus on the prevalence of LD without separation into the specific disorders of Reading, Mathematics, or Written Expression. The prevalence of MD (i.e., when not found in association with other LD) is estimated at approximately one in every five cases of LD. It is thought that 1% of school-age children have MD.

Sleep Terror Disorder. The prevalence of sleep terror episodes (as opposed to Sleep Terror Disorder, in which there is recurrence and distress or impairment) is estimated at 1% to 6% among children. There are limited data on the prevalence of the disorder in the general population.

Sleepwalking Disorder (SD). It is estimated that between 10% and 30% of children have had at least one sleepwalking episode, but the prevalence of SD (marked by repeated episodes and impairment or distress) is far lower, in the range of 1% to 5%.

Stuttering. In prepubertal children, the prevalence of stuttering is 1% and then drops to 0.8% in adolescence.

Bipolar I Disorder. It should be noted that there is still much controversy over the prevalence of Bipolar I Disorder among children and adolescents. The *DSM-IV-TR* estimates that around 10% to 15% of adolescents with recurrent Major Depressive Episodes will develop Bipolar I Disorder. House (1999) noted that manic episodes (required for the diagnosis of Bipolar I) are rare in children. McClellan and Werry (1997) noted, "Historically considered rare, childhood-onset bipolar disorder is now being reported more often, although its frequency remains an area of some controversy" (p. 157). They add that currently, 20% of adult patients with Bipolar I Disorder had their first manic episode in adolescence. These authors note that there is still a great deal of speculation regarding the actual prevalence of Bipolar I in children and adolescents.

Generalized Anxiety Disorder (GAD). In community samples, the one-year prevalence rate for GAD was approximately 3% and the lifetime prevalence rate was 5%. In anxiety disorder clinics, it is estimated that approximately 12% of individuals present with GAD. There is limited data on GAD in children because the *DSM-IV* version of the disorder subsumed the *DSM-III-R* disorder Overanxious Disorder of Childhood (ODC) (Bernstein & Shaw, 1997). The prevalence of ODC has been estimated at 2.9% (Anderson, Williams, McGee, & Silva, 1987) to 4.6% (Costello, 1989). In a national comorbidity survey, Wittchen, Zhao, Kessler, and Eaton (1994) estimated a prevalence of 1.3% for males and 1.5% for females in a 15- to 24-year-old age group.

Social Phobia (SP). Epidemiological research has reported a lifetime prevalence of SP ranging from 3% to 13%. In children, the diagnosis should not be made prior to 2.5 years, as it would be impossible to differentiate the symptoms from developmentally normal stranger anxiety. Anderson and colleagues (1987) estimated the prevalence of SP in New Zealand children to be 0.9%; Kashani and Orvaschel (1990) estimated a prevalence of 1% in a U.S. cohort ages 8, 12, and 17. The median age of onset has been estimated at 12 years (Bourdon et al., 1988).

Posttraumatic Stress Disorder (PTSD). The lifetime prevalence for PTSD ranges from 1% to 14%, and the variability is related to the methodology used and the population sampled. Studies of at-risk individuals (e.g., combat veterans, victims of volcanic eruption, or criminal violence) yield even broader prevalence rates, ranging from 3% to 58%. It should be noted that PTSD is often related to child abuse, which is thought to be underreported due to issues of guilt and shame (Bremner, 1999). Bremner notes that 16% of all women are estimated to suffer from some form of attempted or completed sexual abuse prior to their eighteenth birthday and that a considerable proportion of them will develop PTSD prior to adulthood.

Obsessive-Compulsive Disorder (OCD). OCD was previously thought to be rare in the general population, but studies have estimated a lifetime prevalence of 2.5% and 10-year prevalence of 1.5% to 2.1%. One prevalence study done with adolescents estimated 1% prevalence (Flament et al., 1988). General estimates of lifetime prevalence in community studies of children and adolescents estimate lifetime prevalence between 1% and 2.3%. The same studies estimate a 1-year prevalence of 0.7% for teens and children. The average age of onset ranges from early adolescence to the mid-twenties.

Cyclothymic Disorder. The reported lifetime prevalence of Cyclothymic Disorder is from 0.4% to 1%. Prevalence among clinical populations may range from 3% to 5%.

Schizophrenia. Although Schizophrenia occurs in children, it is relatively rare, but its occurrence increases in adolescents. Often, prodromal signs are noted in retrospect. Because the disorder tends to be chronic, incidence rates are much lower than prevalence rates and are estimated to be approximately 1 per 10,000 per year.

Gender Identity Disorder (GID). There are no recent epidemiological studies to provide data on prevalence of this disorder. European data with access to total population statistics and referrals suggest that roughly 1 per 30,000 adult males and 1 per 100,000 adult females seek sex-reassignment surgery, giving some vague notion of prevalence estimates.

Feeding Disorder of Infancy or Early Childhood. Of all pediatric hospital admissions, 1% to 5% are for failure to thrive, and as many as half of these may reflect feeding disturbances without an apparent predisposing general medical condition.

Nightmare Disorder (ND). It is estimated that between 10% and 15% of children ages 3 to 5 have nightmares of sufficient intensity to disturb their parents, but the prevalence of ND is not known (Rapoport & Ismond, 1996).

Enuresis. The prevalence of Enuresis decreases as children age. At age 5 years, the prevalence is 7% for males and 3% for females; at 10 years, the prevalence is 3% for males and 2% for females; at 18 years, the prevalence is 1% for males and lower among females.

Encopresis. Approximately 1% of 5-year-olds have Encopresis, and the disorder is apparently more common in males than in females.

Anorexia Nervosa (AN). Epidemiological studies among females in late adolescence and early adulthood have found rates of 0.5% to 1% that meet full criteria for AN. Individuals whose symptoms fall below the threshold for the disorder (e.g., Eating Disorder NOS) are commonly encountered. There are limited data concerning the prevalence of this disorder in males. The overall incidence of AN appears to have increased in recent decades.

Bulimia Nervosa (BN). Among adolescent and young adult females, the prevalence of BN is approximately 1% to 3%. It is estimated that

the rate of occurrence of this disorder in males is approximately one-tenth of that in females.

Panic Disorder (PD). Numerous cross-cultural epidemiological studies indicate the lifetime prevalence of PD to be between 1% and 2%. One-year prevalence rates are between 0.5% and 1.5%.

Selective Mutism (SM). SM is thought to be rare; it is seen in fewer than 1% of individuals assessed in the mental health settings.

Stereotypic Movement Disorder (SMD). The information on SMD is limited. The disorder may result in self-injurious behaviors. Estimates of prevalence of such behaviors in individuals with mental retardation vary from 2% to 3% in children and adolescents living in the community.

Major Depressive Disorder (MDD). Adolescent and adult females are twice as likely to suffer from MDD (single or recurrent) than adolescent and adult males. In prepubertal children, boys are more likely than girls to be affected (Cyranowski, Frank, Young, & Shear, 2000). Studies of MDD report a wide range of values for the prevalence in adult populations.

Specific Phobia (SP). It is difficult to estimate the prevalence of SP in adults and children because, although relatively common, this disorder must cause marked distress or impairment to warrant the diagnosis. Lifetime prevalence rates range between 7.2% and 11.3%. There are no prevalence rates specific to children and adolescents.

Autistic Disorder. In epidemiological studies of Autistic Disorder, it is estimated that between 2 and 20 of every 10,000 children will be afflicted. The median is 5 children per 10,000.

Substance Use Disorders (SUDs). The use of psychoactive substances is common among adolescents, with 90% reporting having used alcohol and over 40% reporting having used an illicit substance (Newcomb & Bentler, 1988). A University of Michigan survey (1995) indicated that substance use has increased substantially since 1991. There are no large-scale epidemiological surveys to indicate the level of SUDs in adolescents, but in community surveys, the lifetime prevalence of alcohol abuse or dependence has ranged from 5.3% in 15-year-olds to 32.4% in 17- to 19-year-olds (Bukstein, 1997). The current emotional climate around substance abuse and the legal complications may make it difficult to obtain accurate estimates of prevalence. Where there are estimates for specific substance use in children or adolescents in the *DSM-IV-TR,* those are summarized below. It should be noted that although each subcategory below bears the generic label for disorders related to a substance, for most subcategories, all we have are estimates of use that give us no clue as to how many users would meet the criteria for abuse or dependence. For further caveats to the prevalence of substance use and dependence in general, see Ingersoll and Burns (this volume).

Alcohol-Related Disorders. The first episode of alcohol intoxication is likely to occur in adolescence.

Amphetamine-Related Disorders. A 1997 survey of high school seniors (APA, 2000b) estimated that 16% had ever used amphetamines, with 10% having used in the prior year. It is assumed that the purpose of the use in these instances was to get "high," as opposed to a prescribed use like that for ADHD. A diagnosis of ADHD does increase the risk of substance abuse but treatment with stimulant medication does not increase this risk (Greenhill, 1998).

Cannabis-Related Disorders. A 1995 survey estimated that 42% of high school seniors had ever used a cannabinoid, with 35% using in the prior year.

Cocaine-Related Disorders. The 18- to 25-year-old age group had the highest estimated use in the past year (5% for cocaine and 1% for "crack").

Hallucinogen-Related Disorders. The group with the highest estimate of having ever used one of these drugs (in 1996) was the 18- to 25-year-old group. In this group, 16% reported having ever used a hallucinogen, with 7% reporting having used in the past year.

Inhalant-Related Disorders. The use of inhalants is difficult to estimate, but data from

1996 estimate that the highest use is in the 18- to 25-year-old cohort (11%), with 12- to 17-year-olds reporting the most use in the past year (4%).

Nicotine-Related Disorders. Nicotine intake is thought to typically begin in early adolescence, with 95% of those who continue to smoke at age 20 becoming regular smokers. In 1996, use in the past year was highest in the 18- to 25-year-old cohort (45%).

Opioid-Related Disorders. A 1997 survey of use among high school students estimated that about 2% of high school seniors had ever used heroin, and 10% reported inappropriate use of other analgesics.

Phencyclidine-Related Disorders. According to 1996 data, 3% of Americans 12 years old and older report ever using phencyclidine. The highest proportion using phencyclidine in the prior year was 12- to 17-year-olds (0.7%).

Sedative, Hypnotic, or Anxiolytic-Related Disorders. More than 15% of Americans use these medications in any given year. Most take as directed without any misuse, but 1996 data estimate that 6% of Americans have ever taken these drugs illicitly. The age group with the highest estimated illicit use was 26- to 34-year-olds (3% using "sedatives" and 6% using "tranquilizers"). Those ages 18 to 25 were most likely to have used illicitly in the prior year.

References

American Psychiatric Association. (1987). *Diagnostic and statistical manual of mental disorders* (3rd ed., rev.). Washington, DC: Author.

American Psychiatric Association. (1994). *Diagnostic and statistical manual of mental disorders* (4th ed.). Washington, DC: Author.

American Psychiatric Association. (2000a). *DSM: A brief historical note.* Available: www.psych .org/htdocs/pnews/98-04-03/hx.html.

American Psychiatric Association. (2000b). *Diagnostic and statistical manual of mental disorders* (4th ed., text rev.). Washington, DC: Author.

Anderson, J.C., Williams, S., McGee, R., & Silva, P.A. (1987). *DSM-III* disorders in preadolescent children: Prevalence in a large sample from the general population. *Archives of General Psychiatry, 44,* 69–76.

Barlow, D.A., & Durand, V.M. (1999). *Abnormal psychology* (2nd ed.). Pacific Grove, CA: Brooks/Cole.

Bernstein, G.A., & Shaw, K. (1997). Practice parameters for the assessment and treatment of children and adolescents with anxiety disorders. *Journal of the American Academy of Child and Adolescent Psychiatry, 36*(Suppl.), 69S–84S.

Blazer, D.G., & Kaplar, B.H. (2000). Controversies in community-based psychiatric epidemiology: Let the data speak for themselves. *Archives of General Psychiatry, 57,* 227.

Bourdon, K.H., Boyd, J.H., Rae, D., Burns, B.J., Thompson, J.W., & Locke, B.Z. (1988). Gender differences in phobias: Results of the ECA community survey. *Journal of Anxiety Disorders, 2,* 227–241.

Boyle, M.H., Offord, D.R., Racine, Y.A., Szatmari, P., Sanford, M., & Fleming, J.E. (1997). Adequacy of interviews vs. checklists for classifying childhood psychiatric disorders based on parents' reports. *Archives of General Psychiatry, 54,* 793–799.

Bremner, J.D. (1999). Devastating effects and clinical implications of childhood abuse. *Directions in Psychiatry, 19*(Pt. 2), 147–160.

Bukstein, O. (1997). Practice parameters for the assessment and treatment of children and adolescents with substance use disorders. *Journal of the American Academy of Child and Adolescent Psychiatry, 36*(Suppl.), 140S–156S.

Costello, E.J. (1989). Child psychiatric disorders and their correlates: A primary care pediatric sample. *Journal of the American Academy of Child and Adolescent Psychiatry, 28,* 851–855.

Cyranowski, J.M., Frank, E., Young, E., & Shear, M.K. (2000). Adolescent onset of the gender difference in lifetime rates of major depression. *Archives of General Psychiatry, 57,* 21–27.

Dohrenwend, B.P. (1998). A psychosocial perspective on the past and future of psychiatric epidemiology. *American Journal of Epidemiology, 147,* 222–231.

Eaton, W.W., & Kessler, L.G. (1985). *Epidemiologic field methods in psychiatry: The NIMH epidemiologic catchment area program.* Orlando, FL: Academic Press.

Flament, M., Whitaker, A., Rapoport, J., Davies, M., Berg, C., Kalikow, K., Sceery, W., & Shaffer, D. (1988). Obsessive-compulsive disorder in adolescence: An epidemiological study. *Journal of the American Academy of Child and Adolescent Psychiatry, 27,* 764–771.

Frances, A. (1998). Problems in defining clinical significance in epidemiologic studies. *Archives of General Psychiatry, 55,* 119.

Greenhill, L.L. (1998). Attention deficit/hyperactivity disorder. In B.T. Walsh (Ed.), *Child psychopharmacology.* Washington, DC: American Psychiatric Press.

House, A.E. (1999). *DSM-IV diagnosis in the schools.* New York: Guilford Press.

Kashani, J.H., & Orvaschel, H. (1990). A community study of anxiety in children and adolescents. *American Journal of Psychiatry, 147,* 313–318.

Kazdin, A.E. (2000). Developing a research agenda for child and adolescent psychotherapy. *Archives of General Psychiatry, 57,* 829–835.

Keller, M.B., & Russell, C.W. (1996). Dysthymia. In T.A. Widiger, A.J. Frances, H.A. Pincus, R. Ross, M.B. First, & W. Wakefield Davis (Eds.), *DSM-IV sourcebook.* (Vol. 2, pp. 21–35). Washington, DC: American Psychiatric Press.

Kessler, R.C., Crum, R.M., Warner, L.A., Nelson, C.B., Schulenberg, J., & Anthony, J.C. (1997). Lifetime co-occurrence of *DSM-III-R* alcohol abuse and dependence with other psychiatric disorders in the National Comorbidity Survey. *Archives of General Psychiatry, 54,* 313–321.

Kline, M. (1972). *Mathematical thought from ancient to modern times.* New York: Oxford University Press.

Kohn, R., Dohrenwend, B.P., & Mirotznik, J. (1998). Epidemiological findings on selected psychiatric disorders in the general population. In B.P. Dohrenwend (Ed.), *Adversity, stress, and psychopathology* (pp. 235–284). New York: Oxford University Press.

LaBruzza, A.L. (1997). *Using DSM-IV: A clinician's guide to psychiatric diagnosis.* Northvale, NJ: Aronson.

McClellan, J., & Werry, J.S. (1997). Practice parameters for the assessment and treatment of children and adolescents with bipolar disorder. *Journal of the American Academy of Child and Adolescent Psychiatry, 36*(Suppl.), 157S–176S.

Newcomb, M.D., & Bentler, P.M. (1988). *Consequences of adolescent drug use.* Beverly Hills, CA: Sage.

Rapoport, J.L., & Ismond, D.R. (1996). *DSM-IV training guide for diagnosis of childhood disorders.* New York: Brunner Mazel.

Reiger, D.A. (2000). Community diagnosis counts. *Archives of General Psychiatry, 57,* 223.

Reiger, D.A., Kaelber, C.T., Rae, D.S., Farmer, M.E., Knauper, B., Kessler, R.C., & Norquist, G.S. (1998). Limitations of diagnostic criteria and assessment instruments for mental disorders: Implications for research and policy. *Archives of General Psychiatry, 55*, 109–115.

Shaffer, D., Fisher, P., Dulcan, M., Davies, M., Piacentini, J., Schwab-Stone, M.E., Lahey, B.B., Bourdon, K., Jensen, P.S., Bird, H.R., Canino, G., & Regier, D.A. (1996). The NIMH Diagnostic Interview Schedule for Children version 2.3 (DISC-2.3): Description, acceptability, prevalence rates, and performance in the MECA study. *Journal of the American Academy of Child and Adolescent Psychiatry, 35*, 865–877.

Spitzer, R. (1998). Diagnosis and need for treatment are not the same. *Archives of General Psychiatry, 55*, 120.

Szatmari, P. (1992). The epidemiology of attention-deficit hyperactivity disorder. In G. Weiss (Ed.), *Child and adolescent psychiatric clinics of North America* (pp. 361–384). Philadelphia: Saunders.

University of Michigan. (1995). *1993 Monitoring the future survey.* Ann Arbor: Institute for Social Research.

U.S. Department of Health, Education, and Welfare. (1978). *Epidemiology, health systems research, and statistics/data systems: Report of an ADAMHA workgroup.* Washington, DC: Author.

U.S. Department of Health and Human Services. (2000). *Mental health: A report of the Surgeon General.* Washington, DC: Author.

Wittchen, H-U., Zhao, S., Kessler, R.C., & Eaton, W. (1994). DSM-III-R generalized anxiety disorder in national comorbidity survey. *Archives of General Psychiatry, 51*, 355–364.

23 DIAGNOSTIC EVALUATION OF MENTAL AND EMOTIONAL DISORDERS OF CHILDHOOD

Thomas P. Swales

A wide variety of assessment methods and instruments are appropriate for use with children, including self-report and interviewer-based instruments, parent and teacher questionnaires, and observational systems. The most reliable and valid approach to assessing children for psychiatric disorders incorporates all of these methods into a multimodal assessment.

Before you begin reading this chapter, pull two or three charts from your clinical practice and review them carefully, as if the diagnoses you made were being challenged. Try to answer the following questions:

- Is there a diagnosis from the *Diagnostic and Statistical Manual of Mental Disorders (DSM-IV-TR)* provided for each patient?

- Did you document that you screened for other childhood psychiatric disorders beyond what was diagnosed?

- In reading your notes, would someone find clear examples of how you determined that specific diagnostic criteria were met based on specific examples from the parent and child interviews?

- Was information obtained from the child's teacher and physician?

- How did you monitor improvement (or worsening) in the course of treatment, across sessions?

The objective of this chapter is to provide you with guidelines and resources for improving how you evaluate and diagnose children and adolescents with mental and emotional disorders.

Any diagnostic interview with children or adolescents must include a comprehensive medical, developmental, and social history, typically obtained through interview with the parents. An accurate history provides a base for understanding the presenting problems in the context of a child's life and reveals potential areas for intervention. Medical history is important because it may reveal preexisting or comorbid factors contributing to behavior problems. A medical history should include identification of any major physical problems (head injuries, seizures, infections), past medical or psychiatric hospitalizations, and any prolonged use of medication. Perinatal history should also be explored for prenatal infection or substance abuse, delivery complications, or maternal illness. A developmental history can reveal an experience of delays in language or motor functioning or past treatment for these problems. A social history is complete when it includes information about peer relationships, participation in group organizations, sports and activities, and parental attitude toward discipline and its effectiveness. An educational history not only reveals academic performance, but also indicates the pervasiveness of the problems reported by the parents in the home. Children should also be asked what they like and don't like about school, and what kinds of problems they are experiencing there. A family history (often overlooked) should encompass information regarding medical, neurological, or psychiatric disorders and substance abuse problems.

All mental health professionals rely on the diagnostic criteria in *DSM-IV-TR* (American Psychiatric Association, 2000) to diagnose childhood psychiatric disorders. The diagnostic criteria in the *DSM* also provide a nomenclature and common language that promote meaningful communication among mental health professionals. The *DSM* section on disorders usually diagnosed in childhood or adolescence lists the following diagnoses: mental retardation, learning disorders, motor skills disorders, communication disorders, pervasive developmental disorders, attention-deficit and disruptive behavior disorders, feeding and eating disorders, tic disorders, elimination disorders, and other disorders. Mental health counselors should obtain a history of all of these during their diagnostic interview and refer for appropriate psychological and medical evaluation. However, it is also important that other conditions be routinely screened, including mood disorders, anxiety disorders, Schizophrenia, substance use disorders, and problems related to abuse or neglect. For example, histories of substance abuse, mood disorders, and psychosis must be carefully explored when working with adolescents.

ASSESSMENT TOOLS THAT FACILITATE DIAGNOSIS

Structured and semistructured interviews have been written to diagnose psychiatric disorders in children and adolescents, although these are primarily used in research studies. In these interviews, specific questions are asked of parents and/or children to elicit sufficient information to determine whether or not a specific symptom was present. In structured interviews, patients are asked specific questions that are often read exactly as written, with limited responses typically of yes or no. The National Institute of Mental Health Diagnostic Interview Schedule for Children is perhaps the best-recognized structured interview. This interview can be administered by computer, but the scope of its approximately 3,000 questions would be unrealistic to apply to a real-world clinical setting (*DISC-IV*; Shaffer, Fisher, & Lucas, 1999).

In contrast interviews that are semistructured reflect a more real-world clinical process. These interviews provide open-ended questions and allow for further questions to clarify contradictions or confusion (Angold &

Fisher, 1999). The interviewer has to make clinical judgments regarding which questions to ask based on the child's developmental age, gender, and cultural background. The Kiddie Schedule for Affective Disorders in School-Age Children (K-SADS; Orvaschel, 1995; Orvaschel, Puig-Antich, Chambers, Tabrizi, & Johnson, 1982) is an excellent example of a semistructured interview. Structured interviews are a clear reminder that there is logic in decision making in assessing childhood psychiatric disorders; semistructured interviews highlight the importance of asking the right question to elicit a meaningful response. Semistructured interviews model best practices. Mental health counselors can improve their diagnostic skills, especially during training, by examining these interviews.

All diagnostic interviewing involving children and adolescents must consider the course and timing of symptoms across the developmental life span. For example, if symptoms date back to the preschool years involving inattention, distractibility, and hyperactivity, then it is important to rule out ADHD. In contrast, a rapid onset of problems with no prior difficulties could raise the possibility of a depressive disorder. Even the typical format of a semistructured interview involves gathering background information about developmental and medical history. Typically, information is gathered about the child's school, peer relationships, hobbies and interests, and family relationships. This allows for rapport building and also helps the interviewer to place the child at ease. Second, past treatment is reviewed, including any medical conditions or legal involvement. Third, specific questions are asked to screen for Major Depression and other mood disorders, Schizophrenia and other psychotic disorders, anxiety disorders, and attention-deficit and disruptive behavior disorders.

It does not make sense for mental health counselors to read the *DSM-IV* diagnostic criteria word-for-word. Semistructured interviews indicate the importance of asking several questions of a parent or child to determine if a particular symptom is present and the severity of the problem. For example,

according to *DSM-IV*, the first symptom in a major depressive episode is a depressed mood for most of the day, nearly every day, for two weeks or more. It may make sense to ask questions of both the parent and child, such as: How have you been feeling lately? Have you been feeling sad, down, or cranky? How long does it last? How many days have you felt depressed? Do you feel sad most of the day? These are all examples of follow-up questions that help the mental health professional gauge a depressed mood. Counselors often overlook asking adolescents if they have felt mad, irritable, or cranky, all of which are also signs of depression or Bipolar Disorder. It is also important to ask if there were other times when they felt depressed for days on end, and to find out the longest period when they were depressed. The second symptom in a major depressive episode is a markedly diminished interest or pleasure in daily activities. To assess this feature, practitioners should ask what the child usually does for fun during free time, and if things have changed or become boring: Have you ever had times in the past when you lost interest in most things that you enjoy? Do you know why you have become depressed or lost interest in most things?

Given the wide range of possible psychiatric disorders involving children and adolescents and the high rate of comorbidity, it is important to include in each evaluation a broad survey of possible problems. Behavior checklists completed by the child's parents and teachers are often a first step in screening for childhood psychiatric disorders. Not only do these checklists provide some information on possible problems, but they also quantify how children compare to others of similar age and gender. There are many excellent checklists available, but the most commonly used checklist in clinical settings is the Achenbach Child Behavior Checklist and Teacher Report Form (CBCL, TRF; Achenbach, 1991). Items on the Achenbach are completed for the present time and over the prior two months, and are rated on a 3-point scale where 2 = Very true or often true, 1 = Somewhat or sometimes true, and 0 = Not true. However, it is important to keep in mind that the questions on any checklist are often briefly worded, and as a result, the response may be incomplete. For example, a question worded "Often fidgets" could be interpreted by the reader to refer to fidgeting with hands but perhaps not squirming in a chair. Screening checklists are helpful and important sources of information, but they do not substitute for a thorough clinical interview of the parents and child separately. These checklists can indicate areas for further interview in subsequent sessions.

APPROACHES TO DIAGNOSIS FOR SPECIFIC CHILDHOOD DISORDERS

Unfortunately, there is no one diagnostic interview that can work well with all childhood disorders. Mental health counselors must be prepared to change or modify their standard evaluation practice to address the problem at hand. Additional guidelines are provided for several highlighted disorders that demonstrate the importance of:

- Making direct behavioral observations (e.g., pervasive developmental disorders).
- Obtaining teacher report (e.g., Attention-Deficit/Hyperactivity Disorder).
- Interviewing the parents separately (e.g., Conduct Disorder).
- Using medical laboratory measures (e.g., Substance Abuse and Dependence).
- Thoroughly screening the patient for symptoms of psychosis or medical problems, which warrant immediate attention (e.g., Schizophrenia).
- Interviewing the patient in depth (e.g., mood or anxiety disorders).

When faced with specific diagnostic evaluation challenges involving disorders that are outside the scope of a mental health counselor's usual practice, there are several general handbooks listed in the references that serve as excellent resources for modifying the diagnostic evaluation (e.g., Mash & Terdal, 1997; Netherton, Holmes, & Walker, 1999).

Pervasive Developmental Disorders

Pervasive developmental disorders such as Autism are characterized by severe and pervasive impairment in social interaction and communication, accompanied by abnormal activity and interests, and typically presents before age 3. Neurological and medical disorders are common, as well as mental retardation. A variety of questionnaires and semistructured interviews are available (Trevarthen, Aitken, Papoudi, & Roberts, 1996). However, behavioral observation is often key, and referrals are commonly made for psychological evaluation. To assist clinical observation, instruments such as the Childhood Autism Rating Scales (Schopler, Reicher, DeVellis, & Daly, 1980) are often used to document symptoms and severity. Mental health counselors frequently observe that these children are detached and aloof and may ignore greetings. Language may be absent or odd. Physically, the child may hand-flap, toe-walk, and rock, and may react oddly to tactile or other stimulation.

Attention-Deficit/Hyperactivity Disorder

ADHD is characterized by both inattention and hyperactivity-impulsivity present before age 7 and causing significant impairment in multiple settings. For example, teachers often report that the child is having difficulty in the classroom setting listening, paying attention, and completing work. Hyperactivity may also be present, characterized by physical restlessness and constantly being on the go. In the diagnostic evaluation for ADHD, it is important to consider how the degree of symptoms varies across situations. It is not uncommon for children with ADHD to do more poorly on tasks they find boring. Behavior checklists are particularly important in the evaluation of ADHD, because they provide normative data relative to other children. The hyperactivity index of the Connors Revised Parent and Teacher Rating Scales (Goyette, Connors, & Ulrich, 1978) is commonly accepted as a normative-referenced index that can help discriminate between children with ADHD and comparison groups. The Connors is often repeated on a weekly basis while Ritalin, Adderal, or other psychopharmacological treatment is titrated by a physician to produce maximal behavioral improvement. Many consider that the most important method or "gold standard" by which ADHD should be judged is direct observation of classroom behavior (Abikoff, Gittleman-Klein, & Klein, 1977). Others also consider laboratory-based continuous performance tests helpful. For more information on noninterview-based aspects of the evaluation of ADHD, the reader is referred to Anastopoulos (1999). Clearly, when evaluating for ADHD, it is also important to augment the clinical interview with information directly from the teacher. (For more on ADHD, see Nigg & Rappley, this volume.)

Disruptive Behavior Disorders

Conduct Disorder is often diagnosed through parent interview simply by asking if the child has been displaying any of the behaviors outlined in *DSM-IV*. Conduct Disorder has four main features, which are typically easily elicited through parent interview. First, and most important, is physical aggressiveness to people or animals, which can be readily identified by inquiring about frequent fights at school or in the neighborhood with peers. Also, cruelty to people or animals, as well as use of weapons, are typically elicited through interview. Second, destruction of property should be explored, including firesetting and vandalism. Third, deceitfulness and theft can also be problems, including breaking into a car, house, or building, frequent lying, and stealing from others. Fourth, serious violations of rules involving truancy from home or school should be explored. What makes assessment unique is the importance of obtaining a thorough medical, developmental, and social history, as well as the importance of interviewing both parents together (Breen & Altepeter, 1991).

Substance-Related Disorders

Unfortunately, these disorders are all too common among adolescents with other psychiatric disorders. There are no well-validated measures to screen for substance use disorders in adolescents. Adolescents should be asked specifically about any use of alcohol, marijuana, cocaine, hallucinogens, opioids, inhalants, and stimulants. It makes sense to obtain from adolescents some measure of frequency of use (e.g., days per week or month), amount consumed, and how many total times they have used. Also, it may be helpful to use a timeline follow-back procedure, which involves a structured interview where daily consumption is charted with the aid of a monthly calendar and special events called "memory anchor points." During the interview, the adolescent should be asked about signs of dependence, including any desire to cut down or control use, time spent obtaining drugs or recovering, loss of friends, decrease in school/work performance, and mental or physical problems as a result of use. Laboratory measures, such as urine toxicology screens obtained through the adolescent's pediatrician, are often helpful in cross-validating self-report, as well as information from peers, typically obtained second-hand. Poor schoolwork or missing school because of use, driving while drunk, legal consequences, or fights with friends and family should all be explored. The goal of treatment is to break through the feelings of denial associated with substance dependence and to help the patient recognize the harmful consequences of ongoing use. Only with in-depth assessment can a clear picture of the harmful consequences of use be formed.

Schizophrenia and Other Psychotic Disorders

All children should be screened for the presence of auditory or visual hallucinations and delusions. Children with Schizophrenia generally will present with psychotic symptoms and a deterioration of overall functioning. Unfortunately, mental health counselors can easily overlook inquiring about delusions and hallucinations, with potentially tragic results. Children with early-onset Bipolar Disorder may also present with psychotic symptoms, and at times can be misdiagnosed as having Conduct Disorder. In situations where there is indication of psychosis, a psychiatric evaluation is clearly indicated to aid both in diagnosis and treatment (Werry, McClellan, & Chard, 1991). During the interview, children should be asked if they have ever heard noises that other people couldn't hear, such as the voices of people whispering or talking, or seen something that no one else could see, such as a person. It is important to determine if the child was awake at the time and to also consider the child's age; preschoolers often have imaginary friends. They should also be asked if others are conspiring against them or trying to hurt or poison them.

Depressive Disorders

Children and adolescents may provide more information about symptoms of depression than would be obtained through interview with the parents. All children will experience periods of sadness or unhappiness as a result of specific environmental or internal factors. Clearly, structured interviews highlight the importance of identifying depressive disorders in children and adolescents by conducting a thorough and in-depth interview (see previous). Numerous self-report checklists, such as the Children's Depression Inventory (Kovacs, 1980), have been used to assist not only in the diagnostic evaluation of depression, but also in monitoring symptom change over time. For an excellent review of depression scales and checklists in children, see Compas (1997).

Anxiety Disorders

Childhood fears and anxieties are so common that it is often difficult for any mental health professional to separate clinically significant anxieties and fears from those that are characteristic of normal child development. Consider how common it is for a toddler to experience nightmares, or for an older child to fear heights. By what standard do we determine if these fears justify a psychiatric diagnosis and treatment? As noted in *DSM-IV*, a mental

disorder requires that there be "clinically significant impairment or stress."

Determining the severity of a problem is a difficult clinical judgment. Anxiety disorders are a good example of the challenges in diagnostic evaluation, but the entire spectrum of childhood disorders is filled with the same difficulties. The best strategy to deal with this is to obtain information from multiple sources beyond the child, including the child's family and teachers. With anxiety disorders in particular, it is also important to ask questions to determine if the problem is unremitting or characteristic of a younger child.

To avoid overdiagnosis of Obsessive-Compulsive Disorder and other anxiety disorders, semistructured interviews have also been developed for anxiety disorders in children, such as the Anxiety Disorders Interview Schedule for *DSM-IV*, Child Version (ADIS-C; Silverman & Nelles, 1988). In this instrument, a feelings thermometer is used as a visual prompt to assist younger children in rating their fear or distress. Self-report anxiety scales, such as the Multidimensional Anxiety Scale for Children, can also be helpful in monitoring change over the course of treatment (MASC; March, Parker, Sullivan, Stallings, & Connors, 1997). For an excellent review of assessment of childhood anxiety disorders, see March and Albano (1998).

SUMMARY

The challenges of diagnosing psychiatric disorders in children and adolescents are great. This chapter reviewed many issues in evaluating childhood psychiatric disorders, but in no way is that review complete and comprehensive. Additional training, supervision, and experience in working with children and adolescents will be invaluable for those with further questions. Several recent books serve as excellent references; some have specific guidelines for interviewing children with psychiatric disorders (e.g., Morrison & Anders, 1999) and detailed reviews of childhood psychiatric disorders (Mash & Terdal, 1997). Readers are encouraged to consult these resources as well.

Diagnostic evaluation of childhood psychiatric disorders is a complex undertaking. Reliable and valid diagnostic evaluation must begin with a comprehensive and multimodal assessment. Subsequently, periodic reassessment will also aid the mental health counselor in both monitoring treatment progress and modifying the intervention plan. When evaluating a child for a psychiatric disorder, clinicians specifically should:

1. Obtain a comprehensive history.
2. Interview the parent and child separately.
3. Screen for all major childhood psychiatric disorders.
4. Obtain detailed information about specific symptoms that appear present, and document examples in notes.
5. Use construct-specific instruments tailored to the child's diagnosis to monitor change.
6. Obtain a second opinion when the diagnosis is in doubt.

References

Abikoff, H., Gittleman-Klein, R., & Klein, D. (1977). Validation of a classroom observation code for hyperactive children. *Journal of Clinical and Consulting Psychology, 45,* 772–783.

Achenbach, T.M. (1991). *Manual for the Child Behavior Checklist/4–18 and 1991 profile.* Burlington: University of Vermont, Department of Psychiatry.

American Psychiatric Association. (2000). *Diagnostic and statistical manual of mental disorders* (4th ed., text rev.). Washington, DC: American Psychiatric Association.

Anastopoulos, A. (1999). Attention-deficit/hyperactivity disorder. In S.D. Netherton, D. Holmes, & C.E. Walker (Eds.), *Child and adolescent psychological disorders: A comprehensive textbook* (pp. 118–138) New York: Oxford University Press.

Angold, A., & Fisher, P.W. (1999). Interviewer-based interviews. In D. Schaffer, C.P. Lucas, & J.E. Richters (Eds.), *Diagnostic assessment of child and adolescent psychopathology* (pp. 34–64) New York: Guilford Press.

Breen, M.J., & Altepeter, T.S. (1990). *Disruptive behavior disorders in children: A treatment-focused assessment.* New York: Guilford Press.

Compas, B.E. (1997). Depression in children and adolescents. In E.J. Mash & L.G. Terdal (Eds.), *Assessment of childhood disorders* (pp. 197–229). New York: Guilford Press.

Goyette, C.H., Connors, C.K., & Ulrich, R.F. (1978). Normative data on Revised Connors Parent and Teacher Rating Scales. *Journal of Abnormal Child Psychology, 20,* 221–236.

Kovacs, M. (1980). Rating scales to assess depression in school-aged children. *Acta Paediatrica, 46,* 305–315.

March, J.S., & Albano, A.M. (1998). New developments in assessing pediatric anxiety disorders. In T.H. Ollendick & R.J. Prinz (Eds.), *Advances in clinical child psychology* (Vol. 20, pp. 213–241). New York: Plenum Press.

March, J.S., Parker, J., Sullivan, K., Stallings, P., & Connors, C. (1997). The Multidimensional Anxiety Scale for Children (MASC): Factor structure, reliability, and validity. *Journal of the American Academy of Child and Adolescent Psychiatry, 36,* 554–565.

Mash, E.J., & Terdal, L.G. (1997). *Assessment of childhood disorders.* New York: Guilford Press.

Morrison, J.R., & Anders, T.F. (1999). *Interviewing children and adolescents.* New York: Guilford Press.

Netherton, S.D., Holmes, D., & Walker, C.E. (1999). *Child and adolescent psychological disorders: A comprehensive textbook.* New York: Oxford University Press.

Orvaschel, H. (1995). *Schedule for Affective Disorders and Schizophrenia in School-Age Children, Epidemiologic version 5.* Ft. Lauderdale, FL: Nova Southeastern University.

Orvaschel, H., Puig-Antich, J., Chambers, W., Tabrizi, M.A., & Johnson, R. (1982). Retrospective assessment of prepubertal major depression with the Kiddie-SADS-E. *Journal of the American Academy of Child Psychiatry, 21,* 392–397.

Schaffer, D., Fisher, P.W., & Lucas, C.P. (1999). Respondent-based interviews. In D. Schaffer, C.P. Lucas, & J.E. Richters (Eds.), *Diagnostic assessment of child and adolescent psychopathology* (pp. 3–33). New York: Guilford Press.

Schopler, E., Reichler, R.J., DeVellis, R.F., & Daly, K. (1980). Toward objective classification of childhood autism: Childhood Autism Rating Scale (CARS). *Journal of Autism and Developmental Disorders, 10,* 91–103.

Silverman, W.K., & Nelles, W.B. (1988). The Anxiety Disorders Interview Schedule for Children. *Journal of the American Academy of Child and Adolescent Psychiatry, 27,* 772–778.

Trevarthen, C., Aitken, K., Papoudi, D., & Roberts, J. (1996). *Children with autism: Diagnosis and interventions to meet their needs.* London: Jessica Kingsley.

Werry, J.S., McClellan, J.M., & Chard, L. (1991). Childhood and adolescent schizophrenic, bipolar, and schizoaffective disorders: A clinical and outcome study. *Journal of the American Academy of Child and Adolescent Psychiatry, 27,* 772–778.

24 CHILD MALTREATMENT

Treatment of Child and Adolescent Victims

Cindy L. Miller-Perrin

Child maltreatment is a complex social problem affecting large numbers of children each year. According to the U.S. Department of Health and Human Services (2000), there were 903,000 substantiated victims of child maltreatment in 1998, for a rate of 12.9 per 1,000 children. Of these cases, child neglect was the most common form of maltreatment (53.5%), followed by physical abuse (22.7%), sexual abuse (11.5%), and psychological abuse and neglect (6%). Although not all experts agree on the specific behaviors or events that constitute these forms of child maltreatment, progress has been made in broadly defining them. *Physical abuse* refers to the use of inappropriate physical strategies (e.g., beatings, striking a child with an object, burning a child) resulting in substantial risk of physical or emotional harm to a child. *Sexual abuse* refers to interactions between a child and an adult when the child is being used for the sexual stimulation of the perpetrator or another person (e.g., oral/anal/genital penetration,

fondling, kissing, child pornography). *Child neglect* refers to deficits in the provision of a child's basic needs (e.g., inattention to health care needs, inadequate supervision, inadequate nutrition, clothing, or hygiene). *Psychological maltreatment* refers to "serious mental injury" or acts that communicate to a child that he or she is worthless, unloved, or unwanted. Acts constituting psychological maltreatment include both *emotionally neglectful behaviors* (e.g., inadequate nurture or affection, refusal or delay in psychological care) and *emotionally abusive behaviors* (e.g., verbally belittling, denigrating, threatening, or rejecting children).

SEQUELAE ASSOCIATED WITH CHILD MALTREATMENT

Several behaviors and problems representing the most common potential signs of child maltreatment are presented in Table 24.1.

TABLE 24.1   Potential Signs and Symptoms Associated with Various Forms of Child and Adolescent Maltreatment

Sexual Abuse

Children

Physical complications: genital bleeding, pain, odors; eating or sleep disturbances; somatic complaints; enuresis or encopresis

Affective-behavioral problems: anxiety and fears; nightmares; guilt; anger/hostility; depression; low self-esteem; sexualized behavior and preoccupation (e.g., excessive masturbation, sex play with others, sexual language, genital exposure, sexual victimization of others); aggression; regression/immaturity; hyperactivity

Cognitive deficits: learning difficulties; poor attention and concentration; declining grades

Adolescents

Physical complications: somatic complaints; eating disturbance; sleep disturbance

Affective-behavioral problems: anxiety; anger; depression; guilt; suicidal ideation; low self-esteem; social withdrawal; self-injurious behavior; sexualized behavior; delinquency; running away; substance abuse

Cognitive deficits: learning difficulties; poor concentration and attention; declining grades

Physical Abuse

Children

Physical complications: bruises; head, chest, and abdominal injuries; burns; fractures

Affective-behavioral problems: aggression; hopelessness; depression; low self-esteem; fighting; noncompliance; defiance; property offenses; arrests

Cognitive deficits: decreased intellectual and cognitive functioning; deficits in verbal faculty, memory, problem solving, perceptual-motor skills, and verbal abilities; decreased reading and math skills; poor school achievement; increase in special education services

Social deficits: delayed play skills; infant attachment problems; poor social interaction skills, difficulty making friends, deficits in prosocial behaviors, and deficits in social competence with peers; avoidance of adults

Adolescents

Antisocial behavior: violent interpersonal behavior; delinquency; violent offenses; substance abuse

Other: attention problems; depressed school performance; increased daily stress; low self-esteem

Child Neglect

Physical complications: failure to thrive

Affective-behavioral problems: low self-esteem; aggression; anger; frustration; conduct problems

Cognitive deficits: language deficits; academic problems; intellectual delays; poor problem solving

Social deficits: disturbed parent-child attachment and interactions; deficits in prosocial behavior; social withdrawal and isolation

Psychological Maltreatment

Affective-behavioral problems: aggression; self-abusive behavior; anxiety; shame; guilt; anger and hostility; pessimism; dependency

Cognitive deficits: academic problems; deficits in cognitive ability; poor problem solving

Social deficits: insecure attachments; poor social adjustment

---

Although no one symptom is pathognomic of child maltreatment, the presence of a constellation of symptoms should arouse the suspicion of mental health counselors. Counselors should be mindful, however, that although these behaviors and symptoms appear to be correlated with child maltreatment, researchers have yet to determine the precise nature of causal links between abuse experiences and mental health outcomes.

Because the potential sequelae of child maltreatment can involve multiple aspects of functioning, many patterns of psychiatric symptoms can emerge, resulting in various diagnoses. In *DSM-IV* (American Psychiatric Association, 2000), problems associated with child maltreatment can be coded on Axis I as V-Codes including Physical Abuse of Child, Sexual Abuse of Child, and Neglect of Child. Adjustment Disorder is also a possible diagnosis. Diagnostic considerations should also include Posttraumatic Stress Disorder (PTSD) because both sexual and physical abuse victims are likely to exhibit symptoms consistent with this disorder (e.g., Dubner & Motta, 1999; McLeer, Callaghan, Henry, & Wallen, 1994). Other psychiatric diagnostic patterns commonly noted in victims of child maltreatment include anxiety disorders without PTSD symptoms, mood disorders, Conduct Disorder, ADHD, and Oppositional Defiant Disorder (e.g., McLeer et al., 1994).

TREATMENT CONSIDERATIONS

Working with children and adolescents with an abuse history involves special considerations that should be addressed at the beginning of treatment, including client heterogeneity, developmental issues, and potential impediments to effective treatment.

Client Heterogeneity

Victims of child maltreatment are a diverse group in a number of ways. Victims differ, for example, with regard to their preabuse histories, the nature of their abuse experiences, familial and system responses to the abuse, and available social supports and coping resources. In addition, child maltreatment victims exhibit a range of symptoms of varying intensity. Some children display a variety of symptoms, whereas others demonstrate few or a complete absence of symptoms. Researchers have linked these areas of divergence and shown that factors associated with victims and their abuse often mediate the symptoms that result (e.g., Herrenkohl, Herrenkohl, Rupert, Egolf, & Lutz, 1995).

Given such complexity, it is not surprising that victims of child maltreatment represent a diverse group both in terms of symptom presentation and treatment response. As a result, there is no canned treatment approach that will be appropriate or effective for all clients. Indeed, not all maltreated children will require professional treatment. In addition, some research shows that symptoms for some victims diminish without therapy (Gomes-Schwartz, Horowitz, Cardarelli, & Sauzier, 1990). Professionals should consider the heterogeneity of this treatment population when making treatment decisions, paying particular attention to symptom presentation as well as specific preabuse, abuse, and postabuse characteristics.

Developmental Issues

Research indicates that a child's developmental status is associated with functional outcomes in cases of child maltreatment (see Table 24.1; Becker et al., 1995). Young children, for example, often display difficulties with academic work and attachments (physical abuse) or anxiety and sexualized behavior (sexual abuse). Adolescents, on the other hand, most often demonstrate juvenile delinquency, substance abuse, and low self-esteem. These developmental differences in victim reactions to maltreatment may result from age-related differences in the way victims perceive their abuse experiences (Miller-Perrin, 1998). Mental health counselors should take such developmental differences into account when formulating treatment approaches. Therapists should also consider developmental status when determining specific therapeutic interventions and techniques. Therapists, for example, should talk to children in language they can understand and select approaches consistent with the child's developmental capabilities (e.g., the use of drawings and games for younger children and verbal discussions with older children).

Potential Impediments to Effective Treatment

One challenge to implementing effective treatment interventions with child maltreatment families is the potential for countertransference issues. Therapists working with a parent who has abused a child may have strong negative feelings toward the parent that make it difficult to remain objective and respond in a therapeutic manner. Counselors may also feel uncomfortable when working with children who display challenging behaviors associated with their abuse experience (e.g., sexual behaviors toward the therapist). In addition, studies have revealed that a significant number of professionals who work with victims have a history of child abuse themselves (e.g., Nuttall & Jackson, 1994). These experiences might affect practitioners' views of child maltreatment and its victims, contributing to nonobjective or even distorted perceptions of clients. Practitioners should consult with colleagues regularly to avoid such potential problems.

Other potential challenges in working with maltreating families are difficulties associated with establishing and maintaining therapeutic relationships. Maltreating parents, for example, may be court-ordered to participate in treatment and therefore may lack motivation to change their behavior. In addition, abusive parents often deny that child maltreatment has taken place. Azar and Wolfe (1998) recommend reframing the problem in terms of everyday difficulties such as "trouble handling children," "loneliness," or "stress" to reduce defensiveness. In addition, mutually consensual goal setting may be an effective means of motivating parents for therapy. Special care may also be needed in developing a therapeutic relationship with maltreated children and adolescents who may be reluctant to interact with an adult given their previous history of negative interactions. Therapists should therefore be particularly sensitive to client issues surrounding trust and anxiety about treatment.

Legal issues are another potential impediment to treatment. Mandated reporting responsibilities, for example, should be raised as early as possible in the treatment process with both children and parents. A specific plan for addressing reports to child protective services should be developed with the family's input. To help preserve the therapeutic relationship, clients should be informed before a report is made and given the opportunity to make the report themselves, with the therapist's assistance, if possible. A clinical follow-up to allow families to discuss their reactions to any report of child maltreatment can also be important to maintaining a therapeutic alliance. Child maltreatment also frequently includes legal issues involving the family, such as investigation and prosecution. Families may need to be educated about the role and procedures of local child protective services agencies. Involvement in various legal proceedings could be an additional stressor that families must deal with, and therapists should be aware of the ongoing and potentially stressful nature of such proceedings for both the victim and family (Cohen & Mannarino, 1999).

TREATMENT INTERVENTIONS

Very little research has been conducted on interventions with child and adolescent victims of child maltreatment. As a result, relatively little is known about the success of victim-oriented interventions for the various forms of child maltreatment (see Finkelhor & Berliner, 1995; Oates & Bross, 1995). Although the amount of research examining treatment efficacy is limited, available studies suggest several approaches to intervening in cases of child maltreatment. Due to the complex nature of child maltreatment, interventions should comprise multiple components targeting a variety of problem areas. In addition, because child maltreatment most often occurs within the context of the family, treatment interventions necessarily should focus on the family as well as the child or adolescent victim. Based on each individual client's presentation, mental health practitioners should attempt to incorporate several of the following components into a treatment plan.

Managing Thoughts and Feelings

One major goal of treatment is to help the victim of abuse manage the negative thoughts and emotions that often are associated with child maltreatment, such as guilt, shame, stigmatization, anger, stress, and fear. Therapy should provide victims with the opportunity to diffuse negative feelings by confronting their abuse experience in the safety of a supportive therapeutic relationship. Older children and adolescents often are able to process the abusive experience simply by discussing it with their therapists. For younger children, however, other avenues may be necessary, such as reenacting the abuse through play. Regardless of the client's age, it is necessary to teach strategies for managing the negative emotions that may accompany the processing of the abuse, such as relaxation training, anger management, problem-solving skills, positive coping statements, gradual exposure, stress inoculation, and the use of imagery (see Berliner & Saunders, 1996; E. Deblinger, Lippmann, & Steer, 1996). In implementing any of these strategies, practitioners should be aware that for many victims of abuse, the tendency to avoid activities directed at the past abuse experience (e.g., talking about the abuse, remembering aspects of the traumatic event) can be quite strong.

Another treatment objective is to provide clarification of victim cognitions and beliefs that might lead to negative self-attributions. Cognitive-behavioral approaches are frequently used to help victims change their perceptions about being "different" as well as beliefs that they are somehow to blame for the abuse. Here, therapists often undertake some form of cognitive restructuring to appropriately relocate the responsibility of the abuse to the offender (see Cahill, Llewelyn, & Pearson, 1991; Osmond, Durham, Leggett, & Keating, 1998). Group therapy is a particularly effective modality in which to counter self-denigrating beliefs and to confront issues of secrecy and stigmatization because participants are able to discuss their experiences with peers who also have been abused (Cahill et al., 1991).

Reducing Problem Behavior

Another goal of treatment is the reduction of specific problem behaviors. Although such problems are often addressed through parent training approaches, noted below, individual cognitive-behavioral approaches with children have also been effective in reducing behavioral dysfunctions such as impulsivity, aggression, and sexualized behavior (e.g., Cohen & Mannarino, 1996; Kolko, 1996). Several other therapeutic modalities have demonstrated success in reducing various problem behaviors exhibited by maltreated children, including group approaches as well as dyadic therapy, whereby parents and children are coached to improve parent-child interactions (e.g., Becker & Bonner, 1998; Urquiza & McNeil, 1996). Some preliminary reports also suggest the efficacy of pharmacological interventions for reducing problem behaviors as well as hyperarousal (e.g., Harmon & Riggs, 1996).

Empowering the Child Survivor

Many experts believe that prevention training in the form of self-protection skills is an important component of treatment for clients with a history of child maltreatment. Necessary self-protection skills include teaching children to identify abuse situations, providing them with specific responses to protect themselves from abusive encounters, and encouraging them to disclose any abuse experiences. Such skills are important in light of research that suggests that child maltreatment victims are at increased risk for varied forms of revictimization (Beitchman et al., 1992). Training children in self-protection might prevent future abuse from occurring, contribute to the discontinuation of abuse (e.g., via a victim's disclosure), and may enhance a child's feelings of self-efficacy and self-esteem (Berliner, 1991; I. Deblinger, McLeer, & Henry, 1990). Therapists should also be sensitive and realistic, however, about the degree of control a child might have in threatening situations, particularly those that occur in a child's own home (Cohen & Mannarino, 1999).

Enhancing Developmental Skills

Another primary objective for treatment directed at those who have experienced child maltreatment is to enhance developmental skills (e.g., cognitive and social skills deficits). One of the most common intervention strategies to ameliorate developmental deficits is therapeutic day treatment programs, which typically provide group activities, opportunities for peer interactions, and learning experiences to address developmental delays (Culp, Little, Letts, & Lawrence, 1991). Strategies for enhancing developmental skills, such as problem solving and social skills, can also be implemented during the course of individual therapy (Ammerman & Galvin, 1998). Problem-solving skills training, for example, can teach child maltreatment victims to identify problem situations, generate solutions, and implement appropriate responses. Traditional social skills training can also be implemented, such as didactic instruction, behavioral rehearsal and role-playing, therapist modeling, and films of peers modeling appropriate behavior. Others have used peer prompting, groups, or play therapy to enhance social skills development (Davis & Fantuzzo, 1989; Fantuzzo et al., 1988).

Improving Parent Skills

In treating cases of child maltreatment, mental health professionals should also consider including parent-focused interventions that target the parents of maltreated children. Most parent interventions have focused on physically abusive and neglectful parents and include cognitive-behavioral approaches in the form of skills training (Schellenbach, 1998). Such training involves:

- Teaching parents about normal child developmental processes to correct misperceptions and unrealistic expectations of their children.
- Educating parents about the appropriate use of reinforcement and punishment in shaping child behavior and the importance of consistency in discipline.
- Anger control techniques to reduce negative emotional responses and thoughts and to enhance coping ability.
- Education and training in stress management techniques, such as relaxation training, stress reduction, and coping with stressful parent-child interactions.

Interventions for parents who sexually abuse their children are beyond the scope of this chapter and the reader is referred elsewhere for descriptions (see Chaffin, 1994). Although less common, interventions for the nonoffending parent and siblings in sexually abusive families have been developed and typically focus on education regarding the consequences of child sexual abuse, parental support, instruction in modeling adaptive coping for the child, instruction in parent-child communication, and behavior management skills training (Cohen & Mannarino, 1996; Grosz, Kempe, & Kelly, 2000). Early research evaluating the efficacy of such approaches appears promising for reducing children's externalizing behaviors and self-reported depression and for improving parenting skills (E. Deblinger et al., 1996).

Implementing Adjunct Treatments and Services

Practitioners should also consider implementing various adjuncts to victim-oriented and parent-oriented approaches when treating cases of child maltreatment. Because of the complex and interactive nature of child abuse and neglect, treatment interventions should address a broad range of services not only to address individual needs but to strengthen the functioning of the family embedded in a community. Given the high incidence of marital discord and substance abuse that occurs in maltreating families (Justice & Calvert, 1990; McCurdy & Daro, 1994), possible adjuncts to treatment include marital counseling and alcohol or drug abuse treatment. Maltreating families also are characterized by a lack of social and economic resources. Possible interventions to enhance social support include strengthening informal support networks, using personal networking, volunteer linking, employing neighborhood helpers, and social skills training (Gaudin, Wodarski, Arkinson, & Avery, 1990). Other possible adjuncts to which the practitioner should consider referring families include employment or economic assistance (e.g., through local service organizations, the family's caseworker, or the Salvation Army), money management, home visitation programs, support groups (e.g., Parents Anonymous), crisis hotlines, respite care services, day care or preschool services (e.g., Head Start centers, therapeutic child care centers), and educational classes (Daro & McCurdy, 1994; Hay & Jones, 1994).

SUMMARY

Several forms of maltreatment have emerged from the research literature, including *physical abuse, child neglect, sexual abuse,* and *psychological maltreatment.* Treatment for the various forms of child maltreatment remains a challenge given the complex nature of child maltreatment and the difficulties associated with research in this area. In attempting to address the needs of child maltreatment victims effectively in treatment, mental health professionals should be aware of the following:

- Childhood experiences of maltreatment frequently are associated with myriad problems that may affect the physical, cognitive, social, emotional, and/or behavioral functioning of children and adolescents.
- Therapists face several challenges in working with child maltreatment cases, including the heterogeneity of child maltreatment victims, developmental considerations, and special circumstances that might impede treatment.
- Child-focused interventions should focus on managing thoughts and feelings, reducing problem behavior, empowering the maltreatment survivor via self-protection skills, and enhancing developmental skills.
- Parent-focused interventions should be included and should focus on education about abuse, enhancement of parenting knowledge and skills, parental support, instruction in modeling adaptive coping and parent-child communication, anger management, and stress reduction techniques.
- Several treatment adjuncts and services should also be considered when treating child maltreatment families to address the multidimensional nature of child maltreatment and to enhance the effectiveness of child- and parent-focused approaches.

References

American Psychiatric Association. (2000). *Diagnostic and statistical manual of mental disorders* (4th ed., text rev.). Washington, DC: Author.

Ammerman, R.T., & Galvin, M.R. (1998). Child maltreatment. In R.T. Ammerman & J.V. Campo (Eds.), *Psychological and psychiatric issues in the pediatric setting* (pp. 31–69). Boston: Allyn & Bacon.

Azar, S.T., & Wolfe, D.A. (1998). Child physical abuse and neglect. In E.J. Mash & R.A. Barkley (Eds.), *Treatment of childhood disorders* (2nd ed., pp. 501–544). New York: Guilford Press.

Becker, J.V., Alpert, J.L., BigFoot, D.S., Bonner, B.L., Geddie, L.F., Henggeler, S.W., Kaufman, K.L., & Walker, C.E. (1995). Empirical research on child abuse treatment: Report by the Child Abuse and Neglect Treatment Working Group, American Psychological Association. *Journal of Clinical Child Psychology, 24*(Suppl.), 23–46.

Becker, J.V., & Bonner, B. (1998). Sexual and other abuse of children. In R.J. Morris & T.R. Kratochwill (Eds.), *The practice of child therapy* (pp. 367–389). Needham Heights, MA: Allyn & Bacon.

Beitchman, J.H., Zucker, K.J., Hood, J.E., & DaCosta, G.A. (1992). A review of the long term effects of child sexual abuse. *Child Abuse & Neglect, 16,* 101–118.

Berliner, L. (1991). Clinical work with sexually abused children. In C.R. Hollin & K. Howells (Eds.), *Clinical approaches to sex offenders and their victims* (pp. 209–228). New York: Wiley.

Berliner, L., & Saunders, B.E. (1996). Treating fear and anxiety in sexually abused children: Results of a controlled 2-year follow-up study. *Child Maltreatment, 1,* 294–309.

Cahill, C., Llewelyn, S.P., & Pearson, C. (1991). Treatment of sexual abuse which occurred in childhood: A review. *British Journal of Clinical Psychology, 30,* 1–12.

Chaffin, M. (1994). Research in action: Assessment and treatment of child sexual abusers. *Journal of Interpersonal Violence, 9,* 224–237.

Cohen, J.A., & Mannarino, A.P. (1996). Factors that mediate treatment outcome of sexually abused preschool children. *Journal of the American Academy of Child and Adolescent Psychiatry, 34,* 1402–1410.

Cohen, J.A., & Mannarino, A.P. (1999). Sexual abuse. In R.T. Ammerman, M. Hersen, & C.G. Last (Eds.), *Handbook of prescriptive treatments for children and adolescents* (pp. 308–329). Needham Heights, MA: Allyn & Bacon.

Culp, R.E., Little, V., Letts, D., & Lawrence, H. (1991). Maltreated children's self-concept: Effects of a comprehensive treatment program. *American Journal of Orthopsychiatry, 61,* 114–121.

Daro, D., & McCurdy, K. (1994). Preventing child abuse and neglect: Programmatic interventions. *Child Welfare, 73,* 405–430.

Davis, S.P., & Fantuzzo, J.W. (1989). The effects of adult and peer social initiations on the social behavior of withdrawn and aggressive maltreated preschool children. *Journal of Family Violence, 4,* 227–248.

Deblinger, E., Lippmann, J., & Steer, R. (1996). Sexually abused children suffering posttraumatic stress symptoms: Initial treatment outcome findings. *Child Maltreatment, 1,* 310–321.

Deblinger, I., McLeer, S.V., & Henry, D. (1990). Cognitive behavioral treatment for sexually abused children suffering from posttraumatic stress: Preliminary findings. *American Academy of Child and Adolescent Psychiatry, 29,* 747–752.

Dubner, A.E., & Motta, R.W. (1999). Sexually and physically abused foster care children and posttraumatic stress disorder. *Journal of Consulting and Clinical Psychology, 67,* 367–373.

Fantuzzo, J.W., Jurecic, L., Stovall, A., Hightower, A.D., Goins, C., & Schachtel, D. (1988). Effects of adult and peer social initiations on the social behavior of withdrawn, maltreated preschool children. *Journal of Consulting and Clinical Psychology, 56,* 34–39.

Finkelhor, D., & Berliner, L. (1995). Research on the treatment of sexually abused children: A review and recommendations. *Journal of the American Academy of Child and Adolescent Psychiatry, 34,* 1408–1423.

Gaudin, J.M., Jr., Wodarski, J.S., Arkinson, M.K., & Avery, L.S. (1990). Remedying child neglect: Effectiveness of social network interventions. *Journal of Applied Social Sciences, 15,* 97–123.

Gomes-Schwartz, B., Horowitz, J.M., Cardarelli, A.P., & Sauzier, M. (1990). The aftermath of child sexual abuse: Eighteen months later. In B. Gomes-Schwartz, J.M. Horowitz, & A.P. Cardarelli (Eds.), *Child sexual abuse: The initial effects* (pp. 132–151). Newbury Park, CA: Sage.

Grosz, C.A., Kempe, R.S., & Kelly, M. (2000). Extrafamilial sexual abuse: Treatment for child victims and their families. *Child Abuse and Neglect, 24,* 9–23.

Harmon, R.J., & Riggs, P.D. (1997). Clonidine for posttraumatic stress disorder in preschool children. *Journal of the American Academy of Child and Adolescent Psychiatry, 35,* 1247–1249.

Hay, T., & Jones, L. (1994). Societal interventions to prevent child abuse and neglect. *Child Welfare, 73,* 379–403.

Herrenkohl, E.C., Herrenkohl, R.C., Rupert, L.J., Egolf, B.P., & Lutz, J.G. (1995). Risk factors for behavioral dysfunction: The relative impact of maltreatment, SES, physical health problems, cognitive ability, and quality of parent-child interaction. *Child Abuse and Neglect, 19,* 191–203.

Justice, B., & Calvert, A. (1990). Family environment factors associated with child abuse. *Psychological Reports, 66,* 458.

Kolko, D.J. (1996). Individual cognitive behavioral treatment and family therapy for physically abused children and their offending parents: A comparison of clinical outcomes. *Child Maltreatment, 1,* 322–342.

McCurdy, K., & Daro, D. (1994). *Current trends in child abuse reporting and fatalities: The results of the 1993 annual fifty state survey.* (Available from the National Committee to Prevent Child Abuse, 332 South Michigan Ave., Suite 1600, Chicago, IL 60604)

McLeer, S., Callaghan, M., Henry, D., & Wallen, J. (1994). Psychiatric disorders in sexually abused children. *Journal of the American Academy of Child and Adolescent Psychiatry, 33,* 313–319.

Miller-Perrin, C.L. (1998). Sexually abused children's perceptions of sexual abuse: An exploratory analysis and comparison across ages. *Journal of Child Sexual Abuse, 7,* 1–22.

Nuttall, R., & Jackson, H. (1994). Personal history of childhood abuse among clinicians. *Child Abuse and Neglect, 18,* 455–472.

Oates, R.K., & Bross, D.C. (1995). What have we learned about treating child physical abuse? A literature review of the last decade. *Child Abuse and Neglect, 19,* 463–474.

Osmond, M., Durham, D., Leggett, A., & Keating, J. (1998). *Treating the aftermath of sexual abuse: A handbook for working with children in care.* Washington, DC: Child Welfare League of America.

Schellenbach, C.J. (1998). Child maltreatment: A critical review of research on treatment for physically abusive parents. In P.K. Trickett & C.J. Schellenbach (Eds.), *Violence against children in the family and the community* (pp. 251–268). Washington, DC: American Psychological Association.

Urquiza, A.J., & McNeil, C.B. (1996). Parent-child interaction therapy: An intensive dyadic intervention for physically abusive families. *Child Maltreatment, 1,* 134–144.

U.S. Department of Health and Human Services, Administration on Children, Youth, and Families. (2000). *Child Maltreatment 1998: Reports from the states to the National Child Abuse and Neglect Data System.* Washington, DC: U.S. Government Printing Office.

Resources on Child Maltreatment

Several resources are available to assist mental health counselors in accessing the most current information on child maltreatment, including resource books and online services.

Resource Books on Child Maltreatment

Briere, J., Berliner, L., Bulkley, J.A., Jenny, C., & Reid, T. (1996). *The APSAC handbook on child maltreatment.* Thousand Oaks, CA: Sage.

Child Welfare League of America. (1998). *CWLA standards of excellence for services for abused or neglected children and their families.* Washington, DC: Author.

Karp, C.L., Butler, T.L., & Bergstrom, S.C. (1998). *Treatment strategies for abused adolescents.* Thousand Oaks, CA: Sage.

Lutzker, J.R. (Ed.). (1997). *Handbook of child abuse research and treatment.* New York: Plenum Press.

Miller-Perrin, C.L., & Perrin, R.D. (1999). *Child maltreatment: An introduction.* Thousand Oaks, CA: Sage.

Pearce, J.W., & Pezzot-Pearce, T.D. (1997). *Psychotherapy of abused and neglected children.* New York: Guilford Press.

Wolfe, D.A., McMahon, R.J., & Peters, R.D. (1997). *Child abuse: New directions in prevention and treatment across the lifespan.* Thousand Oaks, CA: Sage.

Online Child Maltreatment Resources

International Society for Prevention of Child Abuse and Neglect
www.child.cornell.edu

Child Abuse Prevention Network
www.child.cornell.edu

National Committee to Prevent Child Abuse
www.childabuse.org

Kempe Center Programs
www.kempecenter.org

National Clearinghouse on Child Abuse and Neglect Information
www.calib.com/nccanch

25 TREATING ANXIETY DISORDERS IN CHILDREN

Christopher A. Kearney and Lisa M. Linning

The concept of anxiety in children has been a focus of mental health professionals for many decades, but the study of how to treat excessive anxiety in children has burgeoned only recently. This chapter discusses the major concepts and terminology used regarding anxiety and anxiety disorders in youth, recent findings that empirically support psychosocial and pharmacological treatments for these disorders, and recommendations for counseling in this area. Resources for further study are also included.

MAJOR CONSTRUCTS AND TERMINOLOGY

Anxiety is a state of general apprehension and discomfort marked by behavioral, cognitive, and physiological symptoms. Common behavioral symptoms in children include avoidance, excessive reassurance seeking, freezing, clinging to others, and crying. Common cognitive or thought-related symptoms include excessive worry about daily and possibly dangerous events, irrational conclusions about oneself and one's environment, and self-deprecation.

Common physiological symptoms include accelerated heart rate, sweating, muscle tension, nausea, stomachaches, headaches, and tremors. A detailed listing of symptoms is available (see Barrios & O'Dell, 1998).

The most common anxiety disorders in children include, alphabetically, Generalized Anxiety Disorder, Obsessive-Compulsive Disorder, Panic Disorder, Posttraumatic Stress Disorder, Separation Anxiety Disorder, Social Anxiety Disorder, and Specific Phobia. However, other syndromes (e.g., Acute Stress Disorder, Selective Mutism) and related problems (e.g., school refusal behavior; see Kearney, 2001) may also apply.

According to the *Diagnostic and Statistical Manual of Mental Disorders* (*DSM-IV*; American Psychiatric Association, 1994), Generalized Anxiety Disorder is marked by excessive and uncontrollable worry as well as physical symptoms (e.g., restlessness) for at least six months. Obsessive-Compulsive Disorder is marked by recurrent, intrusive, bizarre, and uncontrollable thoughts (e.g., contamination) as well as repetitive behaviors or rituals (e.g., handwashing) designed to reduce distress from these thoughts. Panic Disorder is characterized by a series of panic attacks or physical and cognitive symptoms that accelerate and peak within 10 minutes. Fear of subsequent attacks occurs as well. Agoraphobia, or the avoidance of places where a panic attack may occur, is commonly associated with Panic Disorder.

Posttraumatic Stress Disorder involves the presence of specific symptoms following exposure to an extreme stressor (e.g., assault). Key symptoms include physiological hyperarousal, avoidance of stimuli associated with the stressor, and reexperiencing the stressor via memories, dreams, and flashbacks. Separation Anxiety Disorder, the only *DSM-IV* anxiety disorder specific to youth, refers to excessive anxiety about separation from home or major attachment figures (e.g., parents) for at least four weeks. In addition, the child may worry excessively about harm to self or parents while separated. Social Anxiety Disorder refers to persistent fear during interactions with or performances before other people (e.g., public speaking). Socially related

panic-like symptoms and avoidance must last for at least six months. Finally, Specific Phobia is marked by unreasonable fear of a specific object (e.g., animal) or situation (e.g., flying); a severe and immediate anxiety response is triggered following exposure to the phobic stimulus. To meet diagnostic criteria for any of the anxiety disorders, significant interference in daily functioning must be present.

MAJOR FINDINGS AND QUESTIONS REGARDING TREATMENT

The treatment of anxiety disorders in youth has a long history that can be divided into two main phases. The first phase, involving study in the 1960s to 1980s, consisted of many case studies and single-case experimental designs that focused on children with specific fears. The second phase, involving study in the 1990s to the present, consists of a growing number of large-scale interventions that focus on children with different types of anxiety disorders. Both phases involve psychosocial treatment, with a concentration on cognitive-behavioral approaches, and pharmacological treatment, with a concentration on anxiolytic and antidepressant medication. Psychosocial and pharmacological treatments are now discussed separately.

Psychosocial Treatment

Psychosocial treatment for children with anxiety disorders primarily targets the reduction of problematic behavioral, cognitive, and physiological symptoms. The most common approach involves cognitive-behavioral treatment that consists of several components. These treatment components essentially include psychoeducation, systematic desensitization (including relaxation training and exposure), flooding, response prevention, modeling and role play, cognitive restructuring, and parent-based contingency management. Typically, these treatments are administered in conjunction with one another.

Psychoeducation involves educating a child about the nature of anxiety and its response components, and how these components interact in the child to produce an aversive state. Children are informed about the behavioral, cognitive, and physiological components of anxiety, and asked which components usually occur first in their case. In many children, for example, physiological symptoms such as accelerated heart rate lead to cognitive symptoms such as worries about failure or ridicule. Such cognitions may then lead to behavioral avoidance, clinging to others, crying, or other problems. Children are informed of how their cycle of anxiety works and are shown how different treatment components address these aspects of anxiety.

Systematic desensitization was originally designed as a technique whereby one is gradually exposed to fearful stimuli via imagination. Prior to such exposure, a person is taught to relax, often by tensing and releasing different muscle groups. This state of relaxation is then paired gradually with different anxiety-provoking scenes. A person fearful of dogs, for example, would listen to contrived scenes from a therapist regarding various interactions with dogs. As the person listens to such interactions, which should increase anxiety, he or she induces relaxation and, it is hoped, reduces the amount of fear associated with the stimulus (i.e., dog). Over time, the person may listen to more anxiety-provoking scenes, and relax, until no scene produces an aversive reaction. In vivo exposure is usually introduced next; here, one is gradually exposed to real-life situations involving a phobic stimulus. Relaxation is gradually paired with closer approximations to the phobic stimulus until the person can interact with the stimulus (e.g., pet a dog) with no problem.

Flooding is similar to systematic desensitization, but usually involves initial exposure to the most anxiety-provoking scene without prior relaxation training. This approach, based on extinction, assumes that a person will eventually experience anxiety reduction via habituation, or getting more accustomed to a stimulus. The primary advantage of flooding is that it takes less time than systematic desensitization, but the procedure

must be done carefully and following informed discussion with a client to avoid a problematic reaction.

Response prevention is often used with children with Obsessive-Compulsive Disorder and in conjunction with exposure. As a child is exposed to whatever provokes anxiety (e.g., placing hands in dirt), he or she is required to prevent ritualistic or compulsive actions (e.g., handwashing) that would normally follow. Over time, the child comes to realize that anxiety will decline even if no handwashing occurs. Response prevention may also involve the scheduling of checking or other rituals (e.g., certain number per hour) that allows for some compulsive acts but at gradually lower and lower rates.

Modeling and role play are often used with children with social anxiety and involve the observation of others who appropriately engage in a certain activity. For example, children anxious about initiating conversations may watch peers engage in such conversations smoothly and without nervousness. The client may then practice these social skills and interactions repeatedly in an office setting to receive feedback from a therapist. Eventually, as the child becomes more proficient and less anxious, he or she would be assigned real-life tasks such as calling friends or starting conversations with unfamiliar children at school.

Cognitive restructuring targets irrational or illogical conclusions that anxious children often draw about themselves or their environment. For example, many children will overestimate the dangerousness of a situation, overworry about the potential negative consequences of a situation, and/or minimize their own resources for handling a situation. Cognitive restructuring involves techniques to help a child develop healthy patterns of thinking, such as realistically examining the evidence for one's thought, examining plausible alternative thoughts, and assessing one's ability to handle a situation based on past performance. A child who is excessively anxious of failing tests, for example, can be taught that the probability of failure is small, that the consequences for failure on one test are not extreme, and that the child has a long history of success on tests due to his or her excellent study habits.

Contingency management is another important component for treating children with anxiety disorders. The procedure involves training parents and other influential adults to encourage a child to maintain therapeutic homework assignments, assist in exposure-based tasks, reinforce attempts to move forward in the therapeutic process, and discourage dependent and inappropriate behaviors. For example, parents may be asked to establish a series of exposures during the week in which a child must interact with others. As the child does so, parents can monitor progress and practice skills that will help them prevent the child's relapse in the future.

Recent empirical studies support the effectiveness of these treatment components for children with anxiety disorders. For example, Kendall and colleagues (1997) successfully utilized a four-component treatment program for children with anxiety disorders that focused on recognizing anxious somatic feelings, changing unrealistic cognitions or expectations, designing a coping plan, and developing self-reinforcement. Silverman and colleagues (Silverman, Kurtines, Ginsburg, Weems, Rabian, et al., 1999) also found that contingency management, exposure-based cognitive self-control, and education support were useful in ameliorating anxiety disorders in children. Group cognitive-behavioral treatment has also been shown to be effective (Silverman, Kurtines, Ginsburg, Weems, Lumpkin, et al., 1999), and family-based treatment for this population has been successfully designed and tested as well (e.g., Barrett, Dadds, & Rapee, 1996).

A new trend in therapy for this population has focused on prescriptive treatment, or matching different types of treatment to different subtypes of a particular disorder. For example, Eisen and Silverman (1998) successfully used cognitive therapy/exposure for children with more cognitively based Generalized Anxiety Disorder and relaxation training/ exposure for children with more physiologically based Generalized Anxiety Disorder. In similar fashion, Kearney and Silverman (1999)

used prescriptive treatment to address youth with school refusal behavior. Specifically, different treatment packages were assigned on the basis of function, or the reason why a certain child was refusing to attend school.

Pharmacological Treatment

Pharmacological treatments to address youth with anxiety disorders primarily involve antidepressant and anxiolytic medication. Tricyclic antidepressants such as imipramine, desipramine, and clomipramine have been used with mixed results for children with Separation Anxiety Disorder, school refusal behavior, and Panic Disorder. In addition, selective serotonin reuptake inhibitors such as fluoxetine have been used with moderate success for children with obsessive-compulsive and other anxiety disorders. Anxiolytic medications for youth with anxiety disorders primarily include benzodiazepines such as alprazolam and clonazepam as well as buspirone. Use of these medications has led to moderate success in children with Panic and Separation Anxiety Disorder (for reviews, see American Academy of Child and Adolescent Psychiatry, 1997; Kearney & Silverman, 1998; Tonge, 1998).

Major Questions

Several major questions still remain with respect to treating youth with anxiety disorders. Of particular concern is knowing which of the aforementioned treatment components is most effective for treating this population. Exposure to anxiety-provoking stimuli is certainly a key ingredient, but further work is needed to identify the best type of exposure for a particular child. Knowing the best way to combine exposure with other treatment components is crucial as well. Investigations of prescriptive treatment will likely enhance study in this area.

Another key question involves the influence of therapist support. It is possible that educating a child about anxiety and providing therapist support is enough to alleviate a child's anxiety disorder. Evidence for this was recently presented by Last, Hansen, and Franco

(1998), who found that education/support was as effective as cognitive-behavioral treatment for youth with anxiety-based school refusal. However, support may come in the form of reassurance to an anxious child, which may provide short-term but not long-term gains.

Another important treatment question surrounds the best way to prevent anxiety disorders in children. Dadds and colleagues (1997) outlined an early intervention school-based program that utilized cognitive-behavioral and family-based group intervention to prevent the onset and further development of childhood anxiety disorders. Further work is necessary, however, to delineate the best ways of identifying and addressing the needs of children at risk for anxiety disorders.

RECOMMENDATIONS FOR THOSE
WORKING WITH CHILDREN WITH
ANXIETY DISORDERS

Several recommendations from empirical work can be made for counselors regarding the treatment of childhood anxiety disorders. First, as pointed out by Kendall, Panichelli-Mindel, Sugarman, and Callahan (1997), therapists who treat youth with anxiety disorders likely have to adopt several roles. First, as a consultant, the therapist endeavors to avoid the role of expert and encourage a child to develop healthy strategies to handle anxiety-provoking situations. In essence, the therapist tries to build skills to help a child become more independent and appropriate in thinking and decision making. Second, as a diagnostician, the therapist collects information about a child from different sources to compare the child's functioning to normative levels, identify the primary behavior problems, and design a treatment plan. Finally, as an educator, the therapist teaches the child about the nature of anxiety, develops the child's self-control, increases his or her coping skills, and helps the child recognize his or her strengths as well as weaknesses.

Assessing different sources of information is important because anxiety problems are often covert in nature. Whereas many people

easily focus on a child's disruptive behavior, the identification of subtle, anxious behaviors demands input not only from parents but also the child and relevant others who know the child well. In addition, assessment should involve multiple methods of data collection, such as interview, self-report questionnaires, behavioral observation, daily ratings, and formal testing if appropriate. Assessment should also concentrate on problems often associated with anxiety disorders in children, with particular attention to depression.

Counselors should be aware that many children who are anxious are reluctant to talk about their problems or engage in exposure-based tasks that initially raise their anxiety. As such, it is important to go at a pace that is comfortable for a child, inform the child and parents about the rationale for a particular task, and provide frequent encouragement, reinforcement, and feedback. Early in therapy, this may require daily contact with a child to assess for therapeutic compliance, school attendance, level of anxiety, and other relevant issues.

The treatment of anxiety in children should also involve family members. Parents, who may be anxious themselves, can be informed of the nature of anxiety and how to best involve their child in appropriate, interactive situations. Parents should be instructed as well not to "rescue" their child, or allow him or her to prematurely terminate an exposure situation (e.g., attendance at a birthday party). Counselors can also "test" parents by providing them with a hypothetical scenario (e.g., child refuses school due to anxiety) and role-playing appropriate responses.

The treatment of anxiety in children often demands some form of relapse prevention as well. For example, the start of school or attendance at a sleepover can trigger new feelings of anxiety in some children. In these cases, ongoing practice of what was learned in therapy is crucial, and booster sessions may be scheduled with a therapist to enhance appropriate coping and decrease problematic cognitions or behaviors.

Anxiety in children can be a debilitating condition, but one that is amenable to treatment. Indeed, successful treatment of an anxious child is a highly rewarding experience. However, counselors should be well versed in the various techniques available to address this population, and be aware of the rapid changes that are taking place in the field.

References

American Academy of Child and Adolescent Psychiatry. (1997). Practice parameters for the assessment and treatment of children and adolescents with anxiety disorders. *Journal of the American Academy of Child and Adolescent Psychiatry, 36,* 69–84.

American Psychiatric Association. (1994). *Diagnostic and statistical manual of mental disorders* (4th ed.). Washington, DC: Author.

Barrett, P.M., Dadds, M.R., & Rapee, R.M. (1996). Family treatment of childhood anxiety: A controlled trial. *Journal of Consulting and Clinical Psychology, 64,* 333–342.

Barrios, B.A., & O'Dell, S.L. (1998). Fears and anxieties. In E.J. Mash & R.A. Barkley (Eds.), *Treatment of childhood disorders* (2nd ed., pp. 249–337). New York: Guilford Press.

Dadds, M.R., Spence, S.H., Holland, D.E., Barrett, P.M., & Laurens, K.R. (1997). Prevention and early intervention for anxiety disorders: A controlled trial. *Journal of Consulting and Clinical Psychology, 65,* 627–635.

Eisen, A.R., & Kearney, C.A. (1995). *Practitioner's guide to treating fear and anxiety in children and adolescents: A cognitive-behavioral approach.* Northvale, NJ: Aronson.

Eisen, A.R., & Silverman, W.K. (1998). Prescriptive treatment for generalized anxiety disorder in children. *Behavior Therapy, 29,* 105–121.

Kearney, C.A. (2001). *School refusal behavior in youth: A functional approach to assessment and treatment.* Washington, DC: American Psychological Association.

Kearney, C.A., & Silverman, W.K. (1998). A critical review of pharmacotherapy for youth with anxiety disorders: Things are not as they seem. *Journal of Anxiety Disorders, 12,* 83–102.

Kearney, C.A., & Silverman, W.K. (1999). Functionally-based prescriptive and nonprescriptive treatment for children and adolescents with school refusal behavior. *Behavior Therapy, 30,* 673–695.

Kendall, P.C., Chansky, T.E., Kane, M.T., Kim, R.S., Kortlander, E., Ronan, K.R., Sessa, F.M., &

Siqueland, L. (1992). *Anxiety disorders in youth: Cognitive-behavioral interventions.* Boston: Allyn & Bacon.

Kendall, P.C., Flannery-Schroeder, E., Panichelli-Mindel, S.M., Southam-Gerow, M., Henin, A., & Warman, M. (1997). Therapy for youths with anxiety disorders: A second randomized clinical trial. *Journal of Consulting and Clinical Psychology, 65,* 366–380.

Kendall, P.C., Panichelli-Mindel, S.M., Sugarman, A., & Callahan, S.A. (1997). Exposure to child anxiety: Theory, research, and practice. *Clinical Psychology: Science and Practice, 4,* 29–39.

Last, C.G., Hansen, C., & Franco, N. (1998). Cognitive-behavioral treatment of school phobia. *Journal of the American Academy of Child and Adolescent Psychiatry, 37,* 404–411.

March, J.S. (1995). *Anxiety disorders in children and adolescents.* New York: Guilford Press.

Ollendick, T.H., King, N.J., & Yule, W. (1994). *International handbook of phobic and anxiety disorders in children and adolescents.* New York: Plenum Press.

Silverman, W.K., & Kurtines, W.M. (1996). *Anxiety and phobic disorders: A pragmatic approach.* New York: Plenum Press.

Silverman, W.K., Kurtines, W.M., Ginsburg, G.S., Weems, C.F., Lumpkin, P.W., & Carmichael, D.H. (1999). Treating anxiety disorders in children with group cognitive-behavioral therapy: A randomized clinical trial. *Journal of Consulting and Clinical Psychology, 67,* 995–1003.

Silverman, W.K., Kurtines, W.M., Ginsburg, G.S., Weems, C.F., Rabian, B., & Serafini, L.T. (1999). Contingency management, self-control, and education support in the treatment of childhood phobic disorders: A randomized clinical trial. *Journal of Consulting and Clinical Psychology, 67,* 675–687.

Tonge, B.J. (1998). Pharmacotherapy for school refusal. *Behaviour Change, 15,* 98–106.

Resources for Further Study

Resources for further study in this area include the Web sites of the Anxiety Disorders Association of America (www.adaa.org) and the Association for the Advancement of Behavior Therapy (www.aabt.org). Both organizations also publish fact sheets regarding anxiety disorders. Journals that contain many articles on anxiety disorders in children include:

Journal of Clinical Child and Adolescent Psychology

Journal of the American Academy of Child and Adolescent Psychiatry

Journal of Consulting and Clinical Psychology

Journal of Anxiety Disorders

See References for books by these authors:

Eisen and Kearney (1995)
Kendall et al. (1992); March (1995)
Ollendick, King, and Yule (1994)
Silverman and Kurtines (1996)

26 INTERVENTIONS FOR ATTENTION-DEFICIT/ HYPERACTIVITY DISORDER

Joel T. Nigg and Marsha D. Rappley

Actual or suspected Attention-Deficit/Hyperactivity Disorder (ADHD) is among the most common reasons for a school-age child to come to the attention of mental health professionals and primary care physicians (Barkley, 1998; Freid, Makuc, & Rooks, 1998). As documented elsewhere in this volume, the hallmark symptoms of this disorder include active behaviors that disturb classrooms and families (always on the go, can't wait turn, interrupting) as well as off-task behaviors and disorganization that tend to impair academic functioning. The *DSM-IV* (APA, 1994) provides for three subtypes of this disorder. The hyperactive subtype is rare outside the preschool years and is probably a precursor to the combined subtype in most cases (Hart, Lahey, Loeber, Applegate, & Frick, 1995). The inattentive subtype includes children who are sluggish and hypoactive, as well as those who are overactive but shy of cutoffs for the combined type designation (Lahey, Carlson, & Frick, 1997). The combined type is the most common presentation

and is the focus of this chapter. However, intervention for the hyperactive subtype would be nearly identical. In approaching treatment with this population, it is almost always the case that the counselor will also be facing substantial comorbid problems of varying severity (Biederman, Newcorn, & Sprich, 1991). These can include marked oppositional-defiant behaviors that escalate to frank Conduct Disorder in older children, internalizing problems such as significant anxiety and/or depressive symptoms, academic underachievement possibly complicated by a learning disability, and problematic movements or sounds in the context of a tic disorder. Most predictive of poor outcome for ADHD children, and thus important to target during intervention, are aggressive/antisocial behaviors, peer rejection, and reading failure (Farrington, Loeber, & van Kammen, 1990; Moffitt, 1990).

Therefore, in formulating a treatment plan for the child with ADHD, the counselor must look beyond the hallmark symptoms of the disorder and consider interventions that address comorbid problems as well. In some cases, the latter will cause the most impairment for the child. Importantly, various treatments tend to have differential impacts on the symptoms of ADHD per se and on the associated difficulties.[1] Options for interventions for these children thus cover a fairly broad range. However, only a few interventions have demonstrated efficacy or effectiveness and feasibility in most clinical settings. For example, intensive "summer camp" type programs with strict token economies may benefit children with ADHD (Pelham & Hoza, 1996), but until this intervention is disseminated more widely, it will be only in rare circumstances that the counselor will find it feasible to propose such an intervention in a general camp setting. Thus, the most optimal interventions include four broad areas of concern: adequate assessment, behavioral family intervention, classroom intervention, and pharmacological intervention. Information crucial for counselors to bear in mind is noted for each of these in turn. We then conclude with comments on cross-discipline integration.

ADEQUATE ASSESSMENT

Unfortunately, in the press of today's health services delivery systems, it sometimes happens that a child is diagnosed and referred for treatment without adequate prior assessment. An adequate evaluation for ADHD should include at minimum (1) careful developmental history with the parents; (2) standardized rating scales by parents and teachers (see Hinshaw & Nigg, 1999); (3) medical examination to rule out metabolic disorders, vision and hearing disorders, and other conditions; and (4) psychological or neuropsychological administration of psychometric tests to evaluate possible learning disability or other developmental disability. Also, the evaluating professional should have carefully considered such important confound conditions as depression, anxiety, Oppositional Defiant Disorder, and tic disorders (Biederman et al., 1991) and such potentially important situational factors as family discord, inappropriate school placement, and discrete emotional trauma. The treating counselor must review these assessment records before beginning treatment. If the child being referred for treatment has not had an adequate assessment by these standards, then one of the first orders of business is to arrange for additional evaluation to assure that the interventions being planned are appropriate to the mix of problems this particular child is experiencing. Once the assessment picture is complete, a multimodal intervention plan will usually be considered.

BEHAVIORAL INTERVENTIONS IN THE FAMILY

Overview

There is little evidence that individual child psychotherapy, behavioral or otherwise, can ameliorate the core symptoms of hyperactivity/impulsivity, although recent data from the MTA study suggest that an extremely ambitious, state-of-the-art behavioral program (parent training and school behavior plan) can improve ADHD symptoms to an equivalent degree with medication interventions in about three out of four ADHD children (MTA Cooperative Work Group, 1999a). Thus, a well-executed psychosocial intervention may be able to maintain a child if medication (discussed below) is not desirable. Further, chances that a child would improve were increased with the addition of psychosocial treatment (Swanson et al., 2001) to medicine

---

[1] Although empirical information on treatment of ADHD has been accumulating for decades, the field is currently benefiting from a large multisite, multimodal study sponsored by NIMH (Richters et al., 1995), termed the Multimodal Treatment of ADHD Study, or MTA Study. Readers are encouraged to peruse the special issue of *Journal of Abnormal Child Psychology* for December 2000 (V. 28, no. 6) and of the *Journal of the American Academy of Children and Adolescent Psychiatry* for February 2001 (Vol. 40, no. 2), which includes several updates and reports from this project. We note initial findings from that landmark effort as relevant herein.

alone. Also, there is limited evidence for organizational strategies being helpful with inattention/disorganization symptoms, as discussed under school interventions later, and these deserve a trial in most cases. Finally, there is substantial evidence that behavioral parent interventions can improve the ubiquitous oppositional/disruptive behavior of youngsters with ADHD, if not the core ADHD symptoms themselves. Behavioral interventions also increase the success rate of medication alone in relation to critical ancillary problems such as peer relations, internalizing symptoms, and academic progress. Moreover, in anxious ADHD children, psychosocial interventions yield equivalent outcomes to medication alone (MTA Cooperative Work Group, 1999a, 1999b). Furthermore, psychosocial interventions tend to enable a lower dosage of medication to be effective (MTA Cooperative Work Group, 1999a). We emphasize parent training programs in this section.

Parent Training for Behavior Management

The essential components of such programs (Barkley, 1997; Forehand & McMahon, 1981) include the following:

1. Parents are taught to interrupt the pattern of coercive (aggressive) interchange between parent and child that is described by Patterson (e.g., Patterson & Capaldi, 1991). In these interchanges, the child escalates, while parents also escalate their threats, but consequences only follow some of the time. Parents are taught a three-step process in which they issue a command or request, wait one minute while ignoring misbehavior, remind with a warning, wait and ignore once more, and then impose a predetermined consequence.
2. Systematic implementation of positive parent-child interactions that are noncontingent, which strengthens the parent-child bond.
3. Teaching the parent to praise (rather than ignore) appropriate behaviors, while as often as possible ignoring (rather than attending to) misbehavior.

4. Systematic implementation of appropriate disciplinary strategies such as time-out, loss of privilege, and so on when the child's misbehavior cannot be safely ignored. Skills for effectively implementing such consequences as time-out are also taught.
5. The contingency management skills necessary to handle misbehavior are taught. These latter skills entail clear and frequent feedback to the child about his or her behavior, sometimes taking the form of point or token systems. With young children, the points may be recorded on a chart on the refrigerator. With adolescents, in contrast, point systems are unlikely to be appropriate and several modifications of the program are in order, including more active inclusion of the teen in shaping the program and in negotiating with parents around those problems that are negotiable (Robin, 1998).

Such child management skills exceed the communication enhancements taught in typical parenting books and classes and are rarely in the repertoire of even the most sophisticated and dedicated parent. Yet, careful work using one of the well-manualized programs to reduce oppositional and aggressive behaviors is one of the most clearly effective interventions in mental health services. Thus, individual or group work on behavioral parent-child guidance is almost always called for with these children. Counselors who will be conducting front-line treatment of ADHD are exhorted to obtain necessary training to enable them to effectively implement one of the manualized, empirically supported treatment programs in this genre. These include the classic programs outlined by Forehand and McMahon (1981), as well as the user-friendly and widely disseminated modification of those basic programs proffered by Barkley (1997, 1998) and colleagues. These manuals provide detailed materials, including handouts and week-by-week curricula, for systematic parent training. In the most cost-limited form of this intervention, the counselor may meet with the parents weekly for a period of 6 to 12 weeks to teach such a system, then institute periodic booster sessions over the subsequent year to help the parents maintain the gains they have made.

Ancillary Family Counseling

In the case of young children, preschool or early school years, such parent training may be sufficient to improve the situation. However, it is sometimes advisable to combine this work with counseling concerning the disability itself as well as other interventions that are underway (including medications, as we elaborate further in the next section). This is especially true as children get older. Parent attributions and demoralization concerning their own role with the hyperactive child can be a major issue to be addressed with parent education and even family counseling. Parental disengagement, depression, lack of monitoring (especially with adolescent children), and consequent inconsistent response to child misbehavior are among the strongest correlates of poor child outcomes (Patterson & Capaldi, 1991). Thus, in supplementing the behavioral parent training, it is of value for counselors to educate parents about the nature of ADHD, the normal need for additional parent skill building with this disorder, and the long-term value of maintaining their engagement with the child's problems. Thus, motivating parents can also be of value in that one of the strongest predictors of successful treatment, medication or otherwise, is consistent attendance at physician and counselor sessions (MTA Cooperative Work Group, 1999b).

COUNSELING AND PHARMACOLOGICAL INTERVENTION FOR THE CHILD

The Counseling Context

Few topics evoke such strong feelings in parents as the prospect of having their child placed on psychoactive medications. Yet, the impressive effectiveness of stimulant medications (MTA Cooperative Work Group, 1999a) mandates their consideration in a large percentage of cases with impairing ADHD symptoms. Medication achieves the same reduction of ADHD symptoms as ambitious behavioral interventions, at a fraction of the effort and cost; this is a crucial advantage in situations where behavioral interventions are not well supported by insurance or are not available at all. For some parents, the possibility of medical treatment for their child thus is looked to as the last hope in an overwhelming situation, or as a "silver bullet" for difficult and complicated psychosocial problems. For others, medications symbolize an unwarranted effort to control their child.

As a result, counselors are often in an important position to help parents consider their concerns, values, and feelings about the option of medication in the treatment of their child, and to educate parents about the role of the different components of multimodal treatment. Children, also, can have complex feelings about the prospect of medication. These can include relief, fear of stigmatization, misunderstanding medication as "taking drugs," and unrealistic attributions. As a result, similar discussions with children are often warranted, and discussion with both parents and the child are vital in creating a positive plan and shared alliance for approaching the child's behavioral difficulties. These discussions will likely need to address cognitive restructuring of attributions about both the medication itself and the nature of the child's difficulties (Robin, 1998) to reduce blame and self-stigmatization.

Basic Medication Facts

The prescribing of medication falls in the purview of the child's physician, who may be a primary care pediatrician or a psychiatrist. It is useful for the counselor to be aware of the medications commonly used and salient issues that can occur with their use. Because they are the most often effective and have the fewest side effects (Elia, 1993; Rappley, 1997), the most common medications used in the treatment of ADHD are the stimulants: methylphenidate and products related to dextroamphetamine. They stimulate catecholamine activity in the central nervous system, enhancing attentional focus and behavioral control in children and adults. They effectively improve behavioral problems in 70% to 90% of children who take them (Barkley, 1998). Children who fail to respond to the first stimulant will sometimes respond to the second. However, other stimulants, such as magnesium pemoline, are used rarely due to more severe side effects. Other psychotropic medications might be used, such as tricyclic antidepressants, selective serotonin reuptake inhibitors and buproprion, and atypical antispychotics, but with the exception of buproprion, these are generally used to address comorbid problems such as a mood disorder or Obsessive-Compulsive Disorder.

Stimulants are short-acting. Effects on behavior are apparent within 30 to 60 minutes and have worn off within three to six hours depending on the nature of the preparation and the individual child's reaction. They are thus given two to four times per day. Often, exact timing and amount of dosage must be adjusted to achieve the best effect. Monitoring of medication use involves office visits at least every three to four months with review of height, weight, blood pressure, pulse, side effects, and effectiveness of the medication. Common side effects include stomachache, headache, appetite suppression, and sleep disturbance; these often subside in a short time, but persistent appetite suppression may need to be addressed with modified eating regimes to assure adequate weight gain. Less common but notable side effects are dysphoric mood and stereotyped or tic-like behaviors. Although the side effects are similar with the two major types of stimulants, some children will have fewer problems with one than the other (Barkley, 1998). Secondary sleep problems can usually be corrected by adjusting the timing of the dose. "Rebound" is a concern of some parents. It refers to some children's irritable or labile mood as the medication is wearing off, often in the late afternoon. The physician can usually address the problem by tapering the dose. For more detailed information, readers may consult Barkley (1998) or Elia (1993).

Additional Counseling Issues

The counselor may also assist the family with defining the target behaviors and the baseline severity of the problem prior to initiating treatment, particularly with medications. Such definition helps clarify whether the intervention has been effective. Standardized rating scales (see Conners, 1997; Hinshaw & Nigg, 1999) can be useful in this regard. It is valuable to explain the baseline behavioral problems for the child, because behaviors initially reported as baseline problems are often later reported as side effects of the medication in placebo trials. Finally, medications are usually not utilized to maximum effectiveness (MTA Cooperative Work Group, 1999a). Effectiveness can be improved by a systematic double-blind trial of medication. Teachers and parents can complete a short Conners (1997) rating scale daily for one to two weeks to provide data to determine the child's optimal medication and dosage (MTA Cooperative Work Group, 1999a).

SCHOOL INTERVENTIONS

Background

School intervention is generally advised in cases of ADHD for several reasons. Interventions with parents tend to yield larger results at home than at school. Additionally, although medications are the most effective at reducing off-task behavior and improving compliance in school, they are not sufficient alone to ensure appropriate socialization and learning. As reviewed in detail by Pfiffner (1996) and Pfiffner and Barkley (1998), the school context for ADHD children has changed dramatically in the past decade, with recognition by the U.S. Department of Education in 1991 that ADHD could be considered a disabling condition and qualify children for special education services under Section 504 of the Rehabilitation Act (Davila, Williams, & MacDonald, 1991). This recognition has been accompanied by numerous developments in service modules that can be used with ADHD in the school. Thus, if a Section 504 or special education evaluation has not been initiated for the child within the past three years, one of the counselor's first actions will be to ensure that such an evaluation is begun (in most states, these can be compelled by parent written demand). For the counselor, a primary concern will then be assisting school personnel to recognize the intervention options available, advising parents on the range of options the school may be able to consider, and at times, providing technical assistance to school personnel in implementing their program. The key elements of an optimal school program include the following: (1) a school-based behavioral program that delivers consequences within the school setting; (2) organizational strategies in the classroom (Jones, 1994); and (3) peer interventions. We focus on behavioral interventions here because these are most likely to engage the counselor in collaboration with school personnel.

Behavioral Intervention at School

The logic of behavioral interventions in the school setting is very similar to that in the home setting. The teacher faces the task of providing clear behavioral expectations, consistent praise for on-task behavior (resisting the tendency to ignore on-task behavior), and either ignoring or implementing consequences for off-task or disruptive behavior. Depending on the age of the child, this program can be accompanied by a point system to enable children to monitor their progress toward their behavioral goal. Problems with implementing such programs in the school can include: (1) teacher lacks the skills or knowledge to carry out the intervention effectively; (2) teacher lacks time or energy to carry out the intervention; or (3) teacher objects on philosophical grounds to the behavioral intervention. In the first instance, the counselor may need to assist the teacher in locating the appropriate support services to establish a behavioral program. In the second instance, provision of an in-class behavioral aide is advisable; advocacy may be needed to push the school to do so. In the final instance, if an understanding cannot be reached, parents may need to be counseled to seek a different teacher, classroom, or school where appropriate intervention can be delivered. Notably, the situation is more difficult with adolescents; multiple teachers may be involved and their coordination may be quite difficult depending on the resources of the local middle or high school.

Other School Strategies

Under the purview of counseling to assist with organizational strategies, additional interventions often warrant consideration. One domain entails further counseling of the children or teens regarding ADHD and their self-conception and attributions around the intervention being offered to them. A second key area involves "coaching" or case management services to support the school program, thus helping children to track their assignments and responsibilities. Organizational strategies may include an "in" and "out" folder at home and school for completed and to-be-done assignments, a to-do list of assignment tasks for the next hour or for the day, different colored materials and worksheets to help focus attention, and modified work settings to minimize distracting stimulation. For example, some children are able to successfully complete an exam in the hallway, but not in the classroom. Detailed suggestions on working with school settings are provided by Pfiffner (1996), Jones (1994), and Swanson (1992). The counselor can make these options known to parents and school personnel, and in some instances can serve as the coach to help the child implement strategies and troubleshoot any problems with particular strategies that are being tried.

INTEGRATING THE INTERVENTION TEAM

As is apparent from the preceding, the counselor attempting to coordinate treatment for an ADHD child will need to be in contact with the school, the physician, and potentially a consulting psychologist as well as the parents and the child. Extensive collateral contact will thus be essential to successful coordinated intervention. For example, the physician may be unaware of some of the comorbid conditions the counselor has noted, or may assume counseling is addressing particular issues. If all parties are in agreement, it can be prudent in mild to moderate cases to initiate behavioral interventions for a period of several months and evaluate progress prior to determining the necessity for pharmacological intervention. However, in cases of severe impairment or limited resources, the press for immediate medication management may of necessity win out. Coordination of behavioral programming across home and school is vital, as is active education of parents and teachers to the reality that medication alone will not assure an optimal outcome for the child. The counselor may play a crucial role in communicating with both teachers and parents regarding the principles and goals of the behavioral management program. Interventions such as a daily home-school report card can be extremely helpful in facilitating this type of communication and making sure that problems surface and are addressed well before the end of the marking period. Of course, careful attention to confidentiality concerns and clear expectations with family members are essential to success in such collateral communication; whenever possible, letting parents transmit information is thus advantageous.

SUMMARY

Multimodal intervention is most likely to provide the broad benefit in multiple functional areas that most children with ADHD need. Although stimulant medication, when used appropriately, is the most effective intervention to reduce ADHD symptoms, both the probability of improvement and improvement in ancillary problem areas (such as oppositional behavior and peer relations) are enhanced with psychosocial interventions augmenting medication. When medication is not acceptable, well-designed psychosocial intervention can still lead to marked improvement for the child.

Coordination across service providers, as well as counseling the family regarding the progress and options of the interventions, entail crucial roles for counselors and other mental health professionals. After behavior has stabilized, it may be vital to maintain periodic checkup visits to refresh parents on behavior management strategies, revise organizational approaches, and update school planning. If antisocial behavior can be curtailed and academic progress maintained, especially in reading, then the long-term prognosis for children with ADHD is often quite good. Skilled counselors can help to ensure that the children in their care are among those with the positive outcomes.

References

American Psychiatric Association. (1994). *Diagnostic and statistical manual of mental disorders* (4th ed.). Washington, DC: Author.

Barkley, R.A. (1997). *Defiant children: A clinician's manual for assessment and parent training* (2nd ed.). New York: Guilford Press.

Barkley, R.A. (1998). *Attention deficit hyperactivity disorder: A handbook for diagnosis and treatment.* New York: Guilford Press.

Biederman, J., Newcorn, J., & Sprich, S. (1991). Co-morbidity of attention deficit hyperactivity disorder with conduct, depressive, anxiety, and other disorders. *American Journal of Psychiatry, 148,* 564–577.

Conners, C.K. (1997). *Conners Rating Scales–Revised.* Toronto: Multi-Health Systems.

Davila, R.R., Williams, M.L., & MacDonald, J.T. (1991). *Clarification of policy to address the needs of children with attention deficit hyperactivity disorders within general and/or special education.* Washington, DC: Memorandum from the U.S. Department of Education, Office of Special Education and Rehabilitation Services.

Elia, J. (1993). Drug treatment for hyperactive children: Therapeutic guidelines. *Drugs, 46,* 863–871.

Farrington, D.M., Loeber, R., & Van Kammen, W.B. (1990). Long-term criminal outcomes of hyperactivity–impulsivety: Attention deficit and conduct problems in childhood. In L.N. Robins & M. Rutter (Eds.), *Straight and devious pathways from childhood to adulthood* (pp. 62–81). Cambridge, MA: Cambridge University Press.

Forehand, R.L., & McMahon, R.J. (1981). *Helping the noncompliant child: A clinician's guide to parent training.* New York: Guilford Press.

Freid, V.M., Makuc, D.M., & Rooks, R.N. (1998). Ambulatory health care visits by children: Principal diagnosis and place of visit. *National Center for Health Statistics, Vital Health Statistics, 13,* 137.

Hart, E.L., Lahey, B.B., Loeber, R., Applegate, B., & Frick, P.J. (1995). Developmental changes in attention-deficit hyperactivity disorder in boys: A four year longitudinal study. *Journal of Abnormal Child Psychology, 23,* 729–750.

Hinshaw, S.P., & Nigg, J.T. (1999). Behavior rating scales in the assessment of disruptive behavior disorders in childhood. In D. Shaffer, C.P. Lucas, & J. Richters (Eds.), Diagnostic assessment in child and adolescent psychopathology (pp. 91–126). New York: Guilford Press.

Jones, C.B. (1994). Attention deficit disorder: Strategies for school-age children. San Antonio, TX: Psychological Corporation.

Lahey, B.B., Carlson, C.L., & Frick, P.J. (1997). Attention-deficit disorder without hyperactivity. In T.A. Widiger, A.J. Frances, H.A. Pincus, R. Ross, M.B. First, & W. Wakefield Davis (Eds.), DSM-IV sourcebook (Vol. 3, pp. 163–188). Washington, DC: American Psychiatric Press.

Moffitt, T.E. (1990). Juvenile delinquency and attention-deficit disorder: Boys' developmental trajectories from age 3 to age 15. Child Development, 61, 893–910.

MTA Cooperative Work Group. (1999a). A 14-month randomized clinical trial of treatment strategies for attention-deficit/hyperactivity disorder. Archives of General Psychiatry, 56, 1073–1086.

MTA Cooperative Work Group. (1999b). Moderators and mediators of treatment response for children with attention-deficit/hyperactivity disorder. Archives of General Psychiatry, 56, 1088–1096.

Patterson, G.R., & Capaldi, D.M. (1991). Antisocial parents: Unskilled and vulnerable. In P.A. Cowan & M. Hetherington (Eds.), Family transitions (pp. 195–218). Hillsdale, NJ: Erlbaum.

Pelham, W.E., & Hoza, B. (1996). Intensive treatment: A summer treatment program for children with ADHD. In E.D. Hibbs & P.S. Jensen (Eds.), Psychosocial treatments for child and adolescent disorders: Empirically based strategies for clinical practice (pp. 311–340). Washington, DC: American Psychological Association.

Pfiffner, L.J. (1996). All about ADHD: The complete practical guide for classroom teachers. New York: Scholastic.

Pfiffner, L.J., & Barkley, R.A. (1998). Treatment of ADHD in school settings. In R.A. Barkley (Ed.), Attention deficit hyperactivity disorder: A handbook for diagnosis and treatment (pp. 458–490). New York: Guilford Press.

Rappley, M. (1997). Safety issues in the use of methylphenidate: An American perspective. Drug Safety, 17, 143–148.

Richters, J.E., Arnold, L.E., Jensen, P.S., & Abikoff, H.B. (1995). NIMH collaborative multisite multimodal treatment study of ADHD: I. Background and rationale. Journal of the American Academy of Child and Adolescent Psychiatry, 34, 987–1000.

Robin, A.L. (1998). Training families with ADHD adolescents. In R.A. Barkley (Ed.), Attention deficit hyperactivity disorder: A handbook for diagnosis and treatment (pp. 413–457). New York: Guilford Press.

Swanson, J.M. (1992). School based assessments and interventions for ADD students. Irvine, CA: K.C. Publications.

Swanson, J.M., Kraemer, H.C., Hinshaw, S.P., Arnold, L.E., Connors, C.K. Abikoff, H.B., Clevenger, W., Davis, M., Elliott, G.R., Greenhill, L.L., Hechtman, L., Hoza, B., Jensen, P.S., March, J.S., Newcorn, J.H., Owens, E.B., Pelham, W.E., Schiller, E., Severe, J.B., Simpson, S., Vitiello, B., Wells, K., Wigal, T., & Wu, M. (2001). Clinical relevance of the primary findings of the MTA: Success rates based on severity of ADHD and ODD symptoms at the end of treatment. Journal of the American Academy of Child and Adolescent Psychiatry, 40, 168–179.

27 BULLYING

Counseling Perpetrators and Victims

Richard J. Hazler

DEFINING THE PROBLEM

The emerging body of knowledge on repetitive peer-on-peer abuse in the form of bullying has made it clear that the problem can have deadly consequences in acts of revenge against others (Hazler & Carney, 2000), is related to suicidal thinking (Carney, 2000), and can influence suicidal acts (Morita, Soeda, Soeda, & Mitsuru, 1999). These forms of peer-on-peer abuse can be recognized in every counselor's practice because the vast majority of people have been either an abuser, victim, or bystander to these forms of abuse that occur in all parts of our society (Hazler, 1998) and are international in scope (Smith, Madsen, & Moody, 1999).

There is an internationally agreed on definition for bullying situations that emphasizes three key factors. This definition gives counselors direction in evaluating the degree of concern and in developing treatment plans: "Bullying is the *repeated* (not just once) *harming* of another through words, social actions or physical attack. The act of bullying is *unfair* because the bully is either physically stronger or more verbally or socially skilled than the victim(s). An individual (bullying) or group (mobbing) may carry these actions out" (Hazler, Miller, Carney, & Green, in press). These repetitions of what may appear to be minimally hurtful separate actions when individuals do not have a fair chance of defending themselves combine to create conditions that can produce immediate and long-term damage for both the bullies and the victims. Immediate damage for victims is seen in social, academic, and emotional difficulties as well as the potential for suicide or violent aggression against others. Immediate effects for those who bully frequently generally relate to disciplinary actions, social difficulties, and potentially becoming targets of revenge. Long-term damage can be seen in adulthood, when bullies are more likely to have criminal records and victims can suffer social and emotional disabilities. The damage also extends to bystanders, who, recognizing this form of peer-on-peer abuse as a potential threat to themselves, perceive a climate of anxiety and fear over which they have little control. The scope of the problem then extends far beyond individual acts of youth to the immediate climate in schools, families, communities, and eventually to adult development and overall social conditions.

KEYS TO UNDERSTANDING THE PROBLEM

Developmental Component

Harassment and abuse among youth was once thought to be "child's play," as studies utilizing adult estimates of such problems and their impact on youth suggested that the incidence was low, with minimal problems emerging from them. Very different results surfaced when the same problems were studied from the students' point of view. The vast majority of high school students (88%) report having seen harassment and bullying by other students for extended periods of time during their school careers, and 90% of those students believe the bullying caused significant social, emotional, or academic problems for the victims (Hazler, Hoover, & Oliver, 1991). A link between bullying and suicide was later supported by identifying the characteristics of hopelessness, helplessness, isolation, and low self-esteem as key risk factors for both problems (Carney, 2000). This type of information gained more public attention as the mass shootings in schools of the late 1990s and early 2000s highlighted the fact that many of these same personal characteristics were recognizable in the young killers.

The current widely accepted theory recognizes that serious youth violence develops from behaviors that have tended to give adults less concern, such as teasing, trash talking, and bullying at the lower end of the violence continuum. Actions such as antisocial behavior, murder, and suicide at the upper end of this continuum do make headlines, but it is at the lower end of the continuum where the ability to intervene in the development of these problems is most effective.

Dominance aggression is generally considered to be the form of aggression that is most likely to move confrontations that begin as verbal sparring to more serious social and physical behaviors (Weisfeld, 1994). The goal in dominance aggression is to overpower and control the other person in one way or another, thereby confirming one's own power, influence, and self-worth. Neither participant wants to be in the dominated position with the accompanying loser feelings, so each tries to overpower the other, thus continuously raising the personal stakes. What starts out as verbal or physical dominance play can often turn into threats and disputes about reputation and social identity that have a much greater impact on people than anyone planned.

Dominance aggression can first be seen at about the age of 3, when children become motivated to take a toy from another child more for the demonstration of power over that individual than actually having the toy. As intellectual, verbal, and social skills develop with age, the initially physical forms of dominance give way to a more diverse variety of socially tolerated behaviors to exert power and control over others (Weisfeld, 1994). The result is a lessen-

ing of abuse that falls clearly outside of socially acceptable limits as students approach middle school along with an increase of behaviors that cause harm while not receiving recognition or punishment from adults or peers (Smith, Madsen, & Moody, 1999). People learn through social experiences how to avoid being seen hurting another and how to dominate in ways that others will have trouble classifying as problem behaviors. These are the same age levels at which students report the highest levels of bullying and harassment. Peers and adults alike have more difficulty distinguishing play from abuse at these stages, and therefore the problem situations can continue as low-level repeated abuse (Hazler et al., in press; Schafer & Smith, 1996).

Individual and Environmental Characteristics

There are individual characteristics that appear to influence the potential for development and continuation of bullying and harassment. Certainly, someone with less intellectual, emotional, social, or physical ability is at a disadvantage compared to another who has more of these qualities. These inherent advantages or disadvantages that change as children grow and mature will cause youth to experiment with being in powerful or powerless positions, but importantly, it takes more than these initial differences for bullying or victimization to continue. Individual characteristics, developmental factors, and environmental conditions also play critical roles.

A worldwide study of experts on the subject found agreement on several characteristics of bullies and victims that appear to be molded not by heredity, but by developing personality traits and learned behaviors (Hazler, Carney, Green, Powell, & Jolly, 1997). These experts agreed that those who are regular bullies are more aggressive, are easier to anger, are poor interpreters of the actions of others, and demonstrate a lack of empathy for others. These are people smashing their way through relationships to get what they want, paying little attention to their role in their victim's situation or pain. By contrast, the experts viewed victims as overaccepting of their own weaknesses and operating on feelings of poor self-concept, inadequacy, and self-blame. Whereas bullies might need to be punished to help them see their wrongs, victims appear to punish themselves for their self-perceived weaknesses.

The environments of bullies and victims also appear different in ways that would impact both problem development and intervention. Bullies tend to be in homes where there is less time spent as a family unit, more family problems, and inconsistent discipline. Together, these factors may put the young person in a position where a less than supportive model is presented and one that promotes a more random learning of social interaction from peers and outsiders rather than a consistent family. Victims, on the other hand, have a tendency to come from more protective and enmeshed home environments where an overabundance of time is consistently spent in the home or as a family unit. In this case, the child may not have sufficient opportunity to develop critical independence skills necessary to negotiate the more variable nonfamily situations. These influences are often reinforced outside the home when adult and peer bystanders do not intervene to stop bullies from inappropriately abusing victims who can then become social pariahs, as bystanders seek to avoid connections with victims for fear of becoming the bully's next target.

The combination of dominance aggression, inherent individual characteristics, learned behaviors, and environmental influences appear to provide strong support for why virtually all youth report contact with bullying and harassment. The majority of these incidents appear to be brief time periods where productive social learning takes place, resulting in little to no therapeutic intervention being needed. Unfortunately, social learning does not always work effectively or in a timely manner, and some youth suffer serious consequences.

Situational Characteristics and Their Impact

It remains unclear exactly why one young person may react to abuse with violence while another submissively internalizes the pain. What is known is that all victims experience pain that influences how they relate to themselves and others throughout their life. In relation to prevention and intervention efforts, the characteristics of abusive situations and the pain they cause may be best generalized into the categories of isolation, dehumanization, and inevitability (Hazler & Carney, 2000).

Isolation is required for abuse of another to continue over time. Bullies cannot continue to abuse when others effectively step in to control the situation, support the victim, and discredit the bully. Sometimes, this takes the form of the bully manipulating a situation so that a person is physically alone; at other times, it is the creation of an atmosphere where others will not step in to help the victim or confront the abuser. In either case, victims have the tendency to play into the abuser's hands by seeking isolation to avoid more humiliation or greater danger rather than making their inability to handle the situation more public, where support is available.

Dehumanization is related to an abuser's lack of empathy and the victim's sense of unacceptability. Name calling is the most commonly seen application of dehumanization. It is not unique to bullying, but is quite common, as when citizens of a country give hurtful and impersonal nicknames to the enemy when they go to war. The same thing happens in virtually any conflict when the individuals or groups do not want to recognize the humanity of and personal commonalties with their rivals. By implementing a derogatory label, bullies effectively dehumanize their victims, thereby reducing any rationale for treating them as living, breathing, feeling persons like themselves. The impact of this dehumanization is to reduce the responsibility for human caring in the bully and others while also promoting a sense of inadequacy and unacceptability in the victim.

A sense of inevitability emerges in victims, bystanders, and bullies as more attempts to change the situation fail. For bullies, this inevitability promotes continuation, as confidence that an action will lead to the desired result is confirmed. Victim feelings of being less than human and increasingly isolated from others become more and more difficult to fight as the sense grows that there are no socially acceptable ways to improve the situation. Similar feelings of helplessness in victims' inability to make a difference in negative situations also carry over to bystanders. The developing feelings of helplessness, hopelessness, and worthlessness leave youth believing that they have few options beyond dropping out in one way or another. People who see their situation and pain as inevitable feel that they have little to lose when considering leaving the system, cutting emotional ties to others, or attempting to end a life (McDowell & Stillion, 1994). This sense of inevitability becomes a primary concern, as it signifies the point in the victim's process where extreme lashing out at self or others may become seen as the only option.

COUNSELING EMPHASES

The previous findings point professionals to some commonly accepted directions in the counseling of bullies, victims, and bystanders, who are also impacted by the situations. The overall focus of interventions can be generally summarized as follows:

- Most bullying is a transient developmental occurrence as youth experiment with newly recognized ways to exercise power over others (bullying) or as they experience a loss of control to others (victimization). The common developmental nature of these problems emphasizes the need to provide prevention efforts for everyone first. Minimally intrusive interventions are appropriate for the vast majority of transient bullying situations; the most intense disciplinary and therapeutic measures are reserved for those bullying behaviors that continue over time.
- The highly relational nature of bullying gives emphasis to promoting skills, realistic consequences, and reinforcements that focus on social learning and social development.
- Empathy-generating techniques are emphasized because dehumanization is consistent in the implementation of bullying

and a major factor in the development of problematic outcomes.
- Reducing physical, social, and/or emotional isolation are primary goals that increase support for victims, highlight the social unacceptability of bullies, and encourage the productive involvement of bystanders.
- The fact that continuation of a bullying relationship requires consistent patterns of interactions among bullies, victims, and bystanders emphasizes the need for changing any small piece of the pattern. Interventions are directed at breaking the cycle of bullying by disrupting these unhealthy patterns.

Environmental Interventions

The most natural forms of prevention and intervention with bullying behavior are related to the social learning that takes place, not in a counselor's office, but in the young person's real-life social environment. Most bullying prevention and intervention programs are founded on efforts to create an environment that teaches and supports desired behaviors and discourages inappropriate social behaviors such as bullying. The starting place is to produce an environment in a school, treatment facility, home, or other form of community with the following key characteristics:

- Establishes clear policies and promotes direct actions that stop verbal, social, and physical abuse when it occurs.
- Brings widely held member experiences, observations, and beliefs into the open.
- Provides community members with the knowledge and skills needed to understand the impact of their own behaviors and to react effectively to the problem behaviors of others.

A sound structure for an environment that will reduce bullying and its effects begins with policies and responsibilities that are logical, are based on local culture, have widespread public awareness and support, and are implemented consistently. Youth, parents, teachers, and others need to be involved in the development, implementation, and regular reevaluation of policies and procedures for re-acting to abusive situations. Consensus must be developed as to what constitutes verbal, so-cial, or physical abuse, the means of dealing with it, and the understanding that everyone has a distinct role in recognizing and stopping it on an ongoing basis. This foundation allows much of the critical social learning to be imple-mented naturally through a supportive envi-ronment.

Bully-Specific Interventions

Characteristics of those who are found to be consistent bullies are focused around physical and verbal aggressiveness, anger, poor inter-pretation of the actions of others, and a lack of empathy toward others (Hazler et al., in press; Hunt, 1993). The addition of a problematic home environment supports the bully who is more likely to seek self-serving forms of grati-fication than more socially acceptable options. Techniques for dealing with these problems then logically emphasize consistency of conse-quences for inappropriate actions, gaining em-pathy for others, and developing skills in anger management, problem solving, and con-flict resolution.

Having negative consequences for aggres-sive acts is always a foundation of the treat-ment for bullies. The more reality-based and socially appropriate the consequences, the better they serve as social learning tools. The more consistently both adults and peers can implement these at school, at home, and in the community, the better.

Treatment of childhood bullies recognizes the developmental nature of the problem as different from simple aggressiveness, Opposi-tional Defiant Disorder, or Conduct Disorder, although these and other diagnosable condi-tions may exist concurrently with bullying. Bullying behaviors primarily emanate from developmental and situational problems re-lated to social learning. Therefore, counseling these youth to identify and deal more produc-tively with their individual needs, personal difficulties, and lack of skills, particularly as

they relate to the social arena, is a basic tenet of treatment.

Counseling and other techniques that en-courage the development of empathy for vic-tims and others are key to successful work with bullies (Garrity, Jens, Porter, Sager, & Short-Camille, 1996; Hazler, 1996). These ef-forts focus on the dehumanizing techniques of bullies. The more abusers recognize the hurt of their victims in a personalized way, the more difficult it becomes for them to con-tinue causing them pain. Techniques such as reverse role-play, imaging another's world, bibliocounseling, and other methods that get abusers in touch with the lives and pain of others are used to promote a more human-ized picture of others.

Teaching problem solving, anger manage-ment, conflict resolution, and social skills is often an essential part of the treatment for abusers, who generally have problems in these areas. Selecting means and places for abusers to practice these skills with initially low levels of risk is just as important as the use of the skills. One example of a commonly effective environment is to have older stu-dents work in supportive roles with much younger children. The advantage in such an environment is that the much younger child is not threatening to the skills and abilities of the older student. This lack of threat from the younger child reduces the need to demon-strate dominance and allows for the practice of positive social skills with the resulting sup-portive feedback.

Family work for bullies often revolves around increasing understanding, closeness, and consistency of family involvement (Oliver, Oaks, & Hoover, 1994). Encouraging more per-sonal involvement among family members is at the core of treatment. This may be as simple as eating together more often, setting aside fam-ily time, discussing the school day, or review-ing homework regularly.

Victim-Specific Interventions

Techniques for dealing with victims revolve around their often common characteristics, in-cluding feelings of inadequacy, self-blame, poor self-concept, and being incapable, which are reflected in victims' overacceptance of their own weaknesses (Hazler et al., in press; Smith, 1991). Relationships with peers, adults, and even an overinvolved family can serve to reinforce such feelings. These individuals often have much more potential to deal with their victimization than they recognize. Gaining a more realistic picture of their situation and their abusers, enlightening them to their strengths, teaching assertiveness skills, and providing opportunities to practice these skills are the core emphases for individual counseling with victims.

Pain, suffering, sadness, depression, and anger are all likely to be a part of the clinical presentation of a victim. The longer and more consistently the abuse continues, the more contexts in which it occurs, and the more isolated the victim has become, the higher will be the levels of these symptoms. Supportive counseling is therefore the starting place for counseling victims. They need to know first and foremost that there is an individual who can be trusted, who sees them as competent, who understands their feelings and situation, and who has confidence that options can be developed for a seemingly hopeless situation.

Developing a more accurate picture of themselves, their situation, and those involved is an early step in counseling victims because they are likely to overemphasize their personal weaknesses and underemphasize their strengths. The counseling focus is to assist victims in developing a more accurate picture of their abilities and how they relate to what is happening in problem situations.

Having victims develop a more realistic perspective of their abusers can often be as important to counseling as improving their own self-perceptions. Victims as well as bystanders who have experienced dehumanizing actions of bullies often lose a sense of empathy for the abusers. This reduced ability to accurately picture the human side of their tormentors and those who stand by without acting reduces victims' ability to determine actions to effectively deal with abusive situations and increases the potential in victims for thoughts or acts of vengeance. Counseling

is helpful when it increases victims' ability to see abusers and bystanders in a more realistic light, to identify issues they have in common, and to then seek actions that can utilize these factors to improve the situation.

Once a more accurate picture of self, others, and situation is gained, counselors can use a number of specific therapeutic techniques to help the victim. Some commonly used techniques found to have critical value include the following:

- Avoid giving the abusers the emotional payoff they are seeking. This might include the victim who cries or acts sad at each incident as well as the victim who consistently becomes angry and does not turn that anger into effective coping actions.
- Learn techniques for being physically and verbally assertive but not aggressive. Physical techniques involve posture, eye contact, and other physical mannerisms that demonstrate confidence. Verbal skills include speaking up, using "I" statements, showing understanding, and demonstrating confidence.
- Strengthen continuing friendships and make new ones. Developing more friendships, gathering more people around more often, and making closer friendships all serve to reduce isolation, increase personal support, and reduce the likelihood of continued bullying.
- Seek support when necessary. Determining when, where, how, and from whom to seek support is often a lesson needed for victims.
- Encourage family activities that foster independence in addition to the support that some overinvolved families provide. Youth need to develop skills and confidence in their independence beyond their family unit.
- Consider doing the unexpected. Continual abusers are not looking for a fair contest, nor are they looking for surprises. They are seeking consistency in the reactions of their victims. Victims who begin to act in less predictable ways create situations that are not conducive to continual bullying.

- Practice necessary behaviors. Good ideas do not turn into productive actions automatically. Counseling needs to provide opportunities to practice new behaviors through imagery techniques and role play and also by identifying real-life situations where the actions can be practiced with a maximum chance of success and a minimal chance of failure. Most of the necessary behaviors to be learned are useful in many life situations, so that they can be practiced in safer situations in preparation for implementing them in bullying situations.

Joint Bully and Victim Interventions

Bullying and its resulting victimization are best defined as problem relationships, in that they could not persist without a continuing relationship between bully and victim. Because the relationship is by definition an unbalanced one, intervention techniques either seek to reduce the occurrence of the relationship so that one person does not continue to get hurt or to infuse balance by changing the individuals. Only when better balance can be assured should attempts be made to work jointly with bully and victim.

Promoting Issues in Common (PIC) is a general model for dealing with continuing abusive relationships that reflects the basic tenets of when and how to bring bullies and victims together for joint interventions (Hazler, 1996). Three basic stages of PIC emphasize gaining control of the situation, then evaluating the problem and potential for joint efforts, and finally using active joint interventions where and when appropriate. Emphasized throughout is the need for giving direct attention to bully, victim, and bystander needs and only bringing individuals together for joint work when the situation assures a significant degree of success.

The *gaining control stage* emphasizes the initial need to reduce danger in the situation and to act whenever abuse seems to be occurring. Interventions should be as minimally intrusive as possible while still reducing the danger to minimize negative repercussions and improve the chances for joint relationships later.

This is not the time to settle issues between participants. It is the time to reduce tension, give recognition to the seriousness of the situation, follow through with the formal behavioral rules or laws relating to the situation, and assure all participants that more will be done about the situation when things have calmed.

Evaluation is focused around individual discussions with bullies first and then victims, in that order whenever possible. Seeing the abuser first is a common technique that reduces the potential of the abuser's blaming the victim for being a "tattletale." The primary need for individuals at this stage is to be heard and understood in relation to the situation and to other aspects of their life that may be influencing their actions. This is not a time for judging right from wrong, which should be occurring separately with those adults who deal with disciplinary matters. The counselor is looking to develop positive relationships with anyone involved, to understand individual needs, problems, and viewpoints, and to look for areas of potential common concern among participants. Examples of these areas of common concern may include things as simple as participants wanting to avoid being in more trouble or as complex as wanting to be more accepted. If such commonalities are not found, there will be little hope for joint meetings, but as areas of commonality are discovered, they become the focus of potential joint meetings.

Active *interventions* begin with individual care and strengthening of each participant. Only if and when common goals are uncovered and there is sufficient strength in each participant to assure a balanced interaction should joint meetings be planned. The overriding goals for any joint meeting among a bully, a victim, and, potentially, bystanders are to demonstrate equality of participants and produce progress, no matter how small. Early meetings in particular, then, should be highly structured and focused on specific issues that have been previously agreed on individually with the counselor. It is the future of the relationship and how to meet these joint goals that provide the framework, not placing blame for the past.

What should emerge from joint meetings are agreed on actions that are specific enough to be clearly observed and limited enough to create a high possibility for success. General agreements such as "We'll do better" provide little therapeutic value, whereas more specific agreements, such as "We will only call each other by our actual first names and will stay out of each other's way between classes," provide much greater opportunity for both application and evaluation. Subsequent meetings focus first on evaluating the degree of success of carrying out agreements, altering agreements to make them more workable, and, as the situation improves, looking for broader and more generalizable agreements on relating to each other.

Treating bullies and victims jointly is never the first step and sometimes not possible for a long time, if at all. When it is possible, however, it provides a very strong therapeutic tool for the current situation and for the long-term growth of everyone concerned. Learning to effectively improve what once seemed to be insurmountable problems in a relationship teaches major life lessons about working in relationships. These lessons build skills to deal with future problems and also confidence in individuals' ability to overcome difficult situations—if not today, then tomorrow—if sufficient time, energy, and flexibility are included in the process.

References

Carney, J.V. (2000). Bullied to death: Perceptions of peer abuse and suicidal behavior during adolescence. *School Psychology International, 21,* 44–54.

Garrity, C., Jens, K., Porter, W., Sager, N., & Short-Camille, C. (1996). Bully-proofing your school: A comprehensive approach. *Journal of Emotional and Behavioral Problems, 5,* 35–39.

Hazler, R.J. (1996). *Breaking the cycle of violence: Interventions for bullies and victims.* Washington, DC: Accelerated Development.

Hazler, R.J. (1998). Promoting personal investment in systemic approaches to school violence. *Education, 119,* 222–231.

Hazler, R.J., & Carney, J.V. (2000). When victims turn aggressors: Factors in the development of deadly school violence. *Professional School Counseling, 4,* 105–112.

Hazler, R.J., Carney, J.V., Green, S., Powell, R., & Jolly, L.S. (1997). Areas of expert agreement on identification of school bullies and victims. *School Psychology International, 18,* 3–12.

Hazler, R.J., Hoover, J.H., & Oliver, R.L. (1991). Student perceptions of victimization by bullies in schools. *Journal of Humanistic Education and Development, 29,* 143–150.

Hazler, R.J., Miller, D., Carney, J.V., & Green, S. (in press). Adult recognition of school bullying situations. *Educational Research.*

Hunt, R.D. (1993). Neurobiological patterns of aggression. *Journal of Emotional and Behavioral Problems, 2,* 14–19.

McDowell, E.E., & Stillion, J.M. (1994). Suicide across the phases of life. In G.G. Noam & S. Borst (Eds.), *Children, youth, and suicide: Developmental perspectives* (pp. 1–7). San Francisco: Jossey-Bass.

Morita, Y., Soeda, H., Soeda, K., & Mitsuru, T. (1999). Japan. In P.K. Smith, Y. Morita, J. Junger-Tas, D. Olweus, R. Catalano, & P. Slee (Eds.), *The nature of school bullying: A cross-national perspective* (pp. 309–323). New York: Routledge.

Oliver, R., Oaks, I.N., & Hoover, J.H. (1994). Family issues and interventions in bully and victim relationships. *School Counselor, 41,* 199–202.

Schafer, M., & Smith, P.K. (1996). Teachers' perceptions of play fighting and real fighting in primary school. *Educational Research, 38,* 173–181.

Smith, P.K. (1991). The silent nightmare: Bullying and victimisation in school peer groups. *The Psychologist: Bulletin of the British Psychological Society, 4,* 243–248.

Smith, P.K., Madsen, K.C., & Moody, J.C. (1999). What causes the age decline in reports of being bullied at school? Towards a developmental analysis of risks of being bullied. *Educational Research, 41,* 267–285.

Weisfeld, G.E. (1994). Aggression and dominance in the social world of boys. In J. Archer (Ed.), *Male violence* (pp. 42–69). London: Routledge.

28 ASSESSMENT AND TREATMENT RECOMMENDATIONS FOR CHILDREN AND ADOLESCENTS WITH DEPRESSION

Benedict T. McWhirter and Jason J. Burrow

Until recently, depression in childhood and adolescence was not well addressed in the psychological literature or well delineated from other child and adolescent difficulties. Depression was often believed to be simply a sign of other problems and behaviors associated with it, such as anxiety, aggressiveness, delinquency, somatic complaints, substance use, poor peer relationships, poor school performance, school phobia, loss of initiative, and social withdrawal (Miller-Johnson, Lochman, Coie, Terry, & Hyman, 1998). Currently, experts agree that depression in childhood and adolescence is a substantial problem. In fact, the incidence, nature, and treatment of depression during childhood and adolescence have been topics of extensive research in recent years (e.g., Kovacs & Devlin, 1998; Lewinsohn, Rohde, & Seeley, 1998). Depression in youth is now viewed as a significant problem that affects approximately 30% of the adolescent population and between 2% and 5% of younger children (Lewinsohn, Rohde, et al., 1998). One in five young people report a minimum of one episode of major depression by the age of 18 and adolescents seen in mental health centers are most frequently diagnosed with an affective disorder. Additionally, youth who have had depression are likely to have another episode within a few years (Kovacs & Devlin, 1998). Thus, depression is a serious problem faced by many young people.

ETIOLOGY OF DEPRESSION

An extensive discussion of the etiology of depression is important for understanding prevention and treatment but is beyond the scope of this chapter. The most common models for explaining the etiology of depression are biological, behavioral, cognitive, psychodynamic, and family. Biological, behavioral, and cognitive are the only models of depression briefly discussed below due to space constraints. Biological models focus on the role of genetic factors or emphasize biochemical aspects of depression. There is a strong genetic component in the risk of depression (Kovacs & Devlin, 1998), and it has been reported that children of depressed parents are three times more likely to have a major depressive episode at some point during their lives (Garber & Robinson, 1997).

Behaviorists view depression as a result of significant loss and the consequence of inadequate or insufficient reinforcement (Kovacs & Devlin, 1998). Lewinsohn's social learning theory, for instance, suggests that depressive behaviors are determined by the presence or absence of reinforcers and are maintained through the reduction of response-contingent reinforcing events. Depression may be the result of limited positive reinforcement for the individual, which is determined by the number of potentially reinforcing events, the

199

number of these events available in the environment, and the individual's social skills to elicit accessible reinforcers (Lewinsohn & Hoberman, 1985).

Among the cognitive models of depression, Beck and colleagues (1979) suggest that cognition and affect are interactive, and that the prior occurrence of cognition will determine a person's affective response to an event. If cognitions are distorted or inaccurate, the individual's emotional response will be inappropriate. Dysphoria may then be the affective response of one's tendency to cognitively interpret experiences as negative or self-devaluative. Seligman's (1974) "learned helplessness" model contends that depression exists in people who perceive that they have no control over their environment. They develop self-defeating attributions and make internal (feeling responsible for an event), stable (the causes of an event remain constant), and global (event outcomes impact all areas of life) attributions for failure. In contrast, they attribute success to external (caused by others), unstable (causes of events are transitory), and specific (situation-specific) causes.

ASSESSMENT OF DEPRESSION

Assessment of childhood and adolescent depression should include information from multiple sources (e.g., parent, child, and teacher). The specific number of sources needed for accurate assessment depends on the age of the child. Young children may not be able to provide a full clinical picture of their symptoms; thus, information obtained from parents and teachers is typically more necessary than it may be with older children. Adolescents usually provide a more accurate picture of their own depressive symptoms than their parents do. In fact, agreement between parent and adolescent report has been found to be low when diagnosing Major Depressive Disorder in adolescents; typically, parents underreport depressive symptoms as compared to adolescents (Lewinsohn, Rohde, et al., 1998). Thus, counselors should not rely on parent report alone in diagnosing depression.

Self-Report Measures

Screening for current depressive symptoms in children and adolescents is commonly done by administering self-report measures. Some of the most commonly used self-report measures include the Children's Depression Inventory (CDI; Kovacs, 1985a), the Beck Depression Inventory II (BDI II; Beck, Steer, & Brown, 1996), the Center for Epidemiologic Studies Depression Scale (CES-D; Radloff, 1977), and the Children's Depression Scale (CDS; Tischer & Lang, 1983). Self-report measures are used as a quick and efficient method to screen for depressive symptoms in children and adolescents in many settings (e.g., clinic, school). These measures are also used to identify urgent problems such as suicide ideation and risk of self-harm and provide indicators of change during treatment (Lewinsohn, Rohde, et al., 1998). Initial screenings with a self-report measure should typically be followed by an in-depth diagnostic interview.

Diagnostic Interviews

In-depth diagnostic interviews are used to accurately evaluate the number and severity of depressive and other (e.g., anxiety) symptoms in children and adolescents. Some of the more common semistructured interviews include the Interview Schedule for Children (ISC; Kovacs, 1985b), the Child Assessment Schedule (CAS; Hodges, Kline, Stern, Cytryn, & McKnew, 1982), and the Schedule for Affective Disorders and Schizophrenia for Children (K-SADS; Puig-Antich & Chambers, 1978). Semistructured interviews allow counselors some flexibility in assessing the symptoms of depression as well as other disorders. Most of the diagnostic interviews mentioned above assess for a wide range of other disorders (e.g., anxiety, PTSD) in addition to depression. An accurate diagnostic assessment of the child or adolescent is important when considering the high comorbidity of depression with other disorders (Rohde, Lewinsohn, & Seeley, 1991). In choosing which interview to administer it is important to consider the age of the child as well as the psychometric properties of the instrument. Counselors are encouraged to consult the specific reference(s) for each diagnostic instrument to determine the appropriateness for a given client.

Diagnosis

The *Diagnostic and Statistical Manual of Mental Disorders*, fourth edition (*DSM-IV;* American Psychiatric Association, 2000) has added precision to the diagnosis of depression in childhood and adolescence from previous editions. The *DSM-IV* presents differential symptoms of adolescent depression from symptoms commonly experienced by adults. For example, children commonly display irritable mood rather than depressed mood, somatic complaints, and social withdrawal, whereas depressed adolescents typically display psychomotor retardation and hypersomnia. Children may also display depressive symptoms in conjunction with disruptive behavior disorders (e.g., attention-deficit, anxiety), whereas depression in adolescents is commonly associated with disruptive behavior disorders as well as substance-related disorders and eating disorders (Miller-Johnson et al., 1998). Rates of depression are relatively equal between boys and girls, but during adolescence, females have increased rates of depression closely paralleling the gender differences found in adulthood (American Psychiatric Association, 2000).

TREATMENT STRATEGIES FOR CHILDREN AND ADOLESCENTS

Individual

Frequently, individual approaches involve both individual and family sessions, with the focus remaining on the depressed child or adolescent. We focus on cognitive-behavioral approaches here because they have demonstrated effectiveness. For instance, Reinecke, Ryan, and DuBois (1998) conducted a meta-analysis of cognitive-behavioral therapy for depression and dysphoria. All of the 24 studies they analyzed employed cognitive-behavioral interventions and demonstrated positive results in the

treatment and alleviation of depression in adolescents. In young children, however, a cognitive focus may not be as effective because higher-order thinking may not have developed yet.

Cognitive-behavioral treatments for depression flow directly from the cognitive and behavioral models described earlier. For example, Beck and colleagues (1979) developed a therapy with both behavioral and cognitive components designed to reduce automatic negative cognition with the goal of challenging the assumptions that maintain these faulty cognitions. Because depressed clients often have difficulty utilizing cognitive tasks, behavioral strategies should be used first in the therapeutic process. These strategies include scheduling pleasant activities, relaxation training, graduated task assignments, social skills training, and behavioral rehearsal (Reinecke et al., 1998).

Certain behavioral strategies increase an individual's activity level and therefore the frequency of potentially rewarding activities. During depression, there is a tendency to withdraw from pleasurable activities and interactions with others. Behavioral strategies can be used to directly address withdrawal behaviors and encourage children and adolescents to engage in more pleasurable activities such as increasing the number of daily enjoyable activities engaged in. Lewinsohn, Clarke, and Rohde (1994), for example, describe using an instrument called the Pleasant Events Schedule (PES; MacPhillamy & Lewinsohn, 1982) with depressed adolescents in a way that will help them increase the frequency of pleasurable activities.

After these strategies are successfully utilized, emphasis is moved to cognitive interventions that emphasize identifying, testing, and modifying cognitive distortions. Strategies that have been successfully used include (1) recognizing the connections among cognition, affect, and behavior; (2) monitoring negative automatic thoughts; (3) examining evidence related to distorted automatic cognition; (4) substituting more realistic interpretations for distorted cognitions; (5) learning to identify and modify irrational beliefs;

(6) altering biased attentional processes; (7) affect regulation; and (8) impulse control (Brent et al., 1996).

Another cognitive-behavioral treatment approach for children and adolescents is the application of Rational-Emotive Behavior Therapy (REBT) developed by Albert Ellis (Vernon, 1999). REBT was originally developed for adults but has also been used with children and adolescents suffering from a number of disorders including depression. Vernon described the major theoretical ideas behind REBT: (1) Individuals develop beliefs (i.e., rational or irrational) and subsequent emotions and behaviors regarding events that impede their progress toward a goal; (2) an individual's irrational beliefs (e.g., "I fail at everything") must be challenged by the counselor; and (3) comprehensive therapy must focus on long-term change (i.e., core irrational beliefs) instead of a quick fix. For more specific recommendations for implementing REBT with children and adolescents suffering from depression, see Vernon.

In some clinical settings (e.g., schools, managed care) counselors may be limited to a few sessions in which to treat children and adolescents with depression. In such circumstances, a brief counseling model should be used. Littrell and Zinck (1999) describe one brief model that has been used with children and adolescents. Their approach rests on eight characteristics: being time-limited, solution-focused, action-based, socially interactive, detail-oriented, humor-eliciting, developmentally attentive, and relationship-based. This approach can also be implemented with other brief therapy modalities.

Another individual approach that has demonstrated positive results in alleviating depression in adolescents is interpersonal psychotherapy (IPT). This therapy conceptualizes depression as conflict taking place in the context of interpersonal relationships (Mufson & Fairbanks, 1996). There are five areas that form the problem areas and treatment goals in IPT: grief, interpersonal role disputes, role transitions, interpersonal deficits, and membership in a single-parent family (this is a modification for use with adolescents). Goals are to reduce

depression and address the underlying conflict associated with the depression. Examples of techniques used in this approach include exploratory questioning, linking affect and events, clarifying conflicts and communication patterns, and behavior modification strategies. This approach has received promising empirical support (Mufson & Fairbanks, 1996).

Pharmacological interventions are, in some cases, required with depressed clients. Medication usage for depressed youth has followed the trend of adult research. Since the 1960s, tricyclic antidepressants (TCAs) have been prescribed for young patients, although the effectiveness of antidepressants for children and adolescents has not been established through controlled research (Brent et al., 1996). The majority of randomized controlled trials (RCTs) conducted with children and adolescents with a depressive disorder have used TCAs as the psychopharmacological treatment (Birmaher, 1998). Another class of antidepressant medication having fewer side effects, as compared to TCAs, is the class of drugs known as selective serotonin reuptake inhibitors (SSRIs). Birmaher found that very few RCTs have tested the efficacy of SSRIs for the treatment of depression in children and adolescents. One of the SSRIs, fluoxene, has been found to be effective for the treatment of depression in one RCT (Emslie et al., 1997). Birmaher recommends using SSRIs when the child or adolescent suffers from a type of depression not easily treated with counseling or therapy. See also Kutcher (1998) for further information about pharmacological interventions for depression.

Family

The role of the family in the successful treatment of the depressed child or adolescent is crucial. Family counseling has been shown to be very important in the effective treatment of childhood disorders, in part due to the extensive influence families have over young children compared with adolescents (Nichols & Schwartz, 1995). Counselors using only an individually based intervention strategy may, in fact, be doomed to failure because from this perspective the entire family system needs to change. Counselors must be prepared to work with all family members, especially parents who may also suffer from an affective disorder or who may have marital conflict. Concurrent family therapy is, thus, nearly always indicated in working with depressed children and adolescents (Nichols & Schwartz, 1995).

In many circumstances, parent training and education can benefit the family and help prevent depression and other problems. Workshops in parent training can be particularly useful and cost-effective, especially those that focus on developing communication skills, enhancing family interactions, and sharing information about issues (such as birth control, signs of drug use). In families with greater dysfunction, therapeutic programs attending to child abuse and neglect, parental dysfunction, and family violence may also be extremely beneficial.

School Settings

The occurrence of depression among children and adolescents has increased in recent years and is due in part to environmental stressors, in which schools play a major role. This supports the need for early prevention and intervention in the school setting. School prevention and treatment should include a mixture of affective, cognitive, and behavioral strategies that focus on issues such as self-acceptance, problem solving and decision making, and social skills and interpersonal relationships (Vernon, 1989). Group interventions are central to many school-based prevention programs because of their ability to reach a large number of children and their relative cost-effectiveness, adaptability to the classroom format, and usefulness for training skills.

School-based small group intervention programs for depression and other psychosocial problems have not often been rigorously evaluated, but existing outcome studies indicate some positive results. For example, Vernon (1989) developed an effective emotional education curriculum based on REBT. This program targets thoughts, affect, and behavior and has

specific grade-level interventions targeted to the young person's developmental level. Topics such as self-acceptance, feelings, behaviors, problem solving, decision making, and interpersonal relationships are addressed. In addition, Lewinsohn, Clarke, and Rohde (1994) described an eight-week cognitive-behavioral group intervention titled Adolescent Coping with Depression Course (CWD-A). Success for the CWD-A group intervention has been demonstrated in clinical settings, and because its individual sessions are presented in a classlike manner, it may be adaptable to school settings (Lewinsohn, Clarke, et al., 1994). Although the results for group-based interventions for depression are promising, more research on group-based intervention conducted in school settings is needed.

SUMMARY

Depression is a significant and complicated mental health problem among children and adolescents. Its manifestation in childhood varies but in adolescence is more similar to that found in adulthood. Current research supports several treatment approaches as being similarly successful in remitting depression. Readers are encouraged to refer to the references for this chapter for further reading and more detailed coverage of each of the areas reviewed. As indicated by much of the treatment literature cited herein, any successful intervention for child and adolescent depression must focus on the whole ecology of a young person's life—school, family, community, and individual interventions—to be fully successful in reaching out to and helping young people who suffer from depression.

References

American Psychiatric Association. (2000). *Diagnostic and statistical manual of mental disorders* (4th ed., text rev.). Washington, DC: Author.

Beck, A.T., Rush, A.G., Shaw, B.F., & Emery, G. (1979). *Cognitive therapy of depression*. New York: Guilford Press.

Beck, A.T., Steer, R.A., & Brown, G.K. (1996). *Beck Depression Inventory II* (2nd ed.). San Antonio, TX: Psychological Corporation.

Birmaher, B. (1998). Child and adolescent psychopharmacology. *Psychopharmacology Bulletin, 34,* 35–39.

Brent, D.A., Roth, C.M., Holder, D.P., Kolko, D.J., Birmaher, B., Johnson, B.A., & Schweers, J.A. (1996). Psychosocial interventions for treating adolescent suicidal depression: A comparison of three psychosocial interventions. In E.D. Hibbs & P.S. Jensen (Eds.), *Psychosocial treatments for child and adolescent disorders: Empirically based strategies for clinical practice* (pp. 187–206). Washington, DC: American Psychological Association.

Emslie, G., Rush, A.J., Weinberg, A.W., Kowatch, R.A., Hughes, C.W., Carmody, T., & Rintelmann, J. (1997). A double-blind, randomized placebo-controlled trial of fluoxetine in children and adolescents with depression. *Archives of General Psychiatry, 54,* 1031–1037.

Garber, J., & Robinson, N.S. (1997). Cognitive vulnerability in children at risk for depression. *Cognition and Emotion, 11,* 619–635.

Hodges, K., Kline, J., Stern, L., Cytryn, L., & McKnew, D. (1982). The development of a child assessment schedule for research and clinical use. *Journal of Abnormal Child Psychology, 10,* 173–189.

Kovacs, M. (1985a). The Children's Depression Inventory (CDI). *Psychopharmacology Bulletin, 21,* 995–998.

Kovacs, M. (1985b). The Interview Schedule for Children (ISC). *Psychopharmacology Bulletin, 21,* 991–994.

Kovacs, M., & Devlin, B. (1998). Internalizing disorders in childhood. *Journal of Child Psychology and Psychiatry, 39,* 47–63.

Kutcher, S.P. (1998). Affective disorders in children and adolescents: A critical clinically relevant review. In B.T. Walsh (Ed.), *Child psychopharmacology* (pp. 135–147). Washington, DC: American Psychiatric Press.

Lewinsohn, P.M., & Hoberman, H.M. (1985). Depression. In A.S. Bellack, M. Herson, & A.E. Kazdin (Eds.), *International handbook of behavior modification and therapy* (student ed., pp. 173–207). New York: Plenum Press.

Lewinsohn, P.M., Rohde, P., & Seeley, J.R. (1998). Major depressive disorder in older adolescents: Prevalence, risk factors, and clinical implications. *Clinical Psychology Review, 18,* 765–794.

Lewinsohn, P.M., Clarke, G.N., & Rohde, P. (1994). Psychological approaches to the treatment of depression in adolescents. In W.M. Reynolds & H.F. Johnston (Eds.), *Handbook of depression in children and adolescents* (pp. 309–344). New York: Plenum Press.

Littrell, J.M., & Zinck, K. (1999). Application of brief counseling with children and adolescents. In A. Vernon (Ed.), *Counseling children and adolescents* (2nd ed., pp. 122–138). Denver, CO: Love.

MacPhillamy, D.J., & Lewinsohn, P.M. (1982). The Pleasant Events Schedule: Studies on reliability, validity, and scale intercorrelation. *Journal of Consulting and Clinical Psychology, 50,* 363–380.

Miller-Johnson, S., Lochman, J.E., Coie, J.D., Terry, R., & Hyman, C. (1998). Comorbidity of conduct and depressive problems at sixth grade: Substance use outcomes across adolescence. *Journal of Abnormal Child Psychology, 26,* 221–232.

Mufson, L., & Fairbanks, J. (1996). Interpersonal psychotherapy for depressed adolescents: A one-year naturalistic follow-up study. *Journal of the American Academy of Child and Adolescent Psychiatry, 35,* 1145–1155.

Nichols, M.P., & Schwartz, R.C. (1995). *Family therapy: Concepts and methods* (3rd ed.). Boston: Allyn & Bacon.

Puig-Antich, J., & Chambers, W. (1978). *The Schedule for Affective Disorders and Schizophrenia for School-Aged Children (K-SADS).* New York: New York State Psychiatric Institute.

Radloff, L.S. (1977). The CES-D Scale: A self-report scale for research in the general population. *Applied Psychological Measurement, 1,* 385–401.

Reinecke, M.A., Ryan, N.E., & DuBois, D.L. (1998). Cognitive-behavioral therapy of depression and depressive symptoms during adolescence: A review and meta-analysis. *Journal of the American Academy of Child and Adolescent Psychiatry, 37,* 26–34.

Rohde, P., Lewinsohn, P.M., & Seeley, J.R. (1991). Comorbidity with unipolar depression: II. Comorbidity with other mental disorders in adolescents and adults. *Journal of Abnormal Psychology, 100,* 214–222.

Seligman, M.E. (1974). Depression and learned helplessness. In R.J. Friedman & M.M. Katz (Eds.), *The psychology of depression: Contemporary theory and research* (pp. 83–125). New York: Wiley.

Tisher, M., & Lang, M. (1983). The Children's Depression Scale: Review and further developments. In D.P. Cantwell & G.A. Carlson (Eds.),

Affective disorders in childhood and adolescence (pp. 181–203). Jamaica, NY: Spectrum.

Vernon, A. (1989). *Thinking, feeling, behaving: An emotional education curriculum for children: Grades 1–6 and for adolescents: Grades 7–12.* Champaign, IL: Research Press.

Vernon, A. (1999). Applications of rational-emotive behavior therapy with children and adolescents. In A. Vernon (Ed.), *Counseling children and adolescents* (2nd ed., pp. 140–157). Denver, CO: Love.

29 COUNSELING INTERVENTIONS FOR CHILDREN WITH DISRUPTIVE BEHAVIORS

John Sommers-Flanagan, Rita Sommers-Flanagan, and Charles Palmer

In this chapter, we review treatment approaches for young people referred for counseling because of disruptive behavior—children whose main symptoms include misconduct, hostility, aggression, impulsivity, defiance, and disruptive behaviors. These symptoms are commonly associated with Conduct Disorder and Oppositional Defiant Disorder (American Psychiatric Association, 2000). Although children diagnosed with Attention-Deficit/Hyperactivity Disorder (ADHD) and clinical depression also regularly exhibit these challenging behavior patterns (Knox, King, Hanna, Logan, & Ghaziuddin, 2000), specific treatments for children and adolescents diagnosed with ADHD and depression are covered elsewhere in this sourcebook (see Chapter 26 for information pertaining to treatment for youth diagnosed with ADHD and Chapter 28 for treatments for depressed children).

IDENTIFICATION AND TERMINOLOGY ISSUES

As one might guess from the introductory paragraph, assigning psychiatric diagnoses to youth who exhibit disruptive behavior disorders can be a complex and challenging process. To provide effective treatment, counselors should educate themselves regarding factors that can influence the diagnosis and treatment of disruptive youth (see House, Chapter 30). A number of these factors are:

- *Diagnostic comorbidity.* The existence of two or more diagnostic entities within a single individual is very common among youth who display disruptive behaviors; for example, it is estimated that Conduct Disorder and ADHD coexist 45% to 70% of the time, and Conduct Disorder and Oppositional Defiant Disorder coexist in 84% to 96% of cases (Hinshaw, Lahey, & Hart, 1993; Offord, Boyle, & Racine, 1991). Additionally, the coexistence of Posttraumatic Stress Disorder, substance abuse disorders, learning disorders, Reactive Attachment Disorder, anxiety disorders, and depression is surprisingly high among misbehaving youth (Carrion & Steiner, 2000; Sommers-Flanagan & Sommers-Flanagan, 1998).
- *Client deceit.* Young clients who engage in disruptive behaviors frequently minimize,

deny, or blatantly lie to their counselors about their misbehavior; therefore, it is inappropriate to work with these clients without obtaining information about their lives outside the counseling office.

• *Parent and teacher misinformation.* Parents and teachers may be uninformed or misinformed when it comes to specifying the details of young clients' behavior; once again, obtaining information from divergent sources is crucial.

• *Counselor countertransference.* While working with disruptive youth, counselors may be emotionally affected in ways that can interfere with therapeutic objectivity. (Some writers have referred to counseling with difficult adolescents as "blood sport"; Trepper, 1991, p. ix, which suggests that adversarial relationships between young clients and their counselors can develop).

• *Confounding cultural and situational factors.* Often, disruptive behavior disorders are associated with difficult living conditions such as large family size, poverty, overcrowding, homelessness, parental absence or abuse, transportation problems, poor or inadequate housing, and less-than-optimal school settings (Canino & Spurlock, 1994; Kazdin, 1998).

• *Biogenetic conditions.* Although whether heredity or biogenetic factors play a strong role in Conduct Disorder and Oppositional Defiant Disorder is controversial, research clearly points to the importance of biogenetic conditions (e.g., lead toxicity, brain injury) in causing or contributing to impulsive, antisocial, and disruptive behavior.

MAJOR THEORETICAL, RESEARCH, AND PRACTICE PRINCIPLES

There are many different approaches to treating youth with disruptive behavior problems. These approaches include, but are not limited to, family counseling, group and classroom interventions, parent training, and individualized treatment strategies such as behavioral and cognitive-behavioral counseling, residential, hospital, and wilderness-based programs,

hypnosis, biofeedback, and psychotropic medications (Bandoroff & Scherer, 1994; Kazdin, 1996). Most professionals acknowledge that it is very difficult to provide effective treatment for disruptive young clients (Bernstein, 1996; Church, 1994; Kazdin & Wassell, 2000; Meeks, 1980).

Dealing with Client and Parent Resistance

Children and adolescents who behave disruptively often strain their relationships with many important adults (e.g., parents, teachers, probation officers). Consequently, when these young clients arrive at the counselor's office, it is not usually because of their own desire for personal change, but instead because some adult has determined (or hopes fervently) that they might benefit from counseling. Thus, counselors may be immediately confronted with a disinterested and unmotivated client. Most researchers and writers stress that, for treatment with disruptive young clients to be effective, counselors must somehow develop and maintain a positive therapeutic alliance with the client. For example, Hanna, Hanna, and Keys (1999) state: "A counseling technique performed without a properly established empathic and trusting relationship seems to many defiant adolescents to be a threat to their integrity, and just another covert or overt adult attempt at manipulation" (p. 396).

To further magnify the problem, research has shown that parents of children who are most seriously disturbed are often the most resistant to participating in treatment (Reid, 1993). These parents typically drop off their children for counseling, hoping that the counselor will quickly and efficiently "fix" their child. When parental resistance to counseling is high, it may stem from chronic frustration with their child's behavior, apathy and/or depression, substance abuse, poverty, or other family dynamics associated with disengagement.

The key point is that for treatment to proceed with this particular population, parent and child resistance must be addressed. This means that counselors should consider using strategies, incentives, playful activities, humor, and reassurance to reduce resistance and engage parents and children in treatment.

Empirically Supported Treatment Approaches

Despite difficulties engaging disruptive children and their parents in counseling, several treatments hold promise for working effectively with this population. These approaches can be divided into three groups: parent-focused treatments, family-focused treatments, and child-focused treatments. Although this chapter primarily addresses child-focused treatments, we first briefly review parent- and family-focused treatment approaches that have garnered empirical support for reducing children's disruptive behaviors.

A recent meta-analysis indicated that individual cognitive-behavioral treatments are only marginally effective with young children (Bennett & Gibbons, 2000). This is probably because younger children are less cognitively developed and generally more influenced by their family systems. Consequently, the following parent and family approaches to treating children who behave disruptively are especially recommended when counselors are working with young children.

Parent-Focused Treatments. Parent-focused psychoeducational interventions can be effective when parents cooperate with treatment. Parent-focused treatments have their roots in social learning theory. This perspective suggests that children initially learn aggressive and defiant behavior patterns within their family context (Patterson, 1982): "The pioneering research of Patterson and others has found that parents of children with conduct disorders exhibit fewer positive behaviors, use more violent disciplinary techniques, are more critical, more permissive, less likely to monitor their children's behaviors and more likely to reinforce inappropriate behaviors while ignoring, or even punishing, prosocial behaviors" (Webster-Stratton, 1996, p. 437).

Parent-focused approaches seek to modify children's disruptive behaviors by changing family interactions from coercive and aggressive to positive and prosocial. Essentially, this approach involves directly teaching parents to appropriately reinforce prosocial behavior, use effective discipline techniques, provide adequate supervision and monitoring of children's behavior, communicate more effectively, model more appropriate behaviors, and cope with difficult situations, such as divorce or death of a family member (Danforth, 1999). Currently, at least two parent-focused treatments show promising empirical outcomes with disruptive behavior disordered children. These approaches include videotape modeling (Webster-Stratton, 1996) and parent management training (Kazdin & Wassell, 2000).

Family-Focused Treatments. Family therapists (Szapocznik, Kurtines, Santiseteban, & Rio, 1990) argue that interventions for disruptive children must include their families. There are a number of good reasons for this view. Interventions directed toward families avoid identifying and labeling the child as the primary problem and help illustrate that a child's difficult behaviors can be a part of the overall family system dynamics. Family counselors can help identify family patterns that may be contributing to the child's behaviors and help the family find alternative ways to cope and change.

Family therapy is a demanding specialty. Frequently, family therapy, even more rigidly than individual therapy, is defined in terms of specific theoretical frameworks. To competently practice family therapy, extensive education and training in a particular theoretical model may be necessary. Currently, there are two behavioral systems approaches to family therapy that, thus far, have gained empirical support: functional family therapy (Alexander & Parsons, 1982; Morris, Alexander, & Waldron, 1988) and multisystemic family therapy (Henggeler, Melton, & Smith, 1992).

INDIVIDUAL TREATMENTS FOR YOUTH WITH DISRUPTIVE BEHAVIORS: PRINCIPLES AND PROCEDURES

As noted previously, individual treatments for children with disruptive behaviors are more clinically indicated for adolescents or older children (Bennett & Gibbons, 2000). The following principles and procedures are acknowledged as having general theoretical support, as well as limited empirical support.

Engagement

Virtually all approaches to working individually with disruptive behavior disordered youth emphasize the importance of addressing initial client reluctance or resistance, forming a therapeutic alliance, and engaging clients in potentially therapeutic interactions (Bernstein, 1996; Hanna & Hunt, 1999; Meeks, 1980; Sommers-Flanagan & Sommers-Flanagan, 1995, 1997). Strategies for reducing resistance, building an alliance, and engaging young clients in counseling can generally be divided into three categories. First, many clinicians advocate using basic Rogerian relationship variables (congruence, unconditional positive regard, and accurate empathy; Rogers, 1957) to enhance the counselor-client therapeutic alliance. For example, Bernstein (1996) recommends that counselors learn about adolescent culture so that they can quickly express interest and respect to defiant adolescents: "I saw a young man who was rather quiet and indifferent during our first meeting. I noted that he was wearing a Guns and Roses tee shirt and recalled something I had recently read about the rock group. 'Did you hear what happened at the Guns and Roses concert in St. Louis last week?' I queried. 'No, what?' he quickly responded. Suddenly I had his undivided attention" (pp. 41–42).

Second, many clinicians recommend modifying structural, strategic, or situational therapy components to make sitting and talking more comfortable for adolescents (Bernstein, 1996). In their article "Fifty Strategies for Counseling Defiant Adolescents," Hanna et al. (1999) describe numerous structural and strategic modifications that can help young clients talk to and interact with counselors more comfortably. These include:

- Offer a snack.
- Avoid desks.
- Allow clients to occupy their hands while talking.

- Get out of the office.
- Use a variety of media to allow the client to express what is inside without having to rely solely on verbal skills.
- Let clients know how much you have learned from their sessions.
- Treat shocking statements with equanimity and instant reframes.
- Avoid any unnecessary insistence on being verbally respected.

Third, as we discuss in our book, *Tough Kids, Cool Counseling* (Sommers-Flanagan & Sommers-Flanagan, 1997), therapeutic alliances with reluctant young clients can be built partly by implementing specific relationship-building techniques: "Interesting techniques can overcome the youth's initial resistance to forming a therapy relationship and to engaging in therapeutic procedures. In fact, with young clients, interesting techniques may enhance the therapeutic alliance regardless of the particular technique's impact on symptom reduction. Our point is that simply *doing something interesting together* with young clients often enhances the counseling relationship" (p. 35). Specifically, we recommend that counselors have a wide range of potentially therapeutic activities available for use with active and disruptive young clients (e.g., the hand-pushing game, drawing together, arm wrestling, sharing jokes and riddles, passing notes; see Sommers-Flanagan & Sommers-Flanagan, 1997).

Cognitive Behavioral Problem-Solving Approaches

Much of the treatment literature for children with disruptive behavior disorders has focused on how children can be taught to increase their self-control through interpersonal cognitive problem-solving processes (e.g., means-end thinking, consequential thinking, and generating cognitive and/or behavioral alternatives; Spivack & Shure, 1982). Additionally, most treatment approaches integrate behavioral reinforcement and self-reinforcement into their programs. The goal is to help impulsive and disruptive children engage in constructive problem-solving strategies rather than continuing to

rely on impulsive and reactive interpersonal behaviors. For example, in his problem-solving
skills training program, Kazdin (1996) reports
teaching children the following five sequential
problem-solving and self-instructional steps:

1. What am I supposed to do?
2. I have to look at all my possibilities.
3. I had better concentrate and focus in.
4. I need to make a choice.
5. I did a good job; or, Oh, I made a mistake.
   (p. 383)

Emphasizing self-control strategies with
impulsive and disruptive adolescents capital-
izes on strong autonomy and individuation
striving during adolescence (Church, 1994). To
maximize their effectiveness, counselors can
make statements that place therapeutic success
firmly within the youth's control. For example,
"Okay, let's talk about strategies for how you
can get more of what you want out of life"
(Sommers-Flanagan & Sommers-Flanagan,
1997, p. 115).

Other Treatment Approaches

In addition to traditional problem-solving
skills training, other therapeutic approaches
may be integrated into counseling work with
disruptive adolescents. This tendency toward
pragmatic eclecticism with adolescents who
misbehave may be partly due to the somewhat
disappointing results associated with any single approach to treating this population
(Kazdin & Wassell, 2000; Matthys, Cuperus, &
Van Engeland, 1999), or it may simply reflect
the fact that more therapeutic creativity is
called for when working with adolescents (Selekman, 1993). Whatever the case, practitioners may want to utilize solution-focused
(Murphy, 1997), narrative (Lankton & Lankton,
1989), hypnotic (Sommers-Flanagan & Sommers-Flanagan, 1996b), psychodynamic (Bernstein, 1996), and other treatment approaches
with disruptive adolescents.

Finally, in particular, as noted previously,
contact with the young client's parents and
family is often essential. If they proceed carefully, counselors can weave family meetings
into individual therapy with adolescents. The
procedures described below are important
because adolescents can be very sensitive to
rejection and parental alignment (Sommers-
Flanagan & Sommers-Flanagan, 1997).

Family meetings are sessions during
which all relevant family members are in attendance. These meetings are implemented
within the context of the young client's individual therapy. The emphasis in family meetings is on parent-child communication and
parent training, using the child or children
as assistants. Family meetings use a child
empowerment model wherein children have
input regarding appropriate limits, consequences, behavioral choices, and so on.

When conducting family meetings, we utilize the following procedural guidelines:

1. The therapist and child meet prior to the
   family meeting to establish a plan regarding WHAT will be discussed during the family meeting and HOW it will be discussed.
2. Therapist and child have established goals
   for the family meeting. Additionally, they
   may have made predictions regarding how
   the parents will respond to topics that are to
   be discussed and they may have made contingency plans based on those predictions.
3. Therapist and child meet briefly together
   immediately prior to the family meeting
   to review plans and goals for the family
   meeting.
4. The meeting proceeds using a problem-
   solving format wherein a single problem is
   identified, defined, discussed, potential solutions are brainstormed, and family members agree on which potential solution will
   be implemented and how its effectiveness
   will be evaluated.
5. Incentives or rewards may be given to the
   child and/or parents for using effective
   communication skills.
6. Therapist and child meet briefly together
   at the conclusion of the family meeting to
   debrief the session. (pp. 161–162)

Limited and careful family involvement
during individual counseling can serve many
important functions. The counselor can become acquainted with the client's home environment. In addition, the counselor can model

open communication and assist the client in generalizing gains made in counseling to home and school settings.

Treating Underlying Psychiatric Conditions

As noted previously, one of the complicating factors in providing counseling for youth who exhibit Oppositional Defiant and Conduct Disorder symptoms is the fact that their disruptive behaviors may be driven by depression, ADHD, trauma, or other related conditions. The treatment strategies discussed above primarily target disruptive behaviors and may not necessarily provide relief for underlying disorders. Of course, simply changing maladaptive behaviors can, in some cases, begin a healing process that addresses underlying disorders (Sommers-Flanagan & Sommers-Flanagan, 1995). However, it is important to be alert to the multidimensional treatment needs of children with disruptive behaviors.

Biological (Medication) Treatment Alternatives

This is a chapter about nonmedical treatment strategies for disruptive behavior. However, it has become increasingly common for young people who are displaying any kind of disruptive or depressed behavior to be referred to physicians for medical intervention. Counselors often wonder about their responsibilities in this area (see Ingersoll, Chapter 13). Parents and teachers often ask counselors whether a child should be evaluated for psychotropic medications. And counselors often ask themselves that question as well.

We believe all reasonable nonmedical interventions in treating children with disruptive behavioral disorders should be explored before psychotropic drugs trials are initiated (Sommers-Flanagan & Sommers-Flanagan, 1996a). However, there are times when counselors should initiate a medication evaluation or recommend a medication trial. These situations include:

- The young person displays the symptoms in the absence of any clear environmental determinants such as family conflict or developmental difficulties.
- Symptoms include such physiological aspects as sleep disturbance, weight loss or gain, and appetite changes.
- The youth has not responded to counseling interventions of significant duration (8 to 12 sessions).
- The parents or child absolutely refuse counseling interventions.
- There are apparent genetic factors associated with specific symptom patterns.
- The youth's general physical health is in question and he or she has not had a recent physical checkup. (Sommers-Flanagan & Sommers-Flanagan, 1997, p. 224)

In the event that a child is on a psychotropic medication, counseling remains an important treatment component. As behaviorists like to point out, "A pill is not a skill." It is important for counselors to help young people to develop a sense of efficacy that is unrelated to taking medication.

References

Alexander, J., & Parsons, B.V. (1982). *Functional family therapy.* Pacific Grove, CA: Brooks/Cole.

American Psychiatric Association. (2000). *Diagnostic and statistical manual of mental disorders* (4th ed., text rev.). Washington, DC: Author.

Bandoroff, S., & Scherer, D.G. (1994). Wilderness family therapy: An innovative treatment approach for problem youth. *Journal of Child and Family Studies, 3,* 175–191.

Bennett, D.S., & Gibbons, T.A. (2000). Efficacy of child cognitive-behavioral interventions for antisocial behavior: A meta-analysis. *Child and Family Behavior Therapy, 22,* 1–16.

Bernstein, N. (1996). *Treating the unmanageable adolescent.* Northvale, NJ: Aronson.

Canino, I.A., Spurlock, J. (1994). *Culturally diverse children and adolescents: Assessment, diagnosis, and treatment.* New York: Guilford Press.

Carrion, V.G., & Steiner, H. (2000). Trauma and dissociation in delinquent adolescents. *Journal of the American Academy of Child and Adolescent Psychiatry, 39,* 353–359.

Church, E. (1994). The role of autonomy in adolescent psychotherapy. *Psychotherapy, 31,* 101–108.

Danforth, J.S. (1999). The outcome of parent training using the behavioral management flow chart with a mother and her twin boys with oppositional defiant disorder and attention-deficit hyperactivity disorder. *Child and Family Behavior Therapy, 21,* 59–80.

Hanna, F.J., Hanna, C.A., & Keys, S.G. (1999). Fifty strategies for counseling defiant, aggressive adolescents: Reaching, accepting, and relating. *Journal of Counseling and Development, 77,* 395–404.

Hanna, F.J., & Hunt, W.P. (1999). Techniques for psychotherapy with defiant, aggressive adolescents. *Psychotherapy, 36,* 56–68.

Henggeler, S.W., Melton, G.B., & Smith, L.A. (1992). Family preservation using multisystemic therapy: An effective alternative to incarcerating serious juvenile offenders. *Journal of Consulting and Clinical Psychology, 60,* 953–961.

Hinshaw, S.P., Lahey, B.B., & Hart, E.L. (1993). Issues of taxonomy and comorbidity in the development of conduct disorder. *Development and Psychopathology, 5,* 31–49.

Kazdin, A.E. (1996). Problem solving and parent management in treating aggressive and antisocial behavior. In E.D. Hibbs & P.S. Jensen (Eds.), *Psychosocial treatments for child and adolescent disorders* (pp. 377–408). Washington, DC: American Psychological Association.

Kazdin, A.E. (1998). Psychosocial treatments for conduct disorder in children. In P.E. Nathan & J.M. Gorman (Eds.), *A guide to treatments that work* (pp. 65–89). New York: Oxford University Press.

Kazdin, A.E., & Wassell, G. (2000). Therapeutic changes in children, parents, and families resulting from treatment of children with conduct problems. *Journal of the American Academy of Child and Adolescent Psychiatry, 39,* 414–420.

Knox, M., King, C., Hanna, G.L., Logan, D., & Ghaziuddin, N. (2000). Aggressive behavior in clinically depressed adolescents. *Journal of the American Academy of Child and Adolescent Psychiatry, 39,* 611–618.

Lankton, C.H., & Lankton, S.R. (1989). *Tales of enchantment: Goal-oriented metaphors for adults and children in therapy.* New York: Brunner/Mazel.

Matthys, W., Cuperus, J.M., & Van Engeland, H. (1999). Deficient social problem-solving in boys with ODD/CD, with ADHD, and with both disorders. *Journal of the American Academy of Child and Adolescent Psychiatry, 39,* 311–321.

Meeks, J.E. (1980). *The fragile alliance* (2nd ed.). New York: Krieger.

Morris, S.B., Alexander, J.F., & Waldron, H. (1988). Functional family therapy. In I.R.H. Falloon (Ed.), *Handbook of behavioral family therapy* (pp. 107–127). New York: Guilford Press.

Murphy, J.J. (1997). *Solution-focused counseling in middle and high schools.* Alexandria, VA: American Counseling Association.

Offord, D.R., Boyle, M.H., & Racine, Y.A. (1991). The epidemiology of anti-social behavior. In D.J. Pepler & K.H. Rubin (Eds.), *The development and treatment of childhood aggression* (pp. 31–54). Hillsdale, NJ: Erlbaum.

Patterson, G.R. (1982). *Coercive family process.* Eugene, OR: Castalia.

Reid, J.B. (1993). Prevention of conduct disorder before and after school entry: Relating interventions to developmental findings. *Development and Psychopathology, 5,* 242–262.

Rogers, C.R. (1957). The necessary and sufficient conditions of therapeutic personality change. *Journal of Consulting Psychology, 21,* 95–103.

Selekman, M.D. (1993). *Pathways to change: Brief therapy solutions with difficult adolescents.* New York: Guilford Press.

Sommers-Flanagan, J., & Sommers-Flanagan, R. (1995). Psychotherapeutic techniques with treatment-resistant adolescents. *Psychotherapy, 32,* 131–140.

Sommers-Flanagan, J., & Sommers-Flanagan, R. (1996a). The efficacy of antidepressant medications with depressed youth: What psychologists should know. *Professional Psychology, 31,* 145–153.

Sommers-Flanagan, J., & Sommers-Flanagan, R. (1996b). The Wizard of Oz metaphor in hypnosis with treatment-resistant children. *American Journal of Clinical Hypnosis, 39,* 105–114.

Sommers-Flanagan, J., & Sommers-Flanagan, R. (1997). *Tough kids, cool counseling: User-friendly approaches to working with challenging youth.* Alexandria, VA: American Counseling Association.

Sommers-Flanagan, J., & Sommers-Flanagan, R. (1998). Assessment and diagnosis of conduct disorder. *Journal of Counseling and Development, 76,* 189–197.

Spivack, G., & Shure, M.B. (1982). The cognition of social adjustment: Interpersonal cognitive problem solving thinking. In B.B. Lahey & A.E. Kazdin (Eds.), *Advances in clinical child psychology* (Vol. 5, pp. 323–372). New York: Plenum Press.

Szapocznik, J., Kurtines, W., Santiseteban, D.A., & Rio, A.T. (1990). Interplay of advances between theory, research and application in treatment interventions aimed at behavior problem children and adolescents. *Journal of Consulting and Clinical Psychology, 58,* 696–703.

Trepper, T. (1991). Senior editor's comments. In M. Worden, *Adolescents and their families: An introduction to assessment and intervention* (pp. ix-x). New York: Haworth.

Webster-Stratton, C.H. (1996). Early intervention with videotape modeling: Programs with oppositional defiant disorder or conduct disorder. In E.D. Hibbs & P.S. Jensen (Eds.), *Psychosocial treatments for child and adolescent disorders* (pp. 435–474). Washington, DC: American Psychological Association.

Recommended Resources

In addition to the books and articles cited in this chapter and listed in the reference section, counselors may find the following resources helpful.

Books

Hibbs, E.D., & Jensen, P.S. (1996). *Psychosocial treatments for child and adolescent disorders.* Washington, DC: American Psychological Association. This edited volume brings research and application together, considering both theory and empirical data supporting specific treatments for common childhood disorders.

Jongsma, A.E., Peterson, L.M., & McInnis, W.P. (1996). *The child and adolescent psychotherapy treatment planner.* New York: Wiley. This treatment planning guide includes comprehensive coverage of most childhood disorders and presenting problems and includes treatment goals and objectives as well as specific therapeutic interventions for each disorder.

Kelly, F. (1997). *The clinical interview of the adolescent: From assessment and formulation to treatment planning.* Springfield, IL: Thomas. The process and procedures for interviewing difficult adolescents is described in this short book (216 pp.).

Quay, H.C., & Hogan, A.E. (Eds.). (1999). *Handbook of disruptive behavior disorders.* New York: Plenum Press. This handbook provides descriptions of a wide range of treatments for children who exhibit disruptive behaviors.

Sommers-Flanagan, J., & Sommers-Flanagan, R. (1997). *Tough kids, cool counseling: User-friendly approaches with challenging youth.* Alexandria, VA: American Counseling Association. This book has a distinctly applied focus. Suggested techniques and strategies are designed to establish and deepen the therapy relationship with young people who may not be interested in counseling.

Web Sites

This site includes information from Peter Breggin, M.D., about the International Center for the Study of Psychiatry and Psychology. Dr. Breggin is strongly against medication treatment of childhood and adult behavior disorders. www.breggin.com

Wilderness-oriented treatment services for children and adolescents are listed on this site. www.innerharbour.org

Family links, teacher links, and counselor links are featured on this site. www.counselingforchildren.com

This site features information on counseling children with conduct disorder. www.counseling.org/ctonline/archives /conduct

30 EFFECTIVE USE OF *DSM-IV* WITH CHILDREN

Alvin E. House

The ability to accurately and efficiently make a diagnostic classification for children showing emotional and behavioral disorders is rapidly becoming an essential skill for mental health practitioners. Psychiatric classification is the gateway to qualification for third-party reimbursement, federal entitlement programs, and resource management within many service agencies. Mental health counselors must be able to express their understanding of cases and tie their intervention plans to the formal codification of problems found in *Diagnostic and Statistical Manual of Mental Disorders (DSM), International Classification of Diseases (ICD),* Individuals with Disabilities Education Act (IDEA), and related systems.

MAJOR CONSTRUCTS

Mental health diagnosis is the gathering of the data that allow the correct assignment of classification within a system of categories. All presently used clinical systems are categorical. Some subcategories, those of mental retardation for instance, are based on dimensional constructs. The relationships among categories within the *DSM-IV* of the American Psychiatric Association (APA, 1994a) is complex. For effective use of *DSM-IV*, it is essential to understand several key ideas: sign, symptom, syndrome, mental disorder, and relationships: clusters of mental disorders. The client's or an informant's reports of problems are identified as *symptoms*. Symptoms are contrasted with

data such as the clinician's observations or IQ testing results, which are viewed as more objective and referred to as *signs*. Signs and symptoms form the bases of classification based on *syndromes:* covarying groups of signs and symptoms that fit identified patterns. When a syndrome exists and meets other criteria, duration requirements, and clinical significance, a *mental disorder* can be identified.

DSM-IV offers the definition of mental disorder used therein (APA, pp. xxi–xxii). The operative criteria are the presence of either significant distress in the client, significant functional impairment in the client, or a number of special circumstances, for instance, potential loss of liberty. The special circumstances can be seen as particularly salient instances of functional impairment. One fundamental task for evaluators is to determine to their own satisfaction if the child manifests a mental disorder as this concept is used in *DSM-IV*. If the child does not, there are a number of categories of behavior and relationship problems available to classify the difficulty accurately (commonly known as V Codes, although they no longer all begin with the letter V). If the circumstances do qualify as a mental disorder, then the examiner's role is to determine which diagnoses most effectively capture the essential elements of the child's problems.

Another classification system the reader should be aware of describes the categories of eligibility for special education services contained in the IDEA legislation (PL 101–476, 1991) and its subsequent revisions. It is important to recognize that the IDEA categories are not systematically derived from, nor related to, *DSM,* even when the same general labels (e.g., mental retardation) are used. Many children with *DSM-IV* mental disorders would probably qualify for services under IDEA, but this is not automatic and would often need to be justified by the functional significance of the problems.

DSM-IV AND *ICD-9-CM*

Understanding *DSM-IV*

DSM-IV lays out a complex system of many categorical diagnoses, grouped thematically, with certain prescribed relationships among categories. The most essential understanding of *DSM-IV* for accurate diagnosis of childhood disorders is to realize that there is no "child section" of *DSM-IV.* The decision to group several disorders under the rubric Disorders Usually First Diagnosed in Infancy, Childhood, or Adolescence and the placement of this group at the beginning of the manual has often created the misperception that these are the child disorders and the rest of the manual are the adult disorders. Such a view is incorrect. The diagnoses contained in the first chapter of diagnoses can be used for clients of any age. The present attention in both the professional and popular press on adult Attention-Deficit/ Hyperactivity Disorder (ADHD) illustrates this. ADHD is often a problem that continues into adulthood. Autism, learning problems, and mental retardation are also usually lifelong difficulties. Also, many of the diagnoses in this first chapter do not have to begin in childhood; this is simply the typical age of onset. An initial diagnosis of eating problems in young adults, for instance, is well recognized. The diagnosis of Conduct Disorder may be very appropriate to the adult who shows a pattern of violating major societal rules but does not meet the criteria for Antisocial Personality Disorder.

Even more important, the problems afflicting children are by no means constrained to those appearing in the chapter on Disorders Usually First Evident in Infancy, Childhood, or Adolescence. The authors of *DSM-IV* and the two preceding editions recognized that depression in childhood is essentially the same phenomenon as depression in adults; schizophrenia in children is the same basic phenomenon as schizophrenia with onset in early adulthood; anxiety disorders manifested in children show the same core difficulties as anxiety disorders in adults. Depending on the nature of the practice or professional setting, a counselor may see almost as many children with primary difficulties from outside the first chapter of diagnoses in *DSM-IV* as they see of youths whose main problems are found described within that chapter. It is absolutely essential for the effective diagnosis of childhood problems to have a good general knowledge of the layout and workings of the entire *DSM-IV* document.

A second important feature of *DSM-IV* is that multiple diagnoses are allowed and, in some ways, even encouraged to give the most comprehensive picture of the child's situation. This tolerance of multiple diagnoses is not meant to imply the view that separate diagnoses are always independent conditions (see First, Frances, & Pincus, 1995). Often, especially with children, several diagnoses may be viewed as different facets of a common, underlying problem. The different diagnoses are a function of how information has been divided up by *DSM,* not necessarily an argument about how reality is divided up. *DSM* tries to capture, as accurately and objectively as possible, as many of the important clinical details of a case as possible. The current working practice for doing this is to allow multiple diagnoses.

A third defining aspect of the *DSM-IV* concerns the thematic groupings of most of the mental disorders. At the beginning of many thematic chapters, and of many individual diagnoses, appears the phrase: "The essential features of . . ." The importance of this phrase may be missed by the inexperienced user of *DSM-IV.* The information following this expression outlines the general area of difficulty being identified. Specific diagnostic criteria come into play only after a determination is made about the general sort of problem under consideration. Furthermore, the use of the Not Otherwise Specified (NOS) diagnoses, which are available for almost all thematic areas and some more specific diagnostic groupings, is not intended to be a diagnostic blank check. The use of an NOS diagnosis is legitimate if the examiner has determined that "the essential features" are present even though none of the specific diagnostic syndromes can be identified. The need to have access to the essential features of various groups of diagnoses is also why it is necessary to have access to the full text of *DSM-IV* and not only to one of the quick reference volumes (APA, 1994b).

Obtaining Good Data

The first step in understanding a child's problems within the framework of *DSM-IV* is to consider what brings the child to your attention. What are the presenting concerns or complaints that have led to the evaluation? This issue has a complexity with youngsters greater than that seen with adults, the majority of whom are self-referred. The majority of children come to your attention because of adult concerns regarding their behavior (House, 1999). This raises a number of potential questions the examiner must resolve: Is there agreement among the major parties that a problem exists? Is there agreement as to what the problem is? Potential bias on the part of informants can be a major problem in using *DSM-IV* with children. This topic is too broad to consider here beyond the observation that concurrent information from multiple informants tends to strengthen our confidence about outside reports (Mitsis, McKay, Schulz, Newcorn, & Halperin, 2000).

The working perspective of *DSM-IV* is that of the clinician. It is his or her point of view that provides the basis of diagnosis and classification. *DSM-IV* explicitly uses a medical model; it is a system written primarily by physicians for the use of physicians. It is often difficult for professionals from other training disciplines to become comfortable with their judgments being given so much emphasis in a

decision-making process. Accurate use of *DSM-IV* requires a great deal of intellectual honesty. It is your decisions that drive the system, but these judgments are not to be made capriciously or based on any consideration other than the best data available.

The fundamental question for using *DSM-IV* is always: Is there evidence of a mental disorder? If there is evidence of a mental disorder, a variety of heuristic questions can guide the clinician to considering the most likely *DSM-IV* diagnoses and deciding among these. If there is not a mental disorder, the problems that bring the child to attention will be cast in terms of the available V Codes of *DSM-IV* or *ICD-9-CM*. The determination of the presence of a mental disorder is based on evidence of distress or disability affecting the client (APA, 1994a, p. xxi). One of the changes in the fourth edition of *DSM* was to emphasize these foundational criteria by including an explicit requirement to consider the *clinical significance* of any difficulties being evaluated in the diagnostic requirements for most of the clinical disorders. The intent was to establish a sufficiently high threshold for diagnosis so that problematic symptoms that did not reach the level of pathology were not mislabeled as a mental disorder.

In reviewing the case data for initial diagnostic classification, it can be helpful to make use of two opposite heuristic guidelines. First, it is always useful to consider high base rate possibilities. In infants and young children, many examiners find mental retardation, attachment disorders, and specific developmental disorders among the more frequent presenting concerns of caretakers. In children, we see disruptive behavior disorders, learning problems, anxiety disorders, and depression as frequent difficulties. Adolescence often witnesses the emergence of bipolar disorders, substance abuse, panic disorders, and psychotic disorders. With clients at all ages, the clinician should be alert to the possibility of stress and environmental events that may occasion Adjustment Disorder, Acute Stress Disorder, or Posttraumatic Stress Disorder (PTSD). The diagnostician should also be aware of the association reported between adversity during childhood and the emergence of specific diagnostic patterns. For example, mood disorders appear to be common in a population of youth who show delinquent behavior (Pliszka, Sherman, Barrow, & Irick, 2000). The examiner must also remain cognizant of the limitations of associative data. Childhood abuse, for instance, is often an etiological factor in PTSD but is neither necessary nor sufficient for this syndrome to develop (Marshall et al., 2000; Widom, 1999). At all ages, the evaluator should remain open to considering the many relationship and human problems that are not mental disorders but do shape the unique clinical picture, and make appropriate use of the V Codes to communicate these features of the case.

The second heuristic calls our attention to the opposite phenomenon: the possibility of low base rate problems. Autism is rare but should be considered in cases of severe behavior deficit. Tourette's syndrome is not common but should be considered when there is odd behavior or vocalizations, especially in the context of obsessive-compulsive behavior or ADHD. Substance abuse is less frequent in children than adolescents, but does occur in some children and should probably always be in the differential diagnosis. Before concluding the diagnostic decision-making process, it is valuable to consider what elements of the case have not been accounted for and consider whether other diagnoses are warranted. The use of a broad-spectrum problem behavior checklist can be very helpful in eliciting information from caretakers about low-frequency possibilities in an efficient manner (Achenbach, 1991). Adolescents can respond to self-report questionnaires such as the Problem Behavior Checklist, Adolescent Version (Silverton, 1991). Any questions brought up by such screening techniques can be followed up by systematic interview. The systematic consideration of both high and low base rate syndromes associated with the presenting issues will minimize errors. The differential diagnostic decision trees available for *DSM-IV* (First et al., 1995) can also be useful in reviewing potential conceptualizations for a client's presenting problems.

POTENTIAL PROBLEM AREAS

High Comorbidity

A common observation regarding the use of *DSM-IV* with children is the very high frequency of multiple diagnoses. Comorbidity of mental health problems is the typical situation found with youth. Most children who meet criteria for one *DSM-IV* diagnosis will also meet criteria for one or more others. The clinician needs to remain sensitive to this common comorbidity and actively consider probable associated conditions to rule these in or out. Especially frequent comorbidities are between ADHD and Oppositional Defiant Disorder (ODD), between ADHD and Learning Disorders, between ADHD and Conduct Disorders, between the disruptive behavior disorders and mood disorders, within anxiety disorders, between mood and anxiety disorders, and between Mental Retardation and ADHD. *DSM-IV* limits some comorbidities by hierarchical or exclusion rules (APA, 1994a, p. 6). For instance, a diagnosis of Schizophrenia precludes a concurrent diagnosis of ADHD when the problems of impulsivity and inattention occur only during periods of active psychosis. In the same manner, a diagnosis of Conduct Disorder precludes a concurrent diagnosis of Oppositional Defiant Disorder.

ADHD and Mood Disorders. The issue of comorbidity between disruptive behavior disorders and mood disorders in children is an active area of investigation and controversy. A specific aspect of this ongoing discussion is the reported association between diagnoses of ADHD in children who are later diagnosed with Bipolar Disorder. This is a complex and evolving topic, and there is not a consensus regarding how this relationship should best be conceptualized. The reader is encouraged to work at remaining current with the evolving literature. Some authors have offered heuristic guidelines for differential diagnosis (Levin, 2000), and some empirical literature has begun to appear (Sachs, Baldassano, Truman, & Guille, 2000). For the present, a very careful differential diagnosis between Bipolar

Disorder and ADHD should be made in any child or adolescent with atypical features for ADHD or poor response to conventional treatments for ADHD.

Mental Retardation and Other Mental Disorders

It appears that many treatable disorders continue to go unrecognized in children and adolescents who are mentally retarded because these problems are perceived by caretakers and professionals as a "part of the retardation." Mental retardation describes delays in cognitive and behavioral development; it does not explain the presence of behavior problems, emotional problems, abnormal (as opposed to delayed) patterns of habit development, or psychotic symptoms. Because of the natural human tendency to stop asking questions as soon as we have "an answer," careful differential diagnostic consideration of other problems is advised for all youth with known mental retardation.

Common Errors in the Diagnosis of Youth

Among the most frequent diagnostic errors using *DSM-IV* that I have seen are the following.

Placing Diagnoses of Mental Retardation on Axis I. Diagnoses of Mental Retardation, Borderline Intellectual Functioning (this is not a mental disorder but is one of the other conditions that may be a focus of clinical attention), and Personality Disorders and notations of personality traits are all made on Axis II. These are the only diagnostic entries included on Axis II.

Making a Diagnosis of "Impulse Control Disorder." This is not a diagnosis but the title of a group of diagnoses. Impulsivity is not a diagnosis in *DSM-IV*; it is a symptom used in identifying several diagnoses.

Diagnosing Both Conduct Disorder and ODD. As noted above, this combination is excluded by rule.

Missing Comorbid Diagnoses in Children with Mental Reiteration. As previously discussed,

evaluators of children with a known high-frequency disorder should very carefully consider whether additional problems are being overlooked because we "already know what is wrong with the child."

Missing Comorbid Diagnoses in Children with ADHD. There are very high comorbidities between several of the high base rate disorders of youth. The syndromes of ADHD, Conduct Disorder, Learning Disability, and (usually beginning in adolescence) substance abuse are often associated; similarly, Tourette's Disorder may be a low base rate disorder differentially associated with ADHD. The presence of the dramatic and attention-demanding externalizing symptoms of ADHD may distract our attention from other problems the young person is showing, much as the obvious cognitive limitations of the child with Mental Retardation forestalls our consideration of what else may be wrong.

Missing Mood Disorder Diagnoses in Children. A rather pronounced shift has occurred in our perception of depression in children. After decades of minimizing the possibility of pathological low mood in children, the recognition has grown that the clinical syndrome of depression can occur at all ages. Early depression appears to have important prognostic significance in individuals with respect to risk for major depressive, manic, and hypomanic episodes latter in life. There is also increasing recognition of the associations between depression and other internalizing problems in children with acting-out behavior. The child counselor should deliberately investigate the possibility of mood problems in most cases, even if this is not a presenting concern of caretakers.

Failure to Use NOS Diagnoses for Children Who Do Not Really Meet Criteria for a Given Diagnosis. The professional making the diagnosis with *DSM-IV* is given a great deal of flexibility and leeway to classify the individual case in the most clinically meaningful manner. This flexibility, however, should not be taken as license to ignore the system we are claiming to use. It is the responsibility of the individual professional to ensure that each given diagnosis represents the best possible use of the *DSM-IV* system to capture and communicate the essential features of the client's situation. An associated difficulty is the failure to indicate some degree of diagnostic uncertainty in cases where this is, in fact, the case. Although not required by *DSM-IV* convention, specifically identifying the diagnostic criteria supporting each given diagnosis can help prevent these problems.

References

Achenbach, T.M. (1991). *Manual for the Child Behavior Checklist/4–18 and 1991 profile*. Burlington: University of Vermont, Department of Psychiatry.

American Psychiatric Association. (1994a). *Diagnostic and statistical manual of mental disorders* (4th ed.). Washington, DC: Author.

American Psychiatric Association. (1994b). *Quick reference to the diagnostic criteria of DSM-IV*. Washington, DC: Author.

Education of the Handicapped Act Amendment of 1990, Pub. L. No. 101–476, 104 Stat. 1103 (1991).

Fauman, M.A. (1994). *Study guide to DSM-IV*. Washington, DC: American Psychiatric Press.

First, M.B., Frances, A., & Pincus, H.A. (1995). *DSM-IV handbook of differential diagnosis*. Washington, DC: American Psychiatric Press.

House, A.E. (1999). *DSM-IV diagnosis in the schools*. New York: Guilford Press.

Kronenberger, W.C., & Meyer, R.G. (1996). *The child clinician's handbook*. Boston: Allyn & Bacon.

Levin, M. (2000). How can we differentiate between ADHD, bipolar disorder in children? *Brown University Child and Adolescent Psychopharmacology Update, 1*, 4–5.

Marshall, R.D., Schneier, F.R., Lin, S-H., Simpson, H.B., Vermes, D., & Liebowitz, M. (2000). Childhood trauma and dissociative symptoms in panic disorder. *American Journal of Psychiatry, 157*, 451–453.

Mitsis, E.M., McKay, K., Schulz, K.P., Newcorn, J.H., & Halperin, J.M. (2000). Parent-teacher concordance for *DSM-IV* attention-deficit/hyperactivity disorder in a clinic-referred sample. *Journal of the Academy of Child and Adolescent Psychiatry, 39*, 308–313.

Pliszka, S.R., Sherman, J.O., Barrow, M.V., & Irick, S. (2000). Affective disorder in juvenile offenders: A preliminary study. *American Journal of Psychiatry, 157*, 130–132.

Rapoport, J.L., & Ismond, D.R. (1996). *DSM-IV training guide for diagnosis of childhood disorders*. New York: Brunner/Mazel.

Sachs, G.S., Baldassano, C.F., Truman, C.J., & Guille, C. (2000). Comorbidity of attention deficit hyperactivity disorder with early- and late-onset bipolar disorder. *American Journal of Psychiatry, 157*, 466–468.

Silverton, L. (1991). *Problem Behavior Inventory, Adolescent Syndrome Screening Form*. Los Angeles, CA: Western Psychological Services.

Spitzer, R.L., Gibbon, M., Skodol, A.F., Williams, J.B.W., & First, M.B. (1994). *DSM-IV case book*. Washington, DC: American Psychiatric Press.

Widom, C.S. (1999). Posttraumatic stress disorder in abused and neglected children grown up. *American Journal of Psychiatry, 156*, 1223–1229.

Resources and Professional Development

For the counselor working with youth, a number of professional resources can be helpful in gaining skill with *DSM-IV*. Several textbooks explicitly deal with the use of *DSM-IV*, including at least two covering its use with children (House, 1999; Rapoport & Ismond, 1996). The *DSM-IV Case Book* includes a number of child and adolescent cases (Sptizer, Gibbon, Skodol, Williams, & First, 1994), and additional case examples and tables of diagnostic precedence can be found in Fauman (1994). Kronenberger and Meyer's (1996) textbook integrates *DSM-IV* with a broad discussion of assessment and treatment of children and adolescents. I have found group consultation and chart reviews to be a good teaching method for self-development. Finally, a commitment to using *DSM-IV* as carefully as possible to characterize the most essential features of each child's personal situation and problems is possibly the most effective foundation on which to build individual competence.

31 ENLISTING APPROPRIATE PARENTAL COOPERATION AND INVOLVEMENT IN CHILDREN'S MENTAL HEALTH TREATMENT

Linda Taylor and Howard S. Adelman

Counselors and therapists working with children and adolescents are faced with important decisions about the extent to which the family should be involved. Some therapists prefer to work with the family unit; some seldom include family members. The reasons vary. For most, however, the decision about family involvement is based on the needs in each case. Thus, as they first encounter a minor referred for treatment, these therapists focus on assessing not only the individual and contextual considerations related to neighborhood, school, and culture, they also assess the need for and the likelihood of parental involvement.

Why involve parents? Therapists who work regularly with children and adolescents quickly encounter the realities of a lack of parental commitment to seeking out, maintaining, and being involved in the treatment for their youngster. For instance, parent follow-through on child referrals for counseling is estimated at less than 50%, and premature termination occurs in 40% to 60% of child cases (Kazdin, 1997). Clearly, parents must feel a sense of commitment or they will not facilitate their child's enrollment and ongoing participation in treatment. Moreover, parental involvement seems essential when they are the cause of or ongoing contributors to a youngster's problems. Even if this is not the case, family members almost always suffer when their child is not doing well and may need some guidance and support. In addition, in more cases than not, the therapist wants the family to facilitate, nurture, and support desired changes in the youngster. Equally important, what parents learn in the process may generalize to other venues, such as enhancing home involvement in school and parent advocacy.

Many factors shape parental involvement. One set involves the degree to which treatment is seen as positive and accessible. Obviously, negative perceptions and practical barriers can be counterproductive not only to parental connection, but to the youngster's progress. Some families referred for therapy feel uncomfortable with the concept of mental health/mental illness. They may worry that mental health treatment will stigmatize the child either now or by curbing opportunities in the future (Jensen, McNamara, & Gustafson, 1991). Other salient barriers perceived by parents include practicalities of access, feeling that treatment is demanding or not highly relevant to the child's problem, or feeling negatively about the therapist. Dropping out is a likely response when the family's perceptions are that the process is burdensome, unpleasant, or not worthwhile. Conversely, children seem to do better in therapy when parents perceive few negatives related to the process and potential outcomes (Kazdin & Wassell, 1999).

The above concerns are only a small part of the many socioeconomic, language, and racial or ethnic factors that may affect a family's motivational readiness to enroll and maintain a youngster in treatment and to be active participants in the process. The examples cited underscore the importance of directly attending to parental motivation for involvement in child mental health treatment. Two aspects of such motivational considerations are outlined here: using initial processes of therapy to assess and address parental motivational readiness for involvement and maintaining their motivation and involvement throughout treatment.

ACCOUNTING FOR AND ENHANCING MOTIVATIONAL READINESS

It is helpful to think in terms of a range of motivational differences in family involvement. With respect to their youngster's participation in treatment and their own role in the intervention process, parents range from being highly involved (e.g., motivated and active participants who advocate for their children and seek out resources), to marginally involved (e.g., minimally motivated and cooperative), to reluctant to highly resistant (e.g., not at all motivated, uncooperative, avoidant, reactive). Those in this last group often have been pushed to pursue therapy for their youngsters by the school or the justice system.

At all points along the continuum, working with families to establish appropriate cooperation and involvement in their child's treatment often is a critical process objective. To account for motivational differences, a therapist, starting with the first contact, must assess parents' motivation for having their youngster treated and for their own possible involvement. In doing so, the assessment process itself should be designed to enhance the motivation of family members, or at least to minimize conditions that can reduce their motivation. Based on contemporary theories of intrinsic motivation (Ryan & Deci, 2000), this means using practices that can enhance (or at least reduce threats) to feelings of competence, feelings of self-determination, and feelings of relatedness to others.

Using Consent Agreements to Enhance Motivation

When a therapist first encounters family members, there are multiple opportunities to assess their motivation for therapy and to actively engage them. For instance, there are many steps that can be taken during the informed consent process to engender parent involvement. By using the procedure as an intervention step, the therapist provides a natural opportunity for parents to express their questions, concerns, doubts, and fears. A premise of informed consent is that participation is voluntary and that the family can terminate with no penalty or prejudice. If they agree to proceed, the family has taken a first and important step in making a commitment to cooperate with treatment.

In this context, the therapist works from the initial interactions to minimize any sense of coercion and enhance feelings of control and competence by involving parents in decisions. One of the first decisions is whether to have initial meeting(s) with or without the youngster present. The parents' decision provides important assessment data. For example, many who choose to meet without the youngster indicate it is because they don't want to embarrass their child; others feel they can't say things in front of the youngster; still others know that what they have to say will lead to an argument that they want to avoid. At this stage, it is especially important to counter feelings of coercion and intimidation among those who have been pushed to enter therapy. For such cases, when discussing the events or behaviors that led to the referral, it is well to structure the interaction as one of exploring all *their* options for improving the situation, including any changes at school and home they think are worth pursuing. Exploring goals and how to work together on these reassures some families as to the worthwhile nature of the endeavor. Suggesting a short time frame (e.g., three sessions, with a chance to review the progress and concerns after that) provides some families with confidence that the decision to come back is theirs. If there are choices that can be made with respect to a therapist (e.g., age, sex, ethnicity, language), these also should be explored. Families who clearly are not ready or willing to engage in therapy may need the option of holding off for a time so that they can view the need for treatment in a less reactive manner. To this end, the parents must be assured that they will be able to initiate services when they decide help is necessary.

To elicit appropriate involvement, a therapist needs to demonstrate respect for the parents' role and for the efforts they expend related to the youngster's day-to-day experiences. This involves validating those aspects of what they are doing right. Then, the process of opening up discussion about what they might want to change can be initiated as one basis for clarifying why their inclusion in the process is necessary.

Sharing assessment information with them to arrive at an agreed upon definition of the problem(s) and the plan for treatment can be especially helpful. Many times, parents will come in with school reports, testing reports, report cards, and other documents that can, when analyzed and collated, provide a helpful picture of the child's development and a context for the current problem. This establishes for parents a perspective from which to see the need for intervention and for their involvement in the process.

In many settings, the assent of the youngster also must be provided. This is especially important in working with adolescent clients. Modeling for parents how to explain the nature of mental health treatment and eliciting the youngster's response not only can help enhance the youngster's participation, it helps parents further understand the importance of their involvement. Thus, besides protecting client rights, the consent process can reduce feelings of coercion and promote feelings of self-determination, enhance feelings of competence, and foster feelings of positive relatedness between the family and the therapist.

A special problem arises related to children whose parents are divorced or are remarried. Such situations require clarifying the dynamics related to the extended family and the role each member will play in supporting the child's treatment. Setting extended family goals and clarifying respective involvements is essential to increasing the family's communication and problem-solving capabilities in ways that serve the aims of the therapeutic intervention (Lew & Bettner, 1999).

Contracting for Involvement

Many counselors and therapists are fortunate enough to work in agencies or schools that provide service without fees. Whether or not fees are paid by the family, the process of negotiating a "contract" that clarifies treatment arrangements (e.g., costs, expected benefits) can also help clarify mutual expectations about parent involvement. At the outset, the focus with parents who are not highly motivated may just be on agreements about scheduling (e.g., regular appointments, arriving on time) and sharing relevant information. Over time, such initial agreements may be renegotiated to encompass greater degrees of family involvement.

Handling Privacy and Confidentiality Concerns

Families vary widely in how much they want therapists to share information with others. Parents may want their individual discussions with the therapist kept confidential from the youngster and even from each other. There are variations in how much a family wants the school to know. Some parents are uncomfortable with the notion of allowing the youngster and therapist to hold conversations that will not be shared with them. The family's concerns about privacy and confidentiality influence the nature and scope of their involvement.

For many families, initial assurances of privacy and confidentiality are sufficient in enlisting cooperation and participation. For others, discussion of these matters must be done in a way that goes beyond describing the importance and parameters of confidentiality. This is particularly critical in clarifying when confidentiality must be broken. For example, clarifying reporting requirements is unlikely to enhance the involvement of abusive parents.

There is no easy solution to the confidentiality dilemma. One strategy that can pay dividends with respect to parent participation is to reframe the topic in ways that clarify that the intent isn't to play a game of "keeping secrets" from each other or to elicit information to report to the authorities. To the contrary, the intent is to encourage the flow of information that is essential to solving problems, and, when mutual sharing of information is necessary to make things better, the intent is to find ways to facilitate such sharing (Taylor & Adelman, 1998).

Handling Parent Reactions to Initial Contacts and Assessment

In public agencies, enrollment procedures usually require that families complete extensive paperwork. This may include questionnaires asking adolescents and parents to note which of a long list of psychological problems have been experienced. Completing such forms requires literacy skills and candor in self-reporting that may exceed a family's skills or motivational readiness and may reinforce negative feelings about participation. If this appears likely, the therapist must be prepared to make these processes more consumer-friendly, including taking steps to ensure that the level of discourse is a good match for the family's level of literacy, communication skills, and motivation.

Part of the initial assessment usually is a review of the youngster's developmental history. This provides a major opportunity to demonstrate and validate the importance of parent involvement and provides an indication of their willingness and skills for doing so. Because causal attributions for problems often play a major role in shaping behavior, data about such attributions require special attention. If parents blame themselves or each other for the child's problems, the therapist must be ready to explore these perceptions quickly and nonjudgmentally. Extra effort may be required to convince parents that such feelings are natural and that the therapist is not interested in assigning blame but mainly wants to explore causes to find the best way to correct problems.

Carried out effectively, the above practices can help move parents to perceive the therapist as a potential ally rather than an enforcer or an agent of social control. Such a perception allows for a reasonable appreciation of the potential contributions of therapy.

Toward the other end of the continuum, occasionally, families are overly or inappropriately involved in their youngster's therapy. This may not be evident until after the first few encounters. Such parents may be reluctant to allow the youngster to meet alone with the therapist; they may want more frequent appointments than is common practice or may call frequently between appointments; they may self-generate lists or logs of problem behaviors. Such behavior often calls for separate sessions with the parents to clarify what the underlying motivation is and to elicit changes that will facilitate rather than hinder the youngster's progress.

As the above examples suggest, the therapist's concern about parent involvement begins at first contact. Good practice calls for using processes that both assess and enhance motivational factors influencing involvement not only initially, but throughout treatment.

MAINTAINING MOTIVATION AND INVOLVEMENT DURING THE PROCESS

Extrapolating from available research and theory on intrinsic motivation (e.g., Ryan & Deci, 2000), three considerations seem basic for maintaining involvement:

1. Ensuring parents feel a growing sense of relatedness to the therapist.
2. Enhancing parents' valuing of involvement by ensuring that there are a variety of ways they can participate and then facilitating their decision making among desirable options (including ongoing decision making about changing how they are involved).
3. Providing continuing support for learning, growth, and success (including feedback about how their involvement is benefiting the youngster).

These considerations are discussed below with respect to the overlapping topics of therapeutic alliances and assignments, therapy formats, and engaging the family in the evaluation process.

Therapeutic Alliances and Assignments

All therapists create some form of alliance with their child and adolescent clients in order to facilitate change. On the basis of their theoretical models and training experiences, interveners differ in the nature and scope of their alliances with the rest of the family. As already noted, such alliances can determine the course of treatment. Adolescents raise special concerns in this respect. Many teenagers are at a stage of developing separate identities from their families. Therapists are caught in a situation where the youngster may view contacts between the therapist and a parent as undesirable. However, avoiding parents can make them feel excluded and alienated from the process and lead to their abruptly and prematurely withdrawing the youngster from treatment.

Another common problem is that parents may feel threatened by the growing bond between therapist and youngster and by the therapist's interest in eliciting the youngster's perspective on the causes of and potential solutions for the referral problem. The bonding can produce competitive feelings. Eliciting a youngster's perceptions of cause may be seen as buying into ill-informed and self-serving information, especially if the youngster is likely to place blame on the parents. Similar feelings can arise in working with parents who are in conflict with each other.

Interveners must consistently (1) help all concerned parties appreciate the appropriateness and value of various alliances, (2) listen to all perspectives, and (3) validate the feelings that accompany such perceptions. The danger in not doing so is to be seen by parents as a biased, overly permissive, and untrustworthy person. In contrast, when parents understand the process and feel heard and validated, the therapist is more likely to be perceived as an ally. And, should the youngster want to discontinue treatment, the alliance with the parents can prevent premature termination.

There are, of course, instances when parents want the therapist to take over and are satisfied not to form a close alliance. In these instances, the need is to move the youngster and parents to a middle ground as soon as feasible. This requires a constant focus on clarifying and demonstrating to all parties that specific forms of contact are beneficial (e.g., with respect to

making progress and for purposes of anticipating and preventing problems).

The growing use of manualized treatments and use of homework or exercises that the family is called on to facilitate provides many opportunities to involve parents and develop strong, positive alliances. Other occasions arise around the family's role in facilitating, supporting, and nurturing the youngster's progress. In this respect, parents have a special role to play as their child's primary advocate. This role offers many possibilities for the therapist not only to enhance parent involvement, but to increase their positive involvement in other aspects of the youngster's life—especially those venues where problems are being experienced. One example is schooling. Child therapists often find that changes at school are needed to support the treatment process. Whereas direct contacts between therapist and teachers often are helpful, there are benefits to encouraging and preparing the family to become positive advocates. This, of course, is one of the most natural forms of parent involvement. In particular, parents can be taught about the types of special assistance a school might provide (counseling groups, Section 504 accommodations, special education, etc.). Then, the therapist can prepare them with respect to how to approach the school effectively. This includes teaching parents the difference between positive advocacy and the type of adversarial role that often results in youngsters being caught in the middle. Properly done, the results lead to interactions among parents, school staff, and students that are mutually beneficial, encourage special feelings of connectedness, and support treatment processes and results (Friesen & Stephens, 1998).

Therapy Formats

There are a variety of ways in which parents can participate, some of which have been mentioned already. A few other examples will suffice as illustrations.

Youngsters may be seen in groups or individually or with family members included as "collaborative" partners. In many instances, family members will become primary clients with a focus on making family changes (e.g., parents changing their own behaviors to respond differently to their children). This is especially necessary in cases where the family has experienced a shared trauma (e.g., a child has been abused or has experienced a natural disaster or the sudden and violent death of a family member). Shifting from focusing primarily on the child to the whole family can be difficult and calls for recontracting so that the parents understand what will be asked of them and become active participants in the decision making.

Some therapists and agencies find that a family/parent support group provides a useful way to enlist appropriate involvement. Such a format allows for exchanges about common problems and solutions. Not only can participants learn from others, they may experience a growing sense of personal validation, as well as enhance their commitment to treatment processes. These groups may be most helpful when the nature of the youngsters' problems are similar (e.g., crisis situations, specific problem focus, long-standing problems) and when they are composed of parents with the same background.

Homework assignments provide another form of involvement. Such activity is implemented between therapy sessions with reports back to the therapist. For example, parents can assist their child in pursuing problem-solving strategies, can make changes in how they interact with the youngster, and can monitor reduction of symptoms and problems.

Engaging the Family in the Evaluation Process

Evaluation of progress is an additional opportunity to involve parents and provides an essential ongoing perspective on therapeutic processes and outcomes. Research supports the positive impact of including a family-initiated evaluation model on treatment outcome (Stoep, Williams, Jones, Green, & Trupin, 1999). One problem, of course, is that parent and youngster perspectives frequently differ. Moreover, parents often are not inclined to account for the perspectives of the child or adolescent.

Through interactions designed to translate therapist, parent, and youngster perspectives into a shared set of outcome indicators, strong alliances can be created. Again, this involves a focus on clarifying how to ensure that all perspectives are given a serious hearing. It also requires arriving at a working perspective that can be used to generate a feasible solution to a referral problem (Adelman & Taylor, 1994).

CONCLUDING COMMENTS

Therapists who want to enlist parent involvement must be clear about the value of, forms of, and barriers to such involvement. From initial contact, they must include a focus on the family's motivation and incorporate processes that can at least minimize a lowering of motivational readiness and, when necessary, can enhance such motivation. Clearly, this is an area where the full implications for research, theory, practice, and professional training are just beginning to be appreciated.

References

Adelman, H.S., & Taylor, L. (1994). *On understanding intervention in psychology and education.* Westport, CT: Praeger.

Friesen, B.J., & Stephens, B. (1998). Expanding family roles in the system of care: Research and practice. In M.H. Epstein & K. Kutash (Eds.), *Outcomes for children and youth with emotional and behavioral disorders and their families: Programs and evaluation best practices* (pp. 231–259). Austin, TX: ProEd.

Jensen, J.A., McNamara, J.R., & Gustafson, K.E. (1991). Parents' and clinicians' attitudes toward the risks and benefits of child psychotherapy: A study of informed-consent content. *Professional Psychology: Research and Practice, 22,* 161–170.

Kazdin, A.E. (1997). A model for developing effective treatments: Progression and interplay of theory, research, and practice. *Journal of Clinical Child Psychology, 26,* 114–129.

Kazdin, A.E., & Wassell, G. (1999). Barriers to treatment participation and therapeutic change among children referred for conduct disorder. *Journal of Clinical Child Psychology,* *28,* 160–172.

Lew, A., & Bettner, B.L. (1999). Establishing a family goal. *Journal of Individual Psychology, 55,* 105–108.

Ryan, R.M., & Deci, E.L. (2000). Self-determination theory and the facilitation of intrinsic motivation, social development, and well-being. *American Psychologist, 55,* 68–78.

Stoep, A.V., Williams, M., Jones, R., Green, L., & Trupin, E. (1999). Families as full research partners: What's in it for us? *Journal of Behavioral Health Services and Research, 26,* 329–344.

Taylor, L., & Adelman, H.S. (1998). Confidentiality: Competing principles, inevitable dilemmas. *Journal of Educational and Psychological Consultation, 9,* 267–275.

32 UNDERSTANDING AND PROMOTING RESILIENCE WITH OUR CLIENTS

Carl F. Rak

In her most recent book, *Half Empty, Half Full,* Vaughan (2000) discussed the dimensions of assisting clients to develop proactive approaches to their problems and issues. She highlighted that optimism flows from our ability to interpret and remember our experiences in a positive light. Counselors constantly experience the conundrum between pathogenesis and salutogenesis in their work: Do I help the client overcome his or her pathological symptoms and problems, or do I focus on the client's strengths and resiliency? This is not an easily resolved dilemma, and many counselors are limited by misunderstandings surrounding the constructs of salutogenesis and resilience. Salutogenesis represents a focus on the origins of health (Hauser, Vieyra, Jacobson, & Wertreib, 1985), and resilience (Rak & Patterson, 1996) is the capacity of those who are exposed to identifiable risk factors to overcome those risks and avoid negative outcomes. Utilizing resilience in counseling and psy-

chotherapy requires a rich and realistic understanding of the construct. Resilience also has been discussed as the protective or buffering factors that steel an individual in the wake of many of life's stressors.

REVIEW OF THE LITERATURE

Early work in resilience focused on the emergence of buffering and protective factors in adolescents and young adults that assisted them in warding off the overwhelming negative impact of growing up faced with multiple severe risk factors (Garmezy, 1991; Garmezy, Masten, & Tellegen, 1984; Rutter, 1979, 1985; Werner & Smith, 1982, 1992). Each of these longitudinal studies provided evidence that a great majority of youth overcame their crises and lived relatively content and adjusted lives even when exposed to serious risk and traumatic factors. How does this occur, and how does one develop a resilient stance in life? These researchers identified several domains that triggered resilient responses. These include temperament, place in the family, positive school climate, significant positive role models outside the home, positive outlook, being female, adaptable, and tolerant, planning skills, and a warm, close, personal relationship with an adult.

Benson (1997) also identified 40 developmental assets that he divided into two halves: The *external* involves receiving support from adults and environment, feeling a sense of empowerment, knowing boundaries and expectations, finding a constructive use of time; the *internal* involves a personal educational commitment, positive values, social competencies, and a positive identity. Benard (1997) indicated that when tracking youth into adulthood, almost 70% of high-risk children grow up to be not only successful, but also confident, competent, and caring. This body of literature has greatly influenced the shift in much of the mental health literature from examining risk factors to exploring and nurturing the personal strengths of the individual in the midst of crisis.

Lowenthal (1998) further complicated and enriched our understanding of the development of resiliency in children by examining the impact of maltreatment (abuse and neglect) on neurological development and carefully discussing how abuse and neglect can trigger provocative behaviors like mutilation and suicide to initiate numbing responses to lessen fear and anxiety. She postulated that initiating programs aimed to develop and enhance protective factors (resilient) in these children to augment their capacity to ameliorate early negative life consequences remains exceedingly complex and difficult.

Hauser (1999) studied retrospectively 35 adolescent and adult-era interviews to gain a better understanding of resilient individuals' constructions of themselves and their relationships during a time of major disruption. Through a content analysis of the interviews, Hauser and his team found that in the narratives of the participants, there are several reflections when the interviewees speak of one or both of their parents with more compassion

and understanding. Also, the study found that the participants discussed their own parenting episodes with a great deal of complexity that reflected ideas about how they were parented in times of difficulty.

As a result of this research, counselors were encouraged to listen to the stories of their clients to discover the subtle and rich meanings of the proactive influences in their lives and how these forces operated both in the period of turbulence and in the present. It is critical in working with clients that counselors hear not only the narratives of misery, but also the stories of triumph and resilience. In blending both, a counselor develops a fuller understanding of the complex dynamics of clients' lives and how they have interacted over the life span. The critical question remains: How do counselors utilize and promote resilience in their work?

RESILIENCY QUESTIONNAIRE

Rak and Patterson (1996) developed a Resiliency Questionnaire that became a preliminary guide for counselors to frame questions or inquiries in the context of the counseling session aimed at understanding aspects of resilient behavior in a client (see Figure 32.1). The questions were developed from the protective factors identified by Bolig and Weddle (1988), Garmezy et al. (1984), Rutter (1979), Werner (1984), and Werner and Smith (1992). The 25-item Resiliency Questionnaire, intended for latency children and adolescents, covers the personal characteristics and temperament of the individual, family conditions, social-environmental supports, and self-concept aspects of resilience. Each of the dimensions from the research profile that led to the questionnaire will be discussed in detail (Rak & Patterson, 1996).

Personal Factors

Prior research on resiliency concluded that children who demonstrated the following were more likely to develop resilient patterns of behavior: (1) an active, evocative approach toward problem solving, enabling them to negotiate an array of emotionally hazardous experiences;

1. What is your position in the family? Oldest? Youngest? Middle? Oldest girl? Oldest boy?

2. Do you have any memories or recollections about what your mother or father said about you as a young baby? Or anyone else?

3. Did anyone ever tell you about how well you ate and slept as a baby?

4. Do members of your family and friends usually seem happy to see you and to spend time with you?

5. Do you feel that you are a helpful person to others? Does anyone in your family expect you to be helpful?

6. Do you consider yourself a happy and hopeful (optimistic) person even when life becomes difficult?

7. Tell me about some times when you overcame problems or stresses in your life. How do you feel about them now?

8. Do you think of yourself as awake and alert most of the time? Do others see you that way also?

9. Do you like to try new life experiences?

10. Tell me about some plans and goals you have for yourself over the next year. Three years. Five years.

11. When you are in a stressful, pressure-filled situation, do you feel confident that you'll work it out or do you feel depressed and hopeless?

12. What was the age of your mother when you were born? Your father?

13. How many children are in your family? How many years are there between children in your family?

14. What do you remember, if anything, about how you were cared for when you were little by Mom and others?

15. When you were growing up, were there rules and expectations in your home? What were some?

16. Did any of your brothers or sisters help raise you? What do you remember about this?

17. When you felt upset or in trouble, to whom in your family did you turn for help? Whom outside your family?

18. From whom did you learn about the values and beliefs of your family?

19. Do you feel it is your responsibility to help others? Help your community?

20. Do you feel that you understand yourself?

21. Do you like yourself? Today? Yesterday? Last year?

22. What skills do you rely on to cope when you are under stress?

23. Tell me about a time when you were helpful to others.

24. Do you see yourself as a confident person? Even when stressed?

25. What are your feelings about this interview with me?

FIGURE 32.1   A Resiliency Questionnaire. *Source:* Rak & Patterson (1996). Reprinted from *Journal of Counseling and Development*, vol. 74, pp. 368–373. © ACA. Reprinted with permission. No further reproduction authorized without permission of the American Counseling Association.

(2) an ability from infancy on to gain others' positive attention; (3) an optimistic view of their experience in the midst of suffering; (4) an ability to maintain a positive vision of a meaningful life; (5) an ability to be alert and autonomous; (6) a tendency to seek novel experiences; and (7) a proactive perspective. Werner (1986) indicated that a higher portion of resilient children were firstborn, recovered more quickly from childhood illnesses than their peers, and were remembered by their mothers as having been active and good-natured infants. Identifying some or many of these traits in a client will aid the counselor to assess his or her protective capacity in the wake of life's traumas.

Family Factors

In addition to the personality factors, researchers have discovered an array of family factors that contribute to a buffering effect on children in the wake of stressors. The more salient factors are (1) the age of the opposite-sex parent (younger mothers for resilient male participants, older fathers for resilient female participants); (2) four or fewer children in a family spaced more than two years apart; (3) focused nurturing during the first year of life and little prolonged separation from the primary caretaker; (4) an array of alternative caretakers (grandparents, siblings, neighbors) who stepped in when parents were not consistently present; (5) the existence of a multiage network of kin who showed similar values and beliefs and to whom the at-risk youth turned for counsel and support; (6) the availability of sibling caretakers in childhood or another young person to serve as confidant; and (7) structure and rules in the household during adolescence despite poverty and stress (Rak & Patterson, 1996, p. 369). Understanding the existence of the influence of these factors in clients will guide the counselor to a richer understanding of the client's potential for resilience.

Supportive Other Adults

Bolig and Weddle (1988), Beardslee and Podorefsky (1988), and Dugan and Coles (1989) examined role models outside the family circle and their influence as potential buffers for vulnerable children. These supportive adults include teachers, school counselors and administrators, supervisors of afterschool programs, coaches, mental health workers, staff in community centers, clergy, and good neighbors. Resilient children often report a number of mentors outside the family throughout their development. The narratives of children and adolescents are replete with true stories honoring the influence of significant nonfamily adults in their lives. It is critical for counselors to understand that the influence of these significant role models often does not spread to all aspects of a child or adolescent's personality, but is more sharply defined to a set of behaviors or responses in a stressful situation. As we study resiliency, we are able to be more specific and detailed in our understanding of the myriad impacts on young clients. For example, a big brother will assist an at-risk adolescent male with the support, guidance, and tutoring to overcome failing grades and to remain in school; however, this does not guarantee that the adolescent will avoid future danger and trouble with the law.

Self-Concept Aspects

Although our grasp of the construct of self-concept is illusive, researchers have found that the capacity to understand self and self-boundaries in relation to long-term family stressors like psychological illness, to enhance positive self-esteem as a result of adaptive life competencies, and to steel oneself in the wake of stress all act as protective factors. From the research of Beardslee and Podorefsky (1988), who studied 18 young men and women whose parents suffered from major affective disorders, and Marton, Golombek, Stein, and Korenblum (1988), who studied self-esteem, adaptive skills, and an ability to reflect a sense of self and sense of significant attachment figures, it is increasingly clear that the capacity to cope and maintain a sense of self as a victor over adversity enhances a sense of self-competence. Werner (1984, p. 71) best described the conditions:

- At some point in their young lives, resilient children were required to carry out socially desirable tasks to prevent others in their family, neighborhood, or community from experiencing distress or discomfort. Such acts of required helpfulness led to enduring and positive changes in the young helpers.
- The central component in the lives of resilient children that contributed to their effective coping appeared to be a feeling of confidence or faith that things will work out as well as can be reasonably expected, and that the odds can be surmounted.

THREE MODELS FOR UNDERSTANDING RESILIENCE

As the understanding of resiliency grows, it is important to discuss some of the complex limitations of resiliency work with clients. Garmezy et al. (1984) postulated three models to evaluate the relationship between risk and resilience: compensatory, challenge, and conditional. The *compensatory model* weighs environmental risk and protective factors in combination to predict outcomes for children and adolescents. For example, consider the case of an 11-year-old boy who progressed despite several losses and alcoholic parents, partly because of several protective factors present, including involvement with extended family and a somewhat supportive school environment. He later became overwhelmed by several risk factors that occurred within a short period, including the removal of his older sister from the home due to allegations of sexual abuse and the finalization of his parents' divorce. These multiple risk factors greatly increased the probability of adverse outcomes for him.

The *challenge model* postulates that although a negative curvilinear relationship exists between risk and competence, risk factors could be potential enhancers of competence, provided there are only a few. Although the negative relationship between competence and risk is not linear, the model hypothesizes that even with the experience of a few risk factors, an adolescent will have the capacity to cope and overcome their harmful situational impact. An example is a 14-year-old at-risk girl who was removed from her familiar academic program and placed in a program for students with learning problems. Given her history of protective and risk factors, she was able, after a stressful entry period, to adjust to the new environment and thrive using her acquired skills of competence and adaptation.

Finally, the *conditional model* postulates that personal attributes work to modulate (dampen or amplify) the impact of risk factors. The model hypothesizes that, for example, a young adult female in the wake of several life-changing risk factors prospered in part because she had a temperament that made her attractive to others, made her optimistic about her possibilities, and promoted in her a tendency to seek novel experiences.

Thus, understanding resilience and its capacity to ameliorate negative life consequences in the lives of children and adolescents remains exceedingly complex. Counselors and therapists must weigh the interaction between buffering and risk factors to determine where and how to intervene. As Garmezy (1991) suggested, there are many windows from which to view resiliency. In fact, Chambers and Belicki (1988) argued that resilience as a unidimensional concept should be retired.

USING THE QUESTIONNAIRE AS A STRATEGY TO ASSESS RESILIENCE

The Resiliency Questionnaire was developed in the spirit of the interview protocol of Harry Stack Sullivan (1953), which pointedly assessed the life history of clients' relationships and their impressions of those interactions with significant others over the life span. These questions serve as a guide for counselors to assess the client's resilient qualities in the wake of risk factors and the array of stressors that brought the client to counseling. Follow-up questions are necessary to facilitate rich understandings of the client's life space as well as efforts to speak to significant others with client permission to obtain data that the client is unable to supply. In this type of assessment, the counselor utilizes the here-and-now responses

of the client to develop an assessment that minimizes judgment, enhances salutogenesis, and evaluates the client's life space, support systems, and capacity to endure and overcome.

One example of how a counselor uses the questionnaire is the case of Helen, a 14-year-old, who was referred to the school counselor because of a refusal to complete assignments and follow classroom instructions. Many of her teachers were very concerned. She responded positively to items 5, 15, and 20 on the Resiliency Questionnaire. She further elaborated on item 20 by stating, "I know that I am very sad and angry now because of several problems at home." The counselor used her responses on the questionnaire and in the interview to probe her present home situation and assist her with some of those dilemmas. Together, they addressed her troubles at school as a reaction to the stress at home, and the counselor utilized her sense of diligence and duty to correct the problems at school and began to unravel the conundrum in her family life. In another example, a 15-year-old female who was frightened of geometry class was found to be confident and deal effectively with stress in other environments (items 11, 17, 20, and 22). The counselor helped her to transfer these coping skills to the new and unfamiliar academic environment with some success. These are two examples for counselors to implement the Resiliency Questionnaire in their work.

INTERVENTIONS USING A RESILIENCE PERSPECTIVE

With an understanding of the dimensions and complexity of resiliency research, counselors can enrich their work with young clients and adults. It is critical for counselors who work with at-risk clients exposed to several risk factors to understand that only a minority of such children experience moderate to severe difficulty in the process of growing into adulthood. Often, teachers, counselors, and other mental health professionals establish negative self-fulfilling prophecies for children at-risk, making excuses for them and teaching them that they will be unsuccessful. Counselors must find a balance in their work to include the principles of salutogenesis, evaluating the strengths rather than weaknesses, with an empathic understanding that life has been treacherous for many children and adolescents exposed to a multitude of stressors lacking material possessions and a stable home (Rak & Patterson, 1996).

Strategies and interventions that focus on resilience demand an awareness on the part of the counselor of the complexities of resilience and how the dimensions of resilience can operate in children at risk. It is critical for counselors to listen to their clients with an ear toward resilience. That means developing a stance during the assessment process that discovers the client's historical patterns of resilience, whether using the questionnaire or not. This stance moves the counselor away from either listening for problems (pathology) or immediate solutions (solution-focused) and toward a broad understanding of clients' capacity to endure or to buffer themselves from the risk-factors of their troubled lives. The identification of the historical patterns of resilience in clients allows counselors to initiate strategies that reinforce these patterns or create opportunities to teach about it or model behaviors that buttress clients' capacities to self-manage and cope with problems and stressors. Some other strategies to enhance or trigger resilient responses in client are (1) role plays that assist youth in improved self-expression; (2) conflict resolution techniques that help clients work through their interpersonal struggles at home and at school; (3) a nurturing stance by counselors that conveys to youth an empathy and authenticity, realistic reinforcement, and genuine hope; (4) modeling the principles of healthy interaction to clients in counseling; (5) peer support interventions; (6) creative imagery; and (7) bibliotherapy (Rak & Patterson, 1996). Counselors must also be alert to interventions with families and parents that highlight the protective and supportive behaviors within a family system, even in the midst of disorganization and crisis. Thus, by engaging in consultation with parents, counselors can help trigger protective behaviors within families or teach about the dimensions of resilience. Counselors also are encouraged to help clients and their families activate environmental supports that serve as buffers in the wake of overwhelming stressors.

Contrary to recent research perspectives and this author's former thinking, developing a resilience response strategy for counseling is very different from brief solution-focused strategies. Resilience work does not always arrive at solutions for clients, nor does it always resolve the conflicts. Incorporating a resilience focus into one's counseling repertoire demands an even more complex appreciation for how our clients bring us desperation and hope, depravity and resurgence, destruction and salvation. In the quagmire of counseling, if the counselor is capable of focusing on the client's reservoir of historical resilient behaviors along with the history of problems, there is greater hope for a realistic resolution of the client's ongoing life dilemmas. Thus, the counselor is linked to Vaughan's (2000) fundamental message in her work that capturing the origins of resiliency in our clients often results in unlocking the psychological roots of optimism.

References

Beardslee, M.D., & Podorefsky, M.A. (1988). Resilient adolescents whose parents have serious affective and other psychiatric disorders: Importance of self-understanding and relationships. *American Journal of Psychiatry, 145,* 63–69.

Benard, B. (1997). *Turning it around for all youth: From risk to resilience.* Launceston, Tasmania: Resiliency Associates and Global Learning Communities.

Benson, P.L. (1997). *All kids are our kids.* Minneapolis, MN: Search Institute.

Bolig, R., & Weddle, K.D. (1988). Resiliency and hospitalization of children. *Children's Health Care, 16,* 255–260.

Chambers, E., & Belicki, K. (1988). Using sleep dysfunction to explore the nature of resilience in adult survivors of childhood abuse or trauma. *Child Abuse and Neglect, 22,* 753–758.

Dugan, T., & Coles, R. (Eds.). (1989). *The child in our times: Studies in the development of resiliency.* New York: Brunner/Mazel.

Garmezy, N. (1991). Resiliency and vulnerability to adverse developmental outcomes associated with poverty. *American Behavioral Scientist, 34,* 416–430.

Garmezy, N., Masten, A.S., & Tellegen, A. (1984). The study of stress and competence in children: A building block for developmental psychopathology. *Child Development, 55,* 97–111.

Hauser, S.T. (1999). Understanding resilient outcomes: Adolescent lives across time and generations. *Journal of Research on Adolescence, 9,* 1–24.

Hauser, S.T., Vieyra, M.A., Jacobson, A.M., & Wertreib, D. (1985). Vulnerability and resilience in adolescence: Views from the family. *Journal of Early Adolescence, 5,* 81–100.

Lowenthal, B. (1998). The effects of early childhood abuse and the development of resiliency. *Early Child Development and Care, 142,* 43–52.

Marton, P., Golombek, H., Stein, B., & Korenblum, M. (1988). The relation of personality functions and adaptive skills to self-esteem in early adolescence. *Journal of Youth and Adolescence, 17,* 393–401.

Rak, C.F., & Patterson, L.E. (1996). Promoting resilience in at-risk children. *Journal of Counseling and Development, 74,* 368–373.

Rutter, M. (1979). Protective factors in children's responses to stress and disadvantage. In M.W. Kent & J.E. Rolf (Eds.), *Primary prevention of psychopathology: Social competence in children* (Vol. 3, pp. 49–74). Hanover, NH: University Press of New England.

Rutter, M. (1985). Resilience in the face of adversity: Protective factors and resistance to psychiatric disorders. *British Journal of Psychiatry, 147,* 598–611.

Sullivan, H.S. (1953). *The interpersonal theory of psychiatry.* New York: Norton.

Vaughan, S.C. (2000). *Half empty, half full: Understanding the psychological roots of optimism.* New York: Harcourt.

Werner, E.E. (1984). Resilient children. *Young Children, 40,* 68–72.

Werner, E.E. (1986). The concept of risk from a developmental perspective. *Advances in Special Education, 5,* 1–23.

Werner, E.E., & Smith, R.S. (1982). *Vulnerable but not invincible: A longitudinal study of resilient children and youth.* New York: McGraw-Hill.

Werner, E.E., & Smith, R.S. (1992). Overcoming the odds: High-risk children from birth to adulthood. Ithaca, NY: Cornell University Press.

33 SUBSTANCE ABUSE AMONG CHILDREN AND ADOLESCENTS

Michael Windle

In describing substance use and abuse during childhood and adolescence, it is useful to conceive of a continuum of behaviors, ranging from first use or initiation, to escalation to more frequent and higher levels of use, to experiencing substance-related problems, and finally to the expression of a clinical disorder.

Initiation of use marks the age at which an individual first uses a substance. It is an important indicator because earlier initiation has consistently been identified with a greater propensity to subsequently develop serious substance-related problems. *Substance use* refers to the frequency and quantity of using substances. Frequency and quantity of use information helps to distinguish qualitatively different patterns of use, such as abstainers, light users, moderate users, and heavy users. With reference to the use of alcohol, there has been much interest in the study of heavy drinking episodes or "binge drinking," which refers to the consumption of five or more alcoholic beverages on a single occasion.

Substance-related problems refer to adverse consequences associated with substance use and includes events such as missing school because of substance use, passing out from drinking, having encounters with legal authorities, and interpersonal problems (e.g., fighting) with family members or friends over substance use. The clinical diagnosis for an *alcohol or other substance-related disorder* is identical for children and adults and requires meeting explicit criteria. Alcohol disorders, for instance, are characterized by (1) a prolonged period of frequent, heavy alcohol use; (2) a variety of social and/or legal problems associated with alcohol use (e.g., driving while intoxicated, impaired school/work performance); and (3) the expression of dependency symptoms (e.g., unpleasant withdrawal effects when unable to consume alcohol). Controversy exists regarding the adequacy of using adult criteria for alcohol and other substance-related disorders for children and adolescents.

CURRENT FINDINGS ON CHILD AND
ADOLESCENT SUBSTANCE USE AND ABUSE

Age of initiation is an important indicator for three reasons. First, as noted previously, earlier initiation predicts the development of serious substance-related problems. For example, in a nationally representative sample of adults, those who reported initiating alcohol use before age 15 years were four times more likely to develop an alcohol disorder (Grant & Dawson, 1997). Second, there are historical changes in the age of first use of many substances, such that many children are using substances at an earlier age (Office of National Drug Control Policy, 1997). For example, the average age of first use of alcohol was 15.9 years in 1994, relative to 17.4 years in 1987. Similarly, the average age of first marijuana use was 16.3 years in 1994, relative to 17.8 years in 1987. Third, this pattern of an earlier onset of substances is quite dangerous because of the high potency of many substances, including easily accessible solvents and designer drugs such as ecstasy, that may significantly impair development in important biological (e.g., neural growth), psychological (e.g., personal identity), and social (parent and peer relations) domains (e.g., NIDA News Release, 1999).

In relation to human development, there has been empirical support for a range of social events (e.g., perceived peer pressure) and cognitive-developmental processes (e.g., labeling and the elaboration and differentiation of concepts and categories used to organize the world) about alcohol use that are ongoing during the preschool and elementary school years prior to the actual consumption of alcohol. For instance, research by Noll, Zucker, and Greenberg (1990) has indicated that preschool children (ages 3 to 5 years) can identify alcoholic beverages and have already developed certain cognitive concepts and schemas (i.e., integrated beliefs) about drinking behaviors. It is also significant that the actual use of alcohol is initiated by some children during the elementary school years. It has been estimated that 20% to 25% of fourth-graders report having consumed an alcoholic beverage in their lifetime, and this rate increases to slightly more than 50% by eighth grade (Windle, 1999). A more developmental orientation toward substance use and abuse is important because it is increasingly evident that some of the cognitive foundations (e.g., beliefs and attitudes) for substance use, such as intention to use substances, expectancies, and even initiation, have been cultivated or even expressed during the preschool and elementary school years.

Alcohol and other substance use increases substantially during the teen years. Annual surveys of substance use practices among seniors (twelfth-graders) have been completed at the University of Michigan for almost 30 years and are collectively referred to as the Monitoring the Future Studies (Johnston, O'Malley, & Bachman, 1996). These studies have been used to monitor historical trends in substance use among adolescents (e.g., increases or decreases in the use of alcohol, cigarettes, and illicit drugs) and to identify new drugs (e.g., designer drugs) or new patterns of co-occurring substance use that may be relevant for prevention research efforts and the development of social policies. Findings for students who have ever used alcohol in their lifetime (among seniors) has remained relatively stable from 1993 to 1995, hovering at around 80%. The number of seniors engaging in binge drinking, that is, consuming five or more drinks in a single setting in the two-week period preceding the survey assessment, has remained unchanged from 1991 to 1995, with a rate of 28% to 29%. For eighth- and tenth-graders, response to the item "Ever used alcohol in your lifetime" was endorsed by approximately 55% and 71%, respectively, across the years 1993 to 1995. The rates of "Ever been drunk" were stable across the 1991 to 1995 period, with a rate of approximately 26% for eighth-graders and 47% for tenth-graders. It is significant to note that the majority of children have used alcohol by the time they are in eighth grade, and that 26% of them have consumed enough alcohol on a single occasion to characterize themselves as being drunk.

With regard to gender and ethnic group differences, girls typically begin consuming alcohol at a somewhat later age than boys, but by their senior year, nearly as many girls as boys have used alcohol at some point. Nevertheless, on measures of high-volume (heavy) drinking and alcohol-related problems (e.g., driving while under the influence of alcohol, or DWI, infractions), boys still evidence more alcohol-related difficulties than girls. The highest percentage of users of alcohol among teenagers are Caucasians and Native Americans, followed closely by Latinos. The lowest percentage of users of alcohol among teenagers are reported by African American and Asian American teenagers.

The study of alcohol-related problems has indicated that adolescents experience a wide range of adverse social consequences (e.g., legal encounters, fights with family and friends, school difficulties) and dependency symptoms (e.g., passing out when drinking, inability to cut down on substance use). In addition, adolescents who drink or use other substances as a coping mechanism may be at particularly high risk for the development of serious substance problems. The use of alcohol and other substances to self-medicate negative affect may signify current major problems and the adoption of a nonconstructive coping style that will likely perpetuate ongoing difficulties. Children and adolescents with persistent and pervasive problems and/or the adoption of a self-medication coping style are in need of professional assistance, as these are behaviors that portend more dire consequences.

There have been a limited number of studies on the prevalence of substance-related disorders among children and adolescents, and the existing studies are not based on nationally representative U.S. samples (e.g., Martin, Kaczynski, Maisto, Bukstein, & Moss, 1995). Nevertheless, with regard to alcohol disorders, there is consistency in the findings suggesting that those children and adolescents who meet the clinical criteria for an alcohol disorder typically manifest persistent, high-volume drinking and pervasive adverse social consequences and dependency symptoms. Further, these children typically have a history of childhood behavior problems (e.g., conduct disordered difficulties, attentional deficits), long-term troubled family relations, and a pattern of co-existing substance abuse (e.g., marijuana or cocaine abuse). Prevalence estimates of the number of children and adolescents meeting clinical criteria for an alcohol disorder are not known, though some have speculated that the number may exceed two million (e.g., Bukstein, 1995).

ALCOHOL AND SUBSTANCE USE AND RELATED HEALTH PROBLEMS

Higher levels of substance use and substance-related problems among children and adolescents are associated with the three major causes of adolescent mortality: accidents (e.g., automobile, boating), homicide, and suicide. Almost 9 out of 10 teenage automobile accidents involve the use of alcohol (e.g., Windle, 1999). Higher levels of alcohol and other substance use have been associated with higher levels of adolescent suicidal ideation (i.e., thinking about committing suicide) and suicide attempts, and alcohol has been found in high concentrations among adolescents who have completed suicide. Higher levels of adolescent substance use have also been associated with a number of other unhealthy outcomes, including sexual precocity, teenage pregnancy, sexually transmitted diseases, HIV infection, poor school performance, and school dropout.

RISK FACTORS (PREDICTORS) OF SUBSTANCE USE AND ABUSE

Variables that increase the expectation (or probability) that children or adolescents will use or abuse substances are referred to as risk factors. A broad range of risk factors have been identified that contribute to child and adolescent substance use and abuse. Among them are the following.

Societal-community factors may foster youthful drinking behavior via media sources (e.g., television and magazine advertising, movies) and adolescent societal heroes (e.g., rock stars) that explicitly or implicitly convey the message that alcohol consumption and/or other drug use is associated with positively valued characteristics (e.g., popularity with friends).

Early-onset poor school functioning such as persistent behavior problems, including attentional problems, high activity levels, and aggression within the school context, has been a consistent predictor of high levels of teenage alcohol use, as have a low commitment to school achievement, poor attendance, poor grades, and underachievement.

Family factors include the drinking practices of other family members (e.g., parents or siblings), marital conflict, poor family management practices (e.g., failure to monitor children as to where they are, who are they with), harsh (physically abusive) discipline, physical or sexual abuse, and the lack of a warm, open, nurturing relationship with parents.

Peer factors are perhaps the single most highly associated risk factor for adolescent substance use and reflect a tendency for adolescents to select friends and peers according to similarities regarding attitudes, values,

and behaviors. Peer group members may foster alcohol and other substance use practices as drug use becomes a critical component of group identity.

Individual factors have also been identified, including the temperament factors of sensation seeking, rebelliousness, and impulsivity. Research on children of alcoholics (COAs) has supported a genetic susceptibility to alcohol among the offspring of alcoholics, with COA boys at four times the risk of an alcohol disorder in adulthood than non-COA boys (Windle & Searles, 1990).

RECOMMENDATIONS FOR COUNSELING PRACTICE

A common concern by counselors and other health professionals is how to identify early warning signs of substance-related difficulties in children and adolescents. There are some general warning signs, but it is important to caution that these are not exclusive to substance use, but may be attributable to other factors.

Physical signs could include frequent and long-lasting fatigue, increased health complaints, disturbed sleeping and eating patterns, and confusion in thought processes or ideas. *Psychological and emotional signs* could include heightened levels of irritability and mood fluctuations, increases in irresponsible behaviors (e.g., coming home late, forgetting family occasions such as birthdays), increases in seemingly unprovoked hostility and uncooperativeness, a general unwillingness to communicate with parents and other adults (e.g., teachers, school counselors), and increases in depression and withdrawing from interpersonal contact with others (especially adults and other family members). *Social and interpersonal signs* could include changes in friends or peer group toward a more deviant social group, the adoption of styles of dress and musical interests that tend toward the deviant subculture, and encounters with legal authorities (e.g., being a passenger in a car with peers who were stopped for DWI). *School warning signs* could include a drop in grades, increases in the number of unaccounted for absences and times tardy, and increases in disciplinary problems.

It is important to emphasize that many of these signs may be symptomatic of other behaviors or problems. For example, disturbed sleeping and eating patterns may be influenced by disruptive family functioning (e.g., marital conflict), the cessation of a romantic involvement, or anxiety about an upcoming examination or poor performance on a recent examination. As such, it is important to consider the convergence, or consistency, of several warning signs and to rule out alternative explanations when possible.

In addition to these warning signs, there are a broad range of *screening instruments* that may assist in the identification of alcohol and other substance-related problems among children and adolescents (e.g., for review, see Radhert & Czechowicz, 1995). Many of these instruments focus specifically on alcohol and other substance use, whereas others offer a more comprehensive assessment that also includes the measurement of assets and liabilities (e.g., physical health status, legal status, school adjustment, vocational status, family and peer relationships). For the more intensive and extensive clinical diagnosis of a substance-related disorder, there are a number of structured and semistructured interviews based on the *Diagnostic and Statistical Manual of Mental Disorders* (*DSM-IV-TR;* American Psychiatric Association, 2000) that require varying levels of training to administer.

When considering alcohol and other substance use practices among children and adolescents, it is also important to know that more serious levels of use are commonly associated with co-occurring problem behaviors (e.g., poor academic performance, higher levels of delinquency). For those adolescents with problems severe enough to warrant a substance abuse clinical diagnosis, the majority will also have *comorbid psychiatric disorders* (e.g., Major Depressive Disorder). The rate of comorbidity among adolescent substance abusers is greater than among adult substance abusers (e.g., Bukstein, 1995). This suggests that some adolescents are indeed

experiencing severe problems that may require the assistance of substance abuse professionals in the community (e.g., at hospitals or in residential settings).

There is extensive literature on child and adolescent substance use *intervention studies* (e.g., Ashery, in press; Schinke, Botvin, & Orlandi, 1991). Most knowledge- or information-based *school preventive interventions* have not been very successful in modifying the substance use practices of adolescents. An exception to this pattern of findings has been the Life Skills Training Program (Botvin, Baker, Dusenbury, Botvin, & Diaz, 1995), which uses a cognitive-behavioral model to train adolescents in domain-specific skills (e.g., assertiveness skills to resist peer pressure to use drugs, communication and coping skills). *Family-focused interventions* that provide training in parenting skills, listening techniques, and enhanced communication among family members have produced some initial promising results in terms of delaying the onset of substance use among youth and reducing levels of use. Comprehensive *community prevention programs* focus on multilevel interventions that may include components such as individual peer resistance skills training, enhanced family communication, enforced school-level substance prohibitions, and community-level enforcement of laws (e.g., having police enforce laws regarding underage drinking and laws that penalize alcohol outlets for serving minors). The concept behind such comprehensive community interventions is that no single component may be effective, but that the simultaneous intervention across many levels of society may be more effective in producing the desired outcome. Findings to date for these large-scale interventions have been encouraging, though it has been difficult to disentangle which components are most effective in producing the desired changes (e.g., Perry et al., 1996).

References

American Psychiatric Association. (2000). *Diagnostic and statistical manual of mental disorders* (4th ed., text rev.). Washington, DC: Author.

Ashery, R. (in press). *NIDA research monograph on drug abuse prevention through early interventions.*

Rockville, MD: National Institute of Drug Abuse.

Botvin, G.J., Baker, E., Dusenbury, L., Botvin, E.M., & Diaz, T. (1995). Long-term follow-up results of a randomized drug abuse prevention trial in a White middle-class population. *Journal of the American Medical Association, 273*, 1106.

Bukstein, O.G. (1995). *Adolescent substance abuse: Assessment, prevention, and treatment.* New York: Wiley.

Grant, B., & Dawson, D.A. (1997). Age of alcohol onset and its association with *DSM-IV* alcohol abuse and dependence: Results from the National Longitudinal Epidemiologic Survey. *Journal of Substance Abuse, 9,* 103–110.

Johnston, L.D., O'Malley, P.M., & Bachman, J.G. (1996). *National survey results on drug use from the Monitoring the Future Study, 1975–1995: Vol. 1. Secondary school students* (NIH Publication No. 96–4139). Washington, DC: National Institute on Drug Abuse.

Martin, C.S., Kaczynski, N.A., Maisto, S.A., Bukstein, O.M., & Moss, H.B. (1995). Patterns of *DSM-IV* alcohol abuse and dependence symptoms in adolescent drinkers. *Journal of Studies on Alcohol, 56,* 672–680.

National Institute on Drug Abuse News Release. (1999, June 14). Long-term brain injury from use of "ecstasy." Washington, DC: National Institute of Drug Abuse.

Noll, R.B., Zucker, R.A., & Greenberg, G.E. (1990). Identification of alcohol by smell among preschoolers: Evidence for early socialization about drugs occurring in the home. *Child Development, 61,* 1520–1527.

Office of National Drug Control Policy: The National Drug Control Strategy. (1997). [Online]. Available: www.ncjrs.org/htm/chapter2.htm.

Perry, C.L., Williams, C.L., Veblen-Mortenson, S., Toomey, T.L., Komro, K.A., Anstine, P.S., McGovern, P.G., Finnegan, J.R., Forster, J.L., Wagenaar, A.C., & Wolfson, M. (1996). Project Northland: Outcomes of a community-wide alcohol use prevention program during early adolescence. *American Journal of Public Health, 86,* 956.

Radhert, E., & Czechowicz, D. (Eds.). (1995). *Adolescent drug abuse: Clinical assessment and therapeutic interventions.* National Institute on Drug Abuse Research Monograph 156 (pp. 146–171). Rockville, MD.

Schinke, S.P., Botvin, G.J., & Orlandi, M.A. (1991). *Substance abuse in children and adolescents.* Newbury Park, CA: Sage.

Windle, M. (1999). *Alcohol use among adolescents.* Thousand Oaks, CA: Sage.

Windle, M., & Searles, J.S. (Eds.). (1990). *Children of alcoholics: Critical perspectives.* New York: Guilford Press.

Additional Resources

There are a large number of Web sites that offer valuable information on substance use and abuse among children and adolescents. Following are the electronic addresses and a brief description of four sites. Each of these sites provides links to a broad range of other sites that may contain information for specific populations (e.g., Native Americans), advocacy materials for prevention activities, or schedules of training workshops and conferences.

Books

Boyd, G.M., Howard, J., & Zucker, R.A. (Eds.). (1995). *Alcohol problems among adolescents: Current directions in prevention research.* Hillsdale, NJ: Erlbaum.

Bukstein, O.G. (1995). *Adolescent substance abuse: Assessment, prevention, and treatment.* New York: Wiley.

Windle, M. (1999). *Alcohol use among adolescents.* Thousand Oaks, CA: Sage.

Web Sites

The Monitoring the Futures Studies provide updated, annual national surveillance data on youth alcohol and other substance use. www.monitoringthefuture.org

The Web of Addictions provides fact sheets about different addictive substances and hotlines and addresses for support services around the country www.well.com/user/woa

This Web site for the National Association for Children of Alcoholics provides fact sheets for COAs and other families in distress, a substance abuse news summary, and extensive links to other Web pages. www.nacoa.org

This is the Web site for the Center for Substance Abuse Prevention; it provides a wealth of information on child and adolescent substance use prevention programs and the scientific evaluation of such programs. www.samhsa.gov/csap/index.htm

PART IV
Crisis Intervention Issues

34 RESPONDING TO A COMMUNITY CRISIS

Frontline Counseling

Ann Bauer

It is probable that most counselors will have encountered a number of clients working through the grief process. It is possible that a counselor will work with at least a few clients suffering from what Goldman (1996) calls complicated grief. Clients experience complicated grief when their loss has been confounded with tragedy such as murder, suicide, AIDS, and physical or sexual abuse. Unless they choose to put themselves on the front line, it is unlikely that counselors will experience the response of an entire grieving community as it reacts to tragedy and crisis. Because of the immediacy of the exposure to the pain source, this type of work significantly differs from seeing clients individually in an office setting. The pace, intensity, and urgency of crisis response work in some ways parallels the work done by MASH units in the Korean War: Crisis responders are either on or very near the front line; there may be a large number of people all needing help at once, necessitating some form of triage; and sometimes survivors need to be sent on to other helping personnel for long-term support to complete the healing process. Critical decisions are made at a blistering pace, and the sheer number of people in pain can be overwhelming.

This chapter is written to give a thumbnail sketch of crisis response work. It should be a useful refresher for those already trained or in providing the basics for those who have been called to respond. This kind of help differs enough from other helping that it is preferable to have had previous training before beginning work as a crisis responder. The Red Cross and the National Organization for Victim Assistance (NOVA) are excellent sources for that training. However, if you follow the pattern of most crisis responders, your first experience comes to you without the benefit of prior training. If you did not receive training before becoming involved in crisis response work, I encourage you to pursue training afterwards because training will help you sort out and understand what you have experienced. The information in this chapter is drawn for the most part from a combination of NOVA basic and advanced training, the NOVA training manual (Young, 1998), and my personal experience as a crisis responder.

GOAL

According to NOVA, the goal of responding to a psychological crisis is to defuse emotions and reengage the cognitive process, help to organize and interpret the cognitive process, integrate the traumatic event into the life story, and interpret the traumatic event to derive meaning. (Young, 1998). In what can feel like the blink of an eye, the pattern and course of a survivor's life changes radically. The Oklahoma City Memorial vividly illustrates this profound and instantaneous change: Two arches stand at opposite ends of a reflecting pool; symbolizing life before and after the morning bombing, one arch is named 9:02, the other is 9:03. Integrating this profound shift into the understanding of one's life story requires a process that reestablishes, to the degree possible, a sense of safety and security, validates survivors' feelings and reactions, and prepares them for predictable future events.

DEFINITIONS

Understanding the provision of psychological and emotional support to a community in crisis begins in understanding what constitutes a community and what defines a particular event as a crisis. A crisis is an unexpected tragic event that suddenly alters the life pattern of those touched by it and is often associated with loss of life. A community can be as small in size as the extended family of a murder victim or as large as Oklahoma City after the bombing or the state of Florida after Hurricane Andrew. Sometimes, a group of previously unrelated individuals becomes a community as the result of a crisis; for example, friends and family of airplane crash victims can connect as a community and become a support system for each other. Within the larger group, smaller sections can bond in a particular way as a distinct group. The science teacher and her class in Littleton High School in Colorado spent several agonizing hours hiding in a greenhouse from armed students and now call themselves the Greenhouse Group. One of the issues that can emerge in the healing process is an insiders/outsiders question: who can legitimately claim membership in the crisis community can become a hotly debated topic.

Causal Factors

It is helpful to categorize the crisis event by causal factor because the kind of response

people have to a crisis depends in part on the type of crisis that has occurred. After a natural calamity such as a tornado, hurricane, or flood, survivors are usually struggling with essential survival issues such as food, water, and shelter. Help in such cases may be very practical in nature while still addressing emotional needs. Some crisis events are the accidental result of human error, and some are purposefully caused by deliberate human behavior. Deliberately caused tragedies are most apt to evoke anger and rage and leave survivors struggling with the mostly unanswerable question Why? Helping survivors find a productive purpose for the energy of their anger can be a useful approach. Some of the students attending a school that had suffered the tragic loss of two of their junior class were very angry at the local paper that published a front-page graphic picture of the accident and chose to write a letter expressing their outrage. One of the parents of the victims of a school shooting is very active in seeking gun control legislation; MADD (Mothers Against Drunk Drivers) grew out of this active approach to healing. The Mother's Day 2000 "Million Mom March," which pulled together survivors of gun-caused tragedies to protest what they viewed as a lack of adequate gun legislation, is another example.

RESPONSES TO CRISIS

Because survivors are often bewildered by both the events that have occurred to them and their own response to these events, crisis responders can best do their work if they have a clear understanding of common responses to uncommon events. There are some physiological and emotional reactions to a crisis that seem to be typical to the experience of survivors.

Physiological Response

The manner in which the body responds to an emergency is a good place to start, as the physical response strongly colors the mental and emotional reactions people experience. The familiar fight-or-flight response is the result of one nervous system shutting down and another kicking into action. Chemical and hormonal energy flood the muscle system. The cognitive functions shut down, as does the digestive system. Besides suffering severe impairment to critical thinking and decision-making skills, survivors may also vomit or soil themselves. It is important for those working with survivors to understand this biochemical response because clients who have experienced this response will often carry a deep sense of shame for what feels like a loss of control.

Understanding the involuntary nature of this response can be critical in beginning the healing process. Lieberman (1999) suggested an interesting analogy that helps to depict the result of this biochemical response in the brain. He has compared this process to what occurs in a snow globe that has been shaken, when all the little pieces of snow are suspended and swirling rapidly. Survivors offered this metaphor find that it aptly describes the disconnected and confused thinking that immediately follows a crisis. Sometimes as the result of this mental confusion, people behave in ways they later find inexplicable. Sometimes they are frozen in an inability to make any decision or wander aimlessly with no clear direction or plan. This panic reaction can leave a residue of shame that can be relieved best through understanding.

Emotional Response

The initial feeling response to a shocking event is disbelief and denial. The majority of us live with the illusion that bad things happen to other people in other places. We behave as though we can buffer ourselves from risk by eating a certain way or living in a certain place. The sudden loss of this illusion causes thoughts such as "This can't be happening to me, or to my school, or to my community." This sudden loss of a fundamental belief freezes survivors in a state of disbelief and denial. Perhaps because the cognitive and emotional functions are temporarily frozen, memories of crisis events can be sensorial in nature. A sight, a sound, or a smell can become etched in memory, creating neural connections that later function as triggers creating flashback experiences, sometimes years after the crisis event. Once the initial numbness of shock and denial wear off, the activation of the limbic system increases the impact of the emotional responses. These strong emotional responses precede the revival of cognitive functioning.

The two most common emotional reactions are fear and anger. Fear, the most common response of children, becomes terror when confronting the potential loss of one's life. Anger explodes into rage most often when the crisis is caused by deliberate human action, although people can also project this urge to fight on unexpected and undeserving targets. Sometimes, law enforcement becomes the focus because the legal system won't punish the perpetrator to the degree the survivors would like. In one case, surviving students were angry at the bus driver who drove them past the scene of an accident that killed two of their classmates.

There seems to be a strong need to hold someone accountable. Just as the unanswerable question Why? can plague survivors, searching for the answer to the question Whose fault is this? can become both anguished and futile. This need to find a cause can play out in feelings of both reasonable and unreasonable guilt. Sometimes, mistakes are made that lead to tragic consequences; self-forgiveness is critical in such instances. Unreasonable guilt can surprise crisis response workers. Perhaps because of the bargaining nature of some grief responses, people can get stuck in "If only" thoughts and make statements like "If only I had (fill in the blank) this wouldn't have happened." Survivor guilt shows up at times, as in the case of the little girl who was at home sick on the day of a school shooting in which a number of her classmates died; she felt very guilty that she had not gone to school that day even though her absence was legitimate. Shame takes the sense that "I did something wrong" a step further to the position "I am something wrong." Survivors evidence this kind of shame when they wish to hide from outsiders their connection to the traumatic event. One of the teachers in a school that had just experienced a fatal shooting said to a helper with tears in her eyes, "You are going to think we are a bad school."

REENGAGING THE COGNITIVE PROCESS

Because of the shutdown of the cognitive functions, a sense of confusion among survivors is not uncommon. Recall the image of a shaken snow globe; feelings as well as thoughts can be as jumbled as that. The difference lies in the degree of intensity and the way these feelings are untempered and unfiltered by cognitive functions. Active listening fosters healing by validating the experience of these emotions. Besides comfort and reassurance, turning down the volume of powerful feelings sets the stage for the reengagement of the cognitive process. Supporting the reengagement of the cognitive process is one of the critical tasks for crisis responders.

The sooner this process begins, the better. Human beings are not wired to think after a crisis; we are wired to act and react. Unfortunately, many important decisions must be made and problems solved in postcrisis moments. Poor choices can complicate and increase the painful impact of surviving a tragedy. The sooner survivors have access to relatively clear thinking, the sooner they can begin making thoughtful decisions. Crisis responders facilitate this reconnection to thinking by helping survivors turn their experience from jumbled fragments into a coherent story.

The organization of scattered sensations and emotions into a story begins with asking for factual recall of details, such as "Where were you when . . . ," as well as checking for sensory memories: "What did you see, hear, smell, taste, or touch?" The next direction for questioning is to learn which memories stand out since the event. Survivors seem to respond better to the question "How have you reacted?" than "How did you (do you) feel?" If the survivor is blocked about his or her own reactions, sometimes it helps to ask how family members or friends have been reacting since the crisis event. Crisis responders validate the survivor's reactions by using active listening skills such as summarizing and clarifying and

using feeling-focused responses. It is also helpful to point out reactions that are common to survivors of crisis events.

The next step in reengaging the cognitive process is to ask survivors to predict what will happen in the next days or weeks and how they will handle both the practical and emotional concerns. Check for and reinforce healthy coping strategies and reaffirm good choices. This is a good time to employ the problem-solving process as survivors work their way through issues such as upcoming anniversaries, holidays, or decisions about funeral arrangements (see Figure 34.1).

Roles: Facilitator, scribe, helpers

Format: 10 minutes safety and security (group rules, confidentiality)

35 minutes physical sensory perceptions

25 minutes reactions of self, family, and friends

10 minutes preparation for future

10 minutes review and conclude

Allow 15–30 minutes postgroup to talk to individuals, give handouts

Set one (ask as a conglomerate):
  Where were you when it happened?
  Who were you with?
  What did they see, hear, smell, taste, or touch at the time?
  What did they do? How did they react at the time?

Set two (ask as a conglomerate):
  Since the time of the event, what are some of the memories that stand out in your mind?
  What has happened in the past 48 hours?
  How have you reacted?

Set three (ask separately):
  After all that you have been through, what do you think will happen at your job in the next few days or weeks?
  Do you think your family has been or will continue to be affected?
  Do you have any practical concerns about what will happen next?
  (Ask participants how they think they will deal with the issues that have been raised.)

Review notes to identify: descriptions of acute sensory perception; descriptions of shock and disbelief; descriptions of emotional turmoil, coping strategies

---

FIGURE 34.1 Sample Protocol: Group Crisis Intervention. *Source:* NOVA Training Manual. Reprinted by permission. Courtesy of the National Organization of Victims Assistance.

POSITIVE AND NEGATIVE CONVERGENCE

One of the features of a community crisis that creates both hazards and opportunities is the way large numbers of people converge on the crisis site. There may be many emergency and law enforcement personnel. Relatives of potential victims arrive; for example, all the parents of the students enrolled in a school shooting arrive on the doorstep of the school wanting access to their child. Media swarm the scene, as do those wanting to help. Unfortunately, those who are merely curious also arrive in large numbers. NOVA (Young, 1998) sorts this process into two categories: positive and negative convergence. Positive convergence occurs with the arrival of those who will help with the physical and emotional crisis. Negative convergence is fueled by our voyeuristic urge to look at tragedy; media and curiosity seekers fall into this category and impede the helping process. It is not uncommon for survivors to focus anger on the way some members of the media handle a crisis situation. An important rule, central to ethical practice: Do not violate the confidentiality of crisis survivors by repeating what they have said to reporters.

NOVA DEBRIEFING MODEL: GROUP CRISIS INTERVENTION

One way people seek to reestablish a sense of safety and security is by connecting with other survivors. This provides an opportunity for a very effective approach to debriefing that NOVA recommends: group crisis intervention. Instead of working with survivors one at a time, meet with them in groups, asking the same sorts of questions previously recommended, and recording the responses on a flip chart. Working with survivors in a group format provides several benefits: It is an efficient approach in a situation in which survivors and their loved ones may vastly outnumber the crisis responders; it is powerfully validating to survivors to find out that their reactions are shared by others (as in any other support group, listeners gain as much as those who verbalize their reactions);

and people connect to each other in the sharing process, building a support system that can continue to function through the long healing process to come. One caveat: The moderator of a group crisis intervention had better be prepared for the potential that group members may express rage at the law enforcement process or at reporters. It can be a breathtaking experience to be in a room full of hundreds of seriously angry people. Whatever the reaction, it will be strong and may be reinforced in its strength by the presence of others who are experiencing the same reaction. Despite its potential intensity, dealing with survivors in a group format is the recommended approach because of its effectiveness and efficiency (see Figure 34.1).

Because of the potential volatility of survivors' reactions, it is wise to seed the crowd with additional trained mental health workers. Should a survivor become overwhelmed with his or her reactions and run from the room, it is essential that someone follow and check on the person's welfare. This is a good time for some individual attention should the survivor be open to that possibility. In any case, attempts should be made to prevent agitated individuals from driving away until they are relatively calmer.

COMPASSION FATIGUE

The intensity of the survivor's reactions brings us to a final concern for crisis responders and another important way that crisis response work differs from counseling clients in an office setting. Any counselor in any setting can experience what has been called "compassion fatigue." There is something about working with people on the front line that exponentially increases the likelihood that crisis responders will absorb the pain of the people they are helping (Figley, 1995). It may be the intensity of the reactions, the rawness of the pain, or repeated and rapid exposure to people in agony that causes helpers to sustain damage that requires attention and healing. I was surprised by the strength of my own reaction to my initial work as a crisis responder; I spent several months depressed and ashamed of myself for that depression. My own NOVA training provided a cognitive structure that explained my reaction. It was the beginning of my own healing response.

Forward-thinking police and fire departments recognize the vital importance of debriefing their own initial responders to a crisis. Since my initial experience, I now recognize the symptoms and take care of myself by debriefing my experience with someone who understands crisis response work. I strongly advise novice crisis responders to get training and emotional support for their own healing and to talk to someone who is familiar with the debriefing process.

References

Figley, C. (Ed.). (1995). *Compassion fatigue: Coping with secondary traumatic stress disorder in those who treat the traumatized.* New York: Brunner/Mazel.

Goldman, L. (1996). *Breaking the silence: A guide to help children with complicated grief: Suicide, homicide, AIDS, violence, and abuse.* Muncie, IN: Accelerated Development.

Lieberman, R. (1999, November). *Crisis response training.* Paper presented at meeting of the Arkansas School Counselor Association at the University of Arkansas Cooperative Extension Service, Little Rock.

Young, M. (1998). *The community crisis response team training maunal.* Washington, DC: National Organization for Victim Assistance.

Additional Resources

Organizations

National Organization For Victim Assistance
1757 Park Road N.W.
Washington, DC 20010
(202) 232–6682
fax. (202) 462–2255
e-mail: nova@try-nova.org
www.access.digex.net/~nova

American Red Cross
Contact your local chapter (available in White Pages) or call
(800) 435-7669 (English)
(800) 257-7575 (Spanish)

Crisis Intervention: Information for Parents
National Association of School Psychologists
4340 East West Highway, Suite 402
Bethesda, MD 20814
(301) 657–0275
TDD (301) 657–4155
e-mail: NASP8455@AOL.COM

Books for Caregivers

Figley, Charles (Ed.). (1995). *Compassion fatigue: Coping with secondary traumatic stress disorder in those who treat the traumatized.* New York: Brunner/Mazel (ISBN 0876307594). This book focuses on those who provide therapy to victims of Posttraumatic Stress Disorder who themselves often become victim to secondary stress disorder as a result of helping or wanting to help a traumatized person.

Goldman, Linda. (1996). *Breaking the silence: A guide to help children with complicated grief: Suicide, homicide, AIDS, violence, and abuse.* Muncie, IN: Accelerated Development (ISBN 1560324341). Suicide, homicide, AIDS, violent crime, and abuse are each addressed at length, after which the author explains healthy ways to include children in all aspects of the death of a loved one. It includes a list of national support resources and an extensive annotated bibliography.

Kroen, William. (1996). *Helping children cope with the loss of a loved one: A guide for grownups.* Free Spirit (ISBN 1575420007). Using anecdotes about real children and their families, Kroen explains how different ages react to death and offers specific suggestions on how to guide children of different ages through the grieving process.

Books for Children

Buscaglia, Leo. (1983). *The fall of Freddie the leaf.* New York: Holt, Rinehart and Winston (ISBN 0805010645). A warm, wonderfully wise, and strikingly simple story about a leaf named Freddie. Both children and adults will be deeply touched by this inspiring fable illustrating the balance between life and death.

Mellonie, Bryon. (1983). *Lifetimes: The beautiful way to explain death to children.* New York: Bantam (ISBN 0553344021). This book tells about beginnings and endings and living in between. With large, wonderful illustrations, it talks about plants, animals, and people. It shows children that dying is as much a part of life as being born.

Varley, Susan. (1992). *Badger's parting gift.* Mulberry (ISBN 0688115187). All the woodland creatures love Old Badger, and when he dies, they are overwhelmed by their loss. Then they begin to remember, and through their memories, the animals find the strength to face the future with hope.

Books for Teenagers

Hipp, Earl. (1995). Help for the hard times: Getting through loss. Hazeldon. The author believes that the journey through loss begins in the heart. He discusses young people's experiences with loss, helps teens figure out how to go on after loss, and provides them with tools to grieve and ways to keep their losses from becoming overwhelming.

35 TREATMENT FOR VIOLENT CHILDREN AND ADOLESCENTS

Tony D. Crespi

Childhood violence is escalating. The Federal Bureau of Investigation (1999) observed, for instance, that approximately 4.64 million youth under the age of 21 are arrested in a single year, with problems ranging from murder to armed robbery. Garbarino and Kostelny (1997) note a significant change in patterns of family and community violence, with homicides in public view becoming more common. In schools, Goldstein and Conoley (1997) reported that approximately 11% of teachers have been assaulted by students, and an estimated 3 million students, faculty, and visitors to schools were reported as crime victims in a single school year. Elsewhere, Henggeler, Cunningham, Pickrel, Schoenwald, and Brondino (1996) noted that youth are caught in an expanding wake of violence. Today, every state in the country is coping with the problems of childhood violence. In this battle, professional counselors in schools, child guidance clinics, psychiatric hospitals, correctional facilities, and private practice are working to effect change. Still, the tide of violence seems to swell without precedent.

In this context, children are both more likely to be victims of violence and to actively participate in violence. This chapter examines violent behavior in children and adolescents and explores treatment components professionals can utilize to enhance intervention efforts. To date, research has supported counseling initiatives with violent children and adolescents. Of course, it needs to be understood that intervention efforts have generally been small in comparison to the magnitude of the problem. A theme emphasized in this chapter is that more funding is needed for interventions with violent youth.

BACKGROUND

On February 29, 2000, in one of what has become a growing number of tragedies, a 6-year-old boy in a first-grade classroom at Buell

Elementary School in Michigan took out a .32 caliber semiautomatic pistol and shot a fellow classmate. Five other children were in the classroom at the time and witnessed this shocking act of violence (Pfohl, 2000).

Tragically, the 6-year-old girl who was shot died. Of course, the implications of this tragedy continue to extend far past the loss of life. In a basic way, for the families of both children, for the children who witnessed the shooting, and indeed, for the community, life will never be the same: This senseless shooting marked the end of innocence. At Buell Elementary School, following the shooting, a team of school counselors, school social workers, school psychologists, community mental health professionals, a chaplain, and a state trooper began to work collaboratively with the school district and local community to effect change. Children and families received individual, group, and family counseling services. Collaboration and consultation were provided to teachers and the children and community were helped to cope with their grief and loss. In this fashion, mental health professionals thoughtfully addressed the stress and emotional reactions that accompany such tragic incidents and helped children and families establish a sense of emotional stability and emotional strength, rather than succumb to feelings of anxiety or hopelessness.

Tragically, this is not an isolated incident of violence. Fundamentally, childhood violence is reshaping the contours of society, with the implications of violent youth impacting every corner of society. School counselors, for instance, are coping with the fact that children are commonly victim to threats (and thefts) beginning as young as elementary school (Jenkins, 1997). At the same time, at the most extreme end of the continuum, Crespi and Rigazio-DiGilio (1996) noted more youth are actually engaged in homicidal behavior, with at least 30 juveniles sent to Death Row by the beginning of the past decade. More generally, 15 years ago, Elliot, Huizinga, and Morse (1986) observed that assaultive violence among adolescents may be as much as three times greater than current arrest statistics have suggested.

The importance of prevention efforts to reduce childhood violence is clear from conclusive evidence that indicates that adult criminal offenders with violent histories—a population that has reached more than 1 million inmates in state and federal correctional programs (Hammett, Gaiter, & Crawford, 1998)—begin to show dangerously aggressive behavior in childhood (Kemph, Braley, & Ciotola, 1997). Whatever the setting, counselors throughout the country are beginning to come to terms with childhood violence. To be effective, mental health counselors need to do more: to be involved in every facet of the problem, from home and school interventions to providing assistance to police officers and the courts.

COMPONENTS OF EFFECTIVE TREATMENT

The precipitating risk factors that promote violence in children are complex. After all, as a normal aspect of development, almost all children break certain rules, defying a curfew perhaps, or even engaging in shoplifting. Moffitt, Caspi, Dickson, Silva, and Stanton (1996) observed that only about 6% of adolescents refrain entirely from antisocial behavior. Still, the rise in serious aggression, assaultive behavior, arson, vandalism, and violence is growing beyond the boundaries of normal development (Kazdin, 1995).

Fortunately, not all children from the same family actually become violent. Further, there are different types of youth violence that can be distinguished by causes. Tolan and Guerra (1994) note four such causes:

- *Situational violence.* This involves specific situational variables, such as a weekend with unstructured time or exposure to drugs.
- *Relationship violence.* This involves interpersonal violence, such as in close intimate relationships between family members.
- *Predatory violence.* This involves purposeful violence, the intention being for gain, including such incidents as robberies or thefts.

- *Psychopathological violence.* This reflects violence that arises from pathological causes.

In essence, then, not all violent youth are the same. Counseling can help, and mental health professionals need to educate community leaders about the different ways that different treatment modalities can be helpful, and about those elements that distinguish effective from ineffective treatment.

Early Intervention Provides Developmental Assistance

Early intervention programs, which include family support, parent education, and interventions designed to enhance child rearing, seem to decrease juvenile delinquency (Zigler, Taussig, & Black, 1992). Yet, in spite of such data, there is a dearth of support for childhood and adolescent treatment.

The literature on developmental psychopathology in general has noted that antisocial and disruptive behaviors possess increasing stability with age (Zigler et al., 1992). Children who are victims of abuse, neglect, and violence experience significant adjustment problems. In fact, Garbarino and Kostelny (1997) observed that being a child in a stressful environment can lead to long-term mental health problems. Christenson, Hirsch, and Hurley (1997) noted that it is vital to work effectively with families of aggressive children and adolescents, as parenting factors are key determinants in developing aggressive behavior. Of course, this is not new data. More than 25 years ago, Corder, Ball, Haizlip, Rollins, and Beaumont (1976), when comparing and contrasting 30 violent adolescents involved in murder, provided evidence of the importance of addressing family disorganization, marital conflict, parental brutality, and parental alcoholism with violent children.

From an outcome perspective, the families of violent children need to address basic family issues, including parental roles and rules, parental drinking, exposure to violence, and problem resolution strategies. Ideally, counselors need to encourage agencies, clinics, and schools to develop early intervention initiatives that can incorporate these facets into community and agency programming. Done in this way, the cycle of violence can be disrupted.

Schools as Comprehensive Counseling Sites

Even though for more than a decade children have been referred to as one of the most neglected populations in mental health, school-based counseling services for children and adolescents remain below necessary levels (Tuma, 1989). School counselors and school psychologists, two key providers of mental health services for children, are often restricted from providing counseling because of the demands on their time to provide other services. School counselors often have excessively large caseloads and are delegated to handle class scheduling and college advising rather than individual and group counseling to at-risk youth. Similarly, school psychologists often are preoccupied with psychometric duties as opposed to providing direct services. The result is that these mental health counselors are not able to provide necessary primary and secondary prevention services. To maximally help children, school-based mental health personnel need to be given sufficient time, support, and encouragement to develop and provide individual, group, and family interventions.

Mandated Counseling in Institutional Settings

Although the public often assumes that psychiatric and juvenile justice programs for children offer intensive counseling and psychotherapy, the reality is that the typical psychiatric program often emphasizes behavior management interventions to the detriment of counseling services. At the same time, correctional facilities usually operate on a "just desserts" model that minimizes treatment. If children and adolescents are to be maximally helped, however, the full benefit of counseling needs to be emphasized. Therapeutic treatment with children has been demonstrated to be as effective as that conducted with adults, but institutionalized children are less likely to receive such treatment.

Garbarino (1998) noted that institutional settings for young people need to be in places that encourage reflection as well as discipline: "This is what the most traumatized violent youths need, because all that is left for them is to go inward to their deepest core and upward, to make touch with the grandest spiritual realities that they can discover and as a result grow in wisdom in ways that were previously unavailable to them" (p. 366).

Family Counseling

The fact that violent youth come from violent, abusive households (Lewis et al., 1988) appears inadequately understood. Understanding the implications of continued exposure to and involvement in family strife may be a key to disrupting the cycle of violence. Juveniles who kill, for example, have been described for approximately 25 years as emotionally disturbed youth from troubled families, their parents often described as oppressive, violent, or neglectful (e.g., Corder et al., 1976; Sorrells, 1977). Although these data clearly are not new, the implications for adolescent treatment have remained largely unaddressed.

In many ways, children are products of their families (Crespi & Rigazio-DiGilio, 1996). Violent delinquents, in contrast to less violent delinquents, possess a history of familial abuse and violence. Specifically:

- Father figures are typically described as absent, distant, or passive.
- Mothers are typically dominant, overprotective, or seductive.
- Primitive violence is frequently expressed in the home.
- Children typically experience a sense of abandonment and distrust.
- Families are frequently marked by turmoil.
- Homicidal adolescents are frequently mistreated.
- Children frequently experience physical abuse.

- Mothers are frequently seen as afraid of the children. (Crespi, 1996; Crespi & Rigazio-DiGilio, 1996)

Family counseling initiatives, including parent education programs, conflict resolution workshops, and anger management classes, can be helpful in addressing these issues. Although not all insurance carriers readily reimburse providers for these services, mental health treatment initiatives emphasizing family counseling can be invaluable. Children, after all, model what is seen in the home: Violence begets violence. Yet, with treatment, the possibility exists of changing the developmental trajectory.

Violence Prevention Programs

Violence prevention programs, particularly targeted at elementary-age students, seem effective in disrupting the further development of aggression. Aber, Jones, Brown, Chaudry, and Samples (1998) recently found, for example, that a violence prevention initiative with children at risk for future aggression produced notable results when compared to an untreated sample. The 12-year-old Resolving Conflict Creatively Program described by these investigators has been successful in New York schools and is one exemplary model of a well-developed curriculum that can be used by counselors in multiple settings.

Partnerships with Police Departments

Historically, police and mental health professionals have not worked as partners. However, when the two create partnerships, the results can be positive. Such partnerships can foster early interventions with victims, offer opportunities to more readily intervene with perpetrators, and disrupt negative psychological patterns that can occur without a timely response.

The New Haven/Yale Child Study Center Model, also referred to as the New Haven Child Development-Community Policing Program, is a unique program where local police have been working collaboratively with mental health professionals to more effectively help children and families exposed to violence (e.g., Marans, Berkowitz, & Cohen, 1998). The model uses five components:

1. A seminar for police officers on developmental principles.
2. A fellowship linking police with clinical services.
3. A fellowship orienting clinicians to police practices.
4. A consultation service for police, children, and families.
5. A continuing case conference for both police and clinicians.

Developing linkages between mental health professionals and police offers extraordinary possibilities to reduce youth violence.

Social Skills Training

Social skills training programs have had success with at-risk children. The Responding in Peaceful and Positive Ways (RIPP) program, for instance, is one example of a social skills curriculum for young children (Meyer & Farrell, 1998). Designed for students in Richmond, Virginia, the RIPP program uses environmental, intrapersonal, and behavioral objectives delivered through a comprehensive curriculum that uses role playing intended to provide practice opportunities for refining new social skills. The program has 25 sessions using an adult to teach information, attitudes, and skills promoting nonviolence. The model teaches seven steps to reducing violence:

1. Stop.
2. Calm down.
3. Identify the problems and your feelings.
4. Decide your options.
5. Do it.
6. Look back.
7. Evaluation.

Multifaceted Interventions

No single intervention strategy can address all the types of violence or all the types of children who are prone to or victims of violence. Teens who torture other teens represent one type of violence; firesetting represents yet another. For the clinician of the future, the question will be which intervention, for which person, at which moment in time. The knowledge base needed to be helpful, then, is complex. In essence, there are different types of aggressive and antisocial behavior as well as different groups of children who display such behaviors. Consequently, complex treatment and intervention designs will be most effective. Unfortunately, they are more expensive, and some have noted that there is a retreat from addressing the needs of children and families (Roberts, Alexander, & Davis, 1991).

Researchers and practitioners, on the other hand, have suggested a number of effective interventions that can be very helpful with aggressive and violent youth. Ruhl and Berlinghoff (1992) reviewed 15 studies outlining interventions to improve academic performances in children with behavior disorders. Miller (1994) explored family-based interventions for managing childhood aggression, and Patterson, Capaldi, and Bank (1991) and Webster-Stratton (1993) underscored the value of creating an effective home-school partnership with clear school-based interventions for treating childhood aggression as it generalizes into multiple settings.

All in all, highly aggressive children and adolescents can be treated. Some treatments can occur at home, others in school, and yet others in a range of community settings. Oestmann and Walker (1997) note that although aggressive students can pose a serious threat, intervention can prevent more restrictive placement. On the other hand, funding and resources are necessary to deliver the appropriate treatments.

Program Evaluation

Community and school administrators need to be aware of which programs for violent youth are more effective. Retribution programs, for example, where offenders pay fines for their crimes, are generally ineffective (Henggeler, 1989). In contrast, interventions targeted toward preventing precursors to delinquency have been described as effective. School-based mental health services have demonstrated positive gains in reducing antisocial behavior. Despite such success, primary prevention programs, early intervention programs, and psychoeducational initiatives addressing violence are still not widespread in or out of schools (Murphy & Cascardi, 1993).

Mental health counselors and academicians can be key agents in helping community leaders monitor issues by bringing basic methodological expertise to the fore. Communities need to use realistic data in assessing the magnitude of problems and in monitoring effective intervention programs. Mental health counselors need to educate leaders to the importance of using accurate process and outcome evaluation models. Effective data collection can help correct poor intervention models. Sometimes, some interventions are just inadvisable, or even destructive; strip searches are one illustration of an intervention that has yielded negative results (Hyman et al., 1997). Mental health counselors need to help communities learn when and where limits need to be exerted with interventions for children.

SUMMARY

Mental health professionals need to appreciate both the complexity of childhood violence as well as the difficulty developing and receiving support for comprehensive counseling initiatives. It is important to continually keep in mind the important role early counseling initiatives can play in helping violent children break the cycle of violence. Specifically, counselors should:

- Consult with administrators about the importance of providing individual, group, and family counseling programs.

- Provide anger management, behavior management, and parent education classes for parents, community agencies, and schools.
- Consult with community leaders about developing alternative programs for adolescents.
- With colleagues, develop peer supervision groups to discuss the complexities of ethical clinical treatment issues.
- Build professional relationships with local law enforcement agencies surrounding shared interests and common issues.
- Encourage the development of violence prevention programs with elementary-age children.
- Foster social skills training to develop resiliency.

Finally, as has been noted throughout this chapter, mental health professionals need to be advocates for funding the types of treatment programs that have shown some effectiveness in the literature and that can be evaluated in future research.

References

Aber, J.L., Jones, S.M., Brown, J.L., Chaudry, N., & Samples, F. (1998). Resolving conflict creatively: Evaluating the developmental effects of a school-based violence prevention program in neighborhood and classroom context. *Development and Psychopathology, 10,* 187–213.

Christenson, S.L., Hirsch, J.A., & Hurley, C.M. (1997). Families with aggressive children and adolescents. In A.P. Goldstein & J.C. Conoley (Eds.), *School violence intervention: A practical handbook* (pp. 325–365). New York: Guilford Press.

Corder, B.F., Ball, B.C., Haizlip, T.M., Rollins, R., & Beaumont, R. (1976). Adolescent parricide: A comparison with other adolescent murder. *American Journal of Psychiatry, 133,* 957–961.

Crespi, T.D. (1996). Violent children and adolescents: Facing the treatment crisis in child and family interaction. *Family Therapy, 23,* 43–50.

Crespi, T.D., & Rigazio-DiGilio, S.A. (1996). Adolescent homicide and family pathology: Implications for research and treatment with adolescents. *Adolescence, 31,* 353–367.

Elliot, D., Huizinga, D., & Morse, B. (1986). Self-reported violent offending: A descriptive analysis of juvenile violent offenders and their offending careers. *Journal of Interpersonal Violence, 1,* 472–513.

Federal Bureau of Investigation. (1999, May). *Uniform crime reports for the United States.* Washington, DC: U.S. Department of Justice.

Garbarino, J. (1998). Children in a violent world: A metaphysical perspective. *Family and Conciliation Courts Review, 36,* 360–367.

Garbarino, J., & Kostelny, K. (1997). Coping with the consequences of community violence. In A.P. Goldstein & J.C. Conoley (Eds.), *School violence intervention: A practical handbook* (pp. 366–384). New York: Guilford Press.

Goldstein, A.P., & Conoley, J.C. (1997). Student aggression: Current status. In A.P. Goldstein & J.C. Conoley (Eds.), *School violence intervention: A practical handbook* (pp. 3–19). New York: Guilford Press.

Hammett, T.M., Gaiter, J.L., & Crawford, C. (1998). Reaching seriously at-risk populations: Health interventions in criminal justice settings. *Health Education and Behavior, 25,* 99–120.

Henggeler, S.W. (1989). *Delinquency in adolescence.* Newbury Park, CA: Sage.

Henggeler, S.W., Cunningham, P.B., Pickrel, S.G., Schoenwald, S.K., & Brondino, M.J. (1996). Multisystemic therapy: An effective violence prevention approach for serious juvenile offenders. *Journal of Adolescence, 19,* 47–61.

Hyman, I., Weiler, E., Perone, D., Romano, L., Britton, G., & Shanock, A. (1997). Victims and victimizers: The two faces of school violence. In A.P. Goldstein, & J.C. Conoley (Eds.), *School violence intervention: A practical handbook* (pp. 426–459). New York: Guilford Press.

Jenkins, P.H. (1997). School delinquency and the social bond. *Journal of Research in Crime and Delinquency, 34,* 337–368.

Kazdin, A.E. (1995). *Conduct disorders in childhood and adolescence* (2nd ed.). Thousand Oaks, CA: Sage.

Kemph, J.P., Braley, R.O., & Ciotola, P.V. (1997). Description of an outpatient psychiatric population in a youthful offender's prison. *Journal of the American Academy of Psychiatry and Law, 25,* 149–160.

Lewis, D.O., Pincus, J.H., Bard, B., Richardson, E., Prichep, L.S., Feldman, M., & Yeager, C. (1988). Neuropsychiatric, psychoeducational, and family characteristics of 14 juveniles condemned to death in the United States. *American Journal of Psychiatry, 145,* 584–589.

Marans, S., Berkowitz, S.J., & Cohen, D.J. (1998). Police and mental health professionals: Collaborative responses to the impact of violence on children and families. *The Child Psychiatrist in the Community, 7,* 635–651.

Meyer, A.L., & Farrell, A.D. (1998). Social skills training to promote resilience in urban sixth-grade students: One product of an action research strategy to prevent youth violence in high-risk environments. *Education and Treatment of Children, 21,* 461–488.

Miller, G.E. (1994). Enhancing family-based interventions for managing childhood aggression and anger. In M. Furlong & D. Smith (Eds.), *Anger, hostility, and aggression: Assessment, prevention, and intervention strategies for youth* (pp. 83–116). Brandon, VT: Clinical Psychology Press.

Moffitt, T.E., Caspi, A., Dickson, N., Silva, P., & Stanton, W. (1996). Childhood-onset versus adolescent-onset antisocial conduct problems in males: Natural history from ages 3 to 18 years. *Development and Psychopathology, 8,* 399–424.

Murphy, C.M., & Cascardi, M. (1993). Psychological aggression and abuse in marriage. In R.L. Hampton, T.P. Gullotta, G.R. Adams, E.H. Potter, & R.P. Weissberg (Eds.), *Family violence: Prevention and treatment* (pp. 86–112). Newbury Park, CA: Sage.

Oestmann, J., & Walker, M.B. (1997). Interventions for aggressive students in a public-school-based day treatment program. In A.P. Goldstein & J.C. Conoley (Eds.), *School violence intervention: A practical handbook* (pp. 160–188). New York: Guilford Press.

Patterson, G.R., Capaldi, D., & Bank, L. (1991). An early starter model for predicting delinquency. In D. Pepler & K.H. Rubin (Eds.), *The development and treatment of childhood aggression* (pp. 139–168). Hillsdale, NJ: Erlbaum.

Pfohl, B. (2000, June). Children shooting children: Another school tragedy. *NASP Communique, 28,* p. 8.

Roberts, M.C., Alexander, K., & Davis, N.J. (1991). Children's rights to physical and mental health care: A case for advocacy. *Journal of Clinical Child Psychology, 20,* 18–27.

Ruhl, K.L., & Berlinghoff, D.H. (1992). Research on improving behaviorally disordered students' academic performance: A review of the literature. *Behavioral Disorders, 17,* 178–190.

Sorrells, J.M. (1977). Kids who kill. *Crime and Delin-quency, 23*, 312–320.

Tolan, P.H., & Guerra, N. (1994). *What works in reducing adolescent violence: An empirical review of the field.* Boulder, CO: Center for the Study and Prevention of Violence.

Tuma, J.M. (1989). Mental health services for children: The state of the art. *American Psychologist, 44*, 188–199.

Webster-Stratton, C. (1993). Strategies for helping early school-aged children with ODD and CD: The importance of home-school partnerships. *School Psychology Review, 22*, 437–457.

Zigler, E., Taussig, C., & Black, K. (1992). Early childhood intervention: A promising preventative for juvenile delinquency. *American Psychologist, 47*, 997–1006.

36   RESPONDING TO SURVIVORS OF SEXUAL ASSAULT

Patricia Frazier, Jason Steward, Ty Tashiro, and Susan Rosenberger

Approximately 20% of women will be raped in their lifetime (Koss, 1993). Given that an assault history is associated with increased risk of mental and physical health problems, the prevalence of sexual assault in clinical samples is even higher. Thus, knowledge regarding the assessment and treatment of rape survivors is important for clinicians.

This chapter provides a concise summary of research on the effects of adult sexual assault and rape (terms we use interchangeably), factors associated with recovery, and the efficacy of various treatment approaches. Because the vast majority of rape survivors are women, we focus on the assessment and treatment of female survivors. We also include some research on Posttraumatic Stress Disorder (PTSD) more generally, as PTSD is the most common response to sexual assault and because the literature on PTSD is much larger than that on rape. Following this review, we offer specific recommendations regarding the

assessment and treatment of rape survivors. Given space constraints, only new research findings are cited; review articles are listed at the end that interested readers can consult for additional information.

RESEARCH FINDINGS

Effects of Sexual Assault

PTSD is one of the most common responses to having been sexually assaulted. The primary symptoms of PTSD are reexperiencing the event, avoiding reminders of the event, and increased arousal (*DSM-IV*; APA, 2000). The majority of sexual assault survivors meet diagnostic criteria for PTSD in the first few months postassault and approximately half continue to have PTSD one year postassault. Studies comparing PTSD rates across events indicate that rape survivors are more likely than survivors of other traumas to meet diagnostic criteria for PTSD. In addition, PTSD has a high comorbidity rate with other disorders among survivors of rape and other traumas.

Given this high comorbidity rate, it is not surprising that research has documented several other psychological and physical symptoms that are more common in rape survivors than in comparison groups. Depression is among the most prevalent of these, with up to almost half of survivors diagnosed with a depressive disorder. Relatedly, survivors are at higher risk for suicidal thoughts and attempts. Survivors also are at increased risk of experiencing fear, anxiety, negative changes in their beliefs about themselves and the world, sexual dysfunction, social adjustment problems, eating disorders, substance abuse, and physical health problems. Survivors also engage in more health risk behaviors, such as smoking (Brener, McMahon, Warren, & Douglas, 1999).

Despite these problems, many survivors also report positive changes in their lives. The most frequent of these are increased empathy for other survivors, greater appreciation of life, greater recognition of their own strength, and increased assertiveness. These self-reported positive changes tend to be associated with lower distress levels (Frazier, Conlon, & Glaser, 2000).

Factors Associated with Postrape Symptoms

Although survivors are at greater risk for experiencing various psychological and physical problems, there also is great variability in the extent to which survivors are affected by an assault. Knowledge of these factors also is essential to developing a thorough assessment and treatment plan.

Survivor Characteristics. Factors reliably associated with greater postrape distress include prior victimization, which is very common, and prerape psychological problems. Data regarding demographic characteristics are mixed, although there is some evidence that older survivors and those of lower socioeconomic status experience more distress. Research examining differences in postrape distress among women of different ethnocultural groups has not yielded consistent results (Neville & Heppner, 1999).

Assault Characteristics. A recent meta-analysis of factors predicting distress levels following interpersonal violence identified several assault-related factors associated with greater distress, including, in order of importance, subjective distress associated with the event, perceived life threat, and greater force (Weaver & Clum, 1995). Perhaps relatedly, greater dissociation or detachment during a traumatic event is a risk factor for later distress. Greater distress immediately *following* the trauma also is associated with more persistent symptoms.

One assault factor that tends not to be associated with distress levels is the relationship between the survivor and assailant. Specifically, most studies show no differences in distress levels between survivors of stranger and acquaintance rape.

Postassault Reactions. Postassault reactions of the survivor include the attribution made about the cause of the rape and strategies used to cope with the assault. In regard to attributions, several studies show that survivors who engage in more self-blame report more distress. Blaming external factors, such as the rapist or society, also tends to be associated with greater distress. In general, focusing on the past and why the rape occurred is not helpful. Rather, focusing on what one can do in the present to help oneself recover seems more useful (Frazier, 2000). Research on coping strategies suggests that avoidant or disengagement strategies, such as staying home and withdrawing, are associated with more distress. This is consistent with the theory that emotional engagement is necessary for processing the trauma and for recovery.

Postassault reactions from others in the survivor's environment also have been studied. Negative reactions (e.g., blaming) tend to be more correlated with symptoms than are positive reactions (e.g., validation). That is, negative reactions hurt more than positive reactions help. Fortunately, negative reactions are less common than positive reactions, although they do occur, particularly from the police, physicians, and clergy. The effects of these negative "institutional reactions" appear to be mitigated by sustained mental health counseling (i.e., more than one or two visits).

Treatment Efficacy

Much of the research on the treatment of rape trauma focuses on the amelioration of PTSD, as it is the most common response to rape. Thus, below, we review treatments for PTSD, with a specific focus on treatments assessed among samples of rape survivors.

A recent meta-analysis of treatments for PTSD following various traumas revealed that the improvement rate for participants in psychotherapy was 62% compared to 38% for those not receiving psychotherapy (Sherman, 1998). Cognitive-behavioral treatments have received the most research attention and are the treatment of choice among PTSD experts. We briefly describe the three recommended cognitive-behavioral treatments for rape survivors—exposure, anxiety management, and cognitive therapy—and describe the evidence regarding their efficacy.

Exposure treatment consists of the repeated emotional recounting of the traumatic memory (imaginal exposure) or confronting feared situations that have become associated with the trauma (in vivo exposure). The client and therapist create a hierarchy of images/events and the client is exposed to increasingly distressing images/events until they no longer create anxiety. Exposure therapy is designed to activate trauma memories to change their pathological aspects. Factors associated with more successful exposure therapy include high levels of emotional engagement (i.e., fear, anxiety), habituation between sessions, and creation of a more coherent trauma narrative (Amir, Stafford, Freshman, & Foa, 1998; Jaycox, Foa, & Morral, 1998).

Anxiety management focuses on teaching clients skills to reduce anxiety when it occurs. One of the most common anxiety management programs for rape survivors is Stress Inoculation Training (SIT) (Meichenbaum, 1974). Therapists begin SIT by teaching clients that fear and anxiety are learned responses that may occur in three channels: physical, behavioral, and cognitive. Then, clients are taught skills for dealing with anxiety in each channel, such as progressive relaxation (physical), role playing (behavioral), and thought stopping (cognitive).

The goals of *cognitive therapy* are to identify dysfunctional cognitions and replace them with new, more adaptive cognitions. The specific cognitions associated with PTSD in rape survivors include negative thoughts about the self (e.g., incompetence) and the world (e.g., dangerousness) and self-blame. Similarly, cognitive processing therapy, described below, focuses on maladaptive cognitions about oneself and others in five areas: safety, trust, power, esteem, and intimacy (Resick & Schnicke, 1993).

Several studies have examined the efficacy of these treatment approaches for survivors of rape and other traumas (see Foa & Rothbaum, 1998, for a review). Most studies assess individual therapy with nonrecent survivors suffering from chronic PTSD. In studies with rape survivors, both exposure and stress inoculation have been found to be more effective than no or minimal treatment comparison groups. A few studies have shown exposure to be more effective than SIT. Somewhat surprisingly, the combination of SIT and exposure does not appear to produce better results. Although cognitive therapy is effective with survivors of other traumas, no studies have examined the effectiveness of cognitive therapy alone with rape survivors. Cognitive processing therapy, which includes psychoeducation, exposure, and cognitive restructuring, has shown some efficacy, however. More data are needed to determine whether one treatment is superior to others, if combined treatments are more effective (including combinations of psychotherapy and medications), if some treatments are more useful with certain clients, and if different treatments are more effective when implemented at various stages of the therapeutic process. Systematic comparisons of therapy outcomes among PTSD survivors from different cultures also are needed.

SPECIFIC RECOMMENDATIONS

Assessment Recommendations

Trauma Screening. Counselors may work with clients who seek therapy to deal with the aftermath of a recent or nonrecent assault. However, women who have been assaulted may not immediately disclose the assault for various reasons: It is painful, they may not see the relation between the assault and their symptoms, they may fear being blamed, or they may not identify the experience as rape. Therefore, routine screening for traumatic events, including sexual assault, is widely recommended by trauma experts, particularly among clients with depression, anxiety, and substance abuse problems, as these often co-occur with PTSD. Prior trauma history also should be assessed with clients who disclose a specific trauma such as a rape. Screening questions should be behaviorally specific, standardized, and nonleading to reduce both under- and overreporting. Several good brief trauma screening measures are available, including the Traumatic Stress Schedule (Norris, 1992), the Trauma Assessment for Adults (Resnick, 1996), and the Stressful Life Events Screening Questionnaire (Goodman, Corcoran, Turner, Yuan, & Green, 1998).

Clinical Interview. Although clinical interviews are standard procedure in many settings, we briefly outline here some specific areas to assess in working with rape survivors. These include the previously summarized risk and protective factors for postrape distress, such as characteristics of the survivor (e.g., prior psychological functioning), the assault (e.g., objective characteristics, such as injuries, and appraisals, such as perceived life threat), and postassault reactions (e.g., coping strategies, social support, immediate distress levels). The interview also should contain an open-ended assessment of presenting problems and symptoms, including both positive and negative life changes. Foa and Rothbaum (1998) include a sample Assault Information and History Interview covering preassault, assault, and postassault information that they recommend completing with the client during the first treatment session (following an initial evaluation).

Symptom Measures. It also is recommended that the clinical interview be augmented with standardized measures of baseline symptoms, which are essential for measuring progress. Several brief measures of PTSD symptoms are available, such as the Posttraumatic Diagnostic Scale (PTDS) that yields a PTSD diagnosis and a symptom severity score (Foa, Cashman, Jaycox, & Perry, 1997). If indicated, this can be followed by a structured diagnostic interview such as the Structured Clinical Interview for *DSM* (SCID) (First, Spitzer, Gibbon, & Williams, 1996), which is considered the "gold standard" for PTSD assessment. Given that rape survivors are at risk for experiencing various other disorders, additional measures also should be included in the assessment protocol. The Minnesota Multiphasic Personality Inventory (MMPI-2) (Butcher, Dahlstrom, Graham, Tellegen, & Kaemmer, 1989) is useful because it assesses a wide range of symptoms and contains two PTSD scales. The validity scales also are helpful when under- or overreporting of symptoms may be an issue. The Symptom Checklist-90-Revised (SCL-90-R) (Derogatis, 1977) also assesses a wide range of symptoms, and two PTSD scales can be scored from it. Foa, Ehlers, Clark, Tolin, and Orsillo (1999) also have developed a measure of postrape cognitions (e.g., self-blame) that may be useful to include in the assessment battery.

Special Considerations. There are several other issues that should be taken into account when assessing rape survivors. First, informed consent requires that clients be made aware that, although the assessment may be very painful, confronting the trauma is essential for recovery. To foster a sense of safety and control, the process should be explained in detail and clients should be told to inform the counselor if it is too upsetting. When describing the assault itself, Foa and Rothbaum (1998) recommend allowing the client to tell her story without much interruption. Second, hearing clients' stories may also be very difficult for the counselor. It is important to have an accepting attitude without under- or overreacting. Counselors should be aware of their own reactions and ensure that the pacing of the interview reflects the client's needs, not their own. Third, avoidance of traumatic memories may lead clients to underreport traumatic events and symptoms. In addition, they may not remember all events or all parts of each event. Although this is important to keep in mind, these lapses can be difficult to identify, and clients' perceptions of events are more important than factual accuracy. Openly discussing and normalizing fears may help clients overcome avoidance. There is also the possibility of events and symptoms being overreported, particularly when secondary gain may be an issue. Fourth, because they have experienced a trauma involving the intentional infliction of harm, rape survivors may have difficulty trusting the counselor. Thus, it is important to provide a safe environment and to be reassuring and nonjudgmental. Finally, a client's ethnocultural background can affect both the reporting and experiencing of traumatic events and symptoms. The *DSM-IV* (APA, 2000) lists several culture-bound syndromes, some of which involve responses to trauma (e.g., attaques de nervios), and contains guidelines for cultural formulation.

Summary. The assessment protocol should include a clinical interview covering preassault functioning, assault characteristics, and postassault reactions; a brief screening measure for past traumatic events; brief measures of PTSD and other relevant symptoms; and a structured diagnostic interview. Although assessment procedures will vary across settings, the general recommendation is that assessment take place over two sessions. Recommendations vary regarding the order in which various issues should be assessed, but, because building trust and rapport are essential, it makes sense to begin with less-threatening background material in an initial assessment. Clients can complete self-report symptom measures after the first session; these can indicate whether a structured diagnostic interview

also is indicated. More extensive details on the assault itself can be gathered in the first treatment session.

Treatment Recommendations

Treatments of Choice. Based on the available empirical evidence and expert consensus guidelines, psychotherapy (versus pharmacotherapy) is considered the firstline treatment of choice for PTSD. Among psychotherapies, exposure therapy is preferred because more studies have shown it to be effective, it is easier for counselors to implement and clients to follow, and it is thought to yield the quickest results. The recommended level of care for the initial phase of therapy is one-hour, weekly individual sessions (slightly longer sessions for exposure) for approximately three months (Foa, Davidson, et al., 1999).

Although exposure therapy is the treatment of choice, several other factors should be considered in choosing treatment approaches. First, the treatment chosen should reflect the primary symptoms presented by the client: Exposure therapy is recommended for intrusive thoughts and flashbacks, anxiety management for arousal symptoms, and cognitive therapy for guilt and shame. Second, the choice of treatment strategies will depend on the presence of any comorbid disorders. For example, cognitive therapy is recommended for comorbid mood, anxiety, and personality disorders; anxiety management also is recommended for comorbid anxiety disorders. The timing of treatment also depends on the severity of any comorbid disorders. Generally, if the comorbid disorders are mild, they can be treated simultaneously with PTSD; if they are severe, they should be treated first. Third, treatment choices depend on the severity of the PTSD. For moderate to severe PTSD, medications should be considered as an adjunct to therapy. The medications of choice are the selective serotonin reuptake inhibitors (SSRIs), commonly used as antidepressants. Finally, client preference and contraindications for exposure also should be taken into account. Obstacles to exposure include extreme anger, emotional numbing, and overwhelming anxiety (Jaycox & Foa, 1996). In such cases, it may be best to begin with SIT, which is rated by experts as the safest form of treatment. Jaycox and Foa provide additional suggestions.

Improving Compliance. Noncompliance is likely to be an issue when treating rape survivors because of the tendency to avoid confronting the fear associated with the assault. Because compliance and regular attendance are associated with better outcomes, it generally is recommended that special measures be taken to enhance compliance. First, a strong therapeutic alliance is essential and can be facilitated by adopting a nonjudgmental and empathic attitude, being comfortable hearing traumatic memories, expressing confidence in the treatment process, and normalizing the client's reactions to the assault. A second way to increase compliance is to educate the client regarding the process of therapy, the effects of traumatic events, the rationale for the chosen treatment approach, and the importance of persevering through the difficult points of therapy. The treatment rationale may need to be reviewed periodically. Foa and Rothbaum (1998) provide excellent material that can be given to clients to facilitate this process. A third recommendation is to involve a significant other early in the process. Clients may need both emotional and logistical support to complete therapy. Significant others also may need to be educated about trauma and trauma therapy, either through written materials or by attending one session. Support groups for partners may be another option. Finally, given the frequency of avoidance, experts recommend more flexibility in scheduling and no-show/cancellation policies when working with rape survivors.

Lack of Improvement. If a client is not showing improvement with psychotherapy (less than 25% reduction in symptoms), expert guidelines are to add medications or switch to a different treatment modality. If there is a partial response (25% to 75% reduction in symptoms), experts recommend adding medication or another therapy technique (versus switching techniques). In guidelines specific to the

treatment of rape survivors, Foa and Rothbaum (1998) recommend beginning with nine weeks of therapy and adding three weeks if 70% improvement in symptoms has not yet been achieved.

References

American Psychiatric Association. (2000). *Diagnostic and statistical manual of mental disorders* (4th ed., text rev.). Washington, DC: Author.

Amir, N., Stafford, J., Freshman, M., & Foa, E. (1998). Relationship between trauma narratives and trauma pathology. *Journal of Traumatic Stress, 11,* 385–392.

Ballenger, J., Davidson, J., Lecrubier, Y., Nutt, D., Foa, E., Kessler, R., McFarlane, A., & Shalev, A. (2000). Consensus statement on posttraumatic stress disorder from the International Consensus Group on Depression and Anxiety. *Journal of Clinical Psychiatry, 61*(Suppl. 5), 60–66.

Brener, N., McMahon, P., Warren, C., & Douglas, K. (1999). Forced sexual intercourse and associated health-risk behaviors among female college students in the United States. *Journal of Consulting and Clinical Psychology, 67,* 252–259.

Briere, J. (1997). *Psychological assessment of adult posttraumatic states.* Washington, DC: American Psychological Association.

Butcher, J., Dahlstrom, W., Graham, J., Tellegen, A., & Kaemmer, B. (1989). *Minnesota Multiphasic Personality Inventory-2 (MMPI-2): Manual for administration and scoring.* Minneapolis: University of Minnesota Press.

Carlson, E. (1997). *Trauma assessments: A clinician's guide.* New York: Guilford Press.

Derogatis, L. (1977). *Manual for the SCL-90.* Baltimore: Johns Hopkins School of Medicine.

First, M., Spitzer, R., Gibbon, M., & Williams, J. (1996). *Structured Clinical Interview for Axis I DSM-IV disorders, clinician version (SCID-CV).* Washington, DC: American Psychiatric Press.

Foa, E., Cashman, L., Jaycox, L., & Perry, K. (1997). The validation of a self-report measure of posttraumatic stress disorder: The posttraumatic diagnostic scale. *Psychological Assessment, 9,* 445–451.

Foa, E., Davidson, J., Frances, A., Culpepper, L., Ross, R., & Ross, D. (1999). The expert consensus guideline series: Treatment of posttraumatic stress disorder. *Journal of Clinical Psychiatry, 60*(Suppl. 16), 4–76.

Foa, E., Ehlers, A., Clark, D., Tolin, D., & Orsillo, S. (1999). The Posttraumatic Cognitions Inventory

(PTCI): Development and validation. *Psychological Assessment, 11*, 303–314.

Foa, E., & Rothbaum, B. (1998). *Treating the trauma of rape: Cognitive-behavioral therapy for PTSD.* New York: Guilford Press.

Frazier, P. (2000). The role of attributions and perceived control in recovery from rape. *Journal of Personal and Interpersonal Loss, 5*, 203–225.

Frazier, P., Conlon, A., & Glaser, T. (2000). *Positive and negative life changes following sexual assault.* Manuscript submitted for publication.

Goodman, L., Corcoran, C., Turner, K., Yuan, N., & Green, B. (1998). Assessing traumatic event exposure: General issues and preliminary findings for the stressful life events screening questionnaire. *Journal of Traumatic Stress, 11*, 521–542.

Jaycox, L., & Foa, E. (1996). Obstacles in implementing exposure therapy for PTSD: Case discussion and practical solutions. *Clinical Psychology and Psychotherapy, 3*, 176–184.

Jaycox, L., Foa, E., & Morral, A. (1998). Influence of emotional engagement and habituation on exposure therapy for PTSD. *Journal of Consulting and Clinical Psychology, 66*, 185–192.

Koss, M. (1993). Detecting the scope of rape: A review of prevalence research methods. *Journal of Interpersonal Violence, 8*, 198–222.

Koss, M., Goodman, L., Browne, A., Fitzgerald, L., Keita, G., & Russo, N. (1994). *No safe haven: Male violence against women at home, at work, and in the community.* Washington, DC: American Psychological Association.

Meichenbaum, D. (1974). *Cognitive-behavior modification.* Morristown, NJ: General Learning Press.

Neville, H., & Heppner, M. (1999). Contextualizing rape: Reviewing sequelae and proposing a culturally inclusive ecological model of sexual assault recovery. *Applied and Preventive Psychology, 8*, 41–62.

Norris, F. (1992). Epidemiology of trauma: Frequency and impact of different potentially traumatic events on different demographic groups. *Journal of Consulting and Clinical Psychology, 60*, 409–418.

Resick, P., & Schnicke, M. (1993). *Cognitive processing therapy for rape victims: A treatment manual.* Newbury Park, CA: Sage.

Resnick, H. (1996). Psychometric review of "Trauma assessment for adults." In B.H. Stamm (Ed.), *Measurement of stress, trauma, and adaptation.* Lutherville, MD: Sidran Press.

Sherman, J. (1998). Effects of psychotherapeutic treatments for PTSD: A meta-analysis of controlled clinical trials. *Journal of Traumatic Stress, 11*, 413–435.

Weaver, T., & Clum, G. (1995). Psychological distress associated with interpersonal violence: A meta-analysis. *Clinical Psychology Review, 15*, 115–140.

Additional Resources

There are numerous resources available for counselors wanting further information on responding to sexual assault survivors. One of the best is a book by Foa and Rothbaum (1998) entitled *Treating the Trauma of Rape.* Their step-by-step guidelines for conducting various forms of cognitive-behavioral treatment for rape survivors are very helpful. Resick and Schnicke's (1993) treatment manual is a step-by-step guide for cognitive processing therapy. Also very useful, especially for selecting treatment strategies, are the guidelines on the treatment of PTSD from the expert consensus guideline series (Foa, Davidson, et al., 1999), which also are available at www.psychguides.com. The guidelines also contain a list of additional resources, such as the International Society for Traumatic Stress Studies, which has a comprehensive Web site (www.istss.org). More condensed expert consensus guidelines on PTSD also are available (Ballenger et al., 2000). For a recent review of research on the effects of sexual assault and factors associated with recovery, we recommend an article by Neville and Heppner (1999). The book *No Safe Haven*, produced by an APA task force on male violence against women, is an excellent review of research on violence against women more generally (Koss et al., 1994). For further information on assessment, we recommend books by Carlson (1997) and Briere (1997), which both contain extensive reviews of trauma-related measures.

37 SUICIDE RISK ASSESSMENT

James R. Rogers

With approximately 30,000 completed suicides and conservative estimates of around 750,000 suicide attempts annually in the United States, Bonner's (1990) characterization of suicidal crises as representing "therapists' worst fear" and "one of the ultimate tragedies faced by the mental health treatment community" (p. 232) is understandable. In fact, research has shown that mental health clients currently in treatment are at a higher risk for suicide and suicidal behaviors than the general population (Nekanda-Trepka, Bishop, & Blackburn, 1983) and that the probability of losing a client to suicide is relatively high for mental health interns and professional practitioners alike (Kleespies, 1998; Rogers, Gueulette, Abbey-Hines, Carney, & Werth, in press). Additionally, client suicides have been shown to significantly impact practitioners personally in terms of mental health (Kleespies, 1998) and professionally through concerns related to competence and malpractice litigation (Bongar, 1991). Finally, concerns and fears related to working with suicidal clients are exacerbated by the documented lack of systematic training in suicidology within the various mental health-related professional programs (Kleespies, 1998).

Given the high prevalence of suicidal behavior and its impact on the mental health treatment community, it is important that mental health counselors have access to state-of-the-art information related to the assessment of suicidal risk. The purpose of this chapter, therefore, is to provide a brief overview of the current status of suicide risk assessment in the field of suicidology and to provide practitioners with original sources for additional information.

RISK FACTORS AND ASSESSMENT VERSUS PREDICTION

The major terms underlying this discussion are *risk factors*, *assessment*, and *prediction*. The first task, therefore, is to clearly define and differentiate these terms. According to Westefeld et al. (2000), the ambitious goal in the field of suicidology was to develop strategies for predicting suicide. That is, the focus of contemporary suicidology had been pragmatic in nature, with a focus on identifying factors that differentiated between suicidal and nonsuicidal individuals that could be used to target suicidal individuals for preventative interventions (Rogers, 2001). In other words, researchers identified factors that correlated with suicide and suicidal behavior. Characteristics that were identified in this way were subsequently termed *risk factors* or predictors of suicide, despite the fact that their identification was correlational rather than causal in nature. Additionally, although many factors have been individually identified, there has been little empirical attention to their interactions.

Despite the correlational nature of the underlying data, the field moved to incorporate identified risk factors into predictive measurement models. To predict suicidal behavior, however, implies an ability to foretell this low base

259

rate, complex, and multifaceted behavior with a high degree of certainty. According to Maris (1992), the prediction of suicide requires a sophistication in measurement reliability, validity, sensitivity, and specificity unobtainable given the state of psychometric technology and the ethical issues involved in prediction-focused research with suicidal individuals. This realization led Maris (1992) to state, "One might cynically conclude that only suicide 'predicts' suicide" (p. 3). Since the 1990s, the field of suicidology has moved toward the more realistic or reasonable goal of suicide risk *assessment*. Assessment in this sense implies an estimation of the probabilities for completed suicide and other suicidal behaviors as opposed to a point prediction model. Again, however, assessment is predicated on knowledge of the correlates of suicide and suicidal behavior or risk factors.

According to Shea (1999), the focus of suicide risk assessment is to collect data related to suicide risk factors, including suicidal ideation and level of planning, and to use this information for clinical decision making. The data collection activities necessary for a comprehensive suicide risk assessment occur through three major forms: (1) the clinical interview, (2) assessment measures, and (3) third-party sources of collateral information. First, I provide a brief listing of the major suicide risk factors and sources of additional information. This is followed by an introduction to the major forms of data collection in assessment. Finally, I present general information related to the use of this data in the estimation of risk for suicide.

SUICIDE RISK FACTORS

The literature in suicidology has focused on identifying both general risk factors for suicide as well as risk factors for various population subgroups. Relevant subgroups have included adolescents and elderly individuals, groups based on biological sex and sexual orientation, ethnic and cultural groups such as African Americans, Hispanic Americans, Asian Americans, and Native Americans, and groups based on various demographic factors

such as employment status, marital status, and geography (Westefeld et al., 2000). Clearly, a comprehensive listing of the empirically identified risk factors for suicidal behavior for each of these groups is beyond the scope of this chapter. However, the more general risk factors as presented by Maris (1992), Rogers, Alexander, and Subich (1994), and the U.S. Public Health Service (1999) are presented in Table 37.1. Additional sources of information related to these general and subgroup risk factors for suicide include Jacobs (1999), Blumenthal and Kupfer (1990), Berman and Jobes (1992), Maris, Berman, Maltsberger, and Yufit (1992), McBee and Rogers (1997), and Westefeld et al. (2000).

THE CLINICAL INTERVIEW

The clinical interview is a major source of information in the assessment of risk for suicide. As suggested by Kral (1994) and Shea (1999), the most direct "cause" of suicide and suicidal behavior is a decision to act on the suicide idea. Thus, the goal of the clinical interview in

TABLE 37.1   General Suicide Risk Factors

Cultural and religious beliefs
History of psychiatric illness
Alcoholism and drug abuse
Suicidal ideation, talk, and preparation (including presence of a suicide note)
Prior suicide attempts
Easy access to lethal methods
Social isolation
Worthlessness
Hopelessness
Depression
Impulsivity
Hostility
Intent to die
Marital status and family factors
Environmental stress (including actual or anticipated events)
Physical illness
Suicide survivor (history of losing a loved one to suicide)
Future time perspective
Family history of suicide and other social influences
Lack of access to mental health treatment

assessing suicide risk is to create an environment that will allow the counselor to "capture the history, nature, content, and quality of the suicide idea and its experiential meaning for the individual" (Bonner, 2001; p. 86). To effectively engage the suicidal client in this process, Shea suggests that counselors need to consider both the sources of client resistance to engagement and the impact of their own values and beliefs on the interview process.

In terms of sources of client resistance, Shea (1999) suggests that lack of effective engagement in the interview may result from the client's belief that suicide is a sign of weakness, or is immoral or sinful, or because suicide has been defined through his or her experience as a taboo subject. Additional sources of resistance may be a fear of being perceived as "crazy" and subsequently being hospitalized, a sense of helplessness and hopelessness, or a true wish to die. Therefore, it is incumbent on the counselor to be aware of these possible issues and develop interview strategies that can be used to lower those resistances. One step in this direction is for counselors to engage in personal value clarification around those same issues. For example, counselors should explore their own personal, moral, and spiritual beliefs regarding suicide and suicidal behavior as well as their beliefs about the relationship between suicide and mental illness (Shea, 1999).

Finally, Shea (1999) suggests that mental health workers need to be aware of their own tendency to overreact to suicidal clients by placing fears of litigation above client care. This tendency to overreact may result in unnecessarily restrictive interventions, such as involuntary hospitalization, that may in some cases be more detrimental to the client than no intervention at all. Additionally, unnecessarily restrictive interventions may serve to damage the client-counselor relationship and, thus, inhibit therapeutic progress. Alternatively, as suggested by Clark (1998), pro-suicide attitudes of the counselor may lead to underreactions by the mental health practitioner working with suicidal individuals. Although there appear to be no specific data to support either of these positions, it seems reasonable to expect that beliefs and attitudes around these issues could impact treatment decisions and that practitioners should engage in self-exploration around these issues.

ASSESSMENT MEASURES

A number of reviews in the literature examine the usefulness of established personality measures and suicide-specific measures for assessing suicidal risk (e.g., Eyman & Eyman, 1992; Range & Knott, 1997; Rothberg & Geer-Williams, 1992; Westefeld et al., 2000). In general, reviews have not been positive with regard to the independent use of either personality measures or suicide scales in terms of assessing suicide risk. Of the most commonly used personality measures, however, the Minnesota Multiphasic Personality Inventory (MMPI; Hathaway & McKinley, 1949) and its current version the MMPI-2 (Butcher, Dahlstrom, Graham, Tellegen, & Kaemmer, 1989), the Hopelessness Scale (Beck, Weissman, Lester, & Trexler, 1974), and the Beck Depression Inventory (BDI; Beck & Steer, 1987) and its most current revision, the BDI-II (Beck, Steer & Brown, 1996), have been found to be the most useful as screening instruments for suicidality (Westefeld et al., 2000).

In terms of suicide-specific questionnaires or measures, Rothberg and Geer-Williams (1992) provided an analysis of 19 suicide scales related to their psychometric properties and their usefulness in assessing suicidality in five clinical cases. Applying the 19 scales to the clinical cases, the authors found a wide range of estimates of suicide potential for each case. Additionally, they noted the general lack of documented psychometric information on the scales. Westefeld et al. (2000) reviewed 12 suicide-specific measures and concluded that instruments such as the Suicidal Ideation Scale (Rudd, 1989), Suicide Behaviors Questionnaire (Cole, 1988; Linehan, 1981), Reasons for Living Inventory (Linehan, Goodstein, Nielsen, & Chiles, 1983), Suicide Probability Scale (Cull & Gill, 1982), Suicidal Ideation

Questionnaire (Reynolds, 1987), Multiatti-tude Suicide Tendency Scale (Orbach, et al., 1991), Fairy Tales Test (Orbach, Feshbach, Carlson, Glaubman, & Gross, 1983), and the Suicide Status Form (Jobes, Jacoby, Cimbolic, & Hustead, 1997) could provide specific in-formation that could be used as part of a more comprehensive suicide risk assessment and inform treatment decisions. However, these authors cautioned against the use of any of these scales as the sole source of infor-mation for making judgments regarding an individual's level of risk for suicide.

In summary, these results suggest that mental health counselors need to be cautious when using either personality measures or suicide-specific scales for assessing suicidal risk, but when used with caution, they can provide useful assessment and treatment information.

COLLATERAL INFORMATION

Beyond the interview and any assessments using personality or suicide-specific mea-sures, it is important in the data collection pro-cess to attempt to gather information from third parties. This is especially important when it appears that the client may be resistant for any of the reasons mentioned previously. Also, as indicated by Fremouw, de Perczel, and Ellis (1990), the collection of collateral in-formation may be especially important when assessing suicidality in children and adoles-cents. Therefore, mental health practitioners are encouraged to collect any collateral in-formation possible within the limits of the as-sessment setting and the parameters of confi-dentiality. Sources of collateral information for assessment with children and adolescents may include peers, siblings, parents, and teachers and information from previous mental health treatment experiences, including contact with school counselors.

For adults, similar sources of collateral in-formation may be available. As with children and adolescents, it is important to gather information from prior mental health treat-ment contacts the client may have had.

Equally important may be information from significant others in the client's life, includ-ing friends and coworkers. Clearly, however, it may be difficult to efficiently connect with important sources of collateral information, especially when assessment occurs in the context of a one-shot crisis intervention-based suicide risk assessment as opposed to occurring within the context of an estab-lished therapeutic relationship.

ESTIMATING RISK FOR SUICIDE

A major issue in the field of suicidology has to do with the process of synthesizing the infor-mation collected during the process of suicide risk assessment to provide an estimate of risk that can be used to guide treatment decisions. Shea (1999) has characterized this as a very unique process that is difficult to standard-ize. Others have similarly suggested that as-sessment information is filtered through an undefined clinical judgment process that in-cludes the clinician's "gut feeling" regarding the potential of the client to act on his or her suicidal thoughts or plans (e.g., Maris, 1992). Even with little guidance in the field related to this process, the goal is to classify the client into risk categories. For example, Fre-mouw et al. (1990) suggest that mental health practitioners can use assessment data to clas-sify clients into one of four categories: none to low risk, risk, moderate risk, and high risk. Once the classification is determined, these authors provide a decision tree model that can be useful in making subsequent response and treatment decisions.

SUMMARY

Suicide is a major mental health issue in the United States and one frequently encoun-tered by mental health professionals. Despite the documented lack of systematic training in suicidology across the various mental health disciplines, clinicians are expected to be able to adequately assess clients in terms of sui-cide risk. This process requires:

- Knowledge of relevant general and group-specific risk factors.
- An understanding of the unique aspects associated with the clinical interview process as it relates to suicide risk assessment, including personal values clarification.
- An understanding of the benefits and limitations of the use of personality and suicide-specific measures as an important component of suicide risk assessment.
- Attention to possible sources of collateral information to inform the assessment process.
- An ability to synthesize the assessment information and use it to inform clinical judgment regarding suicide risk.

Mental health practitioners are encouraged to use the resources presented in this chapter to extend their knowledge base in suicide risk assessment. Additionally, two relevant Web sites in this area are those of the American Association of Suicidology (www.suicidology.org) and Section VII, Clinical Emergencies and Crises, of the Clinical Psychology Division of the American Psychological Association (www.apa.org/divisions/div12/section7).

References

Beck, A.T., & Steer, R.A. (1987). *BDI, Beck Depression Inventory manual.* San Antonio, TX: Psychological Corporation.

Beck, A.T., Steer, R.A., & Brown, G. (1996). *Beck Depression Inventory* (2nd ed.). San Antonio, TX: Psychological Corporation.

Beck, A.T., Weissman, A., Lester, D., & Trexler, L. (1974). The measurement of pessimism: The Hopelessness Scale. *Journal of Consulting and Clinical Psychology, 42,* 861–865.

Berman, A.J., & Jobes, D.A. (1992). *Adolescent suicide assessment and intervention.* Washington, DC: American Psychological Association.

Blumenthal, S.J., & Kupfer, D.J. (Eds.). (1990). *Suicide over the life cycle: Risk factors, assessment, and treatment of suicidal patients.* Washington, DC: American Psychiatric Press.

Bongar, B. (1991). *The suicidal patient: Clinical and legal standards of care.* Washington, DC: American Psychological Association.

Bonner, R.L. (1990). A "m.a.p." to the clinical assessment of suicide risk. *Journal of Mental Health Counseling, 12,* 232–236.

Bonner, R.L. (2001). Moving suicide risk assessment into the next millennium. In D. Lester (Ed.), *Suicide: Resources for the new millennium* (pp. 83–101). Washington, DC: Taylor & Francis.

Butcher, J.N., Dahlstrom, W.G., Graham, J.R., Tellegen, A., & Kaemmer, B. (1989). *Minnesota Multiphasic Personality Inventory-2 (MMPI-2): Manual for administration and scoring.* Minneapolis: University of Minnesota Press.

Clark, D. (1998). The evaluation and management of suicidal patients. In P.M. Kleespies (Ed.), *Emergencies in mental health practice: Evaluation and management* (pp. 75–94). New York: Guilford Press.

Cole, D.A. (1988). Hopelessness, social desirability, depression, and parasuicide in two college student samples. *Journal of Consulting and Clinical Psychology, 56,* 131–136.

Cull, J.G., & Gill, W.S. (1982). *Suicide Probability Scale.* Los Angeles: Western Psychological Services.

Eyman, J.R., & Eyman, S.K. (1992). Personality assessment in suicide prediction. In R. Maris, A. Berman, J. Maltsberger, & R. Yufit (Eds.), *Assessment and prediction of suicide* (pp. 183–201). New York: Guilford Press.

Fremouw, W.J., de Perczel, M., & Ellis, T.E. (1990). *Suicide risk: Assessment and response guidelines.* Elmsford, NY: Pergamon Press.

Hathaway, S., & McKinley, J. (1949). *The Minnesota Multiphasic Personality Schedule.* Minneapolis: University of Minnesota Press.

Jacobs, D.G. (Ed.). (1999). *The Harvard Medical School guide to suicide assessment and intervention.* San Francisco: Jossey-Bass.

Jobes, D., Jacoby, A., Cimbolic, P., & Hustead, L. (1997). Assessment and treatment of suicidal clients in a university counseling center. *Journal of Counseling Psychology, 44,* 368–377.

Kleespies, P.M. (1998). Introduction. In P.M. Kleespies (Ed.), *Emergencies in mental health practice: Evaluation and management* (pp. 1–6). New York: Guilford Press.

Kral, M.J. (1994). Suicide: A social logic. *Suicide and Life-Threatening Behavior, 24,* 245–255.

Linehan, M.M. (1981). *Suicidal Behaviors Questionnaire.* Unpublished inventory, University of Washington, Seattle.

Linehan, M., Goodstein, J., Nielsen, S., & Chiles, J. (1983). Reasons for staying alive when you are thinking about killing yourself. *Journal of Consulting and Clinical Psychology, 51,* 276–286.

Maris, R. (1992). Overview of the study of suicide assessment and prediction. In R. Maris, A. Berman, J. Maltsberger, & R. Yufit (Eds.),

Assessment and prediction of suicide (pp. 3–24). New York: Guilford Press.

Maris, R.W., Berman, A.J., Maltsberger, J.T., & Yufit, R.I. (Eds.). (1992). *Assessment and prediction of suicide.* New York: Guilford Press.

McBee, S.M., & Rogers, J.R. (1997). Identifying risk factors for gay and lesbian suicidal behavior: Implications for mental health counselors. *Journal of Mental Health Counseling, 19,* 143–155.

Nekanda-Trepka, C.J.S., Bishop, S., & Blackburn, I.M. (1983). Hopelessness and depression. *British Journal of Clinical Psychology, 22,* 49–60.

Orbach, I., Feshbach, S., Carlson, G., Glaubman, H., & Gross, Y. (1983). Attraction and repulsion by life and death in suicidal and normal children. *Journal of Consulting and Clinical Psychology, 51,* 661–670.

Orbach, I., Milstein, I., Har-Even, D., Apter, A., Tiano, S., & Elizur, A. (1991). A Multi-Attitude Suicide Tendency Scale for Adolescents. *Psychological Assessment, 3,* 398–404.

Range, L.M., & Knott, E.C. (1997). Twenty suicide assessment instruments: Evaluation and recommendation. *Death Studies, 21,* 25–58.

Reynolds, W.J. (1987). *The Suicide Ideation Questionnaire.* Odessa, FL: Psychological Assessment Resources.

Rogers, J.R. (2001). Psychological research into suicide: Past, present, and future. In D. Lester (Ed.), *Suicide: Resources for the new millennium* (pp. 31–44). Washington, DC: Taylor & Francis.

Rogers, J.R., Alexander, R.A., & Subich, L.M. (1994). Development and psychometric analysis of the Suicide Assessment Checklist. *Journal of Mental Health Counseling, 16,* 352–368.

Rogers, J.R., Gueulette, C.M., Abbey-Hines, J., Carney, J.V., & Werth, J.L., Jr. (in press). Rational suicide: An empirical investigation of counselor attitudes. *Journal of Counseling and Development.*

Rothberg, J.M., & Geer-Williams, C. (1992). A comparison and review of suicide prediction scales. In R. Maris, A. Berman, J. Maltsberger, & R. Yufit (Eds.), *Assessment and prediction of suicide* (pp. 202–217). New York: Guilford Press.

Rudd, M.D. (1989). The prevalence of suicidal ideation among college students. *Suicide and Life-Threatening Behavior, 19,* 173–183.

Shea, S.C. (1999). *The practical art of suicide assessment: A guide for mental health practitioners and substance abuse counselors.* New York: Wiley.

U.S. Public Health Service. (1999). *The Surgeon General's call to action to prevent suicide.* Washington, DC: Author.

Westefeld, J.S., Range, L.M., Rogers, J.R., Maples, M.R., Bromley, J.L., & Alcorn, J. (2000). Suicide: An overview. *The Counseling Psychologist, 28,* 443–510.

38   COUNSELING INTERVENTIONS WITH SUICIDAL CLIENTS

Rita Sommers-Flanagan, John Sommers-Flanagan, and Katy L. Lynch

Most mental health counselors at some point in their career will face the challenge of working with a suicidal client (Kleepsies, 1993). Undoubtedly, this challenge will be stressful.

This chapter provides mental health counselors with basic information on how to work effectively with suicidal clients. Before devoting the bulk of this chapter to a review of suicide intervention procedures and techniques, we discuss the counselor's personal feelings and attitudes toward suicide and legal liability. For information on suicide assessment, readers should consult Rogers (this volume) or other contemporary sources (Jacobs, 1999; Shea, 1999; R. Sommers-Flanagan & Sommers-Flanagan, 1999).

CAN YOU WORK WITH SUICIDAL CLIENTS?

Counselors, directly or indirectly, can strongly influence what their clients will or will not feel comfortable talking about. This is especially true with regard to suicidality. As Shea (1999) states: "When a clinician begins to understand his or her own attitudes, biases, and responses to suicide, he or she can become more psychologically and emotionally available to a suicidal client. Clients seem to be able to sense when a clinician is comfortable with the topic of suicide. At that point, and with such a clinician, clients may feel safe enough to share the immediacy of their pull toward death" (p. 4). To help clients speak openly about their fears, counselors need to understand their personal biases and reactions toward suicide and suicidal clients. Shea recommends asking the question: "Do I hold and communicate beliefs about suicide that may make a client feel uneasy while talking with me about suicide?" (p. 113).

If you plan to work with suicidal clients, you should ask yourself a number of questions about your attitudes toward suicide. For example, do you think suicide is a sign of weakness, immoral, a sin, crazy or illogical? We recommend that you examine your past with regard to suicidal behavior. Have you or any family members ever contemplated or attempted suicide? Do you have previous experience with suicidal clients that might color your approach to working with suicidal clients in the future?

Having strong philosophical, religious, or personal beliefs about suicide can interfere with your ability to be objective and helpful when working with suicidal clients. If your beliefs make it difficult for you to work effectively with these clients, it is your responsibility to refer them to more appropriate mental health professionals (Wollersheim, 1974).

Finally, some counselors feel strongly that suicide is a right that some clients may wish to exercise. At present, generally both the law and our ethics codes are such that it is our professional responsibility to side with life. Counselors choosing otherwise must seek both legal and collegial input.

LEGAL RESPONSIBILITIES AND LIABILITIES

In most states, mental health professionals have a duty to warn and protect if they have evidence that clients may be dangerous to themselves or others. Therefore, you must actively take steps—sometimes including steps that violate confidentiality—to enhance or ensure your client's safety.

Legal precedent has determined that in cases of suicide or homicide, mental health professionals can be held partly responsible for their client's life or death (Costa & Altekruse, 1994; *Tarasoff v. Regents of the University of California*, 1974). Hence, we recommend that you take the following precautions:

- When appropriate, contact the client's family, friends, or other persons who can provide support and protection.
- Encourage the client and members of the client's support system to remove easily available lethal means from the client's environment. (This should include, but not be limited to, firearms, lethal medications, and sharp or deadly objects.)
- Consult with professional colleagues regarding usual, customary, and highest possible professional practice standards.
- Thoroughly document that you have taken appropriate steps regarding suicide assessment and suicide intervention.

SUICIDE INTERVENTION PROCEDURES AND TECHNIQUES

As suggested by Shneidman (1984), suicidal patients are experiencing deep pain and misery, a cognitive-perceptual narrowing or constriction of their life options or alternatives, and intense pressure or a sense of being compelled toward the suicidal act. It is our duty to make every effort to reduce our clients' psychological pain, open up their mental constriction, and reduce their compulsion toward suicide. Yet it is important to note that this effort, no matter how herculean, will not always be successful. We address the issue of completed suicides later in this chapter.

Stay Calm While Listening with Empathy

Suicidal clients frequently feel isolated; they feel alone with their suicidal thoughts and impulses. Listening compassionately and encouraging them to talk about their psychological or emotional pain and misery is a fundamental intervention. Although we are listening to understand their pain, we should not presume that we fully understand the internal experience of a pain so severe that death seems preferable. To tell clients "I understand" or "I know what you mean" can seem patronizing and serve to further their sense of isolation.

With a suicidal client, it is essential to remain calm while expressing empathy for a client's desperation and suicidal impulses. This is no easy task: "You must deal with your clients' thoughts and feelings in a matter-of-fact manner; this suggests to them that you've dealt with such issues previously, and it reassures them, to some degree, that their experiences are not all that unusual. In some situations, you may want to be openly reassuring and supportive, even acknowledging that suicidal urges are sometimes a natural response" (R. Sommers-Flanagan & Sommers-Flanagan, 1999, p. 262).

Instill Hope and Confidence While Establishing a Therapeutic Alliance

Clients need to know that their counselor is willing to join with them in an effort to reduce or eliminate their suicidal thoughts and impulses. To help build this therapeutic alliance, counselors should express hope and at the same time express empathy. For example,

a counselor might say: "I know that right now you're feeling that life isn't worth living. But I want to tell you something else I know. I know that almost everyone in a situation like yours will eventually feel better and want to live. That's one of the ways depression works. It's horrible and miserable, but eventually it gets better. You probably don't believe me because depression also makes you lose hope for the future, but I want you to work with me to make your misery decrease and your life feel better so that you'll want to live again."

It is unlikely that suicidal clients will immediately respond in a positive way to hopeful, reassuring messages about the future. In fact, with depressed and suicidal clients, counselors usually must repeatedly provide positive, optimistic, and reassuring messages about the future and about the therapeutic relationship. This repetition will need to continue until the client can begin to envision a more hopeful future on his or her own.

Establish a Suicide Prevention Contract and Provide Suicide Hotline/Help Information

Establishing a verbal or written suicide prevention contract is probably the most common initial suicide intervention procedure advocated by suicide prevention specialists. Suicide prevention contracts were originally referred to as "no-suicide agreements" and evaluated by Drye, Goulding, and Goulding (1973), who found these agreements to be strongly effective. Although their initial studies were not particularly well controlled, suicide prevention contracts quickly became standard practice. At this point, using no-suicide agreements is so well established that it is "both routine and a virtual ethical mandate" (J. Sommers-Flanagan & Sommers-Flanagan, 1997, p. 192). In an effort to evoke a more positive mental set, some clinicians, when talking with their clients, refer to no-suicide agreements as "life contracts" (Ingersoll, personal communication, January 20, 2001).

The usual written no-suicide agreement includes a statement similar to the following: "No matter what happens, I will not kill myself, accidentally or on purpose, at any time"

(Drye et al., 1973, p. 172). Care should be taken to word the contract in a very intentional manner. Unless you are able and willing to be available 24 hours a day (which we do *not* recommend), you need to identify alternative support persons and facilities in the agreement. For example, you might state, "In the event I am not available to speak or meet with you when you are feeling suicidal, you agree to contact the suicide hotline and/or be transported to the hospital emergency room for evaluation and support." Be sure to include that clients agree *not* to harm themselves until they have actually met with you or a designated person. We also recommend that you renew or mention no-suicide agreements whenever you see a client until self-destructive urges are no longer active. You may also consider having a witness sign the no-suicide agreement, as social psychology research suggests this may enhance compliance (Cialdini, 1994).

When working with suicidal children and adolescents, the no-suicide agreement should be signed by both the parents and the child. Additionally, research has shown that parents who receive injury prevention education and instructions on limiting access to lethal means of self-injury are more likely to limit their children's access to lethal means (Kruesi et al., 1999). We recommend that counselors not only provide parents of suicidal children with injury and suicide prevention information, but also consider establishing no-suicide agreements with parents specifying that parents will remove all firearms and lethal items from the home (Bailey et al., 1997).

Identifying Alternatives to Suicide

Counselors should avoid arguing with clients over whether suicide is a viable alternative to life. The issue for clients is usually less about wanting to commit suicide and more about their perceived lack of alternatives to suicide. Shneidman (1984) illuminates this issue: "The primary thought disorder in suicide is that of a pathological narrowing of the mind's focus, called constriction, which takes the form of seeing only two choices; either something painfully unsatisfactory or cessation of life" (pp. 320–321).

The primary task of the counselor is to help the client begin viewing suicide as only one of many alternatives. This task can be undertaken in a very straightforward and concrete manner. Specifically, at various points in the therapeutic process, counselors should take out a paper and pencil and brainstorm with the client all the potential life improvements that are likely to make suicide less appealing. Counselors should proceed by saying something such as "I know this seems silly. But let's just make a list of all the alternatives you have that might help you feel better. I realize that suicide is an option, and so we'll put it at the top of the list. So, what else might help you stop or reduce the pain you're feeling now?" Keep in mind that due to the client's depression, suicidality, and associated mental constriction, the client may be unenthused about this procedure and unable to think of any reasonable alternatives to suicide. The counselor may need to lead the way by suggesting various life improvements that might address the client's unmet psychological needs. For example: "How about talking with your husband and a therapist about improving your relationship?"

When engaging in this procedure, counselors should anticipate negative responses to virtually all of the suggestions. Suicidal clients are likely to say "No I couldn't do that" or "That could never work" in response to positive suggestions. If this occurs, counselors should proceed unrelentingly by stating "That's okay. I know it doesn't sound realistic. But we're just making a list, so I'll go ahead and write it down."

Strive to make a list that includes, in addition to suicide, at least 5 or 6, but probably not more than 10, additional alternatives. Because of the mental constriction associated with suicidal thinking, counselors should expect that they may have to generate 80% to 100% of the alternatives. Once the list is generated, it should be reviewed with the client and the client should rank-order, preferably in his or her own hand, all of the items in terms of personal preference. This activity, designed to help reduce the client's mental constriction, often produces surprising results. In particular, clients often rank suicide as third or fourth on their list, which provides the counselor with potentially fruitful areas to focus on in therapy. If the client continues to rank suicide as his or her first or only option, hospitalization should be considered.

Affectively Based Interventions

Rosenberg (1997, 1999) has described a suicide intervention and training model that emphasizes affectively based interventions "designed to engage the client in an exploration of the meaning of the suicidal ideation with the broader and longer term goals of decreasing the ideation and generating life-supporting options" (1999, p. 85). These affectively based interventions include the following:

- "Joining" with life-enhancing parts of the client's self, such as the client's seeking help and presence in the counselor's office.
- Framing client verbalizations about suicide as both an expression of deep miserable feelings as well as a hope that these feelings might diminish without having to resort to suicide.
- Exploring the possibility that suicidal feelings may also reflect feelings of anger—perhaps toward others—that are being turned inward.
- Exploring the possibility that when suicidal feelings seem vengeful or retaliatory, they might be due to having been hurt so deeply by another person that words seem an inadequate method for self-expression.
- Focusing on the finality of death as a solution to emotional distress to "eradicate the feelings of intolerable pain rather than eradicate the self" (Rosenberg, 1999, p. 86).

Setting Limits and Becoming Directive

Limit setting is often an important component of successful suicide intervention. It is particularly important when counselors are working with provocative clients, such as those diagnosed with Borderline Personality Disorder. Marsha Linehan (1993, 1999), based on her work with chronically parasuicidal borderline clients, has outlined a number of techniques that can be used when working with suicidal clients:

- Emphatically instruct the client not to commit suicide: This technique emphasizes the importance of simply telling the client to refrain from suicidal behavior. Of course, it can be used in conjunction with the fact that the client can always commit suicide at some later date, but that he or she is to abstain from suicidal behaviors for now.
- Repeatedly inform clients that suicide is not a good solution and that a better one will be found: Despite their exceptionally convincing arguments, be especially cautious when clients try to "bait" you into agreeing with them that suicide is the best or only solution to a particular problem.
- Give advice and make direct suggestions: There are times when acutely or chronically suicidal clients simply do not "know what to do or how to handle a given situation" (Linehan, 1999, p. 183). When clients are frozen and unable to construct a plan of action, it may be best for the counselor simply to step in and tell the client what to do.

Treating the Underlying Mental Disorder

A number of mental disorders, affective states, and behavioral patterns clearly contribute to suicide risk. In addition to directly addressing suicidal thoughts and impulses, counselors also should focus specifically on underlying conditions or exacerbating behaviors.

Mental disorders most commonly associated with suicide completion include Schizophrenia, Bipolar Disorder, depression, Substance Abuse/Dependence Disorder, Panic Disorder, Posttraumatic Stress Disorder, and Borderline or Antisocial Personality Disorder. The presence of any of these conditions should prompt the counselor to pursue specific treatment formulations, treatment plans, and treatment interventions. In some cases, such as Bipolar Disorder, severe depression, and Schizophrenia, medication may be an important part of the treatment plan. For example, effective treatment of suicidal individuals with Bipolar Disorder should most likely include medication for mood stabilization (Salzman, 1999). Mental health counselors working with suicidal clients benefit from a collegial relationship with a psychiatrist.

COMPLETED SUICIDES

Some suicidal clients will eventually act on their suicidal impulses and either attempt or complete suicide. Obviously, if your client commits suicide, it can cause great psychological and emotional trauma, and you will probably need time to recover from this sad and deeply disturbing event.

Counselors benefit from having a range of resources available to them should their client commit suicide. Sometimes, the best place to begin is with intellectual support. Take solace in the words of Litman (1995): "At present it is impossible to predict accurately any person's suicide. Sophisticated statistical models . . . and experienced clinical judgments are equally unsuccessful. When I am asked why one depressed and suicidal patient commits suicide while nine other equally depressed and equally suicidal patients do not, I answer, 'I don't know'" (p. 135).

The fact is that suicide is unpredictable (see Chapter 37). That does not mean we should not try to predict and prevent it, but it does mean that we must be realistic. Sometimes suicide happens. For many reasons, mental health counselors should create and faithfully attend a professional consultation group. This is especially true for those working with suicidal clients.

References

Bailey, J.E., Kellerman, A.L., Somes, G.W., Banton, J.G., Rivara, F.P., & Rushforth, N.P. (1997). Risk factors for violent death of women in the home. *Archives of Internal Medicine, 157,* 777–782.

Cialdini, R.B. (1994). *Persuasion: Psychological insights and perspectives.* Needham Heights, MA: Allyn & Bacon.

Costa, L., & Altekruse, M. (1994). Duty to warn guidelines for mental health counselors. *Journal of Counseling and Development, 72,* 346–350.

Drye, R.D., Goulding, R.L., & Goulding, M.E. (1973). No-suicide decisions: Patient monitoring of suicidal risk. *American Journal of Psychiatry, 130,* 171–174.

Jacobs, D.G. (Ed.). (1999). *The Harvard Medical School guide to suicide assessment and intervention.* San Francisco: Jossey-Bass.

Kleepsies, P.M. (1993). Stress of patient suicidal behavior: Implications for interns and training programs in psychology. *Professional Psychology, 24,* 477–482.

Kruesi, M.J.P., Grossman, J., Pennington, J.M., Woodward, P.J., Duda, D., & Hirsch, J.G. (1999). Suicide and violence prevention: Parent education in the emergency department. *Journal of the American Academy of Child and Adolescent Psychiatry, 38,* 250–255.

Linehan, M.M. (1993). *Cognitive-behavioral treatment of borderline personality disorder.* New York: Guilford Press.

Linehan, M.M. (1999). Standard protocol for assessing and treating suicidal behaviors for patients in treatment. In D.G. Jacobs (Ed.), *The Harvard Medical School guide to suicide assessment and intervention* (pp. 146–187). San Francisco: Jossey-Bass.

Litman, R.E. (1995). Suicide prevention in a treatment setting. *Suicide and Life-Threatening Behavior, 25,* 134–142.

Rosenberg, J.I. (1997). Expertise research and clinical practice: A suicide assessment and intervention training model. *Educational Psychology Review, 9,* 279–296.

Rosenberg, J.I. (1999). Suicide prevention: An integrated training model using affective and action-based interventions. *Professional Psychology, 30,* 83–87.

Salzman, C. (1999). Treatment of the suicidal patient with psychotropic drugs and ECT. In D.G. Jacobs (Ed.), *The Harvard Medical School guide to suicide assessment and intervention* (pp. 372–382). San Francisco: Jossey-Bass.

Shea, S.C. (1999). *The practical art of suicide assessment.* New York: Wiley.

Shneidman, E.S. (1984). Aphorisms of suicide and some implications for psychotherapy. *American Journal of Psychotherapy, 38,* 319–328.

Sommers-Flanagan, J., & Sommers-Flanagan, R. (1997). *Tough kids, cool counseling: User-friendly approaches to working with challenging youth.* Alexandria, VA: American Counseling Association.

Sommers-Flanagan, R., & Sommers-Flanagan, J. (1999). *Clinical interviewing* (2nd ed.). New York: Wiley.

Tarasoff v. Regents of the University of California, 13 Cal. 3d 177, 529 P.2d 533, 118 Cal. Rptr. 129 (1974).

Wollersheim, J.P. (1974). The assessment of suicide potential via interview methods. *Psychotherapy, 11,* 222–225.

Suggested Readings and Resources

Treating suicidal clients requires that the mental health professional stay current in the treatment and research literature in the area.

Professional Books and Articles

Jacobs, D.G. (1999). *The Harvard Medical School guide to suicide assessment and intervention.* San Francisco: Jossey-Bass. This volume of over 700 pages details a distinctly psychiatric-medical perspective on suicide assessment and intervention.

Juhnke, G.A. (1996). The adapted-SAD PERSONS: A suicide assessment scale designed for use with children. *Elementary School Guidance and Counseling, 30,* 252–258. This short article discusses the adaptation of Patterson et al.'s (1983) SAD PERSONS scale for evaluating school-age children.

Patterson, W.M., Dohn, H.H., Bird, J., & Patterson, G.A. (1983). Evaluation of suicidal patients: The SAD PERSONS scale. *Psychosomatics, 24,* 343–349. This classic article provides an acronym to help clinicians recall suicide predictor variables.

Shneidman, E.S. (1996). *The suicidal mind.* New York: Oxford University Press. In this powerful book, the most renowned suicidologist in the world reviews three cases that illustrate
the psychological pain associated with suicidal impulses.

Self-Help for Suicidal People and Violence Prediction

Convoy, D.L. (1991). *Out of the nightmare: Recovery from depression and suicidal pain.* New York: New Liberty. This self-help book for depressed and suicidal clients seeks to reduce suicidal impulses through a variety of methods.

Ellis, T.E., & Newman, C.F. (1996). *Choosing to live: How to defeat suicide through cognitive therapy.* Oakland, CA: New Harbinger. Based on principles of cognitive therapy, this self-help book helps suicidal people work through their psychological pain and depression and choose life.

Suicide Support Organizations and Web Sites

American Foundation for Suicide Prevention, 120 Wall Street, 22nd Floor, New York, NY 10005 (888) 333-AFSP or (212) 363-3500. www.afsp.org

American Association of Suicidology, Alan L. Berman, Ph.D., Executive Director, 4201 Connecticut Avenue, N.W., Suite 310, Washington, DC 20008 (202) 237-2280. www.suicidology.org

National Crisis Hotline: (888) 284-2433 or (888) suicide.

National Youth Crisis Hotline: (800) 999-9999.

National Organization for People of Color Against Suicide, P.O. Box 125, San Marcos, TX 78667 (830) 625-3576, e-mail: db31@swt.edu.

Suicide Prevent Triangle: SuicidePreventTriangle.org. Lists support groups, suicide self-assessment procedures, software, and educational/resource information on suicide.

39 RESPONDING TO DANGEROUS CLIENTS

Derek Truscott and Jim Evans

An archer competing for a clay vessel shoots effortlessly, with skill and concentration unimpeded. If the prize is changed to a brass ornament, the archer's hands begin to shake. If it is changed to gold, the archer squints as if going blind. It is not abilities that deteriorate, but belief in them does, as the supposed value of an external reward is allowed to cloud the mind. (Chuang-tse, third century B.C.E.)

Even experienced counselors can find their minds clouded when life and death are at stake. *Will my client harm his or her intended victim? Will I be sued, lose my license to practice?* Our belief in our ability can deteriorate rapidly. *Should I warn someone, call the police? Should I try to talk my client out of it, have him or her committed?* Responding to dangerous clients poses a conflict for counselors between ethical and legal duties to our client, a legal duty to protect any potential victim(s) of our client's violent behavior, and fear of disciplinary or civil charges against ourselves.

Prior to the 1976 California Supreme Court decision of *Tarasoff v. Regents of the University of California* (1976), counselors tended not to be concerned about legal liability arising out of their clients' behavior outside of the counseling session. Counselors knew that they had a legal obligation to exercise a degree of care and skill expected of a typical practitioner, and that if they failed to do so and their client was harmed, they could be sued for malpractice. That all changed when Prosenjit Poddar, a 26-year-old graduate student at the University

of California, shot and stabbed Tatiana Tarasoff to death. Ms. Tarasoff's parents sued the psychologist and the psychiatrist who had treated Mr. Poddar on the grounds that they should have warned their daughter that her life was in danger. In 1974, the California Supreme Court initially agreed with the Tarasoffs (*Tarasoff v. Regents of the University of California*, 1974), but that ruling was reheard in 1976 and partially overturned. The later court did acknowledge that a warning may sometimes be necessary to prevent the violent act, but ultimately established that psychotherapists have a legal duty to exercise reasonable care to *protect* the potential victims of their clients' violent behavior. Although relevant only in California, almost every other jurisdiction in the United States and Canada has adopted similar legal reasoning (Truscott, 1993; Truscott & Crook, 1993). The duty to protect generally exists where a client has been (or reasonably should have been) assessed to be a serious threat of physical violence to an identifiable victim or victims.

Although the duty to protect has not necessitated a radical change in counseling practice, it has forced us to more seriously consider our clients' risk for violence and how to respond. This consideration should include how we:

- Keep records.
- Assess violence risk.
- Respond to dangerous clients.
- Assess alliance strength.
- Protect potential victims.

RECORD KEEPING

Thorough records are critical to document that appropriate procedures were followed and reasonable steps were taken in light of the facts. Liability is usually imposed for failing to follow appropriate procedures, especially in gathering or communicating information, not for errors in judgment in light of the known facts. The degree to which relevant information can be obtained will depend on the circumstances of the case. If a client presents with problems related to angry or violent behavior, a thorough assessment of violence-related factors should be undertaken at intake. If concerns arise unexpectedly in the course of counseling, every *reasonable* effort should be made to obtain the information needed without unduly disrupting the counseling process.

ASSESSING VIOLENCE RISK

The low degree of accuracy for predicting violence is well documented in the research literature (Mossman, 1994), but this does not mean that all acts of violence are unforeseeable on the part of counselors. The legal test is one of "reasonable foreseeability" not "certainty." That is, would a prudent counselor have predicted violence on the part of the client? It is the standard of foreseeability that presents the most serious dilemma for counselors because any judgment of liability will be made in hindsight, in which case, the violence will appear more foreseeable. It is prudent, therefore, to treat every threat of violence as serious, without resorting to breaking confidentiality unless all other treatment avenues have been exhausted.

Our ability to make accurate long-term predictions of *any* human behavior, particularly relatively rare behavior such as violence, is poor. This is because human behavior is rarely, if ever, the result of stable individual traits. Rather, it results from an interaction between characteristics of individuals and characteristics of their environment. Virtually anyone is capable of violent behavior despite possessing few violent traits, whereas even the

most violently predisposed individual is not always behaving violently. Stated differently, individual characteristics are neither necessary nor sufficient causes of violent behavior, whereas situational characteristics can be.

Individual characteristics can alter the threshold at which situational characteristics precipitate violence. An individual who possesses many characteristics typical of violence-prone persons would be considered at high risk for violence given relatively fewer situational precipitants. When one is working with a dangerous client, therefore, close attention should be paid to situational variables.

Individual Characteristics

The more closely an individual resembles a fictional modal violent person, the lower the threshold for current risk. The following characteristics typify persons who commit violent acts:

• Male.
• Non-White.
• In late teens or early 20s.
• Has a history of opiate or alcohol abuse.
• Has a low IQ and education.
• Has an unstable residential and employment history.
• Has a history of violent behavior.

Situational Characteristics

Availability of Potential Victim(s)
• Is the intended victim known to your client? (The majority of violent crimes occur between people who know each other.)
• Does your client have a history of aggressing against a particular type of person (e.g., women or coworkers) or in a particular setting?
• Does your client have access to the intended victim?

Access to a Weapon
• Does your client have access to weapons? (They are situationally disinhibiting and lethal.)

- Does your client have combat or martial arts training, or possess great strength (making him capable of inflicting greater harm)?

Alcohol Use

- Has your client been drinking, or is he likely to ingest alcohol soon? (In half of all homicides, the offender was drinking. Alcohol is responsible for more aggression and violence than all other drugs combined.)

Stressors

- Is your client under stress related to family/relationship, peer group, finances, or employment (thereby eroding his frustration tolerance as well as providing motivation for violence)?

RESPONDING TO DANGEROUSNESS

Central to responding to dangerous clients is to do everything reasonably possible to influence the client in a positive way so that violence will not occur. It is most desirable to avoid breaking confidentiality and avoid resorting to initiating actions outside of the counseling room. Overall, this strategy is based on balance theory (Heider, 1958), which is described in terms of two people and an attitude object. This results in three relationships, all of which can either be positive or negative. Only if the situation is imbalanced will social influence occur. In a situation in which a counselor is dealing with a potentially dangerous client, there are three relationships to consider: that between the client and counselor, the client's relationship to violence, and the counselor's relationship to violence. If the client is considering acting in a violent manner, we can assume his or her attitude toward violence is positive. We can also assume the counselor wants to discourage violence and therefore has a negative attitude toward it. If the client has a negative relationship with the counselor, the fact that the client is considering violence will not cause imbalance; the counselor does not approve of

violence and the client does not approve of the counselor. If the counselor does not approve of violence and the client has a positive relationship with the counselor, however, the fact that the client is considering violence will cause imbalance. The only way to resolve this imbalance is to either change the positive relationship with the counselor to a negative one, or to not engage in violence. Thus, it is vital for counselors to maintain a good working relationship with a client who is threatening to engage in violence. This is consistent with decades of counseling research that finds that a strong therapeutic alliance is the cornerstone of a positive outcome in counseling (Bachelor & Horvath, 1999).

Attending to the degree of violence risk and the strength of the therapeutic alliance is central to effective treatment *and* the protection of potential victims. The therapeutic alliance should also be strengthened because acting only to prevent a current violent episode without attending to the therapeutic alliance may enrage a client and thereby increase the risk of violence (Truscott, Evans, & Mansell, 1995), while simultaneously deterring the client from seeking further counseling services for dealing with any future violent impulses. Only if the risk cannot be adequately reduced via the therapeutic alliance should our energies be directed toward other risk-reduction interventions that have a lesser likelihood of success. Counselors responding to dangerous clients, therefore, should attend to two key dimensions: the degree of risk and the strength of the therapeutic alliance. Although both of these dimensions are obviously on continua, we have found it helpful to think of them in a 2 × 2 table. This table is presented in Figure 39.1.

ASSESSING ALLIANCE STRENGTH

A strong therapeutic alliance is present when the client feels a positive affective bond with the counselor and that they are working collaboratively toward shared counseling goals. Note that it is the client's perception of the

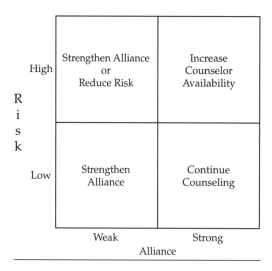

FIGURE 39.1   Model for Responding to Dangerous Clients

alliance that is especially predictive of counseling outcome and should therefore be the focus of an assessment of alliance strength.

Positive Affective Bond

- Has your client expressed, explicitly or implicitly, positive interpersonal feelings toward you?
- Does your client perceive you as warm, supportive, concerned, empathic, compassionate, nonjudgmental, and respectful?
- Does your client trust you to place his best interest first and to continue to work with him in counseling no matter what those interests may be?
- Does your client feel confident that what is being discussed during counseling will be kept confidential?

Working Collaboratively via Shared Tasks

- Does your client agree with the method proposed by you for addressing his concerns?
- To what degree is he committed to addressing his concerns by talking about them?

- Does your client think that what you and he are doing in counseling will accomplish the changes he wants?

Working Collaboratively toward Shared Goals

- What are your client's goals and expectations for seeking help? Are they being addressed?
- Are your client's goals consistent with your goals for him?
- Has your client expressed any opinions about the helpfulness and benefit of counseling so far?

PROTECTING POTENTIAL VICTIMS

Moving from Weak Alliance, High Risk to Strong Alliance, Low Risk

When a client is at high risk for violence and the therapeutic alliance is weak, counselors should make themselves more available through more frequent and/or longer sessions and/or 24-hour telephone access and direct their energies toward strengthening the alliance. If an alliance has not yet been established, the counselor should endeavor to behave in an affiliative, autonomy-granting manner and refrain from responding in a hostile or controlling manner. Counselors should listen with empathy, genuineness, and warmth to clients' narrative of their affect, ideation, and plans (if any) to engender a positive affective bond. The information gained via this process can be helpful when it comes time to formulate risk-reduction interventions, but the primary task of the counselor at this point is to let clients know they have been heard, understood, and accepted.

If a therapeutic alliance had been established and has been weakened or strained, the counselor should openly identify and nonjudgmentally discuss clients' perception of the alliance, clarify any misperceptions, explore any core interpersonal themes that are impacting on the therapeutic relationship, facilitate clients' expression of what they want in and from counseling, and make any necessary adjustments to the therapeutic tasks. The strong reactions the counselor is likely to feel can be used to help understand clients and to help clients understand the reactions they arouse in others. Simultaneously, or in sequence, the counselor should work with clients to alter those aspects of their physical and interpersonal environment that are promoting or maintaining violence.

Once a strong alliance is present, the counselor can then work with clients to reduce the risk of violence by addressing the source of their desperation and collaboratively developing and implementing risk-reduction interventions. The counselor can help clients make their environment less lethal, thereby assisting them in controlling their violent behavior. These interventions will usually be directed toward limiting the clients' access to the means for carrying out any plans they may have made (e.g., removing knives from their home) and/or initiating joint sessions held with a client and others significant to the occurrence of violence. The key process, however, is collaboration with the client.

Moving from Strong Alliance, High Risk to Strong Alliance, Low Risk

If the therapeutic alliance is already strong and the risk is high, counselors should increase their availability and interventions for risk reduction should be developed and implemented collaboratively (as described in the previous section).

Moving from Weak Alliance, High Risk to Weak Alliance, Low Risk

If the alliance cannot be established or strengthened sufficiently, risk-reduction interventions (as described above) can be implemented indirectly by involving significant others with whom the client already has a sufficiently strong alliance (e.g., family members or other health care providers) after obtaining the client's permission. Under these circumstances the counselor may have to "coach" the significant others in implementing interventions and is responsible for follow-up to ensure that the client has been contacted and the risk addressed.

Moving from Weak Alliance, High Risk to Breaking Confidentiality

Only if the alliance cannot be strengthened and risk-reducing interventions cannot be implemented within the boundaries of the therapeutic alliance should third parties be involved without the client's consent. Civil commitment proceedings should be considered, even if there is some doubt as to whether the client meets the appropriate criteria. If time and circumstances permit, the limits of confidentiality and the steps that will be taken should be discussed openly with the client. When third parties are contacted, only that information necessary to prevent the violent act should be divulged.

If the counselor has to break confidentiality, it will likely damage the therapeutic relationship, changing the relationship between the client and the counselor from a positive to a negative relationship. As explained previously, the fact that you do not approve of violence will not be a deterrent to violence if your client does not approve of you. Once again we see the importance of, if at all possible, not breaking confidentially and maintaining the therapeutic alliance if we want to use the counseling relationship to prevent violence. If we cannot do this, we have to be confident that the external measures we implement will be sufficient to prevent the threatened violence.

SUMMARY

Counselors have a legal duty to protect the potential victims of our clients' violent behavior because we are able to influence their behavior. Any influence that we have arises out of a positive therapeutic alliance, and so we must strive above all else to develop and maintain it. Counselors, therefore, should:

- Maintain records of what you did and why.
- Remain alert to violence risk, especially variations in situational influences.
- Develop and maintain a positive therapeutic alliance.
- Alert others only if efforts to influence your client's violence are insufficient.

References

Bachelor, A., & Horvath, A. (1999). The therapeutic relationship. In M.A. Hubble, B.L. Duncan, & S.C. Miller (Eds.), *The heart and soul of change: What works in therapy* (pp. 133–178). Washington, DC: American Psychological Association.

Heider, F. (1958). *The psychology of interpersonal relations.* New York: Wiley.

Mossman, D. (1994). Assessing predictions of violence: Being accurate about accuracy. *Journal of Consulting and Clinical Psychology, 62,* 783–792.

Tarasoff v. Regents of the University of California, 13 Cal. 3d 177, 529 P.2d 533, 118 Cal. Rptr. 129 (1974).

Tarasoff v. Regents of the University of California, 17 Cal. 3d 425, 551 P.2d 334 (1976).

Truscott, D. (1993). The psychotherapist's duty to protect: An annotated bibliography. *Journal of Psychiatry and Law, 21,* 221–244.

Truscott, D., & Crook, K.H. (1993). *Tarasoff* in the Canadian context: *Wenden* and the duty to protect. *Canadian Journal of Psychiatry, 38,* 84–89.

Additional Sources of Information

Bednar, R.L., Bednar, S.C., Lambert, M.J., & Waite, D.R. (1991). *Psychotherapy with high-risk clients: Legal and professional standards.* Pacific Grove, CA: Brooks/Cole.

Botkin, D.J., & Nietzel, M.T. (1987). How therapists manage potentially dangerous clients: Toward a standard of care for psychotherapists. *Professional Psychology: Research and Practice, 18,* 84–85.

Horvath, A.O., & Greenberg, L.S. (1994). *The working alliance: Theory, research, and practice.* New York: Wiley.

Meloy, J.R. (1987). The prediction of violence in outpatient psychotherapy. *American Journal of Psychotherapy, 41,* 38–45.

Monahan, J. (1993). Limiting therapist exposure to *Tarasoff* liability: Guidelines for risk containment. *American Psychologist, 48,* 242–250.

Truscott, D., Evans, J., & Knish, S. (1999). A process model for clinical decision making in high risk outpatient situations: The therapeutic alliance and suicide. *Canadian Journal of Counseling, 33,* 307–316.

Truscott, D., Evans, J., & Mansell, S. (1995). Outpatient psychotherapy with dangerous clients: A model for clinical decision making. *Professional Psychology: Research and Practice, 26,* 484–490.

VandeCreek, L., & Knapp, S. (1993). *Tarasoff and beyond: Legal and clinical considerations in the treatment of life-endangering patients* (2nd ed.). Sarasota, FL: Professional Resource Exchange.

PART V
Counseling Diverse Populations

40 MULTICULTURAL ASSESSMENT

Lisa A. Suzuki and John F. Kugler

Multicultural assessment is the process through which clinicians obtain qualitative (e.g., narrative measures and interview) and quantitative (i.e., test scores) information about a particular individual or group for the purposes of developing a better understanding of life circumstances, making diagnoses, and planning culturally sensitive interventions (e.g., educational, psychological) (e.g., Lonner & Ibrahim, 1996). The complexities of this process and the limitations of current practice have led to a number of controversies regarding unfair usage of particular methods and test instruments. It is important to recognize that all instruments are culturally loaded (i.e., reflect information based on what is valued in the culture in which the test was developed). Even those tests that contain little in terms of language (i.e., nonverbal tests) are considered culturally reduced measures. Given the brevity of this discussion, our focus is on racial/ethnic group differences in the assessment process. Specific attention is given to the following areas: (1) applying qualitative procedures to diverse populations (i.e., clinical interview and narrative assessments), (2) utilizing quantitative personality and cognitive ability tests with diverse populations, (3) identifying moderating variables to be considered in

multicultural assessment, (4) delineating steps in the multicultural assessment process, and (5) listing resources available to assist the clinician.

APPLYING QUALITATIVE PROCEDURES TO DIVERSE POPULATIONS

Qualitative procedures, such as the clinical interview and the mental status exam, are used to obtain background information and indications of an individual's current functioning. These procedures, although traditionally used as part of the intake process, may contain items or questions that fail to account for the complexities of the cultural context in which an individual resides. Takushi and Uomoto (2001) note, "Only when the clinician is willing to explore broad worldviews held by a cultural group, as well as the individual expression of those views, can a foundation be laid for comprehensive understanding of the client and conceptualization of effective treatment interventions" (p. 47). They note that generic interview assessment goals are to (1) establish a therapeutic alliance, (2) clearly define the clinical question, (3) assess the client's strengths (personal, family, and community resources), (4) gather background information, and (5) develop a tentative diagnosis. At each stage of the interview, the therapist must be aware of how cultural factors may be impacting the information that is being obtained.

Various tools have been developed to assist the clinician in obtaining culturally relevant information in the process of evaluation or actual therapy. For example, Berg-Cross and Chinen (1995) created the Person-in-Culture Interview (PICI) to assist in the development of a broader conceptual base for gaining information about an individual within a cultural context. The one-on-one, open-ended interview comprises 24-items. The questions are "constructed so that both cultural and idiosyncratic values will be spontaneously revealed in the course of the interview" (p. 339). The PICI can be used in training as well as part of a therapeutic session. The PICI draws on several perspectives, including psychodynamic, humanistic, family systems, and existential theories.

Narrative instruments also have been developed that focus on culturally relevant themes. One such measure is the Tell-Me-a-Story test (TEMAS; Costantino, Malgady, & Rogler, 1988). The TEMAS is a thematic apperception test in which the clinician presents the examinee with a culturally relevant picture. The pictures are designed for children and adolescents from White and minority cultures (i.e., Hispanic and African American). The children are asked to tell a story about the pictures presented; these stories are then analyzed based on their content. A quantitative scoring system and qualitative theme analysis are used to determine the psychological meaning of the responses within the individual's cultural context.

UTILIZING QUANTITATIVE MEASURES WITH DIVERSE POPULATIONS

Difficulties have arisen in attempts to develop quantitative instruments that can be utilized appropriately with multicultural populations. Racial/ethnic group differences in test scores are common on both cognitive and personality instruments (Dana, 2000; Suzuki, Ponterotto,

& Meller, 2001). However, it is critical to note that within-racial/ethnic group score differences (i.e., differences among individuals from the same racial/ethnic group) clearly exceed between-group differences. Despite acknowledgment of this point, most research has focused on racial/ethnic group differences (e.g., Suzuki & Valencia, 1997).

In the area of cognitive assessment, fairly consistent racial/ethnic group differences have been found in the literature. For example, one of the most controversial areas has been the use of intelligence tests with minorities (Valencia & Suzuki, 2001). In 1994, 52 experts in intelligence and allied fields endorsed a statement to clarify conclusions in the literature ("Mainstream Science," 1994). Part of this statement concerned the average scores obtained by racial/ethnic minority groups. Their summary cited the following test scores: Whites 100; Black/African Americans 85; Hispanics and Native Americans somewhere between Whites and African Americans; and Asians and Jews somewhere above 100 ("Mainstream Science," 1994). Note that these averages are based on tests with a mean of 100 and standard deviation of 15. Overall scores on these measures reveal only partial indicators of group abilities. Examination of the score profiles indicates that Native American and Hispanic groups demonstrate strengths (i.e., scores are higher) in visual reasoning abilities in comparison to verbal reasoning abilities. Asians tend to score high on visual reasoning tasks as well as numerical reasoning. The Black/African American profile of abilities is much less conclusive given within-group score differences (e.g., Suzuki & Kugler, 1995).

Procedures have been developed to assist the clinician in adjusting or identifying potentially moderating factors in the assessment process. For example, in the area of intelligence assessment, Armour-Thomas and Gopaul-McNicol (1998) have developed the biocultural model that integrates preassessment activity areas (i.e., health assessment, linguistic assessment, prior experiences, and family issues) with biological, cognitive process, culturally coded experience, and cultural context with the actual testing procedures. In addition, the model supports the blending of qualitative information and quantitative data to most appropriately judge the overall ability of students from diverse cultural backgrounds. Their work cites training and policy implications to enhance the development of intellectual functioning of children: "We undoubtedly believe that a child's intelligence can be boosted through teaching and coaching, which can be accomplished through several significant groups of people—mental health workers, parents, and teachers. In addition, texts are available that provide information regarding the cultural loading of cognitive instruments (i.e., McGrew & Flanagan, 1998)."

In the area of personality assessment, entire texts have been devoted to understanding racial/ethnic group differences on various personality constructs. These include both objective and projective measures (e.g., Dana, 2000; Suzuki, Ponterotto, & Meller, 2001). It is beyond the scope of this brief discussion to cover all of these instruments; however, it should be noted that subscale and profile differences have been noted on a number of personality instruments with respect to racial/ethnic group membership. A number of articles have been written in attempts to understand the meaning of these differences.

It is critical that clinicians be aware of overall findings for different racial/ethnic groups on quantitative measures. Historically, failure to take into account these differences has led to perceptions of bias in the usage of these measures. As noted in the following sections, this information can prove invaluable in understanding and interpreting the meaning of particular score profiles for minority individuals.

MODERATING VARIABLES TO BE CONSIDERED IN THE MULTICULTURAL ASSESSMENT PROCESS

Given the racial/ethnic group differences on qualitative and quantitative assessment instruments, it is imperative that clinicians take into consideration the multitude of variables that may contribute to these differences. These include but are not limited to socioeconomic status, home environment, educational attainment, hereditary factors, health factors, acculturation, racial identity, geographic residence, and language. All of these areas may in some way be related to clients' worldview and therefore may influence their performance on various measures.

In addition to these variables, it is crucial for the clinician to understand concepts of equivalence that impact the usage of tests for various groups. The different forms of equivalence as summarized by Helms (1997) include functional (i.e., scores have consistent meaning and the construct is evident in different cultural contexts), conceptual (i.e., the content of the items is equally familiar to all racial/ethnic groups), and linguistic (i.e., the item language has equivalent meaning for different groups). The concept of equivalence also pertains to the testing environment and the testing conditions (i.e., procedures).

STEPS IN THE ASSESSMENT PROCESS

The most effective clinician is aware of and attends to the various factors that may be affecting the assessment process. Equally important is the need for the practitioner to remain up-to-date on all state-of-the-art assessment practices and research findings in this area.

Collecting Background Information

A comprehensive, detailed developmental background history of an individual obtained prior to testing comprises the backbone of the assessment process. It is the foundation on which assessment questions are formed and measures are chosen. An effective clinician will engage in a detailed review of an individual's history, thus avoiding misinterpretation of test data. Information regarding family history, developmental milestones, educational and mental health services received, and so on is critical to understanding the biological, environmental, and cultural factors that impact test performance. Understanding the background information may preempt conducting the evaluation. For example, if the individual is a recent immigrant child referred for learning problems, the clinician may decide to wait and see how the child adjusts to the U.S. educational system before testing if there is no evidence of educational problems in the homeland. In addition to interview data, investigating background information may include reviewing past school records and medical reports.

Sometimes, formal assessment is not needed when the basis of a "problem" is understood within a multicultural context. Knowledge regarding the personal history of the client can determine whether a formal evaluation is needed. One case example involved a middle-aged Japanese woman referred for what the family perceived as depression. Given the lack of past history of problems, it was decided that an evaluation would be helpful. During the process of the intake interview prior to formal testing, the evaluator learned that the woman had lived through the tragedy of internment and had recently learned about the U.S. government's attempts at "redress" through financial compensation. The woman had become depressed and angry given that her parents are now deceased and they were the ones who had "lost it all and never regained what they once had." In light of these circumstances, testing was not needed to determine potential causes of the emotional distress.

Selecting Appropriate Instruments

If an evaluation is deemed necessary, the clinician must determine which instruments or procedures will have relevance to the presenting problem. The effective clinician will make efforts to remain up-to-date with new instruments and the accompanying literature. An important issue to be cognizant of is the performance of racial/ethnic groups on particular measures. Group differences are often noted in test manuals despite state-of-the-art standardization samples reflecting national census data. For example, most

norms are based on nationally representative samples with regard to race/ethnicity, gender, educational level, socioeconomic status, and so on.

With regard to quantitative measures, an important place to start is the test manual. Clinicians should begin with understanding the psychometric properties of the instrument. Questions to answer include: How were the test items developed? How was the test standardized? Many test development companies employ a number of procedures to ensure to some extent that the test items are not biased toward particular groups. This includes usage of expert panels to review items, racial/ethnic oversampling (i.e., including more than census proportions of minority groups in development procedures), specific reliability and validity studies conducted with diverse populations, and development of sociocultural norms (Valencia & Suzuki, 2001). Additional resources such as texts written specifically to assist clinicians using various instruments should also be consulted.

Administering the Testing Instruments

When administering the tests, it is critical that the clinician focus close attention on the behavior of the examinee. Issues such as motivation, frustration tolerance, and problem-solving strategies can be observed during this time and used in interpreting the test data obtained. In addition, testing-the-limits procedures (e.g., extended time, usage of paper and pencil for math problems, interviewing the client about a selected answer) can be used to gain additional information about how the individual approaches problems. It is imperative that one never lose sight of the goal of assessment, that is, to obtain a true estimate of the psychological construct being measured for a particular individual.

Knowing the multicultural literature pertaining to the testing of members of a particular cultural group can be valuable. Examiners should be aware of their behavior in cultural interactions. For example, McShane (1989) notes that when testing Native American children, examiners should sit across and to the side of the examinee so that they can observe the child without staring directly at him or her. Effective clinicians are aware of tonal patterns and volume of their speech, as this may have an impact on the test performance of members of particular racial/ethnic groups.

One of the major concerns many clinicians have shared is the lack of instruments available to test individuals for whom English is not a first language. Usage of interpreters and translators is often recommended. However, it is often helpful to meet with interpreters or translators ahead of time to go over the testing procedure and any questions they may have about the process. Interpreters or translators should be familiar with the test items and content. Their feedback regarding the issues of linguistic equivalence is important; for example, at times, items cannot be translated directly given that no equivalent word(s) exist in the client's native language. In addition, their observations regarding the client are important to integrate into the data collected.

Writing up the Assessment Report

The written report should reflect the merging of the qualitative and quantitative test data. Any deviations in standardized assessment procedures (e.g., testing-the-limits) should be noted in the report. In addition, any doubts as to the validity of the results should be mentioned. For example, if the clinician feels that the child being tested was not motivated and did not put forth best effort, this should be reported (e.g., "These results should be considered a low estimate of the overall functioning of this child").

Formulating Recommendations

Based on the results of the testing process, the clinician formulates recommendations and, if called for, a tentative diagnosis. Recommendations are made in light of the overall information obtained, including the background history and behavioral observations. It should be noted that evaluations are based on only a sample of behavior; therefore, any diagnostic impressions may be framed tentatively in the absence of long-term data (i.e., chronic problems). Recommendations should be made in view of the resources and environmental context of the client.

RESOURCES AVAILABLE TO ASSIST THE CLINICIAN

Test Manuals

Test manuals are important resources because they provide information regarding test development strategies and validity and reliability research for a particular instrument. The standardization sample is often the most well-constructed and -controlled sample on which the test is based (e.g., proportional representation based on U.S. census demographics).

Written Volumes

Nearly all assessment texts contain chapters focusing on testing racial/ethnic minorities. Table 40.1 presents recent texts, published between 1998 and 2001, that focus on the various areas of multicultural assessment.

In addition, reference volumes also provide a great deal of summative information helpful to clinicians. For example, the reviews contained in the *Mental Measurements Yearbook* (WinSPIRS, 1989–present) often contain information about test development strategies and norming samples with specific attention to racial/ethnic group representation and potential test bias. This publication is available on CD-ROM as well as in a text format.

Community Experts

Clinicians may find cultural experts helpful in understanding some of the subtle cultural nuances that may impact the assessment process. Professionals who are members of the client's cultural community may be helpful consultants and collaborators in the assessment process. They may be aware of the cultural norms and

TABLE 40.1   References Addressing Multicultural Issues in Assessment (1998–2001)

Title	Author/Editor (Year)	Areas Covered
Handbook of Cross-Cultural and Multicultural Personality Assessment	Dana (Ed.) (2000)	Research practices, acculturation, racial identity, MMPI, Rorschach, TAT, TEMAS, assessment of particular racial/ethnic groups, assessment training
Handbook of Multicultural Assessment (2nd ed.)	Suzuki, Ponterotto, Meller (2001)	General issues in assessment, ethics, quality of life, MMPI, Rorschach, 16PF, CPI, narrative assessments, cognitive assessment, neuropsychological assessment, assessment of family systems, vocational assessment, achievement, and racial identity
Test Interpretation and Diversity: Achieving Equity in Assessment	Sandoval, Frisby, Geisinger, Scheuneman, & Grenier (Eds.) (1998)	Perspectives on test administration, high stakes testing, employment testing, forensic evaluations, language, migration, acculturation, socioeconomic status, visual impairments, deaf and hard of hearing, learning disabilities, assessment training
Psychological Testing of American Minorities: Issues and Consequences (2nd ed.)	Samuda (1998)	Testing controversies, nature and nurture, environmental factors impacting test performance, educational and social consequences, alternatives to traditional standardized tests, compendium of tests for minority adolescents.
Understanding Cultural Identity in Intervention and Assessment	Dana (1998)	Identities of client and providers for various racial/ethnic groups
Specific Tests		
Intelligence Testing and Minority Students: Foundations, Performance Factors, and Assessment Issues	Valencia & Suzuki (2001)	Historical issues, socioeconomic status, home environment, test bias, heredity, special education, giftedness, review of cognitive ability tests
Assessing Intelligence: Applying a Biocultural Model	Armour-Thomas & Gopaul-McNicol (1998)	Intelligence assessment model (see chapter text)
The Black-White Test Score Gap	Jencks & Phillips (Eds.) (1998)	Racial bias in testing; race, genetics and IQ; family background; teacher perceptions/expectations; stereotype threat; other issues related to academic performance

mores that impact test performance. In addition, they may prove knowledgeable regarding community resources that may inform recommendations made for intervention.

Internet Sources

Having access to the Internet can also be invaluable in obtaining the most recent literature with regard to new tests. Most testing companies have Web sites that are easily accessed (e.g., www.psychcorp.com). In addition, some publications are available through special Internet access, thus allowing clinicians greater access to relevant and current literature (e.g., *www.psycinfo.com;* this database allows access to over 1.5 million abstracts). Note that there may be financial charges associated with the use of these databases.

Continuing Education

Workshops and institutes around the country have included attention to multicultural assessment issues. In addition, testing companies offer training services to clinicians and often cover information related to usage of their test with diverse populations. If this material is not provided, clinicians should ask for the information from the test developer.

SUMMARY

The increasing diversity of the U.S. population has led to concerns regarding the usage of various instruments and assessment procedures with groups for which these practices were not initially developed. Over time, testing companies, researchers, and clinicians have responded by creating new measures and challenging the usage of tests. A number of resources are now available to assist mental health professionals in developing multicultural assessment skills. Though this discussion has only highlighted areas with respect to the assessment of racial/ethnic minority group members, the information is applicable to other issues of diversity. There continues to be great need for enhanced sensitivity and awareness of multicultural issues as they impact the assessment process. It is our hope that with new research, more appropriate multicultural assessment practices will be established.

References

Armour-Thomas, E., & Gopaul-McNicol, S. (1998). *Assessing intelligence: Applying a bicultural model.* Thousand Oaks, CA: Sage.

Berg-Cross, L., & Chinen, R.T. (1995). Multicultural training models and the Person-in-Culture interview. In J.G. Ponterotto, J.M. Casas, L.A. Suzuki, & C.M. Alexander (Eds.), *Handbook of multicultural counseling* (pp. 333–356). Thousand Oaks, CA: Sage.

Costantino, G., Malgady, R., & Rogler, L. (1988). *TEMAS (Tell-Me-A-Story) manual.* Los Angeles: Western Psychological Services.

Dana, R.H. (1998). *Understanding cultural identity in intervention and assessment.* Thousand Oaks, CA: Sage.

Dana, R.H. (Ed.). (2000). *Handbook of cross-cultural and multicultural personality assessment.* Mahwah, NJ: Erlbaum.

Helms, J.E. (1997). The triple quandary of race, culture, and social class in standardized cognitive ability testing. In D.P. Flanagan, J.L. Genshaft, & P.L. Harrison (Eds.), *Contemporary intellectual assessment: Theories, tests and issues* (pp. 517–532). New York: Guilford Press.

Jencks, C., & Phillips, M. (Eds.). (1998). *The Black-White test score gap.* Washington, DC: Brookings Institute.

Lonner, W.J., & Ibrahim, F.A. (1996). Appraisal and assessment in cross-cultural counseling. In P.B. Pedersen, J.G. Draguns, W.J. Lonner, & J.E. Trimble (Eds.), *Counseling across cultures* (4th ed., pp. 293–322). Thousand Oaks, CA: Sage.

Mainstream science on intelligence. (1994, December 13). *The Wall Street Journal,* A18.

McGrew, K.S., & Flanagan, D.P. (1998). *The Intelligence Test Desk References (ITDR): Gf-Gc cross battery assessment.* Boston: Allyn & Bacon.

McShane, D.A. (1989, April). *Testing and American Indians, Alaska Natives.* Sponsored by the National Commission on Testing and Public Policy. Symposium concerning the effects of testing on American Indian and Alaska Natives, Albuquerque, NM.

Samuda, R.J. (1998). *Psychological testing of American minorities: Issues and consequences* (2nd ed.). Thousand Oaks, CA: Sage.

Sandoval, J., Frisby, C.L., Geisinger, K.R., Scheuneman, J.D., & Grenier, J.R. (1998). *Test interpretation and diversity: Achievement equity in assessment.* Washington, DC: American Psychological Association.

Suzuki, L.A., & Kugler, J.F. (1995). Intelligence and personality assessment: Multicultural perspectives. In J.G. Ponterotto, J.M. Casas, L.A. Suzuki, & C.M. Alexander (Eds.), *Handbook of multicultural counseling* (pp. 493–515). Thousand Oaks, CA: Sage.

Suzuki, L.A., Ponterotto, J.G., & Meller, P.J. (Eds.). (2001). *Handbook of multicultural assessment: Clinical, psychological, and educational applications* (2nd ed.). San Francisco: Josey-Bass.

Suzuki, L.A., & Valencia, R. (1997). Race/ethnicity and measured intelligence: Educational implications. *American Psychologist, 52*(10), 1103–1114.

Takushi, R., & Uomoto, J.M. (2001). The clinical interview from a multicultural perspective. In L.A. Suzuki, J.G. Ponterotto, & P.J. Meller (Eds.), *Handbook of multicultural assessment: Clinical, psychological, and educational applications* (2nd ed., pp. 47–67). San Francisco: Jossey-Bass.

Valencia, R.R., & Suzuki, L.A. (2001). *Intelligence testing and minority students: Foundations, performance factors, and assessment issues.* Thousand Oaks, CA: Sage.

WinSPIRS. (1989–present). *Buro's mental measurements yearbook* [Computer software].

41 COUNSELING AFRICAN AMERICAN CLIENTS

Lori R. Wicker, Robert E. Brodie II, and Donald R. Atkinson

African Americans are a very diverse group; they come to counseling with different backgrounds, customs, values, traditions, experiences, and presenting problems. Thus, there is no one definitive set of techniques for assessing, diagnosing, and treating African Americans. The purpose of this chapter is to provide information and recommendations that can be integrated with the knowledge and skills clinicians possess so that they are able to provide more culturally sensitive and efficient counseling services to African American clients.

The term African American refers to those individuals who were born in the United States and who are descendents of African slaves. However, there are various other persons of African descent living in the United States, including but not limited to persons or descendents of persons who have voluntarily immigrated from Africa, the West Indies, and South and Central America; these people may not classify themselves as African American. It is important to discuss with your clients how they self-identify ethnically, and use that term when any reference is made to the clients' racial/ethnic background. The term African American will be used throughout this chapter; any reference to Blacks is used to remain consistent with the terminology utilized by the cited authors.

AFRICAN AMERICAN DEMOGRAPHICS

African Americans continue to be a minority in the United States, both numerically and as a function of discrimination. There were 34 million African Americans in the United States in 1998, representing 12.7% of the population. More important to their status as minorities is the fact that they continue to be subjected to racism, discrimination, and oppression in contemporary society. In 1997, for example, 66% of reported racial hate crimes were perpetrated against African Americans. Other, more pervasive evidence of discrimination is reflected in the following demographic data on African Americans (unless otherwise noted, these data come from the U.S. Census Bureau, 1999).

In 1997, the yearly income of 45% of African American families was less than $25,000, which is well below the average U.S. household income of $37,005. Furthermore, 26.5% of African American families lived below the poverty level. In that same year, 47% of European Americans had incomes of $50,000 or more and only 11% lived below the poverty level. Although a significant number of African Americans lived below the poverty level, it is important to acknowledge that there is a growing middle class. In 1997, 25.9% of African American families had an income of $50,000 or more.

Historically, a sizable proportion of African Americans dropped out of high school and very few went on to college. However, this trend is gradually changing; in 1997, only 11.2% of African Americans dropped out of high school, and 59.6% of those who graduated went on to college. Furthermore, the majority of African Americans (77%) now have a high school education, and this number increases to 86% for African Americans between the ages of 25 and 29. A much smaller portion of African Americans hold a bachelor's degree (10.9%) or an advanced degree (4.6%). This is attributed to the fact that although about 60% of African American high school graduates enroll in college, only a small percentage actually complete college; the attrition rate for African American college students is approximately 70% (Steele, 1992).

As a result of low educational attainment, many African Americans occupy low-paying and low-prestige occupations. In 1998, African Americans represented 41.3% of those employed in service and labor occupations. Conversely, African Americans represented only 7.6% of those employed in managerial and professional specialty occupations and 11.1% of those employed in technical, sales, and administrative support occupations. A study by Sigelman and Welch (1993) found that over 50% of African Americans attribute their lower socioeconomic status and overrepresentation in labor and service occupations to discrimination.

The low income and high unemployment rates found in African American communities create a scarcity of resources, which in turn promotes a struggle over the limited resources; too often, this struggle takes the form of criminal activity. This is manifested in a high rate of deaths related to violence among African Americans and their overrepresentation in the criminal justice system, particularly among men. For example, in 1996, 61.7% of every 100,000 homicides involved African American victims (51.5% males, 10.2% female). Additionally, African Americans have approximately a 16% chance of being incarcerated at some time in their life, and of the total number of individuals incarcerated in 1997, 49.4% were African American (Beck & Mumola, 1999).

The elevated school dropout, unemployment, homicide, and imprisonment rates among African American males, combined with the fact that their life expectancy is eight years shorter than that of African American females, impacts the structure of the African American family. For example, in 1998, 46.7%

of African American families were headed by females with no spouse present. The percentage of households headed by females is almost equivalent to the percentage of families headed by married couples (46.6%). Among European American households in that same year, 14% were headed by females with no spouse present and 80.8% were headed by married couples. Although a large number of African American children reside in single-family households, many of the familial roles are carried out by the extended family (e.g. grandparents, aunts, uncles, cousins, and friends). In fact, a large portion of African American children are raised by their grandparents and many households include extended family members. Therefore, clinicians should acknowledge and explore the dynamics of the client's family (i.e., household composition, role of the extended family) as related to the client's presenting issues.

When treating African Americans, clinicians should consider factors related to the client's minority status (i.e., income, level of education). Failure to consider the aforementioned and consequently making comparisons to the European American culture may result in the perception of African Americans as abnormal, deficient, and/or inferior.

SPECIAL HEALTH CONSIDERATIONS

African Americans tend to have certain health problems and diseases at a much higher rate than European Americans, specifically, certain cancers, hypertension, diabetes, obesity, and HIV/AIDS. For example, prostate cancer is more common among African American men than White American men (Office of Research on Minority Health, 1999); one out of every four Black women over 55 suffers from diabetes; and African Americans represent 37% of those with AIDS. An increasingly alarming statistic is that African American women represent 62% of all women with AIDS (Washington, 2000).

The higher rate of these health problems can be attributed to various reasons, including inadequate financial resources, discrimination in the provision of medical services, genetic predisposition, and culturally influenced dietary habits. Environmental stressors such as racism and discrimination contribute to the higher rate of health problems as well. According to Clark, Anderson, Clark, and Williams (1999), increased stress results in increased stress responses (i.e., anger, hopelessness, fear, substance use, overeating) that negatively impact African Americans' mental health and ultimately their physical health (i.e., high blood pressure, respiratory difficulties, heart disease). Furthermore, as a result of the stigmatization of mental illness in the African American culture, psychological difficulty may be expressed somatically (i.e., gastrointestinal difficulties, body aches).

Taken collectively, these data suggest that mental health professionals should promote physical wellness with their African American clients, and give special attention to the affects of stress associated with racism and discrimination on their clients' physical and mental health.

AFRICAN AMERICANS' EXPERIENCE WITH THE MENTAL HEALTH CARE SYSTEM

There is evidence that African Americans underutilize outpatient mental health services (Snowden, 1999), and of those that do choose to utilize outpatient counseling services, a large number do not return after the first session. At the same time, African Americans are overrepresented in public mental health hospitals (Snowden & Cheung, 1990). African American underutilization of outpatient mental health services has been attributed to two general causes: factors within the culture that discourage utilization, and failure by mental health professionals to provide adequate or appropriate mental health services.

Cultural features that have been hypothesized to discourage outpatient mental health utilization include the stigmatization of mental illness, use of alternative sources of help, and distrust of (particularly White) mental health professionals. Nickerson, Helms, and Terrell (1994) have provided support for the stigmatization hypothesis. In a review of

research, these authors found that African Americans often stigmatize individuals with mental illness, avoid using the label of mental illness, and harbor negative attitudes about the usefulness of psychotherapy. In support of the alternative sources of help hypothesis, Cooper-Patrick et al. (1999) found evidence that African Americans are more likely than White Americans to discuss their mental health problems with a physician, and less likely than White Americans to see a mental health specialist for this purpose. Nickerson et al. (1994) also found that African American mistrust of Whites was associated with more negative expectations for counseling and premature termination with White counselors.

A number of authors have pointed to misdiagnosis and mistreatment as evidence that African Americans receive inadequate or inappropriate mental health services. Misdiagnosis includes underdiagnosing (failing to make any diagnosis or judging the symptoms or disorder to be less severe than is merited), making an incorrect diagnosis, and overdiagnosing (judging the symptoms or disorder to be more severe than is merited). Depression has been found to be a common, but often underdiagnosed, mental disorder among African Americans (Paradis, Hatch, & Friedman, 1994). A study by Coleman and Baker (1994) provides an example of incorrect diagnosis. These authors report that reexamination of eight male African American veterans in a VA hospital resulted in a change of diagnosis for seven of them from Schizophrenia to an Affective Disorder. Of particular concern is the fact that African Americans are often misdiagnosed with more severe forms of mental illness than is justified. Whaley (1998) examined differences in paranoid symptom expression by Black, Latino, and White Americans and concluded that cultural mistrust is often misconstrued as psychopathology among Black psychiatric patients.

Overdiagnosis, combined with lack of financial resources, may account for African American overrepresentation in public mental health hospitals; Snowden and Cheung (1990) reported a history of overrepresentation dating back to 1914. Rosenstein, Milazzo-Sayre,

MacAskill, and Manderscheid (1987) found that African American overrepresentation was particularly prevalent for involuntary psychiatric hospitalization, a finding that may reflect a treatment bias among psychologists and psychiatrists. There is other evidence that African Americans receive differential and inferior psychiatric treatment. Flaherty and Meagher (1980) reported that Black schizophrenic inpatients were more likely to be given "as needed" medications and to be placed in restraints and in seclusion and less likely to receive recreation and/or occupation therapy than were White schizophrenic inpatients. More recently, Betts (1997) examined the profiles of patients seen in a psychiatric emergency service and found that Black patients were more likely to be hospitalized and less likely to be assigned to respite care than White patients.

Given the negative ideas, beliefs, and experiences that African Americans associate with the mental health care system, clinicians should make an attempt to demystify the therapeutic process and address client concerns. Further, it is critical that clinicians deliver quality, unbiased service to the African American client.

DIVERSITY CONSIDERATIONS RELATED TO MENTAL HEALTH SERVICE

As stated previously, African Americans are a very diverse population. In fact, four subgroups of African Americans (women, adolescent males, adult males, middle-class men and women) with somewhat separate and unique needs have been identified in Lee (1999). With respect to African American women, mental health professionals are encouraged to consider self-esteem and empowerment issues that may arise from the negative images and stereotypes that exist in society. Mental health professionals are also encouraged to acknowledge issues revolving around fear that mothers may have about the safety of their children and themselves given the high rate of violence and health concerns. A specific issue that impacts the mental health of African American adolescent males is the widely held perception that their future is limited to athletics and entertainment or drug use, violence, and prison. For adult African American men, mental health professionals are encouraged to be aware of self-esteem issues stemming from an inability to fulfill traditionally masculine roles, which may also result in alienation and disconnection from work, family, and community. For middle-class African Americans, mental health issues are often a function of stressors in the workplace, including limited access and glass ceilings, double standards, and exclusion and isolation from White counterparts.

Another important dimension of variability within the African American population is level of racial identity development. According to the Nigrescence model, as cited in Parham, White, and Ajamu (1999), African Americans go through stages of rejecting or embracing Black culture and White culture. African Americans may endorse the precepts of one of the following stages: preencounter (pro-White/anti-Black), encounter (confused White/confused Black), immersion-emersion (pro-Black/anti-White), and internalization (pro-Black/accepting White). The identity stage of the individual can be assessed with the Black Racial Identity Attitudes Scale (RIAS-B) (Helms, 1990). Identification of the racial identity stage of an African American client will help the therapist gain insight into how individuals are reacting to society and how they may conceptualize their presenting issues. Additionally, the client's identity development stage provides information about the degree of social distance that may exist between the therapist and the client, partially determining the degree of rapport and trust that the therapist will be able to establish. Furthermore, the therapist's own stage or state of ethnic identity development may help or hinder the therapy process (Helms, 1990).

It is important for clinicians to recognize the heterogeneity within the African American population and the unique experiences of subgroups when developing treatment plans for African American clients. Further, clinicians will want to consider the impact that the racial identity of their client, as well as their own stage of ethnic identity, has on the therapist-client relationship.

RECOMMENDATIONS FOR CLINICIANS
WORKING WITH AFRICAN AMERICANS

1. Create a "safe environment" for the African American client in the initial session:
   • Explore trust issues surrounding the therapist-client relationship and any negative conceptions the client may have about therapy. For example, ask the client:
     — "What can I do to make you feel comfortable and safe in exploring your issues in therapy with me?"
     — "Are there any concerns about therapy you would like to discuss?"
     — "Are there any questions you would like to ask me?"
2. Increase your knowledge and understanding of the needs and experiences of African Americans:
   • Read relevant literature regarding African Americans.
   • Become familiar with the Afrocentric worldview as reviewed in Parham et al. (1999), which describes traditional norms and values of persons of African descent.
   • Consult with colleagues knowledgeable about working with African Americans.
   • Attend continuing education workshops that focus on issues specific to the counseling, health, and well-being of African Americans.
3. Examine your personal biases toward African Americans as well as your ideas and beliefs about working with them as clients:
   • Examine your opinions about working with African Americans.
   • Assess your qualifications to work with African Americans.
   • Utilize such instruments as the Self-Evaluation of Biases and Prejudices Scale (Jenkins & Ramsey, 1991), which includes questions such as "Do you have cultural

knowledge of African Americans?" and "Would you expect favorable therapy outcomes with African Americans?"
4. In diagnosing and assessing African Americans:
   • Consider cultural biases embedded in psychological assessment instruments, for example:
     — African Americans tend to elevate on certain MMPI-2 scales (Paniagua, 1998).
     — Intelligence test results are generally lower among African Americans. Therefore, when interpreting elevated clinical profiles or lower IQ scores, keep in mind that they do not necessarily reflect pathology and may be the result of a comparison to a White norm.
   • Evaluate culturally related syndromes, ask culturally appropriate questions, and be aware of the potential effect of racism (Paniagua, 1998).
   • Employ structured clinical assessments.
5. Become knowledgeable about counseling models shown most effective with African Americans:
   • A racially and diagnostically homogeneous therapy group such as "Sister Friends" for African American women (Jordan, 1991–1992).
   • A directive therapeutic approach such as cognitive-behavioral therapy (Sapp, 1994).
6. Given the proposed relationship between health and psychological problems for African Americans, increase correspondence with the clients' medical doctor:
   • For example, a client exhibiting symptoms of Obsessive-Compulsive Disorder may seek treatment for dermatitis or eczema as a result of compulsive habits such as engagement in compulsive body washing or house cleaning rituals (Paradis et al., 1994).
7. Refer clients to additional sources of support when appropriate:
   • Legal consultation.
   • Career counseling.
   • Church/community organizations.

References

Beck, A.J., & Mumola, C.J. (1999). Prisoners in 1998. *Bureau of Justice statistics bulletin* (NCJ Publication No. 175687). Washington, DC: U.S. Department of Justice.

Betts, T.A. (1997). *Differential dispositions in a psychiatric emergency service: A function of patient race.* Unpublished doctoral dissertation, Antioch University, New England Graduate School.

Clark, R., Anderson, N., Clark, V., & Williams, D. (1999). Racism as a stressor for African Americans: A biopsychosocial model. *American Psychologist, 4,* 805–816.

Coleman, D., & Baker, F.M. (1994). Misdiagnosis of schizophrenia in older, Black veterans. *Journal of Nervous and Mental Disease, 182,* 527–528.

Cooper-Patrick, L., Gallo, J.J., Powe, N.R., Steinwachs, D.S., Eaton, W.W., & Ford, D.E. (1999). Mental health service utilization by African Americans and Whites: The Baltimore Epidemiologic Catchment Area follow-up. *Medical Care, 37,* 1034–1045.

Flaherty, J.A., & Meagher, R. (1980). Measuring racial bias in inpatient treatment. *American Journal of Psychiatry, 137,* 679–682.

Helms, J.E. (1990). *Black and White racial identity: Theory, research, and practice.* New York: Greenwood Press.

Jenkins, J.O., & Ramsey, G.A. (1991). Minorities. In M. Hersen & A.E. Kazdin (Eds.), *The clinical psychology handbook* (2nd ed.). New York: Pergamon Press.

Jordan, J.R. (1991–1992). Cumulative loss, current stress, and the family: A pilot investigation of individual and systemic effects. *Omega: Journal of Death and Dying, 24,* 309–332.

Lee, C.C. (1999). *Multicultural issues in counseling: New approaches to diversity* (2nd ed.). Alexandria, VA: American Counseling Association.

Nickerson, K.J., Helms, J.E., & Terrell, F. (1994). Cultural mistrust, opinions about mental illness, and Black students' attitudes toward seeking psychological help from White counselors. *Journal of Counseling Psychology, 41,* 378–385.

Office of Research on Minority Health. (1999). Health disparities: Challenge and opportunity. Bethesda, MD: U.S. Department of Health and Human Services.

Paniagua, F.A. (1998). *Assessing and treating culturally diverse clients: A practical guide* (2nd ed.). Thousand Oaks, CA: Sage.

Paradis, C., Hatch, M., & Friedman, S. (1994). Anxiety disorders in African Americans: An update. *Journal of the National Medical Association, 86,* 609–612.

Parham, T., White. J., & Ajamu, A. (1999). *The psychology of Blacks: An African-American perspective* (3rd ed.). Englewood Cliffs, NJ: Prentice Hall.

Rosenstein, M.J., Milazzo-Sayre, L.J., MacAskill, R.L., & Manderscheid, R.W. (1987). Use of inpatient services by special populations. In R.W. Manderscheid & S.A. Barrett (Eds.), *Mental health, United States, 1987* (DHHS Publication No. ADM 87–1518). Washington, DC: U.S. Government Printing Office.

Sapp, M. (1994). Cognitive-behavioral counseling: Applications for African-American middle school students who are academically at-risk. *Journal of Instructional Psychology, 21,* 161–171.

Sigelman, L., & Welch, S. (1993). The contact hypothesis revisited: Black/White interaction and positive racial attitudes. *Social Forces, 71,* 781–795.

Snowden, L.R. (1999). African American service use for mental health problems. *Journal of Community Psychology, 27,* 303–313.

Snowden, L.R., & Cheung, F.H. (1990). Use of inpatient mental health services by members of ethnic minority groups. *American Psychologist, 45,* 347–355.

Steele, C. (1992). Race and the schooling of Black Americans. *Atlantic, 269*(4), 68–78.

U.S. Census Bureau. (1999). *Statistical abstract of the United States: 1999* (119th ed.). Springfield, MA: National Technical Information Service.

Washington, H. (May, 2000). To our health. *Essence, 31*(1), 61, 66, 72, 76, 80, 285, 287.

Whaley, A.L. (1998). Cross-cultural perspective on paranoia: A focus on the Black American experience. *Psychiatric Quarterly, 69,* 325–343.

42 COUNSELING ASIAN AMERICAN CLIENTS

David Sue

The Asian American population is heterogeneous, comprised of 25 or more subgroups, each of whom may have a different set of values, language, food preferences, and history in the United States. The population of Asian Americans is expected to reach 20 million by the year 2020. Some groups, such as Japanese Americans, have been in the United States for generations; others are relatively new arrivals as immigrants or refugees. In fact, the majority of the Asian American population are either immigrants or children of immigrants. The largest ethnic groups of Asian Americans are the Chinese (24%), Filipinos (21%), Asian Indians (13%), Vietnamese (11%), Koreans (10%), and Japanese (10%) (Lee, 1998; Ying, Coombs, & Lee, 1999). Asian Americans tend to be highly educated, with 42% age 25 and older having a college or professional degree, although 66% of Cambodian, Hmong, and Laotian adults in America do not have a high school education (Lee, 1998).

FAMILY CHARACTERISTICS AND VALUES

The orientation of Asian Americans can range from near concordance with Western values to an exaggerated adherence to traditional values. Between- and within-group differences among Asian Americans in terms of values and family characteristics can be quite great. With these caveats in mind, some similar characteristics found in Asian ethnic groups are described. The following are generalizations (Blair & Qian, 1998; D. Sue & Sue, 1999) and must be applied and evaluated carefully when working with specific Asian American clients.

Collectivistic Orientation

The focus is on the family and community rather than the individual. Children are expected to assist, respect, and support the family. The emphasis is on familial obligation (Fuligni et al., 1999). For example, Japanese parents rated "behaves well" as the most important attribute in children's social competence, versus "self-directed" for European American parents (O'Reilly, Tokuno, Ebata, 1986). The implications of this orientation are that assessment, problem definition, goals, and treatment should involve a family and community context.

Hierarchical Relationships

Asian families are patriarchal (the father has the most authority). Communication flows down to the children, who are expected to obey the elders. Parenting styles tend to be more authoritarian than in European American families. Filipino families appear to have more egalitarian relationships. The implication is that family therapists should identify and operate within the cultural structure of the family. Asian American clients may seek direction and suggestions from and be unwilling to disagree with the therapist, who may be seen as an authority figure.

Emotionality

There is less display of emotions between parents and parents and older children than is the case among European Americans. Control over strong emotions is viewed as a sign of maturity. Care and concern is displayed by providing for the needs of family members rather than statements or physical displays of affection. In Western society, the expression of emotions is often considered to be healthy. One must be careful not to characterize the lack of emotional display among Asian Americans as "repression" or a lack of concern.

Academic Achievement

Among all Asian American groups, there is an emphasis on academic achievement. Pressure to succeed can be quite high and the fear of failure appears to account for achievement behavior in Asian American students (Eaton & Dembo, 1997). Children may be under tremendous pressure to obtain good grades. A therapist can help the family define other behaviors in children that are indicators of success.

ASSESSMENT

In traditional psychotherapy, the etiology of a problem is often seen as internal, with little focus on environmental factors. Awareness of and the assessment of the influence of sociopsychological influences on the development of Asians in America are important. Experiences as a minority often are the source of problems or can exacerbate existing psychological conditions. In addition, tests and questionnaires based on European American populations are often used on Asian American populations without consideration of validity issues. Cultural differences can affect responses on assessment. On the MMPI-2, low-acculturated Asian Americans scored significantly higher on nine scales and bicultural Asian Americans had six significantly different scores as compared to their European American counterparts (Tsai & Pike, 2000). The interpretation of the results of personality measures with Asian Americans may reflect a European American bias. Differences are often interpreted as "deficits." The American Psychological Association (1993) "Guidelines for Providers of Psychological Services to Ethnic, Linguistic, and Culturally Diverse Populations" and American Psychiatric Association (2000) *DSM-IV-TR* indicate the need to assess the impact of societal and cultural variables on presenting problems.

Identification of Social Stressors and Social Support

Recent immigrants and other Asian Americans face issues such as language problems, prejudice and discrimination, unfamiliar role expectations, unemployment or underemployment, and conflicting value systems. Among a group of Southeast Asian refugees, depression was related to the experience of racial discrimination (Noh, Beiser, Kaspar, Hou, & Rummens, 1999). Refugees and their family members have high rates of PTSD and depression (Chun, Eastman, Wang, & Sue, 1998). Clinicians need to assess for these situations that may involve trauma and loss and help clients develop strategies for dealing with these issues. Help the client determine whether the problem is a result of environmental factors such as prejudice or bias or involves intrapsychic issues.

Cultural Identity of the Individual and Family Members

The degree of identification with the ethnic group and host culture needs to be assessed for each individual. Those with a traditional ethnic identification may be best helped by an ethnically similar clinician knowledgeable about the specific Asian subgroup. A client with a bicultural orientation can be helped by a clinician who acknowledges cultural differences. Those who have assimilated are often responsive to traditional psychotherapy techniques. Acculturation conflicts between parents and their children, between spouses, and within individuals are relatively common. Among adolescents, many have accepted European American standards of attractiveness and have lower scores on physical self-esteem than their mainstream peers (Pang et al., 1985; Sahey & Piran, 1997). The therapist should help clients be aware of their own cultural norms and values and facilitate means of negotiating a society with different sets of norms.

Cultural View of the Problem

Mind and body are seen as unitary, and psychological problems are often expressed in terms of physical symptoms, although many Asian Americans are also able to acknowledge the impact of stressors on their emotional state. In psychopathology, Asian Americans may demonstrate different symptom patterns as compared to European Americans. Among Vietnamese Americans, depression was accompanied by feelings of shame and dishonor, fear of "going crazy," and demoralization because of the inability to fulfill family obligations. Depression may also be expressed through bodily symptoms such as gastrointestinal distress, headaches, and heart palpitations (Chun et al., 1998). Ignoring somatic complaints or assuming they are the result of emotional issues may not be productive. A clinician should assess and treat both physical discomfort and emotional distress and take appropriate actions to reduce both sets of complaints. The clinician should also be aware that some studies indicate that Asian Americans appear to have different dosage requirements on psychotropic medications, may show more extrapyramidal side effects on drugs such as haloperidol, and require lower doses to achieve therapeutic levels (Chin, 1998).

Awareness of Cultural Differences between Therapist and Client

Therapists are aware of how their cultural background influences their assessment and choice of therapy and ask themselves, "Is it appropriate for me to view this client . . . any

differently than I would if they were from my own ethnic or cultural group?" (American Psychological Association, 1993, p. 46). Therapists should identify their own set of assumptions, stage of ethnic identity, and biases that may determine their reaction to Asian Americans with traditional values.

THERAPY

Asian Americans tend to underutilize mental health services (Snowden & Cheung, 1990; S. Sue & McKinney, 1975). This is believed to be due to variables such as the stigma or shame on the family by an individual seeking therapy, the process of self-exploration and emotional expression during traditional counseling and, the discussion of "private" issues with an "outsider." Among Asian Americans, mental illness is attributed to a lack of will power or self-control. Individuals are expected to have the ability to endure and tolerate difficulties. Coping with problems is accomplished by avoiding "morbid" thoughts. Thus, mental illness is seen as a failure of character in an individual who is unable to exert self-control in dealing with problems (Chang, 1996). To be a credible source of support for Asian Americans, the mental health professional should demonstrate knowledge of and selectively support Asian cultural values for traditional Asian Americans (Kim, Atkinson, & Yang, 1999). Therapists working with Asian American clients may have to adapt their counseling role depending on acculturation level of the client, the locus of the problem, and the goal of helping (Atkinson, Thompson, & Grant, 1993). The following are suggestions for specific psychotherapy approaches for Asian Americans (D. Sue & Sue, 1999).

Individual Therapy

The approach for therapy is partly dependent on the degree of acculturation of the client, although even highly acculturated Asian Americans appear more comfortable with some therapy roles than others. The therapist may have to function as a change agent, consultant, or case manager depending on the specific problems being presented. The following are recommendations for individual therapy:

1. Conduct a thorough assessment of social and environmental concerns and acculturation conflicts that may be related to the presenting problem.
2. Assess the worldview of the client, the problem from his or her perspective, and the goals the client hopes to achieve. Find out successful ways of dealing with past problems.
3. Identify positive assets or strengths within the individual, family, and community and employ them to help the client deal with problems.
4. Be willing to take a more active and directive approach in all phases of the therapy. Different options to solve the problem can be discussed with the client.
5. Try different therapy interventions. Asian American students, even those who are acculturated, appear to prefer the therapist to act as a "consultant" (discussion of options) for problems for environmental issues and to be a "facilitator of indigenous support systems" for intrapsychic problems. These approaches are associated with the Asian values of self-sufficiency and collectivistic values of emotional dependence and group relationships. Traditional psychological approaches that involve emotional exploration were rated low by the Asian American students (Atkinson, Kim, & Caldwell, 1998).
6. Consider using approaches such as solution-focused, brief therapy and cognitive-behavioral approaches, as they may be more culturally acceptable to Asian Americans (Iwamasa, 1993; Leong & Chou, 1996; Tanaka-Matsumi & Higginbotham, 1996). These techniques are concrete, do not require emotional exploration, and allow the clients to exhibit self-control. However, the exercises must be tailored to fit the value structure of the Asian client. For example, in working with Asian clients who have difficulty with assertiveness, the following steps can be employed. First, have the client

consider the possible cultural and societal context for the behavior. (In Asian societies, the emphasis is on harmony, modesty, and indirectness, whereas assertiveness is valued in mainstream American society. Social factors such as minority status, prejudice, and discrimination are also considered.) Second, identify situations where assertiveness would be functional (seeking employment, etc.) and ones in which a more traditional behavioral style would be appropriate (interactions with parents or elders in the community). Third, identify and alter disrupting or anxiety-producing cognitions. Fourth, employ role play and homework exercises to increase assertiveness in specific situations. These strategies are concrete and allow clients to establish self-control.

Family Therapy

Because of the collectivistic orientation of Asian Americans, it would seem that family therapy would be an ideal medium to deal with issues. However, despite the many strengths associated with the Asian family, certain aspects, such as the hierarchical family structure (father is the authority figure who is not to be questioned), the belief that problems with a family member reflect badly on the entire family, and the norm against sharing family conflicts with others, can negatively impact the counseling process. Family therapy approaches have been problematic because they also are based on European American perspectives on ideal communication or relationship patterns within a family. As with individual therapy, these tend to be based on individualistic models that incorporate egalitarian relationships. For example, Bowen (1978) believes that dysfunctional families are the result of fused identity and overdependence among family members. This assumption is in direct opposition to the interdependent nature of Asian American families. Also, in European American perspectives, the expression of emotions within families is considered healthy. Asian American students, however, describe their family's style of expressiveness as one with emotional restraint (Kao, Nagata, &

Peterson, 1997). "Healthy" traditional Asian American families are structured on the sense of duty, obligation, and respect among the members.

Other problematic aspects of European American family therapy approaches involve the use of confrontational techniques, role playing, and nonverbal techniques such as "family sculpting." These approaches would be considered confusing and a possible affront to the parents. Traditionally, family therapists have neglected the effect of such issues as conflicting values, prejudice, and differential acculturation rates on family members. Cultural variations to increase the appropriateness of family therapy for Asian Americans could include some of the following (D. Sue, 1994):

1. Expand systems theories to include societal issues and influences such as prejudice, discrimination, poverty, gender issues, and conflicting value systems. Issues involved in being an Asian American family in this society can be explored.

2. Address their reluctance to come in for therapy. Describe the session as one for which solutions will be sought and explain that family problems are not uncommon in American society.

3. Obtain the perspective of the problem from the father and mother first before communicating with other family members. In a traditionally oriented Asian American family, the clinician could act as the intermediary or negotiator and not have parents and children address one another directly. Conflicts can be reframed. A statement from a son such as "You don't care about me" can be restated as "Your son is wondering what he can do to make you proud of him" (Ho, 1987, p. 52). The goal is to have family members focus on the positive aspects in their relationships. In acculturated Asian families, experimenting with different communication patterns can be attempted.

4. Cast the "identified patient" as conflicting values and socialization experiences. Szapocznik and Kurtines (1993) found that dysfunctional ethnic minority family patterns often revolved around the conflicts produced by different rates of acculturation among family members. For example, an Asian adolescent may be attracted to the independence of his or her peer group. In reaction, the parents may exert their parental control even more rigidly. The task of the family therapist is to loosen the generational-cultural alliances (parent-traditional and adolescent-acculturated). The problem becomes one involving the struggle of family members to adapt to a competing set of values. Advantages and disadvantages of "American" and "traditional" values would be presented. This approach reduces blame on individuals and opens the way to more broadly define appropriate behaviors.

5. Promote filial piety by gently reminding the parents of their obligation to be appropriate role models and educators for their children. They must help their children be successful in a society where different values exist.

6. Help family members broaden the definition of respect and success by focusing on positive interactions and qualities. Instead of attending only to academic achievement in children, parents can learn about other skills and behaviors that they can be proud of.

7. Help family members learn the skills of generating a number of alternative ways of coping with problems and to use these skills in future episodes. The challenge will be to adapt the coping strategies to fit within the cultural context of the family.

CONCLUDING REMARKS

Although there clearly are differences in norms and values between Asian and European Americans, it must be remembered that within-group differences can be quite great. Focusing on traditional Asian values when providing therapy to an Asian American client can lead to stereotyping (Kwon, 1995; D. Sue & Sue, 1999). This danger can be limited by following the suggestions discussed earlier: assessing the worldview and degree of ethnic identity of the client(s) and determining the impact of environmental factors on adjustment.

References

American Psychiatric Association. (2000). *Diagnostic and statistical manual of mental disorders* (4th ed., text rev.). Washington, DC: American Psychiatric Association.

American Psychological Association. (1993). Guidelines for providers of psychological services to ethnic, linguistic, and culturally diverse populations. *American Psychologist, 48,* 45–48.

Atkinson, D.R., Kim, B.S.K., & Caldwell, R. (1998). Rating of helper roles by multicultural psychologists and Asian American students. *Journal of Counseling Psychology, 45,* 414–423.

Atkinson, D.R., Thompson, C., & Grant, S. (1993). A three-dimensional model for counseling racial/ethnic minorities. *The Counseling Psychologist, 21,* 257–277.

Blair, S.L., & Qian, Z. (1998). Family and Asian students' educational performance: A consideration of diversity. *Journal of Family Issues, 19,* 355–374.

Bowen, M. (1978). *Family therapy in clinical practice.* New York: Aronson.

Chang, E.C. (1996). Cultural differences in optimism, pessimism, and coping: Predictors of subsequent adjustment in Asian American and Caucasian American college students. *Journal of Counseling Psychology, 43,* 113–123.

Chin, J.L. (1998). Mental health services and treatment. In L.C. Lee & N.W.S. Zane (Eds.), *Handbook of Asian American psychology* (pp. 485–504). Thousand Oaks, CA: Sage.

Chun, K.M., Eastman, K.L., Wang, G.C.S., & Sue, S. (1998). Psychopathology. In L.C. Lee & N.W.S. Zane (Eds.), *Handbook of Asian American psychology* (pp. 457–484). Thousand Oaks, CA: Sage.

Eaton, M.J., & Dembo, M.H. (1997). Differences in the motivational beliefs of Asian American and Non-Asian students. *Journal of Educational Psychology, 89,* 433–440.

Fuligni, A.J., Burton, L., Marshall, S., Perez-Febles, A., Yarrington, J., Kirsh, L.B., & Merriwether-DeVries, C. (1999). Attitudes toward family obligations among American adolescents with Asian, Latin American, and European backgrounds. *Child Development, 70,* 1030–1044.

Ho, M.K. (1987). *Family therapy with ethnic minorities.* Newbury Park, CA: Sage.

Iwamasa, G. (1993). Asian Americans and cognitive-behavioral therapy. *Behavior Therapist, 16,* 233–235.

Kao, E.M., Nagata, D.K., & Peterson, C. (1997). Explanatory style, family expressiveness, and self-esteem among Asian American and European American college students. *Journal of Social Psychology, 137,* 435–444.

Kim, B.S.K., Atkinson, D.R., & Yang, P.H. (1999). The Asian Values Scale: Development, factor analysis, validation, and reliability. *Journal of Counseling Psychology, 46,* 342–352.

Kwon, P. (1995). Application of social cognition principles to treatment recommendations for ethnic minority clients: The case of Asian Americans. *Clinical Psychology Review, 15,* 613–629.

Lee, S.M. (1998). Asian Americans: Diverse and growing. *Population Bulletin, 53*(2).

Leong, F.T.L., & Chou, E.L. (1996). Counseling international students. In P.B. Pedersen, J.G. Draguns, W.J. Lonner, & J.E. Trimble (Eds.), *Counseling across cultures* (4th ed., pp. 210–242). Thousand Oaks, CA: Sage.

Noh, S., Beiser, M., Kaspar, V., Hou, F., & Rummens, J. (1999). Perceived racial discrimination, depression, and coping: A study of Southeast Asian refugees in Canada. *Journal of Health and Social Behavior, 40,* 193–207.

O'Reilly, J.P., Tokuno, K.A., & Ebata, A.T. (1986). Cultural differences between Americans of Japanese and European ancestry in parental valuing of social competence. *Journal of Comparative Family Studies, 17,* 87–97.

Pang, V.O., Mizokawa, D.T., Morishima, J.K., & Olstad, R.G. (1985). Self-concepts of Japanese-American children. *Journal of Cross-Cultural Psychology, 16,* 99–109.

Sahey, S., & Piran, N. (1997). Skin-color preferences and body satisfaction among South-Asian-Canadian and European-Canadian female university students. *Journal of Social Psychology, 137,* 161–172.

Snowden, L.R., & Cheung, F.K. (1990). Use of inpatient mental health services by members of ethnic minority groups. *American Psychologist, 45,* 347–355.

Sue, D. (1994). Incorporating cultural diversity in family therapy. *The Family Psychologist, 10,* 19–21.

Sue, D., & Sue, D.W. (1999). *Counseling the culturally different* (3d ed.). New York: Wiley.

Sue, S., & McKinney, H. (1975). Asian Americans in the community mental health care system.

American Journal of Orthopsychiatry, 45, 111–118.

Szapocznik, J., & Kurtines, W.M. (1993). Family psychology and cultural diversity. *American Psychologist, 48,* 400–407.

Tanaka-Matsumi, J., & Higginbotham, H.N. (1996). Behavioral approaches to counseling across cultures. In P.B. Pedersen, J.G. Draguns, W.J. Lonner, & J.E. Trimble (Eds.), *Counseling across cultures* (4th ed., pp. 266–292). Thousand Oaks, CA: Sage.

Tsai, D.C., & Pike, P.L. (2000). Effects of acculturation on the MMPI-2 scores of Asian American students. *Journal of Personality Assessment, 74,* 216–230.

Ying, Y-W., Coombs, M., & Lee, P.A. (1999). Family intergenerational relationship of Asian American adolescents. *Cultural Diversity and Ethnic Minority Psychology, 5,* 350–363.

43   COUNSELING LATINO CLIENTS

Rose M. QuinonesDelValle

This chapter focuses on Latino identity development and ethnic identity (Casas & Pytluk, 1995), specific Latino terminology, issues of acculturation, the notion of the conflicted Latino, and specific gender issues. The reader will learn specific counseling approaches applicable to Latino clients.

Effective counseling across cultures begins with self-awareness. In addition to the knowledge obtained through training programs, clinicians must have an understanding of their own culture and cultural biases to work with culturally different clients. Counselors must also be aware of the deficit model and the extent to which they themselves operate from it. The deficit model defines the culturally different individual as lacking, deficient, and as a drain on the society (Bacigalupe, 2000). The deficit model can be seen operating in the following examples: A Latino requiring public assistance is told by the caseworker that until he

or she learns to speak English, no assistance will be available; in a school system, a non-English-speaking child may be placed in a class for students with learning disabilities, instead of being taught English through the use of a tutor or bilingual classes. The deficit model is based on the assumption that the individual in question lacks some major area of social adjustment and is therefore the cause of the problem. When operating from the deficit model, an internal locus of control is projected onto the client and no extenuating circumstance is acknowledged as operating (Ridley, 1995).

In addition to self-awareness and knowledge of the deficit model, the counselor should possess:

- Knowledge and skills in discerning the particular cultural nuances of the presenting client; for example, Puerto Rican women raised in Puerto Rico will be more assertive than counterparts in the United States; a Puerto Rican male raised in the United States has different concepts about manhood than one raised in Puerto Rico.

- The ability to recognize cultural issues that impact the client from the dominant culture, for example, racist attitudes that may affect whether an individual receives public assistance.
- The ability to select a treatment modality that will accommodate the client's culture; for example, use of person-centered approaches may not be as beneficial as family systems approaches.
- The ability to recognize a need for networking and obtaining other resources, such as a folk healer, priest, minister, family members, and other social parties not often considered in the European American tradition.
- Willingness to advocate on behalf of the Latino client. Advocacy is not restricted to outside agencies; rather, it includes advocacy with other professionals such as school personnel or housing authorities. Often, this advocacy takes the form of educating colleagues about stereotypes and unintentional racism (Ridley, 1995), whether personal or institutional.

WHO ARE LATINOS?

The term Latino refers to a heterogeneous group of individuals with cultural similarities derived from their encounters with European colonizers (Spanish, Portuguese, French) and African slaves and the dissimilarities that result from their roots in a variety of indigenous cultures. Of special importance to Latinos are religious practices that are a blend of indigenous, Iberian Catholic, and African spiritualities, such as (1) having an altar in the home; (2) rosary novenas after a loved one dies; (3) calling on the Saints to intervene in daily functioning (a mixture of African and indigenous combined with Catholic rituals); for example, calling on Santa Clara to clear the rain clouds rain away, or San Alejo to keep someone away (Alejo comes from the verb *alejar*, which means to distance or separate); (4) visiting the folk healer while consulting the priest, minister, or physician on matters of the soul or body; an accommodation has taken place among these, evident in modern-day religious beliefs. In recent years, there has been an increasing influence of other Christian sects impacting on Latino groups. This accommodation of language, religions, values, and traditions created the modern Latino.

The modern Latino is known by several different names. *Hispanic* is a generic term used by the U.S. government as a classification for Latino people of 23 cultures found in this hemisphere. *Spanish American* usually refers to individuals who speak Spanish. *Latinos* generally prefer to refer to themselves by their nationalities (Puerto Rican, Cuban, Mexican, etc.). However, those residing in the United States generally prefer Latino over Hispanic. Historically, Latinos have self-referred as *Hispanos*, identifying their connected ties to Spain. *Chicano*, a term used by Mexican Americans in California, was born from the 1960s struggle to affirm their Mexican and Indian culture and their contribution to the American milieu.

In the mid-1990s, according to the U.S. Census Bureau (U.S. Department of Commerce, 1996), 22.3 million Latinos were reported living in the United States, a 53% increase over the 1980 census. Immigration and fertility rates (50%, respectively) accounted for the increase, with estimates of 39 million by 2025. The 2000 statistics show a Latino population increase in every state. Ranked according to population (U.S. Bureau of Census, 2000a), a majority of Latinos are concentrated in states with large metropolitan areas: California (10,459,616), Texas (6,045,430), New York (2,660,685), Florida (2,234,403), Illinois (1,276,193), New Jersey (1,027,277), Arizona (1,084,250), New Mexico (708,407), and Colorado (603,582). Michigan, Pennsylvania, Massachusetts, Connecticut, and Washington also saw significant increases in the Latino population in recent decades. Those states with the smallest Latino population (Maine, North and South Dakota, Vermont) also experienced population gains as much as 55.8%

from the 1991 estimates. However, Latinos reside throughout the country from rural areas to the urban centers (U.S. Bureau of Census, 2000b). Each group has its own distinctions and history (Zayas, Torres, Malcolm, & DesRosiers, 1996). Mexican Americans have been residing in this country since the time of the Spanish, have settled primarily in the Southwest, and have maintained contact with Mexico. Puerto Ricans were granted citizenship in 1917 through the Jones Act. This act facilitated migration to cities like New York; Newark; Philadelphia; Gary, Indiana; Chicago; Boston; and Milwaukee. Puerto Ricans frequently remigrate to Puerto Rico and return to the States. Many Cuban people fled to the United States and settled in Florida after they were exiled when Fidel Castro assumed power in 1959 (Altarriba & Bauer, 1998). In 1980, Castro released 125,000 Cubans from prisons and mental institutions and sent them to the United States. This group, however, did not have as much economic clout as the initial refugees and were not seen by Americans as desirable.

ETHNIC IDENTITY AND WORLDVIEW

According to Knight, Bernal, Garza, and Cota (1993), ethnic identity refers to an individual's self-knowledge and personal ownership in the group's membership and understanding of values, behaviors, and the often proud feelings (called *orgullo* in Spanish) associated with such ethnic membership. As such, it is important for counselors to understand the degree and type of ethnic identity held by their Latino clients (Sue & Sue, 1999). Important aspects of Latino ethnic identity include the following:

- *Familismo.* This term refers to a strong adherence to family values *and loyalty* (Sabogal, Marin, Otero-Sabogal, Marin, & Perez-Stable, 1987). Individual needs are not as important as family obligations. The *compadrazcos* (godparents) are an extension of the family and highly revered. Godparents are included in family affairs and are accorded the same respect and privileges as

the parents by the *aijado/a* (godchild). The *compadre/comadre* can intervene with monetary assistance, moral development, and the parenting of a child if the need arises (Ruiz, 1995). The Latino family is an elaborate system, including godparents, grandparents, aunts, uncles, and *padrinos/madrinas de boda* (best man/maid of honor).

- *Simpatia.* This is a need for promoting social behaviors and pressing for nonadversarial relations; a *personalismo* or magnetism is considered an essential component to smooth relations (Triandis, 1996; Triandis, Bontempo, Leung, & Hui, 1990; Triandis, Marin, Lisansky, & Betancourt, 1984). Political candidates are characterized by their simpatia, which contributes to being viewed as sensitive to constituents' needs.

- *Respeto.* This cornerstone of Latino ethnic identity is paramount in the maintenance of personal respect in interpersonal relations (Marin, 1992). No matter how much education a person has attained, the ability to relate to elders and others is considered more important. It is said, "Ser educado es tener respeto" (to be educated is to know how to respect and treat others). In Spanish, there is a formal and an informal manner of addressing individuals, and proper use of these forms is a clear indication of respeto. Respeto is demonstrated when younger people lower their eyes when speaking to an older person and when younger people address someone of authority or power (parents, older family members, educators) as *usted*.

- *Allocentrism.* This term refers to learning approaches that are cooperative in nature (Duran, 1992). This goes hand in hand with respeto, as cooperation is held in higher esteem than the individual's ego. In the schools, this is characterized by the student who wants to please the teacher and seeks his or her approval.

- *Machismo.* The Latino masculine concept of machismo in this country has been formed through the auspices of Hollywood. Traditionally, the term machismo refers to a man's responsibility to support and protect his family, and it makes him an asset to the family, community, and friends (Bacigalupe, 2000; Morales, 1996). Often, the popular definitions of machismo are the definitions ascribed to the term *machista*, which is essentially sexist, violent, womanizing, and irresponsible. As a result, young Latinos who confuse these concepts may have a perverted sense of self that may bring marital distress and family disintegration.

- *Acculturated.* This term refers to the level of cultural acceptance and integration of the individual simultaneously in two different cultures. For example, the acculturated Latino will be literate in Spanish and English and participate in social activities and navigate socially in both cultures. The acculturated Latino feels certain about his or her culture and operates comfortably in the other (Rogler, Malgady, Constantino, & Blumenthal, 1987).

- *Assimilated.* This term refers to the total acceptance of the host culture and the abandonment of the ethnic identity. This abandonment includes loss of language, customs, traditions, values, and all rudiments of the ethnic Latino.

Whether the ethnic identity of the individual has an impact on gender issues, child rearing, and socialization has not been thoroughly researched (Casas & Pytluk, 1995). However, the issue seems important enough to include in a chapter like this. From a psychological point of view, it would seem that the individual brings to all situations his or her self-concept, and this self-concept encompasses all areas of his or her development (QuinonesDelValle, 1999). Thus, Latino ethnic self-concept, which includes the values of respeto, familismo, and simpatia, colors all aspects of life, including child rearing practices, socialization, and gender roles. This is most apparent in parenting practices. Children, no matter what age, are expected to give their parents respect at all times; lower their eyes when speaking to elders; obey grandparents, godparents, aunts, and uncles; provide for family obligations and needs out of respect; and conduct themselves in a dignified manner. In essence, not to bring embarrassment to the

family due to miseducation when relating to others is of utmost importance (Ruiz, 1995). Ethnic identity also defines the coping repertoire of the individual, as the individual is acting from group and individual identity (Bandura, 1971; Bandura & Walters, 1963; Casas & Pytluk, 1995; Lazarus, 1991; Quinones-DelValle, 1999; Smith, 1991). This occurs when the Latino employs defense mechanisms (seeking support, cautious action, avoidance, assertive action, social joining, and indirect action) that are consistent with the Latino concepts of simpatia, respeto, familismo, and allocentrism (QuinonesDelValle, 1999).

Counselors benefit from knowing that the Latino worldview is similar in many respects to worldviews of other people of color (Bernal & Knight, 1993). Cultural worldview represents the way persons view and relate to the world and others. A particular understanding of the universe, the type of logic used, the relationship with the environment, process of activity (being versus doing), and time orientation are often similar among people of color from different cultural backgrounds (Asante, 1989; Casas & Pytluk, 1995; Jackson & Meadows, 1991; Jackson, QuinonesDelValle, & Toth, 1997; QuinonesDelValle, 1999). Worldview defines for Latinos the manner in which they will act, judge, make decisions, and solve problems (Asante, 1989; Ibrahim, 1991; Ivey, Ivey, & Smimek-Morgan, 1997; Jackson & Meadows, 1991; Myers et al., 1991; Trevino, 1996). The dimensions of a worldview play an integral part in daily functioning (Jackson, 1996; Jackson & Meadows, 1991).

Latino perception of the universe may range from material to spiritual, which provides the context for other philosophical assumptions (Jackson et al., 1997; QuinonesDelValle, 1999). Latinos embrace the essence of people in society and its organizations in the realm of the supernatural, giving meaning to people's lives and orderliness. For example, more traditional Latinos place great emphasis on their relationship to the spirit world. The acculturated individual, more so than the assimilated Latino, will have cognitive knowledge of that relationship. This orientation tells Latinos that maintaining positive relations with people close to one is of greater importance than the acquisition of material goods. This assumption addresses relationships, acquisition of material objects, and the importance attached to them. Relationships are viewed as more important than the acquisition of or mastery of objects, contrary to the Eurocentric perspective.

Latino logic is less polarized and more integrative of extremes. It acknowledges the gray areas; there is always the *pero* (the "but") to be considered when making decisions (Jackson & Meadows, 1991; Jackson et al., 1997; QuinonesDelValle, 1999). Latino cultures emphasize "being" more than "doing" as a means of functioning; this impacts relationships, in that Latinos generally believe that "being" allows for smoother interactions between people. For this reason, time is viewed as less important than relationships. European Americans' tendency to live by the clock is considered rude and not respectful of others. The Latino verbalization "There is still time" epitomizes this philosophy.

The Latino relationship with the environment is closer to harmony than acquisition or mastery. It is essential for Latinos to have this knowledge of themselves and their relationship to the world in order to be grounded. The communion (connection) with nature or the environment is created on a daily basis and is considered in the context of the past and present in a culturally specific interpretation, thus allowing for the future to occur within that context (Berger & Luckmann, 1966; Myers et al., 1991). An example of this communion is evident in the belief that one should leave a place as one found it or improve it. The traditional Latino sees this as a sacred duty.

THE CONFLICTED LATINO

"The conflicted Latino" is a phrase that describes the difficulty of living with the tension between Latino culture and the dominant U.S. culture. The less identification Latinos have with their ethnic group, the more marginal their coping skills and the more confused they become (Phinney, 1995). For example, during the Christmas holidays, the traditional Latino family has festivities that include a religious service, dance, food, and drinks. The offspring are expected to participate in these celebrations; however, the marginal individual may opt for celebrating outside the home. Such individuals may experience guilt and anger over their decision, although the non-Latino counselor may see it as a sign of independence from the family. This conflict of worldviews contributes to the stress of marginality, the confusion of living in two worlds and not adopting either. Marginality disrupts interactions with members of one's own group and those of the host culture (Bernal & Knight, 1993). Latinos who feel powerless and conflicted about their identity will most likely experience maladaptive coping when confronted with issues that affect relationships (Padilla, 1995; Quinones-DelValle, 1999). As a result, the conflicted individual can face low self-esteem and the adjustment problems that go with it (Phinney, 1995).

According to Phinney (1995), the "fitting in" of Latinos in their culture or the dominant culture occurs at an early age and concretizes during adolescence. Thus, through observations of the environment, Latinos decide whether to accept the host culture as their own (assimilate), reject the host culture (remain enculturated), or learn to live in two cultures (acculturate). The ideal is the ability to live and operate in two cultures, each having equal status (cultural pluralism) in society. This choice can be revisited and changed during a person's lifetime. The decision to assimilate, enculturate, or acculturate can be a conscious or unconscious undertaking (Rogler, Cortes, & Malgady, 1991). Usually, individuals make such decisions as they are developing and are reinforced by the ethnic group or chastised for not learning the values of the host culture. This reinforcement for learning those values may be negative or positive (Bandura, 1971; Bandura & Walters, 1963). Whether it is acculturation, enculturation, or assimilation the Latino employs, it is still an attempt to adapt to the environment (Lazarus, 1991).

The conflicted Latino struggles with the essence of his or her identity. This identity includes the tension between one's parentage (ancestors) and external environmental influences that try to create a like individual. That is, the external group environment is attempting to create an individual like itself, while awareness of one's ancestors may pull the individual toward Latino identification. This may sound foreign to the reader, yet this oppressive process takes place throughout the lifetime of the Latino. The conflicted Latino client is often suffering with questions such as:

- How can I fit in?
- When will they accept me?
- What can I do to get respect?
- Will my people accept me?
- Why don't my people act like other Americans?

These questions strike at the heart of a Latino throughout his or her developmental years. In addition to ethnic cultural dictates, there are dictates emanating from the host culture regarding gender roles, filial loyalty versus separation and individuation from the family, and competitive individuality versus Latino family collectiveness. Economic gain for the Latino may take a back seat resulting from institutional barriers such as prejudice or discrimination, Latino reluctance to pursue adjudicative relief, or family reluctance to lose a needed source of income. In addition, poverty, changing roles, lack of opportunity, and racism place Latinos in often precarious situations with their families.

Counseling Issues

By the time Latinos come to a counseling session, they may have exhausted the support system in the community and may be feeling desperate about their problems. In other words, counseling is likely to be construed as a last resort to an overwhelming situation. Typically, before trying counseling, a person will have consulted the extended family, including aunts and uncles, godparents and grandparents; in addition, the folk healer, priest, and minister may have been approached. For this

reason, the counselor may have to deal with representatives of the extended family when interviewing the Latino client for the first time (Carillo, 1982).

The counselor needs to understand that Latinos come to the counseling session with mixed baggage about their sense of self and may not necessarily want to change their worldview. Rather, the need may be for clarification of worldview and the degree to which the client wishes to retain it. Upon learning that a client is Latino, the counselor should confer with others who have specific knowledge about the particular ethnic group the client represents; besides the fact that no two individuals are the same, different cultural groups have different perspectives on issues. In addition, education and economic class impact the ego strength and coping style of the Latino (QuinonesDelValle, 1999) in all areas of development and opportunities available in the society.

Knowledge of the Latino's acculturation level is paramount to understanding the client's therapeutic needs. The processes of acculturation and assimilation are on a continuum and as such have degrees or levels of adaptation. The counselor needs to be aware that assimilation is never truly realized unless the dominant culture accepts the Latino as an equal in all areas.

Counseling and Counseling Suggestions

When working with a Latino client, certain considerations must be acknowledged by the counselor:

- Latinos traditionally do not take advantage of counseling services and are suspect of the counseling process; therefore, it is imperative to make a thorough assessment of the client's concerns and support system, as well as foster the therapeutic alliance.
- Whenever a Latino has an issue of concern, the first line of support is a family member, folk healer, or parish priest/minister. However, when counseling is sought, the Latino may prefer to speak with another Latino counselor. Latino clients may be

looking for a like counselor that understands their conflict firsthand.

- Counselors may find themselves acting as social worker, case manager, or advocate in the process of providing counseling services.

- The counselor may find that Latino clients react better to directive therapies, including cognitive therapy, solution-focused, and family therapy, and may not be receptive to insight-oriented modalities. Whatever modality is utilized, the counselor has to be supportive not only of the client, but that of the client's family throughout the counseling process and cultural context.

- It is not uncommon for family members (sibling, uncle, godparent, grandparent, etc.) to accompany clients on their first visit to meet with the counselor. Family members want to assure themselves that the client is in good hands and that they are not going to lose the connection to their loved one. The counselor should be aware of this phenomenon as a normal component in the treatment of Latinos, unlike the individualistic approach to counseling associated with traditional counseling.

- When working with adolescents, it is important to recognize that peer influences and conflicting cultural influences may be the cause of familial conflict, rather than the family itself.

- Counselors who acquire knowledge of the Latino cultural groups in their geographic region and who have some knowledge of Spanish will be more effective in forming therapeutic alliances with Latino clients. In addition, a knowledgeable counselor queries Latino clients about their ethnic group in a manner that acknowledges differences, for instance, between Mexicans and Puerto Ricans in marital affairs. The counselor should feel confident about the process of soliciting information and be able to convey this confidence to the Latino client, including soliciting information regarding idiosyncracies of ethnic groups. This will create a sense of assuredness about the counselor's skills and foster mutual respect.

- Counselors should address the client as Mr., Mrs., or other title until the client suggests using a first name. Clients may be bilingual, yet their development and thinking may be very ethnically bound.

- Another area the counselor needs to be cognizant of is the manner in which Latinos have been ascribed the negativity surrounding African American and European American relations. Latinos share the bounty of many racial groups within the many cultures; for example, Puerto Ricans may appear to be African, European, indigenous, or a combination of backgrounds; Mexicans may have the same attributes as Puerto Ricans, Cubans, and Dominicans. In essence, a Latino family may consist of all the human shades. The key is not to make assumptions about any Latino cultural group, but to affirm and validate the Latino within the boundaries of his or her culture.

It is important for the counselor to acknowledge the perceived barriers (language, skin color, race) of the host society as impacting on the emotional health of the Latino.

SUMMARY

Counselors need to acknowledge that clear differences exist between Euro-American and Latino clients. In addition to obvious differences, such as language and ethnic influences, there are distinct differences among various Latino cultures and acculturative differences within those groups (Szapocnik et al., 1978). It is also imperative for clinicians to be cognizant of pervasive racism issues in geographic regions and their impact on clients, and to be knowledgeable about multicultural counseling and know how to adapt Eurocentric therapies to the specific counseling needs of the Latino client.

References

Altarriba, J., & Bauer, L.M. (1998, Fall). Counseling the Hispanic client: Cuban Americans,

Mexican Americans, and Puerto Ricans. *Journal of Counseling and Development, 76.*

Asante, K.M. (1989). *Afrocentricity.* Trenton, NJ: Africa World Press.

Bacigalupe, G. (2000). El Latino: Transgressing the macho. In M.T. Flores & G. Carey (Eds.), *Family therapy with Hispanics: Toward appreciating diversity.* Boston: Allyn & Bacon.

Bandura, A. (1969). *Principles of behavior modification.* New York: Holt, Rinehart and Winston.

Bandura, A. (1971). *Psychological modeling: Conflicting theories.* Hawthorne, NY: Aldine/Atherton.

Bandura, A., & Walters, R.H. (1963). *Social learning theory and personality development.* New York: Holt, Rinehart and Winston.

Berger, P.L., & Luckmann, T. (1966). *The social construction of reality: A treatise in the sociology of knowledge.* New York: Doubleday.

Bernal, M.E., & Knight, G.P. (1993). *Ethnic identity: Formation and transmission among Hispanics and other minorities.* Albany: State University of New York Press.

Carillo, C. (1982). Changing norms of Hispanic families. In E.E. Jones & S.J. Korchin (Eds.), *Minority mental health.* New York: Praeger.

Casas, J.M., & Pytluk, S.D. (1995). Hispanic identity development: Implications for research and practice. In J.G. Ponterotto, J.M. Casas, L.A Suzuki, & C.M. Alexander (Eds.), *Handbook of multicultural counseling.* Thousand Oaks, CA: Sage.

Duran, R.P. (1992). Clinical assessment of instructional performance in cooperative learning. In K.F. Geisinger (Ed.), *Psychological testing of Hispanics.* Washington, DC: American Psychological Association.

Ibrahim, F.A. (1991). Contribution of worldview to generic counseling and development. *Journal of Counseling and Development, 70(1).*

Ivey, A.E., Ivey, M.B., & Simek-Morgan, L. (1997). *Counseling and psychotherapy: A multicultural perspective.* Boston: Allyn & Bacon.

Jackson, A.P. (1996). *Cultural World View Inventory.* Kent, OH: Kent State University Press.

Jackson, A.P., & Meadows, F.B. (1991). Getting to the bottom to understand the top. *Journal of Counseling and Development, 70, 72–76.*

Jackson, A.P., QuinonesDelValle, R., & Toth, E. (1997). *Assessment of cultural world view: Psychometric analysis.* Kent, OH: Kent State University Press.

Knight, G.P., Bernal, M.E., Garza, C.A., & Cota, M.K. (1993). A social cognitive model of the development of ethnic identity and ethnically

based behaviors. In M.E. Bernal & G.P. Knight (Eds.), *Ethnic identity: Formation and transmission among Hispanics and other minorities.* New York: State University of New York Press.

Lazarus, R.S. (1991). *Emotion and adaption.* London: Oxford University Press.

Marin, G. (1992). Issues in the measurement of acculturation among Hispanics. In K.F. Geisinger (Ed.), *Psychological testing of Hispanics.* Washington, DC: American Psychological Association.

Morales, E. (1996). Gender roles among Latino gay and bisexual men: Implications for family and couple relationships. In J. Laird & R.J. Green (Eds.), *Lesbians and gays in couples and families: A handbook for therapists.* San Francisco: Jossey-Bass.

Myers, L.J., Speight, S.L., Highlen, P.S., Cox, C.I., Reynolds, A.L., Adams, E.M., & Howley, C.P. (1991). Identity development and worldview: Toward an optimal conceptualization. *Journal of Counseling and Development, 70(1), 54–63.*

Padilla, A.M. (1995). *Hispanic psychology: Critical issues in research.* Thousand Oaks, CA: Sage.

Phinney, J.S. (1995). A three stage model of ethnic identity development in adolescence. In M.E. Bernal & G.P. Knight (Eds.), *Ethnic identity: Formation and transmission among Hispanics and other minorities.* Albany: State University of New York Press.

QuinonesDelValle, R.M. (1999). Cultural world view and coping styles of mainland and continental Puerto Rican women. *Psychology of Women's Quarterly.* Manuscript submitted for publication.

Ridley, C.R. (1995). *Overcoming unintentional racism in counseling and therapy: A practitioner's guide to intentional intervention.* Newbury, CA: Sage.

Rogler, L.H., Cortes, D.E., & Malgady, R.G. (1991). Acculturation and mental health status among Hispanics: Convergence and new direction for research. *American Psychologist, 46, 585–597.*

Rogler, L.H., Malgady, R.G., Constantino, G., & Blumenthal, R. (1987). What do culturally sensitive mental health services mean? The case of Hispanics. *American Psychologist, 42, (6).*

Ruiz, P. (1995). Assessing, diagnosing and treating culturally diverse individuals: A Hispanic perspective. *Psychiatric Quarterly, 66.*

Sabogal, R., Marin, G., Otero-Sabogal, R., Marin, B.V., & Perez-Stable, E.J. (1987). Hispanic familialism and acculturation: What changes and what doesn't? *Hispanic Journal of Behavioral Sciences, 9, 397–412.*

Smith, E.J. (1991). Ethnic identity development: Toward the development of a theory within the context of majority/minority status. *Journal of Counseling and Development, 70,* 181–188.

Sue, D.W., & Sue, D. (1999). *Counseling the culturally different: Theory and practice* (3rd ed.). New York: Wiley.

Szapocznik, J., Scopetta, M.A., & King, O.E. (1978). Theory and practice in matching treatment to the special characteristics and problems of Cuban Americans. *Journal of Community Psychology, 6.*

Trevino, J.G. (1996). Worldview and change in cross-cultural counseling. *The Counseling Psychologist, 24,* 198–215.

Triandis, H.C. (1996). The psychological measurement of cultural syndromes. *American Psychologist, 51*(4), 407–415.

Triandis, H.C., Bontempo, R., Leung, K., & Hui, C.H. (1990). A method for determining cultural, demographic, and personal constructs. *Journal of Cross-Cultural Psychology, 21,* 302–308.

Triandis, H.C., Marin, G., Lisansky, J., & Betancourt, H. (1984). Simpatia as a cultural script of Hispanics. *Journal of Personality and Social Psychology, 47,* 1363–1375.

U.S. Bureau of the Census. (1996). Population profile of the United States: 1991 (P-23, No. 173). Washington, DC: U.S. Government Printing Office.

U.S. Bureau of the Census. (2000a). *Estimates of the population of states by age, sex, race, and Hispanic origin: 1990–1999.* Washington, DC: U.S. Government Printing Office.

U.S. Bureau of the Census. (2000b). *Population estimates program: States ranked by Hispanic population, population division.* Washington, DC: U.S. Government Printing Office.

Zayas, L.H., Torres, L.R., Malcolm, J., & DesRosiers, F. (1996). Clinicians' definition of ethnically sensitive therapy. *Professional Psychology: Research and Practice, 27,* 78–82.

44   COUNSELING AMERICAN INDIAN/ALASKAN NATIVE CLIENTS

John Joseph Peregoy

In response to over 500 years of government intervention, intrusion, and oppression, Kevin Gover, Bureau Chief for the Bureau of Indian Affairs (BIA), used a ceremony commemorating the BIA's 175th anniversary to declare that "it was no occasion for celebration" but was time to acknowledge the BIA's role in "the ethnic cleansing that befell the western tribes" (Howatch, 2000, p. 10). He further acknowledged the sad and inhumane history between the U.S. government and American Indians/Alaskan Natives:

Never again will this agency stand silent when hate and violence are committed against Indians. Never again will we allow policy to proceed from the assumption that Indians possess less human genius than other races. Never again will we be complicit in the theft of Indian property. Never again will we appoint false leaders who serve purposes other than those of the tribes. Never again will we allow unflattering and stereotypical images of Indian people to deface the halls of government or lead the American people to shallow and ignorant

beliefs about Indians. Never again will we attack your religions, your languages, your rituals, or any of your tribal ways. Never again will
we seize your children, nor teach them to be
ashamed of who they are. (Howatch, 2000, p. 10)

This was the first time any U.S. government official has acknowledged the intent,
actions, and outcomes of policies of assimilation and genocide carried out against American Indians and Alaskan Natives. Beginning
a chapter on mental health issues of American Indians/Alaskan Natives (herein after
referred to as Indian/Native) with this quote
emphasizes not only history, but acknowledges continuing failures in education, state
government relations, and fiscal management (or mismanagement, as the case may
be) of the BIA for individual Indians/Na-
tives. This pattern continues to impact the
mental health and social functioning of this
population.

The intent of this chapter is to provide a
primer for non-Native mental health practitioners. It begins with an overview of demographics followed by a discussion of Indian
identity and an examination of stereotypes
and misconceptions of Indians/Natives. Finally, health and mental health issues common
among Indians/Natives are presented along
with a discussion of appropriate considerations in selecting therapeutic interventions
with Indians/Natives.

DEMOGRAPHICS

American Indians and Alaskan Natives are a
heterogeneous group made up of 555 federal
and state recognized tribes. There are 208
tribes not recognized by federal or state governments (BIA, 2000), partly because federal
recognition is a long and arduous task. For example, the Little Shell Band of Montana has
fought in the courts for federal recognition for
more than 27 years.

The U.S. Census Bureau (1995) indicates
that there are about 2.48 million Indians/
Natives. The population is young; 41% are
under 20 years of age, compared to 29% of

the general population. The median age for
Indians/Natives is 22.9 years, compared to
31.1 years for European Americans. About
57% of the population falls in the childbear-
ing years (ages 10 to 44) (Indian Health Service [IHS], 1996). Projections show that by the
year 2050 the Indian/Native population will
reach 4.3 million, nearly doubling today's
number. High school graduation rates are low,
about 66% versus 75% for the general U.S.
population (Pavel, Skinner, Calahan,
Tippeconic, & Stein, 1998). As well, annual income for Indians/Natives is about $12,338,
62% of the national average, with the poverty
rate being about three times the national average (U.S. Bureau of the Census, 1995). Because
the census figures do not take into consideration culturally driven extended family obligations, this figure actually exaggerates
household income for groups like Indians/
Natives that have large extended families.

Mortality rates for American Indians nationally are abysmal, considerably higher than
those for all other races in the United States
(IHS, 1997). For example, deaths from the following were identified, but are by no means
exhaustive: alcoholism is 579% greater; accident is 212% greater; suicide is 70% greater;
and homicide is 41% greater (p. 6).

About 67% of all American Indians and
Alaskan Natives live outside of reservations.
With this shift to the cities, an increase in in-
terethnic and intertribal marriages has occurred. Currently, more than 60% of all
Indians are of mixed background, the result
of intermarriages among African American,
White, Hispanic/Latino, and Asian populations (Peregoy, 1999). Enrolled tribal members living in the city are subject to many of
the same social pressures and urban survival
problems as other ethnic minorities (Trimble, Fleming, Beauvais, & Jumper-Thurman,
1996).

IDENTITY AND INDIANNESS

The issue of who is an Indian/Native and how
one becomes an Indian/Native is an open question for many. The blood quantum definition is

the most common determinant and grew out of government criteria for forcing people onto reservations and providing treaty-obligated services. Blood quantum refers to the degree of Indian/Native blood one has via ancestors and parents/grandparents. For example, Jerry's dad is a full-blood enrolled tribal member and his mother is a White woman of French and English descent; as a result, Jerry's blood quantum is 50% Indian/Native. The blood quantum criteria (also used by tribes to determine tribal membership) varies from tribe to tribe and sometimes from one generation to the next, depending on national and tribal politics. Establishment of Indian/Native identity also has complex political, sociological, and psychological implications.

Several divergent systems for determining identity exist (Minesuah, 1996). First, the BIA has defined being an Indian/Native as possessing a quarter of Indian/Native blood (BIA, 2000); thus, a person who is less than one-fourth Indian/Native is not eligible for services, unless they are enrolled tribal members. The U.S. Department of Education operates under a more liberal definition that includes tribal recognition and enrollment of an individual. A descendent in the first or second degree to a tribal member (child or grandchild of an enrolled member, referred to as descendent), someone who is considered Indian/Native by the Secretary of the Interior for any purpose, and Eskimos, Aleuts, or Alaskan Natives (Indian Fellowship Program, 1989). The Bureau of Census relies on self-identification; people either fill out the census form or tell a census taker that they are Indian/Native. Therefore Indian/Native identity is not only a blood quantum or lineage relationship, but also, more specifically, a relationship of sociocultural affiliation embedded in a reciprocal recognition with the Indian/Native community and tribe. Yet another unrelated system of identifying Indianness exists. These are individuals who identify as an Indian/Native and do not know their history and present community. This provides a state of longing for identity and being that will not come. These people are the want-to-bes—the largest unenrolled tribe.

MYTHS AND STEREOTYPES

This section examines five common stereotypes held about Indians/Natives by non-Indian others:

- All Indians receive financial support from the U.S. government.
- Indians/Natives do not pay taxes.
- Tribes are stingy with one another and do not share their wealth.
- All Indians/Natives look like Jay Silverheels on the 1970s environmental TV commercials, dressed in buckskins with long braided black hair, high cheekbones, and olive-colored skin, possessing great knowledge of how to live an ecologically balanced life.
- All Indians/Natives know all there is to know about all Indian/Native groups and are therefore experts and the envy of all anthropologists.

There are many more myths and stereotypes to be shared; however, it is beyond the scope of this chapter to present these exhaustive misconceptions (see Peregoy, 1999).

Myths about Financial Support of Indians/Natives

The first myth is that the government gives monthly checks to all Indians/Natives. In reality, *no* Indians/Natives receive monthly government checks for being Indian/Native. Some tribal members receive income from their tribes, called *per capita payments:* "Per capita payments are like dividends paid to stockholders in corporate America. These payments are generally made once a year from monies generated by the tribes by leasing land or royalties on natural resources" (Peregoy, 1999). Some Indians/Natives who qualify receive Social Service Assistance just as other citizens do.

Freedom from taxation appears to be another myth that abounds in the non-Indian world. Money made by Indians/Natives working in a free market economy is taxable by both the federal and state governments.

Land holdings held in "trust" by the BIA are not taxable. The early impetus of this trust relationship dates back to the first treaties.

Several tribes have made the news lately because of the 1988 Indian Gaming Regulatory Act (IGRA), which allows tribes to open gaming within reservation boundaries. The news has depicted some tribes as extremely rich due to gaming, but this does not apply to all tribes and the income earned from gaming is not shared across tribes, just as the income of one state or community is not shared with other, poorer communities.

Myths about Appearance, Attitudes, and Behavior

Appearance is often imposed by an outsider, looking in, with the expectation of Indians/Natives dressed in buckskins with long braided black hair, high cheekbones, and olive-colored skin. At a minimum, these assumptions leave no room for the blond, blue eyed Indian/Native or the Black Indians of the Carolinas and Florida (Peregoy, 1999). Intermarriage over the past 500 years has so changed the gene pool, that narrow definitions of physical appearance do not fit the reality of Indian/Native peoples.

The romantic notion that Indians/Natives possess great knowledge of how to live an ecologically balanced life is just that: an unfounded notion. The cultural heritage values ecological balance, but contemporary Indians/Natives do not automatically share such values or have the knowledge they need to live such a life.

Finally, non-Indians often erroneously expect that all Indian/Native people hold the knowledge and practice of sacred ceremonies of all tribes, living or dead. This expectation is grounded in what this author refers to as the "expectation of genetic wisdom" (Peregoy, 1991, p. 114). Simply stated, this is the expectation that an individual Indian/Native is an expert on Indian affairs around the nation, be they spiritual or mundane, across all 555 tribes. Obviously, such an expectation is absurd.

HEALTH AND MENTAL HEALTH ISSUES

The health and mental health status of Indian/Native peoples is generally below that of their White counterparts. Indian/Native women are at higher risk for illnesses like lupus and heart disease, and older women are at greater risk for tuberculosis, pneumonia, and malnutrition. The number of deaths for Indian/Native women due to liver and kidney disease is also higher than for their non-Indian counterparts (IHS, 1996). The primary health/mental health issues in Indian/Native country include depression; alcohol, tobacco, and other drug (ATOD) use; suicide; liver/kidney disease; and tuberculosis.

Alcohol and other drug use in the Indian/Native communities takes a drastic toll. Alcoholism death rates for Indians/Natives range about six times that of the national average (IHS, 1996). In reviewing the 10 leading causes of death in the Indian/Native communities from 1983 to 1993, alcohol use was directly implicated in four (accidents, cirrhosis of the liver, homicides, and suicides). Nearly one-third of all outpatient visits to Indian Health Services (IHS) were related to substance abuse or dependence (IHS, 1997).

Reliable data on extent and pattern of drug use (including alcohol) among Indians/Natives have been scarce and compounded by limits of the generalizability of findings (Abbott, 1998). Research suggests that Indians/Natives are more likely to be either abstainers or heavy drinkers than members of the general population (Barker & Krammer, 1996). Among Navajo, fewer adults drink alcohol (52%) than others in the general population of the United States (May, 1992). The greatest proportion of Indian/Native adults who drink are between the ages of 15 and 29, and there is a reduction in drinking behaviors after the age of 40. A 1996 survey by Barker and Krammer among older urban Indians/Natives found that 72% of those over 59 did not drink, suggesting that this age group did not differ in their alcohol consumption from the general population. Thus, it appears that substance abuse behaviors taper off with age. Yet, for those who drink heavily, it is a killing behavior.

Data available from the 1997 *Trends in Indian Health* indicated that for Indian/Native women, death rates from alcoholism are also high, ranging from 20.1 to 87.6 per 100,000 from tribe to tribe. The rate for all U.S. females is fewer than 10 per 100,000 across all age groups (IHS, 1997). Fetal alcohol syndrome (FAS) is estimated to occur in the general population at about 1 in 750 live births, but May (1994) found that the incidence ranged from 1.3 in 1,000 live births for the Navajo tribe to 10.3 in 1,000 live births for other Southwestern and Plains tribes. Fetal alcohol syndrome and fetal alcohol effects (FAE) on their offspring are consequences for consuming large amounts of alcohol during pregnancy. The child with FAS or FAE suffers from neurosensory and developmental disabilities.

Violence and victimization rates are also high. In 1997, the IHS stated that age-adjusted mortality rates were considerably higher for Indians/Natives than for all other races. Nationally, crime statistics for 1998 showed that the average annual number of victimizations for Indians/Natives age 12 and older are 248% higher than for the rest of the nation. A report by the Bureau of Justice Statistics (Greenfield & Smith, 1999) stated, "Intimate and family violence involve a comparatively high level of alcohol and drug abuse by offenders as perceived by the victims. Indian/Native victims of intimate and family violence, however, are more likely than others to be injured and need hospital care" (p. 8).

Depression is also common, but exact figures on its incidence are difficult to obtain. For Indians/Natives, prevalence estimates suggest that 20% to 60% of the population suffer from depression and other psychiatric disorders (Brucker & Perry, 1998). In one study, Wilson, Civic, and Glass (1995) examined depressive syndromes with 106 Indian/Native patients and found 20.7% scored positive for depressive syndromes and 8.9% met the criteria for major depressive disorder.

Suicide in Indian country is of great concern. Suicide rates in the Indian/Native community are 5 to 10 times higher than the national average. A needs assessment survey on one reservation in the Northwest found that 90% of students, parents, and teachers were concerned about suicide (Schliebner & Peregoy, 1996). Suicide rates are regarded as at least partly due to acculturative and deculturative stress (EchoHawk, 1997). Research is mixed on causation, but several hypotheses have been identified. Psychological factors for depression include an individual's and community's response to the stressors of oppression and other forms of racism. The literature often cites *acculturative stress* as a precipitating or causal factor to depression and other mental health problems, defined as the demands to integrate into and identify with a dominant culture (Berry, Minde, & Mok, 1987). Gloria and Peregoy (1996) have identified *deculturative stress* as stress resulting from the loss or devaluation of historical tradition. They view acculturation as the outcome of processes that occur at multiple levels in a society, and assert that the acquisition of foreign (mainstream) beliefs and values produces high rates of substance abuse, family disruption, criminal behavior, and mental illness; these are attributes of deculturative stress. Deculturative stress is also related to *culture shedding;* this is an adaptation response that includes changing social norms, learning to see gender differently, and a host of other behavioral shifts (Berry, Segall, & Kagitcibasi, 1997): "To be between two worlds forces individuals into conflicts of choice and produces casualties among those who cannot embrace either the old or new" (Braroe, 1988, p. 8).

A little-known issue facing Indian/Native veterans is Posttraumatic Stress Disorder (PTSD) resulting from combat experience, but firm estimates of its prevalence are not available. Approximately 12,500 Indians/Natives served in the Gulf War crisis. Many more served in Vietnam, Korea, and World Wars I and II. Symptoms of PTSD are generally related to the intensity and amount of combat an individual has experienced. For many, the Vietnam War represented a tour of ambiguity. Peregoy (1999) reported anecdotal information of the expectation of White officers for

Indians/Natives to have the innate skills to serve as scouts for reconnaissance missions. Serving on point as scouts put that individual at extreme risk.

The reader should be mindful here of another stereotype—the drunken, depressed Indian. While depression, suicide, and substance abuse rates are extremely high for Indians/Natives, these are not universal afflictions of the population. However, alcohol and drug abuse *are* killing factors for this population and need to be addressed more vigorously by both the local native community and the mental health community.

THERAPEUTIC INTERVENTIONS

Barriers to access for mental health services in the non-Indian community include historical distrust; difficulties in cross-cultural communication stemming from a lack of shared meaning; the use of extended family systems, which can be misunderstood as child neglect or social instability within the family unit; and unfamiliarity of non-Indian counselors with Indian/Native conversational styles (Peregoy, 1999; Sue & Sue, 1999; Trimble et al., 1996). Indian/Native groups may not emphasize personal issues and may refer only peripherally to matters of great importance to the family.

Unfortunately, non-Indian agencies have not demonstrated the ability to cross-culturalize their services to benefit Indian/Native families (Peregoy & Schliebner, 2000). Even though home-based services have significant promise with this population, there is some resistance to providing home-based services on the part of non-Indian providers. This resistance is interpreted by the Indian community as a fear of cultural differences.

What makes for successful interventions with this population? The key to effective therapeutic interventions is to begin by assessing *the level of identity* and *acculturation* of the client before beginning treatment planning. Erroneous assumptions about acculturation have been significant barriers to effective treatment and contributed to

underutilization and early termination by many Indian/Native clients.

An Indian/Native identity is simply defined by how an individual sees himself or herself in the world and answers the question Who am I? Components of an identity include who people associate with for leisure activities, participation in social gatherings and ceremonies, and a connection and awareness of their tribe of origin and/or urban Indian community in which they reside. Those clients who have an Indian/Native ancestor and no affiliation or experience with their tribe would not be likely to have a strong cultural identity. Cultural considerations for this client would not necessarily be needed.

Acculturation refers to contact between two differing cultures; where one cultural group is considered dominant due to numerical, economic, or political power, the other can be considered nondominant (Berry et al., 1997). After contact, both cultures change; however, generally the nondominant group is the one that changes most. Acculturation can occur at the group or individual level. At the individual level, acculturation requires behavior changes, including taking on behaviors and attitudes of the dominant culture. This person has become acculturated, maintaining culture-of-origin ways of being while learning new behaviors and ways of being in the new environment. If individuals maintain elements of their culture and learn the dominant group's social expectations and norms, they are bicultural. When individuals choose to develop bicultural skills (maintaining culture-of-origin practices while learning to replace old behaviors, thus functionally practicing in both cultures), they develop coping strategies that assist in maintaining a functional ego, resulting in less stress in their daily lives (Berry et al., 1997). LaFromboise, Coleman, and Gerton (1993) have suggested that individuals who have bicultural skills are more likely to maintain a stronger level of mental health than monocultural individuals. Choice is a key to the acculturation process. It is appropriate here to distinguish between acculturation and assimilation. The individual who sheds all culture-of-origin beliefs and behaviors and embraces the dominant group, without regard for the culture of origin, has become assimilated. Assimilation does not have the positive association with mental health that a bicultural identity has been hypothesized to have.

In urban areas, it is probably safe to suggest that few traditional people will walk into a non-Indian counselor's door, unless it is a choice out of their control. For those who do come forward, generally speaking, it is important for mental health professionals to become known in the community if they are to be effective with Indian/Native clients. This means two things: becoming active in the Indian/Native community by attending community activities such as Pow-Wows and other social gatherings and making a paradigm shift in what constitutes therapy. A counselor who is making a successful paradigm shift may conduct therapy out of the office, on a basketball court, walking along a creek, or assisting in stripping salmon for smoking and winter stores. In addition to the location of therapy, since traditional people believe in a fundamental relationship to all things on earth, a paradigm shift from linear to systemic thinking assists the counselor in relating to the client's worldview (Garrett, 1999).

Assessment and treatment planning should be driven by identity and level of acculturation. Counselors should look to the client to provide cultural information that is relevant. Also, counselors ought to seek out community leaders for guidance in defining what behaviors are within community norms and those that might be idiosyncratic. A caution is made to the practitioner to not be seduced by what may be perceived as the exotic; this only objectifies the client and diminishes treatment. The following is a case in point:

Junior is a full-blood member of his tribe, born and raised on the St. Regis Mohawk reservation in upstate New York. He moved off the reservation to New York City to make money by working as a high-rise steel construction worker. He still practices traditional ways. Junior has been living in the city, off and on, for about three years. He travels back home about eight times a year. At times, Junior feels he will be pushed off

one of the tall buildings while working by someone he cannot see. Other times, he sees himself walking on air instead of a steel girder. These feelings are transitory but enough of a cause for concern for him to seek mental health services.

In addition to the usual intake topics, to begin successful work with Junior the counselor should inquire about a variety of issues beginning with spiritual orientation and religion. First and second language is another important topic, along with frequency of spiritual practices. These topics can serve as a springboard into understanding the client's identity. During the intake, it is suggested that the counselor explore family-of-origin information to include spiritual practices (Peregoy, 1999). The next step involves exploring stressors and coping strategies. Exploration of Junior's assumptions assist in understanding how he experiences the world. By examining Junior's attendance and participation at ceremonies (via the intake and interview), the therapist can begin to conceptualize both Junior's level of identity development and level of acculturation. By understanding the interplay between these factors, the therapist can then work with the client to develop appropriate goals. If Junior is strongly traditional, the therapist may need to seek guidance from an Indian/Native community organization, or a referral to a traditional healer may be needed. If Junior is a contemporary Indian/Native, then talk therapy, problem-solving skills, and stress management may be the direction to take. Alternatively, it may be that a combination of traditional and contemporary interventions is the most prudent course. In any case, the interventions should be driven by his level of identity and acculturation.

Garrett (1999) has effectively summarized implications for the service provider working with the Indian/Native client: "By understanding that everything has meaning and purpose, our goal in counseling becomes one of helping Native clients to discover purpose, to examine their assumptions, to seek an awareness of universal and personal truths, and to make choices that allow them to exist in a state of harmony and balance within the Circle of Life" (p. 102).

References

Abbott, P.J. (1998). Traditional and Western healing practices for alcoholism in American Indians and Alaskan Natives. *Substance Use and Misuse, 33,* 2605–2646.

Barker, J.C., & Krammer, J.B. (1996). Alcohol consumption among older urban American Indians. *Journal of Studies of Alcohol, 57,* 119–124.

Berry, J.W., Segall, M.H., & Kagitçibasi, C. (1997). *The handbook of cross-cultural psychology: Social and behavior applications* (2nd ed.). Boston: Allyn & Bacon.

Berry, J.W., Minde, T., & Mok, D. (1987). Comparative studies of acculturative stress. *International Migration Review, 21,* 491–511.

Brucker, P.S., & Perry, B.J. (1998). American Indians: Presenting concerns and considerations for family therapists. *Journal of Family Therapy, 26,* 307–319.

Braroe, M.W. (1988). *Indian and White: Self-image and interaction in a Canadian Plains community.* Stanford, CA: Stanford University Press.

Bureau of Indian Affairs. (2000, November 29). *List of federally recognized American Indian tribes and Alaska Natives.* Available: www.doi.gov/bureau-indian-affairs.html

EchoHawk, M. (1997). Suicide: The scourge of Native American people. *Suicide and Life-Threatening Behavior, 27,* 60–67.

Fleming, C.M. (1992). Next twenty years of prevention in Indian country. *Journal of American Indian and Alaskan Native Mental Health Research, 4,* 85–88.

Garrett, M.T. (1999). Understanding the "medicine wheel" of Native American traditional values: An integrative review. *Counseling and Values, 43,* 84–98.

Gloria, A.M., & Peregoy, J.J. (1996). Counseling Latino and other substance abusers/users: Cultural considerations for counselors. *Journal of Substance Abuse Treatment, 13,* 1–8.

Greenfield, L.A., & Smith, S.K. (1999, February). *American Indians and crime.* Washington, DC: U.S. Department of Justice.

Howatch, R. (2000, October). Gover offers historic apology. *American Indian Report: Indian Countries News Magazine 16*(10), 10.

Indian Fellowship Program. (1989). *Final regulations.* 34 CFR, Pt. 263.

Indian Health Service. (1996). *Trends in Indian Health–1996.* Washington, DC: U.S. Department of Health and Human Services, Public Health Service.

Indian Health Service. (1997). *Trends in Indian Health–1997.* Washington, DC: U.S. Department of Health and Human Services, Public Health Service.

LaFromboise, T., Coleman, H., & Gerton, J. (1993). Psychological impact of biculturalism: Evidence and theory. *Psychological Bulletin, 114,* 395–412.

May, P.A. (1994). The epidemiology of alcohol abuse among American Indians: The mythical and real properties. *American Indian Culture and Research Journal, 18,* 121–143.

May, P.A. (1992). Alcohol policy considerations for Indian reservations and border towns. *Journal of American Indian and Alaskan Native Mental Health Research, 3,* 5–59.

Mihesuah, D.A. (1996). *American Indians: Stereotypes and realities.* Atlanta, GA: Clarity Press.

Pavel, D.M., Skinner, R.R., Calahan, M., Tippeconic, J., & Stein, W. (1998, October). *American Indians and Alaskan Natives in postsecondary education.* Washington, DC: U.S. Department of Education, Office of Educational Research and Improvement.

Peregoy, J.J. (1991). *Stress and the sheepskin: An exploration of the Indian/Native perspective in college.* Unpublished doctoral dissertation, Syracuse University, New York.

Peregoy, J.J. (1999). Revisiting transcultural counseling with American Indians and Alaskan Natives: Issues for consideration. In J. McFadden (Ed.), *Transcultural counseling* (2nd ed., pp. 137–170). Alexandria, VA: American Counseling Association.

Peregoy, J.J., & Schliebner, C.T. (2000). Working with diverse cultures: Treatment issues for considerations. In P. Stevens & R. Smith (Eds.), *Substance abuse prevention and intervention: Theory and practice* (2nd ed., pp. 250–276). New York: Prentice Hall.

Schliebner, C.T., & Peregoy, J.J. (1996). *Counseling needs assessment report to a BIA high school in the Northwest.* Unpublished raw data.

Sue, D.W., & Sue, D. (1999). *Counseling the culturally different: Theory and practice* (3rd ed.). New York: Wiley.

Trimble, J.E., Fleming, C.M., Beauvais, F., & Jumper-Thurman, P. (1996). Essential cultural and social strategies for counseling Native American Indians. In P.B. Pedersen, J.G. Draguns, W.J.

Lonner, & J.E. Trimble (Eds.), *Counseling across cultures* (4th ed., pp. 177–209). Thousand Oaks, CA: Sage.

U.S. Bureau of the Census. (1995, November 17). *Population profile of the United States*. Washington, DC: U.S. Government Printing Office. Available: www.doi.gov/bureau-indian-affairs.html.

Wilson, C., Civic, D., & Glass, D. (1995). Prevalence and correlates of depressive syndromes among adults visiting an Indian health service primary care clinic. *American Indian and Alaskan Native Mental Health Research, 6*, 1–12.

45 DISABILITY AND REHABILITATION COUNSELING

E. Davis Martin Jr. and Gerald L. Gandy

Rehabilitation counseling has generally been regarded as a process in which the counselor and the person with a disability work together to understand existing impediments and potentials and to facilitate effective use of personal and community resources as the person adapts to the changes resulting from the disability. It is one of the better ideas set forth by human beings: assisting a person with a disability reclaim lost function or be able to develop function in the first instance. As such, rehabilitation counseling is a dynamic, continuous process; it offers a continuing challenge to the rehabilitation counselor, to the person with a disability, and to the rehabilitation or human service agency.

Rehabilitation counseling has also been viewed as a philosophy, an enduring belief in people (Jacques, 1970). In this context, the concepts of dignity and worth of the person and the importance of attaining personal happiness through acceptance and/or adaptation to disability, healthy interdependence, and usefulness become paramount. Rehabilitation has also been defined as an investment (Berkowitz, 1984); thus, rehabilitation may be viewed from an economic perspective: Factors such as earning power (facilitating entry into the primary labor market), tax savings (and contributions to the tax base), and reduction of disability costs constitute an organizational focus. Still another perspective sees rehabilitation counseling as a series of services incorporated in a restorative or corrective context (Parker & Szymanski, 1998). To some persons, counseling is regarded as a privilege for a select few, partly because of restrictive eligibility criteria and because of the necessity to set priorities for service. Others view it as a right for all citizens. For many, it is equated with equality of opportunity. Finally, rehabilitation counseling has also been viewed in relationship to the ecological movement—the relationship between persons with disabilities and their environment. This concept also relates to the conservation of resources. Maki and Riggar

(1997, p. 19) expressed this relationship to the environment: "that adaptation as a dynamic concept describing the extent to which a person accepts disability as one of his or her many characteristics is a preferred concept to adjustment, which infers a more enduring, static and categoric description when referring to a person's acceptance of their disability."

With such a variety of concepts of rehabilitation—and there are undoubtedly more—it is obvious that definitions will also vary. Thus, the purpose of rehabilitation counseling has been defined as "a comprehensive, individualized process, prescriptive in nature, and directed toward the development or restoration of functional independence and a quality of life" (Maki & Riggar, 1997, p. 19) and as "a comprehensive sequence of services, mutually planned by the consumer and rehabilitation counselor, to maximize employability, independence, integration, and participation of people with disabilities in the workplace and the community" (Parker & Szymanski, 1998, p. 2).

THE REHABILITATION COUNSELOR'S ROLE AND FUNCTION

Jenkins, Patterson, and Szymanski (1992) have indicated that, regardless of employment setting and client population, most rehabilitation counselors assess client needs, develop goals and individualized plans to meet identified needs, and provide or arrange for the therapeutic services and interventions (e.g., psychological, medical, social, behavioral) needed by the clients that may include job placement and follow-up services. Counseling skills are considered an essential component of all of these activities. Research conducted by Leahy, Szymanski, and Linkowski (1993) indicated that the following 10 knowledge domains represent the core competency requirements of rehabilitation counselors: (1) vocational counseling and consultation services; (2) medical and psychological aspects; (3) individual and group counseling; (4) program evaluation and research; (5) case management and service coordination; (6) family, gender, and multicultural issues; (7) foundations of rehabilitation; (8) workers' compensation; (9) environmental and attitudinal barriers; and (10) assessment.

Leahy and Szymanski (1995) noted that a consistent trend in the historical development of rehabilitation practice over the years has been the ever expanding employment settings where practice takes place and the types of population with whom the counselor works during the rehabilitation process. Public (e.g., the state and federal program of vocational rehabilitation), private nonprofit (e.g., rehabilitation centers), and private for-profit (e.g., workers' compensation, insurance rehabilitation, forensic rehabilitation) settings represent the primary employment settings for rehabilitation counselors. However, a number of nontraditional settings have emerged as a result of legislation and other social and economic influences. Such settings include employee assistance programs, disability management programs within employer settings, school-based transition programs, university services for students with disabilities, and medical centers and clinics. Rehabilitation counselors continue to work with clients with physical disabilities but also increasingly with a variety of other populations, including those with developmental, cognitive, emotional, and addiction disabilities, depending on the employment setting in which they practice.

UNIQUE CHARACTERISTICS OF THE REHABILITATION COUNSELING PROCESS

The rehabilitation counseling process has some unique characteristics that help to distinguish the role and function of the rehabilitation counselor. These include the following.

The *continuity of client-counselor relationship* throughout the process constitutes a unique professional role. In many professions, the professional worker is primarily involved with his or her client at a specific point in time in the process. The physician, for example, is often involved with referral, diagnosis, and certification of disability and treatment. The occupational and physical therapist and other members of a rehabilitation team (e.g., psychological or psychiatric) often find their involvement at a specific point in the provision of physical or mental restoration services. Rehabilitation team concepts and team practices necessitate that the rehabilitation counselor becomes the focal point for the person with a disability and his or her family and loved ones. One of the counselor's most important professional concerns is to give meaning to the role and function of all other members of the team who will be actively involved in the client's rehabilitation program. It is the rehabilitation counselor who has the global picture of client impediments and a plan for eliminating, ameliorating, or modifying them. It is the counselor, therefore, to whom the client turns for interpretation of relationships in services and coordination of such services. The continuity of the client-counselor relationship throughout the rehabilitation process is, indeed, one of the unique and essential aspects of the rehabilitation counselor's role as a case manager and coordinator in addition to counseling.

A second unique characteristic of the rehabilitation process is the *comprehensiveness of the diagnostic and case study procedure*. More often than not, disability is not a discrete event in a person's life. The effects of disability manifest a cluster of impediments that impact significantly on medical, psychological, social, educational, economic, and vocational concerns. As such, the rehabilitation counselor becomes involved in all areas of the person's life that impact on the person's functional abilities. The uniqueness of each person is manifested through the interactions of these seemingly discrete elements. The relationship of these different aspects of a person's life has a dramatic impact in terms of vocational choice and ultimately entry into the primary labor market.

A third unique characteristic of the process that impacts on the rehabilitation counselor's role is the *functional emphasis in diagnostic and case study procedure*. In each area of evaluation, the emphasis is on functional ability. The counselor is interested in what the client can do and what experiences can be built upon (e.g., is there a family support system?) and resources that may be exploited in the development of an individualized plan of employment. Certification or diagnosis of disability is the first step in the diagnostic and case study procedure; it is primarily used for eligibility determination but should also be used in a preplanning or prospective manner whenever possible.

A fourth characteristic of the process impacting on counselor role is the *utilization and coordination of services* outside the agency structure: putting together the community and utilizing its resources as a comprehensive rehabilitation center without walls. The counselor coordinates and supplements these services. Management and coordination skill requirements have given special emphasis to the counseling function.

Cassell, Mulkey, and Engen (1997, p. 214) have observed that the "practice of rehabilitation counseling rests on the confluence of two professional resources: counseling and management." Moreover, "no single professional force can be said to predominate, as synergy is only established through concepts and practice surrounding a 'balance' principle." In other words, the rehabilitation process is individualized and is a coordinated, interagency, interdisciplinary method of service requiring knowledge of the community and its many resources—public, private, and voluntary.

PROFESSIONAL ORGANIZATIONS AND CREDENTIALING

Psychologists had a major impact on the development of the profession of rehabilitation counseling (Jacques, 1970; Muthard, 1969; G. Wright, 1980). The Division of Counseling Psychology and the Division of the Psychological Aspects of Disability of the American Psychological Association (APA) were once the major psychological organizations affiliated with the rehabilitation counseling field (Jacques, 1970; G. Wright, 1980). However, rehabilitation counseling began developing a status independent from psychology with the formation of two professional associations, the American Rehabilitation Counseling Association (ARCA) in 1957 and the

National Rehabilitation Counseling Association (NRCA) in 1958 (G. Wright, 1980).

The ARCA developed and remains as a division of the American Personnel and Guidance Association (APGA), now known as the American Counseling Association (ACA) (DiMichael & Thomas, 1985; G. Wright, 1980). The NRCA developed as a division of the National Rehabilitation Association (NRA) (G. Wright, 1980) and includes both professional and lay people involved in the general rehabilitation field. Members not only include rehabilitation counselors and related personnel but also physicians, nurses, psychologists, social workers, administrators, and secretaries. The boards of both organizations created the Alliance of Rehabilitation Counseling in 1993 as a formal collaborative structure to marshal the strengths of both organizations into a unified professional policy and strategic planning voice for rehabilitation counseling, while at the same time respecting the autonomy, heritage, and value of each of the individual organizations (Leahy & Szymanski, 1995).

The accreditation body for rehabilitation counselor education is the Council on Rehabilitation Education (CORE), established in 1972; there were 88 accredited master's programs (and one in candidate status) for the 1999–2000 academic year (Council on Rehabilitation Education, 1999). The Council of Accreditation of Counseling and Related Educational Professions (CACREP), the accrediting body for the general counseling profession, has an ongoing collaborative relationship with CORE, and there is a regular opportunity for joint review of departments that have both accredited programs (Linkowski & Syzmanski, 1993).

The Commission on Rehabilitation Counselor Certification (CRCC) was formed in 1973 (Hedgeman, 1985). The CRCC administers rehabilitation counselor certification examinations for the Certified Rehabilitation Counselor (CRC) credential. There are now over 13,500 CRCs in the United States and several foreign countries (Foundation for Rehabilitation Education and Research, 1997). No formal mechanism exists for collaboration between the CRCC and the National Board for Certified Counselors (NBCC), a generic board, which awards certification for the National Certified Counselor (NCC) credential, but some informal collaboration does occur (Leahy & Szymanski, 1995).

Although rehabilitation counseling has established and maintained a separate national certification mechanism, rehabilitation counselors have joined with counselors in other specialty areas (community, marriage and family, mental health, etc.) to establish a general counselor license at the state level (Leahy & Szymanski, 1995; Sweeney, 1995). License for private practice is the province of respective states and is not the same as certification at the national level. Rehabilitation counseling is part of a generic professional counseling discipline.

MENTAL HEALTH ISSUES RELATED TO PHYSICAL DISABILITIES

Mental health counselors and rehabilitation counselors share the same counseling knowledge and skills in working with clients with mental disabilities. However, rehabilitation counselors normally have additional background and training in regard to working with the mental health issues of clients with physical disabilities, especially in reference to the social and psychological aspects of physical disability. Mental health counselors might want to consider a more collaborative role with rehabilitation counselors in working with clients with physical disabilities, particularly when the mental health issues become more complicated. Regardless, there are some basic issues to be aware of when working with clients with physical disabilities and some of them overlap with clients with mental disabilities.

Acceptance and adjustment to physical disability is a highly individualized process. Severity of disability, on the surface, would seem to be a crucial factor. However, severity of disability or the perception of severity varies from person to person. Persons who have significant physical disabilities (blindness, cerebral palsy, mental retardation, paraplegia, etc.) vary in their reaction(s) to their disability. The perception of severity among others—parents, siblings, loved ones, friends, work and school mates—varies considerably as well. The effect of paraplegia, for example, on one person may be completely devastating from a psychological perspective, but for another be relatively insignificant. These two extremes certainly do not characterize all persons who have a paralysis disability. The majority of persons with disabilities probably fall somewhere between these two extremes. Most people with disabilities, particularly those with physical disabilities, as noted in Henderson and Bryan (1997), "do not view their disabilities as the greatest tragedy in their lives . . . [but] consider their disability as a fact of life, an inconvenience and sometimes a cause of frustration but not the most terrible thing that has happened to them" (p. 90).

Disability can affect personality. The manner in which personality may be affected, however, varies with the particular circumstances and life patterns of an individual (G. Wright, 1980). It should not be assumed that disability will always result in psychological turmoil. Disability, of course, will present frustration, inconvenience, and grief to the person with a disability, but the disability may also present the person with a "potentially powerful stimulant to psychological growth" (Vash, 1981, p. 130):

> I have been disabled since I was sixteen, yet hardly a week goes by, nearly thirty years later, that I don't make some discovery or improvement that in one way or another makes my disability less handicapping. Since I hope that happy process never stops, I have to say that I hope I am never fully "rehabilitated." . . . The core of psychological development is realistic acceptance of one's limitations—be they physical, intellectual, spiritual, or of some other realm. We are not perfect; we are never what we would wish to be—however beautiful, good, gifted, serene, or strong we appear. These imperfections must be accepted without rancor before we can get on with the real and simple business of psychological development—doing the best we can with whatever we've got. (Vash, 1976, pp. 2, 3)

Those who share in the life of a person with a disability may also experience difficulty in coping or relating to the person. This arises not so much from the reality of the disability but more likely because the disability has introduced a new element into the relationship; it has, in essence, changed the relationship. The ability to cope with the changes brought about as a result of the disability then portends the future relationship. Beatrice Wright (1983) has written that "the burden in interpersonal relations will be borne by the person who has the disability. Although the pathology may lie with the group, the person with the disability is the one who is annoyed or hurt most directly. It is he or she who has to 'take it,' who has to handle the ineptitude of others in the ordinary affairs of getting along" (p. 335). Accordingly, it is the people with the disability who must help those who are close to them and, as well, those who are strangers to deal with and adjust to their disability. This may seem to be an overwhelming or at least unfair responsibility placed on the person with a disability; nevertheless, it is a reality that must be faced. Wright discusses issues and literature relevant to mental health issues with physical disabilities in her seminal work, *Physical Disability: A Psychosocial Approach.* An understanding of how disability affects the person with a disability as well as those who come into contact with that person is a basic tenet of her work.

Because disability is a dynamic phenomenon, it is essential that counselors know and understand their own attitudes, both positive and negative, and work toward the elimination of stereotypical responses to persons with disabilities and toward family members as well. Attitudes are subtle and difficult to determine; we do not carry a three-by-five card listing of our attitudes or values. To be an effective counselor with an individual with a disability, a person must know, understand, and appreciate the value systems or philosophies that rehabilitation rests on and those of the consumer or consumer's family. To do so allows the counselor to empower persons with disabilities and, similarly, to empower others who share in the life of the person with a disability.

Counselors must be cognizant of the dynamic nature of disability and must be willing and able to provide an environment that is conducive to success for the person with a disability and for those close to that person. The counselor must assist not only the person with a disability but others whose lives are intertwined with that person to move from a perspective dominated by a comparative-status value orientation to that of an asset-value orientation. Counselors should help clients to seek excellence, not perfection, and to focus on what they can do, not on what they cannot do.

References

American Association of State Counseling Boards. (1996). *The liaison, 3,* 1–9.

Berkowitz, M. (1984). The economist and rehabilitation. *Rehabilitation Literature, 45,* 354–357.

Cassell, J.L., Mulkey, S.W., & Engen, C. (1997). Systematic practice: Case and caseload management. In D.R. Maki & T.F. Riggar (Eds.), *Rehabilitation counseling: Profession and practice.* New York: Springer.

DiMichael, S.G., & Thomas, K.R. (1985). ARCA's journey in professionalism: A commemorative review on the 25th anniversary. *Journal of Counseling and Development, 63,* 428–435.

Foundation for Rehabilitation Education and Research. (1997). *Rehabilitation counseling: The profession and standards of practice.* Rolling Meadows, IL: Author.

Hedgeman, B.S. (1985). Rehabilitation counselor certification. *Journal of Counseling and Development, 63,* 609–610.

Henderson, G., & Bryan, W.V. (1997). *Psychosocial aspects of disability* (2nd ed.). Springfield, IL: Thomas.

Jacques, M.E. (1970). *Rehabilitation counseling: Scope and services* (Guidance Monograph Series). Boston: Houghton Mifflin.

Jenkins, W.M., Patterson, J.B., & Szymanski, E.D. (1992). Philosophical, historical, and legislative aspects of the rehabilitation counseling profession. In R.M. Parker & E.M. Szymanski (Eds.), *Rehabilitation counseling: Basics and beyond.* Austin, TX: ProEd.

Leahy, M.L., & Szymanski, E.M. (1995). Rehabilitation counseling: Evolution and current status. *Journal of Counseling and Development, 74,* 163–166.

Leahy, M.J., Szymanski, E.M., & Linkowski, D.C. (1993). Knowledge importance in rehabilitation counseling. *Rehabilitation Counseling Bulletin, 37,* 130–145.

Linkowski, D.L., & Szymanski, E.M. (1993). Accreditation in rehabilitation counseling: Historical and current content and process. *Rehabilitation Counseling Bulletin, 37,* 81–91.

Maki, D.R. (1986). Foundations of applied rehabilitation counseling. In T.F. Riggar, D.R. Maki, & A. Wolf (Eds.), *Applied rehabilitation counseling.* New York: Springer.

Maki, D.R., & Riggar, T.F. (Eds.). (1997). *Rehabilitation counseling: Profession and practice.* New York: Springer.

Muthard, J. (1969). The status of the profession. In D. Malikin & H. Rusalem (Eds.), *Vocational rehabilitation of the disabled: An overview.* New York: New York University Press.

National Council on Rehabilitation Education. (1996, Winter). Core commission on undergraduate education (CUE). *NCRE Newsletter, 21*(2), 9.

National Council on Rehabilitation Education. (1999–2000). *1999–2000 membership directory.* Logan, UT: Author.

Parker, R.M., & Szymanski, E.M. (1998). *Rehabilitation counseling: Basics and beyond* (3rd ed.). Austin, TX: ProEd.

Sweeney, T.J. (1995). Accreditation, credentialing, professionalization: The role of specialties. *Journal of Counseling and Development, 74,* 117–125.

Vash, C.L. (1981). *The psychology of disability.* New York: Springer.

Wright, B.A. (1983). *Physical disability: A psychosocial approach.* New York: Harper & Row.

Wright, G.N. (1980). *Total rehabilitation.* Boston: Little, Brown.

Suggested Reading

Gandy, G.L., Martin, E.D., Jr., & Hardy, R.E. (1999). *Counseling in the rehabilitation process: Community services for mental and physical disabilities* (2nd ed.). Springfield, IL: Thomas.

46 COUNSELING OLDER ADULTS

Valerie L. Schwiebert and Jane E. Myers

Gerontological counseling as a specialty is relatively new. Although competencies for gerontological counseling have been established (Myers & Sweeney, 1990), there remains a vast disparity between counselors trained to work with older persons and the need for counselors to work with older persons (Myers, 1992, 1995; Ryan & Agresti, 1999). A brief examination of the demographics of the United States underscores the great need for counselors trained to provide services to older persons and their families.

America's population of individuals age 65 and older grew by 74% between 1970 and 1999 (U.S. Census Bureau, 2000.) Although this increase is impressive, it will pale in comparison to the increase in the population of older adults beginning in 2010, when the "baby boomers" reach older adulthood. In 2030, the number of older persons will rise to one in five Americans age 65 or over (Administration on Aging, 1998).

Given the exponential rise in need for services and the extent of underservice of mental health needs among older persons, the training of specialists alone is not enough. All counselors need basic knowledge and skills in working with older persons (Myers & Schwiebert, 1996). Therefore, 16 minimum essential competencies for gerontological counselors were identified (Myers, 1990). These competencies have been recognized by several counseling associations and form the basis for the organization of the discussion to follow.

Competency 1: Demonstrates and actively advocates for positive, respectful, wellness-enhancing attitudes toward older persons and a concern for empowerment of persons throughout the life span.

Ageism is the tendency of individuals to view all older persons negatively and to attribute certain traits to the entire group of older adults. To work effectively with older adults, counselors must first explore their own attitudes and assumptions toward aging. Counselors may wish to think about older persons they know. Counselors may ask themselves: What characteristics do older persons possess that I find positive or negative? How does this affect my perception of older persons? What are my "comfort zones" in talking with older persons?

Examples of aging myths include: All older persons are the same; memory loss is a natural part of aging; and older persons should not be sexually active. Additionally, areas such as sexuality and death and dying may be difficult for counselors until they have come to terms with their own views and values. Overcoming negative stereotypes toward aging and engaging in self-exploration may help counselors formulate effective strategies to combat negative myths associated with aging and to empower older adults.

Competency 2: Demonstrates skill in applying extensive knowledge of human development for older persons, including major theories of aging, the relationship between physical and mental health and aging, the difference between normal and pathological aging processes, gender-related developmental differences, and coping skills for life transitions and losses.

Counselors working with older persons must be able to distinguish between normal and pathological changes associated with the aging process (e.g. depression, memory loss, loss of interest in sexual activity or sexual function). Accurate knowledge of the major theories of aging, physical and mental aspects of normal aging, and transitions and losses of late life are essential if counselors are to overcome their own attitudes of what is "normal" aging. This is critical to formulating effective intervention strategies when working with older adults. For example, a counselor may mistakenly attribute signs of depression in an older person as just a result of the "normal" aging process. This may result in the depression going untreated when it is not a direct result of the aging process and could be resolved.

Theories of later life include Erikson's theory of life span development (1963), Havighurst's theory of aging and education (1972), and Riker and Myers's theory of later life development (1989). Additionally, counselors working with older persons need to be familiar with theories of aging. Examples of these include disengagement theory (Cumming & Henry, 1961), activity theory (Neugarten, Havighurst, & Tobin, 1968), and continuity theory (Rosow, 1963). Finally, counselors working with older adults may wish to review the work of Schlossberg (Schlossberg, Waters, & Goodman, 1995) related to transitions. This work is particularly helpful in understanding transitions of older adulthood, including biological declines, retirement, divorce, death, and grandparenthood, and in serving as a basis for formulating mental health interventions to assist older persons in successfully negotiating these transitions.

Competency 3: Demonstrates skill in applying extensive knowledge of social and cultural foundations for older persons, including characteristics and needs of older minority subgroups, factors affecting substance and medication misuse/abuse, recognition and treatment of elder abuse, and knowledge of social service programs.

Counselors working with older persons must be aware of the cultural context in which aging occurs. This means understanding the trends and changes in society and the impact these changes have on older persons. In addition, population projections indicate that the elderly population will become an increasingly diverse group as non-White populations continue to grow faster and eventually to exceed in number the now majority White population (U.S. Bureau of Census, 2000). Older persons may be confronted with social problems such as poverty, chronic medical conditions, mental health concerns, caregiving issues, loss of independence, stress, elder abuse, and drug misuse and abuse. Counselors must be familiar with the consequences of experiencing these social problems and work to formulate effective intervention strategies to minimize the negative impact of these circumstances. In particular, given the prevalence of elder abuse and mandates for abuse reporting, both ethical and legal obligations require knowledge of elder abuse and its treatment (Welfel, Danziger, & Santoro, 2000).

Competency 4: Demonstrates the ability to function in the multiple roles required to facilitate helping relationships with older persons (e.g., advocate, family consultant) and to mobilize available resources for functioning effectively in each role.

Counselors working with older persons and their families may be called on to function in a variety of roles and to provide a variety of services (Johnson & Riker, 1982), including bereavement counselor, personal counselor, specialist in psychological education, in-service counselor educator, marital and sex counselor, medical support outreach counselor, change agent, advocate, consultant, family counselor, leisure time counselor, and employment counselor, to name but a few.

Competency 5: Demonstrates skill in recruiting, selecting, planning, and implementing groups with older persons.

Counselors working with older persons must be knowledgeable about the special needs of older persons when participating in group counseling. Group work may have advantages for older persons, such as reducing loneliness, increasing socialization, and normalizing the aging process. One major difference in working with groups of older persons is that the development of trust tends to take longer. Additionally, counselors working with older persons in groups may find that reminiscence is a major theme. Life review in the group setting may be particularly helpful to older persons in resolving unfinished business and gaining a sense of ego integrity versus despair (Myers & Schwiebert, 1996).

> Competency 6: Demonstrates skill in applying extensive knowledge of career and lifestyle options for older persons, age-related assets and barriers to effective choices, and resources for maximizing exploration of career and lifestyle options.

Counselors must keep abreast of changing workforce and economic trends to maximize options available to older clients. As life expectancy increases, individuals are working longer, and many individuals may have more than one "career" in a lifetime. Knowledge of both career development theories and transition theories are helpful in providing a framework for working with individuals transitioning between careers or retiring. Counselors may need to assist individuals in redefining themselves outside of the work role, learning how to play, adjusting lifestyle to income, and renegotiating relationships.

> Competency 7: Demonstrates skill in appraisal of older persons, including identifying characteristics of suitable appraisal instruments and techniques, and in using assessment results in developing treatment plans.

Counselors must be able to use standardized assessments or clinical observations and evaluations with older persons. It is also important to remember that assessment is a continuous process, as the older clients' needs change over time. Ideally, assessment results can help older clients enhance life satisfaction and obtain needed services, but improperly used assessments may restrict an older client's ability to function independently. Counselors using more traditional forms of assessment with older persons may find them less familiar with testing, resulting in lowered client performance and increased anxiety. Client physical impairments such as arthritis, hearing or vision loss, and other chronic conditions must also be taken into account when selecting and administering assessment instruments with this population. Validity and reliability as well as the establishment of age-appropriate norms are essential for achieving accurate information and thus for successful assessment with older persons.

> Competency 8: Demonstrates skill in applying extensive knowledge of current research related to older persons and the implications of research findings for helping relationships.

Counselors working with older persons need to be familiar with current research findings related to knowledge of the characteristics, needs, and concerns of older persons and knowledge of counseling services and techniques that are most effective in working with older persons (Myers & Schwiebert, 1996). Some studies have been undertaken, but more documentation of treatment effectiveness is needed. Therefore, counselors working with older persons are called on to undertake ways to evaluate and document the effectiveness of their interventions with this population. Development of successful research designs involving older persons requires the counselor to consider ethical and legal implications, particularly with regard to informed consent (see Schwiebert, Myers, & Dice, 2000).

> Competency 9: Demonstrates skill in applying extensive knowledge of intellectual, physical, social, emotional, vocational, and spiritual needs of older persons and strategies for helping meet those needs.

Wellness theories encourage the counselor to view the older person holistically and from a positive versus a deficit model. Myers,

Sweeney and Witmer (2000) presented a holistic model of wellness and prevention that is specially designed for use by counselors in developing effective interventions. This model includes identification of five major life tasks: spirituality, self-direction, work, friendship, and love. The authors also developed the Wellness Evaluation of Lifestyle (Myers, Sweeney, Witmer, & Hattie, 2000), an assessment instrument that may be helpful in assessing wellness and formulating effective treatment interventions to enhance well-being in later life.

> Competency 10: Demonstrates skill in applying appropriate intervention techniques, in collaboration with medical and other care providers, for physical and mental impairments common to older persons, such as acute, chronic, and terminal illness, depression, suicide, and organic brain syndromes.

Counselors working with older persons are often called on to serve as members of treatment teams and must understand the roles of other service providers. Treatment team members may include physicians, physical and occupational therapists, dietitians, home health care providers, and speech and language pathologists. In addition, counselors must be familiar with medical terminology and physical and mental impairments common to older persons (e.g., suicide, depression, organic brain syndromes).

> Competency 11: Demonstrates extensive knowledge of the formal and informal aging networks, public policy and legislation affecting older persons, and the continuum of care that will allow older persons to maintain their highest level of independence.

Counselors working with older persons must also be familiar with the aging network. This refers to the network of services and programs from which older persons derive personal and social support. These networks are both formal (organized services usually provided through government agencies, professional organizations, and private agencies) and informal (services provided by friends,

family, and neighbors). Counselors must possess the necessary skills to link older persons with the services needed to provide optimal functioning. A list of organizations and their Internet addresses is provided at the end of this chapter.

> Competency 12: Demonstrates skill in applying appropriate intervention techniques for situational and developmental crises commonly experienced by older persons, such as bereavement, isolation, divorce, relocation, sexual concerns, illness, transportation, crime, abuse, and relationships with adult children and caregivers.

Situational and developmental crises may accompany the normal aging process. Grief and bereavement are particularly prevalent among the aging population. Counselors must first explore their own attitudes toward death and dying to be effective in dealing with these issues. Additionally, counselors should be familiar with the stages of normal grief and appropriate intervention strategies for facilitating grief work (Myers & Schwiebert, 1996). Life review may be a particularly helpful strategy in resolving grief and loss issues (see Molinari & Reichlin, 1985). Also, counselors need to be familiar with issues surrounding caregiving and relationships with adult children. Family counseling and communication skills are particularly helpful intervention strategies to consider when working with these issues.

> Competency 13: Demonstrates skill in the use of a wide variety of specialized therapies to assist older persons in coping with both developmental and nonnormative issues, such as creative art therapies, pet therapy, peer counseling, and family counseling.

Although almost any counseling technique can be used with older persons, counseling techniques that meet the special needs of older persons may be most helpful. These include life review, early recollections, integrative counseling, family and group counseling, paraprofessional and peer counseling, self-help groups, creative art therapies, bibliotherapy, music therapy, movement therapy, dance therapy, pet therapy, horticulture therapy, imagery and self-hypnosis, reality orientation, remotivation therapy, and validation therapy. Although not within the scope of this article, readers are referred to *Empowerment for Older Persons* (Myers, 1990), *Adult Children and Aging Parents* (Myers, 1989), and *Competencies for Gerontological Counseling* (Myers & Schwiebert, 1996) for more thorough discussions of these therapies.

> Competency 14: Demonstrates skill in applying extensive knowledge of ethical issues in counseling older persons, their families, and care providers.

Although ethical issues related to counseling all individuals are applicable to older persons, additional consideration of ethical dilemmas is warranted. In a recent article, the Standards Committee of the Association for Adult Development and Aging endorsed specific ethical guidelines for working with older persons (Schwiebert et al., 2000). Readers are encouraged to review this discussion, which highlights additional ethical issues related to working with a variety of older adults, including those with cognitive impairments, those who are the victims of abuse, and those with a terminal illness, as well as issues related to informed consent for research with impaired older adults.

> Competency 15: Demonstrates the ability to act as a consultant to individuals and organizations on issues related to older persons and their families.

Counselors may be increasingly called on to serve as consultants. As the gap widens between professionals trained to meet the needs of this population and the number of older persons requiring service, counselors must use their professional skills and knowledge to train other service providers. The counselor may serve as an educator, trainer, supervisor, professional counselor, or expert witness, to name but a few possible roles (Dougherty, 1990).

> Competency 16: Demonstrates skill in program development for the older population, including needs assessment, program planning, implementation, and evaluation.

Counselors working with older persons may be called on to undertake needs assessments, to plan and implement programs for older persons and their families, and to design evaluations for programs serving this population. Needs assessments and program development may focus on mental health and counseling needs; however, due to the complexity of issues faced by older persons, often counselors will be called on to design programs that address a variety of concerns (e.g., transportation, meals, medicines, health care, socialization, mental health concerns).

SUMMARY

The numbers of older persons in the population continues to increase, yet training for counselors in gerontological issues is not uniformly available. Practitioners working with older adults and their families may benefit from additional training related to each of 16 gerontological competencies. A brief review of these competencies has been provided and a number of resources suggested for additional information. The interested reader is encouraged to seek out Web sites, books, and articles listed below for more information, as well as continuing education opportunities provided through conferences and workshops. It is inevitable that older persons and their families will be among our clientele, and therefore essential that we prepare ourselves to provide effective interventions with this population.

References

Administration on Aging. (1998). *Profile of older Americans*. Washington, DC: Author.
Cumming, E., & Henry, W. (1961). *Growing old: The process of disengagement*. New York: Basic Books.
Dougherty, M. (1990). *Consultation: Practice and perspectives*. Pacific Grove, CA: Brooks/Cole.
Erikson, E. (1963). *Childhood and society*. New York: Norton.

Havighurst, R. (1972). *Developmental tasks and education*. New York: McKay.

Johnson, R., & Riker, H. (1982). Counselors' goals and roles in assisting older persons. *Journal of Mental Health Counseling, 4,* 30–40.

Molinari, V., & Reichlin, R. (1985). Life review reminiscence in the elderly: A review of the literature. *International Journal of Aging and Human Development, 20,* 81–92.

Myers, J.E. (1989). *Adult children and aging parents.* Alexandria, VA: American Counseling Association.

Myers, J.E. (1990). *Empowerment of older persons.* Ann Arbor, MI: ERIC/CAPS.

Myers, J.E. (1992). Competencies, credentialing and standards for gerontological counselors: Implications for counselor education. *Counselor Education and Supervision, 32,* 34–42.

Myers, J.E. (1995). From forgotten and ignored to standards and certification: Gerontological counseling comes of age. *Journal of Counseling and Development, 74,* 143–149.

Myers, J.E., & Schwiebert, V. (1996). *Competencies for gerontological counseling.* Alexandria, VA: American Counseling Association.

Myers, J.E., & Sweeney, T.J. (1990). *Gerontological competencies for counselors and human development specialists.* Alexandria, VA: American Counseling Association.

Myers, J.E., Sweeney, T.J., & Witmer, J.M. (2000). Counseling for wellness: A holistic model for treatment planning. *Journal of Counseling and Development, 78,* 251–266.

Myers, J.E., Sweeney, T.J., Witmer, J.M., & Hattie, J.H. (2000). *The Wellness Evaluation of Lifestyle–Form J.* Manuscript submitted for publication.

Neugarten, B., Havighurst, R., & Tobin, S. (1968). Personality and patterns of aging. In B. Neugarten (Ed.), *Middle age and aging* (pp. 173–177). Chicago: University of Chicago Press.

Riker, H., & Myers, J.E. (1989). *Retirement counseling: A practical guide for action.* New York: Hemisphere.

Rosow, I. (1963). Adjustment in the normal aged. In R. Williams, C. Tibbits, & W. Donohue (Eds.), *Process of aging* (Vol. 2, pp. 195–223). New York: Atherton.

Ryan, N.E., & Agresti, A. (1999). Gerontological training in mental health professions: The results of a national survey. *Journal of Mental Health Counseling, 21,* 352–371.

Schlossberg, N., Waters, E., & Goodman, J. (1995). *Counseling adults in transition.* New York: Springer.

Schwiebert, V., Myers, J.E., & Dice, C. (2000). Ethical guidelines for counselors working with older adults. *Journal of Counseling and Development, 78,* 123–129.

Welfel, E.R., Danziger, P.R., & Santoro, S. (2000). Mandated reporting of abuse/maltreatment of older adults: A primer for counselors. *Journal of Counseling and Development, 78,* 251–266.

Internet Resources

Administration on Aging www.aoa.dhhs.gov

American Association of Retired Persons www.aarp.org

National Center on Elder Abuse at the American Public Human Services Association. (1998). *The national elder abuse incidence study: Final report* [Online]. Available: www.aoa.dhhs.gov /abuse/report/default.htm

National Senior Citizens Law Center www.nsclc .org

SeniorNet www.seniornet.org

Senior Information Network www.seniorinet.com

47 COUNSELING OLDER ADULTS IN INSTITUTIONAL SETTINGS

Nancy A. Orel

The American Psychiatric Association (2000) estimates that 15% to 25% of Americans over the age of 65 display symptoms of mental illness. In institutional settings such as nursing homes, it is estimated that 70% to 90% of the residents suffer from some form of mental illness (Knight, Teri, Wohlford, & Santos, 1995). Mental illness in this population is treatable if detected early; however, the mental health needs of many older adults, especially those in nursing homes, are not being met adequately. Fewer than 5% of nursing home residents receive mental health services.

Most older adults are reluctant to enter nursing homes, but nursing home placement has become an inescapable reality for many. Although the percentage of older adults living in nursing homes at any one time is relatively small (less than 6%), it is estimated that close to 43% of all U.S. residents will spend some part of their lives residing in a long-term care facility (Kemper & Murtaugh, 1991). There are multiple factors that determine nursing home placement. The primary factors include age, gender, previous housing arrangement, level of physical and cognitive functioning, socioeconomic status, societal bias toward institutionalization, and informal support/relationship patterns. The likelihood of placement increases with age. Almost 50% of those age 95 and older live in nursing homes. Generally, the "typical" nursing home resident will be a poor, widowed, White, female over the age of 75 and suffering from chronic disabilities that require assistance with activities of daily living (ADL). The absence of a spouse or other caregiver is the major predictor of institutionalization.

Contrary to the popular myth that older persons are isolated and alienated from their families, approximately 80% of all elderly persons have living children, and 78% to 90% of these live within one hour of an adult child and see their children once a week or more (Lieberman & Fisher, 1995). Families have been labeled the "backbone of long-term care" because they are the major source of home health care for older adults, relinquishing this role only when the financial, emotional, or physical burden becomes intolerable. The decision to institutionalize an aged relative is most often determined by the degree of family burden rather than any particular disease symptomatology.

Considerable evidence indicates that the process of institutionalization is one of the most tumultuous later-life events for *both* the older adult and the spouse or family who is part of the process (Pruchno, Peters, Kleban, & Burant, 1994). In a classic study, 52% of adult child caregivers and 89% of spouse caregivers rated placing an elderly parent or spouse into a nursing home as the most difficult problem they had ever faced (Johnson, 1988).

Increased longevity and the subsequent increase in health care needs have created a phenomenal growth in the population of people using nursing homes. In the decades ahead, mental health practitioners working with families will undoubtedly encounter many adult children and their aging parents struggling with complex issues related to caregiving and long-term care.

The primary purpose of this chapter is to provide an overview of the psychotherapeutic approaches and strategies that have been found to be most effective when working with older adults and their families facing institutionalization. This population requires intervention at three points: during the decision-making process, at the time of relocation into a nursing home, and after placement has occurred. This chapter provides a foundation for practice with elderly nursing home residents and addresses the major problems counselors are likely to encounter.

ISSUES AND INTERVENTIONS PRIOR TO NURSING HOME PLACEMENT

The decision to institutionalize an older relative usually occurs when the family is in the midst of an escalated health concern. Placing an older adult in a nursing home is usually a last resort that occurs only after the family has become physically or emotionally exhausted from providing extensive home care. Because virtually any level of care can be provided in the home if sufficient community and financial resources are available, the decision to institutionalize an aged relative is usually the result of inadequacy—in finances, health, social supports, emotional strength, or other ability to cope.

Professional interventions with the elderly and their families who are considering nursing home placement are warranted. All family members, including the older adult, must be actively involved in the decision-making process. Lack of participation in the decision-making process has been found to lead the excluded member to experience heightened levels of anger, depression, resistance, and resentment (Butler, Lewis, & Sunderland, 1998). The focus of counseling should include (1) encouraging the expression of feelings by all generations through clear, direct, and honest communication; (2) providing support as similarities and differences in the generations' perceptions of conflict and areas of conflict that emerge; (3) helping adult children accept that they may not be able to cope with the needs of their aging parents without some assistance; and (4) supporting elderly parents in coping with feelings related to loss. Ideally, psychotherapeutic interventions should draw on the strengths of the older adult and his or her family. These strengths include cultural expectations of filial obligation, the empowering effects of family solidarity (attachment), and a family's life-long patterns of attachment and coping abilities.

Sidell (1997) has proposed solution-focused brief therapy for families dealing with the stress of placing an older relative into a nursing home. A therapist utilizing solution-focused principles focuses on how the family has already coped with other overwhelming situations, such as caregiving. The family's strengths are tapped and change-focused tasks are assigned so that concrete and measurable goals can be achieved.

For the older adult, the detrimental psychological and physical effects of nursing home placement (e.g., disorientation, depression, increased morbidity) may be inhibited or reversed by making the relocation predictable or controllable. Interventions such as cognitive training techniques that increase the perceived control over the environment have been found to have a positive impact on the physical and mental well-being of nursing home residents (Duffy, 1999). Older adults should also have the opportunity to retain as much autonomy as their physical, psychological, and cognitive levels of functioning allow. Assuming total care and decision-making responsibility for older adults is just as inappropriate as total neglect.

COUNSELING INTERVENTIONS AT THE TIME OF PLACEMENT

Mental health practitioners can be instrumental in assisting family members to cope with the emotional issues associated with the elder's relocation into a nursing home, as well as the strain associated with the elder's adjustment to his or her role as a nursing home resident. Only recently has research begun to explore how older adults and their caregivers are affected by nursing home placement and relocation (Gaugler, Leitsch, Zarit, & Pearlin, 2000). Perhaps this lack of attention reflects the common assumption that after nursing home placement, caregivers no longer experience stress or strain. However, family members continue to experience caregiver burden even after nursing home placement due to (1) their persistent concerns with the well-being of the institutionalized elder, (2) the ambiguity in their roles in institutional care, (3) their uncertainty in knowing how to respond to perceived deficiencies in care, and (4) their stress related to issues of imminent death (Bretscher, 1993; Zarit & Whitlach, 1992).

Relocation into a nursing home is an extremely stressful situation for the older adult. Menniger (1963) labeled the debilitating effects of relocation for the elderly the "institutionalization syndrome." The primary effects experienced include passivity, depression, fear, intellectual ineffectiveness, negative self-image, decreased life satisfaction, and high mortality.

In a classic study of the association of relocation with heightened mortality, Aldrich and Mendkoff (1963) found that "the actual death rate was substantially and significantly higher than the anticipated rate" (p. 189). The most significant increase in mortality occurred in the first three months following relocation into a nursing home, during which it was three times greater than the expected rate. Kasl (1971) provided further evidence that the anticipation of impending institutionalization was itself such a stressful event that this anticipatory period could contribute to increased mortality rate. More recently, Wolinski, Callahan, Fitzgerald, and Johnson (1992) explored the risk factors associated with dying soon after nursing home placement and found that those older adults without close familial ties were at greater risk of dying soon after nursing home placement.

Active family involvement in the older adult's adjustment process is crucial, and mental health practitioners need to encourage that involvement. Research indicates that family involvement can counteract the trauma associated with nursing home placement when the family (1) is actively involved with treatment planning (both initial and follow-up), (2) become partners with staff in the delivery of care, (3) participate in the elder's daily activities (e.g., meals), and (4) provide biographical information that can be used to individualize care (Spencer, 1991; Tobin, 1995).

ISSUES REQUIRING PSYCHOTHERAPEUTIC INTERVENTION AFTER NURSING HOME PLACEMENT

The placement of an aged relative into a nursing home is emotionally problematic for family members. Family members often experience anger, helplessness, hopelessness, failure, grief, guilt, and depression. Guilt may be especially powerful when they experience psychological relief from the burden of providing care and is often expressed behaviorally by withdrawing emotionally or physically from the older adult. This in turn intensifies the older adult's feelings of abandonment and isolation.

Institutionalized older adults experience a profound sense of abandonment and isolation. Other common effects of institutionalization include decreased physical and intellectual functioning; increased morbidity, disorientation, and mortality; declines in psychological well-being; diminished interpersonal competence due to loss of established social networks; attenuation of family ties; feelings of uncertainty related to the future; loss of personal control, independence, and decision making; and changes in lifestyle, socialization patterns, and self-attitude (Solomon, 1993). Most older adults are not acutely aware of the incredible number of losses and changes that are brought about due to nursing home placement. Some of the puzzling behaviors (e.g., oppositional behavior, wandering), confusion, anger, resentment, and depression displayed by newly admitted nursing home residents may be due to this lack of awareness and their inability to find someone to blame for their predicament.

Specific Psychotherapeutic Strategies for Nursing Home Residents

All nursing homes are subject to state or federal standards and the enforcement of these standards are given to the states by the federal government. The legislation that has the most regulatory impact to improve quality of care and quality of life for nursing home residents is the Nursing Home Reform Law of the Omnibus Budget Reconciliation Act of 1987 (OBRA; PL 100-203, 1987). OBRA requires all long-term care facilities to (1) identify the medically related social and emotional needs of each resident; (2) mandate a clear plan to assist each resident in adjusting to the social and emotional aspects of his or her illness, treatment, and stay in the facility; and (3) stipulate provision of a social worker in each nursing home.

These requirements represent an important step toward meeting the emotional and social needs of nursing home residents, but they alone do not guarantee that the multiplicity of concerns of nursing home residents will be addressed. Additionally, OBRA does not address the trauma experienced by family caregivers dealing with the relocation of a relative into a nursing home, nor does it recognize professional counselors as separately reimbursable health care providers. Therefore, only the services of independently practicing psychiatrists, clinical psychologists, and clinical social workers are covered.

Because of Medicare and Medicaid reimbursement restrictions, mental health services provided in nursing homes are primarily delivered through a contractual agreement with the long-term care facility. Patients are referred to the mental health practitioner, and evaluation and treatment *must* be ordered by a physician. The problems most frequently presented for evaluation and treatment include depression, confusion, paranoia, noisiness, restlessness or wandering, combativeness, inappropriate dependency on staff, persistent talk of or wish to die, and critical family members.

In light of the diversity of problems facing institutionalized older adults and the complexity of the setting, treatment must be a multidisciplinary process. Likewise, assessment of nursing home residents is a multidisciplinary process that, according to OBRA regulations, must begin within 14 days of admission into the long-term care facility. This "comprehensive, accurate, standardized, reproducible assessment" of each resident's ability to perform daily life functions is the basis for the development of an interdisciplinary plan of care to assist the resident to attain or maintain the highest level of physical, mental, and psychosocial functioning possible. Physicians, nurses, social service directors, physical therapists, occupational therapists, nurses aids, and administrators are all involved at varying levels in the assessment process and the subsequent delivery of services. Often, the mental health practitioner's primary role is to improve communication and coordinate care. Therefore, mental health practitioners must have a working knowledge of the two major components of this "comprehensive assessment": the Minimum Data Set Plus (MDS+) and the Resident Assessment Protocols (RAPs).

The MDS+ is a standard four-page primary screening and assessment tool that provides functional information about the nursing home resident's ability to perform basic life activities. Selected items from the MDS+, called "triggers," identify potential problems or clinical conditions that need further evaluation (e.g., delirium, depression, anxiety, dementia, psychotropic drug use, urinary incontinence). The RAPs, a standard set of assessment protocols, address these problems or clinical conditions. The RAPs provide the link between the assessment information from the MDS+ and the development of a comprehensive care plan that promotes the resident's highest level of physical, mental, and psychosocial functioning.

In addition to the MDS+ and the RAPs, an effective, comprehensive, and reliable assessment also includes a variety of existing standardized geriatric assessment instruments.

Among the most widely used are the Mini Mental Status Examination (MMSE), the Geriatric Depression Scale (GDS), the Assessment for Involuntary Motion Scale (AIMS), the Delirium Symptom Interview, the Dementia Rating Scale, the Blessed Orientation Memory Concentration Test (BOMC), and the Blessed Information Memory Concentration Test (BIMC) (see Kaszniak, 1996; Lawton & Teresi, 1994; Rubenstein, Wieland, & Bernabei, 1995, for reviews of the assessment procedures and criteria). The choice of a particular assessment tool depends on the unique characteristics of the older adult, the presenting problem, and, in many cases, state and federal regulations.

The information obtained from the comprehensive multidisciplinary assessment provides direction for the appropriate therapeutic intervention. A number of psychotherapeutic interventions may be utilized when counseling nursing home residents and there is no single modality of psychotherapeutic intervention that is preferred for this population. The therapist needs to consider the unique social, physical, and psychological characteristics of the older adult when determining which intervention will be the most effective. Additionally, the nature of the problem(s) and the clinical goals determine the most appropriate intervention strategies. Because psychotherapy must be coordinated with medical care, mental health professionals must be aware of the interplay between physical health and psychological health among older adults (see Morrison, 1997), the common illnesses encountered by older adults and their features, and the effects of psychotropic medications.

Needless to say, the provision of mental health services in nursing homes must adhere to state and federal regulations. For example, OBRA regulations emphasize the use of behavioral and nonpharmacological interventions and recommend that the focus of treatment should be on the use of brief, goal-oriented, structured intervention techniques. Gallagher-Thompson and Thompson (1996) have adapted behavioral approaches successful with younger age groups for older adults. Cognitive-behavioral therapeutic strategies have also been modified for use with older adults, and preliminary research has shown this approach to be successful in treating depression and anxiety (Carstensen & Fisher, 1991). Other therapeutic approaches that have been successfully used with older adults include reality orientation, interpersonal psychotherapy, bibliotherapy, life review, reminiscence, intergenerational therapy, music therapy, art therapy, and group therapy. Because families play such a central role in the lives of both community-based and institutionalized older adults, a family systems approach is the most appropriate perspective to adopt (Gatz et al., 1998).

Although "the similarities in treating older people usually outweigh the differences" (Zarit & Zarit, 1998, p. 187), mental health professionals will often need to modify their therapeutic strategies to adapt them to the needs of older adults who reside in nursing homes. This includes multidisciplinary treatment plans, shorter and more frequent sessions, slower-paced sessions, utilization of techniques that accommodate sensory problems, and environmental modifications.

In addition to the aforementioned adaptations, the following guidelines are offered for mental health practitioners who work with or desire to work with institutionalized older adults and their families:

• Obtain specialized knowledge, skills, and training. Training guidelines have been articulated in the April 2000 report of the American Psychological Association Interdivisional Task Force on Qualifications for Practice in Clinical and Applied Geropsychology: *Training Guidelines for Practice in Clinical Geropsychology.* Also see Schwiebert and Myers (Chapter 46).

• Become familiar with Medicare's prospective payment system and the Standards for Psychological Services in Long-Term Care Facilities (see Lichtenberg et al., 1998), as well as advocate for mental health service utilization in long-term care facilities.

• Recognize the unique ethical and legal concerns that apply specifically to practice with older clients and their caregiving families. These concerns include informed consent, confidentiality, privacy, conflict of interest, end-of-life issues, and advocacy.

• Understand the nursing home setting and how it is organized. Mental health professionals need to establish relationships with the staff (i.e., administrators, nursing director, social service directors, nurses aids) and staff physicians, as well as take an active role in facilitating cooperation and interdependence between family members and nursing home staff.

RECOMMENDATIONS

Successful interventions for older adults require changes in existing social policies, specifically, changes to remove barriers to mental health services for both community-dwelling older adults and residents of nursing homes. These barriers include (1) a lack of sufficient training or general biases against older clients on the part of mental health professionals, (2) third-party reimbursement policies that only minimally cover older adult psychological services, (3) an inability on the part of the older adult to access mental health services, and (4) society's bias toward older adults, which often translates into misdiagnoses or inappropriate placement in nursing homes.

Significant changes are still needed in the way mental health services for nursing home residents are delivered and paid for in the United States. According to the final report of the first multidisciplinary consensus conference convened to improve mental health service in nursing homes (American Association for Geriatric Psychiatry, 2000), legislation is needed to increase funding for mental health treatment and specifically to expand Medicare coverage for professional counselors.

Another important development for mental health professionals is the ongoing initiative by the U.S. Department of Health and Human Services to meticulously investigate claims that practitioners are submitting on behalf of Medicare patients receiving mental health services in nursing homes. Recently, Medicare auditors have questioned the medical necessity of mental health services

performed by psychologists in California, Texas, Florida, Ohio, Washington, New York, and Massachusetts (Foxhall, 2000). Mental health practitioners must comply with all rules and regulations concerning the provision of mental health services for Medicare/Medicaid beneficiaries and must be knowledgeable about claims submission and payment policies. Meticulous documentation is crucial and must include a physician's order requesting psychological evaluation and treatment. Psychological services covered by Medicare are reimbursable only when medically necessary.

The mental health professions need to develop a clearer awareness of the mental health needs of institutionalized older adults and educate the public on what constitutes high-quality long-term care. Systematic research is needed to more thoroughly investigate the concerns, issues, and problems facing older adults and their caregiving families. A research agenda that validates treatment methods (e.g., behavioral, cognitive, interpersonal) specifically for nursing home residents is also needed.

According to the National Advisory Mental Health Council (1993), only 19% of nursing home residents with mental disorders receive counseling services. In spite of the tremendous need for services, many mental health professionals have been hesitant to work with older adults, a hesitancy partially attributable to lack of specialized training in gerocounseling, as well as the historical assumptions, first proposed by Freud (1924), that older adults cannot benefit from counseling. According to Freud, "The mass of material to be dealt with would prolong the duration of treatment indefinitely" (pp. 258–259). Psychotherapy with residents in nursing homes not only has been successful, but is rewarding for those mental health professionals who accept the challenge to work with this population.

References

Aldrich, C., & Mendkoff, E. (1963). Relocation of the aged and disabled: A mortality study. *Journal of American Geriatrics Society, 11,* 185–194.

American Association for Geriatric Psychiatry. (2000, June 26). Providing optimal mental health services in long term care. *First Multi-disciplinary Consensus Conference Convened to Improve Mental Health Services in Nursing Homes* [Proceedings]. Washington, DC: Author. Available: www.aagpgpa.org/pr0627.html.

American Psychiatric Association. (2000). *Diagnostic and statistical manual of mental disorders* (4th ed., text rev.). Washington, DC: Author.

American Psychological Association. (2000, April). *Training guidelines for practice in clinical geropsychology.* Washington, DC: Author.

Bretscher, C. (1993). Nursing home family care. In P. Szwabo & G. Grossberg (Eds.), *Problem behaviors in long-term care* (pp. 229–241). New York: Springer.

Butler, R.N., Lewis, M.I., & Sunderland, T. (1998). *Aging and mental health: Positive psychosocial and biomedical approaches* (5th ed.). Needham Heights, MA: Allyn & Bacon.

Carstensen, L., & Fisher, J. (1991). Treatment applications for psychological and behavioral problems of the elderly in nursing homes. In P. Wisocki (Ed.), *Handbook of clinical behavior therapy with elderly clients* (pp. 337–362). New York: Plenum Press.

Duffy, M. (Ed.). (1999). *Handbook of counseling and psychotherapy with older adults.* New York: Wiley.

Foxhall, K. (2000, January). How would your practice records look to the FBI? *APA Monitor.* Available: www.apa.org/monitor/jan00/pr1.html.

Freud, S. (1924). On psychotherapy. In *Collected papers* (Vol. 1, pp. 249–263). New York: International Psycho-Analytic Press.

Gallagher-Thompson, D., & Thompson, W. (1996). Psychotherapy with older adults in theory and practice. In B. Bonger & L. Beutler (Eds.), *Comprehensive textbook of psychotherapy* (pp. 357–379). New York: Oxford University Press.

Gatz, M., Fiske, A., Fox, L.S., Kaskie, B., Kasl-Godley, J., McCallum, T., & Wetherell, J. (1998). Empirically validated psychological treatments for older adults. *Journal of Mental Health and Aging, 4,* 9–46.

Gaugler, J., Leitsch, S., Zarit, S., & Pearlin, L. (2000). Caregiver involvement following institutionalization: Effects of preplacement stress. *Research on Aging, 22,* 337–359.

Johnson, A. (1988). Relationships among family members and friends in later life. In R.M. Milardo (Ed.), *Families and social networks* (pp. 168–189). Beverly Hills, CA: Sage.

Kasl, S. (1971). Physical and mental effects of involuntary relocation and institutionalization of the elderly: A review. *American Journal of Public Health, 62,* 377–384.

Kaszniak, A.W. (1996). Techniques and instruments for assessment of the elderly. In S.H. Zarit & B.G. Knight (Eds.), *A guide to psychotherapy and aging: Effective clinical interventions in a life-stage context* (pp. 163–219). Washington, DC: American Psychological Association.

Kemper, P., & Murtaugh, C. (1991). Lifetime use of nursing home care. *New England Journal of Medicine, 324,* 595–629.

Knight, B., Teri, L., Wohlford, P., & Santos, J. (Eds.). (1995). *Mental health services for older adults: Implications for training and practice in geropsychology.* Washington, DC: American Psychological Association.

Lawton, M., & Teresi, J. (Eds.). (1994). *Annual review of gerontology and geriatrics: Focus on assessment techniques.* New York: Springer.

Lichtenberg, P., Smith, M., Frazer, D., Molinari, V., Rosowsky, E., Crose, R., Stillwell, N., Kramer, N., Hartman-Stein, P., Qualls, S., Salamon, M., Duffy, M., Parr, J., & Gallagher-Thompson, D. (1998). Standards for psychological services in long-term care facilities. *The Gerontologist, 38,* 122–127.

Lieberman, M., & Fisher, L. (1995). The impact of chronic illness on the health and well-being of family members. *The Gerontologist, 35,* 94–102.

Menniger, K. (1963). *The vital balance: The life process in mental health and illness.* New York: Viking.

Morrison, J. (1997). *When psychological problems mark medical disorders: A guide for psychotherapists.* New York: Guilford Press.

National Advisory Mental Health Council. (1993). Health care reform for Americans with severe mental illness: Report of the National Advisory Mental Health Council. *American Journal of Psychiatry, 150,* 1447–1465.

Omnibus Budget Reconciliation Act of 1987, Pub. L. No. 100–203.

Pruchno, R., Peters, N., Kleban, M., & Burant, C. (1994). Attachment among adult children and their institutionalized parents. *Journal of Gerontology: Social Sciences, 49,* S209–S218.

Rubenstein, L., Wieland, D., & Bernabei, R. (1995). *Geriatric assessment technology: The state of the art.* New York: Springer.

Sidell, N. (1997). Easing transitions: Solution focused principles and the nursing home resident's family. *Clinical Gerontologist, 18,* 21–41.

Solomon, K. (1993). Behavioral and psychotherapeutic interventions with residents in the long-term care institution. In P. Szwabo & G. Grossberg (Eds.), *Problem behaviors in long-term care* (pp. 147–162). New York: Springer.

Spencer, B. (1991). Partners in care: The role of families in dementia care units. In D. Coons (Ed.), *Specialized dementia care units* (pp. 189–204). Baltimore: Johns Hopkins University Press.

Tobin, S. (1995). Fostering family involvement in institutional care. In G. Smith, S. Tobin, E. Robertson-Tchabo, & P. Power (Eds.), *Strengthening aging families: Diversity in practice and policy* (pp. 3–24). New York: Sage.

Wolinski, F., Callahan, D., Fitzgerald, J., & Johnson, R. (1992). The risk of nursing home placement and subsequent death among older adults. *Journal of Gerontology: Social Sciences, 47,* S173–S182.

Zarit, S., & Whitlach, C. (1992). Institutional placement: Phases of the transition. *The Gerontologist, 32,* 665–672.

Zarit, S., & Zarit, J. (1998). *Mental disorders in older adults: Fundamentals of assessment and treatment.* New York: Guilford Press.

48   AFFIRMATIVE ASSESSMENT AND THERAPY WITH LESBIAN, GAY, AND BISEXUAL CLIENTS

Thomas V. Palma

Professional ethics dictate that mental health practitioners and academicians respect and value the self-determination of all people and avoid practices that may prove discriminatory or prejudicial (ACA, 1996; APA, 1992). Despite such edicts, a vocal contingent in the mental health community still endorses a pathological view of homosexuality (Socarides, Kaufman, Nicolosi, Santinover, & Fitzgibbons, 1997). This occurs even though homosexuality is not a mental disorder (APA, 1974) and in the face of empirical evidence that comparable levels of psychological health are evident across heterosexual, homosexual, and bisexual populations (Gonsiorek, 1991; Pillard, 1988).

Sexual minorities are frequent users of mental health services. In fact, 91% of psychologists in private practice report having counseled a Lesbian, Gay, or Bisexual (LGB) person (Hancock, 1995). Consequently, all cli-

nicians are charged to acquire competency in psychotherapy with sexual minorities. Otherwise, they should not practice. Clinicians must evaluate their capacity to provide "therapy that celebrates and advocates the authenticity and integrity of Lesbian, Gay, and Bisexual persons and their relationships" (Tozer & McClanahan, 1999).

Multicultural scholars have long debated what qualities a clinician must possess to demonstrate competency in counseling minority populations. In 1982, Sue et al. postulated that the counselor must have *awareness* of personal beliefs and attitudes, *knowledge* of the worldview/cultural experiences of diverse clients, and *skill* in the development and provision of efficacious therapeutic interventions. A recent factor analysis confirmed the viability of these constructs among counselors in private practice

(Holcomb-McCoy, 2000). Additionally, the study found that an understanding of *identity formation* and multiculturally specific *terminology* contributed to the development of multicultural competency.

Although developed to address therapeutic bias with visible racial and ethnic groups (VREGs), the model has great utility in facilitating therapeutic competency in assessment and therapy with LGB persons (Fassinger & Richie, 1997). This chapter utilizes these competency domains (i.e., terminology, knowledge, awareness, and skills) as a framework for discussion of the theoretical and empirical factors associated with LGB affirmative therapeutic services.

TERMINOLOGY

An important first step is clarifying the terminology and theories that underlie affirmative therapy with sexual minorities. Self-identification as lesbian or gay assumes a primary affectional and erotic attachment to someone of like gender; the bisexual's affectional and erotic attachments are toward men and women (Garnets & Kimmel, 1991). Although theoretical accounts of homosexuality differ, a preponderance of sexual identity formation models perceive homosexuality to be a fixed/stable characteristic (Cass, 1979). These developmental models highlight typical behaviors or cognitive strategies that lead to labeling oneself gay (Cass, 1979, 1996), lesbian (Sophie, 1985/1986), or bisexual (Twining, 1983; Weinberg, Williams, & Pryor, 1994), yet prove unable to reflect the experience of many LGB persons. This limitation is particularly evident when examining the experiences of women and persons of color (Diamond, 2000; Greene, 1994).

Social constructionists reject the essentialist perspective embedded in developmental models, arguing that the labels ascribed to sexual minorities have differed over time and among diverse peoples (Kitzinger, 1995). They assert that one cannot understand what it is to be a Lesbian, Gay, or Bisexual absent the culture and context of the individual.

In response, identity models have begun to incorporate elements of social constructionism. Specifically, developmental models have acknowledged the marked influence of environment (Cass, 1996) and explained the more varied developmental paths by differentiating personal from social elements of sexual identity (McCarn & Fassinger, 1996). Other approaches place greater emphasis on the "process" of sexual identity formation, affirming that personal and cultural factors reciprocally interact to inform the individual in their self-identification as Lesbian, Gay, or Bisexual (Palma, 2000).

Although there is no uniform path by which an individual develops a sexual identity, every sexual minority is adversely impacted by heterosexism and homophobia. Herek (1996) defines heterosexism as the belief system that denies, denigrates, and stigmatizes any nonheterosexual form of behavior, identity, relationship, or community. Such beliefs may perceptually legitimize discrimination and violence directed at sexual minorities and can facilitate a negative self-image among LGB persons.

KNOWLEDGE

Knowledge of the LGB experience has proven difficult, given each groups' lack of visibility. In a population-based sample, Sell, Wells, and Wypij (1995) found that about 20% of women and men indicated affectional and/or sexual attraction to like-gendered persons since the age of 15. Yet, only 4% of women and 6% of men indicated homosexual contact in the prior five years. Although use of diverse sampling techniques and imprecise criteria to identify homosexuality and bisexuality challenge the accuracy of findings, researchers postulate that between 4% and 10% of the population is predominantly Lesbian, Gay, or Bisexual (Norton, 1995).

Intracultural Diversity

The diversity within LGB communities also complicates efforts at understanding. Because they reflect every racial/ethnic, religious, economic, and experiential background, efforts to define specific characteristics or customs proves futile. However, research has delineated gender and racial/ethnic factors that influence the assumption of an LGB identity. This information does inform the scholar and practitioner.

Emergence and Stability of Same-Gender Attraction

Research estimates that men and women most typically acknowledge awareness of same-gender attraction at 10 years of age and act on such inclinations at 13 and 15 years, respectively (Herdt & Boxer, 1993; Pattatucci & Hamer, 1995). A more recent study found that self-identified lesbian and bisexual women acknowledged same-gender attraction at 15 years and their first lesbian contact at 18 years (Diamond, 1998). Oswald (2000) suggests that a woman's reliance on social networks/relationships in establishing notions of self may explain the delay in sexual expression. This may also account for the more fluid nature of sexual identity in women. Although lesbian and bisexual women's affectional patterns appear stable, they often acknowledge opposite-gender sexual behavior and change their sexual identifications one or more times in their lifetime (Diamond, 2000).

Cultural Dynamics and Dimensions of Oppression

Despite a paucity of empirical research, Greene (1994) and Fukuyama and Ferguson (2000) speak to the cultural dynamics and dimensions of oppression experienced by LGBs of color. They acknowledge the near uniform prohibition of a Lesbian, Gay, or Bisexual identity among VREGs. This fuels the perception among people of color that they must choose between identities. The importance of family and inability to disguise one's racial/ethnic heritage often facilitate precedence being given to racial identity. Such precedence frequently coincides with the decision to "pass" as heterosexual. When precedence is given to one's sexual identity, the person of color jeopardizes many familial and cultural supports.

Many of the concerns experienced by LGBs of color are also concerns of sexual minorities with disabilities. They must encounter the social stigma associated with their disability concurrent with the realization of erotic/affectional desire (Saad, 1997). Likewise, their disability may limit access to informational and supportive resources for Lesbians, Gay men, and Bisexuals (O'Toole & Bregante, 1993).

Systemic Heterosexism

Irrespective of gender, race/ethnicity, or disability, the Lesbian, Gay or Bisexual identity is challenged by heterosexist policies and practices in society (Herek, 1996). This is evidenced by the messages of religious leaders who regard lesbians and gay males as "intrinsically disordered" (Ratzinger, 1986), political leaders who compare homosexuality with alcoholism and kleptomania (Fram, 1998), and faith communities who speak of homosexual behavior as sinful (e.g., Baptist, Catholic, Methodist denominations). Prejudice is also reflected in sodomy laws that target sexual minorities or are disproportionately enforced against LGB people (ACLU, 1999), and in U.S. congressional rejection of the Employment Non-Discrimination Act (ENDA) in 1996, 1997, 1998, and 1999. The ENDA would have ended discriminatory practices against LGBs in employment.

These governmental/organizational beliefs inform and reinforce individual attitudinal patterns. Studies consistently find marked antihomosexual sentiment among the general population. Men regard homosexuality more negatively than do women, and each regards a sexual minority of the same gender more negatively than a sexual minority of the opposite gender (Baker & Fishbein, 1998; LaMar & Kite, 1998). These attitudinal patterns are often manifest in the discrimination and violence experienced by a marked segment of the LGB community (Herek, 2000). Negative societal reactions may also be internalized, facilitating a range of emotions, from impaired self-confidence to self-loathing (Gonsiorek, 1993). Such externally mediated forms of oppression have been associated with emotional and psychological difficulties among gay men and adolescents (D'Augelli, 1998; Grossman & Kerner, 1998; Meyer, 1995; Rotheram-Borus, Hunter, & Rosario, 1994).

For LGB individuals on either generational extreme, prejudicial attitudes may present unique challenges. Both experience isolation from the larger gay and lesbian community and may have modest support systems in place. This may complicate the developmental concerns typical of adolescence (Gonsiorek, 1991; Prince, 1995) and of maturity (Adelman, 1990; Berger & Kelly, 1996). Research indicates that youth who identify as gay or lesbian are at greater risk for violence (D'Augelli, Hershenberger, & Pilkington, 1998; Hunter, 1990), abuse of alcohol or drugs (Garofalo, Wolf, Kessel, Palfrey, & DuRant, 1998), and suicide (Remafeldi et al., 1998).

The aforementioned findings should not overshadow the evidence that shows a majority of LGBs exhibit great resilience in the face of subtle forms of prejudice, outright discrimination, and violence. Contemporary research supports the landmark findings of Evelyn Hooker (1957) that no greater levels of pathology are evidenced among gay males than their heterosexual peers. In studies comparing LGBs to heterosexuals, scholars note that sexual minorities exhibited remarkably similar interpersonal patterns (Haas & Stafford, 1998), attachment styles to parents (Ridge & Feeney, 1998), and satisfaction levels in relationships (Kurdek, 1998).

AWARENESS

Prejudicial attitudes toward LGB populations are also evident among mental health professionals. Large numbers of psychologists (Garnets, Hancock, Cochran, Goodchilds, & Peplau, 1991) and counselors (Gibson & Pope, 1993) in clinical practice endorsed beliefs that LGBs are pathological, disordered, or deviant. Research with Lesbians, Gay men, and Bisexuals confirms that such bias is manifest

in the therapeutic setting. Nearly half of LGBs with prior therapy experience reported marked homophobia (i.e., the therapist would not acknowledge or reference their sexual identity, assumed they were heterosexual, or inquired if they wanted to change) and one-fourth regarded prior services as "poor" or "inappropriate" (Nystrom, 1997).

Although studies of counseling/psychology graduate students indicate that the levels of prejudice toward VREG and LGB populations have decreased (McDermott & Stadler, 1988; Palma, 1996), these studies merely reflect the trainees' intent to think and act in nonprejudicial ways. Given that trainees are unlikely to endorse statements that run counter to the nonprejudicial edicts of their profession (i.e., ACA, APA, ASCW), this intent does not necessarily translate into greater self-awareness or multicultural competence. Ethicists acknowledge that without marked awareness of one's values, beliefs, needs, and limitations, the therapist may impede or negatively impact client progress (Corey, Corey, & Callanan, 1998).

Misdiagnosis/Maltreatment

One of the more subtle yet destructive forms of clinical bias is misdiagnosis and establishment of inappropriate treatment goals. Research indicates that a substantial portion of the therapeutic community misuse psychological/psychiatric criteria to maintain a de facto pathological view of same-gender sexual and affectional orientations (Fassinger, 1991; Silverstein, 1991). These clinicians often advocate "sexual reorientation therapies" (Nicolosi & Freeman, 1993), despite the lack of credible evidence to demonstrate the efficacy of treatments to change one's sexual orientation (Haldeman, 1994; Tozer & McClanahan, 1999).

Other mental health professionals are very reluctant to acknowledge pathology among gay and lesbian populations, preferring to view all characterological evidence as a result of environmental stressors. In his seminal article, Gonsiorek (1982) acknowledges that this "antidiagnostic" view may result in malpractice when LGB clients present with symptoms consistent with a marked depression, a thought disorder, neuropsychological impairment, a pervasive characterological pattern of behavior, and so on. He describes three essential steps that will assist the clinician in differentiating the psychopathological condition from the characterological-appearing condition that results from factors associated with the assumption of a Lesbian, Gay, or Bisexual identity: (1) conducting a thorough/careful history with the client, (2) delineating current symptoms and level of functioning, and (3) obtaining a chronological record of events/situations that may have precipitated or resulted from the present symptoms.

SKILLS

The behaviors clinicians demonstrate in therapy are likely to reflect their attitudes toward LGB people. This necessitates the examination of attitudes and the adoption of LGB-affirmative skills in therapy. When clinicians demonstrate skills that respect LGBs, these clients are encouraged to examine and clarify their internal attitudes, drives, and affections. Such support affords greater understanding of heterosexist influences on their sexual identity. Conversely, employing interventions that are less affirmative or perceived as neutral may perpetuate societal oppression (Betz, 1989). Such methods do not effectively counter the heterosexist beliefs that may underlie clients' questioning or reluctance to identify as Lesbian, Gay, or Bisexual.

In therapy, LGB clients often request help for identity-related concerns (e.g., Robert inquires "How do I know if I am gay?"). Yet, far more often, they present with circumscribed issues made more complex by societal heterosexism (e.g., Jean has seen a sudden and marked decline in her academic performance; Derek was again denied a partnership in his law firm). In such instances, the therapist is well advised to assess the relation of such factors to the client's sexual identity. Even when the issue appears unrelated to sexual identity (e.g., James is financially devastated after failure of his

Internet-based company; Susanne's partner is concerned about her "unpredictable mood" and "risk taking" of late), it may be confounded by the client's sexual identity. To accurately diagnose and treat the client, the impetus or factors influencing the presenting issue must be assessed and identity-related concerns must be explored.

A comprehensive psychosocial screening can aid in diagnosis and treatment. This screening requires client self-descriptions of ethnicity/race, sexual identity, religiosity/values, support networks, work/educational history, residency locations, parental/family structure, relationship history, and therapeutic experiences. In addition, as Gonsiorek (1982) suggests, this screening must clarify the issues/symptoms present, their relative onset, and their relation to the individual's identity or past experiences as a Lesbian, Gay male, or Bisexual. This comprehensive screening will inform the therapist as to clients' sexual identification, their level of comfort with their sexual identity, the cultural dynamics present, the relative salience of different cultural factors, the pressures within their environment, prior experiences, and issues present.

Affirmative Therapeutic Skills

In addition, scholars have outlined successful clinical strategies with LGB clients (Garnets et al., 1991). The following affirmative counseling skills are a compilation of these strategies and those informed by this author's clinical experience.

The LGB-affirmative therapist will:

- Acknowledge that a Lesbian, Gay, or Bisexual identity is valid, healthy, and full of possibilities.
- Avoid communication that can be perceived to minimize or exaggerate the impact of discrimination/bias in the lives of LGB clients, or in the assumption and maintenance of their sexual identity.
- Avoid the tendency to classify or describe a same-gendered or multiple-gendered relationship pattern in a heterosexual framework or context.

- Monitor the purpose or intent of clinical inquiry, thereby avoiding the satisfaction of personal curiosities regarding LGB lifestyles in session.
- Examine closely the client's cognitive, affective, and behavioral patterns to more accurately assess concerns/issues and personal well-being.
- Respect clients' willingness or reluctance to communicate their sexual identity and issues related to this identity. This recognizes that sexual identity formation is a lifelong process and that individuals' socialization/experience may place them on a different trajectory for self-identification than other LGB clients.
- Own their personal experience with, knowledge of, and attitudes toward persons with a Lesbian, Gay, or Bisexual identity. Disclosure of this information allows the client to make an informed choice of therapist and provides an environment in which the clinician can seek clarification of terminology or situational factors.
- Dispense with personal notions regarding the origin of or explanations for homosexuality. To do otherwise may shift the focus of the session away from the client's own personal perceptions and feelings toward efforts that seek external validation for or a desire to change one's sexual identity.

SUMMARY

LGB-affirmative therapy acknowledges the individual differences present within Lesbian, Gay, and Bisexual communities as well as their common experience of oppression in society. It allows clients to fully explore their subjective experiences as "reality," recognizing that the therapist's life is neither equivalent to nor particularly informative in the client's identification or experience as a sexual minority. With basic knowledge and awareness of personal values and beliefs, the therapist can provide the sexual minority person an alternative to the destructive experiences often encountered in society. In a respectful and affirming

environment, LGB clients are better able to assess their own motivations and needs, the factors influencing such motivations and needs, and the strategies and resources needed to affect change.

References

Adelman, M. (1990). Stigma, gay lifestyles, and adjustment to aging: A study of later-life gay men and lesbians. *Journal of Homosexuality, 20*(3/4), 7–32.

American Civil Liberties Union. (1999). *Status of U.S. sodomy laws* [Online]. Retrieved May 22, 2000. Available: www.aclu.org/issues/gay /sodomy.html.

American Counseling Association. (1996). ACA code of ethics and standards of practice. In B. Herlihy & G. Corey (Eds.), *ACA ethical standards casebook* (5th ed., pp. 26–59). Alexandria, VA: American Counseling Association.

American Psychiatric Association. (1974). Position statement on homosexuality and civil rights. *American Journal of Psychiatry, 131,* 497.

American Psychological Association. (1992). Ethical principals and code of conduct. *American Psychologist, 48,* 1597–1611.

Baker, J.G., & Fishbein, H.D. (1998). The development of prejudice towards gays and lesbians by adolescents. *Journal of Homosexuality, 36*(1), 89–100.

Berger, R., & Kelly, J. (1996). Gay men and lesbians grow older. In R.P. Cabaj & T.S. Stein (Eds.), *Textbook of homosexuality and mental health* (pp. 305–316). Washington, DC: American Psychiatric Press.

Betz, N.E. (1989). Implications of the null environment hypothesis for women's career development and for counseling psychology. *The Counseling Psychologist, 17,* 136–144.

Cass, V.C. (1979). Homosexual identity formation: A theoretical model *Journal of Homosexuality, 4*(3), 219–235.

Cass, V.C. (1996). Sexual orientation identity formation: A Western phenomenon. In R.P. Cabaj & T.S. Stein (Eds.), *Textbook of homosexuality and mental health* (pp. 227–251). Washington, DC: American Psychiatric Press.

Corey, G., Corey, M., & Callanan, P. (1998). *Issues and ethics in the helping professions.* Pacific Grove, CA: Brooks/Cole.

D'Augelli, A.R. (1998). Developmental implications of victimization of lesbian, gay and bisexual youth. In G. Herek (Ed.), *Psychological* perspectives on lesbian and gay issues: Vol. 4. Stigma and sexual orientation (pp. 187–210). Thousand Oaks, CA: Sage.

D'Augelli, A.R., Hershenberger, S.L., & Pilkington, N.W. (1998). Lesbian, gay, and bisexual youth and families: Disclosure of sexual orientation and its consequences. American Journal of Orthopsychiatry, 68, 361–371.

Diamond, L.M. (1998). Development of sexual orientation among adolescent and young adult women. Developmental Psychology, 34, 1085–1095.

Diamond, L.M. (2000). Sexual identity, attractions, and behavior among young sexual-minority women over a 2-year period. Developmental Psychology, 36, 241–250.

Fassinger, R.E. (1991). The hidden minority: Issues and challenges in working with lesbian women and gay men. The Counseling Psychologist, 19, 151–176.

Fassinger, R.E., & Richie, R.S. (1997). Sex matters: Gender and sexual orientation in training for multicultural competency. In D.B. Pope-Davis & H.L.K. Coleman (Eds.), Multicultural counseling competencies: Assessment, education, training, and supervision (pp. 83–110). Thousand Oaks, CA: Sage.

Fram, A. (1998, June 16). Lott: Gays need help with "problem" [Online]. The Associated Press. Available: seattletimes.nwsource.com/news /nation-world/html98/altgayy_061698.html.

Fukuyama, M.A., & Ferguson, A.D. (2000). Lesbian, gay and bisexual people of color: Understanding cultural complexity and managing multiple oppressions. In R.M. Perez, K.A. DeBord, & K.J. Bieschke (Eds.), Handbook of counseling and psychotherapy with lesbian, gay and bisexual clients (pp. 81–105). Washington, DC: American Psychological Association.

Garnets, L., Hancock, K.A., Cochran, S.D., Goodchilds, J., & Peplau, L.A. (1991). Issues in psychotherapy with lesbians and gay men: A survey of psychologists. American Psychologist, 46, 964–972.

Garnets, L., & Kimmel, D. (1991). Lesbian and gay male dimensions in the psychological study of human diversity. In J.D. Goodchilds (Ed.), Psychological perspectives on human diversity in America (pp. 143–189). Washington, DC: American Psychological Association.

Garofalo, R., Wolf, R.C., Kessel, S., Palfrey, J., & DuRant, R.H. (1998). The association between health risk behaviors and sexual orientation among a school-based sample of adolescents. Pediatrics, 101, 895–902.

Gibson, W.T., & Pope, K.S. (1993). The ethics of counseling: A national survey of certified counselors. Journal of Counseling Psychology, 71, 330–336.

Gonsiorek, J.C. (1982). The use of diagnostic concepts in working with gay and lesbian populations. In J.C. Gonsiorek (Ed.), Homosexuality and psychotherapy: A practitioners handbook of affirmative models (pp. 9–22). New York: Haworth Press.

Gonsiorek, J.C. (1991). The empirical basis for the demise of the illness model of homosexuality. In J.C. Gonsiorek & J.D. Weinrich (Eds.), Homosexuality: Research implications for public policy (pp. 115–136). Newbury Park, CA: Sage.

Gonsiorek, J.C. (1993). Mental health issues of gay and lesbian adolescents. In L. Garnets & D. Kimmel (Eds.), Psychological perspectives on lesbian and gay male experiences (pp. 469–485). New York: Columbia University Press.

Greene, B. (1994). Ethnic-minority lesbians and gay men: Mental health and treatment issues. Journal of Consulting and Clinical Psychology, 62, 243–251.

Grossman, A.H., & Kerner, M.S. (1998). Self-esteem and supportiveness as predictors of emotional distress in gay male and lesbian youth. Journal of Homosexuality, 35(2), 25–39.

Haas, S.M., & Stafford, L. (1998). An initial examination of maintenance behaviors in gay and lesbian relationships. Journal of Social and Personal Relationships, 15, 847–855.

Haldeman, D. (1994). The practice and ethics of sexual orientation conversion therapy. Journal of Consulting and Clinical Psychology, 62, 221–227.

Hancock, K.A. (1995). Psychotherapy with lesbians and gay men. In A.R. D'Augelli & C.J. Patterson (Eds.), Lesbian and gay identities across the lifespan: Psychological perspectives (pp. 398–432). New York: Oxford University Press.

Herdt, G.H., & Boxer, A.M. (1993). Children of horizons. New York: Beacon Press.

Herek, G.M. (1996). Heterosexism and homophobia. In R.P. Cabaj & T.S. Stein (Eds.), Textbook of homosexuality and mental health (pp. 101–113). Washington, DC: American Psychiatric Press.

Herek, G.M. (2000). The psychology of sexual prejudice. Current Directions in Psychological Science, 9, 19–22.

Holcomb-McCoy, C.C. (2000). Multicultural counseling: An exploratory factor analysis. Journal *of Multicultural Counseling and Development, 28,* 83- 97.

Hooker, E. (1957). The adjustment of the male overt homosexual. *Journal of Projective Techniques, 21,* 18–31.

Hunter, J. (1990). Violence against lesbian and gay male youths. *Journal of Interpersonal Violence, 5,* 295–300.

Kitzinger, C. (1995). Social constructionism: Implications for lesbian and gay psychology. In A.R. D'Augelli & C.J. Patterson (Eds.), *Lesbian, gay, and bisexual identities over the lifespan: Psychological perspectives* (pp. 136–161). New York: Oxford University Press.

Kurdek, L.A. (1998). Relationship outcomes and their predictors: Longitudinal evidence from heterosexual married, gay cohabiting, and lesbian cohabiting couples. *Journal of Marriage and Family Therapy, 60,* 553–568.

LaMar, L., & Kite, M. (1998). Sex differences in attitudes toward gay men and lesbians: A multidimensional perspective. *Journal of Sex Research, 35,* 189–196.

McCarn, S.R., & Fassinger, R.E. (1996). Revisioning sexual minority identity formation: A new model of lesbian identity and its implications for counseling and research. *The Counseling Psychologist, 24,* 508–534.

McDermott, D., & Stadler, H. (1988). Attitudes of counseling students in the United States toward minority clients. *International Journal for the Advancement of Counselling, 11,* 61–69.

Meyer, I. (1995). Minority stress and mental health in gay men. *Journal of Health and Social Behavior, 7,* 9–25.

Nicolosi, J., & Freeman, L. (1993). *Healing homosexuality: Case stories of reparative therapy.* Northvale, NJ: Aronson.

Norton, J.L. (1995). The gay, lesbian, bisexual populations. In N.A. Vacc & S.B. DeVaney (Eds.), *Experiencing and counseling multicultural and diverse populations* (3rd ed., pp. 147–177). Muncie, IN: Accelerated Development.

Nystrom, N. (1997). Oppression by mental health providers: A report by gay men and lesbians about their treatment. *Dissertation Abstracts International, 58,* 6A.

Oswald, R.F. (2000). Family and friendship relationships after young women come out as bisexual or lesbian. *Journal of Homosexuality, 38*(3), 65–83.

O'Toole, C.J., & Bregante, J.L. (1993). Disabled lesbians: Multicultural realities. In M. Nagler (Ed.), *Perspectives on disability* (2nd ed.,

pp. 261–271). Palo Alto, CA: Health Markets Research.

Palma, T.V. (1996). Attitudes of counselor trainees toward minority clients: A new look. *Journal of College Student Psychotherapy, 11,* 53–70.

Palma, T.V. (2000). *The culture-rich model of sexual identity formation.* Manuscript presented at the 108th annual convention of the American Psychological Association, Washington, DC.

Pattatucci, A.M.L., & Hamer, D.H. (1995). Development and familiarity of sexual orientation in females. *Behavior Genetics, 25,* 407–420.

Pillard, R.C. (1988). Sexual orientation and mental disorder. *Psychiatric Annals, 18,* 52–56.

Prince, J. (1995). Influences on the career development of gay men. *Career Development Quarterly, 44,* 191–203.

Ratzinger, J.C. (1986). Letter to the bishops of the Catholic church on the pastoral care of homosexual persons. In L. Gross & J.D. Woods (Eds.), *The Columbia Reader on lesbians, gay men in media, society and politics* (pp. 135–138). New York: Columbia University Press.

Remafeldi, G., French, S., Story, M., Resnick, M., Michael, D., & Blum, R. (1998). The relationship between suicide risk and sexual orientation: Results of a population based study. *American Journal of Public Health, 88,* 57–60.

Ridge, S.R., & Feeney, J.A. (1998). Relationship history and relationship attitudes in gay males and lesbians: Attachment style and gender differences. *Australian and New Zealand Journal of Psychiatry, 32,* 848–859.

Rotheram-Borus, M., Hunter, J., & Rosario, M. (1994). Suicidal behavior and gay related stress among gay and bisexual male adolescents. *Journal of Adolescent Research, 9,* 498–508.

Saad, S.C. (1997). Disability and the lesbian, gay or bisexual individual. In M.L. Simski & C.J. Alexander (Eds.), *Sexual function in people with disability and chronic illness: A health professional's guide* (pp. 413–427). Gaithersburg, MD: Aspen.

Sell, R.L., Wells, J.A., & Wypij, D. (1995). The prevalence of homosexual behavior and attraction in the United States, the United Kingdom, and France: Results of national population-based samples. *Archives of Sexual Behavior 24,* 235–248.

Silverstein, C. (1991). Psychological and medical treatments of homosexuality. In J.C. Gonsiorek & J.D. Weinrich (Eds.), *Homosexuality: Research implications for public policy* (pp. 101–114). Newbury Park, CA: Sage.

Socarides, C., Kaufman, B., Nicolosi, J., Santinover, J., & Fitzgibbons, R. (1997, January 9). Don't forsake homosexuals who want help. *The Wall Street Journal*, A12.

Sophie, J. (1985–1986). A critical examination of stage theories of lesbian identity development. *Journal of Homosexuality, 12*(2), 39–51.

Sue, D.W., Bernier, Y., Durran, A., Feinberg, L., Pederson, P.B., Smith, E.J., & Vasques-Nuttail, E. (1982). Position paper: Cross-cultural counseling competencies. *The Counseling Psychologist, 10*, 45–52.

Tozer, E.E., & McClanahan, M.K. (1999). Treating the purple menace: Ethical considerations of conversion therapy and affirmative alternatives. *The Counseling Psychologist, 27*, 722–742.

Twining, A. (1983). Bisexual women: Identity in adult development (Doctoral dissertation, Boston University School of Education, 1983). *Dissertation Abstracts International, 44*, 1340A.

Weinberg, M.S., Williams, C.J., & Pryor, D.W. (1994). *Dual attraction: Understanding bisexuality*. New York: Oxford University Press.

49   COUNSELING WOMEN FROM A FEMINIST PERSPECTIVE

Pam Remer, Sharon Rostosky, and Margaret Laurie Comer Wright

Effective counseling of women, as well as members of other oppressed groups, requires understanding how clients' social contexts contribute to the creation and continuation of their problems in living. Viewing women in their sociocultural contexts allows counselors to understand how gender-role socialization and institutionalized sexism result in the devaluation and oppression of women. This devaluation and oppression of women is often internalized and then reflected in a wide range of the issues that women bring to counseling, including domestic violence, rape, childhood sexual abuse, career underachievement, depression, poor body image, eating disorders, role strain, poverty, sexual harassment, low self-esteem, employment discrimination, and relationship difficulties. In the sections that follow, we first define the constructs most relevant to gender issues in counseling and then describe the principles, goals, and interventions for effective counseling of women. Finally, we make recommendations for ethical psychological practice with diverse groups and suggest directions for future research.

DEFINITIONS

Counseling theories vary in how much emphasis is given to the role of clients' sociocultural contexts. Generally, theoretical frameworks fall on a continuum from *intrapsychic* to *environmentally determined*

(Worell & Remer, 1996). At the intrapsychic end of the continuum are counseling theories that locate the source of clients' problems as internal to clients (i.e., their problems are due to dysfunctional thoughts, behaviors, or feelings). At the environmentally determined end of the continuum are theories that view clients' problems as due to sociocultural environmental factors. At the center point of the continuum are *interactionist* theories, where client difficulties are viewed as being caused by a combination of internal and external variables. Given the gender inequities that exist in institutional domains such as education, work, and health care, traditional intrapsychic conceptualizations are inadequate and even hazardous to the mental health and well-being of women, as they ignore the impact of the sociocultural context (Worell & Johnson, 1997; Wyche & Rice, 1997). Most feminist counseling approaches fall on the interactionist to environmentally determined portions of the continuum, which make them especially appropriate for counseling girls and women. Thus, the recommendations for counseling women that follow are presented from a feminist therapy perspective.

Feminist therapy is founded on the basic assumption that *institutionalized sexism* and *gender-role socialization* have limiting effects on individuals of both genders. Institutionalized sexism is defined as systemic, organized power differences that subordinate women. Gender-role socialization is a multifaceted process of reinforcing specific beliefs and behaviors that a culture considers appropriate based on biological sex. Gender-role socialization is accomplished by a variety of institutions within a society (e.g., families, schools, churches) and occurs across the life span.

Feminist mental health practitioners distinguish between *sex* as a category based on anatomy or reproductive capacity and *gender* as a social category based on implicit and explicit proscriptions for being male or female. In *patriarchal* societies, men and women respectively are assigned dominant and subordinate roles that pervade the social structure. These gendered power relations are often unrecognized, unnamed, and unexamined; nevertheless, they shape individuals' behaviors, experiences, and perceptions of self, others, and the world. Feminist therapy, therefore, conceptualizes women's experiences in light of the gendered social structures that *privilege* or elevate the status of those who are White, male, and heterosexual. These privileges result in special legal, economic, and social benefits for those in power and render women and their realities invisible, marginalized, and devalued.

Feminist mental health practitioners recognize that White male privilege extends to the realm of traditional psychotherapy and challenge the *androcentric*, or male-centered, perspectives that underlie the dominant psychological mental health models (Worell & Remer, 1996). These traditional conceptualizations often lead to blaming victims for the effects of *oppression*, the unjust or cruel exercise of power. Attention to sociocultural contexts also highlights the diversity of women's experiences. For any individual woman, experiences of social oppression based on gender and experiences of social oppression based on race, ethnicity, class, sexual orientation, age, or ability are often interwoven in complex and intersecting ways.

PRINCIPLES AND GOALS OF FEMINIST THERAPY

Although differences exist among the variety of current feminist counseling approaches, they generally share a commitment to a core set of principles (Enns, 1997). The core principle of feminist therapy is that the *Personal is Political*, based on the belief that the "personal" issues women bring to counseling originated in sociopolitical oppression, discrimination, and stereotyping based on gender, race, ethnicity, class, age, abilities, and sexual orientation. In therapy, *consciousness-raising* is used to increase clients' awareness of societal oppression and clients are taught how to identify the external, social sources of their problems. When female clients' issues are viewed through this sociopolitical, contextual lens, even their internal processes (thoughts, feelings, and behaviors) take on a different meaning. Clients' responses to an oppressive environment are not viewed as dysfunctional; instead, they are perceived to be ways of coping with a toxic environment in which one has a subordinate status (Sturdivant, 1980; Wyche & Rice, 1997). For example, depression is considered a logical consequence of being devalued and denied access to power. Low self-esteem may result from internalizing cultural messages that women are inferior to men. Because traditional approaches to assessment and diagnosis decontextualize and pathologize women, feminist therapists challenge these approaches (Santos de Barona & Dutton, 1997).

Because feminist counselors view the origins of women's problems as a combination of internal and external factors, feminist therapy encourages women to work to change unhealthy sociocultural contexts rather than merely adapt to dysfunctional environments. Thus, changing economic, political, legal, educational, religious, and familial institutions that promote and support sexism and other forms of oppression is the ultimate goal of feminist therapy. Feminist therapists work in their communities for social change and encourage their clients to become involved in social change as well. Additional feminist goals related to the personal is political principle are to (1) facilitate clients' replacement of internalized stereotyped gender-role messages and behaviors with more flexible, self-enhancing beliefs and coping strategies; (2) help clients identify and change societal practices that limit, oppress, and harm subordinate groups in society; and (3) empower clients to acquire a full repertoire of behavioral life skills (Worell & Remer, 1996).

The second principle of feminist therapy is a belief in egalitarian relationships. Because a major source of women's problems is the inequitable distribution of power between women and men and between other dominant and subordinate social groups, an important goal of feminist therapy is to effect equal relationships among all people. Consequently, feminist therapists form collaborative relationships with their clients in which clients are treated as experts on themselves and are full partners with therapists in deciding on therapeutic goals and strategies. Counselors inform clients about the therapeutic processes to be employed and self-disclose counselor-held values relevant to the counseling relationship. Female feminist therapists also appropriately self-disclose about relevant experiences from their own lives, which facilitates clients' identification of the "common social conditions that they share as women" (Worell & Remer, 1996, p. 95). Within the feminist therapy perspective of the importance of egalitarian relationships, the goals of counseling include helping clients (1) develop egalitarian relationships, (2) be economically independent, (3) develop skills for confronting sexism in relationships, and (4) identify and claim personal strengths.

Another principle of feminist therapeutic approaches is to understand and appreciate female perspectives, values, and skills. In cultures that are androcentrically biased, traits, values, and behaviors that are stereotypically associated with being female are usually devalued. Paradoxically, in these androcentric cultures, women are socialized to comply with these female stereotypes, yet their mental health is often evaluated according to male-centered norms (Broverman, Broverman, Clarkson, Rosenkrantz, & Vogel, 1970). The resulting double bind means that women are both reinforced and pathologized for overcompliance with feminine stereotypes (Sturdivant, 1980). Feminist therapists help clients challenge androcentric definitions, revalue their female characteristics, and embrace the idea of what Sturdivant calls a "woman-defined-woman" (p. 92). Therapeutic goals consistent with the principle of valuing female perspectives are helping clients to (1) increase self-trust and value themselves as women; (2) trust and value other women; (3) view traditional female values and behaviors positively; (4) engage in self-care; (5) identify, express, and value their own needs; (6) reject definitions of womanhood that are based on androcentric norms; and (7) trust intuition and feelings as sources of knowledge (Worell & Remer, 1996).

FEMINIST THERAPY INTERVENTIONS

As mentioned previously, women may seek therapy for a wide range of issues. Although specific feminist interventions for each of these issues is beyond the scope of this chapter, feminist counselors apply a feminist lens to any presenting problem when working with women. Feminist counselors employ a variety of interventions to meet the goals outlined above. Interventions used in feminist therapy with women may be unique to feminist therapy or may be selected from other theoretical orientations as long as the chosen interventions preserve the three principles of feminist therapy.

Feminist counselors first assess the client's social context and *identity development* as a woman. When the client belongs to multiple oppressed groups, feminist counselors explore each of the client's social identities (e.g., the client's identity as a woman and her identity as a person of color) because these multiple oppressions interactively impact their victims (Santos de Barona & Dutton, 1997; Worell & Remer, in press). Identity development models describe the processes by which an individual's identity is impacted by discrimination and stereotyping of the groups to which he or she belongs. These identity stage models have been created for racial identity (e.g., Cross, 1980; Helms, 1995), gender identity (feminist identity) (Downing & Roush, 1985), and homosexual identity (Cass, 1979; McCarn & Fassinger, 1996; Troiden, 1988). Each model describes the following basic progression: (1) nonawareness of discrimination and concomitant internalization of the oppression, (2) a middle stage of rejection of the oppressing dominant culture, and (3) a final stage of valuing and prizing the positive dimensions of one's social identities and then working to eradicate the toxic elements of the majority culture. Clients who are in the first stage of identity development tend to blame themselves for the problems that have developed due to their membership in oppressed groups. Clients with multiple memberships in oppressed groups may be in different stages of development with their various identities and,

due in part to these differences in awareness, one aspect of their identity may be more salient for them than others. A frequent goal of feminist counseling is to facilitate clients' movement through the stages for all of their relevant identities (Worell & Remer, in press).

In addition, feminist counselors must assess fully the impact of clients' social context (Santos de Barona & Dutton, 1997). Specific strategies include gender-role analysis and power analysis (Worell & Remer, 1996). In *gender-role analysis,* the therapist and client collaborate in (1) identifying gender-role messages experienced by the client, (2) identifying the internalized consequences of those messages to the client, (3) deciding which of those messages the client wishes to change, and (4) developing and implementing a plan for change, such as cognitive restructuring.

Power analysis, which also functions as a combination assessment strategy and intervention, was designed to facilitate women's understanding of their devalued status in society. In power analysis, the counselor educates the client about the various kinds of power and about women's limited access to most kinds of power (Worell & Remer, 1996). The counselor then assists the client in identifying the client's usual means of exerting power and the effectiveness of these strategies. Next, the counselor and client identify the manner in which the client's internalized gender-role messages impact her use of power, thus synthesizing gender-role and power issues for the client. Finally, the client is encouraged to extend and build on her current repertoire of power strategies by experimenting with alternatives. Both gender-role and power analyses are intended to assist the counselor in assessing clients' social contexts and to increase their awareness of the personal and societal consequences of gender-role socialization and institutionalized sexism. In addition, power analysis empowers female clients to challenge and change oppressive environments (Worell & Remer, 1996). Similarly, *assertiveness training* is a feminist intervention that facilitates women's use of personal power to effectively challenge their environments and effect personal and social change.

Bibliotherapy and client participation in *consciousness-raising (C-R) groups* are also feminist interventions designed to increase women's awareness of sexism and other forms of oppression. Bibliotherapy involves reading and processing literature that the therapist has carefully chosen to help the client understand the societal influences that impact her personal experiences. In addition, feminist therapists may strongly encourage their clients to participate in a women's C-R group, a group of women who meet specifically to discuss their experiences as women. A C-R group offers women a supportive forum in which they may share personal gender-role experiences, process the commonalities in women's lives, and see more clearly the association between their experiences and sociopolitical structure (Kravetz, 1980).

Feminist counselors employ *reframing* and *relabeling* techniques and *therapy-demystifying strategies* to achieve the three principles of feminist therapy (Worell & Remer, 1996). When reframing clients' behaviors, feminist therapists consider the sociopolitical and cultural contributions to clients' presenting issues, thus shifting the etiology of the problem from the individual to the external environment. Reframing clients' issues reduces the possibility of blaming the victim. In relabeling interventions, negative labeling (e.g., calling a behavior dysfunctional) of a client's response to sexism is relabeled as a positive coping strategy. Further, "feminine" characteristics, which are devalued when viewed through an androcentric lens, are revalued through a feminist lens. In this way, clients are taught to relabel many of their previously perceived weaknesses as strengths and their "symptoms" as normal coping reactions to an oppressive society, thus valuing the client's perspective as a woman. In addition, feminist therapists attempt to *demystify* the therapeutic process by educating clients about the counseling interventions to be used, by collaboratively evaluating the therapeutic relationship and progress in therapy, and by teaching relevant skills for use in therapy and in other relationships (e.g., assertive communication skills).

In summary, all feminist counseling interventions seek to *empower* clients, or to mobilize the client's personal and collective resources to effect individual, interpersonal, and sociopolitical change. Feminist interventions are also intended to reduce the power differential between the counselor and therapist and to build an egalitarian therapeutic relationship.

ETHICAL PRACTICE WITH WOMEN

Effectively counseling women and members of other disadvantaged groups requires the development of specialized professional knowledge and skills. Specifically, practitioners should seek training that provides opportunities for (1) increasing practitioners' knowledge of current social issues and ethical practice with diverse clients, (2) developing self-awareness of personal biases, and (3) refining conceptual and technical skills. Achieving these training goals is critical for the ethical and competent provision of mental health services to all clients, but here we focus on the importance of these for working with women from diverse social and cultural groups.

Second, feminist mental health practitioners believe that providing ethical and competent mental health services requires that therapists acknowledge and assess the impact of their own values, perceptions, and experiences of both oppression and privilege on their conceptualization and treatment of clients' problems (Johnson & Remer, 1997). Practitioner trainees need to confront their own assumptions and stereotypes regarding other social groups and to reflect on their own stage of identity development. Depending on the social location of the trainee, this may involve self-examination of experiences of both oppression and privilege. For instance, a White female trainee would examine her experiences of gender oppression and White privilege; a Latino trainee with a physical disability might focus on his experiences of ethnic oppression, gender privilege, and discrimination based on ability. An additional example illustrates the complexity of the intersections and interactions of oppressions and privileges. An African American heterosexual female may experience tension between her experiences of racial and gender oppressions. On the one hand, she may share experiences of racial oppression with her African American male brothers at the same time that her African American male acquaintances may gender-stereotype or discriminate against her.

Practitioners who have neglected this important self-examination can negatively impact the counseling processes and outcomes for clients of disadvantaged groups. Consider, for example, a mental health practitioner who is in the first stage of feminist identity development. In the first stage, an individual is unaware of the effects of institutionalized sexism and unquestioningly accepts traditional gender roles and the status quo. A practitioner at this stage will tend to view *all* client problems as individually based and, to the detriment of the client, will not consider the impact of social context. Therefore, counselors who do not undertake this often challenging and difficult personal growth work risk not helping or even harming their clients. Ultimately, working effectively from a feminist framework necessitates that counselors attain the latter stages of feminist identity development, that is, the development of an authentic, positive, flexible feminist identity and commitment to political action aimed toward the creation of a nonsexist society (Downing & Roush, 1985). Finally, counselor trainees need to learn how to rigorously examine and critique theoretical assumptions that are androcentric or ethnocentric (Corey, 2000; Worell & Remer, in press). Likewise, counseling techniques that are based on biased theoretical assumptions should be transformed to align with the three feminist principles stated previously.

An important future direction for the counseling of women is for feminist practitioners to empirically demonstrate the effectiveness of their treatment models and interventions. In the current health care climate, it is imperative that feminist mental health practitioners support all efforts to document the efficacy of what they do. Also,

feminist mental health practitioners should critically examine existing conceptual and treatment models of mental health. Efficacious treatment should not be defined solely as symptom reduction and "adjustment" to toxic environments. Outcomes such as increased well-being and sociopolitical activism should be part of the gauge that empirically establishes effective feminist therapy.

Furthermore, feminist researchers and practitioners recognize that individual change is important, but that ultimately, women and other less-powerful groups will benefit most from social structural changes that eliminate discrimination in our social institutions. To this end, feminist researchers seek to disseminate their scholarship in ways that will help to improve the lives of women and other marginalized groups.

SUMMARY

Effective counseling with women avoids intrapsychic conceptualizations and psychotherapy models that are based on adrocentric, ethnocentric, or heterosexist assumptions and values. This means that clients' concerns and presenting problems need to be identified and assessed within the sociocultural contexts of oppression, discrimination, and sterotyping based on gender, race, ethnicity, class, age, abilities, and sexual orientation. Effective counselors seek to build egalitarian and collaborative therapeutic relationships that value clients' strengths. Ultimately, feminist therapists seek to intervene in ways that produce change in dysfunctional sociopolitical environments.

References

Broverman, I.K., Broverman, D.M., Clarkson, F.E., Rosenkrantz, P.S., & Vogel, S.R. (1970). Sex-role stereotypes and clinical judgments of mental health. *Journal of Consulting and Clinical Psychology, 34,* 1–7.

Cass, V. (1979). Homosexual identity formation: A theoretical model. *Journal of Homosexuality, 4,* 219–235.

Corey, G. (2000). *Theory and practice of counseling and psychotherapy* (5th ed.). Belmont, CA: Brooks/Cole.

Cross, W.E. (1980). Models of psychological nigressence. In R.L. Jones (Ed.), *Black psychology* (pp. 81–98). New York: Harper & Row.

Downing, N.E., & Roush, K.L. (1985). From passive acceptance to active commitment: A model of feminist identity development for women. *The Counseling Psychologist, 13*, 696–709.

Enns, C.Z. (1997). *Feminist theories and feminist psychotherapies: Origins, themes, and variations.* Binghamton, NY: Harrington Park Press.

Helms, J. (1995). An update of Helm's White and people of color racial identity models. In J.G. Ponterotto, J.M. Casas, L.A. Suzuki, & C.M. Alexander (Eds.), *Handbook of multicultural counseling* (pp. 181–198). Thousand Oaks, CA: Sage.

Johnson, N.G., & Remer, P. (1997). Postdoctoral training in feminist psychological practice. In J. Worell & N.G. Johnson (Eds.), *Shaping the future of feminist psychology: Education, research, and practice* (pp. 203–226). Washington, DC: American Psychological Association.

Kravetz, D. (1980). Consciousness-raising and self-help. In A.M. Brodsky & R.T. Hare-Mustin (Eds.), *Women and psychotherapy: An assessment of research and practice* (pp. 268–284). New York: Guilford Press.

McCarn, S.R., & Fassinger, R.E. (1996). Revisioning sexual minority identity formations: A new model of lesbian identity and its implications for counseling and research. *The Counseling Psychologist, 24*, 508–534.

Santos de Barona, M., & Dutton, M.A. (1997). Feminist perspectives on assessment. In J. Worell & N.G. Johnson (Eds.), *Shaping the future of feminist psychology: Education, research, and practice* (pp. 37–56). Washington, DC: American Psychological Association.

Sturdivant, S. (1980). *Therapy with women: A feminist philosophy of treatment.* New York: Springer.

Troiden, R.R. (1988). Homosexual identity development. *Journal of Adolescent Health Care, 9*, 105–113.

Worell, J., & Johnson, N.B. (1997). *Shaping the future of feminist psychology: Education, research, and practice.* Washington, DC: American Psychological Association.

Worell, J., & Remer, P. (1996). *Feminist perspectives in therapy: An empowerment model for women.* Chichester, England: Wiley.

Worell, J., & Remer, P. (in press). *Empowerment therapy with women: Integrating diversity with feminist psychological practice.* New York: Wiley.

Wyche, K.F., & Rice, J.K. (1997). Feminist therapy: From dialogue to tenets. In J. Worell & N.G. Johnson (Eds.), *Shaping the future of feminist psychology: Education, research, and practice* (pp. 57–72). Washington, DC: American Psychological Association.

PART VI
Group and Family Interventions

50 USING BRIEF GROUPS EFFECTIVELY

David Michael Coe

The demands of managed care organizations, agencies, and consumer groups have prompted an increase in the research and practice of brief group counseling. Trends in health care reform are toward improved cost containment, imposed time restrictions, more effective and efficient interventions, and improved consumer satisfaction. Brief group counseling continues to be an effective way to reduce the costs of mental health care, increase access to mental health services, and make efficient use of limited resources.

Brief counseling groups come in many forms. Solution-focused groups and brief focal groups are among the most frequently used forms of brief counseling groups. Solution-focused groups are gaining popularity among practitioners and researchers (Coe & Zimpfer, 1996; Metcalf, 1998; Selekman, 1991). Solution-focused group models are based on writings emanating from within the field of brief marriage and family therapy. Among the most influential solution-focused publications are those of de Shazer (1982), O'Hanlon and Weiner-Davis (1989), and Walter and Peller (1992). Solution-focused approaches seem highly compatible with a group modality and preliminary research has produced promising outcomes (Coe, 2000).

Brief focal groups use treatment approaches selected according to the specific goals of the group. Other techniques are used throughout the group in response to the needs and goals of the participants. Cognitive-behavioral and psychoeducational principles are well suited to a brief focal group model. Brief focal groups are likely to be manual-driven, highly structured, with a precise protocol for each session. This chapter presents a general model of a brief counseling group that draws on the characteristics of solution-focused groups and brief focal groups.

PLANNING A BRIEF COUNSELING GROUP

Implementing an effective brief counseling group requires that clinicians invest considerable time and effort during the planning and development of the group. Proper planning prior to the implementation of a brief counseling group dramatically reduces unexpected complications and improves outcomes. Once the tasks associated with planning a brief counseling group have been sufficiently addressed, brief group counseling can be extremely rewarding for both clinicians and participants. Agencies promoting the use of brief counseling groups can realize substantial benefits as well. Following are general technical and clinical issues involved in planning an effective brief counseling group.

Consultation Issues

Clinicians may need to assume the role of internal consultant. For private practitioners, some of the tasks involved in this stage of group construction are not applicable. It is important that brief group counselors obtain the cooperation, if not the enthusiasm, of the agency administration, staff, and reimbursement sources (see Spitz, 1996, for a thorough analysis of managed care and group psychotherapy). To obtain support from coworkers and administration it is necessary to address bias. Brief counseling groups are not always considered the sole treatment of choice but an adjunctive service. Brief forms of therapy may be perceived as an inferior treatment and a "sellout" to the managed care companies. Reassuring administrative staff and coworkers that brief counseling groups are an effective and efficient form of treatment will reduce resistance, increase cooperation, and improve the chances for success.

Clinicians ought to be prepared to defend their choice of treatment. It may be necessary to provide research data supporting the efficiency and efficacy of the brief group model you plan to use. Fortunately, the number of published research studies is increasing (Budman et al., 1988; Coe, 2000; Eakes, Walsh, Markowski, Cain, & Swanson, 1997; Zimmerman, Jacobsen, Macintyre, & Watson, 1996; Zimmerman, Prest, & Wetzel, 1997).

Leadership Training

Brief group counselors adhere to the standards of practice and ethics espoused by their professional organizations. The Association for Specialists in Group Work (ASGW) requires group counselors to follow the standards of practice and ethical guidelines of the American Counseling Association (1995). In addition, the ASGW has published *Best Practice Guidelines* for group counselors to assist training programs in preparing group workers (Rapin & Keel, 1998). These standards outline the knowledge, skills, ethical standards, and experience group counselors must possess for competent performance. Group leaders can obtain a free copy of these standards by contacting the American Counseling Association. The ASGW is a division of the American Counseling Association and is headquartered in Alexandria, Virginia.

ASSUMPTIONS OF BRIEF GROUP COUNSELORS

Brief group counselors prefer pragmatism, parsimony, and the least intrusive treatment to address problems. They avoid pathologizing jargon and view the participant as the expert on his or her problem. It is the clinician's role to assist participants in selecting limited and achievable goals to maximize their opportunities for successful treatment.

Brief group counselors view problems as temporary and changeable. They assume that there are always times when the problem does not exist and that it is solvable. After the client defines the problem, brief group counselors actively intervene when appropriate to keep the focus of treatment on strengths, skills, resources, and competencies to achieve rapid resolution of the presenting problem(s). One of the hallmarks of brief therapy is using participants' strengths and skills to help them meet their needs and effect change in the here and now rather than attempting to correct underlying causes, resolve conflicts, or effect major personality changes.

Brief group counselors assume that therapy can be brief even though growth is a lifelong process. Small changes occurring during treatment are presumed to lead to further changes after treatment ends, and it is assumed that much of the work of counseling occurs outside of the group setting. It is important that brief group counselors attempt to adhere to these assumptions to create a climate within the group and the agency that promotes and supports the rapid resolution of presenting problems.

Yalom (1996) states that brief counseling groups can be made even more effective by incorporating a focus on interpersonal process. The brief counseling models presented here incorporate interpersonal theory and techniques. Some group models assume that groups pass through several stages of development. Corey and Corey (1992) delineate the stages as pregroup, initial, working, and final stage. Each stage has different characteristics and group and leadership tasks. According to Trotzer (1989), interpersonal techniques are valuable practical tools used to facilitate therapeutic impact for the good of individuals or the group. He lists 19 specific skills, including listening, restatement, reflection, clarifying, summarizing, linking, questioning, and confronting. These skills are used to perform leadership functions such as promoting interaction, intervening, rule keeping, consolidating, enhancing communication, resolving conflicts, and mobilizing group resources. Corey and Corey report similar skills and functions; however, they caution that leadership skills and functions ought to be implemented in a sensitive and timely way with an awareness of the group's stage of development.

NEEDS ASSESSMENT

It is important to perform a formal or informal needs assessment. The results of this assessment help to identify potential participants and substantiate the need for a brief counseling group. Simply asking agency personnel what types of groups they would support and recommend to their clients may be sufficient. Inquiring among consumers about the types of groups they would attend provides useful information. A formal needs assessment may take the form of a written survey of client and coworker needs and preferences. Once you've obtained the cooperation of the agency and selected an appropriate target group, decisions are made regarding the structure of the group.

GROUP COMPOSITION

Brief counseling groups may have a homogeneous composition. In a homogeneous group, participants are included when they are diagnosed as showing signs of the same mental or emotional disorder or because they have identified the same presenting problem(s) and goals. According to Yalom (1996), homogeneous composition promotes several of the therapeutic factors inherent in group work.

Participants gain a sense of hope, universality, and support when others in the group are struggling with the same issue.

In contrast, some research supports heterogeneously composed solution-focused groups (Coe, 2000). In a heterogeneously composed group, participants may have varying diagnoses and presenting problems. Heterogeneous composition offers the opportunity to maximize learning by providing multiple perspectives. Leaders assist participants to identify possible solutions by drawing on the diversity of knowledge, skills, and strategies. Yalom (1996) states that heterogeneous groups imitate a real social universe, thereby pushing the members to develop new methods of interpersonal interaction.

PREGROUP SESSION

Pregroup screening sessions are arranged for each participant. Several important tasks are accomplished during the pregroup session, including diagnosis, participant selection, participant preparation, and goal setting.

Diagnosis

Group leaders use this session to perform a mental status exam leading to a diagnosis according to the criteria delineated in the *Diagnostic and Statistical Manual of Mental Disorders,* fourth edition (American Psychiatric Association, 1994). Most clinical settings require that a diagnosis be rendered to assure compliance with regulatory agencies as well as reimbursement sources. The diagnostic assessment should include a thorough understanding of the potential participant's level of functioning in such areas as work, daily living responsibilities, relationships, leisure activities, health, and spirituality. Brief counseling group leaders assess potential participants from a holistic perspective, focusing on strengths, skills, and resources in addition to limitations and problems.

Goal Setting and Selection

Based on the information shared during the pregroup session, the clinician and potential participant agree on explicit, limited goals. Solution-focused techniques are used to normalize or reframe the problem and identify exceptions, material, and goals. For participants having difficulty setting goals or identifying a solution, asking "the miracle question" often produces useful information (i.e., "How would your life be different if your problem were miraculously solved?"). Participants are selected for inclusion in the group if their needs and goals are compatible with the established goals of the group.

Participant Preparation

During the pregroup screening session, potential participants are provided with a statement of the purpose of the group and group goals. They need to be informed of the types of techniques and procedures that may be used, the qualifications of the group leader, fees, opportunities for follow-up services, personal risks, and any use of recording devices. During the pregroup session, it is important to establish and inform the participants about group rules. The ASGW's *Best Practice Guidelines* (1998) establish minimum ground rules and ethical standards summarized here. It is necessary that group leaders emphasize the need for confidentiality (see Welfel, Chapter 56). The use of alcohol or drugs prior to group sessions is unacceptable. Members should be informed that participation is voluntary and that they may exit at any time. Group leaders must protect participants from physical threats, intimidation, coercion, and undue peer pressure. Members should be informed of any possible risks involved in participation in the group. Many of these issues can be included on a consent form that participants will be expected to sign acknowledging that they were sufficiently informed regarding these issues. Pregroup sessions end with the assigning of a solution-focused task. For example, participants are asked, "Pay attention to times when the problem is less severe, less frequent, or absent." They are instructed to remember these times so they can report them to the group. This information will help with the identification of solutions in subsequent group sessions.

PRACTICAL CONSIDERATIONS

Brief counseling group leaders decide on several practical considerations and inform participants of these during the pregroup screening. These include group size, frequency and duration, length, and location.

Group Size

The size of a brief counseling group may vary. Typically, groups with children have 3 or 4 members, adolescent groups between 8 and 10. A group composed of adults ideally should have about 8 members. This number can be enlarged to 15 members if there is a coleader.

Frequency and Duration

Brief counseling groups typically meet for 1½ hours once a week. For children, adolescents, and inpatient populations, it may be better to meet more frequently and to keep the duration shorter.

Length of Group

Brief counseling groups may be closed or open to new members. In a closed group, all members of the group begin and end the group at the same time. This promotes a sense of cohesion, which facilitates trust and self-disclosure among the participants, leading to increased involvement in the group process. Brief counseling groups average between 8 and 15 sessions in length. Defined starting and ending dates ought to be sufficiently stressed to participants so that they have a clear conception of the time limits. Concern among participants regarding the time-limited nature of the group can facilitate therapeutic processes.

Open groups allow members to enter the group at any time. Group members are able to end the group when they feel they have made sufficient progress toward their goals. This approach seems more in line with brief counseling assumptions because duration of treatment is not imposed. It is the duty of the group leader to address readiness for termination with participants at each session.

Group Location

Leaders should select a comfortable, private room or area where the group will meet. The area ought to be large enough to accommodate the members comfortably while seated in a circle. The location needs to be conveyed to participants and if necessary leaders ought to actually show them the room prior to the starting date to allay any fears they may have.

SELECTING APPROPRIATE TREATMENTS

One of the hallmarks of brief counseling groups is leader flexibility in regard to selecting appropriate treatment interventions. MacKensie (1996) states that brief counseling group leaders need to acknowledge the value of multiple approaches to producing change. Certainly, group leaders need to be well trained in treatment strategies for the target population for whom the group was intended. Seligman (1990) provides a comprehensive and systematic guide for selecting effective treatment for a variety of mental and emotional disorders. McKay and Paleg (1992) provide excellent descriptions of 14 different brief counseling groups on such topics as codependency, anger management, parenting, and surviving sexual abuse. They include an overview of useful treatment strategies and techniques.

Several major techniques, summarized here, have been delineated in the literature (Coe, 2000; Coe & Zimpfer, 1996; de Shazer, 1982, 1984, 1985, 1988; de Shazer et al., 1986; O'Hanlon & Weiner-Davis, 1989; Walter & Peller, 1992):

- *Positive Relabeling.* From the moment of contact with potential participants, the group counselor will begin to relabel participants' identified problems to alter their perception of the problem. The purpose is to provide a new frame of reference describing the problem as something of a less disturbing nature.

- *Normalizing.* This technique consists of construing problems in terms of being common, ordinary, and less pathological. Using linking techniques also helps to promote a sense of universality among members.

- *Joining.* The group leader encourages trust and rapport development by taking time to listen to clients' complaints and expressing the core conditions of empathy, congruence, and unconditional positive regard. Other techniques useful for this purpose include matching the group's language, mirroring the group members' expressions, and using the group members' metaphors. Using energizing and warm-up activities can help to promote rapid cohesion.

- *Assessing Pretreatment Change.* During the first group session, the group counselor will ask members to discuss positive changes that have already occurred in relation to their identified goals.

- *Presuppositional Questioning.* These questions are worded to instill hope, as they imply that change will take place or that it already has occurred. This technique is useful for addressing members' problem behaviors both in and out of the group and for moving the group process forward. As members respond, they begin to use more helpful and hopeful language.

- *Formula First Session Task.* Designed by de Shazer (1985), this task is useful with members who have vague complaints and helps to identify exceptions. Group members are given the instruction, "Between this session and the next, I would like you to observe, so that you can describe to me the next time, what happens (in regard to the identified goal) that you want to continue to have happen."

- *Scaling Questions.* Therapists can obtain a quantitative measurement of clients' progress on their goals by asking participants to rate the amount of their change on a scale from 1 to 10.

- *The Miracle Question.* Counselors can generate a visual description of the member's desired treatment outcome. Members are asked to imagine what will be different in their lives if a miracle occurred while they were sleeping, such that when they awoke their goal had been reached. This task aids participants in gaining self-understanding of their personal values and related goals.

- *Observation Tasks.* Members are asked to observe one another, looking for exceptions. Often, the act of being observed is enough to create changes in behavior. Participants benefit from interpersonal learning and begin to act in ways that are approved of by the group.
- *Cheerleading and Compliments.* These techniques are useful for fostering cooperation and for celebrating exception patterns of behavior. The group leader and participants identify and applaud important strengths and coping strategies of each member.
- *Doing Something Different.* This task is helpful for initiating behavioral changes. The members are instructed to do something different (in relation to the goal area) between sessions, no matter how strange or weird what they do might seem.
- *Pattern Interventions.* These are used to change problem-maintaining patterns of behavior. The counselor instructs members to change the frequency, timing, duration, location, or sequence of events surrounding the problem.
- *Externalizing.* Group leaders discuss problems as something separate from the group members and that oppresses the members and the group. In this way, participants are unified and mobilized to fight back against the problem.

BALANCING PROCESS AND CONTENT

Effective brief counseling groups usually begin by asking participants in a "go-around" to describe what has been better in relation to their specific goals. Homework is reviewed and participants discuss their attempts at trying out new solutions. The focus of the group is on identifying possibilities for solutions. Solution-focused techniques assist participants to identify cognitive and behavioral

solutions. Group members are encouraged to assist each other in identifying alternative solutions, such as new behaviors and ways of viewing the problem.

Effective brief counseling group leaders may employ interpersonal techniques and psychoeducation. Clinicians may follow a manualized approach that emphasizes the presentation of didactic material. Leaders use an array of presentation styles and incorporate handouts or media in addition to formal lectures to present new concepts and skills. Weekly sessions end by processing the material presented and any client issues disclosed during the group. The session is closed with the assignment of new homework and the directive that participants try out some of the solutions they identified or learned during the session. Coe and Zimpfer (1996) outline a complete description of the process and content issues involved in brief solution-focused counseling groups.

SUMMARY

There are many variables involved in designing and implementing a successful brief counseling group. Specifically, it is important that clinicians adequately perform the role of consultant to administration, staff, and reimbursement sources. Brief counseling group leaders need to convey the appropriate attitudes and obtain the necessary skills, training, and supervision to lead brief groups effectively. Important considerations in brief group counseling include the proper preparation of participants, the selection of appropriate treatments, and maintaining the appropriate balance of process and content issues.

Solution-focused counseling has been applied in a variety of settings with diverse populations. Solution-focused counseling has been implemented in both inpatient and outpatient treatment facilities. It has been used with individuals, families, couples, groups, and children. In addition, solution-focused approaches can be combined with other treatment strategies easily and effectively. Because it is considered brief compared to other approaches, it may be more cost-effective, allow faster access to treatment, and be a more efficient use of resources.

References

American Counseling Association. (1995). *Code of ethics and standards of practice.* Alexandria, VA: Author.

American Psychiatric Association. (1994). *Diagnostic and statistical manual of mental disorders* (4th ed.). Washington, DC: Author.

Budman, S., Demby, A., Redondo, J., Hannan, M., Feldstein, M., Ring, J., & Springer, T. (1988). Comparative outcome in time-limited individual and group psychotherapy. *International Journal of Group Psychotherapy, 38,* 63–68.

Coe, D.M. (2000). Solution-oriented group counseling in community mental health: An outcome study (Doctoral dissertation, Kent State University, Ohio, 2000). *Dissertation Abstracts International, 61,* 10A.

Coe, D.M., & Zimpfer, D.G. (1996). Infusing solution-oriented theory and techniques into group work. *Journal for Specialists in Group Work, 21,* 49–57.

Corey, M.S., & Corey, G. (1992). *Groups: Process and practice* (4th ed.). New York: Norton.

de Shazer, S. (1982). Some conceptual distinctions are more useful than others. *Family Process, 21,* 71–84.

de Shazer, S. (1984). The death of resistance. *Family Process, 23,* 79–93.

de Shazer, S. (1985). *Keys to solution in brief therapy.* New York: Norton.

de Shazer, S. (1988). *Clues: Investigating solutions in brief therapy.* New York: Norton.

de Shazer, S., Berg, I.K., Lipchik, E., Nunnally, E., Molnar, A., Gingerich, W., & Weiner-Davis, M. (1986). Brief therapy: Focused solution development. *Family Process, 25,* 207–222.

Eakes, G., Walsh, S., Markowski, M., Cain, H., & Swanson, M. (1997). Family centered brief solution-focused therapy with chronic schizophrenia: A pilot study. *Journal of Family Therapy, 19*(2), 145–157.

McKay, M., & Paleg, K. (1992). *Focal group psychotherapy.* Oakland, CA: New Harbinger.

MacKensie, R. (1996). Time-limited group psychotherapy: Has Cinderella found her prince? *Group, 20,* 95–111.

Metcalf, L. (1998). *Solution-focused group therapy.* New York: Free Press.

O'Hanlon, W., & Weiner-Davis, M. (1989). *In search of solutions: A new direction in psychotherapy.* New York: Norton.

Rapin, L., & Keel, L. (1998). *Association for Specialists in Group Work: Best practice guidelines.* Alexandria, VA: ASGW.

Spitz, H. (1996). *Group psychotherapy and managed mental health care.* New York: Brunner/Mazel.

Selekman, M. (1991). The solution-oriented parenting group: A treatment alternative that works. *Journal of Strategic and Systemic Therapies, 10*(1), 36–49.

Seligman, L. (1990). *Selecting effective treatments.* San Francisco: Jossey-Bass.

Trotzer, J. (1989). *The counselor and the group.* Muncie, IN: Accelerated Development.

Walter, J., & Peller, J. (1992). *Becoming solution-focused in brief therapy.* New York: Brunner/Mazel.

Yalom, I.D. (1996). *The theory and practice of group psychotherapy* (4th ed.). New York: Basic Books.

Zimmerman, T.S., Jacobsen, B.R., Macintyre, M., & Watson, C. (1996). Solution-focused parenting groups: An empirical study. *Journal of Systemic Therapies, 15*(4), 12–25.

Zimmerman, T.S., Prest, L.A., & Wetzel, B.E. (1997). Solution-focused couples therapy groups: An empirical study. *Journal of Family Therapy, 19,* 125–144.

51 EXPLORING DIVERSITY IN THERAPEUTIC GROUPS

Robert K. Conyne, Mei Tang, and Albert L. Watson

Therapeutic groups, encompassing group counseling and group psychotherapy, are a critically important form of group work (Conyne, Wilson, & Ward, 1997). These groups are becoming a mainstay of service delivery for mental health counselors for three broad reasons. First, therapeutic groups possess "therapeutic factors" (Yalom, 1995) that are uniquely suited to client growth, development, and change. These factors include, but are not limited to, the capacity to instill hope, to develop socializing skills, to promote interpersonal learning, to learn from one another, to feel connected to others, and to create existential meaning from life's circumstances. Second, the changing mental health landscape, with managed care's emphasis on cost-effective ways to produce positive outcomes, is compatible with the group approach (McKay & Paleg, 1992; Spitz, 1996). Finally, research has demonstrated that therapeutic groups are effective (Budman, Simeone, Reilly, & Demby, 1994; Fuhriman & Burlingame, 1994; Toseland & Siporin, 1986).

DIVERSITY

Theorists and practitioners recognize the terms *multicultural* and *diversity* as controversial. Following is a brief discussion of some important concepts related to diversity: definition, worldview, acculturation, and racial identity development.

In terms of defining diversity, the Association of Multicultural Counseling and Development (AMCD) reported that the term multicultural limits its focus to race, ethnicity, and culture, whereas the term diversity includes a broader range including but not limited to age, gender, sexual identity, religious/spiritual identification, social and economic class background, and residential location (Ivey, Ivey, & Simek-Morgan, 1997). For that reason we chose the term diversity for this discussion. Other terms are important in understanding the impact of diversity on therapeutic groups.

Worldview is a concept that holds particular significance to multicultural counselors. Worldview is defined as an individual's experiences, including social, moral, religious, educational, economic, and political inputs, that are shared with other members of one's reference group (e.g., cultural group, racial/ethnic group, family).

Acculturation and *racial/ethnic identity development* are important concepts in understanding human behavior. Acculturation is the process wherein an individual relinquishes his or her ethnic values, beliefs, customs, and practices for that of the majority culture (Aponte & Wohl, 2000). Racial/ethnic identity is an individual's self-awareness as a member of a particular racial or ethnic group (e.g., African American, Asian American, White). Both acculturation and racial/ethnic identity may be important factors influencing the relevance of specific counseling interventions.

Developmental models of African Americans were first introduced by Cross (1971) and Jackson (1975). Recent researchers have expanded this concept to Latinos/Latinas (Bernal & Knight, 1993), Whites (Helms, 1995), and biracial groups (Kerwin, Ponterotto, Jackson, & Harris, 1993). Most important, these models of identity development and acculturation may play a significant role in matching clients to appropriate counselors, as well as matching specific clients to other desirable situations, such as heterogeneous groups.

Diversity in Therapeutic Groups

Changing societal demographics demand an understanding of how diversity comprehensively affects therapeutic group work, including group process and dynamics, group leadership, research, and training. Diverse therapeutic groups are being formed that contain heterogeneous members (e.g., by including a range of diversity in the membership) or that are targeted exclusively for people from a homogeneous population (e.g., African Americans, elderly). To be effective, leaders of such multicultural therapeutic groups need to be sensitive to a range of issues, including the concepts of social microcosm and cohesiveness (Sciarra, 1999; Yalom, 1995).

The complexity of a heterogeneous group increases when the group therapist considers how elements of diversity, worldview, acculturation, ethnic/racial identity, and the clients' different levels of development interact. When involved with therapeutic groups possessing such diversity, the group leader should remember to apply the following general guideline: *Create a social ecology in the group that allows for differences to be acknowledged and respected and where commonalities can be recognized and accepted.*

GUIDELINES AND ISSUES FOR EXPLORING DIVERSITY IN THERAPEUTIC GROUPS

Directions from Major Relevant Standards, Principles, and Guidelines

Over the past several years, five relevant sets of standards, principles, or guidelines have been produced by major professional counseling and psychological organizations in the broad areas of diversity and group work. Each of these sets is summarized briefly next.

The American Psychological Association's *Guidelines for Providers of Psychological Services to Ethnic, Linguistic, and Culturally Diverse Populations* (APA, 1990) encourages using a systematic sociocultural framework with clients when diversity in values, interaction styles, and cultural expectations is considered.

The Association for Specialists in Group Work's *Professional Standards for the Training of Group Workers* (ASGW, 2000) indicates that group leaders need to use personal contextual factors (e.g., family of origin, neighborhood of residence, organizational membership, cultural membership) in interpreting behavior of members in the group and that diversity-competent group work is necessary for observing and participating in group activities.

The Association for Specialists in Group Work's *Best Practice Guidelines* (ASGW, 1998) contains a broad, overarching perspective regarding diversity, stating that leaders of therapeutic groups need to practice with broad sensitivity to member differences, including but not limited to "ethnic, gender, religious, sexual, psychological maturity, economic class, family history, physical characteristics or limitations, and geographic location" (p. 242).

The Association for Multicultural Counseling and Development's *Multicultural Counseling Competencies* (AMCD, 1996) addresses general counselor competencies (including counselor attitudes and beliefs, knowledge, and skills) that are pertinent to counseling within the principles of self-awareness, awareness of worldview, and diversity-appropriate intervention strategies.

The Association for Specialists in Group Work's *Principles for Diversity-Competent Group Workers* (ASGW, 1999) is compatible with the AMCD's *Multicultural Counseling Competencies*. These ASGW principles center on the application of the diversity principles to group leadership. Necessary group leader attitudes, knowledge, and skills are identified within the principles of group leader self-awareness, awareness of group members' worldview, and diversity-appropriate intervention strategies within the group. Example applications of selected principles follow.

Application Example of Group Leader "Awareness of Self" Principle. Leaders of diverse groups will be confronted with challenges arising from differences between themselves and many of their group members. Such challenges may be manifested in any of the following dimensions: race, ethnicity, culture, Socioeconomic Status (SES), gender, sexual orientation, abilities, religion and spiritual beliefs, values, and biases. Diversity-competent group leaders need to be comfortable, tolerant, and sensitive about such differences. To reach that goal, group leaders must first become aware and comfortable with themselves as multicultural beings.

Application Example of "Awareness of Group Member's Worldview" Principle. Increasingly, therapeutic groups will involve members who are "out of the mainstream" due to such sociopolitical factors as their immigration status, low SES, experienced racism, sexism, or other forms of oppression, and feelings of powerlessness that may result from such conditions. Group leaders need to become aware of the different views of the world that members may possess and how these views can affect the member, the leaders, other members, and group processes. Diversity-competent group leaders must learn how to include appropriately these worldviews into their practice, rather than to ignore or minimize them. Consistent with other best practices in group work, they collaborate and work with the unique resources of members.

Application Example of "Diversity-Appropriate Intervention Strategies in the Group" Principle. Members from diverse backgrounds will bring into group interaction a variety of verbal and nonverbal behaviors. For example, a perceived reluctance to verbally engage in the group may represent a cultural value, as may be the case initially with many Asian group members. Therefore, diversity-competent group leaders are able to engage in a variety of verbal and nonverbal group leading functions dependent on the type of group and on the multiple, self-identified diversity status of various group

members. These group leaders are not limited to one method or approach to group leadership, and they recognize that any approach might be culture-bound. They can ameliorate the negative effects of inappropriate interventions due to being culture-bound by drawing from other culturally pertinent skill sets.

RECOMMENDED GROUP LEADER STRATEGIES

Based on the issues and professional association guidelines presented above, the following 10 strategies are recommended for leaders working with diversity groups.

Leaders of diverse groups need to:

1. Demonstrate core competencies and best practices in group work leadership.
2. Develop awareness of both the group members' and their own cultural backgrounds, and of those experiences that have influenced attitudes, values, and reactions about group interaction.
3. Be aware of how the cultural identity of group members and of themselves affects attitudes and expectations toward group intervention.
4. Educate themselves about how socialcultural factors (e.g., racism, oppression, discrimination, and stereotyping) affect themselves and members in a group setting.
5. Assess group goals during the planning stage to determine whether a homogeneous or heterogeneous group best fits the purpose, also giving consideration to issues of structure and group size.
6. Be especially cognizant of group dynamics, such as the power relationship existing between the minority and majority members, verbal and nonverbal cues from members (which might be different from the group leader's frame of reference), and intensity of intermember conflict.
7. Acknowledge the individuality of every group member rather than stereotyping individual members by their ethnic group characteristics.

8. Avoid being either overly protective or confrontive of minority group members to avoid any unnecessary projection.
9. Distinguish between which behaviors in the group are "symptomatic" and which are "cultural."
10. Develop culturally appropriate skills that facilitate the positive cultural identity of each member and constructively use the anxiety generated by cultural differences.

Regarding recommendation 9, for example, some group members might be quiet in groups because of their cultural tradition (i.e., to be reserved). However, if group workers interpret such behaviors as being noncompliant due to their lack of knowledge of culture, clients' culturally appropriate behavior can be mistakenly viewed as "symptomatic." Conversely, overgeneralizing ethnic group characteristics to individual clients should be avoided (recommendation 7). Group leaders can encourage members to share their general understanding of each member's culture, followed by examining how this general understanding of culture may (or may not) apply to the group member.

ISSUES FOR EXPLORING DIVERSITY IN THERAPEUTIC GROUPS

The professional association documents summarized earlier provide guidelines to which leaders of therapeutic groups involving diversity can refer. Therapeutic group work with diverse populations represents a new service modality, and most mental health practitioners have limited knowledge, and limited skill, in providing this service (D'Andrea & Daniels, 1996). Many specific issues remain to be addressed, including those that are presented next.

Uncharted Territory

It is ironic to discuss the lack of empirical research on multicultural group counseling in the year 2000, considering that Kurt Lewin's T-groups were implemented in the late 1940s and

early 1950s, a half century ago, to reduce interracial tension between communities and community leaders (Merta, 1995; Sciarra, 1999). But although the empirical research available on multicultural group counseling is scant and the knowledge base is limited (D'Andrea & Daniels, 1996), the past decade has witnessed an increase in multicultural group counseling research (see, e.g., Fenster, 1996; Fukuyama & Coleman, 1992; Gainer, 1992).

Diversity and related issues are concerns for therapeutic group leaders. Issues such as worldview, degree of acculturation, and racial identity may become barriers to group leaders and clients, as well as barriers between individual clients. The competing worldview regarding the nature of police (e.g., police serve and protect versus intimidate and harass) is one example that could alienate both group leaders and group members. To avoid such situations, it is imperative that group leaders recognize and appreciate perspectives different from their own.

Theoretical Assumptions

Vasquez and Han (1995) observed that therapy groups are generally driven by Eurocentric assumptions about what constitutes therapeutic and effective interventions. As an example, Vasquez and Han explored Yalom's (1985) curative (therapeutic) factors, which were mentioned at the beginning of this chapter. Some therapeutic factors, such as socializing techniques and skills, imitative behavior, interpersonal learning, assertiveness, and expression of negative feelings may be therapeutic for some members of the dominant culture, but often are not for those whose culture considers family or group belonging as primary, with individualism being secondary. For these group members, such direct expression would be considered impolite, presumptuous, and unacceptable.

What can leaders of multicultural therapeutic groups do, given these circumstances? First, recognize and understand the limitations discussed above. Second, explore nontraditional approaches, such as an ecological one, that consider the effects of the client environment on behavior and vice versa. Third, as part of professional development, routinely consult with professionals who possess an alternative frame of reference (e.g., Afrocentric, feminist), and enhance multicultural group competencies and best practices through relevant continuing education.

Racial Identity Development

The racial heterogeneity/homogeneity of specific groups of people has received considerable attention. Examples of these groups include Asian Americans (Fukuyama & Coleman, 1992), African Americans (Gainer, 1992; Rollock, Westman, & Johnson, 1992), Hispanics (Arredondo, 1991; Baron, 1991), and American Indians (Sage, 1991). However, Helms (1995) suggested that the stage of racial identity development of group members, rather than race, may be a better determinant of the quality and effectiveness of culturally diverse group counseling. Helms and Cook (1999) suggested that whereas Yalom (1985) attributed many group member conflicts to early family experience, conflicts arising from racial and cultural phenomena may serve as a more comprehensive indicator.

Prejudice, Racism, and Power

People of color often carry an unusual burden throughout life. This burden, whether individual or institutional in form, frequently is manifested but unaddressed in therapeutic groups. Blacks and Hispanics, for example, regardless of their personal demeanor and accomplishment, often are told that they possess numerous moral, intellectual, and psychological deficits and that they are disproportionately responsible for societal ills, such as AIDS, crime, violent behavior, and sexual promiscuity (Fenster, 1996). Even in racially heterogeneous settings, these attitudes and beliefs influence the behavior of people of color as well as Whites. Many of these attitudes are rooted in prejudice and racism. The lack of comfort of both people of color and Whites in addressing them tends to empower White

people and disempower people of color. In therapeutic groups, inclusion and exclusion issues can take on special importance by members who are routinely excluded from various societal opportunities.

White Privilege

Many sensitive White people are concerned with racism and discrimination and the limiting effect these factors exert on the person of color. However, it is more rare when White people realize the benefit or privilege they derive from such acts. Generally, when subtle or overt racism/discrimination occurs, someone benefits. White privilege (Kivel, 1996; McIntosh, 1988; Terry, 1970) may be particularly difficult to address in multicultural therapeutic groups because of the denial of it that many Whites experience and the resentment felt by people of color related to that denial.

White privilege might occur in the form of tangible benefits such as those described above or in the form of intangibles, which include attitude, perceptions, and behavior. Several specific benefits of White privilege are described by Kivel (1996). He suggested that Whites are given more attention, more respect, and more status than people of color. Being White means that one will be accepted, acknowledged, and given the benefit of the doubt. Even when Whites get into trouble, authority figures expect them "to be able to change and improve, and therefore will discipline or penalize [them] less or differently" (p. 29). An important implementation to multicultural therapeutic group work is that leaders need to learn to hear clients differently, to see them differently, and to respond differently.

SUMMARY

Diversity in therapeutic groups is a reality, mirroring societal demographic trends. Group leaders need to accept and plan for this condition, which will cause many to challenge their basic orientation to group leadership and to adopt more diversity-competent approaches. In this chapter, we have reviewed basic information related to therapeutic groups, diversity, and diversity in groups. We also have identified a set of issues that we think are important to address, along with strategic recommendations and selected resources.

References

American Psychological Association. (1990). *APA guidelines for providers of psychological services to ethnic, linguistic, and culturally diverse populations*. Washington, DC: Author.

Aponte, J., & Wohl, J. (2000). *Psychological intervention and cultural diversity*. Needham Heights, MA: Allyn & Bacon.

Arredondo, P. (1991). Counseling Latinas. In C.C. Lee & B.L. Richardson (Eds.), *Multicultural issues in counseling: New approaches to diversity* (pp. 143–156). Alexandria, VA: American Association for Counseling and Development.

Association for Multicultural Counseling and Development. (1996). *Multicultural counseling competencies*. Washington, DC: Author.

Association for Specialists in Group Work. (1998). Best practice guidelines. *Journal for Specialists in Group Work, 23*, 237–244.

Association for Specialists in Group Work. (1999). Principles for diversity-competent group workers. *Journal for Specialists in Group Work, 24*, 7–14.

Association for Specialists in Group Work. (2000). *Professional standards for the training of group workers*. Alexandria, VA: Author.

Baron, A. (1991). Counseling Chicano college students. In C.C. Lee & B.L. Richardson (Eds.), *Multicultural issues in counseling: New approaches to diversity* (pp. 171–184). Alexandria, VA: American Association for Counseling and Development.

Bernal, M., & Knight, G. (1993). *Ethnic identity: Formation and transmission among Hispanics and other minorities*. Albany: State University of New York Press.

Budman, S., Simeone, P., Reilly, R., & Demby, A. (1994). Progress in short-term and time-limited group psychotherapy: Evidence and implications. In A. Fuhriman & G. Burlingame (Eds.), *Handbook of group psychotherapy* (pp. 319–339). New York: Wiley.

Conyne, R., Wilson, F.R., & Ward, D. (1997). *Comprehensive group work: What is means and how to teach it*. Alexandria, VA: American Counseling Association.

Cross, W., Jr. (1971). The Negro-to-Black conversion experience. *Black World, 20*, 13–27.

D'Andrea, M., & Daniels, J. (1996). What is multicultural group counseling? Identifying its potential benefits, barriers, and future challenge. *Counseling and Human Development, 28*, 1–16.

Fenster, A. (1996). Group therapy as an effective treatment modality for people of color. *International Journal of Group Psychotherapy, 46*, 399–416.

Fuhriman, A., & Burlingame, G. (Eds.). (1994). *Handbook of group psychotherapy: An empirical and clinical analysis*. New York: Wiley.

Fukuyama, M., & Coleman, N. (1992). A model for bicultural assertion training with Asian-Pacific American college students. *Journal of Specialists in Group Work, 17*, 210–217.

Gainer, K. (1992). Internalized oppression as a barrier to effective group work with Black women. *Journal for Specialists in Group Work, 17*, 235–242.

Helms, J. (Ed.). (1995). *Black and White racial identity: Theory, research, and practice*. Westport, CT: Greenwood.

Helms, J., & Cook, D. (1999). *Using race and gender in counseling and psychotherapy: Theory and process*. Needham Heights, MA: Allyn & Bacon.

Ivey, A., Ivey, M., & Simek-Morgan, L. (1997). *Counseling and psychotherapy: A multicultural perspective*. Needham Heights, MA: Allyn & Bacon.

Jackson, B. (1975). Black identity development. *MEFORM: Journal of Educational Diversity and Innovation, 2*, 19–25.

Kerwin, C., Ponterotto, J., Jackson, B., & Harris, A. (1993). Racial identity in biracial children: A qualitative investigation. *Journal of Counseling Psychology, 40*, 221–231.

Kivel, P. (1996). *Uprooting racism*. Gabriola Island, British Columbia: New Society.

McIntosh, P. (1988). *White privilege: Unpacking the invisible knapsack*. Wellesley, MA: Wellesley College, Center for Research on Women.

McKay, M., & Paleg, K. (Eds.). (1992). *Focal group psychotherapy*. Oakland, CA: New Harbinger.

Merta, R. (1995). Group work: Multicultural perspectives. In J.G. Ponterotto, J.M. Casas, L.A. Suzuki, & C.M. Alexander (Eds.), *Handbook of multicultural counseling* (pp. 567–585). Thousand Oaks, CA: Sage.

Rollock, D., Westman, J., & Johnson, C. (1992). A Black student support group on a White university campus: Issues for counselors and therapist. *Journal of Specialists in Group Work, 17*, 243–252.

Sage, G. (1991). Counseling American Indian adults. In C.C. Lee & B.L. Richardson (Eds.), *Multicultural issues in counseling: New approaches to diversity* (pp. 23–35). Alexandria, VA: American Association for Counseling and Development.

Sciarra, D. (1999). *Multiculturalism in counseling.* Itasca, IL: Peacock.

Spitz, H. (1996). *Group psychotherapy and managed mental health care: A clinical guide for providers.* New York: Brunner/Mazel.

Terry, R. (1970). *For Whites only.* Grand Rapids, MI: Eerdsmans.

Toseland, R., & Siporin, M. (1986). When to recommend group treatment: A review of the clinical and group literature. *International Journal of Group Psychotherapy, 36,* 171.

Vasquez, M., & Han, A. (1995). Group interactions and treatment with ethnic minorities. In J. Aponte, R.Y. Rivers, et al. (Eds.), *Psychological interventions and cultural diversity* (pp. 109–127). Boston: Allyn & Bacon.

Yalom, I. (1985). *Theory and practice of group psychotherapy.* New York: Basic Books.

Yalom, I. (1995). *Theory and practice of group psychotherapy* (2nd ed.). New York: Basic Books.

Fenster, A. (1996). Group therapy as an effective treatment modality for people of color. *International Journal of Group Psychotherapy, 46,* 399–416.

Garvin, C.D., & Reed, B.G. (1983). Gender issues in social group work: An overview. *Social Work with Groups, 6,* 5–18.

Marsiglia, F.F., Cross, S., & Mitchell-Enos, V. (1998). Culturally grounded group work with adolescent American Indian students. *Social Work with Groups, 21,* 89–102.

Merta, R. (1995). Group work: Multicultural perspectives. In J.G. Ponterotto, J.M. Casas, L.A. Suzuki, & C.M. Alexander (Eds.), *Handbook of multicultural counseling* (pp. 567–585). Thousand Oaks, CA: Sage.

Storck, L. (1997). Cultural psychotherapy: A consideration of psychosocial class and cultural differences in group treatment. *Group, 21,* 331–349.

Tsui, P., & Schultz, G. (1988). Ethnic factors in group process: Cultural dynamics in multiethnic therapy groups. *American Journal of Orthopsychiatry, 58,* 136–142.

Yu, A., & Gregg, C. (1993). Asians in groups: More than a matter of cultural awareness. *Journal for Specialists in Group Work, 18,* 86–93.

Resources

Selected Suggested Readings

Brook, D., Gordon, C., & Meadow, H. (1998). Ethnicity, culture, and group psychotherapy. *Group, 22,* 53–80.

Brown, A., & Mistry, T. (1994). Group work with "mixed membership" groups: Issues of race and gender. *Social Work with Groups, 17,* 5–21.

Conyne, R.K. (1999). *Failures in group work: How we can learn from our mistakes.* Thousand Oaks, CA: Sage.

Davis, L.E. (1984). Essential components of group work with Black Americans. *Social Work with Groups, 7,* 97–109.

DeLucia, J., Coleman, V., & Jensen-Scott, R. (1992). Group counseling with multicultural populations [Special issue]. *Journal for Specialists in Group Work, 17,* 194–254.

Selected Internet Resources

Association for Specialists in Group Work
  www.coe.colstate.edu/asgw
American Group Psychotherapy Association
  www.agpa.org
American Psychological Association Division 49
  www.info.pitt.edu/~cslewis/GP2/Hello.html
Center for the Study of Group Processes
  www.uiowa.edu/~grpproc/index.html
APA division 45 homepage
  www.apa.org/about/division/div45.html
Association for Multicultural Counseling and Development
  www.amcd-aca.org
Race and ethnicity studies online resource
  www.georgetown.edu/crossroads
  /asw/race.html

52 SOLUTION-FOCUSED FAMILY COUNSELING

Cynthia J. Osborn, John D. West, and
Megan L. Petruzzi

A number of individuals and groups have informed the practice of using solutions in the process of family counseling, and the group at the Brief Family Therapy Center (BFTC) in Milwaukee, Wisconsin (Berg, 1994; Berg & Miller, 1992; de Shazer, 1985, 1988, 1991), has been especially helpful in this process. Other authors have also written on the use of solutions in counseling and the reader will find some of these references at the end of this chapter.

SOME BASIC ASSUMPTIONS

Various authors (Berg & Miller, 1992; de Shazer, 1985; O'Hanlon & Weiner-Davis, 1989; Walter & Peller, 1992) have discussed assumptions that are part of solution-focused counseling. Berg and Miller noted, however, that the work of the BFTC "has been to eschew discussions about theory and principles in favor of practical ... 'how to' type descriptions of the solution-focused approach" (p. 1). The following six assumptions about the process of change in counseling appear congruent with solution construction:

1. Walter and Peller (1992) described members in a treatment group as those who share a desire to do something about a problem. Members of a treatment group, therefore, may comprise a subsection of the family (e.g., mother, son, and aunt) and may also include members external to the family (e.g., teacher, minister, parole officer).

2. From a solution-focused perspective, counseling requires a cooperative relationship between counselor and clients (Berg & Miller, 1992; Walter & Peller, 1992). This means that clients need to be willing to consider changes in their own behavior and the counselor must show an appreciation for clients' stories and not get too far ahead of them when exploring possibilities for the future.

3. Identifying goals in counseling (O'Hanlon & Weiner-Davis, 1989; Walter & Peller, 1992), rather than focusing only on problems, plays an important role in solution construction. As O'Hanlon and Weiner-Davis noted, "If you don't know where you're going, how will you know when you get there? How will you even know if you're headed in the right direction?" (p. 164).

4. A family's resources and strengths are considered helpful in movement toward goals (Berg & Miller, 1992; O'Hanlon & Weiner-Davis, 1989; Walter & Peller, 1992). Using clients' resources to support changes allows clients to use small changes to help develop larger ones (de Shazer, 1985; O'Hanlon & Weiner-Davis, 1989; Spiegel & Linn, 1969; Walter & Peller, 1992).

5. Various authors (de Shazer, 1985; O'Hanlon & Weiner-Davis, 1989; Walter & Peller, 1992) have discussed the issue of meanings people bring to behavior. "Meaning is informed by participant observers," Walter and Peller noted that an "event does not have meaning in itself that is discovered by someone outside of the event"

(p. 25). Goals, resources, and strengths, therefore, need to be meaningful and important to family members; in other words, it is not enough that they are meaningful and important to the counselor.

6. Walter and Peller's (1994) thoughts on terminating therapy constitute a final assumption: "Ending therapy does not have to wait until the problem is totally solved or the goals totally reached. When clients think that they are on track or that they now have things they can do on their own, they no longer need a therapist" (p. 113). The complete resolution of a problem could require a considerable amount of time, and some problems may never be completely resolved. Assisting families in "getting back on track" (Walter & Peller, 1994) so that difficulties are successfully managed may represent a workable goal.

These assumptions provide a guide for considering how the counselor might approach family counseling; they are not intended as all-encompassing descriptions of solution-focused family counseling.

THEORETICAL CONSIDERATIONS IN SUPPORT OF SOLUTION-CONSTRUCTION

The model of solution construction in clinical work continues to evolve: There is no one way to construct solutions, nor one "right" or "correct" way to conduct counseling from this perspective (Berg & Miller, 1992; Miller & de Shazer, 1998). A consideration of the theoretical underpinnings associated with solution-focused family counseling, therefore, is warranted.

A Family's Shared Desires

Family members can arrive at a counseling session with different interpretations of the presenting complaint. From a solution perspective, such variability is expected and acceptable, and consensus regarding what brought members to the session may not be necessary (de Shazer, 1988, 1994; Miller & de Shazer, 1998). What *is* crucial is a shared desire for positive change among family members present and an agreement about the direction or goal(s) for counseling (see Hopwood & Taylor, 1993; Lipchik & Kubicki, 1996).

A pragmatic feature of the systemic perspective in solution construction is that participation of *all* family members does not appear to be necessary for positive goal attainment (de Shazer & Berg, 1985). The counselor works with whoever is motivated to change and is able to attend a counseling session. In her work with families, Lee (1998) depicted a solution approach as one that "works with any member who is motivated to come to therapy and assumes that a small change in one part of the family system will lead to changes in other parts" (p. 13). Indeed, Lee's research with 59 families at the BFTC over a three-year period indicated, in part, that "neither the number of family members involved nor who attended the therapy sessions was related to goal attainment" (p. 12). More specifically, the participation of one or both parents did not make a difference in terms of successfully addressing the presenting concern (i.e., a child's emotional or behavioral problem).

Family and Counselor Collaboration

The importance of the family and counselor collaboration has been stressed throughout the solution-focused literature (Berg & Miller, 1992; Walter & Peller, 1992). Friedman and Lipchik (1999) depicted the counselor's ability to remain connected with the client system as "the underpinning for the whole collaborative process, the grease that keeps the axles turning" (p. 329). Ways to facilitate family engagement and cooperation include accepting family members' perspectives of "the problem" and reinforcing that members bring with them a certain level of expertise regarding what will be helpful for them (Furman & Ahola, 1995).

Listening, joining, and affirming the client system (i.e., "connection") constitute the first phase of a time-effective and competency-based perspective (Friedman, 1997). Booker and Blymyer (1994) observed their clients to be "actively interested in change, especially when they discover that they set the therapeutic agenda" (p. 59). The importance of this is demonstrated in Lee's (1998) study in which 54.4% of the 59 families reported six months after concluding counseling that "being supported/validated" was the most helpful element of counseling.

Goal Formulation with the Family

Developing a clear focus and goal is considered essential in brief therapy "so as to facilitate concentration of therapeutic energy on the clinical area of greatest interest" (Eckert, 1993, p. 244). Indeed, a major technical error related to negative outcomes in brief counseling is the clinician's failure to structure or focus the sessions (Budman & Gurman, 1983; Koss & Shiang, 1994). In their work with 39 individual clients, Beyebach, Morejon, Palenzuela, and Rodriguez-Arias (1996) noted the correlation ($r = .35$, $p < .05$) between establishing clear goals and a greater sense of expected success on the client's part.

The process of goal formulation begins with the counselor's careful questioning of family members about what they want to have happen as a result of participating in counseling. For example, the "miracle question" represents an appropriate starting point for soliciting from clients their ideas and desires about the helpfulness of counseling (De Jong & Miller, 1995; de Shazer, 1988; Lipchik, 1988; Walter & Peller, 1992). Clients are asked to imagine a time in the future when the problem that brought them to counseling has been miraculously solved (usually while they were sleeping and, hence, without their knowledge). Client responses are then met with "a whole series of satellite questions designed to take the client's attention away from difficulties and to focus it on imagining a future when the problem is solved" (De Jong & Miller, 1995, p. 731). Beyebach et al. (1996) described the usefulness of future-oriented techniques such as the miracle question as "not only in helping clients clarify their goals for psychotherapy but also in promoting commitment to achieving those goals" (p. 324).

Resource Utilization with the Family

A focus on solutions represents a practical (Miller & de Shazer, 1988) and parsimonious (Berg & Miller, 1992) approach to counseling. This simply means that "therapy proceeds with the most straightforward assumptions and strategies and adds complexity only as needed" (Berg & Miller, 1992, p. 9). A vital element of solution construction with families is *utilization*, a term Milton Erickson (1954) coined and defined as the involvement with and "acceptance of what the [family] represents and presents" (p. 127). This implies that such resources as talents and abilities, past successes and accomplishments, "inside stories" and opinions, and cultural values that family members bring can be factored into the therapeutic process.

An example of resource utilization is inquiring during the initial session about positive change that has occurred since the counseling appointment was made. Several researchers (Beyebach et al., 1996; Lawson, 1994; Weiner-Davis, de Shazer, & Gingerich, 1987) have observed this phenomenon of "presession change" in 59.75% to 66.66% of individual clients seen in the first session. Positive change reported by clients prior to the initiation of counseling represents "tangible evidence for clients that they are already doing something that makes a desired difference" (Lawson, 1994, p. 247). The counselor can then encourage clients to continue engaging in presession positive behaviors to enhance the therapeutic process.

Ending Family Counseling

Research suggests that clients prefer fewer sessions (Garfield, 1986) and are likely to engage and remain for the duration of counseling when they understand in advance that counseling will be brief (Steenbarger, 1994). De Jong and Hopwood (1996) reported that over a 10-month period, 275 clients participated in counseling at the BFTC for an average of 2.9 sessions. Furthermore, 45% of clients contacted seven to nine months after their last counseling session stated that their treatment goal had been met, and an additional 32% reported that there was some progress made toward their treatment goal. Similarly, Beyebach et al. (1996) reported an average of five sessions at a private brief family therapy center over a three-year period, with 71% of clients reporting either the complete disappearance of their complaints or a clear improvement. With a solution-focused approach, therefore, improvement can take place in a relatively short period of time.

Our preference for the term *solution construction* as opposed to *problem resolution* is exemplified when thinking about how to conclude counseling. Working toward solutions does not imply that complaints need to be eradicated before counseling is considered complete. Helping clients "get back on track" (Walter & Peller, 1994) may occur when the problem and solution have been "compartmentalized" (Booker & Blymyer, 1994), meaning that only selected pieces of the complaint are focused on and the construction of a solution is therefore realistic and feasible. Counseling may end when family members agree that they have identified enough resources to tackle the demands of daily living on their own, without regularly scheduled counseling sessions.

SELECTED PROCEDURES FOR FOCUSING ON SOLUTIONS

To illustrate how the theory presented in this chapter can be applied to the clinical setting, four procedures are highlighted. The procedures are consistent with helping families construct solutions during family counseling.

Maximizing Collaboration

From the perspective of solution construction, establishing a positive therapeutic working relationship is primarily the counselor's responsibility (Berg & Miller, 1992; de Shazer, 1985). This begins by entering the counseling session with the expectation of cooperation (de Shazer, 1985), viewing clients as "hidden" customers for positive change (Berg & Miller,

1992), and honoring the client's needs and wishes so that "the goal of therapy is to meet the client's goal" (de Shazer, 1990, p. 278). In this manner, the counselor sets the stage for therapeutic collaboration and continually regards the process as dynamically and intricately interactive (de Shazer, 1985).

A useful counselor posture intended to solicit client cooperation is that of "not knowing," wherein the counselor conveys a genuine intrigue and desire to be informed by the client in the absence of preconceived opinions and expectations about the client (Anderson & Goolishian, 1992). In his work with adolescents, Selekman (1993) described a "Curious Columbo" approach, referring to the television detective who portrayed himself as naive and unaware to those suspected of a crime. The intention is to engage clients in a process of "mutual puzzling" (Anderson & Goolishian, 1991) about possible solutions so that the client is a partner in constructing positive change. Coping questions (Berg, 1994; Berg & Miller, 1992) such as "How did you ever manage to refrain from stepping into conflict?" communicate genuine interest and encourage client reflection and investigation. This is further enhanced when the counselor adjusts counseling to fit the client's readiness for change so that the counselor is in tune with the client and not one or two steps ahead of the client's movement toward change (de Shazer, 1988; Walter & Peller, 1992).

Using Exceptions to Formulate Desired Goals

Exceptions to the problem have been identified as "those things in the client's life which, to the client, represent satisfactory functioning" (Molnar & de Shazer, 1987, p. 353). Identifying exceptions has been referred to as the "key component" of a solution mindfulness in counseling (Berg, 1995) and is credited as representing an ingredient for goal development in counseling (de Shazer, 1991).

Change has been depicted as inevitable and positive change always a possibility (Walter & Peller, 1992). Identifying and highlighting past, current, and future (i.e., imagined) exceptions to the presenting family complaint allows members to envision an alternative to what might have been experienced as a constant or continual problem. Miller and de Shazer (1998) stated that encouraging family members to identify personal and social resources and helping them notice how they are already managing their problems is actually the counselor's ethical responsibility.

To illustrate the use of exceptions in goal formulation, the mother of a 16-year-old daughter, Laura, complains that their every conversation turns into an argument. To elicit exceptions, the family might be asked to identify times when the problem (i.e., the argumentative relationship) is or was not occurring (e.g., "When was a time that the two of you were able to communicate with each other without arguing?"). Perhaps Laura and her mother identify times when they had scheduled enjoyable outings into their weekly routine. Once an exceptional outing has been described, the counselor could ask Laura and her mother to practice or recreate in the next week the behaviors that contributed to the recalled outings being enjoyable. Walter and Peller (1992) noted that exceptions can be "bridged" in this manner into a goal so that Laura and her mother might also be asked, "If you continue to do these things, will you be on track to getting what you want out of coming here?"

Using the Family's Resources

Once family members have articulated a desired outcome, the family's shared resources may be identified and amplified. Franklin, Corcoran, Nowicki, and Streeter (1997) recommended using the client's own language, meanings, and exceptions to determine the anchors on a scale when asking "scaling questions" (see Berg, 1994; Molnar & de Shazer, 1987). Franklin et al. noted, "Anchors are important because they define the meaning of the numbers on a rating scale . . . and therefore must be collaboratively constructed with the client, using the client's own words and experience" (p. 253).

Laura and her mother could be asked to describe their differing responses to one another

and select their own wording for anchors on a 10-point scale. Laura might select the anchors of "yelling and not listening" (to represent a 0 on the scale) and "completely calm, cool, and collected in reasoning with Mom" (to represent a 10 on the same scale). Laura's mother might select the anchors of "feeling impatient and nagging" (to represent a 0 on the scale) and "feeling patient and reasoned" (to represent a 10). The counselor could then ask Laura and her mother to place themselves on their scales when they were in conflict two weeks ago and then again last weekend when they experienced a quarrel-free Sunday afternoon. Laura, for example, may place herself at a 4 during a conflict two weeks ago and at a 7 last Sunday. Eliciting and recognizing Laura's resources can be facilitated by asking her, "What did you do to make it possible for you to move from a 4 to a 7 in response to your mother's requests for help in the garden?" Laura may have remembered how "Mom and I enjoyed being together at other times, and being in the garden one hour didn't need to spoil the entire day." Laura can be commended for her ability to understand the relationship with her mother as being larger than working in the garden, and she might be asked to apply this same reasoning ability the next time her mother asks for help. The counselor can follow up in a similar manner with the mother. Questioning in this fashion elicits the clients' own experiences as resources for identifying exceptions and goals.

Getting Back on Track

Cummings and Sayama (1995) conceptualized time-sensitive and effective counseling as taking place intermittently and across the life span, meaning that clients participate in counseling on an "as needed" basis, staying for a brief number of sessions (e.g., four to six consecutive weekly sessions) and returning at a later date if and when needed. Imagine that Laura and her mother have reported fewer quarrels at home and more times completing housework together over the past four weeks. To help determine "when to stop meeting like this" (de Shazer, 1991), several questions can be generated and discussed. These "on track" questions are intended to assist Laura and her mother to figure out when they have maximized the helpfulness of counseling and to help them understand when they can expect to maintain gains from counseling on their own: "If, when the two of you leave here today, you are back on track to improving your relationship, what will the two of you be doing differently? Although your relationship might not be perfect, what might you notice that would indicate you don't need to return to talk with me?" In follow-up discussion with the counselor, responses from Laura and her mother might suggest a time-limited perspective on counseling and a recognition that they will see themselves as managing their relationship without regularly scheduled counseling sessions.

SUMMARY

This chapter is not intended to represent a comprehensive framework for solution-focused family counseling; rather, it is presented as an introductory overview. For further reference, the reader is encouraged to locate the Web page of the Brief Family Therapy Center (www.brief-therapy.com) and of the Institute for the Study of Therapeutic Change (www.talkingcure.com).

References

Anderson, H., & Goolishian, H. (1991). Thinking about multi-agency work with substance abusers and their families: A language systems approach. *Journal of Strategic and Systemic Therapies, 10,* 20–35.

Anderson, H., & Goolishian, H. (1992). The client is the expert: A not-knowing approach to therapy. In S. McNamee & K.J. Gergen (Eds.), *Therapy as social construction* (pp. 25–39). Newbury Park, CA: Sage.

Berg, I.K. (1994). *Family-based services: A solution-focused approach.* New York: Norton.

Berg, I.K. (1995). Solution-focused brief therapy with substance abusers. In A.M. Washton (Ed.), *Psychotherapy and substance abuse: A*
practitioner's handbook (pp. 223–242). New York: Guilford Press.

Berg, I.K., & Miller, S.D. (1992). *Working with the problem drinker: A solution-focused approach.* New York: Norton.

Beyebach, M., Morejon, A.R., Palenzuela, D.L., & Rodriguez-Arias, J.L. (1996). Research on the process of solution-focused therapy. In S.D. Miller, M.A. Hubble, & B.L. Duncan (Eds.), *Handbook of solution-focused brief therapy* (pp. 299–334). San Francisco: Jossey-Bass.

Booker, J., & Blymyer, D. (1994). Solution-oriented brief residential treatment with "chronic mental patients." *Journal of Systemic Therapies, 13,* 53–69.

Budman, S.H., & Gurman, A.S. (1983). The practice of brief therapy. *Professional Psychology: Research and Practice, 14,* 277–292.

Cummings, N., & Sayama, M. (1995). *Focused psychotherapy: A casebook of brief, intermittent psychotherapy throughout the life cycle.* New York: Brunner/Mazel.

De Jong, P., & Hopwood, L.E. (1996). Outcome research on treatment conducted at the Brief Family Therapy Center, 1992–1993. In S.D. Miller, M.A. Hubble, & B.L. Duncan (Eds.), *Handbook of solution-focused brief therapy* (pp. 272–298). San Francisco: Jossey-Bass.

De Jong, P., & Miller, S.D. (1995). How to interview for client strengths. *Social work, 40,* 729–736.

de Shazer, S. (1985). *Keys to solution in brief therapy.* New York: Norton.

de Shazer, S. (1988). *Clues: Investigating solutions in brief therapy.* New York: Norton.

de Shazer, S. (1990). Brief therapy. In J.K. Zeig & W.M. Munion (Eds.), *What is psychotherapy? Contemporary perspectives* (pp. 278–282). San Francisco: Jossey-Bass.

de Shazer, S. (1991). *Putting difference to work.* New York: Norton.

de Shazer, S. (1994). *Words were originally magic.* New York: Norton.

de Shazer, S., & Berg, I.K. (1985). A part is not apart: Working with only one of the partners present. In A. Gurman (Ed.), *Casebook of marital therapy* (pp. 97–110). New York: Guilford Press.

Eckert, P.A. (1993). Acceleration of change: Catalysts in brief counseling. *Clinical Psychology Review, 13,* 241–253.

Erickson, M.H. (1954). Special techniques of brief hypnotherapy. *Journal of Clinical and Experiential Hypnosis, 2,* 109–129.

Franklin, C., Corcoran, J., Nowicki, J., & Streeter, C. (1997). Using client self-anchored scales to measure outcomes in solution-focused therapy. *Journal of Systemic Therapies, 16,* 246–265.

Friedman, S. (1997). *Time-effective psychotherapy: Maximizing outcomes in an era of minimized resources.* Boston: Allyn & Bacon.

Friedman, S., & Lipchik, E. (1999). A time-effective, solution-focused approach to couple therapy. In J.M. Donovan (Ed.), *Short-term couple therapy* (pp. 325–359). New York: Guilford Press.

Furman, B., & Ahola, T. (1995). Solution talk: The solution-oriented way of talking about problems. In M.F. Hoyt (Ed.), *Constructive therapies* (pp. 41–66). New York: Guilford Press.

Garfield, S.L. (1986). Research on client variables in psychotherapy. In S.L. Garfield & A.E. Bergin (Eds.), *Handbook of psychotherapy and behavior change* (3rd ed., pp. 213–256). New York: Wiley.

Hopwood, L., & Taylor, M. (1993). Solution-focused brief therapy for chronic problems. In L. VandeCreek, S. Knapp, & T.L. Jackson (Eds.), *Innovations in clinical practice: A sourcebook* (Vol. 12, pp. 85–97). Sarasota, FL: Professional Resource Exchange.

Koss, M.P., & Shiang, J. (1994). Research on brief psychotherapy. In A.E. Bergin & S.L. Garfield (Eds.), *Handbook of psychotherapy and behavior change* (4th ed., pp. 664–700). New York: Wiley.

Lawson, D. (1994). Identifying pretreatment change. *Journal of Counseling and Development, 72,* 244–248.

Lee, M.Y. (1998). A study of solution-focused brief therapy: Outcomes and issues. *American Journal of Family Therapy, 25,* 3–17.

Lipchik, E. (1988). Purposeful sequences for beginning the solution-focused interview. In E. Lipchik (Ed.), *Interviewing* (pp. 105–117). Rockville, MD: Aspen.

Lipchik, E., & Kubicki, A.D. (1996). Solution-focused domestic violence views: Bridges toward a new reality in couples therapy. In S.D. Miller, M.A. Hubble, & B.L. Duncan (Eds.), *Handbook of solution-focused brief therapy* (pp. 65–98). San Francisco: Jossey-Bass.

Miller, G., & de Shazer, S. (1998). Have you heard the latest rumor about . . . ? Solution-focused therapy as a rumor. *Family Process, 37,* 363–377.

Molnar, A., & de Shazer, S. (1987). Solution-focused therapy: Toward the identification of therapeutic tasks. *Journal of Marital and Family Therapy, 13*(4), 349–358.

O'Hanlon, W.H., & Weiner-Davis, M. (1989). *In search of solutions: A new direction in psychotherapy.* New York: Norton.

Selekman, M.D. (1993). *Pathways to change: Brief therapy solutions with difficult adolescents.* New York: Guilford Press.

Spiegel, H., & Linn, L. (1969). The "ripple effect" following adjunct hypnosis in analytic psychotherapy. *American Journal of Psychiatry, 126,* 53–58.

Steenbarger, B.N. (1994). Duration and outcome in psychotherapy: An integrative review. *Professional Psychology: Research and Practice, 25,* 111–119.

Walter, J.L., & Peller, J.E. (1992). *Becoming solution-focused in brief therapy.* New York: Brunner/Mazel.

Walter, J.L., & Peller, J.E. (1994). "On track" in solution-focused brief therapy. In M.F. Hoyt (Ed.), *Constructive therapies* (pp. 111–125). New York: Guilford Press.

Weiner-Davis, M., de Shazer, S., & Gingerich, W. (1987). Building on pretreatment change to construct the therapeutic solution: An exploratory study. Journal of Marital and Family Therapy, 13, 359–364.

53 ASSESSMENT IN COUPLE AND FAMILY COUNSELING

Michael J. Sporakowski, Anne M. Prouty, and Christopher Habben

Several years ago, David Olson (1994), in an address following his acceptance of the International Association of Marriage and Family Counselors' Distinguished Research Award, discussed the whys and why nots "behind doing assessment." He used a format (à la David Letterman's "Top Ten") in listing his sometimes tongue-in-cheek reasons for not doing assessment. This listing included: Assessment confuses my reality; it may prevent me from seeing the truth; it interferes with my therapeutic interventions; it is only needed by novices; it represents too positivistic an approach; and it is too much work. On the more constructive side, he indicated: You cannot *not* do assessment; it is a process, not an outcome; it can generate dialogue on relevant issues; assessment can be therapeutic and empowering; it can link diagnosis with intervention; and outcome-based assessment is vital in being competitive in the therapeutic marketplace. This chapter is intended to help the counselor have a better understanding of the functions of assessment and an increased familiarity with some resources for relationship assessment.

FUNCTIONS OF ASSESSMENT

The first and likely most obvious function of assessment is the gathering of *information*. This occurs at three levels. At the first level, *basic information* for record keeping is acquired and usually includes information about presenting problems, source of referral, information provided by the referral agent, and demographic information. The next level includes a relationship chronology, and the third involves obtaining information about perceptions and expectations—about relationships and about counseling.

A second function of assessment is *diagnostic*. The assessed status of a marriage might indicate poor overall adjustment but with major problems in several specific areas, for example, sex and money matters, which may be the focus of intervention. A couple relational assessment might be helpful in deciding on the type and frequency of sessions, who would be involved, and for what purposes.

A third assessment function is ongoing *evaluation* of the counseling process and outcomes. Depending on the counselor's and client's agreement, this might occur in each session or at set points during the process—at the termination of counseling, or as needed, depending on the ground rules that have been established. It might also include a follow-up session at a specified time posttermination.

METHODS AND TECHNIQUES

This section briefly presents *some* of the assessments available to couple and family counselors for a variety of tasks. It is not our intention to be comprehensive in this presentation, but to provide examples (see Table 53.1)

TABLE 53.1 Frequently Utilized Couple and Family Instruments

Author(s)	Instrument	Instrument Name	Instrument Measures	Description
		Couple/Relational		
Bienvenu, 1970	MCI	Marital Communication Inventory	Assessment of marital communication	*46 items* Questionnaire
Olson, Fournier, & Druckman, 1987	REPARE-ENRICH	Prepare (Premarital Instrument) Enrich (Marital Instrument)	Assesses 14 areas of couple relationship and assesses typology based on relational cohesion and adaptability	*125 items* Likert response items
Schumm, Paff-Bergen, Hatch, Obiorah, Copeland, Meens, & Bugaihis, 1986	KMS	Kansas Marital Satisfaction Scale	Marital satisfaction	*3 items* Likert response items
Snyder, 1979	MSI	Marital Satisfaction Inventory	Marital satisfaction	*280 items* True-false questionnaire
Spanier, 1976	DAS	Dyadic Adjustment Scale	Overall measure of dyadic adjustment	*32 items* Likert response items yes/no questions
Straus, Hamby, Boney-McCoy, & Sugarman, 1996	CTS2	Revised Conflict Tactics Scale	Scales assess negotiation, psychological aggression, physical assault, sexual coercion and injury	*78 items* Likert response items
Taylor & Morrison, 1984	TJTA	Taylor-Johnson Temperament Analysis	Individual temperament and couple analysis	*180 items* Three-point scale
		Family Assessment		
Epstein, Baldwin, & Bishop, 1983	FAD	Family Assessment Device	Family functioning via six dimensions of problem solving, communication, roles, affective responsiveness, affective involvement, behavior control, and general functioning	*60 items* Likert response items
Moos & Moos, 1981	FES	Family Environment Scale	Relationship, personal growth, and system maintenance in family	*Real Form: 90 items true-false* *Ideal Form: 90 items true-false* *Expected Form: 90 items true-false*
Olson, Portner, & Lavee, 1985	FACES III	Family Adaptability and Cohesion Evaluation III	Family adaptability, cohesion, and communication	*20 items* Likert response items

373

of the types of assessments available and some of the ways in which they *might* be utilized.

Histories

Using an oral history as a means of assessment is suggested by Hartman and Fithian (1974). The value of a detailed history lies in conceptualizing the focus of treatment, tying information gathered to the theoretical underpinnings of the treatment process, and assisting in understanding the context in which the problems occur. The Structured Initial Interview (Hiebert, Gillespie, & Stahman, 1993) helps sort out the complexities of couple histories, relationship patterns, and the dynamics—both subtle and repetitive resistive—occurring in dysfunctioning systems seeking conjoint treatment of the relationship.

Genograms (McGoldrick & Gerson, 1985) show generational levels of family history and functioning over time. They may be used as part of the counseling process in the office or as a homework assignment. Births, deaths, marriages, divorces, illnesses, and other conditions may also be part of the recorded material. In addition to the generic genogram, several variations have been published that look at specific familial dynamics and presenting problems.

Observational Methods

Behrens, Meyers, Goldfarb, Goldfarb, and Fieldsteel (1969) developed the Family Interaction Scales for use in assessing families during a home visit. The scales are labeled Family investment in selves in home, Family group patterns of interactions, Interaction of husband and wife as marital partners, Interaction of husband and wife as parents, Parent-child interaction, Child-parent interaction, and Child-child interaction. Ratings on these scales provide three referent points: organization and structure of families, affect, and reality orientation.

DeFrank-Lynch (1979) provided a collection of activities both adults and children can participate in for assessing family structure, boundaries, closeness, cooperation, decision making, and role behavior. Although formal scoring procedures are not used, observation of the activities provide the counselor with insights into family functioning.

Symbolic Representations

Many early psychodynamic assessments were used to view individual internal perceptions and/or apperceptions of family relationships. The Thematic Apperception Test (TAT) (Winter, Ferreira, & Olson, 1965), Adult-Child Interaction Test (A-CIT) (Alexander, 1955), a variation on the TAT format, and the Blacky Pictures (Blum, 1950) all purported to offer assessments and insights into various aspects of family functioning. These included individual personality in couple interaction using six of the TAT cards (Araoz, 1972), adult-child and child-adult interactions (A-CIT) on eight cards, and psychosexual development in a family setting, using 11 cartoons depicting a family of dogs as the stimuli (Blacky Pictures).

Assessments such as Kinetic Family Drawings (Burns & Kaufman, 1970) and the Projective Storytelling Cards (PST Cards) (Caruso, 1988) have been used to elicit themes regarding family dynamics and encourage participation in therapy, especially of children. The PST Cards, 25 in number, may also be of help in assessing children and adolescents who are victims of abuse. Photographs of family transitions, critical events, and developmental stages were used by Kaslow and Friedman (1977) to help therapists stimulate client memories, identify family myths, and become aware of family status hierarchies.

Temperament, Personality, and Character Type

A number of personality assessments are useful for individual, couple, and family assessment. The Interpersonal Checklist (LaForge & Suczek, 1955) was one of the earliest instruments used in this grouping. Luckey's (1960) research and clinical work asked individuals to rate their spouse and their view of how they believed their spouse would rate them. These ratings were then plotted and compared, and used in discussing areas of conflict and agreement in couple interactions.

The Taylor-Johnson Temperament Analysis (TJTA), 16PF, and Myers-Briggs Type Indicator (MBTI), and the Neuroticism Extroversion Openness Personality Inventory-Revised (NEO-PI-R) have been adapted for couple counseling and profiling. The TJTA (Taylor & Morrison, 1984) focuses on typical (not pathological) personality characteristics, such as nervous versus composed, active-social versus quiet, sympathetic versus indifferent, and, dominant versus submissive. The innovative aspect of this assessment method is its use of criss-cross profiling for couples, which allows comparisons of self and other perceptions and thus discussions of couple members' abilities to accurately portray self and other. The profile itself might be creatively used as a self-administered picture, without actual testing and scoring, saving time and effort in visually representing the individual and couple member traits described. Part of the latter task could involve discussions of similarity of profiling and areas of disagreement. The MBTI (Briggs & Myers, 1977; Hammer, 1987) and 16PF (Karson & O'Dell, 1976) offer similar possibilities for counselors and clients. These assessments and the NEO-PI-R (Couple Compatibility Report) (Costa & McCrae, 1992) are currently available in computerized scoring formats with relationship profiling as a special feature.

Marital Adjustment, Happiness, and Quality

Assessments in this group range in length from the brief (the four-item Kansas Marital Satisfaction Scale; Schumm et al., 1986) to the somewhat lengthy (Marital Satisfaction Scale; Snyder, 1979). Probably the most widely used scales today are the 32-item Dyadic Adjustment Scale (DAS; Spanier, 1976), the 14-item Revised DAS (Busby, Crane, Larson, & Christiansen, 1995), and the 15-item Locke-Wallace Short Marital Adjustment Scale (SMAS; Locke & Wallace, 1959). The utility of these scales runs from simple, single-dimension statements of adjustment, to more complex commentaries on specific problem areas, to scales

assessing multiple dimensions within the marriage (e.g., sexual adjustment, parenting satisfaction). If the focus of the counseling is to be on greater depth of couple interaction, the longer assessments may prove more helpful (Prouty, Markowski, & Barnes, 2000). Olson, Fournier, and Druckman's (1987) two instruments, PREPARE (premarital) and ENRICH (marital), are dyadic assessment tools based on Olson's circumplex model of familial dynamics.

Family Adjustment

The most recent version of the Family Adaptability Scale (FACES III) (Olson, Portner, & Lavee, 1985) measures two primary factors, adaptability and cohesion, and may be used clinically as an indication of communication. The Family Environment Scale (Moos & Moos, 1981) also assesses family cohesion; it includes expressiveness, conflict, independence, control, moral-religious emphasis, achievement orientation, active-recreational orientation, intellectual-cultural orientation, and organization. The Personal Authority in the Family Systems (PAFS) Questionnaire (Bray, Williamson, & Malone, 1984) has theoretical roots in transgenerational theories of family therapy. The 132-item instrument is designed to assess individuation, fusion, triangulation, intimacy, personal authority, and intergenerational intimidation. A fourth measure, the Family Assessment Device (FAD) (Epstein, Baldwin, & Bishop, 1983), is designed to identify family problems. This 53-item scale assesses family functioning in six areas: behavior control, roles, affective responses, problem solving, communication, and affective involvement.

Family Stress and Conflict

Holmes and Rahe (1967) gave us one of the enduring approaches to assessment of stress with a life events accumulation instrument, the Social Readjustment Rating Scale. By examining events such as vacations, marriages, deaths, financial debt, and the like, they came up with a measure useful in predicting likelihood of major illnesses. Later, Lazarus and Folkman (1984) talked about the "hassles and uplifts" of daily experience and developed a Ways of Coping Scale, 67 items long, to help assess methods for adapting to stress. McCubbin, working in the health domain, expanded on the earlier life events work and developed a more family-focused Family Inventory of Life Events (McCubbin & Thompson, 1987), acknowledging the theoretical importance of the accumulation of stress over time. At a more specific level, Abidin (1990) published his 120-item Parenting Stress Index, an instrument assessing adaptability, acceptability, attachment, social isolation, and relationship with spouse. All of these measures could prove useful in determining levels of stress brought to the counseling situation and in assessing the stress-reduction effects of the treatment.

The revised Conflict Tactic Scale (CTS2) (Straus, Hamby, Boney-McCoy, & Sugarman, 1996) measures psychological and physical violence within dating, cohabiting, or married dyads. As opposed to the original scale, this version includes two new subscales with questions covering sexual coercion and injury.

Skills and Abilities

The Marital Communication Inventory (Bienvenu, 1970) consists of a 46-item checklist relating to communication issues in an intimate dyadic relationship. Its utility can be found in a total score for comparison with normative data or as a stimulus for discussions of perceptions and specific problem areas. A second assessment, the Parenting Skills Inventory (Nash, 1984), is an 85-item checklist providing ratings of parenting skills and abilities for role support, role image, objectivity, expectations, rapport, communication, and limit setting, as well as an overall score. A profile is derived indicating "good," "satisfactory," or "needs work" levels of functioning. Single- as well as two-parent families may take this instrument, as adjustments are made for either status in its scoring. The instrument is useful as a behavior describer and discussion facilitator and is available both in paper-and-pencil

versions and in a computer administered, scored, and profiled version.

Obviously, there are other areas of assessment that might be of interest to the couple and family counselor. Assessing sexual functioning, adjustment to divorce, and evaluation of custody and abuse situations are other contemporary topics of interest, though not detailed in this chapter. Included in the reference section are several major citations helpful in finding other assessments. Most notable for their comprehensiveness are the works of Fredman and Sherman (1987), Kramer and Conoley (1992), L'Abate and Bagarozzi (1993), and Touliatos, Perlmuter, and Straus (1990).

INNOVATIVE APPROACHES TO ASSESSMENT

Many of the assessment techniques described in this chapter may be used in nonstandard ways for constructive counseling reasons. If the purpose of the assessment is to foster dialogue about relationships, comparisons of scores to normative data may not be beneficial to the client's relationship. The criss-cross technique mentioned in use with the TJTA might be applied to other assessment situations. Perception of self and other is frequently integral to observing and understanding interpersonal relationships. Such innovation may have its drawbacks from theoretical and methodological perspectives, but may provide creative insights into relationships without the necessity of test taking.

Many assessment instruments are now available in computerized formats for administration, scoring, and interpretation purposes (Erdman & Foster, 1986). The couple and family counselor with an interest and some computer skills may find it challenging and fruitful to develop computer programs for assessments he or she has created or frequently uses if they are not currently available, tailoring them to specific counseling tasks or environments. Caution must be exercised in recognizing and coping with the legalities of such activities, so that the computer is not viewed or used as a diagnostician, but as a tool to assist the counselor in observing, recording, and interpreting client characteristics and behaviors.

CONFIDENTIALITY ISSUES

Assessment in couple and family counseling raises all the typically discussed professional and ethical issues discussed in the writings of Huber and Baruth (1987) and Van Hoose and Kottler (1985), but, because of its interpersonal nature, it may give rise to others that require attention. Specifically, spouse and family members may wish to see the assessment results of their spouse, children, or parents. Early in the counseling/assessment process, the purposes and utilization of the assessment procedures must be discussed with all involved and ground rules agreed on regarding how the information can be used, by whom, and under what conditions.

SUMMARY

Assessment offers glimpses of behavior, personality, and relationships and is part of an ongoing process in counseling, concluding perhaps only when counseling ends. Assessment in couple and family counseling offers many choices. We assume that assessment is a vital piece of the counseling matrix and that it may take many forms depending on the theory, practice, clients, and personal and professional development of the counselor. The challenge to be current yet thoroughly grounded in assessment is great, though manageable, through workshops, supervision, consultation, and professional readings.

References

Abidin, R.R. (1990). *The Parenting Stress Index* (3rd ed.). Charlottesville, VA: Pediatric Psychology Press.

Alexander, T. (1955). *The Adult-Child Interaction Test*. Champaign, IL: Child Development.

Araoz, D.L. (1972). The Thematic Apperception Test in marital therapy. *Journal of Contemporary Psychotherapy, 5*(1), 41–48.

Behrens, M.L., Meyers, D.I., Goldfarb, W., Goldfarb, N., & Fieldsteel, N.D. (1969). The Henry Ittleson Center Family Interaction Scales. *Genetic Psychology Monographs, 80,* 203–295.

Bienvenu, M.J. (1970). Measurement of marital communication. *Family Coordinator, 1,* 26–31.

Blum, G.S. (1950). *The Blacky pictures.* Ann Arbor, MI: Psychodynamic Instruments.

Bray, J.H., Williamson, D.S., & Malone, P.E. (1984). Personal authority in the family system: Development of a questionnaire to measure personal authority in intergenerational processes. *Journal of Marital and Family Therapy, 10,* 167–178.

Briggs, K.C., & Myers, I.B. (1977). *Myers-Briggs Type Indicator.* Palo Alto, CA: Consulting Psychologists Press.

Burns, R.C., & Kaufman, S.H. (1970). *Kinetic Family Drawings (KFD): An introduction to understanding children through kinetic drawings.* New York: Brunner/Mazel.

Busby, D.M., Crane, D.R., Larson, J.H., & Christiansen, C. (1995). A revision of the Dyadic Adjustment Scale for use with distressed and nondistressed couples: Construct hierarchy and multidimensional scales. *Journal of Marital and Family Therapy, 21,* 289–308.

Costa, P.T., & McCrae, R.R. (1992). *NEO Personality-Revised.* Odessa, FL: Psychological Assessment Resources.

Caruso, K.R. (1988). *Projective Storytelling Cards.* Torrance, CA: Children's Professional Products.

DeFrank-Lynch, B.J. (1979). *Family assessment: A collection of tools and techniques for assessing family dynamics.* Branford, CT: Institute for Human Development.

Epstein, N.B., Baldwin, L.M., & Bishop, D.S. (1983). The McMaster Family Assessment Device. *Journal of Marital and Family Therapy, 9,* 171–180.

Erdman, H.P., & Foster, S.W. (1986). Computer-assisted assessment with couples and families. *Family Therapy, 13,* 23–40.

Fredman, N., & Sherman, R. (1987). *Handbook of measurements in marriage and family therapy.* New York: Brunner/Mazel.

Hammer, A.L. (1987). *MBTI relationship report: Couples counseling.* Palo Alto, CA: Consulting Psychologists Press.

Hartman, W.E., & Fithian, M.A. (1974). *Treatment of sexual dysfunction: A bio-psycho-social approach.* New York: Aronson.

Hiebert, W.J., Gillespie, J.P., & Stahman, R.F. (1993). *Dynamic assessment in couple therapy.* New York: Lexington Books.

Holmes, T.H., & Rahe, R. (1967). The Social Read-justment Rating Scale. *Journal of Psychosomatic Medicine, 11,* 213–218.

Huber, C.H., & Baruth, L.G. (1987). *Ethical, legal and professional issues in the practice of marriage and family therapy.* Columbus, OH: Merrill.

Karson, S., & O'Dell, J.W. (1976). *Clinical use of the 16PF.* Champaign, IL: Institute for Personality and Ability Testing.

Kaslow, F.W., & Friedman, J. (1977). Utilization of family photos in family therapy. *Journal of Marriage and Family Counseling, 3,* 19–25.

Kramer, J.J., & Conoley, J.C. (Eds.). (1992). *The eleventh mental measurements yearbook.* Lincoln, NE: Buros Institute of Mental Measures.

L'Abate, L., & Bagarozzi, D. (1993). *Sourcebook in marriage and family evaluation.* New York: Brunner/Mazel.

LaForge, R., & Suczek, R.F. (1955). The interpersonal dimensions of personality: III. An interpersonal checklist. *Journal of Personality, 24,* 94–112.

Lazarus, R.S., & Folkman, S. (1984). *Stress, appraisal, and coping.* New York: Springer.

Locke, H.J., & Wallace, K.M. (1959). Short marital-adjustment and prediction tests: Their reliability and validity. *Marriage and Family Living, 21,* 251–255.

Luckey, E.B. (1960). Marital satisfaction and its association with congruence of perception. *Marriage and Family Living, 22,* 49–54.

McCubbin, H.I., & Thompson, A.I. (Eds.). (1987). *Family assessment inventories for research and practice.* Madison: University of Wisconsin.

McGoldrick, M., & Gerson, R. (1985). *Genograms in family assessment.* New York: Norton.

Moos, R.H., & Moos, B.S. (1981). *Family Environment Scale manual.* Palo Alto, CA: Consulting Psychologists Press.

Nash, L. (1984). *The Parenting Skills Inventory.* La Canada, CA: Parenting Plus.

Olson, D.H. (1994). Top 10 reasons for not doing assessment (á la David Letterman). *Family Digest, 6*(2/3), 2.

Olson, D.H., Fournier, D.G., & Druckman, J.M. (1987). *Counselor's manual for PREPARE/ENRICH* (Rev. ed.). Minneapolis, MN: PREPARE/ENRICH.

Olson, D.H., Portner, J., & Lavee, Y. (1985). *FACES III.* St. Paul: Family Social Science University of Minnesota.

Prouty, A., Markowski, M., & Barnes, H. (2000). Using the Dyadic Adjustment Scale in marital therapy: An exploratory study. *Family Journal, 8,* 250–257.

Schumm, W.R., Paff-Bergen, L.A., Hatch, R.C., Obiorah, F.C., Copeland, J.M., Meens, L.D., & Bugaighis, M.A. (1986). Concurrent and discriminant validity of the Kansas Marital Satisfaction Scale. *Journal of Marriage and the Family, 48,* 381–387.

Snyder, D.K. (1979). Multidimensional assessment of marital satisfaction. *Journal of Marriage and the Family, 41,* 813–823.

Spanier, G.B. (1976). Measuring dyadic adjustment: New scales for assessing the quality of marriage and similar dyads. *Journal of Marriage and the Family, 38,* 15–28.

Straus, M., Hamby, S., Boney-McCoy, S., & Sugarman, D. (1996). The revised Conflict Tactics Scales (CTS2): Development and preliminary psychometric data. *Journal of Family Issues, 17,* 283–316.

Taylor, R.M., & Morrison, L.P. (1984). *Taylor-Johnson Temperament Analysis manual.* Los Angeles: Psychological Publications.

Touliatos, J., Perlmuter, B.F., & Straus, M.A. (Eds.). (1990). *Handbook of family measurement techniques.* Newbury Park, CA: Sage.

Van Hoose, W.H., & Kottler, J.A. (1985). *Ethical and legal issues in counseling and psychotherapy.* San Francisco: Jossey-Bass.

Winter, W.D., Ferreira, A.J., & Olson, J.L. (1965). Story sequence in analysis of family TATs. *Journal of Projective Techniques and Personality Assessment, 29,* 392–397.

54 FAMILY COUNSELING COMPETENCIES

Melanie A. Warnke

Mental health counselors who offer couple and family counseling are obliged to deliver only those services they can provide competently. The American Counseling Association (ACA), one of its divisions, the International Association of Marriage and Family Counseling (IAMFC), and the Council for Accreditation of Counseling and Related Education Programs (CACREP) view couple and family counseling as a specialty area within the profession of counseling. Counselors providing couple and family services are expected to have professional counseling competence as a foundation for couple and family counseling competence. Competence is a complex concept; there is no consensus for defining competence in counseling. Although counselors are responsible for identifying their personal areas of competence, this chapter provides some guidelines for considering couple and family counseling competence among professional counselors who are appropriately credentialed to practice in their states. Competence can be examined from two different yet overlapping perspectives: boundaries of practice, or the types of services counselors provide based on their preparation, and quality of services (Ritchie & Warnke, 1999). The concepts of boundaries of practice and quality of services apply to mental health professionals who are not professional counselors (e.g., psychologists and social workers). However, each profession has its own education, training, and experience recommendations for establishing couple and family therapy competence. In addition, the Ameri-

can Psychological Association and the National Association of Social Workers have codes of ethics that should be consulted by members of these professional associations.

BOUNDARIES OF PRACTICE

Boundaries of knowledge and skills for practice in couple and family counseling are established through graduate education, training, supervised experiences, professional credentials, and professional experiences (ACA, 1995; IAMFC, 1993). Counselors who are establishing couple and marriage counseling as a new area of competence practice only after appropriate education, training, and supervised experience (ACA, C.2.b.). Membership in professional organizations does not establish competence. Counselors are expected to have competence applicable for all counselors regardless of specialization in addition to competence in couple and family counseling. (For further discussion of professional counselors' practicing within their limits of competence, see Welfel, Chapter 72.)

Couple and family counseling is not a therapeutic technique, but an approach to understanding human behavior (Miller, Scott, & Searight, 1990). Counselors need a strong foundation of family systems-based knowledge and skills to practice couple and family counseling. The IAMFC (1993) and the American Association for Marriage and Family Therapy (AAMFT; as cited in Crespi, 1988) have stated that individuals who provide couple and family counseling services should have minimum educational attainment of master's degrees.

There are hundreds of degree and postdegree couple and family counseling/therapy programs in the United States (Crespi & Gillen, 1995). The number of departments at universities (e.g., counseling, psychology, social work, family studies) offering couple and family counseling/therapy training has increased significantly in the past three decades. During this time, there has also been a proliferation of independent family institutes. Many of the independent institutes are associated with particular schools of couple and family therapy (Liddle, 1982). Independent institutes do not regularly offer graduate degrees; nondegree training at these institutes can provide exceptional specialized training, but they should not be considered equivalent to degree-granting training programs.

Counselors who wish to demonstrate couple and family counseling competence through their training in graduate degree programs should follow an organized program of study. One or two courses in systems theory and/or techniques do not qualify as an organized program of study for obtaining specialization in couple and family counseling. The IAMFC ethical code (1993) states that in addition to the core counseling requirements for all accredited counseling programs, students in marriage and family counseling specialization programs are expected to have specific marriage and family knowledge and skills enumerated by CACREP. CACREP (2001) identified four specific curricular areas in which students in 60-semester-hour marriage and family counseling programs must gain knowledge and experience: foundations in marriage and family counseling, contextual dimensions of marriage and family counseling, knowledge and skills for the practice of marriage and family counseling, and clinical instruction.

The foundations in marriage and family counseling area of CACREP training standards (1994) includes the content of marriage and family counseling history as well as philosophical and etiological assumptions; marriage and family professional organizations,

training standards, and credentialing; ethical, legal, and professional issues associated with marriage and family practice; roles of marriage and family counselors in various settings; and implications of clients' cultural/lifestyle diversity. The contextual dimensions area of marriage and family counseling curricula focuses on how family functions are influenced by factors such as family life cycle stages, healthy family functioning, families of origin, human sexuality, social definitions of demographic factors, and social trends. The knowledge and skills for the practice of marriage and family practice area include family systems theories; schools of marriage and family therapy; marriage and family therapy research; and developmental, preventative, and dysfunction remediation interventions. During their clinical instruction in practica and internships, students in marriage and family counseling programs are expected to provide counseling that includes working with couples and families utilizing systemic approaches.

AAMFT (1990) identified core areas of a course of study required for individuals wishing to obtain clinical member status from the organization: (1) marital and family therapy studies—systems theory, family development, and gender and cultural issues; (2) marital and family therapy—couple and family interventions/treatments and advanced theories; (3) human development—personality development, pathology, and sexuality; (4) professional studies—ethical and family law issues; (5) research—research design and statistics; (6) clinical practicum—one-year minimum of supervised experience with couples and families; and (7) clinical experience—two-year minimum of supervised post-master's degree marriage and family therapy professional experience. Many of the counselors who provide couple and family counseling will not complete the requirements necessary to become an AAMFT clinical member because this association's training standards are based on an assumption that marriage and family therapy is a discipline unto itself, but the standards do provide suggested guidelines for preparation of clinicians who are primarily interested in providing couple and family services.

Criteria for educational programs and clinical membership status are modified regularly to meet the needs of clients and mental health professions. Counselors need to keep updated about AAMFT and CACREP standards so they can compare their education, training, supervised practice, and professional experiences to stated standards from these professional organizations. Educational programs provide opportunities for knowledge and skills acquisition, but couple and family counselors recognize that they must maintain their competence by keeping current through attending institutes, classes, workshops, conferences, or conventions and by reading current literature. Counselors may also keep current by voluntarily meeting the initial certification and re-certification requirements of the National Academy for Certified Family Therapists, a national credentialing body.

Working within one's boundaries of practice by developing and maintaining specialized knowledge and skills in couples and family counseling is essential for establishing professional competence, but it is not sufficient for establishing competence. How well counselors provide couple and family services is the second perspective for evaluating competence.

QUALITY OF CARE

Many ethical principles, standards, and dilemmas are based on how professional groups conceptualize and treat clients' difficulties. Because couple and family counselors view problems as nonlinear and interactional and because counselors' therapeutic relationships are with two or more individuals who have intimate and intense relationships prior to treatment, clinical and ethical issues are often more complex than issues experienced in the course of individual counseling (Beamish, Navin, & Davidson, 1994; Searight & Merkel, 1991). To recognize these complex quality of care clinical and ethical issues, counselors need the appropriate education, training, and experience in couple and family counseling. Competent couple and family

counselors continually examine and take steps to provide services that, first, do not harm and, second, benefit families and individual family members (Zygmond & Boorhem, 1989). Ethical codes of AAMFT (1998) and IAMFC (1993) focus on members' therapeutic relationships with couples and families, but they do not provide clear guidelines for all quality of care ethical dilemmas that occur in the process of providing counseling to couples and families. A variety of quality of care issues must be viewed from a family systems framework when counselors provide couple and family counseling. A few of these issues are presented to emphasize the need to consider clinical and ethical issues from a systems orientation. Professional counselors who offer couple and family services are, of course, expected to follow all of the ethical guidelines of the ACA (1995) and the IAMFC (1993) as well as any other ethical standards identified by applicable state credentialing boards. Because quality of care issues are very complex and the ethical codes as well as the professional literature are ambiguous at times, the reader should not expect this chapter to provide simple answers to the issues presented. References are provided for further exploration.

Determining Who the Client Is

Determining whether the costs and benefits of counseling should be evaluated at the couple/family level or the individual member level is related to the ethical issue of determining who the client is. The preamble and ethical code of the IAMFC (1993) suggest precedence is given to the well-being of the family as a whole. The AAMFT ethical code (1998) states that marriage and family therapists consider the welfare of family units and individuals. The professional literature (Beamish et al., 1994; Miller et al., 1990; Patten, Barnett, & Houlihan, 1991; Searight & Merkel, 1991; Smith, 1999; Stevens et al., 1999) has explored ethical issues of setting priorities when a family unit's well-being may be in conflict with the well-being of individual family members.

Informed Consent

The importance of informed consent with couples and families has been addressed by the ethical codes of AAMFT (1998) and IAMFC (1993) and others (Beamish et al., 1994; Kaplan & Calkin, 1995; Smith, 1999). (For more general discussion of providing accurate informed consent, see Chapter 65.) Informed consent is complicated when some family members do not have the legal right to consent to treatment and when couple and family counseling treatment outcomes may be less predictable than individual counseling outcomes. Informed consent includes describing techniques used in treatment. Whether it is ethical to use deceptive and manipulative strategies and whether clients should be informed of the potential use of these strategies as a component of consent to treatment have been debated in the literature (Miller et al., 1990; Solovey & Duncan, 1992; Stevens et al., 1999; Zygmond & Boorham, 1989). Informed consent is also related to clients' right to refuse treatment. A number of authors (Beamish et al., 1994; Miller et al., 1990; Patten et al., 1991; Searight & Merkel, 1991) have discussed the clinical and ethical implications of counselors refusing to treat families unless all members participate and of counselors engaging nonattenders when not all family members participate in treatment.

Confidentiality

Competent counselors explain clients' rights to confidentiality and limits to confidentiality during the process of informed consent. (For additional discussion of clients' rights and limits to privacy, see Welfel, Chapter 64.) In couple and family counseling, confidentiality must be addressed at two levels: at the level of sharing information with individuals outside of the counseling sessions and at the level of sharing information obtained from one family member with another family member when both are being seen in couple or family counseling. Ethical codes of AAMFT (1998) and IAMFC (1993) specify that in most circumstances, practitioners do not share information with individuals outside of the counseling sessions unless all legally competent individuals involved in the counseling sign a waiver to release the information. The IAMFC ethical code states, "Unless alternate arrangements have been agreed upon by all participants, statements by a family member to the counselor during an individual counseling or consultation contact are not disclosed to other family members without the individual's permission" (p. 75). Counselors can divulge to other family members information obtained from one individual if this policy about "family secrets" has been communicated and agreed on by counseling participants as a part of informed consent. Debates continue about the ethics of maintaining, disclosing, or selectively disclosing this type of information to other family members (Beamish et al., 1994; Kaplan & Culkin, 1995; Miller et al., 1990; Patten et al., 1991; Smith, 1999; Stevens et al., 1999).

Counselor Values

"Counselors are aware of their own values, attitudes, beliefs, and behaviors and how these apply in a diverse society, and avoid imposing their values on clients" (ACA, 1995, p. 1). Couple and family counselors who fail to respect their clients' values and impose their own values about issues such as family normalcy or dysfunction, preservation of coupled relationships, gender roles, and extramarital relationships are practicing incompetently (see Miller et al., 1990; Patten et al., 1991; Zygmond & Boorhem, 1989).

Evaluating Quality of Care Provided

Competent couple and family counselors evaluate the clinical and ethical implications of their practice. They utilize a systems orientation for understanding quality of care issues such as determining who the client is, providing informed consent, describing rights and limitations of confidentiality, deciding whether to see families when at least one member refuses to participate, and monitoring whether they are imposing their values on clients.

SUMMARY

The competence of counselors who provide couple and family services is evaluated from two overlapping perspectives: boundaries of competence and quality of services. Boundaries of practice are associated with counselors' graduate education, training, supervised experiences, credentials, and professional experience. CACREP's (1994) standards of curricular experiences for marriage and family counseling specialization are critical guidelines counselors can utilize for comparing their preparation. To provide quality couple and family services, counselors need a strong foundation of preparation; however, counselors with adequate preparation can practice incompetently by not providing quality service (Ritchie & Warnke, 1999). Competent counselors monitor themselves and take steps to provide services that, first, do not harm and, second, benefit families and individual family members. Couple and family counselors will judge and be judged in terms of their competence based on whether they practice within their boundaries of preparation and how well they provide services.

References

American Association for Marriage and Family Therapy. (1990). *AAMFT membership requirements.* Washington, DC: Author.

American Association for Marriage and Family Therapy. (1998). *AAMFT code of ethics.* Washington, DC: Author.

American Counseling Association. (1995). *Code of ethics and standards of practice.* Alexandria, VA: Author.

Beamish, P.M., Navin, S.L., & Davidson, P. (1994). Ethical dilemmas in marriage and family therapy: Implications for training. *Journal of Mental Health Counseling, 16,* 129–142.

Council for Accreditation of Counseling and Related Educational Programs. (2001). *CACREP accreditation standards and procedures manual.* Alexandria, VA: Author.

Crespi, T.D. (1988). Specifications and guidelines for specialization in family therapy: Implications for practicum supervisors. *International Journal of Family Psychiatry, 9,* 181–191.

Crespi, T.D., & Gillen, J.J. (1995). Professional licensing in marriage and family therapy: Autonomy and opportunity for health care providers. *Family Therapy, 22,* 185–192.

International Association of Marriage and Family Counselors. (1993). Ethical code for the International Association of Marriage and Family Counselors. *Family Journal: Counseling and Therapy for Couples and Families, 1,* 73–77.

Kaplan, D., & Calkin, M. (Eds.). (1995). Family ethics: Lessons learned. *Family Journal: Counseling and Therapy for Couples and Families, 3,* 335–338.

Liddle, H.A. (1982). Family therapy training: Current issues, future trends. *International Journal of Family Therapy, 4,* 81–97.

Miller, T.R., Scott, R., & Searight, H.R. (1990). Ethics for marital and family therapy and subsequent training issues. *Family Therapy, 17,* 161–171.

Patten, C., Barnett, T., & Houlihan, D. (1991). Ethics in marital and family therapy: A review of the literature. *Professional Psychology: Research and Practice, 22,* 171–175.

Ritchie, M., & Warnke, M.A. (1999). Competence of marriage and family counselors. In P. Stevens (Ed.), *Ethical casebook for the practice of marriage and family counseling* (pp. 73–82). Alexandria, VA: American Counseling Association.

Searight, H.R., & Merkel, W.T. (1991). Systems theory and its discontents: Clinical and ethical issues. *American Journal of Family Therapy, 19,* 19–31.

Smith, R.L. (1999). Client confidentiality in marriage and family counseling. In P. Stevens (Ed.), *Ethical casebook for the practice of marriage and family counseling* (pp. 83–92). Alexandria, VA: American Counseling Association.

Solovey, A.D., & Duncan, B.L. (1992). Ethics and strategic therapy: A proposed ethical direction. *Journal of Marital and Family Therapy, 18,* 53–61.

Stevens, P., Baltimore, M., Birdsall, B., Erickson, S.H., Miller, L.D., Thomas, A., & Frame, M.W. (1999). The ethical code illustrated. In P. Stevens (Ed.), *Ethical casebook for the practice of marriage and family counseling* (pp. 43–70). Alexandria, VA: American Counseling Association.

Zygmond, M.J., & Boorhem, H. (1989). Ethical decision making in family therapy. *Family Process, 28,* 269–280.

PART VII
Practice Management

55 PRACTICING EVIDENCE-BASED MENTAL HEALTH

Using Research and Measuring Outcomes

Thomas L. Sexton and Monique C. Liddle

As mental health care enters and continues through the twenty-first century, accountability has become an important core issue. Mental health practitioners are asked to be accountable for their conduct and practice to their clients and to the profession itself. However, with the growth of managed mental health care organizations, practitioners negatively view the important role of accountability because accountability has become synonymous with managed care. Accountability portrayed by managed care is seen by many mental health practitioners as "intrusive, restrictive, and not in the ultimate best interests" of clients (Henry, 1998, p. 131). In actuality though, accountability results not from managed care but from an increase in the quantity and quality of clinical research available to guide clinical decision-making. Sexton, Whiston, Bleuer, and Walz (1997) argue that research has improved to the point that it is now a necessary clinical aid. However, negative perceptions of managed health care, the understandable time constraints of practitioners (Whiston, 1996), and the lack of a practical model of research-based mental health care have interfered with the successful integration of research and practice. We suggest that professional accountability, when defined as Evidence-Based Mental Health (EVB-MH) practice, can be both practitioner-friendly and provide accountable and effective counseling services to clients.

In this chapter, we outline a practical model of EVB-MH practice that can serve the dual masters of client needs and clinical accountability and thus guide the mental health practitioner through the world of accountability in a way that is beneficial to clients. In addition, we provide examples of the ways in which general trends, specific protocols, and outcome assessment can positively improve mental health practice. Even though we provide specific examples, one of the hallmarks of EVB-MH practice is that the integration of research and practice is a dynamic one. Thus, this chapter is not intended as a compendium of available resources. Instead, we hope to provide a model that can be used by practitioners to facilitate the consistent integration of research evidence, specific process and outcome assessment, and clinical judgment into accountable and improved mental health services.

WHY EVIDENCE-BASED MENTAL HEALTH PRACTICE?

In today's world of mental health, accountability and research-based practice are not a choice but an ethical and professional mandate (Sexton, 2001). Practitioners have an ethical mandate to engage in EVB-MH practice by using general research trends, specific protocols, and personal assessments to inform treatments and interventions to provide the best care for clients. To "do no harm" (as mandated by the APA, ACA, and AAMFT codes of ethics), mental health practitioners have a professional responsibility to "maintain a reasonable level of awareness of current scientific and professional information in their fields of activity, and undertake ongoing efforts to maintain competence in the skills they use" (APA, 1992). To do so, practitioners (1) can be familiar with general trends in research, (2) learn effective protocols for certain presenting problems, and (3) measure their own outcomes to determine if their techniques and interventions truly are effective for their clients. Consequently, EVB-MH practice is the epitome of the practitioner "practicing reflectively" (Wampold, 2000, p. 18). The scientifically informed practitioner is a necessary component of ethically effective and appropriate clinical practice.

From our perspective, EVB-MH practice is different from the current models of the empirically validated/supported treatment (EVT/EST) movement. This movement, initiated by the Task Force on the Promotion and Dissemination of Psychological Procedures early in the 1990s, attempted to identify treatments that were "well established" scientifically or "probably efficacious" (see Chambless et al., 1996) to provide a foundation of accountability for the field. Despite the best intentions by the task force and others, the practicing community has not embraced the EVT/EST movement for several reasons. Primarily, practitioners view the field as dominated by the managed health care system, which is seen as not in the best interests of their clients (Henry, 1998, p. 131).

We suggest that although ESTs might be useful guides for mental health practice, what they lack is a practical yet systematic model for integrating the useful research trends and specific protocols into practice. As an alternative, EVB-MH is a practitioner-friendly framework that is a practically and clinically useful combination of research, practice, and clinical judgment. Accordingly, EVB-MH practice is a reciprocal relationship between science/research and practice: Science/research informs practice, and practice informs the formulation of research questions (science). The practitioner and the scientist are part of a necessary interconnected and mutually interdependent system.

EVIDENCE-BASED MENTAL
HEALTH PRACTICE

EVB-MH has three primary considerations: (1) using the general trends from meta-analyses and critical review studies that identify broad trends relevant for practice; (2) identifying specific protocols that offer direct and specific guidance for intervening with specific clients in specific settings; and (3) measuring outcomes on a local level to continually inform the clinician's practice. These components, explained next, serve as increasingly specific levels of guidance for mental health practitioners to use in making clinical decisions. For example, general trends help orient the practitioner to broad trends in the research, which helps to improve practice with varying clients and treatment plans. These broad and common trends in practice are not sufficient, but are a necessary component to evidence-based practice. Specific protocols are more directive in that they identify specific treatments for specific clients with particular problems. Constant measuring of outcomes provides additional, distinct information of an individual practitioner's work. In this role, mental health practitioners become their own researchers, providing unique data to improve their practice, thus enabling the practitioner's accountability.

In the following sections, we outline the level of guidance that is a part of EVB-MH practice. Our goal is to provide you with a schema for utilizing EVB-MH practice, not to provide a specific treatment for a specific type of client in a specified context. Thus, our intent is to provide examples of how available and future research literature can be organized systematically into increasingly specific categories that pragmatically can inform practice. These categories are not mutually exclusive. Each category is necessary for effective practice, and the categories are interdependent.

General Trends

At the broadest level of guidance, EVB-MH practice calls for practitioners to be aware of, use, and seek general research-based trends that inform practice. General trends are not meant to provide specific guidance to practitioners regarding certain aspects of the clinical process. Instead, they are general findings regarding a wide range of clients with broad categories of actions. Examples of broad trends are psychotherapy in general, group therapy, family counseling, and examination of common factors within therapy. Broad trends answer the questions, Does it work? and What are the major categories of actions necessary for success?

Many of the research trends available to inform practice focus on the well-documented common factors in mental health practice. Sexton, Schofield, and Whiston (1997) state that the "counseling relationship remains unequivocally the *most* significant factor in successful counseling" (p. 10). Literature has cited the therapeutic alliance, identified transtheoretically, as a core component to positive therapeutic outcomes (Asay & Lambert, 1999). In addition, the literature has not been able to support empirically constructs once perceived important to effective outcomes. For example, the practitioner's empathy and support toward the client are considered primary factors in establishing therapeutic alliance; however, broad trends in the research state that empathy is a useful factor in successful mental health practice only when it is perceived by the client (i.e., client-perceived empathy). Thus, this broad trend would suggest that practitioners assess what the client considers empathetic and then demonstrate those behaviors. It is only when this match occurs that empathy, a critical part of the therapeutic relationship, increases the likelihood of successful intervention.

The research literature has gained significant information regarding the time needed to work successfully with clients. For example, the benefits of counseling can be achieved typically in 5 to 10 sessions (see Hubble, Duncan, & Miller, 1999; Kadera, Lambert, & Andrews, 1996). As such, practitioners can make an assessmeant when their clients match this trend and develop intervention methods to accommodate brief counseling. Accordingly, 20% to 30% of clients require longer treatments, and thus, practitioners can assess and identify which clients will require the appropriate treatment. Practitioners can be aware of client variables that can better predict outcome rather than assuming that successful outcome is only the result of interventions used.

Where would practitioners locate additional information that examines trends regarding the therapeutic relationship and other general trends related to psychotherapy? Typically, scientific journals provide such trends through qualitative and quantitative literature reviews (meta-analysis). However, most general trends are found in book chapters or a book series that is dedicated specifically to broad trends. An example is Bergin and Garfield's (1994) *Handbook of Psychotherapy and Behavior Change*. This book has been in print for over 30 years and has kept abreast of general trends in the field. Lambert and Cattani-Thompson (1996) and Hubble, Duncan, and Miller (1999) are also excellent sources for additional information.

Specific Protocols

Although informative, such broad and general findings do not help practitioners know exactly which intervention program to apply to which client. Successful intervention programs contain, in some fashion, the critical common factors while adding the unique intervention methods to further enhance successful intervention with specific client problems. We now know that certain systematic intervention programs are more successful in certain client areas (Alexander, Sexton, & Robbins, 2001; Roth & Fonagy, 1996). For example, the systematic research reviews by Gurman, Kniskern, and Pinsof (1986) concluded that family-based interventions were successful across a variety of client problems, including adolescent behavior problems, antisocial children, and schizophrenic behaviors. Further, career counseling is effective for a variety of concerns, including indecision and facilitating career maturity (Whiston, Sexton, & Lasoff, 1997).

In general, four criteria need to be met for a program to be considered a useful, research-based protocol (Elliott, 1998):

1. A strong research record that demonstrates the effectiveness of the program.
2. Independent research replications.
3. Multisite replications needs to demonstrate that the program is effective in a variety of practice settings with varying types of clients as applied by different interventionists.
4. Replicable as demonstrated by a clear articulation and description (e.g., a manual).

Treatment manuals, a critical component of specific mental health intervention protocols, serve as a mechanism to transfer the technology of effective programs into practice. Treatment manuals have been found to increase the intervention delivery consistency among practitioners (Crits-Christoph & Mintz, 1991), resulting in a significant positive relationship between practitioner compliance with the manual and positive outcome (Luborsky, Singer, & Luborsky, 1975). Treatment manuals vary in their makeup. Useful manuals direct the practitioner toward specific process goals, providing guiding therapeutic principles and requiring the practitioner to respond contingently to the interpersonal events in a given counseling session to reach the manual-prescribed goals.

Measuring Outcomes

For research evidence to be applicable to individual practitioners in their settings, mental health practitioners ought to measure the outcomes of their work and utilize the results to revise their practices. Outcomes typically are considered as an end of therapy and counseling to measure whether the client benefited

from treatment. We recommend measuring outcomes as an integral part of the entire treatment and therapeutic process. Therefore, once treatment goals have been identified, the practitioner can first identify specific interventions, then monitor and assess if they are working, and then readjust interventions if necessary. Measuring outcomes occurs in the beginning, middle, and end of the therapeutic process to assess if the interventions are helpful to clients while they are in therapy.

The EVB approach, therefore, assumes that the practitioner is a "local clinical scientist" (Stricker & Trierweiler, 1995). The local clinical scientist is "a vibrant scientist-professional" who utilizes psychological theory to provide assistance to clients and consistently questions his or her conceptualization and clinical interventions with the attitude of a scientist (p. 999). Stricker and Trierweiler further state that practitioners, as local clinical scientists, ought to utilize a model that "encourages critical, scientific thinking and the application of scientific knowledge to clinical issues, [and] . . . is consistent with conducting research" (p. 999). Therefore, both clinical practice and laboratory research become many methodologies that add to disciplinary knowledge (Stricker & Trierweiler, 1995). It is precisely in this way that EVB-MH practice is an inherent property of practitioners as local clinical scientists.

Ogles, Lambert, and Master (1996) identify four specific applications of measuring outcomes for practitioners. In assessing pretreatment severity, for example, practitioners can measure the severity of depression or anxiety prior to treatment or therapeutic interventions. Another way to assess change is from session to session. An example of an instrument for this area is the Outcome Questionnaire (OQ-45), identified in the following paragraph. A third option is for practitioners to assess "pre- and posttreatment change" (Ogles et al., p. 48). This option is ideal for practitioners who cannot administer an instrument after each session. Once a client's symptoms have been identified and measured initially, the same instrument can be administered after treatment. Finally, Ogles et al. identify an application in which practitioners can evaluate the "clinical significance of change occurring in psychotherapy" (p. 48). Data from norm groups are compared with the client's end-of-treatment level of functioning. There are additional applications for measuring outcomes; this list is meant to provide practitioners with an initial introduction.

Once practitioners have an idea of what they would like to measure, identification of instruments becomes the next step in measuring outcomes. Lambert and Brown (1996) and Ogles et al. (1996) identify several standardized scales that practitioners can use to assess clinical outcomes. Following is a brief excerpt of some of their inventories and scales. Lambert and Brown (1996) and Ogles et al. (1996) include: the Beck Depression Inventory—a self-report of depressive symptoms; the Symptom Check List-90r; the Outcome Questionnaire (OQ-45), which measures three areas of client functioning—symptomatic distress, interpersonal problems, and social role adjustment; the Hamilton Anxiety Rating Scale, which assesses levels of anxiety as rated by a clinician; the State-Trait Anxiety Inventory—a "self-report instrument that differentiates between general feelings of anxiety (trait anxiety) and current feelings of anxiety (state anxiety)" (p. 40); the Inventory of Interpersonal Problems—a self-report that measures "distress arising from interpersonal sources" (p. 42); the Dyadic Adjustment Scale—a self-report that measures relationship satisfaction; and the Child Behavior Checklist, which assesses competencies and behavioral problems of children between ages 4 and 16. These scales are available and easy to use. For further detailed information regarding these instruments, please refer to Lambert and Brown and Ogles et al.

CONCLUSION AND IMPLICATIONS

Faced with increasing demands regarding practice, mental health practitioners must have a basis from which to make clinical decisions that are both therapeutic and accountable. In the past, the field has relied on theoretical congruency as the basis of practice. With the improvement in the quality and quantity of research, empirically based protocols have become the "gold standard" of practice. Both of these models, though different, place the source of clinical decision making outside the practitioner. We suggest an alternative, evidence-based model that is intended to empower the practitioner. In our EVB-MH practice model, it is the mental health practitioner who integrates research knowledge in a way that fits the clinical question at hand. Broad trends are used for general questions, individual protocols for specific applications, and ongoing local evaluation for answers about individual practice sites. As the practitioner integrates these sources of information, clinical decisions improve, become increasingly evidence-based, and retain a sense of clinical responsivity.

It is easy to understand why many in the field are not only uncomfortable with managed health care, but are concerned with whether its primary concern is the client. The literature is saturated with the conclusion that therapy works (see Lambert & Bergin, 1994). Practitioners now are called to do that which will inform positively their practice and will satisfy the demands of managed health care: using research and measuring outcomes. Managed health care thus becomes a tertiary concern for practitioners. The guidelines outlined in this chapter are ultimately for the benefit of our clients, for the benefit of how we, as practitioners, facilitate therapeutic change, and to demonstrate how evidence-based mental health practice does benefit clients. This perspective of accountability properly places it within the field of mental health and secondarily addresses concerns of managed care. Instead of managed health care dictating to the field what works, using research and measuring outcomes provides practitioners with the content of what is managed by managed health care.

References

Alexander, J.F., Sexton, T.L., & Robbins, M.A. (2001). The developmental status of family therapy in family psychology intervention science. In H.A. Liddle (Ed.), *Family psychology intervention science.* Washington, DC: American Psychological Association.

American Psychological Association. (1992). Ethical principles of psychologists and code of conduct. *American Psychologist, 47,* 1597–1611.

Asay, T.P., & Lambert, M.J. (1999). The empirical case for the common factors in therapy: Quantitative findings. In M.A. Hubble, B.L. Duncan, & S.D. Miller (Eds.), *The heart and soul of change: What works in therapy* (pp. 33–55). Washington, DC: American Psychological Association.

Bergin, A.E., & Garfield, S.L. (Eds.). (1994). *Handbook of psychotherapy and behavior change* (4th ed.). New York: Wiley.

Chambless, L.D., Sanderson, W.D., Shoham, B., Bennett-Johnson, S., Pope, K.S., Crits-Christoph, P., Baker, M., Johnson, B., Woody, S.R., Sue, S., Beutler, L., Williams, D.A., & McCurry, S. (1996). An update on empirically validated therapies. *The Clinical Psychologist, 49*(2), 5–18.

Crits-Christoph, P., & Mintz, J. (1991). Implications of therapist effects for the design and analysis of comparative studies of psychotherapies. *Journal of Consulting and Clinical Psychology, 59*(1), 20–26.

Elliott, D.S. (1998). Editor's introduction. In D. Elliott (Series Ed.) *Book three: Blueprints for violence prevention.* Golden, CO: Venture.

Gurman, A.S., Kniskern, D.P., & Pinsof, W.M. (1986). Research on marital and family therapies. In S.L. Garfield & A.E. Bergin (Eds.), *Handbook of psychotherapy and behavior change* (3rd ed., pp. 565–624). New York: Wiley.

Henry, W. (1998). Science, politics, and the politics of science: The use and misuse of empirically validated treatment research. *Psychotherapy Research, 8,* 126–140.

Hubble, M.A., Duncan, B.L., & Miller, S.D. (1999). *The heart and soul of change: What works in therapy.* Washington, DC: American Psychological Association.

Kadera, S.W., Lambert, M.J., & Andrews, A.A. (1996). How much therapy is really enough: A session-by-session analysis of the psychotherapy dose-effect relationship. *Journal of Psychotherapy: Practice and Research, 5,* 1–22.

Lambert, M.J., & Bergin, A.E. (1994). The effectiveness of psychotherapy. In A.E. Bergin & S.L. Garfield (Eds.), *Handbook of psychotherapy and behavior change* (pp. 143–189). New York: Wiley.

Lambert, M.J., & Brown, G.S. (1996). Data-based management for tracking outcome in private practice. *Clinical Psychology: Science and Practice, 3,* 172–178.

Lambert, M.J., & Cattani-Thompson, K. (1996). Current findings regarding the effectiveness of counseling: Implications for practice. *Journal of Counseling and Development, 74,* 601–608.

Luborsky, L., Singer, B., Luborsky, L. (1975). Comparative studies of psychotherapies: Is it true that "everyone has won and all must have prizes"? *Archives of General Psychiatry, 32*(8), 995–1008.

Ogles, B.M., Lambert, M.J., & Masters, K.S. (1996). *Assessing outcome in clinical practice.* Boston: Allyn & Bacon.

Roth, A., & Fonagy, P. (1996). *What works for whom?* New York: Guilford Press.

Sexton, T.L. (2001). Evidence-based counseling intervention programs: practicing "Best Practices." In D. Locke, J. Meyers, & E. Herr (Eds.), *Handbook of counseling* (pp. 512–599). Thousand Oaks, CA: Sage.

Sexton, T.L. Schofield, T.L., & Whiston, S.C. (1997). Evidenced-based practice: A pragmatic model to unify counseling. *Counseling and Human Development, 30,* 1–18.

Sexton, T.L., Whiston, S.C., Bleuer, J.C., & Walz, G.R. (1997). *Integrating outcome research into counseling practice and training.* Alexandria, VA: American Counseling Association.

Stricker, G., & Trierweiler, S.J. (1995). The local clinical scientist: A bridge between science and practice. *American Psychologist, 50,* 995–1002.

Wampold, B.E. (2000). Outcomes of individual counseling and psychotherapy: Empirical evidence addressing two fundamental questions. In S.D. Brown & R.W. Lent (Eds.), *Handbook of counseling psychology* (3rd ed., pp. 711–739). New York: Wiley.

Whiston, S.C. (1996). Accountability through action research: Research methods for practitioners. *Journal of Counseling and Development, 74,* 616–623.

Whiston, S.C., Sexton, T.L., & Lasoff, D. (1997). Career-intervention outcome: A replication and extension of Oliver and Spokane. *Journal of Counseling Psychology, 45,* 150–165.

56 ADVERTISING, MARKETING, AND FINANCING A MENTAL HEALTH PRACTICE

Howard B. Smith

Mental health counselors in private or group practice settings have many decisions to make about how they will assure the best chance of success with their business venture. To expect that all one needs to do is hang out the proverbial shingle and wait for the clients to call is a fatal mistake. It is essential to remember that we are entering a marketplace that is somewhat unique. One must consider all of the stakeholders. The most obvious, of course are the practitioner and the client. However, today there are very few mental health practitioners who operate their business strictly on a private pay basis. With the presence, and some would say dominance, of managed care organizations and insurance companies in the mental health care marketplace today, practitioners must acknowledge the role they play. Third-party reimbursement is the order of the day, and if one is to succeed in a practice setting, there must be a significant amount of planning directed to third-party payers.

This chapter attempts to offer a primer on how the mental health care provider going into private practice can do so in a way that will have the best chance of ensuring success. I address the issues of advertising, marketing, and financing a private or group practice. I encourage the reader to consider the material from each of the three stakeholder positions: the practitioner, the client, and third-party payers, including insurance companies, self-insured businesses or industries, and managed care organizations.

ADVERTISING

Advertising is a subset of marketing. However, there are some distinctions that need to be made between the two to put each into a proper perspective. Lawless (1997) distinguished among advertising, direct mail, and public relations and publicity by noting that publicity, public relations, and the like enhance advertising and other marketing activities. They keep the practitioner's name in front of the public. It is important for the person opening a practice to understand how to use both public relations/publicity and advertising/marketing. One must consider the advantages and disadvantages of each, which is another way of saying that getting the word out about your practice requires some careful planning.

Public relations might include holding free sessions on parenting adolescents at a local church or writing a small column for the local newspaper on a regular basis covering selected topics, such as midwinter blues, depression, or physical exercise and attitude. These are low cost in terms of capital outlay but there are associated costs in terms of time.

Yet another form of publicity can come from involvement with local, state, or national professional associations (Lawless 1997). Mental health professionals can volunteer to sit on a committee, run for office, or head a task force. These are newsworthy items that keep practitioners in front of the potential client and referral population.

The codes of ethics for several mental health provider groups provide limited guidance on how we may advertise. For example, the American Psychological Association (APA) has an extensive statement in its *Ethical Principles of Psychologists and Code of Conduct* (1992). Standard 3.03 warns against making false or deceptive statements in advertising or public statements. Psychologists can claim only degrees that "(1) were earned from a regionally accredited educational institution or (2) were the basis for psychology licensure by the state in which they practice." Standard 3.06 also warns psychologists against soliciting to provide services to persons who are unduly vulnerable to their influence.

Sections C.3 and C.4 of the *ACA Code of Ethics and Standards of Practice* (1995) tell us that professional counselors can list highest degrees earned, credentials they possess, specialties, locator information, and a professional-level membership in a professional association. We are entitled to be individuals when it comes to promoting our business by capitalizing on a "slick" approach. However, sometimes a simple graphic along with the necessary information on business cards can make our presentation appear professional, which is preferred over being unique. In advertising a practice, being unique reaches a point of diminishing returns rather rapidly. Poor attempts at being clever are worse than no attempt at all.

Examples of advertising may be simple ads in the local newspaper or distributing a flyer or brief brochure to medical doctors and attorneys to display in their waiting rooms. Richards (1990) warns counselors against assessing the value of these forms of advertising in terms of "dollar-spent/dollar-received" benefit. Again, the value in these examples of advertising is to get one's name and the name of one's practice in front of as many potential clients and referral sources as possible. One should consider these when starting a practice as well as using them as an ongoing marketing device throughout the duration of the practice. They are especially valuable when adding a new practitioner to staff or a specialty area to the service and when changing or expanding an office location.

Advertising to third-party payers calls for different strategies. Browning and Browning (1996) list seven methods to get one's name included on an approved referral list. Practitioners can call the managed care company and ask the provider relations department to send them provider application materials. Second, practitioners can prepare a practice profile summary letter and include with it proof of licensure and certification, professional liability insurance coverage, and vita or resume. Third, practitioners may want to consider using a two-step approach: sending a brief overview letter that refers the reader to the practice profile sheet. The fourth method is to contact employee assistance managers at local companies and ask them how to become a preferred provider with their managed care organizations. Fifth, practitioners with staff privileges at a local hospital can find out who handles liaison work between the hospital and managed care plans. Sixth, if a potential client who is on a managed care plan for which you are not on the list of preferred providers comes to you for help, you can ask for a one-time-only approval status and use that to cultivate a relationship that leads to full status. Last, Browning and Browning suggest that practitioners contact the CEO or top official at a company and send him or her a package introducing themselves and describing how including their practice would be an asset to the company (such as close geographic proximity or extended evening or weekend hours) (pp. 30–34).

Similarly, Frager (2000) suggests sending CEOs a simple, one-page letter expressing interest in participating in the company's provider network. This letter must convince them of your knowledge of the managed care company and show why they need to include you as a provider and what you can do for them. The goal is to convince managers of network development that their company needs your practice on their panel.

MARKETING

Unfortunately, few graduate programs in mental health educate their students about how to market their newly acquired skills. They often have a job placement service, but getting a job and marketing your own practice in an open market are distinctly different functions. Both Richards (1990) and Lawless (1997) agree that the marketing of a new practice may be the most confusing area for private practitioners. In essence, you are selling yourself through the services you provide. Therein lies the problem. As Richards states, "The product is an illusive one: it cannot be statistically reviewed, tabulated, or compared to another product, as consumers often do with the products they buy" (p. 129).

There is often a barrier to overcome when it comes to selling ourselves. We hesitate to come across as self-promoting. We sense that we have a nebulous ethical dictum opposed to anything that gives our own well-being a higher priority than our clients'. After all, if we tell people they need our services, what does that say about our concept of them? We cannot guarantee results of any kind other than to do our best, distinguishing between being responsible *to* and responsible *for*. We are responsible *to* our clients to be and stay adequately prepared to deliver the best quality services of which we are capable. But in the final analysis, *they* are responsible *for* how they feel and what they do with our counsel.

If mental health counseling is to be of service to the public at all, practitioners must realize that there are ethical ways to market their services. Marketing is not manipulation. Marketing is what you do naturally when you know who you are and where you want to be in the future. Marketing includes everything you do that applies to your professional practice, from printing business cards to the way you answer the phone and how you send out statements for services delivered (Lawless, 1997). It also includes the way you write your reports. Zuckerman (1993, 1997) states that a bit of guidance in organizing your thoughts and preparing reports not only makes your report preparation easier, it makes the reports look better. If these reports are to go before a court or back to the school or business, they too are a form of marketing because they make a statement about your practice. Richards (1990) says

that even the name you select for your practice, if it does not include your own name, is of critical importance. Channeling these details into a consistent pattern that exudes the quality and statement you want to make about who you are as a professional and how you present yourself constitutes the marketing plan.

Effective marketing requires a marketing plan. This plan includes the advertising and public relations issues discussed above, but it goes much further than that. Developing this plan necessitates analyzing how you will run your practice. For example, what services will you offer? Will you guarantee that the first appointment can be made within 24 hours of the client's call? Do you have extended hours to accommodate work schedules? Is your office accessible to people with special challenges? Do you offer bilingual services? These are only a few considerations offered by Lawless and Wright (2000).

Marketing costs money. It is easy to overlook the value of marketing when money is tight; however, that is exactly when marketing is essential. In a sense, it is like a personal savings account: Unless you discipline yourself to set aside a fixed amount of revenue to market your practice, you will not get the results from marketing that you will need to succeed. Further, without a marketing plan, the dollars spent for marketing will not be effective and may well be wasted.

Developing a marketing plan requires a great deal of consideration and strategic thinking about what you want people to think about your practice. Even for existing practices, the process of developing a marketing plan has benefits, as it forces practitioners to reevaluate and rethink some of the choices they have made to this point.

Different audiences may require different emphases if you want to best reach them. For example, if your target client population is families, churches, synagogues, and mosques may be good places to leave brochures. You may want to make a presentation to the local clergy association and describe your belief in family values. A yellow page ad should mention your expertise, experience, and special training in this area.

FINANCING

How one addresses the financial aspects of running a practice is of critical importance. Without a synergistic business plan, the best advertising, the best publicity, and the best marketing will probably end in frustration and failure. At the very least, practitioners will not be maximizing their efforts. Again, the business aspect of a practice is an area that is rarely, if ever, addressed by counselor education programs. Unless one has taken some undergraduate courses in business along the way, one could find oneself at a disadvantage in the private practice arena.

Practitioners have options in managing the financial end of the practice. First, practitioners can contract with a business manager or a certified public accountant to handle the financial aspects of the practice. Establishing a relationship with an attorney may also be practical. Contracting for these services reduces practitioners' need to understand and keep track of all of these aspects and allows them to concentrate their efforts on doing what they are trained to do: provide quality mental health counseling services. For this option to be successful, however, one needs to execute extreme caution in selecting the professionals with whom one enters into agreement. Do they have a good reputation in the community? Be sure to check out references and spend some time in getting to know the persons under consideration. Ask them the same kind of questions you wish your clients would ask you: What is your training? Where did you get your degree? Do you have experience working with a mental health professional in private practice? What sort of reports can I expect from your services? How long have you been in this community? May I check with your professional organization to learn more about your certification or credentials? Are you bonded? In addition, being a mental health professional, you need to be comfortable in the relationship you have with these people. You must have an extremely high level of trust in them and their ability to give you good advice. An alternative to putting a business manager on retainer is to hire a bookkeeper or a bookkeeping firm to take care of the accounting. Their ability to keep and maintain records could be all the help you need.

Each of these alternatives have positive and negative aspects. The key to success here is making sure that who is doing your books understands the documentation and tracking of records necessary to operate a private practice in mental health counseling. Remember, however, that if you hire employees you have the responsibility of overseeing them, training them in confidentiality protection, and monitoring their compliance. You are ultimately responsible for the confidentiality of the client data.

Yet another option is to carry out the financial or business end of the practice yourself. If you already have knowledge of state laws regarding taxation and licensing of businesses and already know how to construct a realistic budget, you may be able to get by very well without a business manager. If you are short of business acumen, however, forgoing such services could end up putting you out of business.

If you are just starting a practice (as opposed to buying into an existing practice), you may need capital other than your own savings or personal loans. The Small Business Administration may be of some assistance in this area, if not for a loan, at least for advice and recommendations for securing the adequate resources needed. They can be found on the Internet at www.sba.gov. There may be other special loans available as well. This could be especially true if you have recently experienced a natural disaster in your community with an attendant surge in mental health needs. Spending some time researching these possibilities could save you several percentage points on startup capital.

To generate the financial revenue you need to survive, you will need to be very aggressive and diversified in the services you offer. A few suggestions have been mentioned above regarding offering free presentations and advertising effectively. You may also have to make cold calls on prospective sources of clients. For example, if you have training in working with children, you could meet with the school superintendent and explore whether there is a possibility of contracting with the school to provide services in addition to what the school counselor can handle. You could also visit with local judges to see if they would be willing to refer couples to you prior to dissolving a marriage or in an attempt to save the relationship.

Developing and offering programs for employee assistance to businesses and industries is another proven and effective practice builder for many professionals. This is especially true if the business or industry is self-insured. Again, you may need to do some research to show that mentally and emotionally healthy employees are more efficient and productive than are troubled employees. You could prepare a list of services you offer for management training programs, such as stress management, identifying and intervening with a troubled employee, and wellness programs such as smoking cessation and blood pressure checks. If you are successful in offering such programs you may even consider subcontracting to other allied health professionals.

One day you may need to consider adding staff to cover the client load. You could hire additional mental health professionals and pay them a salary or develop a scale for splitting the income they generate in which they keep a certain percentage of the income after you subtract a percentage to cover overhead, secretarial services, and other expenses you will incur. You should remember to change your professional liability coverage to accommodate additional staff members.

A second way to expand is to develop working agreements or accords with members of other mental health professions and allied health professionals. This adds to the multidisciplinary nature of your staff, something that managed care organizations like to see. For example, you might want to contract with a psychiatrist who would be available to see your clients one half-day each week to assess psychopharmacology needs. And, in the event that you do not have committal or admission privileges in your state for clients who need that service, the psychiatrist can do that for you. Another alternative is to contract with a nearby medical clinic to cross-refer clients. Physicians can serve the physical and pharmacological needs of your clients and you can provide the mental health services needs for their clients. If there is potential for a number of rehabilitation clients, you might contract with a rehabilitation counselor and perhaps a physical therapist or sports medicine professional as well.

All of these suggestions have advantages and disadvantages. None is the magic bullet that guarantees a successful practice. But together, they have the potential of helping us establish an effective and profitable practice under the right circumstances.

References

American Counseling Association. (1995). *The ACA Code of Ethics and Standards of Practice.* Alexandria, VA: Author.

American Psychological Association. (1992). *Ethical Principles of Psychologists and Code of Conduct.* Washington, DC: Author.

Browning, C.H., & Browning, B.J. (1996). *How to partner with managed care: A "do-it-yourself kit" for building working relationships and getting steady referrals.* New York: Wiley.

Frager, S. (2000). *Managing managed care: Secrets of a former case manager.* New York: Wiley.

Lawless, L.L. (1997). *How to build and market your mental health practice.* New York: Wiley.

Lawless, L.L., & Wright, G.J. (2000). *How to get referrals: The mental health professional's guide to strategic marketing.* New York: Wiley.

Richards, D.L. (1990). *Building and managing your private practice.* Alexandria, VA: American Counseling Association.

Zuckerman, E.L. (1993). *The clinician's thesaurus: A guidebook for wording psychological reports and other evaluations* (3rd ed.). Pittsburgh, PA: Clinician's ToolBox.

Zuckerman, E.L. (1997). *The paper office: Forms, guidelines, and resources* (2nd ed.). New York: Guilford Press.

57 COUNSELORS DEALING WITH THE MEDIA

Judith A. DeTrude

Counselors interact with the media for multiple reasons, one reason being the dissemination of information to the public to educate people about mental health issues and create awareness of preventive mental health practices. There are some limited ethical codes (ACA, 1995) defining the expectations of counselors/therapists when working with the media, but for most instances when counselors/therapists interact with the media, there remain few specific guidelines to help prepare professionals in this endeavor.

This chapter provides some specific case examples that describe the experiences of professionals interacting with the media and offers some general guidelines on how to be prepared for such interactions. *Media* in this chapter is defined as newspapers (any written interaction), TV, and radio. Although the term covers a wide range of technology, there are basic principles for media interaction that are applicable to all the modes listed previously.

NEWSPAPERS: WRITTEN INTERACTIONS

Newspapers are an ideal source for practitioners to use to promote their private practice, get known in a community, and provide a public service to educate the public on specific mental health issues. Advertising in newspapers or newsletters to promote one's private practice or a workshop seems to be very basic and easily adheres to the ethical codes established by most professions. These state that counselors/therapists must accurately present their credentials and must not claim competencies that they do not possess (ACA, 1995). One noted example of this occurred in a local newsletter when a counselor wrote a column on mental health issues and was listed as a "licensed psychotherapist." There is no licensure for psychotherapists in that state, and it is the responsibility of the professional to correct that label with the editorial staff. The advertising aspect in newspapers or written communications seems to be less of a problem than the next areas of communication.

Professionals can find themselves facing an ethical dilemma when asked to write an educational or "advice" column for a newspaper on mental health issues. This is the standard format where readers are encouraged to send in questions and the professional will respond. For example, "My teenage daughter spends so much time in her room, has seemed to isolate herself from her usual group of friends, and has lost interest in those activities that used to be so much fun for her. I am concerned that she is depressed. What can I do to help her?"

The responsible therapist might describe the symptoms of depression and also list resources that are available in the community to help people who might be suffering from depression. The response might be: "Depression in teenagers can often be seen in the following ways, but these are only general guidelines and often people react very differently to being depressed. It is very important to have a clinical diagnosis conducted by a mental health professional to discover if someone is depressed. Some general characteristics of people who might be depressed are . . ." This response does not make an inference from the mother's description, because the therapist does not want to be diagnosing a client through a newspaper.

The irresponsible therapist would directly refer to the mother with these words: "It seems that your daughter . . ." This situation immediately places the counselor/therapist in the vulnerable position of diagnosing a client who has never been seen and responding to the observations of a secondary person rather than direct clinical interaction with the teenager. It would be easy to identify this teenager as depressed, but it is crucial to avoid diagnosing by ensuring that all responses remain generic.

As a way of avoiding this potential ethical trap, a professional may offer to write columns on mental health that concentrate on issues but are not responses to letters. In this manner, the professional is protected from being seen as specifically responding to an individual's concerns and can therefore focus on general mental health issues for educational purposes. A column on depression providing the statistics of the illness in the general population, the symptoms, and resources can serve the purpose of responding to public concerns and at the same time protect the professionalism of the writer.

Writing a generic mental health column for a newspaper also contains some controls that protect the professional from being misunderstood. The major control is the professional's ability to proofread the column before it is published. If the newspaper wants to reserve the right to edit without the professional's having final approval, this is a clear indication that one's writing can be changed in a manner that could be detrimental to one's practice and the message conveyed. Participation in the editorial review process is something all writers should insist on before agreeing to write information columns.

Counselors/therapists may also find themselves being quoted in a newspaper if they are present during a community crisis or if their opinions are solicited by phone. In most of these situations, they have not been prepared for this interaction and will be expected to spontaneously address an issue. An example is when several teenage suicides take place in a community. A therapist specializing in suicide receives a call from the newspaper asking for an opinion on these recent suicides. As in the above situation, therapists can remain generic and provide information and clinical data on teenage suicide. But one factor that is quite different in this situation is the lack of editorial review, as the paper will most likely want to get these comments into their next issue. Therapists can request a copy of their comments faxed for review, but this may not be possible due to the newspaper's deadline. Another option is to send the newspaper printed material on teenage suicides that does not specifically address these community suicides. A third and often the most ethical option is to decline to respond to this request without a guarantee of how the information might be interpreted or changed by the time it is published.

COUNSELORS ON THE RADIO

The radio increases the ethical complications a professional may encounter. Radio talk or call-in shows are popular with the public. Even though a talk show host makes a disclaimer that the show is not therapy, the show's introduction presents the host as "a licensed . . ." or "professional . . .", so all the public knows is that this person is a mental health professional. Often, the public does not distinguish between advice or talking and counseling. Thus, a deception is practiced on anyone calling in to talk with these professionals. It is highly unlikely that a counselor/therapist will become the star of a radio call-in program, but the caveat for professionals is quite strong in avoiding those situations that are set up to create sensationalism for the listening audience.

Interviewers may contact professionals for information on certain subjects; as with newspaper requests, these requests may be controlled or spontaneous. An example of a controlled situation is a request made to this author for suggestions on how to leave work at home when families go on vacations. The initial request was made and was then followed by the questions that were to be used by the interviewer. This allowed the interviewee to do some research and prepare selective responses to the questions. Once the interview was completed, the radio station sent a transcript to the interviewee for editorial comment. In this situation, information was provided and the professional remained in control of the process.

Therapists should not respond to an interviewer spontaneously without any advance reading of the questions. In such a situation, professionals should request an editorial review. If the interviewer refuses this, professionals would be wise to skip the interview, as the tape could be altered to imply information that the professional did not give during the actual interview.

COUNSELORS, CLIENTS, AND TV APPEARANCES

TV interaction can also be spontaneous or a planned appearance. Again, the professional's responsibility is to impart mental health knowledge to the public. But the sensation created by TV talk shows is certainly to be avoided. One only has to read the comments of Harkaway (1989) and Pittman (1989) to understand how the professional therapist has expectations going into the appearance that are often completely opposite those of the producers. The visiting professional in these situations has little control over what happens during the interaction with clients or the talk show host, and for the purposes of show ratings, the escalations of the interactions in the audience are encouraged. The visiting professional has to either accommodate this escalation and risk breaching ethical codes or be overrun by the hosts (Harkaway, 1989). These programs are usually "lose-lose" situations for the counselor/therapist and are best avoided when possible. It is rare for therapists

to have any editing privileges, but this is certainly the first request any visiting professional should make.

It is also important to recognize the danger that can befall "clients" or "unsuspecting" participants on these programs. In an interview with Matt and Paula (DeTrude, 1996), who participated as clients on a major talk show, the couple described being demoralized by their appearance. The husband (Matt) went to "Romance School" and was given a homework assignment that matched neither his nor his wife's ideas of romance. During a preinterview with the therapist prior to the televised show, they were asked to rank Matt's romantic abilities in the relationship. The couple was fairly consistent in their rankings, but the editing turned the questions around to make them seem to be a troubled couple. They did not know this had been done to their interview and were confronted with this editing during their interview in front of the audience. Matt unfortunately broke his arm before completing the homework assignment, and when the couple arrived at the program and saw the therapist, they pointed this out right away. Her response was "No problem." When the couple was on the air, the therapist responded to the broken arm and lack of homework completion with "Isn't this a typical man, looking for an excuse and not able to come up with a new romantic idea for the wife?"

As counselors, we can imagine the devastating effects on this couple after such an appearance. This couple received phone calls from people they had not seen or heard from in years inquiring if they were all right, and they had to explain to their families that they really did have a good marriage. As professionals, we have a duty to protect clients from this abuse if we know they are going to interact with the media, and that protection also applies to being present for them once they have completed the interaction.

An example of a spontaneous interaction with a TV show occurred when a tragic accident took the life of a young woman in high school and critically wounded another young woman. Two other teens in the car survived with scratches. The friends of the teens went to the site of the accident to place flowers and grieve. A high school counselor went to the site to support the students and was accosted by the media for comments on the accident. The counselor avoided making any comments and immediately got away from the TV crews. The crews, anxious for "sensational coverage," hid in the trees as the students placed remembrances at the site in hopes of securing comments from the students and get a clearer picture of their mourning. The counselor then had to act as a protector to get the students away from the intrusive cameras and reporters. This is an example of a counselor acting responsibly to media requests, as the school district would not want the counselor to spontaneously respond to a TV interview, nor would the counselor want to comment on such a sensitive accident.

In another example, a request was made by a local TV station for a university counselor to comment on the adjustments of freshmen students entering college. The questions were sent prior to the interview, parameters were established for how long the responses were to be, and the interview was immediately available for editing by the interviewee before the tape was taken back to the TV station. There were no surprises during the TV program, as the interviewers had taken multiple steps to protect the professionalism of the interview. This serves as an example that it is possible to interact with the media and still work within the established ethical guidelines of the mental health profession.

ETHICAL CODES AND RECOMMENDATIONS

It is unusual for graduate counseling programs to prepare counselors/therapists to interact with the media. The ethical codes of the American Counseling Association (ACA) (1995) and the American Association for Marriage and Family Therapy (AAMFT) (1998) do not provide lengthy guidelines for this type of activity, but there is a separate division of APA (1992) that specializes in media psychology, and consequently, more psychologists appear on talk shows due to this training and affiliation. The ACA Code of Ethics C.5.d (1995) under Media Presentations states: "When Counselors provide advice or comment by means of public lectures, demonstrations, radio or television programs, prerecorded tapes, printed articles, mailed material, or other media, they take reasonable precautions to ensure that (1) the statements are based on appropriate professional counseling literature and practice; (2) the statements are otherwise consistent with the Code of Ethics and the Standards of Practice; and (3) the recipients of the information are not encouraged to infer that a professional counseling relationship has been established." C.6.b, Personal Public Statements (ACA, 1995), also states: "When making personal statements in a public context, counselors clarify that they are speaking from their personal perspectives and that they are not speaking on behalf of all counselors or the profession." The AAMFT Code of Ethics 3.8 (1998) states: "Marriage and family therapists, because of their ability to influence and alter the lives of others, exercise special care when making public their professional recommendations and opinions through testimony or other public statements."

Secondary to the previous ethical concerns described for media appearances are those of physical appearance, which include how to dress and speak and correct posture. A criminal justice program at a university (Hartley, 1995) incorporates this type of training for the students due to the interaction with the media that occurs for law enforcement personnel. The suggestions used in this training are applicable and good suggestions for counselors/therapists in this position:

1. Get to know your media; personal contacts are very important for developing stories or getting your information told to the media.
2. Remember: It is a reporter's business to ask questions—even those that you may not want to answer. Be prepared for the questions—preparation can be the key in any interview or news conference situation.
3. Positive relationships built during normal (day-to-day) activities will be valuable

during emergency situations. People who have worked together on a regular basis every day will work better together when the community is facing a crisis.

Additional interview tips provided by Hartley are:

1. Be prepared: Know what you plan to talk about!
2. It is important that you, or the person you plan to have speak to the news media, know the subject matter involved thoroughly.
3. If you don't know the answer to the question asked, say no! Never say "No comment."
4. Avoid using jargon or acronyms.
5. Don't rush your answers—buy some time on a question by giving some background information on the issue before you directly answer the question.
6. Remember that even if the interview is being taped, your remarks could be edited in such a fashion to cause problems. Think through each answer.
7. Watch your body language—hand movements, involuntary smiles, squinting. They can be damaging on the air.

By incorporating these suggestions along with the following recommendations for media appearances, the professional can do as much as possible to protect the interaction. Some of these recommendations are:

1. *Provide training in counseling programs.* McCall (1990) suggested practicing media skills such as using brief language understandable to a lay audience, making rapid judgments of the real nature of the caller's problems, and developing sensitivity to topics that might be of interest. Some techniques that can be utilized in training are asking students to read articles on ethical dilemmas in media interactions; staging a mock appearance on a TV talk show or news interview; watching or listening to TV and radio broadcasts where professionals appear; interviewing professionals who have made media appearances; practicing reviewing tapes following editing; and giving and receiving feedback on nonverbal behavior.

2. *Develop clear expectations with the show's producers via written contracts.* The expectations between the counselor who is making the media appearance and the producer must be congruent prior to any media involvement. It is recommended that these agreements be written. The following are some areas for consideration:
   a. *Assure* that credentials will be accurately represented. Counselors should provide producers with copies of their credentials.
   b. *Realistically assess* one's area of training and experience. Agree to address only those areas within one's level of competence.
   c. *Agree* that a preshow assessment for guests is required. This should reduce the risk that one will be dealing with guests whose concerns fall outside one's realm of expertise. "Preassessments also allow the professional to ensure that the guests have appropriate expectations about what will and will not occur" (Heaton & Wilson, 1995, p. 248).
   d. *Provide* adequate time to cover a topic or issue completely (Heaton & Wilson, 1995).
   e. *Agree* that no diagnosis and treatment or provision of therapy will be done on the air.
   f. *Debrief* following a taping.
   g. *"Do not allow* tapes to be reproduced later without the consent of participants" (Keith-Spiegel & Koocher, 1985, p. 215).

3. *Differentiate between personal and professional opinion.* Broder (1989) posits that a professional has the right to present his or her opinions and values, but the professional clearly explains those that are professional and those that are personal.

4. *Offer general information about a particular problem rather than specific advice.* It is impossible for professionals to be experts on everything, but there are certain areas that professionals need to be well versed in, such as marriage, child care and discipline,

phobias, depression, sexual relations, contraception, addictions, career changes, and homosexuality (McCall, 1990).

5. *Be prepared and know the subject matter thoroughly.*

6. *Respect the dignity and worth of all individuals.* This includes being sensitive and informed about diverse groups of individuals, including the effects of statements and discussions in various media formats.

7. *Educate media professionals about the ethical guidelines of counselors in the media.* Offer to meet with media representatives and provide consultation and in-service training.

8. *Offer workshops.* Present ethical concerns and media skill training at professional counseling conferences or publish articles in professional journals and newsletters.

9. *Consult with colleagues.* Prior to agreeing to interact with the media, seek out professionals who have had experience in this area. "Engage a group of one's peers to monitor and make suggestions for improvement and change" (Keith-Spiegel & Koocher, 1995, p. 215).

SUMMARY

Counselors want to be responsible educators on mental health issues, and most of this education has occurred at professional workshops and community activities. Media interactions and appearances are new arenas for counselors and are both challenging and rewarding. Ethical codes can serve as broad guidelines, but it is not possible for the codes to address every ethical dilemma. As counselors become involved with the media, it is their professional responsibility to self-monitor all of their actions to ensure they are acting ethically and within the expectations of their profession.

References

American Association for Marriage and Family Therapy. (1998). *Code of ethics.* Washington, DC: Author.

American Counseling Association. (1995). *Code of ethics and standards of practice.* Alexandria, VA: Author.

American Psychological Association. (1992). *Ethical principles of psychologists and code of conduct.* Washington, DC: Author.

Broder, M. (1989). *Suggestions for media mental health professionals* [Prepared by the Guidelines Committee of the Association for Media Psychology, Division 46]. Washington, DC: American Psychological Association.

Harkaway, J. (1989). Circus maximus. *Family Networker, 13,* 43–46, 78–79.

Hartley, R. (1995). *Managing media relations.* Huntsville, TX: Sam Houston State University, Criminal Justice Center.

Heaton, J., & Wilson, N. (1995). *Tuning in trouble: Talk TV's destructive impact on mental health.* San Francisco: Jossey-Bass.

Keith-Spiegel, P., & Koocher, G. (1985). *Ethics in psychology: Professional standards and cases.* New York: Random House.

McCall, R. (1990). Ethical considerations for professional psychologists working in the media. In C. Fisher & W. Tyron (Eds.), *Annual advances in applied psychology: Ethics in applied psychology* (Vol. 4, pp. 163–185). Norwood, NJ: Ablex.

Pittman, F. (1989). In the lion's den. *Family Networker, 13*(46), 78–79.

58 COUNSELORS AS EXPERT WITNESSES

Larry S. Stokes and Theodore P. Remley Jr.

Counselors as expert witnesses offer testimony in court in the form of expert witness opinions regarding plaintiffs or defendants. Expert witnesses are persons with specialized knowledge, experience, or expertise in a particular area that is relevant to a court proceeding. Expert witnesses are allowed to state their professional opinions and are limited to testimony within the scope of their expertise. Fact witnesses can be any citizen subpoenaed to court to provide factual information related to a legal proceeding. Such witnesses may relate only what they saw, did, or said, but are not allowed to give their opinions.

QUALIFICATIONS

Counselors are increasingly finding themselves with opportunities to testify as experts in cases involving personal injury, wrongful death litigation, divorce, child custody, child abuse, workers' compensation, and vocational issues (La Forge & Henderson, 1990). Some expert opinions allowed by courts include issues of competency, potential for rehabilitation, psychological injury, parental fitness, abuse, and suicide. Counselors are serving as experts on issues such as prediction of dangerousness, fitness to stand trial, legal insanity, and Post-traumatic Stress Disorder. Because the field of mental health is so complex, judges have recognized the need to limit the opinion evidence of a mental health professional to the witness's demonstrated areas of expertise. Mere possession of credentials does not make a mental health professional an expert on all matters

falling under the rubric of mental health (Freckelton, 1999).

Rule 702 of the Federal Rules of Evidence (FRE, Rule 702 et seq.) outlines the standard for admitting expert testimony: "If scientific, technical, or other specialized knowledge will assist the trier of fact to understand the evidence or to determine a fact in issue, a witness qualified as an expert by knowledge, skill, experience, training or education, may testify thereto in the form of an opinion or otherwise."

There are no specific credentials required for a person to be designated as an expert witness. A judge, after hearing a person's credentials, decides whether an individual will be "qualified" as an expert witness. Experts are evaluated based on their qualifications, including but not limited to:

- Education, training, and practical experience.
- Professional and technical expertise.
- Job position and function.
- Publications, books, articles, and research in a particular field.
- Licenses, certifications, or registrations.

Some judges will not admit testimony from unlicensed or uncertified professionals, and even if such professionals are qualified and allowed to testify, juries may not give testimony from uncredentialed witnesses much weight. On the other hand, licenses and certifications are no substitute for practical experience. The weight given to scientific evidence in a legal proceeding will depend on how effectively the expert presents the evidence to the jury (Meyer, 1999). Cooper, Bennett, and Sukel (1996) examined how the comprehension of highly complex testimony and the credentials of legal witnesses affected persuasion in the jury decision process. The results of their study indicated that jurors are more persuaded by a highly credentialed expert witness than a less credentialed expert witness, but only when the testimony is highly complex. When the testimony is less complex, jurors rely primarily on the content of the testimony. Thus, credentials may be persuasive to jurors, but the presentation of the testimony is often more important.

When counselors agree to serve as experts, it is important to formalize business relationships so that the counselors and their attorney clients understand the parameters of their agreement. Counselors can refuse a case for any reason, including time, inclination, or conflict of interest. If counselors are hired as expert witnesses, they are a consultant to the attorney and may assist in:

- Suggesting case strategies.
- Educating the attorney about the specific area of information.
- Suggesting sources of information, such as articles and research papers.
- Investigating and testing.
- Preparing deposition or trial questions for direct or cross-examination.
- Assisting to prepare other witnesses.

Experts may be requested by their attorney clients to critique the work of an opposing expert witness by reviewing his or her report and deposition testimony. Experts may also be asked to observe the live testimony of an opposing expert witness to offer advice to the attorney who hired them.

Once experts have done more than discuss the case with the attorney or have reviewed documents, it may not be ethical for them to work for the other side (Poynter, 1987). Some courts have ruled it impermissible to hire an expert previously engaged by the other side. As counselors are making decisions on whether to reject or accept a case, they should depend on their judgment about the case and evaluate the credentials and integrity of the requesting attorney. If at any time counselors realize that an attorney who has retained them is incompetent, unreasonable, or dishonest, it is recommended that the counselors end the relationship.

Fees should be discussed before the engagement begins. It is typical to charge an hourly professional rate for time and expenses. Such expense items can include mileage reimbursement fees; consulting fees; other experts' fees; airfare, travel, and lodging fees; meals; specific resources purchased; and preparation of demonstrative evidence. When working with a new attorney client, retainers are often requested. Retainers are an advance payment for future work. To determine a retainer amount, a good practice is to estimate the cost to perform testing and analysis as well as testimony, and collect a portion of that amount.

ASSESSMENTS AND EVALUATIONS

Counselors in forensic settings who offer services as expert witnesses investigate a particular case by evaluating and analyzing information. Usually, the findings are documented in a written report that expresses opinions and conclusions. When counselors are called on to testify in depositions and trial, their objective is to explain and defend the conclusions reached. Counselors functioning as expert witnesses may recommend aspects of litigation strategy and often suggest other experts who may assist in case preparation and presentation.

Expert witnesses must be unbiased and objective. As a result, a mental health professional who has provided counseling services to a client should not agree to provide expert testimony because that professional is biased by the nature of the counseling relationship. Mental health professionals who are requested by their clients to provide expert testimony in a legal proceeding should decline because their role is to provide counseling, not evaluation. In addition, the mental health professional usually does not have sufficient information to form an expert opinion regarding a matter at issue in the court proceeding. Mental health professionals in a client-counselor relationship who are subpoenaed to court to testify should refuse to give opinions, stating that they "do not have sufficient information to form a professional opinion regarding the matter."

As an expert witness, the counselor is not hired to give an opinion but to arrive at an opinion after thorough evaluation and investigation (Poynter, 1987). The facts on which an expert's opinion is based must come from observation of the facts, knowledge of a particular field, and assumed facts supported by evidence submitted in the case. It is important to remember that the expert is a consultant in his or her field of expertise, not a professional expert witness. The opposing counsel will sometimes attempt to show that an expert witness is a "hired gun" and a professional expert witness. Therefore, it is important to maintain objectivity and an unbiased opinion at all times.

Deutsch and Sawyer (1989) have suggested that regardless of the particular approach used by the counselor, the client interview, assessment, standardized tests, and review of the relevant records are necessary components of an evaluation process. Evaluations without the subject present are possible; however, evaluations without direct contact are far less informative. An interview provides the professional with personal observations, behavior patterns, ability to assess motivation, and an opportunity to administer standardized tests when appropriate. Maxmen and Ward (1995) have noted that assessment is a specific task that is distinct from therapy. The authors explained that the patient interview is usually the principal source of data; however, additional sources can be friends, family, physical examinations, laboratory tests, psychological studies, staff observations, and standardized interviews. The primary objective of an interview is to obtain information that will determine the patient's diagnosis, prognosis, psychodynamics, and treatment. Deutsch and Sawyer outlined three basic steps that should be followed during the interview: orientation and rapport building, direct observation of the subject's behavior and performance, and information gathering.

Direct observation supplies information about the subject's orientation, thoughts, attitudes, personal insights, and general approach to the evaluation. The information obtained in the initial interview should be divided into identifying information, general case information, and information regarding the presenting problem and nature of the litigation.

Client assessment is a comprehensive, usually interdisciplinary, process of evaluating an individual's physical, mental, and emotional abilities, limitations, and obstacles to identify an optimal outcome for the client (Power, 1991). Client assessment is a method of acquiring information to assist individuals to identify their functional competencies and limitations (Hershenson, Power, & Waldo, 1996). In selecting assessment measures, counselors should have an understanding of standardized tests and how they are developed. Selection of assessment approaches should include consideration of validity, reliability, and norms.

In forensic settings, the counselor should inform the individual being evaluated that there is no client-counselor relationship and should explain limits to confidentiality. The counselor should inform the individual that he or she is being seen for assessment purposes only, how the counselor will be involved in the litigation process, and whether a report will be rendered. It is important to differentiate between the counselor role and that of a forensic expert, so that the individual being evaluated knows the exact nature of the relationship.

EXPERT REPORTS

Expert reports can be verbal or written. An initial report will probably be verbal; an attorney usually does not want an opinion on paper until all the facts of the case have been discovered. The attorney may then request a written report. A formal written report includes the expert's opinions and bases for those opinions. Reports should indicate the purpose for the assessment, methods used in the assessment process, pertinent dates, documents reviewed, tests utilized, and a thorough explanation of the conclusions. The report should be impartial, objective, and thorough. If utilized, the report should include citations of the work of other experts, articles, and books supportive of the conclusions.

DEPOSITION AND TRIAL TESTIMONY

Depositions are sworn statements recorded before the trial, which become part of the evidence in a case. Direct examination is the testimony taken by an attorney who has called the witness to the stand. Cross-examination refers to questions presented by the opposing counsel, the purpose of which is to challenge the information and opinions presented during direct examination.

There are two purposes for depositions: discovery and impeachment (Poynter, 1987). In a discovery deposition, the opposing attorney is trying to find out what an expert utilized to arrive at the opinion: the methods and conclusions. For impeachment, the opposing attorney tries to make the expert commit to information, so that the expert's testimony can be refuted at trial. Impeachment of an expert witness is accomplished by presenting alternative conclusions or examples of faulty methods. The following steps are recommended to ensure that expert witnesses are thoroughly prepared for a deposition and for direct and cross-examination:

- Conduct a complete and thorough review of all records of the case, including historical events and important facts (Davis, Yazak, & Kelling, 1990).
- Obtain information describing validity and reliability of any tests that may have been used (Blau, 1984).
- Review the literature and identify the authority supporting each position taken.
- Update your curriculum vitae, highlighting relevant education, employment, experience, licenses and certifications, professional memberships, and publications (La Forge & Henderson, 1990).
- Meet with the attorney who has retained you to review your role in the trial and prepare for testimony.

When giving deposition or trial testimony, suggestions include the following:

- Listen to the questions and pause before answering.
- Look directly at the attorney asking the question.
- Answer all questions as directly and as completely as possible.
- Use common terms whenever possible, and let the key points in your testimony stand out.
- Tell the complete truth.

There are several types of questions used to present expert testimony under direct as well as cross-examination. Types of questions include open-ended, close-ended, leading, hypothetical, and catch-all questions. Open-ended questions allow experts a great deal of latitude to tell their story in their own style or fashion. Close-ended questions control the answers by asking for only yes or no responses. Leading questions are those where experts are given a statement to which they are asked only to agree or disagree. Hypothetical questions are based on an assumed set of facts. Catch-all questions ask experts to tell all they know about a subject. As can be expected, it is virtually impossible to tell all one knows while in the witness box.

DIRECT AND CROSS-EXAMINATION

Direct examination is the telling of the story and conclusions from the expert's point of view. It begins with establishing the witness's education, background, and experience in his or her field of expertise. It is important to establish educational attainment, work experience, certifications or licenses held, professional affiliations, research conducted, and publications. A review of the method utilized and basis for conclusions should follow. This review can include a summary of records inspected, interview methods utilized, and the testing, analysis, and research that was performed. Direct examination usually includes a series of open-ended questions that ask the expert to tell what was done and the conclusions reached.

The reason attorneys hire expert witness is to provide a knowledgeable person who will assist the trier of fact to understand the technical aspects of a case and who will attempt to persuade the judge or jury to accept an explanation of the technical facts (Brodsky, 1999). Counselors in forensic settings can prepare and present court testimony through the use of learned skills, which can be markedly improved through practice. Four elements of effective expert witness testimony are suggested:

1. *Dynamic communication.* Findings introduced in a dynamic manner assist the judge or jury by making the testimony content meaningful.
2. *Audience involvement.* Portraying your knowledge with pleasure and adventure helps to connect with the trier of fact.
3. *Clear communication.* Simple, direct, and clear language assists the trier of fact to understand the complexity of the issues.
4. *Authenticity.* Presenting yourself at your natural best is recommended.

Cross-examination is a challenge. The cross-examining attorney wants to discredit the expert and the foundation for the expert's opinions or conclusions. An effective way to cross-examine an expert is to get the expert to agree with parts of the examiner's case. If the opposing attorney can persuade the expert to agree with aspects of the opposing expert's conclusions, an appearance of agreement among the experts is presented.

Some attorneys try to demonstrate partiality by showing that an expert works exclusively for the same attorneys or always testifies on behalf of the plaintiff or defense. If bias on the part of an expert witness can be established, credibility is diminished (Ingraham & Mauriello, 1991). A good way to respond to this effort to make an expert appear biased is to demonstrate to a judge or jury that the expert would have been willing to work for either side.

Fees for expert testimony can also be offered into evidence as producing bias. A common trick in questioning is for the opposing attorney to ask the expert, "How much are you being paid for your testimony today?" A good response to that question is to say, "I am not being paid for my testimony today; however, I am being paid for my time."

A witness may be asked whether he or she participated in a pretrial conference with the opposing attorney. This is meant to imply that the witness has been instructed in what to say. It is customary and preferred to meet with the attorney so that any new or additional information can be supplied and a strategy or a plan for direct examination can be developed. Answering that expert witnesses usually do meet with attorneys who retain them to discuss their testimony is appropriate.

A cross-examiner may pose several questions in a row that produce a series of "I don't know" answers. This can result in the witness's credibility being impeached by appearing to lack knowledge about the subject. Varying responses to avoid a number of "I don't know" answers is a good strategy. Another method of diminishing an expert's credibility is to point out inconsistencies in the expert's testimony. This can make the expert appear confused or dishonest. Experts must be careful to be consistent throughout their testimony.

Another tactic is for a cross-examiner to provoke the witness to display frustration or anger, which serves to reduce the appearance of professionalism and expertness. Some helpful tips include:

- Never argue with the opposing attorney, and do not defend yourself.
- Never look at your attorney while you are being cross-examined; jury members may think you are waiting for a signal.
- Remember, you are not a professional expert witness; you are a professional counselor working as an expert witness.
- Maintain flexibility.
- Remain dispassionate and do not take any comments or criticisms personally.

It is the function of the direct-examining attorney after cross-examination to rehabilitate the expert witness. Asking questions that rebuild the judge's or jury's confidence in their knowledge base and to reestablish their expertise is the method usually used to rehabilitate expert witnesses after a damaging cross-examination.

DAUBERT AND BEYOND

In 1993, the U.S. Supreme Court issued its ruling in *Daubert v. Merrell Dow Pharmaceuticals,* which changed the elements of admissibility of expert testimony. Until the *Daubert* decision, the rule for admissibility was governed by the *Frye* (1923) standard, which indicated that general acceptance of the methodology within the relevant scientific community determined whether an expert would be qualified by a judge to testify. Four criteria that must now be met have emerged from the *Daubert* decision:

1. *Reliability of the methodology.* This criterion applies to scientific validity. It is not the conclusion or opinion that has to be scientifically reliable or valid, but the method used to arrive at the conclusion.
2. *Relevance.* Before the expert testimony can be admitted, the court must determine that the information to be presented will assist the trier of fact by providing relevant issues, facts, and information.
3. *Reasonable reliance.* Facts must be based on information that is reasonably relied on by experts in the field.
4. *Nonprejudicial.* The value of the testimony must be weighed so that it does not confuse, mislead, or prejudice the trier of fact.

With the advent of these criteria, judges are required to make preliminary assessments of the expert evidence to determine if it is scientifically valid and meets the other three criteria (Brodsky, 1999). In an effort to exclude "junk science," the judge must determine whether the expert's proposed testimony meets the test for scientific knowledge. The following assessments of the testimony will be made by the judge:

- If the underlying theory or methodology can be and has been tested.
- If the methodology has been subjected to peer review and publication.

- If the known and potential error rates are acceptable, and the methodology meets related standards and safeguards.
- If there is widespread acceptance in the scientific community of the technique or methodology.

The initial *Daubert* opinion addressed scientific evidence; *Kumho Tire Company v. Carmicheal (1999)* outlined the same criteria for nonscientific experts, which could include counselors. Sometimes, hearings are conducted to limit or exclude testimony that does not meet the criteria. Either side may request a hearing and sometimes, for strategic reasons, do so to have an opportunity to observe the opposing expert.

The *Daubert* and subsequent *Kumho Tire* decisions do not apply in all state courts. Brodsky (1999) reported that approximately 23 states have adopted the *Daubert* guidelines, but at least 15 states still follow the *Frye* general acceptability rule. In addition, not all experts are subject to *Daubert* rules. Brodsky reports that some courts have determined that various technical and professional experts are not subject to the full scientific reliability standard, only to general acceptability. To pass *Daubert* challenges, Brodsky suggests that experts master scientific knowledge and research that has appeared in peer review journals that supports the methodology used by the expert.

Although experts are called on to give opinions, they are not allowed to speculate. If counselors are well read and knowledgeable in their field of expertise, trust their theory and methodology, and believe their conclusions are reliable and valid, their opinions are not speculation.

SUMMARY

Counselors increasingly are finding themselves with opportunities to provide expert witness testimony in litigated cases, and the standard for qualification and acceptance as an expert is continually being raised. The general acceptability rule for expert testimony is gradually being replaced by decisions such as those in *Daubert* and *Kumho Tire.* A thorough knowledge of underlying theory or methodology, as well as evidence of peer review and publications describing validity and reliability in methods that have achieved widespread acceptance in the community, are essential to the testimony of counselors in forensic settings. Once a counselor enters the forensic arena and offers expert witness testimony services, the counselor may be subject to the same scrutiny as any other scientific expert witness.

To maintain credibility when giving expert witness testimony, counselors must remain unbiased and objective, conduct a thorough assessment and evaluation, and avoid becoming defensive when challenged. Experts must maintain credibility so that judges and juries will give substantial weight to their opinions.

Counselors who have provided counseling services to a client should not agree to provide expert testimony because of the biased nature of the counseling relationship and potential for ethical violations. The lack of confidentiality should be explained to the person being assessed or evaluated to differentiate between the counselor role and that of a forensic expert who is conducting an evaluation. The Committee on Ethical Guidelines for Forensic Psychologists (1991) has outlined four ethical goals for expert witnesses:

1. Assume a special responsibility to be fair and accurate.
2. Avoid partisan distortion or misrepresentation.
3. Actively disclose all sources of information.
4. Be prepared to distinguish between expert testimony and legal issues and facts.

Brodsky (1999) proposed a four-level hierarchy of witness obligations: truth of the findings, obligations to the court, responsibility to the party being evaluated and to both sets of attorneys, and obligations to oneself and one's profession. Credibility on the witness stand can be maintained by expert witnesses by listening carefully, answering completely and truthfully, and staying faithful to their methods and conclusions.

References

Blau, T.F. (1984). *The psychologist as expert witness.* New York: Wiley Interscience.

Brodsky, S.L. (1999). *The expert expert witness: More maxims and guidelines for testifying in court.* Washington, DC: American Psychological Association.

Committee on Ethical Guidelines for Forensic Psychologists. (1991). Specialty guidelines for forensic psychologists. *Law and Human Behavior, 15,* 655–665.

Cooper, J., Bennett, E.A., & Sukel, H.L. (1996). Complex scientific testimony: How do jurors make decisions? *Law and Human Behavior, 20,* 379–394.

Daubert v. Merrell Dow Pharmaceutical, Inc., 509 U.S. 579, 113 S. Ct. 2786 (1993).

Davis, A., Yazak, D., & Kelling, G., Jr. (1990). Cross-examination of expert witnesses: What to expect from the opposing counsel. *Journal of Applied Rehabilitation Counseling, 27,* 53–58.

Deutsch, P.M., & Sawyer, H.W. (1989). *A guide to rehabilitation.* New York: Matthew Bender & Company.

Federal Rules of Evidence, Rule 702.

Freckelton, I. (1999). The diagnostic expertise of forensic psychologists. *Psychiatry, Psychology and Law, 4,* 73–77.

Frye v. United States, 293 F. 1013 (D.C. Cir. 1923).

Hershenson, D.B., Power, P.W., & Waldo, M. (1996). *Community counseling: Contemporary theory in practice.* Boston: Allyn & Bacon.

Ingraham, B.L., & Mauriello, T.P. (1991). *The police investigation handbook.* New York: Mauriello Bender and Company.

Kumho Tire Company Ltd. et al. v. Carmichael et al. (1999), 11th Cir. U.S. Ct. App. No. 97–1709.

La Forge, J., & Henderson, P. (1990). Counselor competency in the courtroom. *Journal of Counseling and Development, 68,* 456–459.

Maxmen, J.S., & Ward, N.G. (1995). *Essential psychopathology and its treatment* (2nd ed.). New York: Norton.

Meyer C. (Ed.). (1999). *Expert witnessing: Explaining and understanding science.* New York: CRC Press.

Power, P.W. (1991). *A guide to vocational assessment* (2nd ed.). Austin, TX: ProEd.

Poynter, D. (1987). *The expert witness handbook: Tips and techniques for the litigation consultant.* Santa Barbara, CA: Santa Barbara Publishing.

PART VIII

*Personal Care and
Interprofessional Relations*

Coping with the Demands of the Profession

59 IMPAIRMENT IN THE MENTAL HEALTH PROFESSIONS

Holly A. Stadler

The personal freedom of clinical practice coupled with a general absence of oversight and accountability creates the opportunity for practitioners who are operating in a dysfunctional capacity to go unnoticed or unattended for extended periods of time (Stadler, Willing, Eberhage, & Ward, 1988). Professionals who have been trained to think independently and to work through situations on their own may not recognize or be willing to admit that their clinical capacities have fallen below a reasonable standard of effectiveness. (Kottler and Schofield, in this volume, underscore the stresses inherent in the mental health professions.) Mental health professionals who promote and encourage introspection and self-care in their clients often are reluctant to examine those same areas in themselves.

Because of the harm that can come to clients in such circumstances, the topic of practitioner impairment has always been a concern in the health care professions. However, only in the past 30 years has particular attention been paid to understanding the incidence and etiology of clinical impairment. Some professional groups have taken active steps to promote identification and remediation of impaired colleagues. The American Medical Association (AMA) was an early leader in the development of legislative models for "Sick Doctor" statutes. What began as a peer assistance movement has developed into an extensive network of physician effectiveness committees supported by state medical societies (Collins, 1998).

The efforts of the American Psychological Association began in the 1980s with a task force on services for distressed psychologists. In 1994, an Advisory Committee on Impaired Psychologists prepared a manual for state associations. Although 21 states and Canadian provinces report the existence of functioning programs for impaired psychologists, there is still much need for serious action to address the problem (Coster & Schwebel, 1997).

Finally, the American Counseling Association (ACA) has yet to act decisively to confront the issue of impairment among its members. A 1991 task force failed to produce any formal policies or procedures to assist impaired counselors (Sheffield, 1998). The ACA Ethics Committee responds to concerns about impairment if complaints are filed against a member of the organization. Each of the organizations mentioned does address impairment in their ethical codes, acknowledging that practitioners should refrain from conducting clinical work when they are not competent to practice.

DEFINING IMPAIRMENT

Kilburg (1991) has described a continuum of professional functioning that ranges from peak, through normal and distressed, to impaired and eventually disabled. He notes that distressed, impaired, and disabled performance is often an indicator of failure to physically, emotionally, socially, behaviorally, or professionally self-regulate. Some examples of impairment include burnout, chemical dependency and codependency, mental illness, sexual impropriety, legal problems or malpractice distress, family and relationship problems, and physical illness and disability.

Inconsistency in defining and conceptualizing impairment has been used to explain several seemingly intractable problems related to the topic of impairment. The slow progress of policymaking by professional societies and licensing boards, enabling behavior by colleagues of impaired practitioners, and the mismanagement of treatment of impaired practitioners have been attributed at some point to lack of definitional and conceptual clarity.

Definitions proposed by Lalotis and Grayson (1985) have been widely quoted, as they seek to differentiate impairment from incompetence and unethical behavior. They use the term impairment when referring to interference in professional functioning due to chemical dependency, mental illness, or personal conflict. In their conceptualization, incompetence refers to those circumstances in which a practitioner has never attained a reasonable standard of competence or has failed to maintain it because of knowledge or skill deficits or impairment. Unethical behavior refers to causing injury or harm to a client while performing in a professional role. These authors contend that unethical or incompetent practice may not necessarily be due to practitioner impairment but may result from a long-standing character disorder, professional naivete, or ignorance. Regardless of definition, it is clear that professional distress is multifaceted, encompassing a variety of problems of differing origins.

INCIDENCE

A study of psychologists (Thoresen, Miller, & Krauskopf, 1989) found them to be a healthy group, reporting high levels of satisfaction with their professional and life situations. In contrast to this positive information about psychologist well-being are other data that give cause for alarm regarding practitioners' capacity for self-regulation. Another study of psychologists (most studies of incidence use psychologists or physicians as respondents to surveys) indicated that 56.7% of the respondents reported that they continued to work when they were too distressed to be effective (Pope, Tabachnick, & Keith-Spiegel, 1987). More than 5% of these respondents revealed that they conducted therapy while under the influence of alcohol. Kitchener (2000) has concluded that estimates of impairment vary widely. For example, studies have identified relationship or marital problems in 20% to 82% of the psychologists sampled. She points out that fewer psychologists are impaired by substance abuse, ranging from 9% to 11% of those sampled. Depression and suicide also are found among psychologists, with 61% of one sample reporting having experienced a depressive episode, 29% describing themselves as having been suicidal, and 4% reporting suicide attempts. One study found reason for concern in the rate of suicide among male psychologists (Orr, 1997).

Few data are available on the incidence of impairment among counselors. Welfel (1998) does describe a sample of school counselors, 33% of whom report high emotional exhaustion. Likewise, we know little about the incidence of physical impairment among therapists. The research of Thoresen and his colleagues (1989) cited 10% of psychologists reporting recurring physical ailments ranging from allergies to cancer.

RISK FACTORS

Particular aspects of the work of counselors and psychotherapists are thought to contribute to the potential for distress and impairment. There are characteristics of clients that appear to promote distress. Unfortunate as it is, we must recognize that client suicide is an occupational hazard in the mental professions. Twenty-two percent of psychologists and 61% of psychiatrists have experienced client suicide (Chemtob, Bauer, Hamada, Pelowski, & Muraoka, 1989). Work with suicidal clients is very stressful for the professional and has significant impact on both professional and personal lives. Other research has noted that work with difficult clients is the most troubling aspect of clinical practice (Sherman, 1999).

Certain types of client problems are experienced as stressful by therapists. For example, clients with substance abuse problems are frequently chronically disabled and difficult to assist. The high recidivism rate of these clients increases the emotional intensity and stress of this work (Elman & Dowd, 1997). Counselors who work with clients with HIV disease find it stressful knowing that, as yet, clients cannot be cured of the disease (Mirsalimi & Roffe, 1991). Farrenkopf (1992) has identified characteristics of sex offenders that contribute to distress in mental health professionals. These clients often are self-centered, lack empathy, and are manipulative; they frequently minimize or externalize personal responsibility for their behavior and lack the internal motivation to change while resisting external influences to change. Encounters with these clients may leave female practitioners feeling vulnerable, threatened, paranoid, and vigilant. Male practitioners may experience a sense of collective guilt after repeated exposure to accounts of abusive male behavior. Treating victims of various types of trauma and abuse can lead to compassion fatigue and secondary Posttraumatic Stress Disorder (Welfel, 1998). Long-term exposure to clients' traumatic experiences can undermine therapists' own sense of trust and safety as well as their feelings of power and efficacy.

Beyond the stress of working with particular types of clients, there are common themes in the work environment that contribute to practitioner distress. Psychiatric hospitals and psychiatric wards are the most frequent settings where patient suicides occur (Chemtob et al., 1989). Some clinicians have observed that their work stress is related to the lack of time they have to meet work-related obligations and to the restructuring of clinical practice brought on by managed care (Sherman, 1999). Other work stress occurs when confronting hostile institutions and making do with fewer resources while needs escalate (Welfel, 1998). The potential for burnout is increased in organizations where there is a lack of positive feedback, where there is role ambiguity, and where the therapist lacks autonomy and control.

Finally, personal characteristics of therapists themselves may be risk factors for impairment. Contrary to the popular notion that practitioners can keep their personal distress from affecting their work performance, Sherman (1999) found that high distress in clinicians correlated positively with more work impairment and inversely with satisfaction with personal life events.

In contrast to the largely atheoretical examination of risk factors related to impairment and burnout, Glickauf-Hughes and Mehlman (1995) have developed an interesting object relations thesis to explain some issues common to therapists. They discuss how, in their early years, many therapists learned to be self-reliant and to achieve without needing or acknowledging help. Through childhood experiences in providing the primary nurturing or parenting function in the family, the child learns to become acutely aware of the needs and feelings of others. This background is good preparation for a profession that involves listening and attuning oneself to client's indirect messages and unspoken needs. However, Glickauf-Hughes and Mehlman argue that in learning to perform these nurturing and parenting functions, the child sacrifices his or her own needs, and as an adult does not know his or her true self, having become expert at the art of not experiencing feelings. The pseudointimacy of the therapeutic encounter may feel safe for the therapist with dependency needs who seeks intimacy without personal vulnerability. With these types of risk factors in mind, let's turn to some of the warning signs of impairment.

WARNING SIGNS

How do we recognize the signs of distress and impairment in ourselves and others in our profession? Studies of psychologists have described emotional exhaustion and fatigue as evidence of personal problems. Relationships deteriorate and the impaired therapist becomes isolated and withdrawn, disillusioned with the profession, anxious and depressed. Decreasing tolerance of human frailties can result in emotional distance in therapy (Farrenkopf, 1992). Alcoholism is a clear warning sign of impairment and more prevalent among male therapists, although drug abuse among therapists does not appear to be a very common concern (Mahoney, 1997).

Prolonged exposure to clients' traumatic material can even affect a therapist's memory system (McCann & Pearlman, 1990). Clinicians have described internalizing memories of clients' traumatic imagery in addition to experiencing flashbacks, dreams, and intrusive thoughts. Vicarious experiencing of trauma may disrupt the therapist's basic assumptions about the world, that it is benign and meaningful and that people are trustworthy. Therapists may begin to restrict their movement, feeling powerless, vulnerable, and overcome by the capriciousness of unexpected life events.

Research on impaired physicians is more plentiful than on mental health professionals, and there is much to be learned from these colleagues. This research has indicated that work performance problems are usually the last signs of impairment to appear (Fleming, 1994). Family dysfunction and marital problems have been described as warning signs of impairment in physicians, in addition to legal and health problems. Colleagues might notice behavior changes in the impaired practitioner as well as mood changes, increased anger,

cynicism, and an antagonistic demeanor. Relationship problems at work, a careless appearance, change in dress habits, and the smell of alcohol or heavy cologne used to mask that odor may also be warning signs. When work performance begins to change it may be noticed as changing work habits, tardiness or unusual work schedule, procedural errors, and poor record keeping (Fleming, 1994).

When clinicians get to the point of exploiting clients (Tremlow, 1997), it is usually the result of reaching a critical mass of boundary problems (see Herlihy in this volume for a detailed discussion of boundary issues). Boundary problems could range from special considerations given to certain types of clients to active fantasies about clients. In these cases, it is likely that earlier warning signs were ignored or rationalized without significant intervention having taken place.

PREVENTION OF BURNOUT AND IMPAIRMENT

Knowing the risk factors and warning signs of impairment can guide us in developing personal and institutional practices to prevent its occurrence. In Kilburg's (1991) plan for the prevention of burnout, therapists should become aware of the risk factors previously described and keep up to date on issues related to burnout and impairment. He believes that clinicians must develop their own prevention strategies, which could include strengthening coping skills and a periodic assessment of personal risks and impairment status.

In developing a personal prevention plan, therapists should take note that 84% of the psychologists in Pope and Tabachnick's (1994) survey reported having had psychotherapy. Eighty-six percent of these indicated that they found therapy to be helpful. Forty-six percent of female therapists and 30% of male therapists in this study had therapy in the prior year.

The resources and activities for therapist self-care and the prevention of impairment might include pleasure reading, physical exercise, hobbies, recreational vacations, prayer/meditation, and volunteer work (Mahoney, 1997). Other self-care strategies include developing strong interpersonal support from family, friends, companions, and peers. Self-awareness and self-monitoring combined with self-regulation are essential components of a personal wellness plan for mental health professionals (Coster & Schwebel, 1997). Kitchener (2000) has delineated the three watchwords of nurturing personal well-being: rest, relaxation, and exercise. Being able to recognize one's own vulnerabilities and seeking help and support when stress becomes overwhelming are the underlying themes of any comprehensive wellness plan.

Personal wellness strategies that might be implemented in the work environment should be directed to reducing stress and enhancing collegial and supervisory support. Team building and working with colleagues to institute change in the immediate workplace can enhance a sense of empowerment and reduce stress. Involvement in professional and civic activism and continuing professional development are avenues for renewal and can offset the ennui and loss of interest that may develop when one notices that clinical work has become repetitive (Kilburg, 1991).

When personal prevention and remediation efforts fail and personal problems continue, it is the clinician's ethical responsibility to cease participation in professional activities that could harm clients and to get help (American Counseling Association, 1995; American Psychological Association, 1992; Kitchener, 2000). Caring colleagues should demonstrate their professionalism and concern for the welfare of all involved by encouraging self-care and self-regulation and by taking steps to intervene when direct assistance becomes necessary.

INTERVENTION

When therapists do become impaired, protecting consumers is of paramount importance, but other considerations also come into play. These considerations are centered primarily on assisting therapists to return to productive practice and to resume making the contributions to society that are the outcomes of a productive practice. When therapist impairment has deteriorated to the point of ethical violation, several responses are available. Some approaches stress treatment and then a return to practice; others focus on punishment for the violation or both treatment and punishment. Clarifying whether an ethical violation was due to incompetence or impairment is important, as this distinction serves as a guide for appropriate intervention and consequences (Kitchener, 2000).

In helping an impaired therapist to return to productive practice it is important to remember the needs of those who have been affected by the therapist's impairment (e.g., families, friends, colleagues, and clients) (Brown, 1997). When impairment has included therapeutic boundary violations, special attention is warranted for past and present clients who have been subjected to those violations. Colleagues who have been betrayed by this misconduct are likely to need assistance in managing their reactions.

The medical profession has the most well-developed system for assistance to impaired physicians. They have encouraged the development of treatment programs specifically for medical professionals. Critical aspects of a complete remediation program are monitoring and follow-up of therapists after treatment. Discipline enforcement is not a popular topic among professionals because it confronts us with the reality of impairment and its consequences. Walzer and Miltimore (1993) have proposed a system for practice oversight for impaired physicians involving monitoring of practices, procedures, and case records. This system provides further oversight through supervision, integrating teaching and training with discussion of therapy notes and work with selected clients. In their proposal, monitors and supervisors would be empowered to intercede should work performance be faulty. When a licensing board becomes involved in mandating remediation, it is typically the function of a treating therapist to provide initial diagnostic and prognostic consultation, as well as progress reports and further recommendations. The ultimate goal of remediation, monitoring, and supervision for the therapist is to develop "more mature, ethical, and educated level of skill and professionalism to attain a level of performance that is acceptable under the standard of care" (Walzer & Miltimore, 1993, p. 571).

SUMMARY

Much work remains to confront the problem of impairment in the ranks of mental health professionals in a proactive and comprehensive manner. Counseling and psychology professional groups and licensing organizations must take greater responsibility for prevention of impairment and for intervention when impairment is recognized. As professionals, we must take responsibility for our own self-care, recognizing the occupational hazards of a career in the mental health professions and being vigilant for warning signs of impairment in ourselves and our colleagues. To retain the public trust and honor our commitment to ethical practice, we can no longer sweep these problems from sight.

References

American Counseling Association. (1995). *ACA code of ethics and standards of practice*. Alexandria, VA: Author.

American Psychological Association. (1992). Ethical principles of psychologists and code of conduct. *American Psychologist, 47*, 1597–1611.

Brown, L. (1997). Remediation, amends or denial. *Professional Psychology: Research and Practice, 28*, 297–299.

Chemtob, C., Bauer, G., Hamada, R., Pelowski, S., & Muraoka, M. (1989). Patient suicide: Occupational hazard for psychologists and psychiatrists. *Professional Psychology: Research and Practice, 20*, 294–297.

Collins, G.B. (1998). New hope for impaired physicians: Helping the physician while protecting patients. *Cleveland Clinic Journal of Medicine, 65*, 101–106.

Coster, J., & Schwebel, M. (1997). Well-functioning in professional psychologists. *Professional Psychology: Research and Practice, 28*, 5–13.

Elman, B.D., & Dowd, E.T. (1997). Correlates of burnout in inpatient substance abuse treatment therapists. *Journal of Addictions and Offender Counseling, 17*, 56–65.

Farrenkopf, T. (1992). What happens to therapists who work with sex offenders? *Journal of Offender Rehabilitation, 18*, 217–223.

Fleming, M.F. (1994). Physician impairment: Options for intervention. *American Family Physician, 50*, 41–44.

Glickauf-Hughes, C., & Mehlman, E. (1995). Narcissistic issues in therapists: Diagnostic and treatment considerations. *Psychotherapy, 32*, 213–221.

Kilburg, R.R. (Ed.). (1991). *How to manage your career in psychology*. Washington, DC: American Psychological Association.

Kitchener, K. (2000). *Foundations of ethical practice, research, and teaching in psychology*. Mahwah, NJ: Erlbaum.

Lalotis, D., & Grayson, J. (1985). Psychologist heal thyself: What is available for the impaired psychologist? *American Psychologist, 40*, 84–89.

Mahoney, M. (1997). Psychotherapists' personal problems and self-care patterns. *Professional Psychology: Research and Practice, 28*, 14–16.

McCann, I.L., & Pearlman, L.A. (1990). Vicarious traumatization: A framework for understanding the psychological effects of working with victims. *Journal of Traumatic Stress, 3*, 131–149.

Mirsalimi, H., & Roffe, M.W. (1991). *Psychosocial correlates of burnout and depression in HIV counselors* (Report No. CG 024809). East Lansing, MI: ERIC Document Reproduction Service No. ED354 467.

Orr, P. (1997). Psychology impaired? *Professional Psychology: Research and Practice, 28*, 293–296.

Pope, K.S., & Tabachnick, B. (1994). Therapists as patients: A national survey of psychotherapists' experiences, problems and beliefs. *Professional Psychology: Research and Practice, 25*, 247–258.

Pope, K.S., Tabachnick, B., & Keith-Spiegel, P. (1987). Ethics of practice: The beliefs and behaviors of psychologists as therapists. *American Psychologist, 42*, 993–1006.

Sheffield, D.S. (1998). Counselor impairment: Moving toward a concise definition and protocol. *Journal of Humanistic Education and Development, 37*, 96–106.

Sherman, M. (1999). Distress and professional impairment due to major life events and work factors among applied psychologists. *Dissertation Abstracts International: Section B: The Sciences and Engineering, 59*(7-B), 3750.

Stadler, H., Willing, K., Eberhage, M., & Ward, W. (1988). Impairment: Implications for the counseling profession. *Journal of Counseling and Development, 66,* 258–260.

Thoresen, R., Miller, M., & Krauskopf, C. (1989). The distressed psychologist: Prevalence and treatment considerations. *Professional Psychology: Research and Practice, 20,* 153–158.

Tremlow, S.W. (1997). Exploitation of patients: Themes in the psychopathology of their therapists. *American Journal of Psychotherapy, 51,* 357–375.

Walzer, R.S., & Miltimore, S. (1993). Mandated supervision, monitoring, and therapy of disciplined health care professionals: Implementation and model regulations. *Journal of Legal Medicine, 14,* 565–596.

Welfel, E. (1998). *Ethics in counseling and psychotherapy: Standards, research and emerging Issues.* Pacific Grove, CA: Brooks/Cole.

60 ETHICAL ISSUES RELATED TO INTERPROFESSIONAL COMMUNICATION

Harriet L. Glosoff

Various models of interdisciplinary work have long been an integral part of working in medical, rehabilitation, community mental health, and educational settings. Most practitioners recognize the necessity of joining forces with other professionals to best serve the complex medical, psychological, and social needs of children with special education problems, patients who are elderly, clients with physical disabilities or severe physical illnesses such as AIDS or cancer, and those with substance abuse disorders. In fact, the codes of ethics of all mental health professions direct their members to interact with other professionals in a variety of ways to best serve their clients. Further, mental health professionals have an ethical obligation to conduct these interactions in a manner respectful to their colleagues and true to standards of their own profession. On the surface, this appears to be an easy mandate. After all, counselors, social workers, psychologists, and marriage and family therapists all are trained to work in the best interest of the clients. In reality, however, political and economic rivalries, internal identity conflicts, and guild interest may interfere with clinicians living up to the spirit of their professional codes of ethics. Terms and ethical guidelines associated with models of interdisciplinary communication, problems that interfere with effective interprofessional treatment, and suggestions for becoming more effective are presented in this chapter.

TERMS ASSOCIATED WITH INTERDISCIPLINARY MENTAL HEALTH TREATMENT

Terms such as *interdisciplinary, multiprofessional,* and *interprofessional* often are used interchangeably in the literature and this chapter to describe such interactions. There is a wide continuum of arrangements that involve interdisciplinary communication. At one end of this continuum is a model of delegation, where one person, operating from a position of authority, delegates to another professional specific aspects of a client's treatment while maintaining ultimate responsibility for that client's overall treatment. Models of collaborative teamwork lie on the other end of the continuum, where two or more professionals work together to generate and implement treatment plans. In effective teamwork, one person is usually identified as a team leader, but decisions are based on consensus.

Referring, conferring, consulting, coordinating, and *teamwork* are other terms typically associated with ways in which mental health professionals work interprofessionally. Most mental health clinicians are trained to refer clients to and take referrals from other professionals. For example, counselors often work with clients who are exhibiting signs of clinical depression. They may refer such clients to a psychiatrist to determine the possible benefits of medication and to rule out any organic basis for the symptoms. *Conferring* often is considered an informal comparing of observations. For example, a school counselor confers with teachers about a student who is exhibiting behavioral problems to discuss general observations. Bope and Jost (1994) presented *consulting* as a slightly more structured communication between professionals. In consulting, one professional solicits another's opinion, most often to make a decision or to plan a course of action. Using the same example, the teacher may consult with the counselor to seek specific ideas about the most effective interventions to be used to approach the student's parents. The goal of *coordination* of services is to ensure that all service providers are operating from the same plan of action and are aware of each of their roles and functions in helping their shared client. Finally, *teamwork* is the most structured form of collaboration and is rooted historically in the delivery of health care and educational services. Bope and Jost defined teams as "groups of professionals that consult, confer, and cooperate

formally and deliberately over a considerable period of time" (p. 62).

Following is a discussion of ethical guidelines related to interprofessional collaboration. Issues related directly to client contact or care are addressed first, followed by those more closely related to contact among professionals.

ETHICAL GUIDELINES RELATED TO
CLIENT CARE

Almost all mental health professions' codes of ethics provide guidance regarding interdisciplinary interactions. These refer to interactions with other practitioners who hold the same academic degree but have different areas of specialization (e.g., a counseling psychologist consulting with a clinical psychologist or a school counselor conferring with a rehabilitation counselor) as well as clinicians from different disciplines (e.g., a counselor referring a client for a psychiatric evaluation). It is critical for clinicians to be aware of and address ethical issues related to referrals, confidentiality of information, and respect for other professionals (Remley & Herlihy, 2001).

Referrals

The codes of ethics of the National Association of Social Workers (NASW, 1999), the American Counseling Association (ACA, 1995), the American Psychological Association (APA, 1995), and the American Psychiatric Association (1980) all direct their members to consult with or refer clients to other professionals when this is in the best interest of the client. Some examples of this include when other professionals' specialized expertise would most fully serve a client's need or when practitioners believe that they cannot effectively work with a client. Further, these codes mandate that professionals be knowledgeable about referral sources. Although practitioners are not typically held legally accountable for the behavior of a professional to whom they have referred a client, they can be considered ethically responsible for harm suffered by a client if they knowingly referred that client to someone who has a negative reputation or who does not have the expertise to effectively serve the person referred (Remley & Herlihy, 2001). For example, Mark is close with Sue, a local psychiatrist. Sue has confided to Mark on several occasions that she does not enjoy seeing clients anymore and is feeling burned out and ineffective in her work. It would be unethical for Mark to refer clients to Sue until she addresses this problem.

Codes of ethics provide further guidance to mental health professionals regarding the "dos" and "don'ts" of making ethical referrals. For example, the ACA *Code of Ethics* (1995) specifies that counselors may not use their places of employment or institutional affiliations to recruit clients for their own private practices. The NASW *Code of Ethics* (1999) notes that social workers are to take appropriate steps to facilitate the referral and the transfer of responsibility. Ethical mental health professionals are also aware of their obligation to make reasonable arrangements for the continuation of needed treatment and to ensure that clients are not abandoned or neglected in the referral process (e.g., see Standard 1.7 of the *Code of the Ethics* of the American Association for Marriage and Family Therapy [AAMFT], 1998, and Standard A.11.a. of the ACA code).

All mental health professions consider "fee splitting" or receiving fees solely for making a referral as unethical practice. For example, section 1.27 of the APA *Ethical Principles*, Standard D.3.b. of the ACA *Code of Ethics*, and Standard 2.06(c) of the NASW *Code of Ethics* clearly state that their members are prohibited from giving or receiving payment for a referral when they are not actually providing any professional service. Welfel (1998) pointed out that it is not uncommon for someone who owns an established mental health practice to receive fees from other professionals based on a percentage of their income, in return for the use of office space and secretarial services. This would be considered unethical if two practitioners have totally separate practices and fees are exchanged based on the number of referrals made. It would, however, be ethical if one person subcontracts with another for overhead expenses associated with seeing clients, such as for the use of treatment rooms and secretarial services (Welfel, 1998).

Confidential Information

Mental health professionals often must share information with other professionals about clients that is confidential. Once again, most codes of ethics provide guidance in how to do so in the most ethical manner. Although clients may give verbal permission for their counselors to speak with a potential referral source or with other team members, it is best to obtain this permission in writing. For example, the ACA code specifically requires this before records are transferred (Standard B.4.e.). As part of the informed consent process, clients should be informed about any limits to confidentiality, including if treatment involves a one-time or continuous review by other professionals.

In addition, most codes of ethics direct mental health professionals to disclose only information pertinent to the purpose for which the communication is made. For example, the information shared during a discussion about a potential referral will address the reason for the referral but typically not include the client's name. Once it is decided that it is an appropriate referral, with the client's consent, all pertinent information should be communicated to the new provider (e.g., NASW, Standard 2.06[b]).

ETHICAL GUIDELINES REGARDING OTHER PROFESSIONALS

The ethical guidelines reviewed so far address some of the "mechanics" of interdisciplinary communications or what mental health professionals are expected to do as part of the referral or collaboration process to protect clients. Ethical standards that speak to responsibilities to other professionals direct mental health professionals to form relationships with other professionals based on respect, honesty, and fairness (Welfel, 1998). Although these concepts may be aspirational in nature, there are ethical standards that delineate specific behaviors associated with cooperative and respectful practice. For example, the ACA *Code of Ethics* and APA's *Ethical Principles* both state that on learning that clients are already receiving mental health services, practitioners are to discuss this with the client, obtain appropriate releases of information, discuss with the other professional the best course of treatment, and coordinate efforts if both are to see the client. Welfel stated that if clients do not consent to communications between the two (or more) mental health professionals involved, it is up to each professional to decide whether continuing treatment with the client under such a restriction may potentially be more harmful than helpful. If the professional decides that it will be harmful, he or she should discuss this with the client, and if the client is still unwilling to permit communication between the service providers, request that the client see only the other professional. If faced with such a situation, it is important for professionals to remember their ethical obligation to not abandon their client, to terminate their relationship smoothly, and to facilitate the client's working solely with the other professional.

Another important aspect of respect among colleagues relates to how they conduct themselves publicly when referring to other professionals as well as how they conduct themselves directly with their colleagues. For example, social workers are to "treat colleagues with respect and should represent accurately and fairly the qualifications, views, and obligations of colleagues" (NASW, 1999, Standard 2.01[a]). APA's Principle B directs psychologists to "promote integrity in the science, teaching, and practice of psychology" and to be honest, fair, and respectful of others in this process. The ACA code and the *Guidelines for Psychiatrists in Consultative, Supervisory, or Collaborative Relationships with Nonmedical Therapists* (American Psychiatric Association, 1980) are more specific on the issue of respect. The guidelines specify that "no professional should attempt to define the functions and responsibilities of any other profession" (p. 1489) and that psychiatrists are to recognize the unique skills and competencies of other professionals. Section C.6.a. of the ACA code states that counselors are to respect approaches to counseling that differ from their own. The code further directs that counselors should be knowledgeable of the traditions and practices of other professional groups.

PROBLEMS RELATED TO INTERPROFESSIONAL WORK

Clearly, there is a great degree of overlap across ethics codes published by the various mental health professions regarding the need to refer, to consult, and to cooperate with colleagues in the best interests of clients. One interpretation of this overlap is that there is a shared value among the different professions regarding the need to act in the best interest of clients. From the wording of most codes of ethics, however, it strikes this author as a value of tolerating others to serve clients. This is different from a value based on an appreciation of how the very differences among disciplines may facilitate professionals' development and strengthen their own professional identities as helping to serve clients most effectively.

Leach, Glosoff, and Overmier (in press) examined the codes of ethics published by psychological associations in 23 countries (other than the United States). They found that the majority of these (68%) included standards that explicitly addressed the need to respect, trust, and become knowledgeable about colleagues within and outside of the field of psychology. For example, the *Code of Conduct* of the Hong Kong Psychological Society (1991) states, "Psychologists respect the professional standards of other disciplines, and great care shall be taken to develop and strengthen harmonious interdisciplinary relations" (Standard 3.6). This author believes that the direction to create harmonious relationships with colleagues from professions other than psychology is much stronger than simply stating that we should not speak poorly of people with degrees different from our own.

There are a number of factors that influence the beliefs, attitudes, and behaviors of mental health practitioners and the types and effectiveness of interprofessional relationships in which they may engage. Licensing, reimbursement issues, and ways in which mental health practitioners are socialized into their respective professions all affect whether professionals choose to work collaboratively and with whom. Following is a brief discussion of some of these factors.

Diverse Professional Identities

Every time two or more professionals interact, they each bring their own set of professional norms and values along with their professional knowledge and skills (Waugaman, 1994). Not all professions, however, include teaching their members to work in teams, especially with members of other disciplines. This may lead to professionals valuing only the models in which they were trained and looking at those used by other professionals with disdain or suspicion. This, in turn, often causes professionals to limit their contacts and referrals to only members of their discipline (Welfel, 1998). If they do so without ever discussing other options with their clients, they rob them of their right to choose for themselves.

Using the title of the degree conferred as the *sole* criterion for referring clients seems a shallow way to make decisions about potential sources of referrals—similar to the proverbial judging a book by its cover. It is an especially problematic method to use because the assumptions we make in judging other professionals may not be accurate. In the long run, doing so may prevent us from getting to know who might actually have the combination of knowledge, skills, and personality to most effectively meet someone's mental health needs. For example, Steve may assume that all counselors are trained to work only with functionally well clients who are experiencing normal developmental problems. He may not know that Tamika, who is a counselor in the same building as he, has had extensive supervised experience and great success in treating individuals with Posttraumatic Stress Disorder. Instead, he refers a client to a clinical psychologist whose office is across town from where the client lives.

Relationships among professionals can become strained due to philosophical differences.

Different models of training and epistemological assumptions about mental health and mental illness may lead to tension among mental health professionals working together (Berg, 1986). For example, some mental health professions are oriented more toward theoretical issues, others toward practical matters. Some may conceptualize clients' problems in terms of pathology, and others may approach clients' issues from a wellness perspective. Professionals who hold such divergent views may believe that their view is the only valid one. In such cases, it is likely that discussions will be based on defensive and offensive stances and that each professional will honestly believe that he or she is acting in the best interest of the client. It is unlikely that productive brainstorming would occur that may yield the most effective results for the client. In fact, depending on how the professionals view the nature of mental health, they may or may not involve the client as part of their team.

Internal Conflicts within Professions

For interdisciplinary work to be effective, the role of each professional must be clearly understood by all involved, including the client. One factor that may influence the difficulty of this task is how secure each professional is with his or her professional identity. Professions, like people, go through developmental stages. At various points in time, professional associations struggle with internal conflicts regarding their profession's identity, rifts between groups that would like to emphasize clinical practice and those that wish to focus on research, internal groups trying to create hierarchies of what type of practitioner may be considered the "most true" professional, and demands from external sources to become accountable in new or different ways. Similar to adolescents who may take a militant stance on an issue to avoid cognitive dissonance brought on by considering another's point of view, professionals who are insecure or operate from a sense of inferiority may also hold fast to "their right way" of conceptualizing clients' issues. They may present with a narrow self-definition and excessive professional pride to protect their identity (Kapp, 1987). They may also see the need to consult others as a reflection of their own inabilities and may fear being seen by others as incompetent. This, in turn, may lead to professionals practicing outside their scope of expertise.

Political Conflict and Economic Rivalry

Conflict may occur when members of one profession perceive that their own professional identity or their rights are being threatened or when members of different professions have conflicting ideas regarding what may be "best" for the clients involved (Julia & Thompson, 1994). Even when professionals agree on what interventions may be most effective in a given case, there are often disagreements regarding which professionals are competent to provide these services (Welfel, 1998). As funding sources for mental health services have gotten tighter over the years, there seems to be an increasing number of turf battles among professions that center on issues of dwindling resources rather than attending to the best interests of those seeking services.

Professionals are socialized or indoctrinated into a specific profession. This indoctrination may include subtle messages that one profession is superior to others, often based on arbitrary variables not supported by research, such as the name of the degree granted or positions taken by associations that master's-level clinicians shouldn't practice independently. These messages may override the standards cited in the codes and create dissonance for practitioners. Remley and Herlihy (2001) offered that two professionals may testify at a state legislative session on opposite sides of a mental health provider issue one day. The next day, these same professionals may find themselves members of a treatment team needing to work together in the best interest of a shared client. In such situations, it seems essential to put political differences aside, to focus on their client's need, and to discover what skills and knowledge each of them brings to the table.

Historically, psychiatry was the first "core provider" of mental health services noted in federal legislation and regulations. These laws directly and indirectly mandate which disciplines are eligible for reimbursement for federally funded services. States and private insurance companies have typically referred to federal statutes and regulations when formulating their criteria for recognition of providers of mental health services. This, in turn, determines who can be reimbursed for the provision of services. Psychology was the first nonmedical profession to be considered eligible to provide independent mental health services under federal- and state-funded programs. Social work was the first master's-level profession recognized for purposes of reimbursement. Over the past 25 years, the "newer" mental health professions of counseling and marriage and family therapy have also made gains in this arena. Each time one group of professionals has attempted to broaden its scope of practice through legislation or regulations, other professional associations have contested on grounds of inadequate training. As pointed out earlier, this may make it difficult for people from different professions to learn to value each other's expertise in relation to what a particular client may need.

RECOMMENDATIONS

Kapp (1987) contended that health and human service professionals need to be taught the wisdom of interprofessional cooperation as well as the technical tools of their trade. Educators of psychologists, counselors, social workers, marriage and family therapists, and psychiatrists are responsible for teaching their students about their ethical obligation to not only make referrals, but to learn about their colleagues from other professions. Educators can model this by asking colleagues from other fields to speak in their classes and by collaborating with them on research and writing projects. This may convey a true sense of valuing what other professions have to offer consumers and may help instill this attitude in their students.

As in learning to become culturally competent mental health practitioners, it is important to recognize our own biases and assumptions about practitioners who may appear to be the same as or different from us. To do so, professionals are encouraged to get beyond the titles on diplomas and to engage in a process of cultural sensitization similar to processes used to facilitate cross-cultural communication in counseling (Dombeck, 1997). To this end, it is important to talk to colleagues about their beliefs, their approaches to treatment, and their areas of expertise rather than operate from the information published by professional associations. Berg (1986) suggested that professionals practice self-monitoring of their attitudes about other professions and their own sense of anxiety and recognize how this may distort their perceptions of the worth of their colleagues. In addition, using the very communication skills professionals are trained to use with clients may lead to more effective interdisciplinary communications. For example, before reacting to what one believes one has heard during an interdisciplinary communication, it is helpful to paraphrase and confirm that is what the other person meant to convey. This seems especially important in situations fraught with stress due to underlying political or professional tension.

Similar to the use of informed consent practices with clients, delineating expectations regarding roles, functions, and responsibilities when first entering into an interdisciplinary relationship can help prevent problems later on. The more secure professionals are in their own identity and the more they can clearly articulate their perspectives, the better able they may be in dealing with different points of views presented by colleagues. This, in turn, may facilitate professionals' ability to draw on their different perspectives, values, and experiences when trying to make treatment decisions. When a decision made by a team or by other professionals working with a shared client raises ethical concerns, most codes of ethics recommend that these concerns first be addressed directly with the individuals involved. Effective interdisciplinary relationships do not, however, mean that mental health professionals should engage in treatment that they believe is ineffective or in other ways unethical. If disagreements cannot be resolved, ethical professionals pursue other avenues, such as reporting a colleague to a licensing board, to address their concerns consistent with client well-being.

SUMMARY

The appropriate use of interdisciplinary relationships is basic to good client care (American Psychiatric Association, 1980). Regardless of the difficulties involved, interdisciplinary interactions are essential when working with clients to resolve complex emotional, physical, psychological, social, economic, and spiritual needs. It is also one way to counteract feelings of isolation that many practitioners face in their own work (Glosoff, 1997; Kapp, 1987). Because of this, mental health professionals need to find ways to participate in respectful interprofessional relationships to best serve their clients and themselves.

References

American Association for Marriage and Family Therapy. (1998). *Code of ethics.* Washington, DC: Author.

American Counseling Association. (1995). *Code of ethics and standards of practice.* Alexandria, VA: Author.

American Psychiatric Association. (1980). Guidelines for psychiatrists in consultative, supervisory, or collaborative relationships with nonmedical therapists. *American Journal of Psychiatry, 137,* 1489–1491.

American Psychological Association. (1995). *Ethical principles of psychologists and code of conduct.* Washington, DC: Author.

Berg, M. (1986). Toward a diagnostic alliance between psychiatrist and psychologist. *American Psychologist, 41,* 52–59.

Bope, E., & Jost, T. (1994). Interprofessional collaboration factors that affect form, function, and structure. In M. Castro & M. Julia (Eds.), *Interprofessional care and collaborative practice* (pp. 61–69). Pacific Grove, CA: Brooks/Cole.

Dombeck, M. (1997). Professional personhood: Training, territoriality, and tolerance. *Journal of Interprofessional Care, 11,* 9–21.

Glosoff, H.L. (1997). Multiple relationship issues in private practice. In B. Herlihy & G. Corey

(Eds.), *Boundary issues in counseling: Multiple roles and responsibilities* (pp. 113–120). Alexandria, VA: American Counseling Association.

Julia, M., & Thompson, A. (1994). Group process and interprofessional teamwork. In M. Castro & M. Julia (Eds.), *Interprofessional care and collaborative practice* (pp. 35–41). Pacific Grove, CA: Brooks/Cole.

Kapp, M.B. (1987). Interprofessional relationships in geriatrics: Ethical and legal considerations. *The Gerontologist, 27*, 547–552.

Leach, M., Glosoff, H.L., & Overmier, B. (in press). International ethics codes: A follow-up study of previously unmatched standards and principles [CD-Rom]. In J.B. Overmier & J.A. Overmier (Eds.), *Psychology: IUPsyS Global Resource* (ed. 2001). Brighton, England: Psychology Press.

National Association of Social Workers. (1999). *Code of ethics.* Washington, DC: Author.

Remley, T.P., Jr., & Herlihy, B. (2001). *Ethical, legal, and professional issues in counseling.* Upper Saddle River, NJ: Merrill.

Waugaman, W.R. (1994). Professionalization and socialization in interprofessional collaboration. In M. Castro & M. Julia (Eds.), *Interprofessional care and collaborative practice* (pp. 23–31). Pacific Grove, CA: Brooks/Cole.

Welfel, E. (1998). *Ethics in counseling and psychotherapy.* Pacific Grove, CA: Brooks/Cole.

61   WHEN THERAPISTS FACE STRESS AND CRISIS

Self-Initiated Coping Strategies

Jeffrey A. Kottler and Margot Schofield

You sit in your office insulated from the rest of the world. Phone calls, spontaneous visitors, interruptions of any kind are rarely tolerated once you are in session. You are bound to keep virtually all proceedings within your domain confidential, holding inside you secrets that have never been shared before. Unless you arrange for consultation or supervision, the only people you talk to on a regular basis are the lost and the lonely, those who often have no place else to go and nobody else who will listen to them. These are people who are acutely distressed, who experience excruciating pain, and who may be extremely annoying for others to deal with. Some of them stay up late at night plotting ways to get underneath your skin; others can't help themselves but are just doing their best to defend themselves against perceived attacks. And these are just your colleagues—your clients are far worse.

Just kidding.

Sort of. Actually, seeing clients may be the least stressful part of your job. You also have mountains of paperwork to take care of—progress notes, treatment plans, quarterly summaries, insurance forms, logs, billing forms, scheduling information, appointment cards, letters to compose, and e-mail messages to respond to. Then there are the organizational politics, departmental squabbles, interpersonal conflicts, and power struggles that are often so much a part of organizational life.

If you are not feeling some degree of stress in your life, and not noticing the ways your personal life is affected by your work, then you are probably not paying very close attention. In addition, therapists who fail to address their stress and personal issues become not only depleted but impaired (Belson, 1992; Bernier, 1998; Kottler, 2000; Kottler & Hazler, 1996; Maslach, 1982; Sussman, 1995). They hide in their work as a way to avoid dealing with their own unresolved problems (Guy, 1987; Kottler, 1993). Most frightening of all, they develop a host of stress-related disorders that may be variously described as compassion fatigue (Figley, 1995), secondary trauma (Carbonell & Figley, 1996), malignant empathy (Breggin, 1997), vicarious trauma (Pearlman & Saakvitne, 1995), burnout (Bernier, 1998; Maslach, 1982), or rustout (Kottler & Zehm, 2000). This is especially the case without continual self-monitoring and restorative efforts.

THE NATURE OF CRISIS AND STRESS IN A THERAPIST'S LIFE

In addition to the effects of work on our personal lives, there is a corresponding influence of the ways events at home impact our work. Any crisis you experience related to your health, your family, your friends, your financial situation, your safety, or your career is also going to have some impact on your work (Kottler, 1993; Rabin, Feldman, & Kaplan, 1999).

The clients you see constantly push your buttons. They present problems that you have not fully resolved yourself. They struggle with issues related to death, personal meaning, mediocrity, fears, personal responsibility, temptation, impulsiveness—the same things that you face on a daily basis. They test you, try to manipulate you, and deceive you. Sometimes, they even try to hurt you.

In spite of the demands that you appear confident, poised, in control, and always the consummate expert, you must live with your own doubts and fears. Much of the time, you aren't completely sure what is going on with a particular case; you are winging it, doing the best you can. You are applying theories that you don't fully understand, treating disorders

that seem intractable, working with people who are so complex that you could never fully get a handle on who they are even if you had the rest of your life. Furthermore, you are working under tremendous time pressures. The client is impatient and wants instant results: "I would prefer we wrap this up today, but if necessary, I don't mind coming back another time." Supervisors are monitoring your progress, urging you to be more efficient. Third-party and managed care groups are looking over your shoulder, second-guessing your treatment decisions, and demanding that you function more cost-effectively.

You have your own life as well. You have family, friends, dreams, fantasies, ambitions, and chores to do. You don't have enough money or time. Everyone wants a piece of you. And you have problems of your own: Life is passing you by; you are getting older. And as a therapist, there is no place to hide. Every day you must face your worst fears.

The question is not whether you will face stress and crises in your life, but rather how you will deal with them. The good news, however, is that with some preventative work, in addition to remedial, self-initiated interventions as needed, you can enjoy a satisfying career and superior personal life unmatched by any other professional. What other job offers such opportunities to apply everything you learn at work to your personal life? And what other type of work allows you to apply everything you learn in your personal life to make yourself a more effective professional?

COMMON SOURCES OF STRESS IN A THERAPIST'S LIFE

Stress refers to the physiological, psychological, emotional, and behavioral changes people experience when they feel threatened or overwhelmed by life circumstances (Auerbach & Gramling, 1998). It represents a discrepancy between the demands of your job and your ability to respond in an effective manner (Rabin et al., 1999). Therapist stress arises from the same situations that challenge our clients: discrete events, ongoing role strains, daily hassles, contextual factors, and lifestyle issues (Kasl, 1983).

The symptoms of therapist stress manifest themselves in a host of ways, from counter-transference and burnout to severe decompensation (Kottler, 2000; Yassen, 1995). They include difficulties in cognitive functioning (confusion, memory deficits, irrational beliefs, perfectionism), emotional conditions (depression, sadness, anxiety, numbness), behavioral problems (withdrawal, isolation, inappropriate risk taking), and physical maladies (headaches, sleep disruption, addictions, lowered resistance).

Most of the sources of stress and crisis in a therapist's life originate in four main areas (Kottler, 1992). In *work environment stress,* we are faced with demanding time pressures, excessive paperwork, rules and restrictions on our freedom, organizational politics, colleagues who are less than supportive, as well as supervisors who may be less than competent. There is *event-related stress* that emanates from our personal lives, including such things as health issues, developmental transitions, and legal or financial problems. A third set of challenges arises from *client-induced stress,* the sort sparked by angry outbursts, accusations of incompetence, suicidal threats, premature termination, and so-called difficult clients. Finally, there is *self-induced stress* that results from our own feelings of perfectionism, excessive rumination about cases, emotional depletion, unhealthy lifestyle, self-doubt, physical exhaustion, and fears of failure.

Among these broad areas, most of the attention in the literature has been focused on work-related stress and burnout (Cushway & Tyler, 1994; Sowa, May, & Niles, 1994; Vredenburgh, Carlozzi, & Stein, 1999). This means that little guidance is offered to us in our struggles to cope with our own personal issues that are sparked by clinical work.

Several factors are most commonly associated with stress in a therapist's work. These include maintaining the therapeutic relationship, identifying and working with difficulties in the therapeutic process, professional doubts, involvement with clients, and personal depletion (Hellman, Morrison, & Abramowitz,

1987). In addition, certain types of clients are experienced as more stressful than others (Bloomfield, 1997; Kottler, 1992). These include those who are angry, sadomasochistic, and suffering from major personality disorders, sexual abuse, and eating disorders. Perhaps most debilitating of all for therapists is dealing with clients who are actively suicidal (Cooper, 2000; Fox & Cooper, 1998).

Among personal factors that are often reported by therapists as sources of stress in their lives, frequently mentioned are little time available for one's family, difficulty switching roles from therapist to family member, setting unrealistic standards for one's own relationships, and family members tired of being treated or talked to like clients (Wetchler & Piercy, 1986). For those who practice family therapy on a regular basis, additional situations often cited include the added complexity of dealing with several individuals, differing expectations or desires about required changes, differing motivation levels among family members, attempts to get the therapist to side with particular family members, being confronted with one's own family-of-origin issues, and a sense of outrage about some family dynamics, such as child abuse or domestic violence (Barker, 1997).

SIDE EFFECTS OF BEING A THERAPIST
THAT EXACERBATE STRESS

Although all therapists face stress in their lives to some degree, individuals differ in their responses and the coping strategies they use depending on their attitudes, sense of personal mastery, hardiness, social supports, work experience, and self-care (Funk, 1992; Sowa et al., 1994; Varma, 1997). Personality factors also play a role because professionals seem more vulnerable if they are prone to passivity, impatience, low frustration tolerance, and poor impulse control (Maslach, 1982). Among all the factors mentioned, an internal locus of control seems particularly important to help therapists stop the downward spiral that often occurs when usual self-care strategies are abandoned (Koeske & Kirk, 1995).

Most of these dangers and side effects can be addressed if therapists monitor closely their ongoing personal and professional functioning levels and take proactive steps to counteract symptoms, and sources of stress, before things get out of hand.

STRATEGIES FOR WORKING THROUGH STRESS

Several strategies have been found consistently helpful to therapists in their efforts to reduce stress levels in their lives and work. Many of these methods are familiar to us because they are similar to what we recommend for our own clients.

Self-Care

Unless we take care of ourselves, we are not much good at taking care of others. In surveys of coping strategies preferred by therapists, activities frequently mentioned include increased social support, regular exercise, and supervision (Cushway & Tyler 1994; Jensen, 1995). Yet, among the options selected, surprisingly only 1% of clinicians actually sought therapy themselves for their problems (Arvay & Uhlemann, 1996).

Self-Awareness

Promoting greater self-awareness is a key strategy in improving quality of life and in coping with stress, not only in clients' lives but in our own. Through early recognition of signs and symptoms, we have a greater capacity to choose how to respond to the stressors. Strategies for developing self-awareness have been developed in most therapeutic systems and include personal therapy, dream analysis, relaxation, meditation, yoga, journaling, and participation in group work, particularly those groups with a strong experiential focus.

It may be useful to reflect on questions such as the following, as well as to talk about them to trusted confidantes:

- What haunts you the most and continues to plague you during vulnerable moments?

- In what ways are you less than fully functioning in your personal and professional life?
- What are some aspects of your lifestyle that are unhealthy?
- What are your most difficult, conflicted, and dysfunctional relationships?
- How does all of this impact your work with clients?

Intimacy

Intimacy is often a two-edged sword for therapists. The intimacy associated with therapy is often what draws us to this work in the first place as one of our greatest rewards. However, such intense relationships, often scheduled back-to-back, also create a number of problems. That is one reason it is important not only to balance our caseload, but also to maintain solid friendships, love relationships, and collegial affiliations.

It is part of our training and experience to be relationship experts, highly skilled at building trust and intimacy rather quickly. Ideally, we use those same abilities to establish more satisfying love relationships with those who matter most: our family and friends.

Personal Therapy

It is one of the great ironies (and hypocrisies) of our profession that we are often unwilling to seek help ourselves (Guy, Poelstra, & Stark, 1989). What sort of confidence must we have in our craft if we don't believe therapy is suitable or appropriate when we are encountering difficulties? What sort of modeling are we demonstrating for the rest of the world when we appear so reluctant to solicit for ourselves what we think is so important for others?

Personal therapy can take a number of different forms in addition to traditional methods. For those of us who are unusually resistant to "talking cures" because of a tendency to intellectualize, overanalyze, and act as spectators rather than participants in the process, other therapeutic experiences such as transformative travel or adventure-based activities can be helpful (Kottler, 1997; Kottler & Montgomery, 2000).

Stress Management Techniques

Just as we might teach them to our clients, it is critical to have at our disposal ways for metabolizing stress and dealing with crisis situations. Some clinicians find it useful to keep a journal as a way to work through personal struggles and dump intense emotional material. Others employ variations of relaxation training, yoga, meditation, deep breathing, martial arts, and cognitive monitoring. One key seems to involve doing whatever is possible to remain flexible in response to changing circumstances. There will always be shifting environmental stressors to which we must adapt.

Difficult Clients

Therapists are most likely to experience stress when they encounter clients who are angry, manipulative, seductive, or resistant (Caldwell, 1992; Kottler, 1992). Other chapters in this volume discuss this challenge at greater depth. A key strategy in managing intense anger in clients is to remain calm and in control of one's own emotions—not to take things personally (of course, this is easier said than done). This helps to provide reassurance and containment of the client's diminished control, and avoids the escalation of the emotions that may result from the client's vigilance toward any perceived threat. It also serves to reduce anxiety among all participants in the relationship (Novaco & Chemtob, 1998).

In each of these situations, as well as any other stressful events that are part of a therapist's life and work, it is far better to prevent them before they get out of hand. As with any other mental health issue, the best coping strategies are those that help clients (and their therapists) to rehearse methods ahead of time, recognize the earliest signs of difficulty, and apply practiced interventions (Miller, 1998; Rowe, 1999).

Practicing What You Preach

One of the most important benefits of our profession is that we have not only permission but a mandate to apply to ourselves what we do with others. What sort of hypocrite would we be if we did not demonstrate in our own lives what we claim is so important for our clients?

Many therapists frequently report that the best part of our job includes all the ways we can apply our knowledge and skills to improve our own personal functioning. Depending on preferred theoretical orientations and therapeutic strategies, this can include such things as disputing our own irrational beliefs (I must help everyone all of the time), creating more meaning in our lives (There is value in the pain I sometimes face), taking greater personal responsibility (I am experiencing the consequences of my own choices), demonstrating greater flexibility (What can I try instead of what is not working?), and uncovering consistent patterns (How is what I am experiencing now related to what I have faced before?). It is also helpful to listen to the advice we offer to others:

- Examine your own fears of failure.
- Confront tendencies toward perfectionism.
- Be realistic about what can and cannot be done.
- Diversify your life as much as possible.
- Build a better support system.
- Set clearer limits and boundaries.
- Get help when you need it.

Obviously, the better we are at applying our favorite interventions to ourselves, the more skilled we become using them with others. Just as important is all the practice we get every day helping clients deal with their crises and challenges. If we are paying attention, this can only make us better able to face our own stress.

References

Arvay, M.J., & Uhlemann, M.R. (1996). Counsellor stress in the field of trauma: A preliminary study. *Canadian Journal of Counselling, 30,* 193–210.

Auerbach, S.M., & Grambling, S.E. (1998). *Stress management: Psychological foundations.* Upper Saddle River, NJ: Prentice-Hall.

Barker, P. (1997). Stress in psychotherapists who work with dysfunctional families. In V.P. Varma

(Ed.), *Stress in psychotherapists* (pp. 87–100). London: Routledge.

Belson, R. (1992, September/October). Ten tried-and-true methods to achieve therapist burnout. *Family Therapy Networker*, 22.

Bernier, D. (1998). A study of coping: Successful recovery from severe burnout and other reactions to severe work-related stress. *Work and Stress, 12*, 50–65.

Bloomfield, I. (1997). Stress in psychotherapists working outside the National Health Service. In V.P. Varma (Ed.), *Stress in psychotherapists* (pp. 210–229). London: Routledge.

Breggin, P.R. (1997). *The heart of being helpful: Empathy and the creation of a healing presence.* New York: Springer.

Caldwell, M.F. (1992). Incidence of PTSD among staff victims of patient violence. *Hospital and Community Psychiatry, 43*, 838–839.

Carbonell, J.L., & Figley, C.R. (1996). When trauma hits home: Personal trauma and the family therapist. *Journal of Marital and Family Therapy, 22*, 53–58.

Cooper, G. (2000, March/April). When clients kill themselves. *Family Therapy Networker*, 16.

Cushway, D., & Tyler, P.A. (1994). Stress and coping in counselling psychologists. *Stress Medicine, 31*, 169–179.

Figley, C.R. (1995). Compassion fatigue: Toward a new understanding of the costs of caring. In B.H. Stamm (Ed.), *Secondary traumatic stress* (pp. 3–28). Lutherville, MD: Sidran Press.

Fox, R., & Cooper, M. (1998). The effects of suicide on the private practitioner. *Clinical Social Work Journal, 26*, 143–157.

Funk, S.C. (1992). Hardiness: A review of theory and research. *Health Psychology, 11*, 335–345.

Guy, J.D. (1987). *The personal life of the psychotherapist.* New York: Wiley.

Guy, J.D., Poelstra, P.L., & Stark, M.J. (1989). Personal distress and therapeutic effectiveness: National survey of psychologists practicing psychotherapy. *Professional Psychology: Research and Practice, 20*, 48–50.

Hellman, J.D., Morrison, T.L., & Abramowitz, S.I. (1987). Therapist experience and the stresses of psychotherapeutic work. *Psychotherapy, 24*, 171–175.

Jensen, K. (1995). The stresses of counsellors in training. In W. Dryden (Ed.), *The stresses of counselling in action* (pp. 184–196). London: Sage.

Kasl, S.V. (1983). Pursuing the link between stressful life experiences and disease: A time for reappraisal. In C.L. Cooper (Ed.), *Stress research: Issues for the eighties* (pp. 79–102). New York: Wiley.

Koeske, G.F., & Kirk, S.A. (1995). Direct and buffering effects of internal locus of control among mental health professionals. *Journal of Social Service Research, 20*, 1–28.

Kottler, J.A. (1992). *Compassionate therapy: Working with difficult clients.* San Francisco: Jossey-Bass.

Kottler, J.A. (1993). *On being a therapist.* San Francisco: Jossey-Bass.

Kottler, J.A. (1997). *Travel that can change your life.* San Francisco: Jossey-Bass.

Kottler, J.A. (2000). *Doing good: Passion and commitment for helping others.* Philadelphia: Accelerated Development.

Kottler, J.A., & Hazler, R. (1996). Impaired counselors: The dark side brought into light. *Journal of Humanistic Education and Development, 34(3)*, 98–107.

Kottler, J.A., & Montgomery, M. (2000). Prescriptive travel and adventure-based activities as adjuncts to counselling. *Guidance and Counselling, 15(2)*, 8–11.

Kottler, J.A., & Zehm, S. (2000). *On being a teacher: The human dimension.* Thousand Oaks, CA: Corwin Press.

Maslach, C. (1982). *Burnout: The cost of caring.* Englewood Cliffs, NJ: Prentice Hall.

Miller, L. (1998). Our own medicine: Traumatized psychotherapists and the stresses of doing therapy. *Psychotherapy, 35*, 137–146.

Novaco, R.W., & Chemtob, C.M. (1998). Anger and trauma: Conceptualization, assessment, and treatment. In V.M. Follette & J.I. Ruzek (Eds.), *Cognitive-behavioral therapies for trauma* (pp. 162–190). New York: Guilford Press.

Rabin, S., Feldman, D., & Kaplan, Z. (1999). Stress and intervention strategies in mental health professionals. *British Journal of Medical Psychology, 72*, 159–169.

Rowe, M.M. (1999). Teaching health-care providers coping: Results of a two year study. *Journal of Behavioral Medicine, 22*, 511–527.

Sowa, C.J., May, K.M., & Niles, S.G. (1994). Occupational stress within the counseling profession: Implications for counselor training. *Counselor Education and Supervision, 34*, 19–29.

Sussman, M.E. (Ed.). (1995). *A perilous calling: The hazards of psychotherapy practice.* New York: Wiley.

Varma, V.P. (Ed.). (1997). *Stress in psychotherapists.* London: Routledge.

Vredenburgh, L.D., Carlozzi, A.F., & Stein, L.B. (1999). Burnout in counselling psychologists: Type of practice setting and pertinent demographics. *Counselling Psychology Quarterly, 12,* 283–302.

Wetchler, J.L., & Piercy, F.P. (1986). The marital/family life of the family therapist: Stressors and enhancers. *American Journal of Family Therapy, 14,* 99–108.

Yassen, J. (1995). Preventing secondary traumatic stress disorder. In C.R. Figley (Ed.), *Compassion fatigue* (pp. 178–208). New York: Brunner/Mazel.

62   TREATMENT FAILURES

Opportunities for Learning

Laura J. Veach

The only people who never fail are those who never try.

—Ilka Chase

Failure is instructive. The person who really thinks learns quite as much from his failures as from his successes.

—John Dewey

Clinicians working in mental health settings commonly experience treatment failure. One of the challenges of a discussion of treatment failure is operationally defining the term failure. For example, a client may suddenly drop out of treatment, an event many clinicians classify as treatment failure, yet the client may continue to make positive life changes as a result of the counseling prior to dropout. In his work on single-session therapy, Talmon (1990) cites a high frequency of single-session therapy that has been well documented over the past 30 years in numerous settings using various therapeutic approaches. In his own research, Talmon found that 78% of clients

who had attended only one counseling session reported positive outcomes. During one-year follow-up interviews, clients reported that "they got what they wanted . . . and felt better or much better about the problem that had led them to seek therapy" (p. 9). However, in addiction treatment, for example, research clearly indicates that better client outcomes are achieved with clients who complete treatment (Bell, Williams, Nelson, & Spence, 1994; Fals-Stewart & Schafer, 1992; Manu, Burleson, & Kranzler, 1994).

Treatment failure can best be defined as (1) lack of progress, (2) worsening of symptoms, and (3) client dissatisfaction with the course of counseling. In addition, this chapter focuses on examining outcomes from the mental health professional's viewpoint. For the purposes of this chapter, failure is best viewed on a continuum ranging from more positive, desired outcomes of treatment to more negative outcomes. The more negative the outcome, the greater the degree of failure.

Four major terms relate to treatment failure: noncompliance, premature termination, dropout, and relapse. *Noncompliance* is an aspect of a relatively unsuccessful treatment experience in which the client is unwilling to complete specific therapeutic assignments. The client may continue to attend sessions but does not comply with the defined plan of care. Examples include the client who attends counseling sessions with a stated goal of sobriety yet drinks alcohol surreptitiously. Clients who are mandated to attend treatment by family, loved ones, courts, or employers are at greater risk for noncompliance (Clark, 1999).

Premature termination is defined as agreeing to a particular number of sessions, but ending counseling prior to that point *with notification* to the clinician and often in opposition to the clinician's objections. The client may have made significant progress and may acknowledge the need for further care, yet chooses to terminate counseling for other reasons. Some researchers have argued that therapists have different and varying criteria for classifying early termination and that the determination of how much counseling is sufficient really should rest with the client, not the clinician (Samstag, Batchelder, Muran, Safran, & Winston, 1998).

Dropout status is defined as leaving treatment *without notification*. This action by the client can be alarming for the counselor, especially if the client has a history of harmful behavior to self or others.

Relapse is a term often used with regard to substance use disorders and severe mental illness, referring to a client's return to the use of mood-altering substances or processes. The mental health professional often defines relapse as failure, the most negative outcome. This term can refer to the worsening or reappearance of undesired symptoms in a client. Examples include a person with Schizophrenia who fails to continue a prescribed treatment protocol, resulting in a psychotic episode, or a patient with Bipolar Disorder who attempts suicide.

Several possible causes of treatment failure have been hypothesized, but most research examines treatment completers and ignores failures (Sexton, Whiston, Bleuer, & Walz, 1997). When failure is examined, *resistance* is often cited. Resistance refers to the various ways in which a client passively opposes therapeutic change (Young, 2001). Clients who dislike their clinician are likely to experience negative outcomes in the treatment experience (Young, 2001). Differences in class, race, gender, ethnicity, communication style, religious preference, therapeutic approach, and appearance can spark resistance and failure. Clinicians who use the initial stage of counseling to build rapport and move slowly into treatment interventions may reduce the risk.

Empirical studies of the relation between particular therapeutic approaches and failure have had mixed results (Byrne, 1995; Sexton et al., 1997). Some findings do support the importance of the client-counselor interaction as an important factor for reducing treatment failure (Sexton et al., 1997). Research by Samstag et al. (1998) found that the client's experience of the therapeutic relationship with the clinician could be an important predictor of outcome. Certainly, more research into specific factors contributing to negative outcomes is needed.

SOURCES OF TREATMENT FAILURE

Four possible sources—client, counselor, system, and society (Young, 2001)—should be carefully reviewed either to prevent failure or to better understand what happened. Several *client characteristics* increase the risk of treatment failure. One occurs when the client enters counseling with an expectation of instant remedies. This risk can be minimized when, at the initiation of services, clinicians carefully assess client expectations for counseling. Another source of treatment failure is an inability or unwillingness of the client to trust the counselor. Clients who have a history of betrayal are particularly vulnerable to treatment failure because they have difficulty trusting the counselor. In this circumstance, the clinician needs to identify past trauma and normalize the mistrust the client is experiencing.

Other sources increasing the risk of treatment failure include clients who demonstrate overcontrolling behaviors such as dominating sessions or dictating treatment guidelines. In addition, clients who have biologically based disorders, personality disorders, or substance use problems are more likely to experience treatment failure. When working with clients with these diagnoses, clinicians who wish to minimize the risk of treatment failure need to be fully competent in and sensitive to the complex issues such diagnoses present.

Next, sources of treatment failure may relate to the *mental health professional*. Treatment failure is tied to incompetent practice; whenever clinicians practice in areas in which they are underqualified there is an increased risk of treatment failure. In addition, when otherwise competent counselors utilize an intervention that proves unsuccessful or one that does not match the client's needs, negative outcomes can result. Some mental health professionals who experience a higher incidence of negative outcomes need to examine their own resistance in meeting clients where they are (i.e., starting with an understanding of the client's worldview). Failure to attend to a client's worldview is evidence of insensitivity to issues of cultural diversity. Not surprisingly, unethical practices, treatment by impaired professionals, and the use of shaming messages from the clinician (e.g., the clinician comments on incomplete counseling assignments in a negative, scolding manner) are also tied to treatment failures.

The managed behavioral health care *system* has been cited as an important negative influence on treatment effectiveness (Acuff et al., 1999; Murphy, DeBernardo, & Shoemaker, 1998; Phelps, Eisman, & Kohout, 1998). In the third-party and managed care reimbursement system, limits of authorization for care are seen by clinicians as major problems. Clinicians argue that payors set limits arbitrarily, with little sensitivity to individual client levels of progress. Because clients often do not have the personal resources to self-pay for services, they feel little choice but to terminate even if not significantly improved. In addition, current compromises in confidentiality with managed care organizations (MCOs) may increase negative outcomes as clients become reluctant to reveal personal information vital to effective treatment (Davis & Meier, 2001; Welfel, 1998). When clinicians spend inordinate amounts of time on record keeping, they have less time to develop, provide, or monitor the impact of services on clients. In this environment, it is not surprising that treatment failure occurs.

Two other systemic issues negatively affect treatment: poor communication and delays in providing treatment when sought. Poor communication from a referral source to the client or the clinician is a frequent problem. An employer who mandates counseling yet provides clinicians no information about precipitating factors for the referral illustrates this problem. This lack of collateral information can slow the development of a strong therapeutic alliance and reduce the effectiveness of interventions used. Long waits for treatment also raise the risk of treatment failure because clients often lose motivation during the waiting period.

Finally, *social* attitudes and policies influence the incidence of negative outcomes. First, the stigma associated with seeking mental health treatment makes many people reluctant to ask for professional help. Some delay initiation of services until the problem has gotten to unmanageable levels. So, when treatment is sought, more intense treatment is needed and more attention is required to establish a satisfactory therapeutic alliance than might be the case if no stigma were attached to mental health care. The cost of counseling, both in dollars and in time, also adds to client reluctance. The expense is substantial, sources of insurance reimbursement are shrinking, and client ability or willingness to self-pay for services is low. The stigma and costs of counseling also reduce support for counseling from external resources, such as employers, family, schools, and courts, and thereby indirectly contribute to treatment failure.

LESSONS FROM FAILURE

How do we learn from our failures? Negative outcomes should be systematically reviewed to learn from these events. As Coyne (1999) states, "Reliance on clinical judgment as the sole source of evaluation is no longer the standard of practice . . . outcome measurement is the new standard" (p. 12). Currently, United Way expects agencies receiving their funding support to conduct outcome studies and offers step-by-step models for developing an outcome measurement system (Hatry, van Houten, Plantz, & Greenway, 1996). Quality of care accrediting organizations, such as the Joint Commission on Accreditation of Healthcare Organizations (JCAHO) and the Commission on Accreditation of Rehabilitation Facilities (CARF), also provide specific quality of care standards in behavioral health and have extensive information on outcome measurement criteria.

Outcome data are clinicians' most reliable source of information on the value of their work. How can clinicians know what is or is not working effectively without reliable, objective outcome data? An honest look at unsuccessful work, as painful as that process can be, is an essential ingredient to confidence in the quality of the care provided. Needless to say, data demonstrating the positive effects of counseling are equally valuable in understanding treatment failure.

In clinical practice, several obstacles exist to the systematic collection and study of outcome data, not the least of which is time or budget constraints (Ogles, Lambert, & Masters, 1996). To streamline the process, clinicians should follow five basic steps. First, clinicians should determine the three most important treatment outcomes to measure (e.g., mood stability, family change, symptom reduction, dropout rate, premature termination rate, relapse incidence). Then, they should carefully evaluate both time and cost. Can data already collected (e.g., number of dropouts) be utilized? Third, they must identify study participants and weigh advantages and disadvantages of the plan. Disadvantages of collecting outcome data may include counselor time requirements, increased work to elicit data, and decisions about missing data (Ogles et al., 1996). Fourth, consulting current literature or specialists in outcome evaluation is helpful. For example, academicians

might be interested in collaborating on outcome studies as a part of their research agenda. Time spent in the initial design stage can reduce many problems once the outcome study has begun. Finally, and most important, counselors need to assess how the information will be used to change counseling practice. By targeting a small number of areas to measure, clinicians enhance the final aspect of outcome measurement, namely, taking the information collected and administering pertinent changes.

Strategies to Improve Client Outcomes and Reduce Failure

1. Utilize data to (a) understand trends of noncompliance, premature termination, dropout, and relapse; (b) implement changes directly related to data analysis; and (c) continue ongoing evaluation and focus on answering the question, "How do I know clients are better off after receiving the counseling than they were before?" (Hatry et al., 1996).
2. Evaluate clinical (not administrative) supervision and training needs and obtain needed expertise.
3. Examine thoroughness of diagnostic workup and consider supplemental assessment tools. Most dropouts occur early in the treatment process (Samstag et al., 1998).
4. Review treatment plans carefully with client for clarity and completeness. One study found more extensive treatment plans were significant in predicting improved retention of clients in treatment (Veach, Remley, Kippers, & Sorg, 2000).
5. Utilize cocounselors in group counseling settings if at all possible (Coyne, 1999).
6. Attend to self-care issues; address burnout factors consistently. Follow practice guidelines for ethical standards of care.

When learning from cases with negative outcomes, it may be helpful to focus on the specific aspects of failure:

- *Noncompliance.* Consider changing past strategies employed to address noncompliance. For example, in the case of a client diagnosed with Borderline Personality Disorder who is continuing to engage in self-injury, involve a clinician who specializes in Dialectical Behavioral Therapy (DBT) and seek training in this clinical approach, which has extensive outcome analysis to support its effectiveness (Linehan, 1993).

- *Premature termination.* Consider factors that contribute to premature termination. Do follow-up interviews indicate a trend of positive or negative outcomes with premature discharges from treatment? Are positive changes evident? Does the client feel pressured to end treatment prematurely? This may happen when the MCO case manager authorizes only a few visits and the client's financial problems prevent him or her from paying for future visits out of pocket. The counselor must carefully weigh the best alternatives in this scenario. Should the denial be appealed? Should payments be extended?

- *Dropout.* Conduct follow-up studies either by phone or letter. Solicit input from the former client regarding the effectiveness of counseling: what went well, what was unsatisfactory, and what beneficial changes occurred as a result of counseling.

- *Relapse.* This is perhaps the most serious aspect of treatment failure and often the greatest area of concern for the counselor. Charges of malpractice may occur when clients believe relapse led to harm. A lawsuit may cite that failure to treat the client effectively resulted in harm (e.g., suicide). One element of a plaintiff's case against a counselor includes client injury after "the counselor failed to conform to the required duty of care" (Remley & Herlihy, 2001, p. 146). Although difficult to prove malpractice, suing mental health professionals has substantially increased since 1990 (Remley & Herlihy, 2001). Carefully study each incident of relapse by reviewing the written plan of care and decide whether further intervention may be beneficial. Consult a clinical supervisor regarding the effectiveness of the approach in each relapse case. Note any trends and address these accordingly.

SUMMARY

Treatment failures regularly occur in mental health settings. It is important for the clinician to reduce the risk of failure by means of the following:

- Devise a standard of care to regularly examine and learn from client outcomes, including positive and negative outcomes.
- Utilize positive accomplishments to serve as resources for addressing negative outcomes.
- Seek clinical supervision/consultation on a regular basis.
- Continue ongoing professional development.
- Practice within the boundaries of competence.
- Provide timely written treatment plan information to clients.
- Identify areas for change based on outcome data and implement changes with ongoing evaluation.
- Keep abreast of current literature and research findings.
- Utilize quality-of-care resources, such as credentialing organizations (e.g., JCAHO).
- Advocate for clients with MCOs and work for public policies that reduce obstacles to treatment.
- Follow ethical guidelines.

References

Acuff, C., Bennett, B.E., Bricklin, P.M., Canter, M.B., Knapp. S.J., Moldawsky, S., & Phelps, R. (1999). Considerations for ethical practice in managed care. *Professional Psychology: Research and Practice, 30,* 563–575.

Bell, D.C., Williams, M.L., Nelson, R., & Spence, R.T. (1994). An experimental test of retention in residential and outpatient programs. *American Journal of Drug and Alcohol Abuse, 20,* 331–340.

Byrne, R.H. (1995). *Becoming a master counselor: Introduction to the profession.* Pacific Grove, CA: Brooks/Cole.

Clark, D.A. (1999). Case conceptualization and treatment failure: A commentary. *Journal of Cognitive Psychotherapy: An International Quarterly, 13,* 331–337.

Coyne, R.K. (1999). *Failures in group work: How we can learn from our mistakes.* Thousand Oaks, CA: Sage.

Davis, S.R., & Meier, S.T. (2001). *The elements of managed care: A guide for helping professionals.* Belmont, CA: Wadsworth.

Fals-Stewart, W., & Schafer, J. (1992). The relationship between length of stay in drug-free therapeutic communities and neurocognitive functioning. *Journal of Clinical Psychology, 48,* 539–543.

Hatry, H., van Houten, T., Plantz, M.C., & Greenway, M.T. (1996). *Measuring program outcomes: A practical approach.* Alexandria, VA: United Way of America.

Linehan, M.M. (1993). *Cognitive-behavioral treatment of borderline personality disorder.* New York: Guilford Press.

Manu, P., Burleson, J.A., & Kranzler, H.R. (1994). Patient predictors of irregular discharge from inpatient substance abuse treatment. *American Journal on Addictions, 3,* 122–128.

Murphy, M.J., DeBernardo, C.R., & Shoemaker, W.E. (1998). Impact of managed care on independent practice and professional ethics: A survey of independent practitioners. *Professional Psychology: Research and Practice, 29,* 43–51.

Ogles, B.M., Lambert, M.J., & Masters, K.S. (1996). *Assessing outcome in clinical practice.* Boston: Allyn & Bacon.

Phelps, R., Eisman, E.J., & Kohout, J. (1998). Psychological practice and managed care: Results of the CAPP practitioner survey. *Professional Psychology: Research and Practice, 29,* 31–36.

Remley, T.P., & Herlihy, B. (2001). *Ethical, legal, and professional issues in counseling.* Upper Saddle River, NJ: Merrill-Prentice Hall.

Samstag, L.W., Batchelder, S.T., Muran, J.C., Safran, J.D., & Winston, A. (1998). Early identification of treatment failures in short-term psychotherapy: An assessment of therapeutic alliance and interpersonal behavior. *Journal of Psychotherapy Practice and Research, 7,* 126–143.

Sexton, T.L., Whiston, S.C., Bleuer, J.C., & Walz, G.R. (1997). *Integrating outcome research into counseling practice and training.* Alexandria, VA: American Counseling Association.

Talmon, M. (1990). *Single-session therapy: Maximizing the effect of the first (and often only) therapeutic encounter.* San Francisco: Jossey-Bass.

Veach, L.J., Remley, T.P., Kippers, S., & Sorg, J. (2000). Retention predictors related to intensive outpatient programs for substance use disorders. *American Journal of Drug and Alcohol Abuse, 26,* 417–428.

Welfel, E.R. (1998). *Ethics in counseling and psychotherapy: Standards, research, and emerging issues.* Pacific Grove, CA: Wadsworth.

Young, M.E. (2001). *Learning the art of helping: Building blocks and techniques* (2nd ed.). Upper Saddle River, NJ: Prentice-Hall.

Additional Recommended Resources

Heppner, P.P., Kivlighan, D.M., & Wampold, B.E. (1992). *Research design in counseling.* Pacific Grove, CA: Brooks/Cole.

Luborsky, L., Crits-Christoph, P., Mintz, J., & Auerbach, A. (1988). *Who will benefit from psychotherapy? Predicting therapeutic outcomes.* New York: Basic Books.

Walz, G.R., & Bleuer, J.C. (1993). *Counselor efficacy: Assessing and using counseling outcomes research.* Ann Arbor, MI: ERIC Counseling and Personnel Services Clearinghouse.

Web Sites

The Commission on Accreditation of Rehabilitation Facilities
www.carf.org

The Joint Commission on Accreditation of Healthcare Organizations
www.jcaho.org

National Guideline Clearinghouse (a resource for evidence-based clinical practice guidelines)
www.guidelines.gov

National Institute of Mental Health
www.nimh.nih.gov

PART IX
Ethical and Legal Issues

63 ETHICS COMPLAINTS

Procedures for Filing and Responding

Carmen Braun Williams

Mental health professionals are required to adhere to codes of ethics and state licensing regulations while engaged in mental health practice. These codes serve at least two primary functions: They establish guidelines for responsible mental health delivery and protect consumers from unethical and illegal conduct by counselors. It is the responsibility of all mental health professionals to be very familiar with and knowledgeable about the codes, statutes, and laws that govern their practice.

Most codes of ethics, including those of the American Counseling Association (ACA, 1995), the American Psychological Association (APA, 1992), and the National Association of Social Workers (NASW, 1999), reflect parameters that are both aspirational and mandatory. For example, the preamble for each of the aforementioned codes is intended to guide the mental health professional "toward the highest ideals" of the profession (APA, 1992, Preamble). These ideal values and perspectives are grounded in a specified set of ethical principles and standards of practice. Although ethics codes and standards of practice provide a yardstick against which ethical practice can be measured, because they tend to be general they cannot be relied on to completely solve many of the complex ethical questions that arise in practice.

Many factors mitigate the ability of professional ethics codes to address specific issues. One factor is the diversity of settings, populations, and functions that characterize professional practice (Pedersen, 1995). Counselors engage in psychotherapy, supervision, case management, research, and education, and perform these roles in business settings, educational institutions, agencies, and private practice. Thus, the language of professional ethics codes is necessarily broad to address a multitude of practice arenas (Herlihy & Corey, 1996; Welfel, 1998). The advantage of broadly based codes of ethics is that they allow counselors flexibility when confronting unique or complex circumstances. The disadvantage, especially for professionals seeking specific direction when faced with complicated ethical questions, is that codes of ethics alone often are insufficient in supplying answers. Consequently, determining the most ethical course of action when difficult situations arise means relying on additional resources and following clear and sequential steps in a careful deliberation process (Corey, Corey, & Callanan, 1998; Forester-Miller & Davis, n.d.; Herlihy & Corey, 1996; Kenyon, 1999; Steinman, Richardson, & McEnroe, 1998; Welfel, 1998).

In addition, in some instances, statements in professional codes of ethics conflict with legal statutes, emphasizing even more the need for counselors to seek out additional guidance (Corey et al., 1998; Herlihy & Corey, 1996). Most mental health professional associations have ethics committees, typically at both the national and state levels, a primary function of which is to educate members about their code of ethics. This frequently takes the form of responding to ethics inquiries. For example, a member can call or write to the national or state office and inquire as to whether a certain course of action would constitute an ethical violation. Responses to these inquiries typically detail relevant sections of the code in an effort to offer direction. Such consultation can be very helpful, especially in clarifying ambiguities in the ethical decision-making process.

Despite ethics codes, laws, and other sources of information and guidance, even well-intentioned counselors make mistakes. Certainly many, if not most, therapeutic mistakes can be handled within the context of the counseling relationship and resolved satisfactorily at that level. However, some mistakes are more egregious and may constitute an ethical violation. These situations may come to the attention of counselors through direct observation or reports by students, clients, and colleagues. Professional ethics codes require counselors to take action when they learn of potential ethics violations yet provide options for the kind of action to be taken. Options include consulting with ethics committees, as described above, and consulting with colleagues or others knowledgeable about ethics in an effort to determine whether the behavior observed or reported constitutes a violation of the code of ethics.

If these consultations strengthen a counselor's belief that an ethical violation has occurred, ethics codes require counselors to take appropriate action "when they possess reasonable cause that raises doubts as to whether counselors or other mental health professionals are acting in an ethical manner" (ACA, 1995a, p. 16). Ethics codes offer two courses of action in these cases: an informal course in which the counselor approaches and attempts to resolve the issue directly with the other counselor, and a formal course of action in

which the counselor files a complaint with the appropriate ethics committee. One factor that always must be considered first as counselors weigh their options is whether a client's confidentiality would be violated. Counselors in most circumstances cannot act on information about another mental health professional without the client's consent. Welfel (1998) identified additional factors for counselors to weigh in determining whether to pursue formal or informal avenues, including the seriousness of the potential violation.

The remainder of this chapter outlines procedures for filing formal ethics complaints. Information about how to respond if a complaint is filed against you also is reviewed.

PROCEDURES FOR FILING FORMAL COMPLAINTS

Professional ethics committees serve not only an educational function, as described above, but also an adjudicative purpose. Explicit rules and procedures for filing, investigating, and deciding the outcome of complaints guide the adjudication process by these administrative bodies. Thus, these written procedures facilitate a process by which unethical mental health practice is monitored and sanctioned, and in this manner, work to protect the public. The careful process by which complaints are evaluated also serves to protect mental health professionals from groundless and/or unsubstantiated accusations of unethical practice.

The scope of ethics committees' rules and procedures includes specifying procedures for evaluating the validity of allegations of unethical conduct; specifying procedures for conducting hearings when requested by accused members; identifying options for sanctioning members found in violation of ethics codes; and codifying appeals procedures. The task of ethics committees is to adhere carefully to each step in the adjudication process and allow ample time during the actual case adjudication procedure for thorough deliberation of each case presented.

The ACA *Policies and Procedures for Processing Complaints of Ethical Violations* (ACA, 1997), guides its Ethics Committee's case adjudication process. According to this document, the ACA Ethics Committee is directed to compile "an objective, factual account of the dispute in question" and promote a consistent, unbiased, and confidential peer review process that furthers the interests and objectives of the professional association and its members (pp. 17–18). Adherence to these policies and procedures obligates Ethics Committee members to attend only to the factual details of cases (i.e., to separate facts from emotional appeals and unsubstantiated statements). In keeping with these guidelines, committee members are required to recuse themselves from cases if they believe their objectivity would be compromised.

Ethics complaints usually begin with a telephone call to the ethics committee office by current or former clients, colleagues, other mental health professionals, state, divisional, or other affiliated professional ethics committees, or any other individual who believes an ethical violation has occurred. Complaints also may be initiated by ethics committee chairpersons if they have evidence to believe that a violation may have occurred. Initiating such *sua sponte* complaints may take place when the committee receives a report of a conviction of malpractice, suspension, or expulsion from a state organization, or revocation of the counselor's license.

A complaint must be presented via written communication, signed, and marked as confidential to the ethics committee office if it is to move forward. It must contain the names and addresses of the complainant(s), accused person(s), and any other persons knowledgeable about the situation and cited in the report. A critical preliminary step in the process is determining whether the person being accused is a member of the organization or was a member at the time the alleged violation occurred. If the accused person is not a member of the professional organization to which the complaint is directed, the ethics committee has no jurisdiction and the person filing the complaint is so informed.

When a written complaint has been received, it is reviewed by one of the two ACA Ethics Committee Cochairpersons in ACA cases, or the APA Ethics Office director

and APA Committee chair in APA cases. Complaints sent to the NASW are forwarded to the appropriate state chapter. At the state level, a Committee on Inquiry (COI) conducts the initial review of cases involving social workers. The initial review of ACA, APA, and NASW complaints is designed to make several determinations: Was the individual a member of the organization at the time of the alleged violation? Would the behavior described, if true, constitute an ethical violation? Is there sufficient information to determine whether a violation may have occurred? Have codes additional to those identified by the complainant been violated? When did the alleged violation occur? Some organizations, such as the APA and NASW, impose time limits on filing complaints, although these restrictions may be waived if the alleged misconduct is serious. The ACA Ethics Committee, though imposing no time limits, requires information about the time frame in which the behavior occurred to determine which version of the ACA *Code of Ethics* applies.

In ACA and APA cases where insufficient information exists to make a fair determination about whether a violation may have occurred, the committee may request further information from the complainant or other persons. A deadline is imposed for the receipt of information and failure to conform to the time limit may result in dismissal of the case. If the behavior described, even if true, would not constitute an ethical violation, the case is dismissed. Some ethics committees make a determination about the ability to decide a case based on the information provided. For example, the APA, when drafting its *Ethics Committee Rules and Procedures* (APA, 1996), included a section allowing the investigator and chair the prerogative not to open a case if they believe the alleged misconduct would be impossible to prove. Many complaints do not move to the point of formal adjudication due to these constraints.

If a case is accepted by the ACA, complainants are provided with a copy of the appropriate version of the ACA *Code of Ethics*, the *Policies and Procedures*, a verification affidavit, and a formal complaint form asking them to verify sections of the code they believe relevant and add sections they believe the person they are accusing has violated. The APA Ethics Committee follows a similar procedure. Complainants are informed that the accused member will be contacted and are asked to sign several releases at this point to allow the case to proceed. Complainants must grant permission to provide copies of the complaint and supporting documentation to the accused person. If the complainant is or was a client of the accused person, he or she is asked to grant permission to the accused counselor to provide confidential information so that the accused has the opportunity to adequately defend himself or herself. In doing so, complainants waive their rights to file future ethics complaints pertaining specifically to the accused individual's release of confidential information about the complainant.

When these materials are received by the ACA Ethics Committee, copies are sent via certified mail to the charged member, along with two other documents: notification of his or her right to request a hearing and the time limit in which to do so, and ACA Ethics Committee policies regarding disclosure of serious violations and sanctions to state and national certification and licensing boards. Members choosing to decline their right to a hearing must sign a waiver to that effect. Similarly, APA members are issued a charge letter and afforded the opportunity to respond to the complaint and request a hearing. Unlike ACA policy, APA rules explicitly stipulate that members' responses to complaints must be written personally rather than by a legal representative or other third party.

Charged members are given a time limit in which to respond in writing to complaints, although a written request for an extension may be granted by the committee. Members are asked to address as fully as possible each section of the code they have been accused of violating and include any evidence and supporting documentation they wish the ethics committee to consider. Both the ACA and APA Ethics Committee have the option of requesting further information from the accused member or others to aid them in their process of deliberation.

The NASW, on the other hand, has a policy whereby cases reviewed and accepted by the COI at the state level move immediately to adjudication. That is, in cases involving social workers, the investigative process is bypassed. A Hearing Committee, appointed by the COI and composed of three NASW members, is conducted in the state in which the accused member resides and practices. Testimony by both the complainant and accused NASW member is heard, and a decision is made about whether or not a violation of the NASW *Code of Ethics* has occurred (M. McGlowne, personal communication, September 28, 2000).

In ACA and APA cases, when the materials compiled by the accused member have been received within the time limit, the complainant is notified via certified mail and both parties are given a tentative date of adjudication. It is worth noting that ACA and APA cases may move to adjudication whether or not the accused member has responded to the charges once the time limit has expired. ACA has the option of suspending accused individuals' membership and denying them any benefits associated with professional membership until they cooperate with the ethics proceedings. Members of ACA and APA are not permitted to drop their membership to avoid the adjudication process.

The ACA Ethics Committee meets at least three times yearly for the purpose of adjudication. Committee members are provided copies of the complaint, supporting documentation, the accused member's response, and supporting evidence and documents at least 15 business days prior to formal adjudication proceedings. Adjudication meetings normally are attended by the full committee, the ACA Ethics Committee liaison, and the ACA Ethics Committee student representative. A vote of at least four committee members is needed to conduct business. The liaison and student representative are nonvoting members of the committee. The ACA legal counsel is available to attend adjudication meetings at the request of the committee.

The adjudication process consists of discussion, deliberation, and decisions regarding each of the ethics codes the member has been accused of violating. Following deliberation, the committee makes a determination about the outcome of a case. A vote is taken on each ethics code in question. The committee may decide to dismiss the complaint in its entirety or particular charges within the complaint, or determine that one or more sections were violated and impose one overall sanction or a combination of sanctions.

Available sanctions for ACA members include remedial measures, suspension, expulsion, or other corrective action. The APA *Rules and Procedures* includes a more detailed list of outcomes, divided into sanctions and directives. Available sanctions for APA members include reprimand, censure, expulsion, and stipulated resignation (whereby the member is offered the opportunity to resign). Directives include cease and desist orders, supervision, education or training, evaluation and treatment, probation, or other corrective action. Permanent expulsion from ACA membership requires a unanimous committee vote. Recommendations for expulsion of APA members are forwarded to the APA Board of Directors for review. Accused members have the right to appeal Ethics Committee decisions. After the time period has elapsed and an appeal has not been filed, the complainant is notified of the outcome.

Expulsion of ACA and APA members is a relatively infrequent outcome. According to ACA records, two members were expelled between 1996 and 2000 (APA Ethics Committee, 2000; Brown & Espina, 2000; Shumate & Espina, 1999); 28 APA members lost their membership in 1999 (APA Ethics Committee, 2000). Suspensions and expulsions of ACA members are reported to several bodies: the American Association of State Counseling Boards (AASCB), ACA divisions to which the guilty member belongs, the state branches in which the member lives and practices, the National Board for Certified Counselors via the AASCB, and the ACA Insurance Trust. They also are published in the ACA newsletter *Counseling Today*. The APA and NASW similarly report serious ethical violations to relevant regulatory and professional agencies. These professional organizations and regulatory bodies, upon notification of a decision to suspend or expel, may take independent action against the member found in

violation of professional ethics codes. States vary as to how reports from professional organizations are handled. Nevertheless, a serious ethical violation could lead to further disciplinary action at the state level, including revoking a practitioner's license. Ethics committee actions other than suspension or expulsion are not made public. A case is closed when the sanction has been completed or, in decisions of no violation, when the complainant and accused member have been notified.

RESPONDING TO A COMPLAINT FILED AGAINST YOU

The prospect of being accused of an ethics violation is upsetting to most mental health professionals. It may be comforting to know that most counselors will never confront this situation. The ACA and APA receive many times more inquiries and correspondence concerning potential ethical violations than actual cases that reach the adjudication stage. Comparisons among ethics inquiries, complaints, and actual adjudicated cases are published annually in the spring edition of the ACA *Journal of Counseling and Development* and August edition of *American Psychologist*. Hundreds of informal ethical inquiries are received yearly by these professional associations. Only 5 formal complaints against ACA members were filed and investigated during the 1999–2000 fiscal year (ACA Ethics Committee, 2000). The APA Ethics Committee received a total of 70 complaints in 1999 (1 per 1,265 members, or .08% of the membership) (APA Ethics Committee, 2000). Even though many complaints do not proceed past initial review, should you find yourself faced with an accusation of unethical conduct, you ought to take the complaint seriously and cooperate fully with the process, even if you believe the allegations to be unfounded.

If a formal complaint is filed against you, ACA, APA, and NASW ethics codes require you to cooperate with complaint procedures. All organizations have a staff person in the ethics office available to provide information to the accused member (and complainant) about each step in the complaint process (although the NASW process takes place through state chapters). It is important to keep in mind that notification of a formal complaint does not equate with a guilty verdict, although the stress for the accused member can be great even at this early stage in the process. When responding to the complaint, you need to compile and attach as much relevant evidence and documentation as possible, and it is wise not to malign the person who has brought the complaint forward. Some counselors choose to consult with an attorney or another mental health professional at this point to help them prepare their response. In fact, the legal counsel associated with a malpractice insurance policy exists for this very reason. Therefore, professional counselors should immediately contact their policy carrier if they receive notice of a complaint against them.

The need to take the accusation seriously applies even if the complaint is informal. The latter case typically involves being confronted about a possible violation by another mental health professional. It is important in these circumstances to be willing and available to meet with the other person, to listen to his or her concern, and to respond genuinely and nondefensively. It certainly is appropriate to correct any misinformation others may have about your actions, assuming confidentiality issues have been addressed. However, it also is important to take responsibility for your errors. Most complaint and adjudication procedures are designed to be rehabilitative, not punitive. If ethical errors of a less serious nature (i.e., those that do not cause harm to another person or the profession) can be addressed at an informal level and result in corrective behavior, then the process works to everyone's advantage.

Timelines for responses are provided by ethics committees and should be followed unless a waiver is granted. Members also have the right to appeal decisions with which they disagree. Ethics cases can take as long as a year to be processed depending on how responsive the complainant and accused are and whether legal action is occurring simultaneously (in which case, ACA will put a case on hold until litigation is completed). It can be a long while before a decision is forthcoming despite ethics committees' intentions to act as expeditiously as possible without compromising the process. While awaiting the outcome of a complaint against you, it may be comforting to know that ethics committees are required to follow rigorous procedures in an effort to render decisions that are as fair and objective as possible.

SUMMARY

Professional association codes of ethics, state licensing regulations, and legal statutes have jurisdiction over the practices of mental health providers. These regulatory entities help to ensure that consumers are protected against unethical and illegal conduct. Codes of ethics, because they must address a wide range of professional activities, are broadly based and often insufficient in providing answers to complicated ethical dilemmas. Also, certain sections of ethics codes may be in conflict with legal statutes. For these and other reasons, even well-intentioned counselors may find themselves uncertain about the most ethical route to take in difficult circumstances. Ethical errors in judgment can and do take place, and when counselors become aware of these breaches, they are obligated to take action.

Counselors may find themselves faced with the task of confronting other mental health professionals or responding to a complaint filed against them. Ethics committees for professional organizations have very specific rules and procedures for handling complaints of ethical violations. Written reports of suspected ethical violations to professional ethics committees are thoroughly reviewed and investigated in an effort to balance protection of the public with protection of counselors from unsubstantiated accusations of misconduct.

References

American Counseling Association. (1995). *Code of ethics and standards of practice.* Alexandria, VA: Author.

American Counseling Association. (1997). *Policies and procedures for processing complaints of ethical violations.* Alexandria, VA: Author.

American Counseling Association Ethics Committee. (2000). *Ethics committee member manual FY-2001.* Alexandria, VA: ACA.

American Psychological Association. (1992). *Ethical principles of psychologists and code of conduct.* Washington, DC: Author.

American Psychological Association. (1996). *American Psychological Association ethics committee rules and procedures.* Washington, DC: Author.

American Psychological Association Ethics Committee. (2000). Report of the ethics committee, 1999. *American Psychologist, 55,* 938–945.

Brown, S.P., & Espina, M.R. (2000). Report of the ACA ethics committee: 1998–1999. *Journal of Counseling and Development, 78,* 237–241.

Corey, G., Corey, M.S., & Callanan, P. (1998). *Issues and ethics in the helping professions* (5th ed.). Pacific Grove, CA: Brooks/Cole.

Forester-Miller, H., & Davis, T.E. (n.d.). *A practitioner's guide to ethical decision making.* Alexandria, VA: American Counseling Association.

Herlihy, B., & Corey, G. (1996). *ACA ethical standards casebook* (5th ed.). Alexandria, VA: American Counseling Association.

Kenyon, P. (1999). *What would you do? An ethical case workbook for human service professionals.* Pacific Grove, CA: Brooks/Cole.

National Association of Social Workers. (1999). *Code of ethics.* Washington, DC: Author.

Pedersen, P. (1995). Culture-centered ethical guidelines for counselors. In J.G. Ponterotto, J.M. Casas, L.A. Suzuki, & C.M. Alexander (Eds.), *Handbook of multicultural counseling* (pp. 34–49). Thousand Oaks, CA: Sage.

Shumate, S., & Espina, M.R. (1999). Report of the ACA ethics committee: 1997–1998. *Journal of Counseling and Development, 77,* 243–245.

Steinman, S.O., Richardson, N.F., & McEnroe, T. (1998). *The ethical decision-making manual for helping professionals.* Pacific Grove, CA: Brooks/Cole.

Welfel, E.R. (1998). *Ethics in counseling and psychotherapy: Standards, research, and emerging issues.* Pacific Grove, CA: Brooks/Cole.

64 PROTECTING CLIENTS' RIGHTS TO PRIVACY

Elizabeth Reynolds Welfel

Mental health professionals are obligated by both law and professional ethics to protect the privacy of client information. Two major terms are associated with this obligation: *confidentiality* and *privilege.* Confidentiality is the broader term and is defined as the responsibility of the mental health professional to keep secret all materials and statements clients supply to counselors and the records produced from counseling. With the exception of employees under the direct supervision and control of a mental health professional, no person may have access to client data unless a client releases it or a law or ethics code permits it. This obligation includes both clinically relevant information (such as diagnosis) and other personal information (such as name or place of birth) as long as that knowledge was gained as a result of a professional contact. It also extends past the death of a client. The terms *content* confidentiality and *contact* confidentiality are used to refer to these responsibilities. Confidentiality applies to all clients regardless of age or level of functioning. When working with minors or others who are not competent to make decisions for themselves, professionals must obtain releases from parents or other appointed legal guardians unless there is an ethical or legal allowance for disclosure without such consent.

Violations of confidentiality, both inadvertent and conscious, are the most frequently identified form of unethical behavior reported by practicing mental health professionals (Pope & Vetter, 1992), though most of these violations never get brought before ethics boards. Some of these undetected violations probably stem from unauthorized counselor communications with family members or friends about their cases (Welfel, 2002), others from inappropriate disclosure to colleagues. According to the ethics codes of mental health professions, clinicians may not discuss identifying client data even with colleagues or supervisors without client consent unless necessary to follow the law or to protect client welfare. Sometimes, mental health professionals reveal client data through carelessness—files left unattended, comments made in places that are not as private as they appear, or poorly disguised statements used as case illustrations in classes or professional meetings. With the emergence of forms of electronic communication, the confidentiality of client records is jeopardized when care is not taken to ensure that materials transmitted via facsimile or e-mail are protected from unauthorized use. The burden to maintain the privacy of such materials falls on the professional who is transmitting them.

Privilege has a more narrow definition. It refers to the legal right of clients to prevent mental health professionals from offering testimony or written documents in a legal proceeding involving that client. Privilege, or privileged communication, as it is also called, is established by state or federal statute or case law. The right of a client to assert privilege depends on which mental health professionals are identified in the laws. State statutes and court rulings vary widely, though most identify psychiatrists and psychologists as professionals whose clients may assert privilege. Social workers, mental health counselors, psychiatric nurses, and psychology assistants with a license to conduct counseling and psychotherapy are not routinely mentioned. Therefore, these professionals must read the laws in the states in which they practice to ascertain whether privilege applies to their work. If a licensed mental health profession is named in the privileged communication statute or included through case law, that professional is *obligated* to assert privilege if subpoenaed to provide testimony or records unless the client provides a release of information. In the absence of a signed client release, the proper response to a subpoena is to inform the court that the requested information appears to be privileged and to decline to provide materials while awaiting the court's ruling on the applicability of privilege in this case. Needless to say, mental health professionals who have received subpoenas for client data should seek legal advice to assist them. If a judge ultimately orders that privilege does not hold in the current case, the clinician has three options: to submit the requested testimony or records as ordered, to appeal the order to a higher court, or to risk a contempt-of-court charge.

Privileged communication in federal court was clarified in the U.S. Supreme Court decision *Jaffee v. Redmond* (1996). In this case, a licensed clinical social worker working in Illinois was ordered to give testimony in a federal proceeding about communications her client made in session. Her client was a police officer charged with violating the civil rights of a citizen whom she had shot and killed during a robbery. This police officer sought counseling after the shooting to help her cope with the incident, as required by police policy. Lower courts had ordered the social worker to testify in the absence of a clear federal statute relating to privilege for therapists (although Illinois had granted the clients of licensed clinical social workers privilege in state court). The social worker continued appeals until the case reached the Supreme Court. That body ruled that there was an important public interest to be served in having client disclosures to therapists kept private. Their holding specifically referred only to psychologists and social workers as having privilege in federal courts. However, a subsequent ruling in a federal court in California applied this privilege to a licensed marriage and family counselor (*Speaker v. County of San Bernadino*, 2000). The latter court argued that privilege should be applicable *because the client believed he was dealing with a psychotherapist.* The perception of the client that the disclosures would be privileged was the crucial factor in that court's ruling along with the obvious public policy value of having counseling services available to police officers under stress. Clearly, the federal court decisions in these cases highlight the seriousness of the obligation of the mental health professional to protect client rights to privacy. Mental health professionals who fail to honor privilege place themselves in jeopardy for litigation against them in either state or federal courts.

LIMITS OF CONFIDENTIALITY

Jaffee v. Redmond also asserted that privilege is not absolute and that there are situations in which the public interest might be better served by disclosures of client data even without client permission. This finding parallels the trend in state courts and legislatures. Eight broad categories of limitations currently exist. Even though breach of confidentiality is allowed or mandated in these cases, the disclosure should always be as limited in scope as possible to satisfy the requirements.

Client Requests for Release of Information

As part of their rights as citizens, clients have control over information about themselves. If they decide to have information from counseling or psychotherapy released to themselves or another party, clinicians are free to release that information under most circumstances. A written release form retained in the client's chart is the best way to document such client requests. If clinicians believe that a release of information is not in client's best interest, they are obligated to discuss those reservations with the client and seek a mutually agreeable resolution. When personal client data are released to others, mental health professionals should ascertain that the receiving parties are qualified to understand the information and that the data will continue to be treated as confidential. These restrictions exist because unqualified individuals are at significant risk for misunderstanding the information and thereby misserving the client. According to Tranel (1994), mental health professionals who are uncertain about the competence of the receiving professionals should obtain a curriculum vitae or similar documentation to verify qualifications. When clients or others seek the release of raw data from psychological tests, clinicians should act cautiously. They should first seek a resolution that meets the client's need without the inclusion of raw test data. If that effort fails, they should get legal advice about state statutes governing the release of raw test data, as state laws vary considerably on this matter. Mental health professionals must honor their obligations to maintain the security of copyrighted test materials.

Court Orders for Confidential Information

As already discussed, when a court orders a mental health professional to release information, the clinician is obliged to respond either by presenting the information or testimony to the court or by filing an appeal of the order to a higher court. When the court employs a mental health professional to evaluate a person involved in a legal proceeding, privilege does not usually apply. Either the persons subject to the evaluation have waived their right to confidentiality prior to the court's employment of the clinician, or the court did not recognize any such right to confidentiality in the first place.

Client Litigation

If a client sues a clinician for actions related to the professional service (such as breach of contract or negligence), that clinician has the right to defend himself or herself against the charges. Because no clinician could mount an adequate defense without referring to client information, the confidentiality of client contact and disclosures does not apply. In other words, by virtue of bringing the case against the mental health professional, the client is waiving the right to confidentiality. In parallel fashion, when clients bring ethics charges against clinicians, ethics committees routinely ask clients to sign waivers of confidentiality. Without such signed waivers, ethics committees do not move forward with an investigation of the complaint.

When clients who are involved in personal injury or discrimination cases are claiming psychological damage, they may refer to their involvement in counseling or psychotherapy as evidence of that damage. Because the employer has the right to defend against such charges and because the client voluntarily brought these charges to the court, confidentiality of client disclosures is not typically honored and clinicians must testify and provide documents that the court seeks.

Limitations Based in State and Federal Statutes

Federal and state statutes mandate that mental health professionals report suspicion of child abuse and neglect. The definitions of reportable actions and the procedures for reporting vary by state, but the obligation to report takes precedence over other obligations to confidentiality. Moreover, the penalties for failing to report often include criminal charges (see Chapter 68 for more information on child abuse reporting). Every state also has a statute regarding elder abuse, though not all of them mandate reporting. The wide variability in state laws on this issue places an extra obligation on mental health professionals to explore the specific language in their state's law (see Chapter 69 for more information on elder abuse).

Dangerous Clients

Communications from clients who are dangerous to themselves or others are not protected by the same level of confidentiality as most other material disclosed in counseling. In many states, mental health professionals have a *duty to warn and protect* when they have reason to believe a client is dangerous. When clients threaten others or themselves and clinicians judge the danger to be clear and imminent, clinicians must do their best to protect the intended victim from that danger. Sometimes, the best way to achieve that protection is to warn the victim of the danger; at other times, the optimal approach is to intensify treatment so that the client is kept safe and the urge to do harm is reduced. (For a more detailed discussion of clinicians' responsibility with dangerous or suicidal clients, see Chapters 38 and 39.)

Confidentiality with Clients with HIV Disorders

Clients with life-threatening communicable diseases such as HIV disorders sometimes act in ways that put others at risk for infection, either by using unsafe practices such as sharing needles in intravenous drug use or having unprotected sexual contact. The ethical dilemma for professionals lies in balancing their responsibility to the client against their obligation (if any) to the third parties at risk for infection. There has been a vigorous debate in the literature about the confidentiality of such disclosures, but only the American Counseling Association's code of ethics (1995) specifically mentions this issue. That code states that professionals "are justified" but not mandated in disclosing confidential information to a third party under the following circumstances:

- The third party is identifiable.
- The counselor has good reason to believe the client has a disease that is both communicable and fatal.
- The client has not already informed the third party and is not intending to inform him or her in the immediate future.

Generally, the stance of the professional associations is toward protecting the rights of the client and breaching confidentiality only as a last resort. The American Psychological Association (1991), the American Psychiatric Association (1988), and the National Association of Social Workers (1990) have opposed efforts to apply the duty-to-warn principle to this circumstance. These organizations emphasize the importance of using the therapeutic relationship to help the client make a responsible choice about his or her behavior and to assist the client in voluntarily disclosing his or her HIV status to the affected third parties. People with HIV disorders have been subject to many forms of discrimination and prejudice. As a result, mental health professionals need to work assiduously to avoid public disclosure of their conditions if at all possible.

It is important to note that because of this history of discrimination, a number of states have passed legislation regarding disclosures about HIV status to third parties. Some statutes explicitly prohibit clinicians from making such breaches of confidentiality. Therefore, mental health professionals need to stay abreast of state laws on this topic.

Confidentiality with Minors and Others Not Competent to Consent to Treatment

A mental health professional working with minors is obligated to honor confidentiality in most of the same ways as with adults. Permission must be secured before information is released, records should be protected from access by unauthorized persons, and the identity of minor clients should be kept confidential. However, because minors generally do not have legal status to consent to treatment independently, parents or guardians must give consent and thereby have rights to the information discussed in treatment (see Lawrence & Kurpius, 2000, for a fascinating discussion of the history and current status of the legal rights of minors). Preadolescent children expect that their parents will know about what happens in counseling, and so parents' access to the counselor and counseling records is typically not an obstacle to providing effective service to this age group.

Adolescents, however, are reluctant to share personal information without some assurance of confidentiality from disclosure to parents. In short, parents' legal right to access to counseling records frequently conflicts with the clinician's responsibility to promote the welfare of the adolescents. In some states, legislatures have enacted statutes that give adolescents the legal right to privacy regarding certain types of communications. In Ohio, for example, minors over the age of 14 may seek treatment from a mental health professional without parental consent for a limited period of time. Federal law also offers adolescents some degree of confidentiality regarding counseling for substance abuse and reproductive issues. In the absence of such legal rights, mental health professionals need to seek from parents a waiver of their rights to full disclosure of therapeutic content so that the professional may help the child (see Chapter 31 for a full discussion of strategies for involving parents in treatment for minors). In any case, if a clinician has reason to believe that disclosure of the content of a child's communications will place the child at risk for harm, the clinician is bound to place the best interests of the child above the parents' right to information.

Group and Family Counseling and Therapy

Participants in group and family therapy have the same rights to confidentiality from mental health professionals as do individual clients. However, mental health professionals do not have control over the actions of group or family members who may reveal to others material discussed in sessions. Therefore, responsible practice requires that group and family therapists act energetically to minimize the risk of such violations of confidentiality by:

- Careful screening of participants.
- Explicit informed consent that delineates the risks to confidentiality.
- The use of signed contracts for confidentiality to reinforce the importance of the matter.

- Implementation of frequent reminders to participants of the paramount importance of confidentiality to effective sessions.

When professionals conduct simultaneous individual and group or family sessions, they are ethically bound to keep the material disclosed in individual sessions private unless they have consent from the individual to mention that issue in a group or family session. To avoid the appearance of coercion in obtaining that consent, a clinician should avoid asking an individual for permission to discuss a topic from a one-on-one session during a group or family session.

SUMMARY

Mental health professionals need to keep in mind that confidentiality is the foundation of effective practice. Without confidence that their communications will be handled confidentially, clients will be unlikely to seek service. Specifically, clinicians should:

- Guard client data carefully and closely supervise employees with access to them.
- Keep thorough records of any incidents in which client data are shared with others and monitor release of information closely.
- Consult with supervisors about complex, confusing, or serious confidentiality questions.
- Build a professional relationship with an attorney competent in mental health law.

- Keep current with changes in ethical standards and federal and state laws regarding privilege and confidentiality.

References

American Counseling Association. (1995). *Code of ethics and standards of practice.* Alexandria, VA: Author.

American Psychiatric Association Ad Hoc Committee on AIDS Policy. (1988). AIDS policy: Confidentiality and disclosure. *American Journal of Psychiatry, 145,* 541–542.

American Psychological Association. (1991). *Legal liability related to confidentiality and the prevention of HIV transmission.* Washington, DC: Author.

Jaffee v. Redmond, 116 S. Ct. 1923, WL 315841 (U.S. Ill., June 13, 1996).

Lawrence, G., & Kurpius, S.E.R. (2000). Legal and ethical issues involved when counseling minors in nonschool settings. *Journal of Counseling and Development, 78,* 130–135.

National Association of Social Workers. (1990). *Acquired Immune Deficiency Syndrome/Human Immunodeficiency Virus: A social work response* (Policy statement). Washington, DC: Author.

Pope, K.S., & Vetter, V.A. (1991). Prior therapist-patient sexual involvement among patients seen by psychologists. *Psychotherapy, 28,* 429–438.

Speaker v. County of San Bernadino, No. ED CV 94-0141RT (C.D. Cal. Feb. 1, 2000).

Tranel, D. (1994). The release of psychological data to nonexperts: Ethical and legal considerations. *Professional Psychology: Research and Practice, 25,* 33–38.

Welfel, E.R. (2002). *Ethics in counseling and psychotherapy: Standards, research and emerging issues.* (2nd ed.). Pacific Grove, CA: Brooks/Cole.

65 ACCURATE AND EFFECTIVE INFORMED CONSENT

Mitchell M. Handelsman

The basic idea of informed consent is really quite simple: Counselors are obligated to provide sufficient information to their clients and research subjects so that they can make intelligent, reasoned choices (though not necessarily the choices the counselors would make) about whether to participate in treatment, consultation, research, or any other professional activity. However, the implementation of this simple concept raises ethical, legal, clinical, and logistical issues. Although it is neither possible nor desirable to lay out a "cookbook" set of rules about informed consent, this chapter explores several issues that counselors may find useful when making decisions about how to fulfill their obligations of informed consent. First, I present four general themes that provide a context for approaching informed consent. Then, I explore the specific components of informed consent and their implementation.

THEMES

Understanding the Multifaceted Justification for Informed Consent: Ethical, Clinical, and Legal Dimensions

The most basic ethical justification is the principle of autonomy (Beauchamp & Childress, 1994), which states that people are self-governing and have the right to make decisions about health care, mental health care, and other aspects of their lives. Thus, consenting to—or refusing—counseling services constitutes an exercise of the right of self-determination. Because potential clients are not expert in counseling, they must trust counselors to provide sufficient information on which to base a good decision. Thus, the obligation falls to the counselor to provide adequate, relevant, and accurate information, and to respect clients' decisions to accept or refuse services (Appelbaum, Lidz, & Meisel, 1987; Lidz et al., 1984). The ethical principles of beneficence (do good) and nonmaleficence (do no harm) also justify consent to the extent that a good informed consent process leads to better outcomes and avoids potential risks.

The ethical principles of beneficence and nonmaleficence are directly related to the clinical justification for consent: The conversations and shared decision making that stem from a good consent process may lead to a more trusting and effective professional relationship (Appelbaum et al., 1987). Indeed, empirical studies of reactions to therapists have shown that a consent procedure in a first counseling session leads to higher ratings of therapists' expertness and trustworthiness (Sullivan, Martin, & Handelsman, 1993). And a complete consent process may decrease the risk of malpractice exposure (Bennett, Bryant, VandenBos, & Greenwood, 1990; Moline, Williams, & Austin, 1998).

Along with ethical and clinical justifications, a knowledge of legal considerations is essential to designing good consent policies. The legal doctrine of informed consent has a long history in medicine, with many of the most important court cases occurring since the

1950s (Appelbaum et al., 1987; Haas, 1991). As psychology and the other mental health professions have defined themselves more and more as health care professions, the legal doctrine has been applied to these professions. Recently, several states—including Colorado, Ohio, and Washington—have passed laws requiring mental health professionals to disclose information about their services to clients. Thus, counselors can anticipate more legal obligations, which may or may not complement their ethical and clinical responsibilities.

Applying a Process versus an Event Model of Consent

To the extent that counselors see informed consent primarily as a set of legal and ethical rules, they may be tempted to think of informed consent as an *event* that happens before services are provided. For example, the APA (1992) *Ethics Code* implies an event model when it states that psychologists "provide . . . appropriate information beforehand about the nature of . . . services" (Standard 1.07). However, good informed consent is much more of a *process* than an event (Appelbaum et al., 1987). Indeed, each time clients come to a session they are consenting (behaviorally) to that particular session. As issues, goals, risks, and benefits change over time, clients continue to need updated information to make decisions that are just as informed, reasoned, and beneficial as their initial ones. These decisions may be about such issues as whether to come at all, what material to cover in the next phase of treatment, and what activities may be involved in the consulting relationship.

In contrast to the APA code, the ACA (1995) code implies a process model when it discusses counseling plans in section A.1.c.: "Counselors and clients regularly review plans to ensure their continued viability and effectiveness, respecting clients' freedom of choice." Clients may respond to different types of information at different points in therapy (Braaten & Handelsman, 1997). Thus, a process model, revising and reviewing information and consent over time, actualizes the ethical principles of autonomy and beneficence more fully.

Incorporating Consent into the Counseling Process

Adopting a process model of consent leads naturally to viewing consent as part of, not a burdensome add-on or precursor to, whatever professional service is being provided. In fact, an informed consent process in therapy may itself be therapeutic, because increasing clients' autonomy, having them make better decisions, is often a goal of treatment (Haas, 1991). Counselors who take a narrow and detached view of consent (e.g., getting the required signature on a form that has been reviewed by an attorney) may lose sight of the full ethical and practical benefits of consent. By making consent an integral part of the professional relationship, they can avoid this trap.

Universalizability

The ethical concept of universalizability states that we should adopt an ethical stance with which we would feel comfortable if we (or a loved one) were the client (Beauchamp & Childress, 1994). When developing and implementing consent policies, counselors may want to ask themselves, "What would I like a counselor to do when I am (or my loved one is) a client?" Many would like their counselors to educate them not only about the counselor's own services, but about alternatives. A good informed consent process changes the interests of counselors from a totally substantive approach of looking at the issues that clients come in with, to a process approach of helping clients make the best decisions about their needs and goals. Thinking about consent from clients' perspectives may help counselors implement consent in a more comprehensive and clinically sensitive way.

COMPONENTS OF INFORMED CONSENT: THEORY AND IMPLEMENTATION

Informed consent has been incorporated into both the APA (1992) and ACA (1995) ethics codes and covers activities including assessment, evaluation, treatment, counseling, teaching, consultation, and research (Table 65.1 lists

TABLE 65.1   Ethical Codes and Standards Relevant to Informed Consent

APA Code

Principles

  B   Integrity
  D   Respect for People's Rights and Dignity

Standards

1.07   Describing the Nature and Results of Psychological Services
1.21   Third-Party Requests for Services
1.25   Fees and Financial Arrangements
4.01   Structuring the Relationship
4.02   Informed Consent to Therapy
4.03   Couple and Family Relationships
5.01   Discussing the Limits of Confidentiality
6.10   Research Responsibilities
6.11   Informed Consent to Research
6.12   Dispensing with Informed Consent
6.13   Informed Consent in Research Filming or Recording
6.16   Sharing and Utilizing Data

ACA Code

Sections

  A.1.c. Client Welfare; Counseling Plans
  A.3. Client Rights
  A.6.a. Dual Relationships; Avoid When Possible
  A.10.a. Fees and Bartering; Advance Understanding
  A.10.c. Fees and Bartering; Bartering Discouraged
  A.12.b. Computer Technology; Explanation of Limitations
  B.1.g. Right to Privacy; Explanation of Limitations
  B.3. Minor or Incompetent Clients
  D.2.c. Consultation; Understanding with Clients
  E.3.a. Informed Consent; Explanation to Clients
  F.2.a. Counselor Education and Training Programs; Orientation
  G.2. Informed Consent (Research and Publication)

Standards of Practice

  SP-2 Disclosure to Clients
  SP-6 Advance Understanding of Fees
  SP-33 Assessment Explanations to Clients
  SP-39 Evaluation Information

all the relevant sections of both codes). The most explicit statement of the components of consent is in Standard 4.02 of the APA (1992) Code, Informed Consent to Therapy, which lists the following major aspects: the client's capacity to consent, the information provided to clients, the voluntariness of the client's consent, and the documentation of consent. In addition, Standard 4.02 and several others emphasize the importance of clients understanding the information provided. In this section I explore each of these components.

Competence (Capacity) to Consent

Clients must have the cognitive capacity to understand and to consent: "When persons are legally incapable of giving informed consent, psychologists obtain informed permission from a legally authorized person" (APA, 1992, Standard 4.02). Both codes mention minors, who by definition do not have the legal right to consent. Others who may be incompetent to consent include clients with developmental disabilities and older adults who have cognitive impairments.

Working with children or other incompetent clients does not absolve counselors of all informed consent obligations. The APA code (1992, Standard 4.02c) specifies that psychologists "(1) inform those persons ... in a manner commensurate with the person's psychological capacities, (2) seek their assent to those interventions, and (3) consider such persons' preferences and best interests." *Assent* is obtained when a client agrees to services even though that agreement is not legally recognized. The ACA code (1995, Section A.3.c.) does not mention assent, but does mention the obligation that "counselors act in these clients' best interests."

Counselors need to avoid the temptation to presume diminished competence only because of the presence of a mental illness, or because of the stress involved in seeking counseling services. Also, counselors need to beware of making the content of the decision the basis for a judgment of competence. For example, the fact that a person refuses services, or in some other way makes a "foolish" decision, is not evidence of diminished capacity. Also, incapacity is not necessarily an all-or-none concept. For example, individuals adjudicated legally incompetent to handle their finances may still be deemed competent to make health care decisions. Although gray areas always exist, a good guideline may be that clients are not ethically incompetent unless they are legally incompetent.

Information

Clients must trust professionals to provide adequate, relevant, and accurate information about the services being rendered. Inadequate information makes the consent less valid. Neither the APA nor the ACA ethics code provides definitive guidance about what information must be conveyed; they merely mention several types of information to be provided. The APA code (1992) highlights the nature of the relationship and services, the role of the professional, confidentiality and its limits, financial arrangements, the use of test results and conclusions, and supervision or student status. The code also states, "Psychologists make reasonable efforts to answer patients' questions and to avoid apparent misunderstandings about therapy" (APA, 1992, Standard 4.01d). The ACA code (1995) adds the disclosure of "goals, . . . limitations, potential risks and benefits of services, . . . the implications of diagnosis," and the clients' right to refuse services and "the consequences of such refusal" (Section A.3.a.). To provide more specific guidance, many authors have published lists of what information should be included in an informed consent process or in written contracts for treatment (Bennett et al., 1990; Haas, 1991; Moline et al., 1998).

Counselors also need to be aware of the policies that their agencies might have and of the legal requirements for disclosure of information. Managed care arrangements create an additional obligation for counselors to inform clients of the limitations of their coverage and the relationship between the counselor and the managed care organization (Appelbaum, 1993; Haas & Cummings, 1991).

How much information must counselors provide? Because clients cannot become familiar with all possible aspects of professional services, counselors must decide how much information is enough. In medicine, three legal standards exist for such a decision (Beauchamp & Childress, 1994). Under the *professional standard* (*Natanson v. Kline*, 1960), physicians are obligated to disclose to clients "what is customary and usual in the profession" (Appelbaum et al., 1987, p. 41). This standard is too conservative and does not fulfill the ethical obligations of autonomy and beneficence. In addition, it does not recognize the therapeutic relevance of consent.

A more accepted approach is the *reasonable person* standard (*Canterbury v. Spence*, 1972), which obligates physicians to disclose information that a reasonable person, in the client's situation, would find relevant (i.e., would be a factor in the decision to accept or refuse services). The *subjective* standard, which is generally not accepted, states that physicians are obligated to disclose information that the particular client would find relevant (Appelbaum et al., 1987).

The latter two legal standards are more client-oriented and thus more useful to counselors. Consistent with these client-oriented standards and with the concept of universalizability, Nagy (2000) recommended that practitioners "consider telling [clients] what you might want a good friend to know . . . if he or she were about to consult a psychologist for the first time" (p. 89).

Voluntariness

The concept of voluntariness is a key component, but the least defined of all the components of consent (Appelbaum et al., 1987). We know that valid consent cannot be coerced, and consent can be withdrawn at any time (Bennett et al., 1990). However, defining voluntariness is often quite difficult. For example, is consent voluntary when a person needs services but the insurance carrier pays only for one type of treatment? Difficulty in defining voluntariness and coercion also occurs frequently in forensic settings in which the consequences of refusing services may be severe. At the same time, the requirement to provide information is not lessened by the possibility of a nonvoluntary consent. In fact, Kitchener (2000) argued that "in court-ordered evaluations, psychologists bear a heavy social responsibility and have special obligations to inform clients about their role and the evaluation process" (p. 64).

Documentation

The APA code requires that "consent be appropriately documented" (1992, Standard 4.02d), but gives no other guidance. One way to document consent is to have a written, signed consent form in the file. Disclosing information in writing and having clients sign the form that becomes part of the record is ethically desirable and good clinical practice (Bennett et al., 1990). Many sources have examples of such written forms (e.g., Moline et al., 1998; Zuckerman, 1997).

No written consent form will be comprehensive in the information it conveys, if only because each counseling relationship will contain some idiosyncratic components. Thus, having a copy of a signed consent form in the chart is not enough to fulfill the process model of consent. Counselors need to document the initial conversation that took place, including questions that were addressed and additional information that was conveyed. For the purpose of facilitating the conversation between counselors and clients, Handelsman and Galvin (1988) suggested using a form that consists of a series of questions that clients may want to ask their therapists. The documentation would include which questions were asked and how they were answered. And, of course, it is also a good idea to document the ongoing conversations throughout the relationship, not just at the beginning. In other words, document the process, not just the event.

Understanding

Both the ACA and APA codes repeatedly mention that information be conveyed in language that the client can understand. This requirement is especially important when working with people who are not well-educated, whose first language is not English, or who are from different cultural backgrounds. However, given clients' level of anxiety about coming to a counselor, counselors need always to make their information as accessible as possible.

To the extent that therapists have relied on written forms to convey information to clients, the empirical data on the readability of these forms are not encouraging. Studies have shown that most forms are written at the level of an academically oriented magazine

and may not be understandable at all (Handelsman, Kemper, Kesson-Craig, McLain, & Johnsrud, 1986; Handelsman et al., 1995).

Forms can be made more understandable and accessible in several ways. First, readability can be improved by decreasing the number of words in sentences and the number of syllables in words. For example, the sentence "Confidentiality is a right legally guaranteed to psychotherapy clients" could be rephrased "I will keep what you say between us." Word processing software packages have readability measures built in. Second, forms can be personalized, for example, by referring to "you and me" rather than "client and counselor." Research has shown that such personalized and readable forms, in addition to being more understandable, may lead to more favorable perceptions of counselors (Handelsman & Martin, 1992; Wagner, Davis, & Handelsman, 1998). Third, clients can be given a copy of the form for their own reference (Nagy, 2000). This strategy may increase the recall (Morrow, Gootnick, & Schmale, 1978) and thus the value of the information. Finally, as with all aspects of informed consent, written forms can be thought of as part of the relationship and as part of a process.

SUMMARY

Informed consent is an obligation with ethical, legal, and practical dimensions and implications. An effective consent procedure, however, is not merely an ethical burden; it can be clinically valuable. As counselors develop their policies, they are encouraged to:

- Think of informed consent as a process rather than an event.
- Incorporate the consent process into the treatment.
- Provide information that they or their loved ones would want.
- Provide information and solicit assent for clients who are not competent to consent.
- Provide all useful information that a reasonable person would want to know, and answer questions.

- Document the consent and the conversations that take place.
- Make information, especially on written forms, readable and personalized.
- Give clients a copy of the form for their reference.
- Revisit the information, and the consent, throughout the professional relationship.

References

American Counseling Association. (1995). *Code of ethics and standards of practice.* Alexandria, VA: Author.

American Psychological Association. (1992). Ethical principles of psychologists and code of conduct. *American Psychologist, 47,* 1597–1611.

Appelbaum, P.S. (1993). Legal liability and managed care. *American Psychologist, 48,* 251–257.

Appelbaum, P.S., Lidz, C.W., & Meisel, A. (1987). *Informed consent: Legal theory and clinical practice.* New York: Oxford University Press.

Beauchamp, T.L., & Childress, J.F. (1994). *Principles of biomedical ethics* (4th ed.). New York: Oxford University Press.

Bennett, B.E., Bryant, B.K., VandenBos, G.R., & Greenwood, A. (1990). *Professional liability and risk management.* Washington, DC: American Psychological Association.

Braaten, E.B., & Handelsman, M.M. (1997). Client preferences for informed consent information. *Ethics and Behavior, 7,* 311–328.

Canterbury v. Spence, 464 F.2nd 772 (D.C. Cir. 1972).

Haas, L.J. (1991). Hide and seek or show and tell? Emerging issues of informed consent. *Ethics and Behavior, 1,* 175–189.

Haas, L.J., & Cummings, N.A. (1991). Managed outpatient mental health plans: Clinical, ethical, and practical guidelines for participation. *Professional Psychology: Research and Practice, 22,* 45–51.

Handelsman, M.M., & Galvin, M.D. (1988). Facilitating informed consent for outpatient psychotherapy: A suggested written format. *Professional Psychology: Research and Practice, 19,* 223–225.

Handelsman, M.M., Kemper, M.B., Kesson-Craig, P., McLain, J., & Johnsrud, C. (1986). Use, content, and readability of written informed consent forms for treatment. *Professional Psychology: Research and Practice, 17,* 514–518.

Handelsman, M.M., & Martin, W.L., Jr. (1992). Effects of readability on the impact and recall of written informed consent material. *Professional Psychology: Research and Practice, 23,* 500–503.

Handelsman, M.M., Martinez, A., Geisendorfer, S., Jordan, L., Wagner, L., Daniel, P., & Davis, S. (1995). Does legally mandated consent to psychotherapy ensure its ethical appropriateness? The Colorado experience. *Ethics and Behavior, 5,* 119–129.

Kitchener, K.S. (2000). *Foundations of ethical practice, research, and teaching in psychology.* Mahwah, NJ: Erlbaum.

Lidz, C.W., Meisel, A., Zerubavel, E., Carter, M., Sestak, R.M., & Roth, L.H. (1984). *Informed consent: A study of decision making in psychiatry.* New York: Guilford Press.

Moline, M.E., Williams, G.T., & Austin, K.M. (1998). *Documenting psychotherapy: Essentials for mental health practitioners.* Thousand Oaks, CA: Sage.

Morrow, G.R., Gootnick, J., & Schmale, A. (1978). A simple technique for increasing cancer patients' informed consent to treatment. *Cancer, 42,* 793–799.

Nagy, T.F. (2000). *Ethics in plain English.* Washington, DC: American Psychological Association.

Natanson v. Kline, 350 P.2d 1093 (Kan. 1960).

Sullivan, T., Martin, W.L., Jr., & Handelsman, M.M. (1993). Practical benefits of an informed consent procedure: An empirical investigation. *Professional Psychology: Research and Practice, 24,* 160–163.

Wagner, L., Davis, S., & Handelsman, M.M. (1998). In search of the abominable consent form: The impact of readability and personalization. *Journal of Clinical Psychology, 54,* 115–120.

Zuckerman, E.L. (1997). *The paper office* (2nd ed.). New York: Guilford Press.

66 RESPONSIBLE DOCUMENTATION

Kathryn C. MacCluskie

If it isn't written down, it doesn't exist.

—Source unknown

Some counselors and other mental health workers may tend to neglect paperwork, viewing it as a necessary but odious and time-consuming aspect of their jobs. This is an understandable perception, given the fact that human contact, for many counselors, is far preferable to sitting alone at one's desk doing paperwork. Nevertheless, responsible case documentation is essential to competent provision of services to clients. Wiger (1999b) noted that most therapists receive little training in proper documentation, but when they do, they report feeling much more at ease about requesting third-party payments.

Case documentation refers to written documents that chronicle the course of a client's treatment, beginning with initial contact with the counselor, through the termination summary completed when the client discontinues treatment. In addition to intake information and progress notes, it also encompasses many other forms, such as consent to treatment, release of information, a financial agreement, treatment plan, and copies of any correspondence pertaining to the client, sent either to or from the counselor.

This chapter covers important terms related to documentation, reasons why good documentation is important, the key elements that should be documented in a client's chart, and current issues related to documentation.

IMPORTANT TERMS

There are several common terms and phrases associated with case documentation and third-party reimbursement. The following definitions (as cited in Wiger, 1999b) are excerpted from the Blue Cross/Blue Shield requirements for mental health benefit eligibility. Although these definitions are specific to Blue Cross/Blue Shield, they are an excellent representation of current commonly accepted standards for eligibility for mental health services. *Medical necessity* means that the client is experiencing symptoms that result in significant impairment ... as he or she attempts activities and responsibilities of daily living, caused specifically by a mental disorder. A related term, *therapeutic necessity,* means that specified therapeutic services are indicated, such services being warranted by the diagnosis and severity of impairment, and such services having been empirically demonstrated to be efficacious interventions for the diagnosis. The intensity with which treatment continues must be consistent with the documented intensity or severity of symptoms with which the client presents. Furthermore, there needs to be documentation of client progress corresponding to the therapeutic services at a rate consistent with the intensity and severity of the symptoms. The latter two conditions will be impossible for the counselor to prove unless information has been recorded and documented as an ongoing record of the client's response to treatment.

WHY KEEP GOOD RECORDS?

There are a multitude of reasons for good record keeping. It could be argued that, ultimately, *any* justification for competent documentation leads to the same desired outcome of providing maximum therapeutic benefit to all clients. The reasons I address in this chapter fall under the categories of ethical mandates, legality, interinstitutional communication, and quality assurance.

Ethical Mandates

Wiger (1999a) noted, "Without good documentation, there is no clear record of the course and progress of therapy. Sloppy clinical procedures are not only unfair to the client, but they may border on malpractice" (p. 1). Many mental health specialty areas have specific guidelines for record keeping, including the American Association for Marriage and Family Therapy, the American Counseling Association, the American Psychological Association, the American Psychiatric Association, the Association for Specialists in Group Work, and the National Association of Social Workers (Moline, Williams, & Austin, 1998). For example, the American Psychological Association *Code of Ethics,* Section 1.24 Records and Data, states, "Psychologists create, maintain, disseminate, store, retain, and dispose of records and data relating to their research, practice, and other work in accordance with law and in a manner that permits compliance with the requirements of this Ethics Code." The American Counseling Association Section B.4.A. states, "Counselors maintain records necessary for rendering professional services to their clients and as required by laws, regulations, or agency or institution procedures." All six sets of ethical guidelines have explicit articles requiring accurate and timely documentation of client care.

Legal Reasons

Smith (1996) noted that maintaining complete, current records and conscientious awareness of confidentiality are means of reducing the likelihood of clients filing malpractice complaints. Furthermore, if a malpractice complaint does occur, adequate and secure record keeping lessens the likelihood that the clinician will, in fact, be found guilty of negligence. Thus, adequate case documentation can be a good defense against legal liability in cases of alleged neglect or malpractice. Welfel (1998) observed that "most scholars find the current [record keeping] standards valuable for maintaining quality care to clients and for protecting professionals whose work is challenged by disciplinary boards, lawsuits, or third-party payers" (p. 311). The client record is the primary evidence a counselor has regarding how a client's treatment began, transpired, and was concluded.

Documenting Abuse. In the category of adequate record keeping are two situations in which a service provider is at heightened risk for liability. One is documentation of a client disclosure that would require the counselor to break confidentiality. Child abuse constitutes a mandatory report in every state and the District of Columbia (see Chapter 68). Many states also have mandatory reporting laws covering dependent or elder abuse as well, with reporting requirements similar to those for child abuse (see Chapter 69).

Beyond the mandatory phone call from the counselor to the protective services agency, there also must be documentation of the client's disclosure and the counselor's report to protective services in writing. There may be specific forms used for reporting abuse generated by Child Protective Services. A copy of the written report should always be retained for the client's chart. If a preliminary phone call is made to protective services prior to filing the written report, the phone call also should be documented.

Duty to Warn. Another high-risk situation is one in which the counselor has a duty to warn a potential victim (see Chapter 38). These laws may vary across states. When a client indicates intent to perpetrate harm toward another specific individual, there is an identifiable victim, and the mental health professional must warn the victim and the police in Arizona, California,

Kentucky, Louisiana, Maryland, Montana, and Utah. In Minnesota, law enforcement is notified when the victim cannot be reached. In Colorado, the client does not need to say he intends to kill a victim in order for the therapist to break confidence. Some states allow a choice of responses to meet the duty to protect (Indiana, Massachusetts, Michigan, New Hampshire, and Tennessee). Mental health professionals need to be aware of the laws in their state.

Documenting Suicidality. Finally, when a counselor has determined that a client's risk for attempted suicide is high, the counselor must take steps to ensure the client's safety. Ideally, the counselor might persuade the client to make the disclosure of suicidal intent to someone in the client's support system. This is an ideal situation because the counselor has not been forced to break the client's confidence. However, if a client refuses to do this or self-admit to a more restrictive setting, the counselor has no choice but to break confidence and take steps to ensure the client's safety. This might involve notifying a family member, helping the family member initiate involuntary hospitalization papers, or arranging for family members to stay with the client constantly, in lieu of being hospitalized.

Every aspect of the counselor's interaction with a suicidal client needs to be accurately and objectively documented. If a therapist broke a client's confidence because the client was determined to be at high risk for suicide (or harming another person), and the counselor had no documentation of the evidence used to determine the risk, the counselor could be liable for breach of confidence. When a therapist carefully records client symptoms, verbalizations, behaviors, and diagnostic impressions, the likelihood of a breach of confidence suit is lessened considerably.

The possibility always exists that case records will be subpoenaed or court-ordered. It is generally advisable to write notes, summaries, and so on as though they will be scrutinized closely. Perhaps more likely than a subpoena, sometimes clients or a client's family member (e.g., a parent or spouse acting on a client's behalf) expresses interest in reviewing a client's treatment records. Although the counselor or the counselor's employer are the owners of the paper documents, the client has "property interest" in his or her treatment records, and increasingly, courts are ruling that clients have the right to review their own records (Vandecreek & Knapp, 1997).

Documenting for Institutional Communication

There are numerous organizational entities that might require documentation to communicate about a client or service processes: insurance companies or other third-party payers (e.g., Medicaid); governing bodies (e.g., County Board of Mental Health); accrediting bodies (e.g., Joint Commission of Accreditation of Healthcare Organizations, JCAHO); and internal agency requirements (i.e., quality assurance) to ensure compliance with the first three groups.

Quality Assurance

In manufacturing, there is an aspect of production called quality control, in which random samples of the product are taken off an assembly line and inspected in detail to monitor the quality of assembly. Quality assurance in agencies serves precisely the same purpose.

Some agencies use a system of internal review, where certain staff members are designated as quality assurance (QA) workers. QA workers might have a portion of their work week allocated for chart review, in which they randomly select client charts and scrutinize them carefully. Those selected charts are inspected for proper inclusion of appropriate documents, such as consent to treatment, treatment plans, releases of information that are up to date, and dates of billed service that should coincide with dates of service documented in the progress notes.

QA serves several important functions. First, when outside accrediting bodies such as JCAHO visit the agency and audit records, if the internal QA people have done their jobs well, site visits should go well. Employees in public agencies have a material interest in maintaining agency accreditation because the accreditation status might affect the agency's eligibility for funding from the county, state, or federal government or eligibility to maintain a contract with a third-party payer.

External accreditation is also important because it indicates that the agency has met certain minimum criteria for service delivery. When clients present at that agency for service, they know that the agency has been endorsed by a large, widely respected body that scrutinizes health care agencies. Additionally, agencies are better able to negotiate contracts with third-party providers if they have been endorsed by accrediting bodies such as JCAHO.

KEY DOCUMENTATION

This section deals with the basic elements of a client's chart and related documenting issues. The American Psychological Association *Record Keeping Guidelines* (1993) stipulate minimum elements in a client record: "(1) identifying data; (2) dates of service; (3) types of service; (4) fees; (5) any assessment, plan for intervention, consultation, summary reports, and/or testing reports and supporting data as may be appropriate; and (6) any release of information obtained" (p. 3).

Initial Assessment and Treatment Plan

Many agencies have their own internally generated forms for completing an initial interview with a client. There is consistency across authors as to what information should be contained in an initial intake (Faiver, 1986; Moline et al., 1998; Moyers & Hester, 1999; Wiger, 1999a, 1999b). The treatment plan should, by definition, address the concerns the client indicates are most pressing. Sometimes, a client is unable to clearly articulate the specific nature of his or her problem(s). The therapist's job is to help the client understand, in language the client is familiar with, what the crux of the problem is. The treatment plan should target the problems the client identifies, but also should involve a collaborative effort between

counselor and client to subsequently define the corresponding treatment goals. Depending on the therapist's theoretical orientation, treatment planning should occur in the first few meetings between the client and counselor. For an example of a treatment plan, see Chapter 14.

Progress Notes

Progress notes can take several forms. Formats vary slightly in how categories of client status are recorded, and agencies or third-party payers may have specific requirements as to the particular format to be used. The purpose of the progress note is to document the manner in which the treatment plan is being implemented, specific interventions employed in each session, the status of the client's current symptoms as they relate to the presenting complaint, and the plan for the subsequent session. Every contact a counselor has with a client should have a corresponding progress note entry. Two commonly used formats for recording client progress are the DAP and the SOAP. The DAP (Wiger, 1999b) stands for Data (an objective account of what transpired in the session; this would include an objective behavioral description of what the client did and said); Assessment (the counselor's interpretation of the implications of the data in the context of the presenting problem and treatment plan); Plan (based on the data and assessment, the plan describes what the counselor intends to accomplish in the next session). The SOAP format (Tuthill, 1997) stands for Subjective (the client's complaint); Objective (the objective evidence for care seen on each visit); Assessment (assessment of the client's condition); Plan (plan for treatment on that visit).

There also need to be case note entries for each contact the counselor has with collaterals (other individuals involved with the client). This might include other mental health professionals, medical personnel such as physicians, attorneys, teachers, family members, and employers. For each person contacted or with whom the counselor has communication, there must be a release of information signed by the client and granting the counselor permission to communicate with the collateral person.

Correspondence

Any correspondence or other material received by the client, such as written homework assignments, journaling, artwork, and letters, should be filed in the client record. As well, any correspondence the counselor writes to or about the client should be kept in duplicate form in the client's file.

Termination Summary

There needs to be a summary of the client's treatment, beginning with a brief overview of the presenting problems, treatment goals, methods used, and client's response to the treatment, when a client's chart is closed and archived. Regardless of whether the client successfully achieved the identified goals on the treatment plan, when a client's chart is archived, there needs to be notation as to the justification for closing/terminating services. Some agencies have a policy about how to terminate a case for lack of contact, with specific guidelines as to how much time must transpire before the chart can be closed.

A key element of documentation, beyond the actual content of the record, is the manner in which the content is recorded. There are two related issues here. One is objectivity, and the other is retrievability. Of primary consideration is that the documentation be as objective as possible. Although there is no such thing as absolutely objective documentation, therapists should strive to avoid interpretation of client behavior or affect. Instead, it is preferable to describe client behavior in such a manner that a reader not present in the room would be able to generate an accurate mental image of how the client presented. Direct quotes can be quite helpful. Consider the following three examples of a case notation:

1. The client was depressed in this session.
2. The client sat slumped in his chair with a sullen facial expression and downcast eyes.
3. The client sat slumped in his chair with a sullen facial expression and downcast eyes, and he stated, "I feel like I'm carrying the world on my shoulders."

All three examples give the reader information about the client's depression, but the third example clearly offers the reader more information than the first. Additionally, a client reading his or her own records is less likely to be offended by a behavioral description than a therapist's interpretation.

The main concern related to retrievability is legibility of handwriting. Weiner (1995) observed that illegible writing in a client's chart suggests carelessness, which could be extrapolated to indicate general carelessness in providing services to a client. In a court of law, if a therapist was being sued for negligence, such carelessness would likely be a contributing piece of evidence of neglect.

CURRENT ISSUES RELATED TO DOCUMENTATION

This section reviews some current issues, many unresolved, related to case documentation.

Release of Information to Third-Party Payers

There is controversy about how much information third-party payers are legally permitted to demand. At the time this volume went to press, there was a lawsuit as to how much information an insurance company needs to have to justify continued coverage for health care (Rabasca, 2000). In New Jersey, the lawsuit involved a psychologist suing an insurance company for being dropped from the company's provider list after the psychologist refused to release detailed client records. His lawsuit was based on two facts: New Jersey state law directly stipulates that psychologists should not release progress notes to insurance companies, and his contract with Magellan stipulates that he will obey the law at all times.

Electronic Format

Electronic progress notes and charting may become a commonplace arrangement in the years to come. There are clear advantages to electronic format, the most obvious being accessibility to the records by other health care providers and reduction of physical storage space. However, there are also disadvantages, such as who has access to the records. With a paper chart, a counselor or an agency can maintain tight control over the physical location and security of the chart. With an electronic chart, it is much more difficult to maintain that same level of security, and any number of people skilled in computer use might be able to access confidential chart information. There is additionally the problem of therapists or other readers of the electronic chart being able to enter the computer program and edit the existing chart, whereas with a paper chart, it is often easy to detect if the chart has been modified after the original documentation.

Faxing progress notes, reports, and other case information has become commonplace. It is important for therapists to note that they are ultimately responsible for the security and confidentiality of those notes. When a fax is sent, the control of the security leaves the therapist's hands, although legally, the therapist is still responsible (Welfel, 1998).

Progress versus Process Notes

Several authors (Moline et al., 1998; Vandecreek & Knapp, 1997) differentiate between progress notes and process notes and strongly advise against including process notes as part of the client's case record. *Progress notes* are the actual notation about what transpired in a particular treatment session. They tend to be descriptive of the treatment procedure and the counselor's observations.

In contrast, a *process note* refers to a counselor's personal opinions and internal, emotional reactions to a client or some aspect of the client's care. Process notes can be very helpful to the counselor and possibly the client because the counselor needs to be aware of his or her own countertransference to the client. Material generated through process notes can help counselors process their own feelings with a supervisor or colleague, and can also help counselors generate hypotheses about issues related to the client's diagnosis or treatment. However, process notes should not be

part of the client's record, but should be stored in a separate location, such as a personal journal kept at home.

Release of Information to Consumers of Mental Health Services

Terminology, labels, and language used in communication about clients will influence others' impressions of the client. The therapist should strive to use language free of prejudice and make every attempt to be as objective and behavioral in descriptions and diagnoses as possible. When communicating with other professionals about the client, the therapist must strive for equilibrium between maintaining the client's confidentiality and the need for other professionals and colleagues to have information that will benefit the client and that may enable other professionals to provide optimal care for the client (du Plessis & Hirst, 1999).

SUMMARY

Numerous rationales for responsible case documentation have been presented. Adequate record keeping is essential for reasons of quality services to clients. Many mental health specialty areas have ethical codes with specific guidelines for record keeping. There are also legal ramifications for competent record keeping, some of which include documenting therapist's justification for breaking confidentiality in duty-to-warn cases and mandatory reporting of abuse. There are typically documentation requirements imposed by third-party payers and accrediting bodies as well.

Although agencies and third-party payers vary with respect to the amount and form of the records maintained, case documentation should always be done in an objective, professional manner. When describing client verbalizations or nonverbal behavior, clinicians are well advised to write a concise behavioral description of what they observed. Similarly, statements by clinicians about conclusions they made should be written in professional language, and those conclusions should be preceded by the objective client data (either behavioral observations, collateral information, or background information) that provide the basis for the conclusions.

References

American Psychological Association. (1993). *Record keeping guidelines.* Washington, DC: Author.

du Plessis, P., & Hirst, F. (1999). Written communication about clients. In R. Bor & M. Watts (Eds.), *The trainee handbook: A guide for counselling and psychotherapy trainees* (pp. 87–106). London: Sage.

Faiver, C. (1986). The mental health status examination: Revised. In P.A. Keller & L.G. Ritt (Eds.), *Innovations in clinical practice: A source book* (Vol. 5, pp. 279–285). Sarasota, FL: Professional Resource Exchange.

Moline, M.E., Williams, G.T., & Austin, K.M. (1998). *Documenting psychotherapy: Essentials for mental health practitioners.* Thousand Oaks, CA: Sage.

Moyers, T.B., & Hester, R.K. (1999). Credentialing, documentation, and evaluation. In B.S. McCrady & E.E. Epstein (Eds.), *Addictions: A comprehensive guidebook* (pp. 414–420). New York: Oxford University Press.

Rabasca, L. (2000). Two APA members sue managed-care companies on behalf of patient welfare. *APA Monitor, 31,* 30.

Scott, R.W. (2000). *Legal aspects of documenting patient care* (2nd ed.). Gaithersburg, MD: Aspen.

Smith, S.R. (1996). Malpractice liability of mental health professionals and institutions. In B.D. Sales & D.W. Shuman (Eds.), *Law, mental health, and mental disorder* (pp. 76–98). Pacific Grove, CA: Brooks/Cole.

Tuthill, A.R. (1997). Record keeping: New rules make it more important than ever. *California Chiropractic Association Journal, 22,* 22–24.

Vandecreek, L., & Knapp, S.J. (1997). Recordkeeping. In J.R. Matthews & C.E. Walker (Eds.), *Basic skills and professional issues in clinical psychology* (pp. 155–172). Boston: Allyn & Bacon.

Weiner, I.B. (1995). How to anticipate ethical and legal challenges in personality assessment. In J.N. Butcher (Ed.), *Clinical personality assessment* (pp. 95–103). New York: Oxford University Press.

Welfel, E.R. (1998). *Ethics in counseling and psychotherapy: Standards, research, and emerging issues.* Pacific Grove, CA: Brooks/Cole.

Wiger, D.E. (1999a). *The clinical documentation sourcebook: A comprehensive collection of mental health practice forms, handouts, and records* (2nd ed.). New York: Wiley.

Wiger, D.E. (1999b). *The psychotherapy documentation primer.* New York: Wiley.

67 MANAGING BOUNDARIES

Barbara Herlihy

Questions regarding the boundaries of the therapeutic relationship have been quite troublesome for mental health professionals. Two terms, *boundaries* and *dual* or *multiple relationships,* are closely related but have different meanings. A boundary might be described as a border or frame around the professional relationship that defines the roles and responsibilities of each member of the therapeutic dyad. Although the therapeutic relationship can be intense and may involve a great deal of emotional intimacy, it is a professional relationship. Therefore, it needs to have certain limits that might not exist in a personal relationship. Limits on the frequency and location of meetings, on physical contact, and on the exchange of gifts are just a few examples (Remley & Herlihy, 2001). Katherine's (1991) definition of a boundary as a limit that promotes and preserves integrity serves as a reminder that the purpose of boundaries is to provide structure and safety for clients.

The need to establish and maintain boundaries in the therapeutic relationship has been recognized since the beginnings of psychotherapy practice. Early psychoanalysts believed that maintaining the analytic framework, which included a range of procedural elements such as the schedule for sessions and stylistic elements such as the analyst's relative anonymity, was itself a therapeutic factor (Corey, 2001). Modern-day counselors of all theoretical orientations acknowledge the need to carefully maintain therapeutic boundaries, although there is a range of opinion regarding where those boundaries should be set and how flexible they should be.

Most professionals agree that boundaries need to be consistent and yet flexible enough for counselors to be able to respond to the unique needs of each client. Some writers (Gabbard, 1995; Smith & Fitzpatrick, 1995) have used the term "boundary crossing" to describe a departure from usual practice that is done to benefit a particular client at a particular time. For instance, a counselor might have a policy of not accepting gifts but would make an exception for a token gift when a client's cultural values would lead the client to see refusing the gift as an insult. Most mental health professionals probably make occasional, minor departures from their customary practices when they believe that clients' best interests will be served. Although infrequent boundary crossings that can be clinically justified are unlikely to be problematic, practitioners would be unwise to let them become routine. When a pattern of blurring the professional boundaries

develops, a dual relationship is created that is potentially harmful to the clients involved. A gradual erosion of the boundaries of a professional relationship can lead therapists down an insidious path and leave them vulnerable to charges brought in court or before an ethics committee or a licensing board (Remley & Herlihy, 2001).

A dual or multiple relationship exists whenever helping professionals take on two or more roles, simultaneously or sequentially, with a person who is seeking their help (Herlihy & Corey, 1997). Various types of dual relationships involve the blending of the professional relationship with another professional relationship (such as serving as someone's counselor and supervisor), a personal/social relationship (counselor and friend), a business relationship (counselor and employer), or a sexual relationship.

The codes of ethics of all the major mental health professions caution practitioners about dual relationships, yet the codes do not attempt to prohibit all dual relationships. Rather, they advise their members to refrain from entering into those dual relationships that are likely to impair professional objectivity or harm or exploit the other person involved. This type of wording points up two characteristics of dual relationships that make them troublesome for mental health professionals: They are not always harmful, and they are not always avoidable.

Dual relationships are not always harmful. Instead, they exist along a continuum, from those that are extremely exploitative and harmful to clients to those that are relatively benign. Nonetheless, a possible dual relationship always carries the *potential* for harm. Therefore, it is crucial that counselors are able to assess the risk factors in any dual relationship they consider entering. The first and perhaps primary risk of harm arises from the power differential in the therapeutic relationship. Clients invest a great deal of trust in their counselors and they make themselves vulnerable when they disclose their personal problems, fears, and struggles. Mental health professionals exploit this vulnerability and trust when they use the relationship to meet their own needs for friendship, affiliation, or sexual gratification. Second, dual roles may carry conflicting responsibilities for the professional involved. For instance, the nonjudgmental acceptance that is vital to the role of counselor is in conflict with the responsibility for evaluation that is inherent in the role of supervisor or employer. Third, clients' expectations will differ according to the role the professional is playing at a given time. For example, assume that Sue is a counselor who has unwisely entered into a counseling relationship with her friend Melinda. Melinda, as a friend, has felt free to call Sue at home in the evenings and to invite her out to lunch. In her client role, however, these behaviors are inappropriate. Clients in such relationships are likely to feel confused and ultimately hurt and betrayed. Their dependency on the professional may leave them feeling trapped in the dual relationship, thus compounding the harm.

A second troublesome characteristic of dual relationships is that they are not always avoidable. Much has been written about the dilemmas faced by rural practitioners (Brown, 1994; Forester-Miller, 1997; Schank & Skovholt, 1997; Sleek, 1994) who might have few if any clients if they could not provide counseling services to people with whom they were already acquainted in some capacity. "Small worlds" can exist in urban environments as well. Clients often seek out psychotherapists who hold values similar to their own. Thus, a therapist's cultural or ethnic identity, sexual orientation, membership in a religious congregation, political affiliation, or substance dependence recovery status can increase the potential for dual relationships to occur (Herlihy & Corey, 1997; Lerman & Porter, 1990). In addition, some roles that mental health professionals play, such as the role of supervisor to students and novice practitioners, seem to involve an inherent duality (Borders, 1992).

Although professionals may be unable to avoid some dual relationships and might choose to enter into others that carry little risk of harm, one type of dual relationship—sexual intimacies with clients—is universally acknowledged to be devastating to clients. It is explicitly forbidden by the codes of ethics of all the major mental health professions. At one time, sexual relationships, primarily between male therapists and female clients, were not uncommon occurrences that went largely unacknowledged. This is no longer true, due to a series of events including (1) the pioneering efforts of researchers such as Gartrell, Herman, Olarte, Feldstein, and Localio (1987) to bring this practice to light and Pope (1988) to describe the harmful effects on clients as a "patient-therapist sex syndrome"; (2) the efforts of professional associations to create and impose sanctions against offenders; and (3) a trend toward criminalizing the behavior. The authors of one study (Anderson & Kitchener, 1996) concluded that instances of sexual intimacies between therapists and clients have decreased in frequency over the past two decades.

Professional associations have taken somewhat differing stances on the issue of posttherapy sexual relationships. The National Association of Social Workers (NASW) (Code of Ethics, 1999) does not specify a time limit or waiting period between the termination of a professional relationship and the initiation of a sexual relationship. Other associations, including the American Counseling Association (ACA) and the American Psychological Association (APA), prohibit their members from engaging in sexual intimacies with former clients for at least two years after termination of the professional relationship (ACA Code of Ethics and Standards of Practice, 1995; APA Ethical Principles of Psychologists and Code of Conduct, 1992). Some professionals have misinterpreted these guidelines to mean that posttermination sexual relationships are always acceptable after two years have elapsed. More accurately, sexual intimacies even after more than two years have passed should occur only under exceptional circumstances, and it is always the responsibility of the professional involved to ensure that no harm is done.

The mental health professions have reached a clear consensus regarding the impropriety of sexual intimacies with clients.

However, questions related to nonsexual dual relationships and boundary crossings remain controversial. Some practices that involve a boundary crossing, but that do not by themselves constitute a dual relationship, have been debated in the professional literature. These practices include touching or physical contact with clients, therapist self-disclosure, accepting gifts, socializing with clients or former clients, and bartering. The position that mental health professionals take toward these behaviors will vary depending on a number of factors, such as their theoretical orientation, the setting in which they practice, the nature of their clientele, and current social mores.

The views of mental health professionals toward the propriety of therapeutic touch or nonerotic physical contact with clients have fluctuated over time, along with changes in societal values (Smith & Fitzpatrick, 1995). In the Freudian era with its Victorian notions of sexuality, therapeutic touch was prohibited and was presumed to have a negative effect on transference and countertransference. During the 1960s and 1970s, the era of the human potential movement, therapeutic touch was a more accepted practice. Today, mental health practitioners (and their malpractice insurance carriers) are more sensitive to the possibility of lawsuits and are more cautious about making physical contact with clients. Generally, therapists would be well advised to consider the potential risks, including the possibility (which can vary according to the client's age, sex, diagnosis, or culture) that a client might misinterpret or sexualize such a gesture, and should proceed only after first securing the client's permission.

The extent to which counselors engage in self-disclosure depends on factors such as their theoretical orientation and their skill and comfort in using this technique (Remley & Herlihy, 2001). Self-disclosure becomes a boundary issue when it is done to meet a counselor's own needs for understanding, approval, intimacy, or other personal needs. When self-disclosure is used inappropriately or excessively, a role reversal occurs in which the client becomes the therapist's emotional caretaker. Counselors need to self-monitor their use of this technique, keeping in mind Simon's (1991) finding that inappropriate therapist self-disclosure, more than any other kind of boundary crossing, is likely to precede therapist-client sexual intimacies.

Although many practitioners include the information in their professional disclosure statements that they do not accept gifts from clients, clients will not always understand or respect this boundary. When a client offers a gift, counselors often feel uncomfortable refusing out of a concern that the client may feel hurt, offended, or rejected. In some instances, the gracious acceptance of a token gift may be an appropriate and justifiable boundary crossing; at other times, offered gifts will need to be refused. Perhaps the best way for counselors to avoid awkward interchanges is to think through the criteria they would use in determining whether to accept or refuse a gift. Factors to consider might include the monetary value of the gift, the client's motivation for offering it, the therapist's motivation for accepting or refusing it, the stage of the therapeutic relationship, the cultural meaning of gifts to the client, and the implicit message the counselor would be sending in an acceptance or refusal. Consideration for the client's welfare must always be paramount in decision making regarding this issue.

There is consensus among mental health professionals that a friendship and a therapeutic relationship with a client cannot exist simultaneously. A friendship is characterized by mutual support and reciprocated personal disclosures, whereas the emotional intimacy in a therapeutic relationship is one-way. Yet, individuals who choose to become mental health service providers are not expected to forfeit their social lives to avoid all nonprofessional contact with clients (Glosoff, 1997). Therapists who practice in rural settings or who belong to "small world" communities probably can expect out-of-the-office encounters with clients to occur routinely. Such unplanned meetings need not be problematic if counselor and client have discussed in advance how the client prefers to handle these encounters. On the other hand, clients sometimes will invite their therapists to social events, ask them to meet for lunch, or ask them to attend an event that has special meaning for the client, such as a graduation or a wedding. The mental health professional's response to these kinds of requests may depend, again, on a number of factors, such as theoretical orientation or the client's more general respect for the therapeutic boundaries.

Mental health practitioners seem to find the practice of developing posttherapy social relationships much less objectionable than posttherapy sexual relationships. In one study, Salisbury and Kinnier (1996) found that fully 70% of counselors surveyed believed that a posttherapy friendship could be acceptable, and that 33% of them had actually developed friendships with former clients. The codes of ethics are silent on this issue, leaving it up to individual professionals to decide their own stance toward the practice. Factors that should be considered include the amount of time that has passed since the termination of the professional relationship, the possibility that the former client might want to return for further counseling, the length and nature of counseling, the client's issues and diagnosis, any transference and countertransference issues, the client's ego strength, the circumstances surrounding termination, and whether the professional's needs for friendship may be superseding considerations for client welfare. Practitioners should also keep in mind that the power differential that existed in the therapeutic relationship is not automatically negated by termination. Friendships between counselors and former clients never begin on an equal footing.

As a general rule, bartering is a practice that should be avoided due to its inherent potential for conflicts, exploitation, and distortion of the professional relationship. Professional codes of ethics, including those of ACA, APA, and NASW, stop short of prohibiting this practice, however. Instead, they specify circumstances under which it might be acceptable, including when the relationship is not exploitative (ACA, APA), when the client requests or initiates it (ACA, NASW), when it is an accepted practice

among other professionals in the community (ACA, NASW), when it is not clinically contraindicated (APA), when it is considered essential for the provision of service (NASW), or with the client's informed consent (NASW).

Given that, aside from sexual relationships with current clients, boundary issues and dual relationship questions have few universally agreed-on answers, it is imperative that mental health professionals have a process for reasoning through the issues that will arise inevitably in their work. Herlihy and Corey (1997) have offered a decision-making model that includes these steps:

1. Determine whether the potential dual relationship is avoidable or unavoidable.
2. If it is avoidable, the potential risks and benefits should be assessed. Kitchener and Harding (1990) have suggested that practitioners faced with a possible dual relationship might assess the potential for harm by considering that (a) the greater the incompatibility of the client's expectations of the counselor in the two roles, the greater the risk of harm; (b) the greater the divergence between the responsibilities of the counselor in the two roles, the greater the potential for divided loyalties and loss of objectivity; and (c) the greater the power differential between the two individuals involved, the greater the potential for exploitation of the person in the vulnerable position.
3. Discuss the potential problems and benefits with the client. In most instances, the decision regarding whether to enter into a dual relationship can be made *with* the client rather than *for* the client.
4. Decide. If the risks seem to be high, decline to enter the relationship, explain the reasons for the decision to the client, and refer if necessary.

If the dual relationship is entered into, either by choice or because it cannot be avoided, steps that can be taken to protect the client from harm include securing the client's fully informed consent and discussing boundary issues with the client on an ongoing basis, seeking consultation throughout the dual relationship, documenting decisions and the rationale for those decisions, and self-monitoring against a loss of objectivity. When a dual relationship is unusually complex or when the risk of harm seems high, obtaining supervision for one's work with the particular client is a prudent step.

Much has been written about managing therapeutic boundaries. Katherine's (1991) book provides an excellent introduction to boundaries in general. *Boundary Issues in Counseling* (Herlihy & Corey, 1997) discusses dual relationship issues in various settings and with various clientele. Several articles that address boundary issues in specific modalities (e.g., family therapy, group work) and within specialty areas of practice (e.g., substance dependency counseling, pastoral counseling) can be found in specialty journals.

Although consensus may never emerge around some boundary and dual relationship issues, mental health professionals can protect their clients' welfare by:

1. Determining, before problems arise, where they want to draw their professional boundaries with their clients. For instance, is it okay for clients to call between scheduled sessions? Should they contact you in an emergency, or should they utilize a service that exists in the community?
2. Working to ensure that clients understand the limits to the relationship. Written professional disclosure statements, face-to-face discussions at the onset of therapy, and periodic revisiting of the issues are easily implemented strategies.
3. Being consistent yet flexible, and having a clear rationale for any exceptions made.
4. Taking proactive steps to protect the client when exceptions are made, such as seeking consultation or working under supervision.
5. Self-monitoring for any patterns that might develop.
6. Keeping up with current thinking by studying revisions in codes of ethics, reading the literature, and attending continuing professional development activities.

References

American Counseling Association. (1995). *Code of ethics and standards of practice*. Alexandria, VA: Author.

American Psychological Association. (1992). *Ethical principles of psychologists and code of conduct*. Washington, DC: Author.

Anderson, S.K., & Kitchener, K.S. (1996). Nonromantic, nonsexual posttherapy relationships between psychologists and former clients: An exploratory study of critical incidents. *Professional Psychology: Research and Practice, 27,* 59–66.

Borders, L.D. (1992). Duality within the supervisory relationship. In B. Herlihy & G. Corey (Eds.), *Dual relationships in counseling* (pp. 122–124). Alexandria, VA: American Association for Counseling and Development.

Brown, L. (1994). Boundaries in feminist therapy: A conceptual formulation. *Women and Therapy, 15*(1), 29–38.

Corey, G. (2001). *Theory and practice of counseling and psychotherapy* (6th ed.). Pacific Grove, CA: Brooks/Cole.

Forester-Miller, H. (1997). Rural communities: Can dual relationships be avoided? In B. Herlihy & G. Corey (Eds.), *Boundary issues in counseling* (pp. 99–100). Alexandria, VA: American Counseling Association.

Gabbard, G.O. (1995, April). What are boundaries in psychotherapy? *Menninger Letter, 3*(4), 1–2.

Gartrell, N., Herman, J., Olarte, S., Feldstein, M., & Localio, R. (1986). Psychiatrist-patient sexual contact: Results of a national survey: I. Prevalence. *American Journal of Psychiatry, 143,* 1126–1131.

Glosoff, H.L. (1997). Multiple relationship issues in private practice. In B. Herlihy & G. Corey (Eds.), *Boundary issues in counseling: Multiple roles and responsibilities* (pp. 114–120). Alexandria, VA: American Counseling Association.

Herlihy, B., & Corey, G. (Eds.). (1997). *Boundary issues in counseling: Multiple roles and responsibilities*. Alexandria, VA: American Counseling Association.

Katherine, A. (1991). *Boundaries: Where you end and I begin*. New York: Simon & Schuster.

Kitchener, K.S., & Harding, S.S. (1990). Dual role relationships. In B. Herlihy & L. Golden (Eds.), *Ethical standards casebook* (4th ed., pp. 145–148). Alexandria, VA: American Counseling Association.

Lerman, H., & Porter, N. (1990). The contribution of feminism to ethics in psychotherapy. In

H. Lerman & N. Porter (Eds.), *Feminist ethics in psychotherapy* (pp. 5–13). New York: Springer.

National Association of Social Workers. (1999). *Code of ethics.* Washington, DC: Author.

Pope, K.S. (1988). How clients are harmed by sexual contact with mental health professionals: The syndrome and its prevalence. *Journal of Counseling and Development, 67,* 222–226.

Remley, T.P., Jr., & Herlihy, B. (2001). *Ethical, legal, and professional issues in counseling.* Upper Saddle River, NJ: Merrill.

Salisbury, W.A., & Kinnier, R.T. (1996). Posttermination friendship between counselors and clients. *Journal of Counseling and Development, 74,* 495–500.

Schank, J.A., & Skovholt, T.M. (1997). Dual-relationship dilemmas of rural and small-community psychologists. *Professional Psychology: Research and Practice, 28,* 44–49.

Simon, R.I. (1991). Psychological injury caused by boundary violations: Precursors to therapist-patient sex. *Psychiatry Annals, 21,* 614–619.

Sleek, S. (1994, December). Ethical dilemmas plague rural practice. *APA Monitor,* 26–27.

Smith, D., & Fitzpatrick, M. (1995). Patient-therapist boundary issues: An integrative review of theory and research. *Professional Psychology: Research and Practice, 26,* 499–506.

68   REPORTING SUSPECTED CHILD ABUSE

Seth C. Kalichman

Millions of children are reported for child abuse and neglect in the United States each year, and reported cases represent a small minority of all abused children. Along with almost every human service profession, mental health practitioners are required by law to report known or suspected child abuse in all 50 of the United States. Professionals file nearly half of child maltreatment reports, with the majority originating from hospitals, schools, day care centers, and mental health/social service agencies (Kalichman, 1999). However, it is well established that mental health professionals often choose not to report suspected child abuse, commonly because they (1) feel that they can protect children better than the child protection system and (2) fear that reporting will cause irreparable damage to their services. Failure to report suspected child abuse is a violation of the law and therefore constitutes unethical behavior. On the other hand, failure to act in the best interest of one's client, such as triggering state intervention, is also unethical. For many mental health professionals, mandated reporting of suspected child abuse therefore represents an ethical dilemma.

This chapter briefly reviews the history and major elements of most mandatory child abuse reporting laws. The ethical issues posed by mandated reporting are also reviewed. Finally, practical suggestions for managing child abuse reports within clinical contexts are offered.

HISTORY OF CHILD ABUSE REPORTING LAWS

The advent of child abuse reporting laws followed a heightened awareness of suspicious injuries of children observed by medical professionals, particularly pediatricians and emergency room physicians. Kempe, Silverman, Steele, Droegemueller, and Silver (1962) first described the battered child syndrome and published the single most influential article on child maltreatment. As a new medical diagnosis, the battered child syndrome was characterized by "injury to soft tissue and skeleton" (p. 105) and was accompanied by "evidence of neglect including poor skin hygiene, multiple soft tissue injuries, and malnutrition" (pp. 105–106). Kempe et al. also provided detailed radiological features and clinical manifestations that were often discrepant with available information from case histories alone. Thus, several specific features, most of which were relevant to the medical examination of children, objectively defined the battered child syndrome.

The battered child syndrome and Kempe et al.'s (1962) commentary regarding physician reluctance to report abuse stimulated initiatives to develop mandatory reporting legislation. The first of three model reporting statutes was drafted in 1963 by the Children's Bureau of the National Center on Child Abuse and Neglect. Two subsequent statutes were drafted in 1965, one proposed by the American Medical Association and the other by the Program of State Governments. By 1966, an unprecedented legislative proliferation occurred with all states in the United States except Hawaii, which later followed, enacting laws mandating physicians to report suspected child abuse. The intent of the first reporting statutes was to identify cases of the battered child syndrome known to physicians that would not be recognizable by nonmedical observers (Paulsen, 1967).

Legislatures subsequently broadened most aspects of these early statutes, including the range of professionals and types of maltreatment meeting legal standards for required reporting. In the late 1960s and early 1970s, several groups of professionals were added to the rolls of mandated reporters. Definitions of abuse were also broadened to include emotional and nutritional maltreatment, as well as sexual abuse and exploitation.

States themselves have broadened and expanded their own reporting laws, with California amending its reporting statute more than 15 times in the 20 years following its passage (Meriwether, 1986). The expansion of reporting laws has not, unfortunately, taken into account the unique circumstances of professionals who were added to the roster of mandated reporters. Because the battered child syndrome originally described cases that were most likely seen by emergency room physicians, radiologists, and pediatricians, first-generation reporting statutes understandably targeted medical professionals. When reporting laws were expanded to include nonmedical professionals, there was also an expansion of definitions of abuse and conditions under which reporting was required. But reporting laws do not differentiate among mandated reporters who differ in their professional training, circumstances of practice, and conditions under which suspicions of maltreatment arise. Thus, a single standard for reporting is applied across professions, circumstances, and settings.

ELEMENTS OF REPORTING LAWS

Mandatory child abuse reporting laws (1) define abusive situations; (2) delineate reportable circumstances, the degree of certainty that reporters must attain, the age limits of reportable children, and details of who must report; (3) outline the sanctions for failing to report; and (4) provide immunity from civil and criminal liability for reports filed "in good faith." Although most reporting statutes share general features, state-reporting laws can also differ in important ways. The greatest degree of variability among laws is the way in which abuse is defined and conditions under which reporting is required. Three elements of reporting laws therefore appear to pose the greatest challenges to professionals: Who is required to report? What is required to be reported? and When is reporting required?

Who Is Required to Report?

The first laws that required professionals to report suspected child abuse were directed exclusively at medical professionals; however, this situation was fairly short-lived. Soon, a variety of helping professionals were added to the list of mandated reporters. Expanding mandated reporters continued over the years. For example, several states now mandate commercial film developers to report suspected abuse, usually specifying suspected sexual abuse and sexual exploitation that may be indicated by sexually explicit photographs of children. In addition, professionals who care for or supervise children in various settings have been added to the list of mandated reporters. Animal humane officers have even been designated mandated reporters in some states because of the common association between cruelty to animals and child abuse. Nearly universally, states require mental health professionals, including psychologists, counselors, social workers, and psychiatrists, to report suspected abuse. Other professionals who may be required to report suspected child abuse include pharmacists, dentists, and religious healers. Finally, it has become increasingly common for states to require that any person who suspects child abuse is required to report. When all states are considered, there are nearly 40 different professions specified in mandatory reporting laws (Wurtele & Miller-Perrin, 1992).

What Is Required to Be Reported?

A great deal of confusion exists concerning definitions of child maltreatment, much of which is the product of language used for divergent purposes. As a matter of classification, definitions serve diagnostic functions in medicine as well as other human service professions. However, both medical and social service definitions of abuse may differ from legal definitions. With respect to legal definitions of abuse, there are three functions for which abuse is typically defined: (1) criminal acts, (2) determination of child dependency, and (3) identifying cases that warrant reporting. Whereas legal definitions will overlap across these three areas of law, there are often distinguishing characteristics.

Legal definitions of child abuse focus on one of two features: the behavior of the abusive adult or the effects of abuse on children (Meriwether, 1986). Focusing on the perpetrator's behavior results in a set of circumstances or behaviors that lead to abusive conditions. On the other hand, focusing on the consequences suffered by victims of abuse emphasizes signs and symptoms. In either case, definitions of abuse can be broad, such as the circumstances of abuse and the signs of serious injury, or narrow, such as genital fondling or subdural hematoma.

Delineating what constitutes child abuse and neglect, both professionally and legally, directly affects whether cases are reported. Although research has shown differences in tendencies to report different types of abuse (Giovannoni, 1989; Kalichman & Craig, 1991; U.S. Department of Health and Human Services, 1988; Wilson & Gettinger, 1989; Zellman & Antler, 1990), there is little research to support the idea that signs or circumstances of different types of abuse, or narrow or broad definitions of abuse, differentially affect reporting decisions. One study, however, has found relationships between broad/narrow definitions of child abuse and both reporting and substantiation rates. Rycraft (1990) evaluated legal definitions of abuse and found that states with broad and nonspecific definitions have the highest reporting and substantiation rates. On the other hand, states with narrow and specific definitions of abuse have among the lowest rates. Rycraft concluded that definitions of child abuse are a determining factor in reporting decisions as well as the final dispositions of reported cases.

When Is Reporting Required?

Professionals mandated to report child abuse are required to do so under explicit conditions defined by law. The circumstances that specify when reporting is required are a source of controversy (Meriwether, 1986; Wurtele & Miller-Perrin, 1992). State laws, following the first model statutes, do not require reporters to have knowledge or any degree of certainty that abuse has occurred or will occur. Most often, laws use such language as "reason to believe" or "having reasonable cause to suspect" abuse. Few states provide any further description of conditions required for reporting. However, states that do define conditions for reporting may define "reasonable suspicion" as "It is objectively reasonable for a person to entertain such a suspicion, based upon facts that could cause a reasonable person in a like position, drawing when appropriate on his or her training and experience, to suspect abuse" (California Crime Prevention Center, 1988, p. 1). Still, what constitutes reasonable suspicion, as it may be differentiated from clinical hunches, professional impressions, and intuition, remains open to question. Understanding reporting laws and their implications for child welfare vary among persons involved in the child abuse reporting and child protection processes (Brooks, Perry, Starr, & Teply, 1994). Deisz, Doueck, George, and Levine (1996) found that the reasonable cause standard for reporting was interpreted differently by mental health professionals compared to child protection workers. Mental health professionals generally applied more expansive and broadened concepts of reportable situations under this standard, whereas child protection workers were more restrictive in their concept of reasonable cause to suspect abuse (Levine, 1998).

ETHICAL ISSUES IN MANDATED REPORTING

Requirements to report suspected child abuse stem from two broader professional obligations: the duty to protect and the duty to warn. Professionals must protect those they serve from potential harm. Physicians and other providers, for example, must report violent injuries such as those sustained by gunshot, knifing, poisoning, and any other wounds believed to result from suspicious acts. Reports of domestic violence often are also required. Health care providers are required to report a number of diseases to public health officials. Mandatory reporting laws exist to protect the public. Reporting potential child abuse does not require informed consent, and reporting laws supersede assurances of professional confidentiality. Laws that require reporting suspected child abuse therefore occur in a broader context of standards for protecting vulnerable persons from harm.

Mandated reporting of suspected child abuse also occurs within the context of professional obligations to protect persons from harm. Professionals are bound to a protective duty through ethical codes, standards of practice, and the law. Aside from required reporting of suspected child abuse, professionals must report suspected elder abuse and abuse of disabled persons. For example, New Jersey has defined abuse of adults as "the willful infliction of physical pain, injury, or mental anguish; unreasonable confinement; or the willful deprivation of services which are necessary to maintain a person's physical and mental health" (Wulach, 1998, p. 231). New York, on the other hand, only requires reporting adult abuse when it occurs in nursing homes or residential care facilities (Wulach, 1993). In California, institutionalized elder abuse is broadly defined to include assault, deprivation of food or water, sexual assault, negligent care, abandonment, fiduciary abuse, and isolation, all of which require reporting (Caudill & Pope, 1995). The duty to report therefore extends to other vulnerable populations, and many of the principles of mandated reporting of suspected child abuse extend to these other situations. (See Chapter 69 for more information on elder abuse reporting.)

Because reporting suspected child maltreatment involves breaking confidentiality to protect vulnerable persons, reporting requirements fall under the rubric of the duty to protect. Obligations to warn third parties of potential danger has been widely debated, particularly with reference to the case of *Tarasoff v. Board of Regents of the University of California* (1976; Koocher, 1988).

Duty to warn is also the mechanism that pits professional standards of confidentiality against the necessity of protecting others. It is in that sense that reporting suspected child abuse is considered a special case of duty to warn. Reporting abuse necessarily involves breaching confidentiality, preventing personal harm, and placing legal constraints on professional actions. Reporting also appears most akin to duty to warn when the source of the information is an adult suspected of being abusive, where potential harm may come to a third party. Also, like other types of duty to warn, reports of suspected child abuse can be used in prosecution of a crime (Leong, Eth, & Silva, 1992). In contrast to other instances of duty to warn, however, a child welfare agency receives the warning and responds on behalf of the child. Mandatory reporting is also different from most other cases of duty to warn because reporting suspected abuse is, for the most part, a legal obligation with ethical implications, whereas most other situations of duty to warn are ethical obligations with legal implications.

INFORMED CONSENT

Professional standards in mental health practice specify that information revealed by clients should remain confidential and that persons should be informed, when appropriate, of the legal limits of confidentiality. Clients, no matter their age, have a right to be informed of the limits of confidentiality before they disclose information in confidence. Informing minors about limited confidentiality, however, is complicated by their willingness to discuss issues that could anger their parents. In one survey, Beeman and Scott (1991) found that 70% of practicing psychologists obtained informed consent

from adolescent clients, including consent for limited confidentiality. Beeman and Scott also found that professionals viewed limiting confidentiality as the single most important element of informed consent for both adolescents and adults. However, treating minors requires parental consent, raising the possibility of parents interfering with the treatment process, especially when the parent is abusive. Parents may badger children about what they are saying in therapy, or tell children that the social service workers will take them away for "telling family secrets." Still, professionals state that including limited confidentiality in informed consent is necessary and has the potential benefit of enhancing a sense of autonomy that can help build therapeutic relationships (Beeman & Scott, 1991).

Psychologists who have previously experienced problems resulting from breached confidentiality are more likely to inform clients about limited confidentiality compared to psychologists who have not experienced such problems (Baird & Rupert, 1987). Fifty-nine percent of practicing psychologists in one survey believed that their clients were at least somewhat aware of professionals' requirements to report suspected child abuse (Brosig, 1992). This finding suggests that professionals may not believe it is necessary to inform clients of limited confidentiality with respect to mandated reporting. Although there are no standards for informing clients of limited confidentiality, there are some noteworthy suggestions.

The psychologists' ethics code states that informing persons of confidentiality and the limits of confidentiality should occur at the outset of professional and scientific relationships. Specifically, the code states, "Unless it is not foreseeable or is contraindicated, the discussion of confidentiality occurs at the outset of the relationship and thereafter as new circumstances may warrant" (APA Standard 5.01b). Keith-Spiegel and Koocher (1998) stated this position, suggesting that professionals discuss the limits of confidentiality as early in relationships as possible, such as during initial interviews.

PRACTICAL GUIDELINES FOR REPORTING SUSPECTED CHILD ABUSE

Comprehensive suggestions for managing reports of suspected child abuse are provided elsewhere (e.g., Kalichman, 1999). Following is a brief synopsis of practical guidelines for reporting suspected child abuse.

Exploring the Situation

Role conflict occurs when professionals act outside of their competence and capacity to investigate child abuse. For example, school psychologists without previous contact with a family should not delay reporting so that they can first talk with family members about their suspicions of abuse. Similarly, therapists will assume an investigative role if they contact a teacher before they are willing to report. Reporting decisions should be based on information gained in the course of usual professional activities, such as evaluating, teaching, or counseling. Within these roles, professionals can further explore their concerns about a child but without performing their own investigation.

Directly asking children and parents about abuse, such as "Is someone touching you in a way that makes you feel uncomfortable?" or "Were marks left after hitting your child?" can confirm abuse. However, parents' denial of abuse may merely reflect their unwillingness to admit abuse, therefore offering less than conclusive information Children and adults who respond to direct questions about abuse by becoming quiet or by refusing to answer may be communicating important information. Thus, how professionals process this information determines the inferences they draw about the situation and their decisions to report. Professionals must therefore establish their own thresholds for reporting, erring either in terms of overreporting or underreporting.

Consultation

When an evaluation and exploration of a case remains ambiguous as to whether to report, it is appropriate to consult a fellow mandated reporter. Professionals should identify potential colleagues in advance who would be qualified to discuss abuse and could offer insights. In essence, the standard for "reasonable suspicion" is whether a reasonable person would suspect maltreatment. Consulting a colleague therefore offers the strongest check on an individual's level of suspicion. Seeking advice can also occur in conjunction with case conferences and staff meetings. Through frank discussions it may become apparent that a case constitutes reasonable suspicion. On the other hand, consultation may help a professional decide not to report. Once again, when reporting decisions are not reached after consultation, the next course of action is to make preliminary contact with a child protection worker.

Preliminary Contact

Mandated reporters can contact a child protection worker for initial feedback about a case before reporting, particularly feedback about whether certain indicators of abuse are reportable. Professionals may discuss cases with an initial intake worker who receives reports or a case worker with whom the professional has had previous experience. Even in the most ambiguous cases, input from child protection workers will most likely resolve the decision to report or not to report suspected abuse.

SUMMARY

Mandated reporting can create professional role conflict and ethical challenges for mental health professionals. Psychologists, counselors, social workers, and other mental health practitioners rely on clinical hunches and intuition to guide many of the directions they take in their course of treatment. These subjective judgments are often difficult to distinguish from reasonable suspicions of abuse. Because reporting laws are intended to cast a broad net in identifying a maximum number of abused children, it is expected that nonabusive persons will be investigated. In addition, a large volume of reports has resulted in an overburdened child protection system. Mental health professionals therefore serve their clients and society best when they develop sound bases for reporting and effective methods of reporting individual cases. Practitioners and their clients benefit from a clear and complete informed consent process, well-defined thresholds for reporting cases of suspected child abuse, and procedures for managing ambiguous cases of suspected abuse.

References

Baird, K.A., & Rupert, P.A. (1987). Clinical management of confidentiality: A survey of psychologists in seven states. *Professional Psychology: Research and Practice, 18,* 230–234.

Beeman, D.G., & Scott, N.A. (1991). Therapists' attitudes toward psychotherapy informed consent with adolescents. *Professional Psychology: Research and Practice, 22,* 230–234.

Brooks, C.M., Perry, N., Starr, S., & Teply, L. (1994). Child abuse and neglect reporting laws: Understanding interests, understanding policy. *Behavioral Sciences and the Law, 12,* 49–64.

Brosig, C.L. (1992). *Child abuse reporting decisions: The effects of statutory wording of reporting requirements.* Unpublished master's thesis, Loyola University of Chicago.

California Crime Prevention Center. (1988). *Child abuse prevention handbook.* Sacramento: Author.

Caudill, O.B., & Pope, K.S. (1995). *Law and mental health professionals: California.* Washington, DC: American Psychological Association.

Deisz, R., Doueck, H.J., George, N., & Levine, M. (1996). Reasonable cause: A qualitative study of mandated reporting. *Child Abuse and Neglect, 20,* 275–287.

Giovannoni, J. (1989). Definitional issues in child maltreatment. In D. Cicchetti & V. Carlson (Eds.), *Child maltreatment* (pp. 3–37). New York: Cambridge University Press.

Kalichman, S.C. (1999). *Mandated reporting of suspected child abuse: Ethics, law, and policy* (2nd ed.). Washington, DC: American Psychological Association.

Kalichman, S.C., & Craig, M.E. (1991). Professional psychologists' decisions to report suspected abuse: Clinician and situation influences. *Professional Psychology: Research and Practice, 22,* 84–89.

Keith-Spiegel, P., & Koocher, G.P. (1998). *Ethics in psychology: Professional standards and cases* (2nd ed.). New York: Random House.

Kempe, C., Silverman, F., Steele, B., Droegemueller, W., & Silver, H. (1962). The battered child syndrome. *Journal of the American Medical Association, 181,* 4–11.

Koocher, G.P. (1988). A thumbnail guide to "duty to warn" cases. *The Clinical Psychologist, 41,* 22–25.

Leong, G.B., Eth, S., & Silva, J.A. (1992). The psychotherapist as witness for the prosecution: The criminalization of *Tarasoff. American Journal of Psychiatry, 149,* 1011–1015.

Levine, M. (1998). Do standards of proof affect decision making in child protection investigations? *Law and Human Behavior, 22,* 341–347.

Meriwether, M.H. (1986). Child abuse reporting laws: Time for a change. *Family Law Quarterly, 20,* 141–171.

Paulsen, M.C. (1967). Child abuse reporting laws: The shape of legislation. *Columbia Law Review, 67,* 1–49.

Rycraft, J.R. (1990). Redefining abuse and neglect: A narrower focus could affect children at risk. *Public Welfare, 49,* 14–21.

Tarasoff v. Regents of the University of California, 17 Cal. 3d 425, 551 P.2d 334 (1976).

U.S. Department of Health and Human Services. (1988). *Study findings: Study of National Incidence and Prevalence of Child Abuse and Neglect.* Bethesda, MD: Westat.

Wilson, C.A., & Gettinger, M. (1989). Determinants of child abuse reporting among Wisconsin school psychologists. *Professional School Psychology, 4,* 91–102.

Wulach, J.S. (1993). *Law and mental health professionals: New York.* Washington, DC: American Psychological Association.

Wulach, J.S. (1998). *Law and mental health professionals: New Jersey.* Washington, DC: American Psychological Association.

Wurtele, S.K., & Miller-Perrin, C.L. (1992). *Preventing child sexual abuse: Sharing the responsibility.* Lincoln: University of Nebraska Press.

Zellman, G., & Antler, S. (1990). Mandated reporters and child protective agencies: A study in frustration. *Public Welfare, 48,* 30–37.

69 DEFINING AND RECOGNIZING ELDER ABUSE

Paula R. Danzinger

The population of the United States is aging. By the year 2050 it is estimated that approximately one in five Americans will be over the age of 65 (Administration on Aging, 1996). As the population gets older, mental health counselors will be seeing a greater number of older adults in their practice settings. Included in this clientele will be an increasing number of abused older adults.

Although abuse of children is recognized as a serious and frequent occurrence, abuse of older adults often goes unrecognized and unacknowledged. Several factors appear to account for the invisibility of this problem: questions about what constitutes elder abuse, lack of skill in recognizing elder abuse, and lack of understanding of the steps that need to be taken when elder abuse is present. This chapter addresses these issues.

TYPES OF ABUSE

There are several different types of abuse perpetrated on older adults. These include physical abuse, psychological or emotional abuse, financial abuse or financial exploitation, sexual abuse, abandonment, neglect, and self-neglect.

Physical Abuse

Physical abuse is characterized by the use of physical force that may result in bodily injury, physical pain or impairment, or even death. Physically abusive acts include slapping, hitting, burning, and hitting with objects. The following is an example of physical abuse:

> Mary is an 85-year-old woman living in her 61-year-old son's house. Mary is bedridden and incontinent. She is often left alone with her daughter-in-law, who has been given the role of primary caregiver. The daughter-in-law is often short-tempered with Mary and will slap her in the face when Mary asks for food or to have her clothing changed.

Psychological or Emotional Abuse

This abuse is characterized by the infliction of anguish, emotional pain, or distress and may occur in conjunction with other types of abuse or by itself. Examples of psychological or emotional abuse are verbal belittling and humiliation, infantilizing the elder, threats of institutionalization, and verbally aggressive threats and insults. The following is an example of emotional abuse:

> Amos is an 88-year-old man living with his daughter's family. He is confined to a wheelchair and cannot leave the house on his own. His grandson is 19, unemployed, and living at home. When there is no one else in the house the grandson will shout at Amos and tell him he is a dirty, worthless old man. When his friends are over he will push and pull Amos's wheelchair to show how smooth the wheels are, frightening Amos. When Amos asks him to

stop, he belittles Amos, calling him a chicken and a smelly baby.

Financial Abuse or Financial Exploitation

This abuse is characterized by illegal or improper use of an older adult's funds, property, or assets. It may also involve schemes designed to defraud older adults, such as Internet, telemarketing, and mail fraud (Hanson, 2000). Examples of financial exploitation are theft of Social Security checks, the use of threats to have the older adult sign a new will, and investment scams that target older adults. An example of financial exploitation follows:

> Trudy is a 75-year-old, disabled widow living on a fixed income. Her nephew helps her by grocery shopping for her and occasionally taking her to the doctor. Her nephew tells her that he needs $30,000 for a new business he is thinking of starting. He tells Trudy that if she doesn't give him the money, he will be very busy soliciting other funding for his project and will not have time to buy her groceries. Trudy withdraws her savings and gives it to her nephew.

Sexual Abuse

Nonconsensual sexual contact of any kind constitutes sexual abuse. These contacts include touching of genitals, inappropriate sexual remarks, forcing the older person to watch sexually explicit movies, or sexual intercourse. The following is an example of sexual abuse:

> Susan is a 78-year-old woman living in a nursing home. She is cognitively alert but is mostly bedridden. Her roommate suffers from dementia. Each afternoon, one of the aides comes to her room and lifts her bed sheets and nightgown and proceeds to "examine" her genital area. The aide then "examines" her roommate in a similar manner.

Abandonment

Abandonment is characterized by the desertion of an older adult by an individual who has assumed responsibility for providing care for that person. The following is an example of abandonment:

> John has been living with his 96-year-old uncle, who suffers from dementia and has lost his speech. John's financial resources are marginal and his support system is limited. He feels he can no longer care for his uncle but does not know what alternatives he has. He takes his uncle to a medical clinic in a neighboring town and leaves the uncle there.

Neglect

Characterized by the refusal or failure to fulfill any part of a person's obligations or duties to care for an older adult, neglect may be intentional or may occur due to lack of social supports or inadequacies in the family system. Intentional neglect may include willfully withholding food or medications, providing inadequate heat or clothing, and refusal to take the older person to doctor appointments. Unintentional neglect may take the same form as intentional neglect, but is the result of ignorance on the part of the caregiver or the caregiver's inability to provide care (Lachs & Pillemer, 1995). The following is an example of neglect:

> Teresa cares for her 92-year-old mother in her home. Teresa is mentally handicapped and is barely able to live on her own. She often leaves her mother alone for one or two days at a time. Teresa is on government assistance and has limited resources. When her money is running low, she stops giving her mother food until the next paycheck comes. She has not taken her mother to the doctor since her mother was treated for a broken hip six years before.

Self-Neglect

In self-neglect, the behaviors of the older adult threaten his or her health and safety. Self-neglect may include failure to follow medical advice, abuse of drugs or alcohol, cluttered and unsafe homes, failure to eat properly, and self-injurious behavior such as cutting or hitting oneself (Lustbader, 1996). The following is an example of self-neglect:

> Juan is an 86-year-old who lives alone in an old house in a run-down neighborhood. He lives on a fixed income and often spends his money on a bottle of liquor rather than food. He has stacks of newspapers that are as high as the ceiling in some parts of the house. His family fears that the house is a firetrap. Juan has refused his family's offers of help.

RECOGNIZING ABUSE

Barriers to Recognizing Abuse

It is often difficult to determine whether an older adult is being abused. Many factors come together to make detecting abuse problematic. The first factor may be the older adults themselves. Reporting that they are abused may be threatening to them for a number of different reasons. They may be afraid that they will be left alone if the abuser is their primary caregiver. They may fear being institutionalized or being subjected to even worse treatment if their living arrangements are changed (Welfel, Danzinger, & Santoro, 2000). In addition, if their abuser is an adult child or a spouse, they may feel protective toward that person and hesitate to expose the abuser to legal punishment.

Family members often do not want to report abuse of their older members because they are often the abusers. According to the Administration on Aging (1998), 47% of the abuse of older adults is perpetrated by adult children of the abused, 19% by spouses, and another 24% by other relatives. Family members may fear the consequences of the abuse and feel shame at their behavior, whether they are the abuser or just have knowledge of the abuse (Welfel et al., 2000). In addition, noncaregiver family members may be concerned that if the abuse is discovered, the elder will be removed from the caregiver's care and that they will be called on to provide for the elder, either financially or physically.

Another factor in the underreporting of elder maltreatment is that most elder maltreatment is not visible or observable. When an older adult is seen to have bruises or other signs of physical abuse, it may be explained by accidental self-injury. Other types of abuse such as emotional/psychological abuse or financial abuse have no visible signs.

Older adults, especially the very old or the frail old, are less visible than other age groups. They are often housebound and, unlike victims of child abuse, are not seen by outside people on any regular basis. In addition, many people feel an aversion to older people and tend to shy away from meaningful interaction with them that might lead to the discovery of abuse.

Even when the older adult is seen by health professionals, the signs of abuse may be missed. Mental health professionals have been shown to have a bias against older adults and tend to view them as being less competent than younger adults (Danzinger & Welfel, 2000; James & Haley, 1995). Due to this bias, the signs of abuse may be attributed to other factors supported by stereotypes of older people, such as that elderly people fall a lot and bruise themselves or that the older patient or client is confused and unreliable as a source of information. The counselor often will rely on reports by caregivers or family members rather than the self-report of the older person.

Who Are the Abused?

According to the Administration on Aging (1998), older women are more likely to be abused, and older men are more likely to be abandoned. Women are at a much higher risk for emotional and psychological abuse and financial exploitation than men are, though the reasons for these differences are not clear.

The very old (80 years or older) are at the highest risk for abuse of all kinds, especially neglect, physical abuse, emotional and psychological abuse, and financial exploitation. Minorities account for fewer than 10% of victims, with African American elders experiencing the highest proportion of abuse among minorities.

Who Are the Abusers?

Women are slightly more likely to be perpetrators of neglect of older adults, and men are more likely to be perpetrators of all other types of abuse. Most perpetrators are younger than their victims, with most of those being under the age of 60. Approximately 90% of the perpetrators of elder maltreatment are related to the victims in some way, with data suggesting that adult children are the most likely to be the perpetrators across all types of abuse (Administration on Aging, 1998).

Risk Factors

There are a number of factors that can put an older person at risk for being a victim of elder maltreatment. First, many caregivers are thrust into that position because of the unavailability of other caregiving resources. Many of them have little or no experience caring for an older, vulnerable adult, nor do they want to be caregivers. The stress of caring for a dependent adult, in combination with the normal stresses of day-to-day life that caregivers experience, can be overwhelming (Quinn & Tomita, 1997). Many caregivers have little if any support in their homes or in the community. Anger, frustration, feelings of being inadequate, lack of knowledge of services available, and feelings of having nowhere to turn can lead to abusive behaviors.

The degree of frailty of the older person is another risk factor. Disability on the part of the older adult makes defending himself or herself or seeking help more difficult. Lachs and Pillemer (1995) suggest that the cognitive impairment of the elder can heighten the risk of elder maltreatment. Dementia may cause the elder to exhibit aggressive behaviors toward the caregiver or to display disruptive behaviors, leading to abusive treatment by the caregiver.

In addition to factors that are unique to caregivers, other factors that may lead to any type of domestic violence put elders at higher risk for abuse. These factors include the caregiver's history of violence, substance abuse, and mental/emotional disorders, as well as lack of adequate financial resources and abuser personality traits.

Signs of Abuse

Although detecting abuse may be difficult, there are signs and symptoms that may help mental health counselors recognize that an older adult is being abused. General signs that a client is being abused include frequent, unexplained crying, unexplained fear of or suspicion of particular person(s) in the household, and an older adult's report of being mistreated. In addition to these general signs, each type of abuse has its own indicators:

- Signs of physical abuse:
  - Bruises, bone fractures, and open wounds. Both the caregiver and the elder might explain these injuries as being the result of accidental self-injury, but a pattern of repeated injuries should be investigated.
  - Indication of overmedication or undermedication.
  - Caregivers attempting to isolate the older adult by refusing to allow visitors or by refusing to bring the elder to scheduled appointments.
- Signs of psychological or emotional abuse:
  - Extreme emotional upset.
  - Emotional agitation.
  - Extreme withdrawal.
- Signs of financial exploitation:
  - Sudden change in bank accounts.
  - Abrupt changes in the older adult's will.
  - Unexplained disappearance of funds.
  - Self-report of elders that they are giving money away or purchasing unneeded and unwanted goods.

- Signs of sexual abuse:
  —Unexplained venereal disease.
  —Bruises around the genital area.
  —Unexplained vaginal or rectal bleeding.
  These signs are difficult to detect and involve self-report from the older adult or evidence from medical sources.
- Signs of abandonment:
  —Desertion of older adult in a public place.
  —Self-report by elders that there is no one caring for them.
- Signs of neglect:
  —Dehydration.
  —Malnutrition.
  —Untreated health conditions.
  —Unkempt or dirty appearance (dirty clothes, body).
  —Unsafe living conditions.
- Self-neglect:
  —Any of the signs for neglect when the older adult lives alone.
  —Cuts, bruises, or open wounds.

REPORTING OF ABUSE

Counselors who do not have older adults as clients may mistakenly believe that elder abuse is not an issue that they will be dealing with directly. Counselors may obtain information about elder abuse from many different sources. Their client may be the abused older adult or may be the abuser, who may tell the counselor about frustration and anger with an older adult living in his or her home. A school counselor may have a student who reports that life at home is problematic because of the issues surrounding Grandma living with the family. A client may come to a session upset because he or she suspects that the older man living next door is suffering abuse by his son with whom he lives. Information about abuse may come from any number of sources, and counselors must know what to do if they suspect elder abuse is occurring.

Although counselors are aware that all 50 states plus the District of Columbia, Puerto Rico, and the Virgin Islands have laws mandating the reporting of child abuse to appropriate authorities, counselors may not know that 45 states plus the District of Columbia, Puerto Rico, and the Virgin Islands have laws mandating the reporting of elder abuse that occurs in any setting. The remaining five states strongly encourage reporting abuse that occurs in domestic settings and mandate reporting of abuse that occurs in an institutional setting.

The procedures for reporting elder abuse differ by state, but there are some general statements that can be made about the process. Reporting is mandated when a counselor has evidence that would cause a competent professional to suspect abuse, but the counselor is not obligated to prove that the abuse is occurring (Welfel et al., 2000) and reporters of elder abuse have immunity from civil or criminal liability if the report is made in good faith. After a report is made, the designated protective services agency (e.g., Department of Human Services in Ohio) will begin an investigation, usually within 24 to 72 hours. Competent adults are given the right to refuse protective services, and intervention against an older adult's wish can be accomplished only by court ruling, with the protective services agency bearing the burden of proof.

States differ as to age requirements for elder abuse, with some laws applying to "vulnerable" adults and some applying to any adult over the age of 60 or 65. States also differ as to the types of abuse that are reportable, all states specify physical abuse, but only 73% require reporting of self-neglect. Because the laws vary so widely from state to state, counselors need to investigate the specific requirements mandated in their state.

SUMMARY

Abuse of older adults is an increasing problem in our society. Mental health counselors need to have an understanding of the problem and its causes and know the appropriate steps to take if abuse is suspected.

The following are guidelines for mental health counselors dealing with older adults.

- Abuse of older adults occurs among men and women of all racial, ethnic, and socioeconomic groups.
- The perpetrator is often an adult child or spouse of the abused, but paid or informal caregivers may also be involved.
- Physical, functional, or cognitive problems in the older adult may make caregiving more frustrating and problematic and may place the older adult at greater risk.
- Financial dependency of the caregiver or other family problems may impair the ability to provide adequate care.
- Mental illness, alcoholism, or drug abuse in the older adult or in the caregiver may be associated with abuse and neglect.
- A past history of abusive relationships may predispose the victim to future mistreatment.
- Inadequate housing or unsafe conditions in the home may increase the likelihood of abuse or neglect.
- The counselor presumes the client is mentally competent and in control of decision making until facts prove otherwise.
- The client should actively participate in defining the problem and deciding the most appropriate course of action.
- Clients may exercise the freedom of choice and the right to refuse services as long as they have the capacity to understand the consequences of their actions.
- If abuse is suspected, counselors should document information carefully.
- Counselors should offer the client options and choices.
- Counselors should encourage that the client plan for safety and support.
- Finally, counselors can assist the client with referrals to local services.

For further information and resources for elder abuse, counselors may visit the National Center for Elder Abuse (NCEA) Web site at www.gwjapan.com/NCEA/ or the Administration on Aging Web site at www.aoa.gov.

References

Administration on Aging. (1996). *Aging in the 21st century* [Online]. Available: www.aoa.anns.gov/aoa/stats/aging21.

Administration on Aging. (1998). *The national elder abuse incidence study: Final report.* Retrieved May 15, 2000. Available: www.aoa.dhhs.gov/abuse/report/default.htm.

Danzinger, P.R., & Welfel, E.R. (2000). Age, gender and health bias in counselors: An empirical analysis. *Journal of Mental Health Counseling, 22,* 135–149.

Hanson, L.J. (2000). Senior citizens are the most targeted by Internet, telemarketing, and mail fraud. *APF Reporter, 19.* Retrieved May 15, 2000. Available: www.aliciapatterson.org/APF1903/Hansen/Hansen.html.

James, J.W., & Haley, W.E. (1995). Age and health bias in practicing clinical psychologists. *Psychology and Aging, 10,* 610–616.

Lachs, M.S., & Pillemer, K. (1995). Abuse and neglect of elderly persons. *New England Journal of Medicine, 332,* 437–443.

Lustbader, W. (1996, Spring). Self-neglect: A practitioner's view. *Aging,* 51–60.

Quinn, M.J., & Tomita, S.K. (1997). *Elder abuse and neglect: Causes, diagnosis, and intervention strategies* (2nd ed.). New York: Springer.

Welfel, E.R., Danzinger, P.R., & Santoro, S. (2000). Mandated reporting of elder abuse: A primer for counselors. *Journal of Counseling and Development, 78,* 284–292.

70 THE RESPONSIBLE USE OF TECHNOLOGY IN MENTAL HEALTH PRACTICE

Elizabeth Reynolds Welfel and Kathleen T. Heinlen

The emergence of computer capabilities and electronic forms of communication has significantly affected the practice of counselors and therapists. Not only do mental health professionals regularly keep client records on their computers, but they also use facsimile (fax) machines to transmit client documents, send e-mails to clients and colleagues, participate in professional listservs, and occasionally conduct supervision via computer or participate in videoconferences about client care. They are also exploring the use of the Internet and World Wide Web to provide clinical services directly without benefit of any face-to-face client contact (Bloom & Walz, 2000; Heinlen, Welfel, Richmond, & Rak, 2000; Maheu & Gordon, 2000) and are seeking to become part of the growing telehealth movement (Jerome et al., 2000; Nickelson, 1998). Many of these media have the potential to improve communication between therapists and clients, increase the accessibility of mental health care, and foster fuller consumer knowledge of the scope of mental health services available. Internet-based services also have the potential to demystify and destigmatize the therapeutic process, thereby encouraging reluctant individuals to make contact.

This potential can be realized only if mental health professionals recognize the problems that can arise from irresponsible, ill-informed, and premature use of these media. There are four major risks involved in the use of technology for client services: (1) errors in diagnosis and treatment related to limited face-to-face client contact, (2) breach of confidential client disclosures and records, (3) inadequate client consent for treatment, and (4) difficulties in protecting clients at risk. The body of this chapter offers suggestions for using technology responsibly in professional practice. The statements of the codes of ethics of the professional associations (American Counseling Association, 1995; American Psychological Association, 1992; National Association of Social Workers, 1999) regarding client rights to privacy and consent to treatment form the foundation for these recommendations.

FACSIMILE MACHINES

Once therapists send documents via facsimile they have relinquished control over the information contained therein. If the receiving fax machine is in the exclusive control of the recipient (and the fax number was dialed correctly), sending a fax is no more likely to jeopardize client privacy than use of the postal service or overnight delivery. However, facsimile machines are usually widely accessible. Sometimes, faxes are transmitted at inconvenient times, increasing the risk that others will read them. For these reasons, we offer several strategies to protect the privacy of data when using fax machines:

- Use a cover sheet explicitly stating that the faxed material is confidential and meant to be read only by the recipient listed there.

- Prearrange a time to send the fax and get confirmation of receipt by telephone. Not only does this verify the correct fax number and ensure that the recipient will retrieve the fax quickly, but it also immediately alerts both professionals if the material does not get transmitted as intended.
- Develop a policy that sensitive personal client information (such as HIV status) is not transmitted via fax.
- Educate and monitor office personnel regarding appropriate handling of client facsimile transmissions.
- Devise special written client releases for fax transmissions, or add wording to existing forms to cover the use of the fax.

COMPUTER-BASED CLIENT RECORDS

Clinicians commonly create and store records of client service on computer hard drives and floppy disks (Rosen & Weil, 1996). Aside from test results, signed releases, and insurance papers, the entire set of client records for a practice or agency may be contained on a handful of floppy disks or a minute amount of memory on a hard drive. The capacity to compress so much data into an easily accessible format is a convenience for clinicians. However, this very capacity makes that data vulnerable to loss, theft, or unauthorized duplication at a level impossible with paper records. As the number of computers in networks expands, so too does the risk of unauthorized access to confidential data. Consequently, therapists ought to use the following precautions when storing client records on computer:

- Avoid using a computer to which others have access. If no other options exist, use a floppy disk, not a hard drive, for the creation and storage of all client records.
- Use code numbers or pseudonyms to identify files and floppy disks so that the nature of their contents is not immediately obvious should their security be compromised.
- Maintain a paper file for each client and identify a number or code name of the files

and disk on which additional client records are stored.
- If computers are networked, utilize all appropriate procedures to protect against viewing or theft of files by others in the network.
- Regularly update virus protection and create backup copies of all files. Keep these in a secure location separate from the original floppies (which, of course, are also stored in a secure place).

USE OF E-MAIL, CHAT ROOMS, AND INTERNET-BASED COMMUNICATIONS

A small but increasing number of clinicians are utilizing Internet-based resources to communicate with clients and colleagues. Estimates suggest that a large percentage of these involve communications with clients via e-mail between sessions or consultations with colleagues about practice issues. A growing number are involved in supervision via e-mail and chat or interact with insurers and managed care companies via e-mail. Currently, hundreds of clinicians are offering Web-based assessment and treatment services for clinical issues via e-mail and chat (Heinlen et al., 2000; McMinn, Buchanan, Ellens, & Ryan, 1999). As with any new phenomenon, terminology is in flux and a number of different names are in use to refer to Web-based services: WebCounseling, cybercounseling, e-mail counseling, Internet counseling, online therapy, and telehealth services. For the purposes of this chapter, we use the term WebCounseling. Currently, WebCounseling primarily consists of e-mail exchanges (both synchronous and asynchronous) and communication via synchronous chat rooms. Videoconferencing is a rarely used option (Rabasca, 2000), but this method may become more viable when technical problems are resolved (Sussman, 1998).

These services seem to be multiplying faster than the evidence supporting their clinical utility or safety. In fact, early evidence reveals substantial ethical problems with WebCounseling sites (Heinlen et al., 2000), ranging from large gaps in informed consent, confidentiality, and the protection of vulnerable clients to unsubstantiated advertising claims for their efficacy. These findings suggest that a disturbing number of professionals have initiated WebCounseling without sufficient knowledge of the medium or reflection about its capabilities. Not surprisingly, given the potential benefits and risks to the public, several professional associations have issued guidelines to assist mental health professionals considering this medium, including the National Board of Certified Counselors (1997), the American Counseling Association (1999), and the National Association of Social Workers (2000). Concerned professionals have also banded together to form their own organization and produced recommendations for responsible Web-based services (International Society for Mental Health Online, 2000). Although these standards differ somewhat in the particulars, all emphasize the following aspects of responsible Web-based practice.

Confidentiality

In addition to the ordinary limits of confidentiality in face-to-face practice (see Chapter 56), the state of current technology further reduces confidentiality for Internet-based communications. Hackers easily gain access to unsecured sites, and current security protections (such as encryption) reduce, but do not eliminate, the threat of invasion from determined hackers. In addition, e-mail communications do not travel directly from the counselor's computer to the client's; they pass through many other computers on their way to the recipient. Moreover, some Internet service providers (such as America Online) retain copies of *all* e-mail communications sent through them for one year. The use of passwords and encryption limits unauthorized access, but that is not the only threat to client privacy. For example, a client who uses a workplace computer to send or receive e-mail from a WebCounselor has no guarantee of confidentiality because an employer has full legal rights (and technological capacity) to view employee e-mail. A counselor or client may also inadvertently leave a message onscreen that others can view. Therefore, current standards universally recommend that WebCounselors offer prospective clients a full description of the limits of confidentiality, both those derived from traditional practice, such as mandated reporting of child abuse, and those that derive from Internet technology, such as the limits of computer security. Unfortunately, our research suggests that many WebCounselors are either unaware of these technological limitations to confidentiality or are unmotivated to explain them to prospective clients (Heinlen et al., 2000).

Uncertain Effectiveness of WebCounseling and Implications for Consent

Because Web-based services offer none of the visual, auditory, or kinesthetic cues found in face-to-face counseling, diagnosis and treatment in this medium rely exclusively on what clients reveal in their typed comments. WebCounselors have no access to independent verification of any information received, not even the basic demographic characteristics of the client. Therefore, the likelihood of misunderstanding of text-based communications is substantial. Moreover, there is no theory or model for WebCounseling in the professional literature to clarify good practice, nor is there any substantial empirical evidence of its capacity to benefit clients (Heinlen et al., 2000). For all these reasons, WebCounseling services must be considered an experimental medium. Consequently, those using the Web for clinical interventions have a double burden in conducting informed consent: Not only are they responsible for explaining the typical aspects of treatment to clients (such as fees for service and credentials of the provider), but they must also carefully describe the untested nature of the service the client is considering. Clients should be warned that there is no independently published evidence of prior effectiveness of WebCounseling and no evidence that this service will not harm them. A number of current WebCounseling sites either fail in these aspects of informed consent or make claims for the medium that cannot be justified (Heinlen et al., 2000). Others present contradictory information. On the one hand, they describe the benefits of WebCounseling (such as anonymity of service and help with problems embarrassing to discuss in person), and on the other hand, they use legal disclaimers that deny *all* responsibility for the effects of their service.

Most WebCounseling sites rely on nonsynchronous (time-delayed) e-mail as the medium for service. In this case, clients also need information about the length of time between submission and reply and the avenues available to them in the event of technology failure or other interruption in service.

Because a high proportion of Web users are minors, WebCounselors should develop procedures for verifying the age of the prospective client and for obtaining parental consent for minors. Many WebCounselors deal with the issue by including a statement that people must be over 18 years of age to use the service. This is one step in the right direction, but because of the ease with which Web users can disguise their identity, additional steps need to be taken to verify client age.

Competence

Because WebCounseling is considered experimental, clinicians cannot know whether their competencies in face-to-face practice transfer to the Web. Therefore, professionals need to be cautious about claiming competence in any aspect of WebCounseling and about treating clients with significant mental illness or distress. Research raises some troubling questions about the degree to which those professionals currently on the Web comprehend these limitations. For example, a number of WebCounselors identify multiple areas of competence and some claim to be able to offer online treatment for sexual abuse, anorexia nervosa, major depression, and Posttraumatic Stress Disorder (Heinlen et al., 2000). In light of current evidence, such claims seem inconsistent with current ethical standards and detrimental to client welfare.

Client Records

WebCounselors need to devise a system of client records for their work in this medium that contains identifying client information, billing information if needed, copies of any paper documents exchanged, and hard copies of e-mail exchanges. They ought to explain fully to clients the nature of the records kept and the length of time they will be preserved. As with any other office records, they ought to have another professional identified who can gain access to client records if they experience a sudden incapacity.

Responsibilities to Vulnerable Clients

Professionals seeing face-to-face clients who are dangerous to themselves or others have a well-established duty to protect these clients from harm, either through intensifying therapeutic interventions or through involving others outside the therapeutic dyad to help keep the person safe (see Chapter 38). Both of these methods are difficult, if not impossible, to implement for Web-based clients. Web clients are not physically accessible to the WebCounselor, and there are no established protocols for evaluating the severity of the risk of suicide or harm to others or even the veracity of client statements. For these reasons, ethical guidelines recommend the identification of a local professional contact for the WebClient so that if the identifying information provided to the WebCounselor is accurate, a nearby therapist or law enforcement officer may be able to intervene. They also advise WebCounselors to provide the client with contact information so that the WebCounselor can be reached when offline. Because these measures have an uncertain level of effectiveness, the most prudent course of action is to advise clients who feel themselves at risk of suicide or harm to others to seek other sources of support. A number of Web sites in our research directed clients at risk to call 911, go to the local hospital, or call the police. Aside from one site that advertised itself as a resource for people who felt suicidal, most WebCounselors energetically discouraged people already feeling suicidal from making initial contact with them, asserting that WebCounseling was not an appropriate source for help with such crises (Heinlen et al., 2000). The guidelines strongly support the latter stance.

Legal Issues

Legal protections for clients and professionals who use the Web for clinical services are uncertain. The global nature of the Web undermines the jurisdiction of states to police the actions of Web-based providers (Maheu, Callan, & Nagy, in press; Nickelson, 1998). Moreover, consumers have little hope of addressing grievances against WebCounselors by suing for damages because the applicability of civil law is just as uncertain (Shapiro & Schulman, 1996). Some state licensing boards are asserting that only individuals with licenses in their states can legally offer services to residents of that state, but the ultimate impact of such statues is not yet clear (Koocher & Morray, 2000).

Consequently, professionals considering the use of this medium for clinical services are well advised to check with their attorneys and state licensing boards to determine whether any statutes, case law, or regulations govern its practice in their jurisdictions. It may also be prudent to have an attorney knowledgeable about the Web review all Web site content before it is posted.

Finally, mental health professionals should be aware that professional liability insurers vary in their willingness to insure Web-based services. Because offering services without benefit of liability coverage is inadvisable, an early step in the process of evaluating the feasibility of a WebCounseling site should be communication with the insurer to verify coverage. A final check with the insurer should take place once all the site materials are developed to confirm that the insurer understands the details of the site and is agreeing to cover any claims arising from its use.

General Cautions about the Practice

Many psychologists and counselors view Web-Counseling as unquestionably unethical (Kirk, 1997; McMinn et al., 1999). There has been significant debate in the professional organizations about whether publishing standards for WebCounseling was wise given the dearth of evidence of its safety or effectiveness. To some, it appeared as a premature endorsement of a dangerous development that could give the public a false sense of security about Web-Counseling. Others have taken the position of cautious acceptance of a movement that cannot be halted by organizational opposition. Regardless of how this debate ultimately gets resolved, it is important to acknowledge that many professionals offering WebCounseling services are failing to observe some of the most basic ethical tenets of the professions. Some promise absolute confidentiality, others claim immediate results, and still others make disparaging statements about face-to-face services to sell WebCounseling to visitors to their sites (Heinlen et al., 2000). A number require payment in advance. This evidence raises important questions about the motivation of those offering these sites. They seem more interested in self-promotion and personal profit than in promoting the welfare and dignity of the public. Such a perspective not only places them and their clients at risk, but it also jeopardizes public confidence in the mental health professions. Therefore, any mental health professional considering the use of WebCounseling services needs to begin the process with some self-examination:

- Is my interest in the Web based primarily on a desire to better serve the public, and not a search for supplemental income?
- Do I understand the boundaries of my competence in this arena?
- Do I have the personal and professional resources needed to be diligent about my Web-based practice?
- Can I cope with the legal uncertainties of practice on the Web?
- Am I really prepared to be as accessible as WebCounseling demands?

The process of developing a Web site that complies with regulations and ethical guidelines is not simple and requires a substantial investment of time and money. The frequency with which WebCounseling sites emerge and then fade away (Heinlen et al., 2000) suggests that this is not a quick fix for an ailing practice or a simple way to additional income.

If the Web is to actualize any of the potential so often claimed by proponents, those involved have a duty not only to be diligent in the development and maintenance of their sites, but also to be committed to systematic research on the process and outcomes of Web-Counseling. Without such evidence, this medium will remain an experimental approach used by the few, disdained by the many, with little broad impact on public mental health.

USE OF PROFESSIONAL LISTSERVS

Some professionals are using listservs and Web discussion groups to communicate with other professionals about issues of interest to them. Topics range from advice about practice management and frustrations with third-party payment systems to discussions about new theory and research and consultations on case management. When mental health professionals are sharing client information in these media, their practices must be consistent with standards in the codes of ethics. Specifically, if they are sharing identifiable client data, they must have a signed client release for such disclosures before they are made. This release should explain to clients what the professionals know about the audience receiving the disclosures and the risks of breach of confidentiality on the Web.

Even when sharing nonidentifiable client data for which a signed release is not mandated, there are ethical issues to consider. The most important consideration is whether the data are truly disguised so that the client cannot be identified. Second, the professional needs to assess whether the feedback gained from the disclosure will be expert enough to be helpful. If participation in the listserv has been restricted to a group of competent professionals, then the feedback received may be useful. If not, the disclosure may prove to be a waste of time. Third, as with any consultation, all advice obtained must be independently evaluated by the clinician to judge its fit with the needs of the particular client.

SUMMARY

Many of the problems that practitioners experience with the use of technology for client services derive from their ignorance or misunderstanding of the limitations of technology. Practitioners need to educate themselves about the risks to client privacy, the uncertain value of Web-based services, and the importance of client consent to any use of technology for client data.

References

American Counseling Association. (1995). *Code of ethics and standards of practice.* Alexandria, VA: Author.

American Counseling Association. (1999). *Ethical standards for Internet on-line counseling.* Alexandria, VA: Author. Available: www.counseling.org/gc/cybertx.htm.

American Psychological Association. (1992). *Ethical principles of psychologists and code of conduct.* Washington, DC: Author.

Bloom, J.W., & Walz, G. (Eds.). (2000). *Cybercounseling and cyberlearning: Strategies and resources for the Millennium.* Alexandria, VA: American Counseling Association.

Heinlen, K.T., Welfel, E.R., Richmond, E.N., & Rak, C.F. (2000). *The scope of webcounseling: A survey of services and compliance with NBCC Standards for the ethical practice of webcounseling.* Manuscript submitted for publication.

International Society for Mental Health Online. (2000). *Suggested principles for the online provision of mental health services.* Available: www.ismho.org.

Jerome, L.W., DeLeon, P.H., James, L.C., Folen, R., Earles, J., & Gedney, J.J. (2000). The coming age of telecommunications in psychological research and practice. *American Psychologist, 55,* 407–421.

Kirk, M.A. (1997, January). Current perceptions of counseling and counselor education in cyberspace. *Counseling Today, 19,* 17–18.

Koocher, G.P., & Morray, E. (2000). Regulation of telepsychology: A survey of state attorneys general. *Professional Psychology: Research and Practice, 31,* 503–508.

Maheu, M.M., Callan, J.E., & Nagy, T.F. (in press). In S.F. Bucky (Ed.), *Call to action: Ethical and legal issues for behavioral ethics and law in the practice of psychology.* New York: Plenum Press.

Maheu, M.M., & Gordon, B.L. (2000). Counseling and therapy on the Internet. *Professional Psychology: Research and Practice, 31*, 484–489.

McMinn, M.R., Buchanan, T., Ellens, B.M., & Ryan, M.K. (1999). Technology, professional practice and ethics: Survey findings and implications. *Professional Psychology: Research and Practice, 30*, 165–172.

National Association of Social Workers. (1999). *Code of ethics*. Washington, DC: Author.

National Association of Social Workers. (2000). *Online therapy and the clinical social worker*. Washington, DC: Author.

National Board for Certified Counselors. (1997). *Standards for the ethical practice of web counseling*. Available: www.nbcc.org/ethics/wcstandards/htm.

Nickelson, D.W. (1998). Telehealth and the evolving health care system: Strategic opportunities for professional psychology. *Professional Psychology: Research and Practice, 29*, 527–535.

Rabasca, L. (2000, April). Taking telehealth to the next step. *APA Monitor, 31*, 36–37.

Rosen, L.D., & Weil, M.M. (1996). Psychologists and technology: A look at the future. *Professional Psychology: Research and Practice, 27*, 635–637.

Shapiro, D.E., & Schulman, C.E. (1996). Ethical and legal issues in e-mail therapy. *Ethics and Behavior, 6*, 107–124.

Sussman, R.J. (1998). Counseling online. *CTOnline*. Available: www.counseling.org/ctonline/sr598/sussman.htm.

71   COUNSELING SUPERVISION

Essential Concepts and Practices

Rodney K. Goodyear, Ferdinand Arcinue, and Michele Getzelman

Most counseling practitioners eventually become supervisors. This career step is satisfying and confers status. But it also helps protect the public and serves the profession, for supervisors ensure that more novice practitioners deliver competent client services even as they develop their skills. Supervision is therefore essential to the maintenance and enhancement of the counseling profession.

The root meaning of supervision, "to oversee," applies across all occupations and contexts in which supervisions occurs. Counseling supervision, though, has specific meaning and therefore requires an elaborated definition. Bernard and Goodyear (1998) defined it as: "[An] intervention provided by a more senior member of a profession to a more junior member or members of that same profession. This relationship is evaluative, extends over time, and has the simultaneous purposes of enhancing the professional functioning of the more junior person(s), monitoring the quality of professional services offered to the client(s) she, he, or they see(s), and serving as a gatekeeper of those who are to enter the particular profession" (p. 27).

As an area of inquiry, supervision has matured sufficiently that book-length coverage (e.g., Bernard & Goodyear, 1998; Watkins, 1997) is necessary for an adequate review of its conceptual and empirical literature. Given the space constraints of this chapter, we selectively address concepts and issues most likely to be useful to counseling supervisors.

MAJOR FINDINGS FROM THEORY, RESEARCH, AND PRACTICE

In this section, we cover the following topics: models for practice, the supervisory relationship, and supervision formats. Knowledge of this material is an essential prerequisite for supervisory practice.

Models for Practice

Kurt Lewin's assertion that "there is nothing so practical as a good theory" certainly applies in supervision. Practitioners seeking theory to inform their supervision have several (nonindependent) options. One is to extrapolate directly from their counseling model so they might engage in, say, client-centered or cognitive-behavioral supervision. It is true that virtually all supervisors must be influenced to some extent by the theories they use as counselors. But supervision is *not* counseling and requires different or at least additional concepts. We believe that supervisors vary on a continuum from those whose work is totally and consistently informed by their theory of counseling to those whose work is simply "flavored" by it.

A second theoretical option focuses on trainee developmental processes (see, especially, Stoltenberg, McNeill, & Delworth, 1998). Chagnon and Russell (1995) pointed out that models of this type are grounded in two basic assumptions. The first is that in the process of moving toward competence, supervisees move through a series of stages that are qualitatively different from one another. The second is that each of the supervisee's stages requires a qualitatively different supervisory environment for optimal supervisee satisfaction and growth to

occur. For example, the very beginning trainee is likely to approach supervision with dichotomous (right versus wrong) thinking, seeking the correct way to respond to the client; the supervisor is pulled to behave as a teacher who will give the "right" answer. More advanced trainees begin to appreciate that there is a range of possible responses to the client and are more open to exploring in supervision their own reactions to the client.

A third option is to employ one of the social role models (cf. Holloway, 1992), all of which describe supervision in terms of component functions or roles. Bernard and Goodyear (1998) summarized the roles various authors had suggested. The three most common were *counselor*, *teacher*, and *consultant*; a fourth, *evaluator* or *monitor*, was suggested by a smaller subset of authors. The behavior of the supervisor in each role is suggested by its label.

Bernard (1997) has probably best described the use of these supervisory roles. In her discrimination model, the supervisor shifts among the roles of teacher, consultant, and counselor; within each of these roles, the supervisor can focus on the supervisee's issues of personhood (e.g., personal reaction to the client, including countertransference), technical skills and strategies, and conceptualizations about the client and the counseling process. The effective supervisor employs all these roles and foci, moving fluidly from one to the other in response to the supervisee's immediate training need.

The Supervisory Relationship

Like counseling, supervision occurs within the context of a relationship, and many relationship processes and issues are common to both interventions. For example, supervisors and supervisees develop working alliances just as counselors and clients do. But there also are important differences. Perhaps the most important is that whereas the relationship often *is* the intervention in counseling, supervision is an educational process in which the supervisee is learning new skills. If supervision consisted only of the supervisor-supervisee relationship, the supervisee would be unlikely to develop many of the skills and conceptualizations necessary for practice. Another difference is that supervision is an evaluative process, which affects trust and other relationship phenomena in ways discussed later.

Yet another difference is that supervision involves three people (the client, therapist/supervisee, and the supervisor). This contributes to two particular relationship phenomena that merit attention: parallel processes and interpersonal triangles.

Parallel Processes. Parallel process refers to the phenomenon in which the dynamics in supervision replicate those that occurred or are occurring between the supervisee and client: "Supervisees unconsciously present themselves to their supervisors as their clients have presented to them [and] the process reverses when the supervisee adopts attitudes and behaviors of the supervisor in relating to the client" (Friedlander, Siegel, & Brenock, 1989, p. 149). For example, a supervisee whose client was confused may present in an uncharacteristically confused manner during supervision.

There are at least two ways in which this phenomenon can be useful in supervision. First, by exploring the parallels between supervisor-supervisee interactions and those occurring between supervisee and client, the supervisee can obtain important information about the client's dynamics. Second, the supervisee can learn to behave toward the client as the supervisor has behaved with him or her in supervision (i.e., to "model" the supervisor's behavior). Psychodynamic supervisors and supervisees are more likely than their nonanalytic counterparts to perceive the existence and importance of parallel processes. We believe, however, that the phenomenon can be useful to any supervisor.

Interpersonal Triangles. Client, counselor, and supervisor constitute a triangle, which Bowen (1978) emphasized to be the most fundamental relationship unit. Triangles constitute a type of social geometry in which two members will tend to form a coalition against a third; the third has an important function, though, in stabilizing that coalition. Usually,

a coalition can be considered to exist when two members of a triad discuss a third in secrecy: This is the prototypical supervisory situation. The purpose is benign, but the effect is a supervisor-supervisee coalition.

Some supervisors and therapists use triangle-related phenomena strategically. For example, the counselor might say something like this to the client: "My supervisor is convinced that your problem is X and that I should be doing Y about it. Just between us, though, I think her response is pretty insensitive to the issues you are facing." This sets up the supervisor as an oppressor and strengthens the client-counselor coalition (i.e., "bond"). Whether supervisors and supervisees choose to use such strategies, it *is* important that supervisors maintain awareness of triangle-related phenomena.

Diversity Issues

Counseling has distinguished itself among the mental health professions with its emphasis on issues of diversity. It would be a serious oversight for us to neglect to address that issue in this chapter.

In their recent review, Goodyear and Guzzardo (2000) were able to find only eight studies of cross-cultural or cross-racial supervision, even using very liberal inclusion rules. What was clear from even this very scant research base, though, is that supervisors need to recognize that within the majority of cross-cultural supervisory dyads, the supervisors are White, whereas the supervisees are racial or cultural minorities.

This suggests that in addition to the power differential that supervisors have by virtue of their position, most of these supervisors *also* are working with supervisees who are sensitive to social power that traditionally has accrued to White people. It is important, therefore, for the supervisor to raise with the supervisee the issue of racial or cultural differences as a first step toward developing a constructive relationship based on mutual respect.

But if there are few studies of cross-cultural supervision, there are even fewer studies of the role of gender in supervision (Goodyear & Guzzardo, 2000). Two studies, though, examined actual within-session behaviors and confirmed that social role interactions of men and women in the everyday world affects the professional interactions that occur in supervision. For example, when a male supervisee made a statement that coders rated as high in power, supervisors were more likely to support it than if a female supervisee had made it; interactions in male-male supervisory pairings were more task- (versus relational-) oriented than the interactions between female supervisors and male supervisees.

Dealing with diversity-related issues is often difficult in counseling. But it becomes even more complicated in supervision because of supervision's nature as a three-person system (with its attendant coalitions and parallel processes). To illustrate, consider how differently the dynamics might be in each of the following situations: (1) a Black client, with both the supervisor and supervisee White; (2) a White client, with the other two Black; (3) a Black supervisor, with the other two White. Each could result in dramatically different dynamics, at least with respect to the issue of race and culture.

Supervision Formats

The most common supervision format is dyadic, in which supervisor and supervisee meet to review case notes. This, though, is but one format and by some measures the least effective. In a variant on that first format, for example, the dyadic supervision can center on reviews of the supervisee's audio- or videotapes of the counseling session. Another format is for the supervisor and supervisee to work together as a cotherapy team. Yet another is some form of live supervision, usually involving observation through one-way glass. A particular strength of these last two formats is that they permit close monitoring, therefore allowing supervisees to be assigned clients with more pathology than otherwise would be suitable.

Group supervision, one of the most frequently used formats (Bernard & Goodyear, 1998), merits special mention. It is economical of the supervisor's time. It also exposes supervisees to a broadened range of clients, vicarious learning opportunities, and a learning environment that involves the support of others at similar levels of development. Although there are disadvantages (e.g., not all supervisees will get the same amount of time during any session; improperly handled group dynamics can be harmful to some group members), the benefits overall outweigh the negatives.

Supervision formats differ in the extent to which they (1) allow immediate (versus delayed) feedback to the trainee, (2) provide access to actual in-session behavior, and (3) protect clients. Supervisors should consider each when choosing a format.

ISSUES IN SUPERVISION PRACTICE

Although material in the previous section is relevant to supervision practice, that which we address in this section should be foremost in the thinking of anyone assuming supervisory responsibilities. These are: qualifications to supervise, vicarious liability, and evaluation in supervision.

Qualifications to Supervise

We believe supervisors should meet two fundamental criteria. First, they should have sufficient training, knowledge, and skill to competently provide any professional service their supervisee undertakes. Second, they should have received specific training in supervision theory and practice, whether in a graduate-level course or during continuing education workshops. An increasing number of states (e.g., California, Ohio, and Texas) are stipulating that licensed mental health professionals receive such training if they are to practice as supervisors.

Also, because client protection and professional liability issues are involved, a licensed professional should assume ultimate responsibility for the supervisee's work. This does not, however, preclude having an unlicensed person as part of a hierarchical training arrangement. For example, there is a role in graduate training programs for more advanced students or interns to supervise while having a licensed person supervising the supervision they provide.

Vicarious Liability

Perhaps the most sobering concept for a new supervisor to learn is that of "vicarious liability." That is, the supervisor has responsibility for any unethical behavior or malpractice in which his or her supervisee engages; this liability exists even if the supervisee has failed to reveal problem behavior (e.g., there have been cases in which, unbeknownst to the supervisor, the supervisee was engaging in sexual contact with the client; the supervisor still was held accountable). In the famous *Tarasoff* case, for example, suit was brought against both the therapist and his *supervisor*. There are at least two practice implications of this: (1) Maintain awareness of supervisee behavior (which, as we discuss below, requires mutual trust); and (2) Document supervisory sessions (there is an example of a supervision record form in Bernard & Goodyear, 1998).

Evaluation

Evaluation is a defining aspect of supervision and differentiates it from counseling, which it sometimes resembles. Evaluation enables the supervisor simultaneously to ensure that the client receives quality care and to provide growth-producing feedback to the supervisee. We address three important issues related to supervisory evaluation: effects on the supervisory relationship, accuracy, and the special problem of impaired or incompetent trainees.

Effects on the Supervisory Relationship. The goals of client protection and supervisee development can conflict. When this occurs, client well-being always has primacy. Trainees therefore often experience it as a paradox that effective supervision requires them to disclose their actions, thoughts, and feelings, yet these disclosures also can be "used against them" as the basis for negative evaluations, client reassignments, or sanctions that might even include dismissal from the training program. It

is unsurprising, then, that supervisees adopt various strategies to manage the impressions the supervisors have of them. Ladany, Hill, Corbett, and Nutt (1996), for example, found that anxiety about evaluation was one reason supervisees selectively revealed information to supervisors.

Evaluation, then, can limit supervisees' trust in the supervisor, which is crucial to effective supervision. Because of vicarious liability, supervisors need to trust that supervisees are being forthcoming about their behavior; at the same time, for supervisees to profit from supervision, they need to trust that they can make disclosures to the supervisor without fearing that unpleasant surprises will occur as a consequence. "Trust is efficient": Vigilance against untrustworthy acts from either party not only takes energy and time, but it also compromises the supervision.

Trust is not an all-or-nothing phenomenon and always exists to some degree. It also is not something that develops instantaneously, but rather is earned over the course of many interactions and interpersonal risks taken together. One means to maximize trust is for the supervisor to be as straightforward and clear as possible about expectations (what criteria will be used in evaluation?) and about evaluation methods (e.g., what data will be used and when will it be gathered? What sort of feedback will be given?).

Evaluation Accuracy. Supervision's integrity rests on the accuracy with which supervisees' functioning is assessed. Yet supervisor biases and blind spots can affect supervisee evaluations. Some supervisors probably do give supervisees unfairly negative evaluations based on personal bias or dislike; this is reprehensible and should be guarded against. Interestingly, though, Goodyear and Guzzardo's (2000) review suggests that the greater likelihood is of an unwarranted *positive* evaluation. There are data showing, for example, that supervisors inflate evaluations of supervisees when they like them. To the extent that the supervisor can use objective measures, bias is reduced.

We should note as well that supervisors should seek evaluative feedback from their supervisees so that they can improve their practice. The appendixes of Bernard and Goodyear (1998) have instruments that might be used to evaluate both supervisor and supervisee.

Impairment or Incompetence. A specific issue related to evaluation concerns identifying and responding to trainees who are impaired or incompetent. Bernard and Goodyear (1998) defined impairment as having a serious deficit in the areas of personal functioning (awareness of self, management of personal stress, etc.), knowledge and application of professional standards (ethics, professional behavior, mental health law), and competency (clinical skills, appropriate interventions, assessment, etc.). More recently, Forrest, Elman, Gizara, and Vacha-Haase (1999) distinguished incompetence from impairment. They suggested that the incompetent trainee has never achieved satisfactory levels of functioning, whereas the impaired trainee has shown a decline from a previous level of functioning.

Because the supervisor is legally and ethically responsible for supervisee functioning, there is a responsibility to identify impaired or incompetent trainees and take appropriate action, whether it is remediation of some sort or even removal from the training program.

Additional Information

It has been possible in this chapter to cover only a select few of the topics from the substantial supervision literature. For supervisors who want to learn more about additional topics or who want expanded discussions of the material we have presented here, we offer some suggested resources.

Two books that provide a broad overview of supervision are those of Bernard and Goodyear (1998) and Watkins (1997). As well, Chapter 11 of Bernard and Goodyear contains a comprehensive list of supervision books that had been published to date. From among them, we particularly recommend the now-classic Mueller and Kell (1972) and two model-driven books: Holloway (1995) and Stoltenberg et al. (1998).

Statutes and regulations for the licensure of mental health professionals all stipulate how much supervision is required, conditions under which supervision should occur, and supervisors' qualifications. Links to the licensure laws in the various states can be found at the Mental Health Licensure Resources Web site maintained by Larry E. Long Jr.: www.tarleton.edu/~counseling /coresour/lllpc.htm.

Some professional associations specify criteria for becoming supervisors. Those criteria can be found on the Web site for the American Association for Marriage and Family Therapy (AAMFT; www.aamft.org/about /asrequire.htm) and for the National Board for Certified Counselors (NBCC; www .nbcc.org/acs/overview.htm).

References

Bernard, J.M. (1997). *The discrimination model.* In C.E. Watkins (Ed.), *Handbook of psychotherapy supervision* (pp. 310–327). New York: Wiley.

Bernard, J.M., & Goodyear, R.K. (1998). *Fundamentals of clinical supervision* (2nd ed.). Boston: Allyn & Bacon.

Bowen, M. (1978). *Family therapy in clinical practice.* New York: Aronson.

Chagnon, J., & Russell, R.K. (1995). Assessment of supervisee developmental level and supervision environment across supervisor experience. *Journal of Counseling and Development, 73,* 553–558.

Forrest, L., Elman, N., Gizara, S., & Vacha-Haas, T. (1999). Trainee impairment: A review of identification remediation, dismissal, and legal issues. *The Counseling Psychologist, 27,* 627–686.

Friedlander, M.L., Siegel, S.M., & Brenock, K. (1989). Parallel process in counseling and supervision: A case study. *Journal of Counseling Psychology, 36,* 149–157.

Goodyear, R.K., & Guzzardo, C.R. (2000). Psychotherapy supervision and training. In S.D. Brown & R.W. Lent (Eds.), *Handbook of counseling psychology* (3rd ed., pp. 83–108). New York: Wiley.

Holloway, E.L. (1992). Supervision: A way of teaching and learning. In S.D. Brown & R.W. Lent (Eds.), *Handbook of counseling psychology* (2nd ed., pp. 177–214). New York: Wiley.

Holloway, E.L. (1995). *Clinical supervision: A systems approach.* Thousand Oaks, CA: Sage.

Ladany, N., Hill, C.E., Corbett, M.M., & Nutt, E.A. (1996). Nature, extent, and importance of what psychotherapy trainees do not disclose to their supervisors. *Journal of Counseling Psychology, 43,* 10–24.

Mueller, W.J., & Kell, B.L. (1972). *Coping with conflict: Supervising counselors and therapists.* New York: Appleton-Century-Crofts.

Stoltenberg, C.D., McNeill, B., & Delworth, U. (1998). *IDM supervision: An integrated developmental model for supervising counselors and therapists.* Jossey-Bass: San Francisco.

Watkins, C.E., Jr. (Ed.). (1997). *Handbook of psychotherapy supervision.* New York: Wiley.

72   RESPONSIBLE INTERACTIONS WITH MANAGED CARE ORGANIZATIONS

Elizabeth Reynolds Welfel

Mental health professionals who accept managed care clients are frustrated by that system and overwhelmingly view it as negatively affecting their autonomy to make treatment decisions, income, and job satisfaction (Acuff et al., 1999; Murphy, DeBernardo, & Shoemaker, 1998; Phelps, Eisman, & Kohout, 1998; Sank, 1997). The professional literature also identifies several unethical practices by some mental health professionals who interact with managed care (Bilynsky & Vernaglia, 1998; Cooper & Gottlieb, 2000; Danzinger & Welfel, 2001; Murphy et al., 1998; Phelps et al., 1998; Rothbaum, Bernstein, Haller, Phelps, & Kohout, 1998; Watt & Kallmann, 1998; Wineburgh, 1998). Most prominent among these are:

- Giving inaccurate diagnoses to meet managed care requirements for reimbursement even when they believed alternative (unreimbursable) diagnoses better described the client's concerns.
- Tailoring treatment to the parameters acceptable for managed care organization

(MCO) reimbursement even when believing that other treatment plans were preferable.
- Failing to disclose to clients the extent of disclosure of confidential client information to MCOs for fear of scaring them away.
- Complying with "gag orders" that limit informed consent to treatment even though such orders are in direct conflict with ethical standards and legal restrictions.
- Using treatment approaches approved by MCOs without sufficient training or supervised experience in order not to lose MCO clients.
- Terminating treatment (without a specific referral to alternative care) when reimbursement ends even if they believe clients may benefit from additional services but may be unable to pay for them.
- Declining to challenge MCO-recommended treatments they believe unhelpful or appeal denials of reimbursement for services they see as necessary for fear of alienating the MCO and being removed from provider lists.

What makes the managed care environment a risky place for clinicians who want to practice ethically, and what can they do to avoid these pitfalls? The simplest explanation is that managed care imposes a new and more extensive conflict of interest on the clinician than do traditional forms of reimbursement for professional services (Cooper & Gottlieb, 2000). In managed care interactions, when professionals act in ways they believe are beneficial to clients, they feel as though they are jeopardizing the financial stability of their practices. An underlying reason for the problems mental health professionals have in coping with managed care is the divergence in philosophies and ethics of care.

A note of caution is in order here before professionals get defined as heroes and MCOs as villains. The mental health ethic is not as altruistic as it appears because practitioners also receive their highest profits when clients pay directly or traditional insurers reimburse them for comprehensive diagnosis and care. In parallel fashion, the business ethic is not as self-interested as it seems because in the long run, the profitability of any company is ensured only when it provides an effective service that actually benefits subscribers. Otherwise, employers would look elsewhere for insurance coverage for their employees.

Managed care is based on utilitarian principles that emphasize the welfare of subscribers as a group and the financial viability of the organization over the welfare of the individual. The ethic governing their operation is the business ethic of obtaining the highest possible level of profitability within the parameters of law and consumer rights. For-profit companies view making a profit not just as a practical goal to keep the company viable or a marker of the success of its managers, but an *ethical responsibility* to both employees and shareholders. By doing well financially, MCOs are truly "doing good" in their framework. Mental health professions emphasize an opposing principle: the promotion of the autonomy and welfare of the individual client above all other considerations. Clearly, mental health professionals want and need to make money, but they see financial compensation primarily as a reward for effective service, not an overarching goal or an ethical duty. Moreover, when the welfare of the client conflicts with the opportunity to make a profit, the mental health professions without exception sacrifice profit and align with the interest of the client.

Second, the utilitarian philosophy means that MCOs focus on capitated risks to groups and never waver from seeing the welfare of the individual in relation to the impact of that individual's care on other subscribers and the viability of the company. In other words, a defining feature of the system is a generalized and restrictive approach to care: Whenever care is provided to one person, that either limits care to others or reduces the profitability of the MCO. In traditional mental health care, professionals acknowledge the influence of the group on the costs and accessibility of care, but the welfare of the group and the economics of care invariably take second place to the best interests of the individual client.

Third, the group orientation of managed care results in an emphasis on standardization of care and defined protocols for services for particular diagnoses. The momentum to define "treatments of choice" or "best practices" for disorders such as substance abuse and depression has come at least partly from third-party payors who want standards for treatment that transcend individual differences. In contrast, clinicians center their attention on treating *individuals* with mental health problems and on adapting treatment to the unique circumstances of the individual. This difference, coupled with their economic incentive, leads to managed care's focus on alleviating obvious presenting problems in opposition to the clinician's emphasis on thorough assessment of the presenting problem in a context of general functioning and cultural and social factors. Put another way, managed care sees its role as eliminating symptoms that inhibit normal functioning quickly and efficiently, whereas clinicians generally interpret their role as promoting client well-being and identifying and treating both the presenting problems and the issues underlying current symptoms. In managed care systems, the independence that the clinician once had to define the content, duration, and structure of treatment is significantly diminished.

Unfortunately, most clinicians are not free to elect nonparticipation with MCOs. Because MCOs dominate the marketplace, most mental health professionals jeopardize the financial viability of their practice or agency if they refuse to accept MCO reimbursement for services, although some have experimented with this option (Bittner, Bialek, Nathiel, Ringwald, & Tupper, 1999). According to Kiesler (2000) 88% of Americans and virtually 100% of Californians with private insurance are enrolled in managed care plans. Moreover, a substantial proportion of governmental programs such as Medicare and Medicaid are using managed care systems to pay for mental health care.

To avoid these ethical problems and meet their fiduciary responsibilities to clients, clinicians should better understand the contracts they sign and the additional ethical and legal duties that managed care has imposed.

NEGOTIATING FAIRER CONTRACTS

In spite of the evidence that the mental health needs of many Americans are unmet (U.S. Department of Health and Human Services, 2000), MCOs experience an oversupply of mental health professionals seeking to contract with them to provide client services. This abundant supply of mental health professionals coupled with MCOs' dominance in the marketplace leaves many clinicians feeling powerless to negotiate the terms of their contracts with MCOs. Although their power to amend contract language is limited, there are steps they can take to protect their interests and their clients' welfare. The first and most fundamental is to understand the provisions of the contracts they are signing. A "why bother to attend to the details, I can't change anything anyway" attitude is particularly dangerous for two reasons. First, MCO contracts often identify duties that professionals may not realize they have, such as reporting to the MCO any malpractice claim or

disciplinary actions against them. Second, MCO contracts vary in language, and some contracts have provisions that are much more dangerous to mental health professionals than others. For example, some contracts have two-way indemnification clauses, meaning that in the event of a client lawsuit, the therapist agrees not to hold the MCO liable and the MCO agrees not to hold the therapist liable. Others have one-way indemnification: The therapist agrees to protect the MCO from liability but not the other way around (Frager, 2000). This can be a very important difference in the event of legal action.

This "why bother" attitude toward MCO contracts is symbolic of a broader misperception: that all MCOs are identical. Not only are there a variety of MCO structures and policies, but there is also a continuum of compliance with professional standards for MCOs. Clinicians need to investigate the companies to determine the adequacy of their commitment to professional guidelines, such as those of the National Committee on Quality Assurance (NCQA, 2000b). This body also publishes an annual "report card" on MCOs to help professionals and consumers evaluate the quality of services offered by particular organizations (NCQA, 2000a). The National Alliance for the Mentally Ill (NAMI, 2000) has also examined the quality of care by MCOs and published its findings for public review.

Prior to signing a contract with any behavioral health organization, a mental health professional should know the following:

- The type, frequency, and extent of patient data required for authorization of care and utilization review.
- The procedures used to protect the privacy of patient data and the extent to which the MCO shares patient data with other organized systems of care.
- The qualifications and training of those with access to patient data regarding confidentiality.
- The criteria used to determine "medically necessary treatment" and the frequency with which those criteria are updated.

- The information communicated to subscribers about their mental health benefits.
- The content of the release of information forms the MCO wants used with their subscribers.
- The procedures for appealing denials of care.
- The provisions for removing mental health professionals from provider panels, specifically whether they can remove clinicians "without cause."

When clinicians have answers to these questions, they will be better able to determine whether the policies and procedures of the MCO are consistent with their ethical obligations to promote the welfare and dignity of their clients.

SEPARATING CLINICAL DECISION MAKING
FROM REIMBURSEMENT ISSUES

Needless to say, managed care systems write contracts that protect their interests and risks of liability. One aspect of contracts that clinicians may not fully understand is the language in managed care contracts that places the responsibility of making sound clinical judgments squarely and completely in the hands of the clinician. Here is the type of language typically included:

> Nothing contained in this agreement shall be construed to require providers to recommend any treatment they deem professionally unacceptable. The MCO agrees not to interfere with the rendition of services by the provider, it being understood that the traditional provider and patient relationship will be maintained.

> Providers agree that the determination by an MCO that a particular treatment is not a covered service shall not relieve providers from providing or recommending such care as they deem appropriate, nor shall such benefit determination be considered a medical determination by the MCO.

This means that MCOs are legally separating reimbursement from clinically needed treatment. They are placing the full responsibility for treatment decisions on mental health professionals, are relieving themselves from any responsibility for clinical decision making, and are declaring that clinicians are obligated to recommend the care they think best regardless of the reimbursement implications of that recommendation. If clinicians fail to act in that way, they are accepting the same responsibility for that failure as clinicians working with clients with other payment arrangements.

Therefore, when clinicians make comments such as "The MCO wouldn't let me continue treatment even though it was clearly in the client's best interest," they are probably misunderstanding the contracts they have signed. According to the language cited above, clinicians are agreeing to always act in the best interests of clients regardless of the MCO's determination of what is a covered service.

Realistically, of course, without insurance coverage, many clients are unable or unwilling to pay for mental health services. The tendency of mental health professionals to account for these realities as they develop plans for care is quite understandable and often motivated by a desire to give clients as much care as possible within reimbursement restrictions. Professionals put themselves at risk, though, when they design care with reimbursement as a primary consideration. Instead, they must independently determine the treatment plan(s) they believe appropriate and then consider reimbursement issues secondarily. Moreover, the decision to undertake a treatment plan that is reimbursable over one that is clinically appropriate should be the decision of the client, made with clear consent after being informed about all the treatment options. The following sections explain the components of adequate informed consent for MCO clients resulting from this contract language and the implications for policy and procedures to avoid the appearance of abandoning clients (also see Chapter 66).

CONDUCTING EXTENSIVE INFORMED CONSENT WITH CLIENTS

A competent informed consent procedure leaves MCO clients with a clear understanding of the limits of confidentiality of the information they disclose to clinicians, the restrictions of reimbursement likely to be imposed by the MCO, the distinction between clinically needed treatment and reimbursable treatment, and their right to appeal denials of care. Both Morriem (1991) and Appelbaum (1993) argue that clinicians have a *duty to disclose* the financial implications of managed care on the costs of their treatment. Specifically, a thorough informed consent will give clients answers to the following questions or recommendations for strategies to obtain answers from the MCO:

- If I authorize release of information to an MCO, what information are they likely to ask for?
- How much detailed information will they seek about my problems?
- How often will they need information about my treatment?
- Do I have any control over the amount of information released to them? If I release only partial information about my problems, will that jeopardize the likelihood of reimbursement?
- To whom, exactly, is this information released, and what happens to it once the MCO has it? Will it remain confidential?
- Will the MCO want access to the records of my treatment even after treatment is finished?
- Will the MCO have a role in determining how much treatment I receive or the kind of treatment I get?
- If my MCO offers coverage for mental health care, does that mean that this particular treatment will automatically be covered if it falls within that maximum?
- Can I deal directly with the MCO about my treatment if I want?
- Can I change my mind about consent to release information to them if I give it now?

- Can I protest any decisions the MCO makes that I disagree with?
- Can I continue care even if the MCO does not reimburse it? How much will it cost me?

APPEALING ADVERSE DECISIONS BY THE MCO

A legal precedent has been established that implies a duty for clinicians to challenge denials of reimbursement by an insurer if they judge the requested services to be necessary and appropriate (Appelbaum, 1993). This precedent comes from a California case, *Wickline v. State* (1986), in which a cancer patient claimed injury from an MCO denial of payment for hospital services. In that case, her physician failed to advocate on her behalf by appealing the MCO denial. The ruling stated, "The physician who complies without protest with the limitations imposed by a third-party payor, when his medical judgment dictates otherwise, cannot avoid his ultimate responsibility for the patient's care." Does this mean that a clinician must appeal every denial of care? Such a standard is unrealistic and unjustified. Appelbaum's recommendations are sound ones:

- At least a first-level appeal should be undertaken whenever the clinician judges the treatment to be necessary for the well-being of the client.
- Further appeals should be pursued only with the agreement of the client.
- The probability of success of the appeal, the client interest in the treatment, and the availability of alternative care should all be considered when deciding whether to appeal denials beyond the initial level (p. 253).

DEVELOPING POLICIES AND PROCEDURES TO AVOID ABANDONING CLIENTS

When appeals are unsuccessful, both the ethics codes and legal standards declare that clinicians have a duty not to discontinue treatment for lack of sufficient payment when an emergency exists. A client who is a danger to self or others is the most obvious example of a client for whom discontinuing care would be unethical and negligent. Care should be continued until the emergency is resolved or competent alternative care can be obtained. Clinicians do not have a duty to provide unlimited care without payment for clients in less-threatening circumstances. If a nonemergency client exhausts insurance benefits, then the clinician's obligation is limited to finding a low-cost referral source and conducting a small number of sessions to responsibly complete termination and ensure a smooth referral to other professional services. It is important to note, however, that most codes of ethics either strongly encourage or mandate mental health professionals to accept some work on a pro bono or lowered fee structure as part of the duty of the profession to serve the public interest without constant consideration of personal profit. As noted above, clients should be fully informed about the implications of nonpayment on their rights to services at the initiation of those services.

SUMMARY

Clinicians working with MCOs face the burden of a conflict of interest between their own investment in not alienating the MCO from whom they need referrals and the interests of their individual clients, which frequently call for challenge of MCO policy and procedure for reimbursement of mental health care. Clinicians in this precarious situation must remember that the ethical and legal standards of care obligate them to place the client's welfare as the highest priority and to advocate on behalf of the client for any services they believe clinically necessary. Specifically, clinicians who wish to act responsibly must (1) negotiate fair contracts that protect them and their clients; (2) undertake full and fair informed consent with clients regarding the impact of managed care on the privacy, structure, and duration of services available; (3) appeal denials of care they believe inappropriate; and (4) avoid abandoning clients for lack of payment.

References

Acuff, C., Bennett, B.E., Bricklin, P.M., Canter, M.B., Knapp, S.J., Moldawsky, S., & Phelps, R. (1999). Considerations for ethical practice in managed care. *Professional Psychology: Research and Practice, 30,* 563–575.

Appelbaum, P.S. (1993). Legal liability and managed care. *American Psychologist, 48,* 251–257.

Bilynsky, N.S., & Vernaglia, E.R. (1998). The ethical practice of psychology in a managed-care framework. *Psychotherapy, 35,* 54–68.

Bittner, S., Bialek, E., Nathiel, S., Ringwald, J., & Tupper, M. (1999). An alternative to managed care: A "guild" model for the independent practice of psychotherapy. *Journal of Marital and Family Therapy, 25,* 99–111.

Cooper, C.C., & Gottlieb, M.C. (2000). Ethical issues with managed care: Challenges facing counseling psychology. *The Counseling Psychologist, 28,* 179–236.

Danzinger, P.R., & Welfel, E.R. (in press). The impact of managed care on mental health counselors: A survey of perceptions, practices, and compliance with ethical standards. *Journal of Mental Health Counseling, 23.*

Frager, S. (2000). *Managing managed care: Secrets from a former case manager.* New York: Wiley.

Kiesler, C.A. (2000). The next wave of change for psychology and mental health services in the health care revolution. *American Psychologist, 55,* 481–487.

Morriem, E.H. (1991). Economic disclosure and economic advocacy: New duties in the medical standard of care. *Journal of Legal Medicine, 12,* 275–329.

Murphy, M.J., DeBernardo, C.R., & Shoemaker, W.E. (1998). Impact of managed care on independent practice and professional ethics: A survey of independent practitioners. *Professional Psychology: Research and Practice, 29,* 43–51.

National Alliance for the Mentally Ill. (2000). Stand and deliver: Action call to a failing industry. Available: www.nami.org/update/reportcard.htm.

National Committee on Quality Assurance. (2000a). *NCQA health plan report card.* Available: www.ncqa.org/update/reportcard.htm.

National Committee on Quality Assurance. (2000b). *Standards for the accreditation of managed care organizations.* Available: www.ncqa.org/pages /communications/publications/mcopubs.htm.

Phelps, R., Eisman, E.J., & Kohout, J. (1998). Psychological practice and managed care: Results of the CAPP practitioner survey. *Professional Psychology: Research and Practice, 29,* 31–36.

Rothbaum, P.A., Bernstein, D.M., Haller, O., Phelps, R., & Kohout, J. (1998). New Jersey psychologists' report on managed mental health care. *Professional Psychology: Research and Practice, 29,* 37–42.

Sank, L. (1997). Taking on managed care: One reviewer at a time. *Professional Psychology: Research and Practice, 28,* 548–554.

U.S. Department of Health and Human Services. (2000). *Mental health: A report of the Surgeon General.* Washington, DC: Author.

Watt, J.W., & Kallmann, G.L. (1998). Managing professional obligations under managed care: A social work perspective. *Family Community Health, 21,* 40–49.

Wickline v. State, 228 Cal Rptr. 661 (Cal. App. 2d, 1986).

Wineburgh, M. (1998). Ethics, managed care and outpatient psychotherapy. *Clinical Social Work Journal, 26,* 433–443.

APPENDIX

Ethics Codes and Guidelines in Mental Health Disciplines

American Association of Sex Educators, Counselors and Therapists. (1993). *1993 code of ethics.* Chicago: Author. Available: www.aasect.org /codeofethics.cfm

American Counseling Association. (1995). *Code of ethics and standard of practice.* Alexandria, VA: Author.

American Counseling Association. (1999). *Ethical standards for Internet on-line counseling.* Alexandria, VA: Author. Available: www.counseling .org/gc/cybertx.htm

American Mental Health Counselors Association. (1998). *Code of ethics for mental health counselors.* Alexandria, VA: Author. Available: www .amhca.org

American Psychiatric Association. (1998). *Principles of medical ethics with annotations especially applicable to psychiatry.* Washington, DC: Author. Available: www.psych.org

American Psychological Association. (1981). *Specialty guidelines for the delivery of services: Clinical psychologists, counseling psychologists, organizational/industrial psychologists, school psychologists.* Washington, DC: Author.

American Psychological Association. (1992). *Ethical principles of psychologists and code of conduct.* Washington, DC: Author.

American Psychological Association. (1993a). *Guidelines for ethical conduct in the care and use of animals.* Washington, DC: Author.

American Psychological Association. (1993b). *Guidelines for providers of psychological services to ethnic, linguistic and culturally diverse populations.* Washington, DC: Author.

American Psychological Association. (1993c). *Record keeping guidelines.* Washington, DC: Author.

American Psychological Association. (1994). Guidelines for child custody evaluations in divorce proceedings. *American Psychologist, 49,* 677–680.

American Psychological Association. (1997). *Services by telephone, teleconferencing and Internet.* Washington, DC: Author. Available: www.apa .org/ethics/stmnt01.htm

American Psychological Association, Committee on Legal Issues. (1996). Strategies for private practitioners coping with subpoenas or compelled testimony for client records or test data. *Professional Psychology: Research and Practice, 27,* 245–251.

American Psychological Association, Committee on Professional Practice and Standards. (1995). Twenty-four questions (and answers) about professional practice in the area of child abuse. *Professional Psychology: Research and Practice, 26,* 377–383.

American Psychological Association, Committee on Psychological Testing and Assessment. (1996). Statement on the disclosure of test data. *American Psychologist, 51,* 644–648.

American Psychological Association, Committee on Women in Psychology. (1989). If sex enters into the psychotherapy relationship. *Professional Psychology: Research and Practice, 20,* 112–115.

503

American Rehabilitation Counseling Association. (1987). *Code of professional ethics for rehabilitation counselors.* Arlington Heights, IL: Author.

American School Counselor Association. (1992). *Ethical standards for school counselors.* Alexandria, VA: Author. Available: www.schoolcounselor.org/ethics/index.htm

Association for Counselor Education and Supervision. (1990). Standards for counseling supervisors. *Journal of Counseling and Development, 69,* 30–32.

Association for Counselor Education and Supervision. (1993). Ethical guidelines for counseling supervisors. *Counselor Education and Supervision, 34,* 270–276.

Association for Specialists in Group Work, Executive Board. (1989). *Ethical guidelines for group counselors.* Alexandria, VA: American Counseling Association.

Association of State and Provincial Psychology Boards. (1991). *ASPPB code of conduct.* Montgomery, AL: Author.

Canadian Counseling Association. (1999). *Code of ethics.* Ottowa, Canada: Author. Available: www.ccacc.ca/coe.htm

Canadian Psychological Association. (1991). *Canadian code of ethics for psychologists–Revised.* Ottawa, Canada: Author.

Committee on Ethical Guidelines for Forensic Psychologists. (1991). Specialty guidelines for forensic psychologists. *Law and Human Behavior, 15,* 655–665.

International Association of Marriage and Family Counselors. (1993). *Ethical code for the International Association of Marriage and Family Counselors.* Alexandria, VA: Author.

National Association of School Psychologists. (1992). *Principles for professional ethics.* Silver Springs, MD: Author.

National Association of Social Workers. (1999). *Code of ethics.* Washington, DC: Author.

National Association of Social Workers. (2000). *Online therapy and the clinical social worker.* Washington, DC: Author.

National Board for Certified Counselors. (1997). *Standards for the ethical practice of Web counseling.* Available: www.nbcc.org/ethics/wcstandards/htm

National Board for Certified Counselors. (2000). *National Board for Certified Counselors: Code of ethics.* Alexandria, VA: Author.

National Career Development Association. (1987). *National Career Development Association ethical standards.* Alexandria, VA: Author.

AUTHOR INDEX

Abbey-Hines, J., 259
Abbott, P.J., 309
Abelsohn, D., 35
Aber, J.L., 248
Abidin, R.R., 376
Abikoff, H., 166
Abramowitz, J.S., 108
Abramowitz, S.I., 428
Achenbach, T.M., 164, 216
Achopler, E., 165
Acuff, C., 434
Adelman, H.S., 222, 224
Administration on Aging, 320, 480, 481
Adson, D.E., 122
Agency for Healthcare and Policy Research, 114, 115, 116, 117
Agras, W., 55, 108, 124
Agresti, A., 320
Ahrens, A.H., 52
Ahrons, C.R., 35
Aitken, K., 165
Ajamu, A., 289
Albano, A.M., 167
Alden, L., 137
Aldrich, C., 328
Aldwin, C.M., 45
Alexander, J.F., 207, 389
Alexander, K., 249
Alexander, R.A., 260
Alexander, T., 374
Ali, A., 53
Allmon, D.J., 137
Alpert, J.L., 171
Altarriba, J., 300
Altekruse, M., 265

Altepeter, T.S., 166
Altman, R., 90
Altschuler, G.C., 26
Amada, G., 28
Amato, K., 32, 34, 36
Amchin, J., 78
American Academy of Child and Adolescent Psychiatry, 180
American Association for Geriatric Psychiatry, 331
American Association of Marriage and Family Therapists, 280, 382, 401, 421
American Counseling Association, 381, 398, 401, 417, 420, 421, 422, 441, 442, 443, 444, 445, 450, 454, 455, 456, 460, 467, 468, 484, 486
American Psychiatric Association, 4, 69, 70, 71, 72, 74, 76, 77, 78, 88, 89, 112, 113, 114, 115, 116, 128, 143, 155, 157, 160, 162, 163, 202, 252, 256, 293, 294, 326, 359, 420, 422, 425, 451
American Psychological Association, 77, 78, 170, 359, 394, 401, 417, 420, 441, 442, 443, 444, 445, 451, 454, 455, 456, 460, 462, 463, 467, 468, 475, 484
Amir, N., 108, 254
Ammerman, R.T., 173
Amorim, P., 81
Anastasi, A., 105

Anastopoulos, A., 166
Andenas, S., 45
Anders, T.F., 167
Anderson, H., 368
Anderson, J.C., 158
Anderson, N., 288
Anderson, S.K., 467
Andreasen, N.C., 145
Andres, R., 54
Andrews, A.A., 389
Andrews, J., 139
Angermeyer, M.C., 145
Angle, B., 96
Angold, A., 164
Antler, S., 473
Aponte, J., 358
Appel, L.J. 54
Appelbaum, P.S., 453, 454, 456
Applegate, B., 183
Araoz, D.L., 374
Archer, J., Jr., 25, 26, 27, 28, 29
Archer, R.P., 103
Arkinson, M.K., 174
Armstrong, H.E., 137
Arredondo, P., 362
Arvay M.J., 429
Asante, K.M., 301
Asay, T.P., 389
Asher, S.J., 32
Ashery, R., 235
Ashford, J., 88
Ashforth, B.E., 19, 20
Association for Specialists in Group Work, 359
Astin, A.W., 26
Atkinson, D.R., 294, 295
Auerbach, A., 437

505

SUBJECT INDEX